Mass Media
Mass Culture

AN INTRODUCTION

Fiji p.59

The McGraw-Hill Series in Mass Communication and Journalism

Mass Media
Mass Culture

AN INTRODUCTION

JAMES R. WILSON
California State University, Fresno

STAN LE ROY WILSON
Professor Emeritus
College of the Desert

Fifth Edition

Boston Burr Ridge, IL Dubuque, IA Madison, WI New York San Francisco St. Louis
Bangkok Bogotá Caracas Lisbon London Madrid
Mexico City Milan New Delhi Seoul Singapore Sydney Taipei Toronto

Cover images:
"Princess Diana" by Ken Goff/Timepix, "Toni Morrison" by James Keyser/Timepix, "The Beatles" by Terence Spencer/Life Magazine/Timepix, "Edward R. Murrow" Lisa Larsen/Life Magazine/Timepix, "Elvis" by Robert W. Kelley/Life Magazine/Timepix, "Cindy Crawford" by Albert Ferreira/DMI/Timepix, "Peanuts" by Photofest, "Sammy Sosa" by John Lacono/SI/Timepix, "Stephen King" by Ted Thaj/Time Magazine/Timepix, "Ellen DeGeneres and Anne Heche by Patsy Lynch/Timepix. "Lucille Ball" by Loomis Dean/Life Magazine/Timepix

McGraw-Hill Higher Education

*A Division of The **McGraw-Hill** Companies*

MASS MEDIA/MASS CULTURE

Published by The McGraw-Hill Companies, Inc. 1221 Avenue of the Americas, New York, NY, 10020. Copyright © 2001, 1998, 1995, 1993, 1992, by The McGraw-Hill Companies, Inc. All rights reserved. No part of this publication may be reproduced or distributed in any form or by any means, or stored in a database or retrieval system, without the prior written consent of The McGraw-Hill Companies, Inc., including, but not limited to, in any network or other electronic storage or transmission, or broadcast for distance learning. Some ancillaries, including electronic and print components, may not be available to customers outside the United States.

This book is printed on acid-free paper.

1 2 3 4 5 6 7 8 9 0 VNH/VNH 0 9 8 7 6 5 4 3 2 1 0

ISBN 0072314621

Editorial director: *Phillip A. Butcher*
Sponsoring editor: *Valerie Raymond*
Developmental editor: *Amy Shaffer*
Marketing manager: *Kelly M. May*
Project manager: *Karen J. Nelson*
Production supervisor: *Rose Hepburn*
Senior designer: *Jennifer Hollingsworth*
Supplement coordinator: *Mark Sienicki*
Media technology producer: *Kimma Stark*
Cover and interior designer: *Michael Warrell*
Compositor: *GAC Indianapolis*
Typeface: *10.5/12 Goudy*
Printer: *Von Hoffmann Press, Inc.*

Library of Congress Cataloging-in-Publication Data

Wilson, James R. (James Ross)
    Mass media/mass culture : an introduction / James R. Wilson, Stan Le Roy Wilson.
  — 5th ed.
      p.   cm.
    ISBN 0-07-231462-1
    Includes bibliographical references and index.
    1. Mass media and culture.   I. Wilson, Stan Le Roy.   II. Title
P94.6.W55   2001   00–55892
    302.23dc—21

www.mhhe.com

About the Authors

James Ross Wilson is a professor of mass communication and journalism at California State University, Fresno. He earned his master's degree from CSUF and his bachelor's degree from what was then known as Fresno State College. In addition to teaching classes in broadcast news writing, management, audio and video production, and pop culture, Wilson serves as general manager and faculty adviser for the student-run campus radio station, KFSR-FM. • Wilson spent 20 years working in radio broadcasting as a news reporter, news director, program director, and station manager before joining the faculty at CSUF in 1983. He also trained military personnel for work in the Armed Forces Radio and Television Service while assigned to the Department of Defense Information School at Fort Slocum, New York.

Stan Le Roy Wilson is professor emeritus of mass communication at the College of the Desert in Palm Desert, California. He holds a doctorate from the University of Southern California and earned his bachelor's and master's degrees from California State Universities, Fresno and Stanislaus. Prior to his 34-year teaching career at California State universities and community colleges, he worked as a newspaper and radio journalist and as a public relations consultant. • Wilson has held leadership positions in state and national journalism and mass communication organizations, and in 1995 in Washington, D.C., he was inducted into the Community College Journalism Association's Hall of Fame. In addition to his professional career, Wilson has had an active political life, serving 17 years on the Palm Desert City Council with four terms as mayor. He left teaching in January 1995 following his election to the Riverside County Board of Supervisors, where he currently is serving his second four-year term representing the largest geographic region in one of the nation's largest counties.

Walkthrough

Since its inception, *Mass Media/Mass Culture* has presented the fundamentals of mass communication and, at the same time, shown the importance and relevance of mass media in our society. Reflective of the dynamic nature of the field of mass communication, many new features, examples and references are incorporated into the fifth edition. This text differs from many in the field by giving students a reason why the study of mass communication is important to them: its powerful impact on our lives and the culture in which we live.

Approach of the Book

This textbook teaches media literacy by explaining the relationship between mass communication and our popular culture. It also uses a unifying theme to transmit information about how the media have evolved the media progression theory developed by John Merrill and Ralph Lowenstein. This concept traces how the various mass media move through three stages of evolution—the elitist, popular, and specialized stages. A timeline showing various media at differing stages in their evolution appears in each of the media chapters.

If at times the tone of this book seems critical, it does not stem from an anti-media bias, but rather from an effort to stimulate critical thinking by presenting the whole media picture—warts and all. The reader can be assured that the authors are not anti-media. Before becoming teachers of mass communication, both of us worked in the fields of print and broadcast journalism. As the sons of a newspaper publisher, we have been associated with mass communication our entire lives. We believe, however, that we can get a higher level of performance from the media if we actively scrutinize them and call out for improvements.

Cultural History of **Recorded Music**		Elitist	Popular	Specialized
1877	Thomas A. Edison invents the "talking machine."	•		
1902	Enrico Caruso begins recording opera.	•		
1905	Columbia introduces two-sided disks.	•		
1920s	African-American music helps recording industry expand its sales.		•	
1920s	Jazz music evokes charges that music is corrupting young people.		•	
1920s	Covering (white musicians playing African-American music) leads to development of "white swing".		•	
1925	Electric phonograph replaces hand-cranked machines.		•	
1927	Jukebox becomes popular.		•	
1930s	Recording industry declines due to Great Depression and radio's free music.		•	
1930s	Big band era keeps recording industry alive.		•	
1940s	Frank Sinatra gains fame appealing to youthful bobby-soxers.		•	
1950s	Specialization of radio introduces African-American rhythm-and-blues to white audiences.		•	
1954	Sam Phillips of Sun Records discovers Elvis Presley, who becomes the king of rock and roll.			•
1955	The motion picture industry, reaching out for a youth audience, uses Bill Haley and the Comets' "Rock Around the Clock" as the theme song for *The Blackboard Jungle*.			•
1955–1963	Rock and roll becomes firmly entrenched in the new youth subculture.			•
1960s	Led by the Beatles and the "British Invasion", rock music begins carrying less innocent messages that reflect changing American subcultures.			•
1970	The Beatles disband.			•
1970s	Disco palaces invade American culture.		•	•
1976	Punk rock emerges in Britain.			•
1981	Warner-Amex introduces MTV cable channel; popularizes music videos.			•
1985	U.S. Senate committee holds hearings on rock music lyrics; suggests a rating system to warn listeners of explicit lyrics.			•
1986	Michael Jackson pays a reported $40 million to $50 million for the rights to Beatles' music.			•
1988	CDs replace LPs as most popular format of recorded music.			•
1990	Jury finds Florida music store owner guilty of obscenity for selling rap music.			•
1990	Court finds Judas Priest innocent of causing the suicides of two Nevada youths by placing subliminal messages in their music.			•
1990s	Alternative or grunge rock provides popular protest to the show-biz glitz of the music industry.			•
1996	Gangsta rap star Tupac Shakur is gunned down in Las Vegas; his first posthumous album jumps to number one of the charts			•
1999	MP3 digital audio file format for computers causes concern for recording industry			•
2000	Time Warner announces plans to combine its music operations with Britain's EMI Records, creating a joint operation valued at $20 billion from almost 25 percent of global music sales.			•

277

Timeline

Each of the media chapter (6–12) includes a cultural history timeline. These timelines trace the evolution of the medium through the elitist, popular, and specialized stages.

Globalization of Information on the World Wide Web

The collapse of space, time and borders may be creating a global village, but not everyone can be a citizen.

—1999 United Nations Human Development Report

Key People and Concepts

Satellite News Gathering (SNG)

MP3 Technology

Slate

MSNBC

1996 Communications Decency Act

Child Online Protection Act (COPA)

Speed vs. Accuracy

Freedom of the Press and the Internet

Internet-Addiction Disorder (IAD)

Chapter Three

A new chapter 3, *Globalization of Information on the World Wide Web*, examines the Internet's impact on other mass media as well as issues that arise from its global reach.

Key People and Concepts

Each chapter leads off with a new feature, *Key People and Concepts*, designed to highlight what is important in each chapter and to give students a point of reference.

Practicing Media Literacy Boxes

Practicing Media Literacy boxes, found throughout the text, pose a critical thinking question to challenge students to reflect on the concept just covered.

NEW TECHNOLOGY AND COMMUNICATION

Practicing Media Literacy
What do you think can be done to keep erroneous information from being spread on the Internet?

It's hard to believe that 100 years from now, as historians look back on the beginning of the 21st century, the names of Steve Jobs and Bill Gates may have as much significance to them in the field of global communication as past innovators Johann Gutenberg and Samuel F. B. Morse have to today's historians.

But the world of communication has changed drastically, primarily due to such computer innovators as Jobs and Gates. Any many of those changes came in just the final third of the 20th century.

For example, when the Apollo 11 spacecraft made the first manned landing on the surface of the moon in 1969, the on-board computer that helped Neil Armstrong and Buzz Aldrin to land and takeoff from the moon's surface was extremely limited when compared with home computers of the year 2000.

The fixed memory—what is now referred to as ROM—held about 72,000 bytes, which is only 1/20th of the storage capacity of a single 3.5-inch floppy disk used with today's computer system. In addition, the Apollo 11's total random access memory, or RAM, was about ... late ...

The News Media: *Keeping the Culture Informed*

Were it left to me to decide whether we should have a government without newspapers, or newspapers without a government, I should not hesitate a moment to prefer the latter.

Key People and Concepts

Convergence

Authoritarian Theory

Libertarian Theory

Expanded Chapter Five

Expanded chapter 5 (formerly chapter 3), *The News Media: Keeping the Culture Informed*, addresses the responsibilities of the news media.

witty comedy team of George Burns and Gracie Allen, and the puppets Cecil the Seasick Sea Serpent, Howdy Doody, and Kukla, Fran, and Ollie.

Most of these entertainers had started their careers in **vaudeville** and made the
transition to radio. Now they were transmitting recreations of the early days of vaudeville into the living rooms of the United States. The content of popular cultural
entertainment had changed little since the 19th century. Only the delivery system had
changed.

Red Scare

During the early 1950s, House and Senate committees that investigated the alleged
infiltration of Communists into the movie industry (see Chapter 9) also scrutinized
television and radio. Their search was greatly aided in June 1950 by the right-wing
publication *Red Channels*, which listed the names of some 150 radio and television industry personnel who were accused of being either sympathetic to or associated with
the Communist movement. Many people on the list found themselves suddenly out of
work and their careers destroyed as a fearful industry took the easy way out to avoid
controversy. Many network executives referred to the list to see if certain performers,
writers, and directors were "acceptable" for use in their programs. **Blacklisting** was
now a fact of life in the broadcasting industry. Some of the better-known names cited
were actors Orson Welles, Howard Duff, and Edward G. Robinson; composer Aaron
Copland; musicians Leonard Bernstein, Burl Ives, and Lena Horne; and radio–
television newsmen William L. Shirer and Howard K. Smith. Smith was listed because
a Communist newspaper had praised his reporting of a particular news event. While
many feel that broadcasters have an important role in society, this segment of society

vaudeville _____

blacklisting

Marginal Terms

Marginal terms run along side the text to
reinforce concepts and to provide land-
marks to use when studying the chapter.

Boxes

All boxed material is now presented according to themes: *Media Literacy* boxes connect the concepts to real
world events; *Media Watch* boxes detail actions and reactions of media practitioners; *Profile* boxes introduce
important media people; and *How It Works* boxes, found in the media chapters, give glimpses into the
media industries.

Box 2.1
MEDIA LITERACY
Popular Culture and Mass Media Myths about Romantic Love by Dr. Mary-Lou Galician

Dr. FUN!'s Mass Media Love Quiz is based on
the research of Dr. FUN!—otherwise known as
Dr. Mary-Lou Galician of Arizona State University. This material is copyrighted and all rights are
reserved. Test yourself: Answer True or False to each
statement to indicate your own personal belief.

1. Your perfect partner is cosmically predestined
for you and nothing/nobody can ultimately separate you.
2. There is such a thing as "love-at-first-sight."
3. Your true "soulmate" should KNOW what you're
thinking or feeling (without your having to tell).
4. If your partner is truly meant for you, sex is easy
and wonderful.
5. The man should NOT be shorter, weaker, younger,
poorer, or less successful than the woman.
6. To attract and keep a man, a woman should look

recordings and the radio, advertising, and even the
news—so we shouldn't feel too badly if we wind up
with some unrealistic expectations. Remember: Mass
media rely on simplification, distortions of reality, and
dramatic symbols and stereotypes to communicate their
messages.

Unfortunately, "false-love" images and scripts of
coupleship put pressure on BOTH women and men—
to measure up to *Playboy* centerfolds and Prince
Charmings. Some media-constructed unrealistic expectations can even lead to depression and other dysfunctions, several can be downright dangerous. So it's smart
to become aware and change our unhealthy views.

With this in mind, let's look more closely at the
mass media myths in my quiz:

1. A partner who is "perfect" would be less than fully
human, but media myths glorify the unrealistically
ideal. While you're seeking your one-and-only Mr.

Box 6.3
HOW IT WORKS
Book Publishing

A lot happens between the time a writer signs a
contract to publish a book and the moment a
finished product reaches a bookstore. The
process can take 18 months or longer and involve many
people. Although the process varies depending on the
size and clout of the publishing house, here is what usually happens.

First, an *author* must contact an acquisitions editor.
The author usually has an outline or overview of the
book and some sample chapters. Sometimes an agent
does the contacting and negotiates a contract.

The *acquisitions editor's* job is to look for potential
authors and work out contract agreements. Contracts
usually call for an advance and a percentage of the
book's sales to be paid to the author. The acquisitions
editor also manages one or more "lists" of books in a
particular discipline or area, overseeing projects and
making sure books are proceeding as planned.

The *production editor* manages the book during the
various stages of production, which include copyediting, design, typesetting, proofreading, and printing.
Usually the book is typeset and printed by outside
firms.

The *marketing department* is responsible for advertising the book and getting reviews for promotional
purposes. Marketing activities include writing advertising, catalog, and back-cover promotion copy; developing thematic promotion campaigns for books; and
getting authors booked for lectures or guest appearances
on television and radio talk shows.

The *fulfillment department* is responsible for getting
the book to bookstores and making sure additional
copies are printed when supplies run low. In the case of
textbooks, sales representatives are responsible for visiting schools or college instructors and telling them
about the book.

Box 16.2
MEDIA WATCH
Violence and Popular Music

The popularity of rap music did not diminish during the final years of the 20th century. This, despite the fact that many organizations and public
figures had been protesting the violent and abusive
content of many of the songs. For example, a variety of
police, politicians, and community leaders have expressed anger at the popular gangsta recordings and
videos that they say show youths and young adults, predominantly African Americans, rapping about shooting police officers, drinking large bottles of beer,
smoking marijuana, carrying guns, and treating women
in an abusive manner. They claim that young fans of
such recording artists as Tupac Shakur, Snoop Doggy
Dogg, DRS, Eazy-E, Ultramagnetic MCs, and Mista
Grimm are exposed to negative and one-sided images
of African-American life.

Although the rappers defend their work by saying
they are rapping only about what is happening in the
street, African-American leaders claimed the music
reflects only a small percentage of African-American
life and the recordings and videos distort the black
experience and reflect on it negatively. Leaders in the
Inglewood (California)–based organization Stop
the Violence–Increase the Peace Foundation claim
the videos are making heroes out of gang members.
Parents claim the music is undoing years of good child
rearing.

Executives at MTV, BET, and The Box claimed the
controversy was just a fabrication and young viewers are
smart enough to distinguish between music the rap and
real life. They passed it off as just being "show business."
However, as the controversy intensified, the three cable

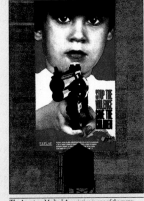

*The American Medical Association is one of the many
organizations expressing concern that violence in the
media—from radio and recordings to movies and
television—is a serious public health issue, similar to
smoking and drunk driving.*

Box 5.4
PROFILE
Philanthropist Ted Turner   Doing What He Enjoys

One billion dollars. That's what media mogul
Ted Turner pledged in 1997 to create a new
foundation to benefit United Nations causes,
such as cleaning up land mines around the world, helping refugees in war-torn nations, and fighting disease
and hunger. Turner's pledge was to donate $100 million
in stock every year for 10 years.

In making the announcement, Turner expressed
pride that the money was going to "the poorest people
in the world, the people who need it the most." It was
obvious that Turner didn't need it. When he made the
announcement of the grant, Turner said his net worth
at the start of 1997 was $2.2 billion, but added that a
surge in his stock in Time Warner during the next nine
months had boosted his worth to $3.2 billion.

While Rupert Murdoch may be one of the most
powerful media moguls on earth, he certainly has competition from this Southern media baron who has developed his own media empire, making it one of the
largest in the world with the 1996 merger with Time
Warner. This competition has also developed into a
very strong media rivalry. Sportsman and media mogul
Ted Turner was the uncontested king of cable television
during the latter part of the 20th century. The four-time
Yachtsman of the Year and 1977 winner of the Americas Cup yacht race is the owner of the Atlanta Braves
and the Atlanta Hawks, as well as Turner Broadcasting
System, Inc., until its merger with Time Warner.

Turner's venture into cable television began when
he purchased Atlanta television station WTBS and
turned it into a superstation by expanding its range via
satellite and cable TV. After Warner-Amex beat him to

*Cable tycoon Ted Turner is said to be worth
billions and he's now becoming a philanthropist.*

to broadcast via satellite from Baghdad, Iraq, primed
the all-news network for the Gulf war. When war broke
out and the United States began bombing Baghdad,
CNN newsmen Bernard Shaw, John Holliman, and Peter Arnett were on hand to describe it live from the
window of a Baghdad hotel.

Independent TV stations and even CBS, ABC,
and NBC began carrying CNN reports and attributing
their war news to Ted Turner's "nitwork." The number
of CNN viewers skyrocketed, and the increased audience allowed the news network to raise its advertising
rates from $3,800 for a 30-second spot to $138,000. Ted
Turner wore that "I told you so" smile all the way to the
bank.

Resources for the Student

CD-ROM

Each new *Mass Media/Mass Culture* text comes with a free CD-ROM, *Making the Grade*, designed to help students master the material. *Making the Grade* includes these features:

* Study questions with feedback
* An Internet Primer
* A Guide to Electronic Research
* A Study Skills Primer
* Learning Assessment Tools

PowerWeb

AN ONLINE READER AND RESOURCE SITE.
Each new book also comes with a passcard to a website made available in partnership with Dushkin/McGraw-Hill, publisher of the popular *Annual Editions* series. The site includes:

* Articles on mass communication issues, refereed by content experts
* Real-time news on mass communication topics
* Weekly course updates
* Interactive exercises and assessment tools
* Student study tips
* Web research tips and exercises
* Refereed and updated research links
* Daily news
* Access to the Northernlight.com's Special Collection of journals and articles

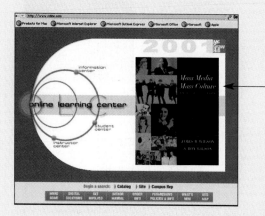

Online Learning Center

In direct support of *Mass Media/Mass Culture*, *5th edition*, students will find these additional resources at www.mhhe.com/wilson:

* More self-test questions
* A message board
* Chapter summaries
* The chapter, "The Selling of American Politics" (revisions will follow the 2000 election)
* An online glossary
* A media journal
* INTERLINK: A Guide to the Internet for Mass Communication Students

Resources for Instructors

Resources

To facilitate teaching the course, the following supplements are available:
- An Instructor's Manual with Test Questions, written by James Wilson
- Computerized Test Questions
- The McGraw-Hill Video
- Text-specific website, the *Online Learning Center*, includes:
    Teaching material from the Instructor's Manual
    PowerPoint slides
    A video guide to relate McGraw-Hill videos to text chapters

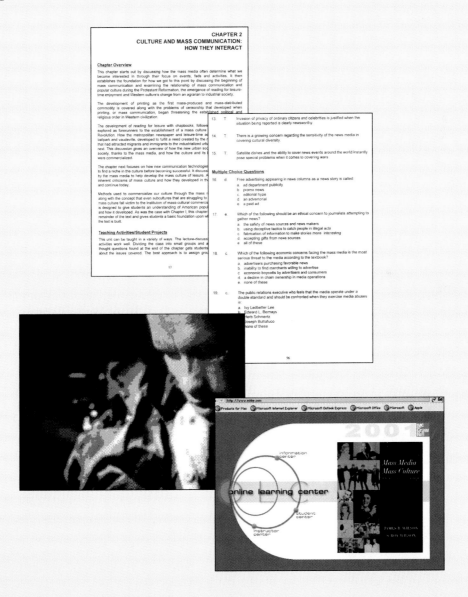

Preface

ORGANIZATION OF THE BOOK

This new edition of *Mass Media/Mass Culture* is organized into four sections:

The first section, *Culture and Communication*, is designed to give readers an overview of the basic definitions, concepts, forms of journalistic communication, and legal parameters necessary to establish the foundation for a study of the interrelationship of media and culture.

Chapter 1, *Culture and Communication: Basic Concepts*, defines and explains popular culture, the communication process and the EPS (media progression) cycle. It includes discussions of such terms as gatekeeping, agenda setting, and information processing.

Chapter 2, *Culture and Mass Communication: How They Interact*, reviews the impact of mass communication on our culture since the introduction of movable type by Gutenberg in the fifteenth century. Rapid changes in mass culture since the Industrial Revolution are highlighted, as are modern-day cultural impacts and trends.

Chapter 3, *Globalization of Information on the World Wide Web*, reviews the development of the Internet from an historical perspective. It also examines the impact of the Internet on other mass media and takes a look at the international problems that have been created by the World Wide Web and its infiltration into our global cultures.

Chapter 4, *Legal Controls on the Media*, examines the various laws and regulations that attempt to control media operations in the United States. These controls are examined in the context of the importance of the First Amendment to our American democracy and current trends in libel case judgments.

Chapter 5, *The News Media: Keeping the Culture Informed*, discusses the role and responsibilities of the news media in an informed society. It discusses the styles and problems of journalists in gathering and disseminating news and information. It also discusses the four theories of the press that have been operating throughout the world since the beginning of mass communication.

The second section, *Development of Print Media*, begins a chapter-by-chapter look at the mass media by focusing on the oldest forms of mass communication: the print media.

Chapter 6, *Books: The Permanent Medium*, explores the development of the most permanent medium, books. It traces the medium from early clay tablets to today's mass market paperbacks and specialized publications. It also focuses on the impact books have had on Western civilization, as well as on the historical evolution of censorship. Book publishing of the future is examined by looking at some of the new technological changes on the horizon. As in all media chapters, the interrelationship of books and culture is discussed.

Chapter 7, *Newspapers: Past, Present and Future*, examines the historical development of newspapers and then focuses on the conflict between the need for the industry to make money and its historical obligation in a free society to keep people informed. The chapter also looks at potential changes that are on the horizon for newspapers as the electronic revolution expands. Highlighted in this chapter is a discussion on how our changing culture is impacting this medium.

Chapter 8, *Magazines: The Specialized Medium*, examines the evolution of magazine publishing and how magazines have found a niche in our culture by serving highly specialized interests. The rapid expansion of new magazines in the 1980s and the changes that have occurred in the 1990s are also examined. The chapter also looks at some technological changes that are occurring in the industry and how our culture has been impacted by the ever-changing field of magazines.

The third section, *Development of Electronic Media*, moves the reader into the era of phenomenal changes resulting from the development of the electronic media in the late 19th century and throughout the 20th century.

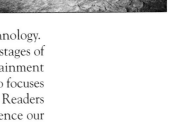

Chapter 9, *Motion Pictures: Cultural Reflections*, begins this electronic media examination by tracing the development of motion pictures from Edison's mechanical kinetoscope to today's special effects wizardry first introduced by George Lucas and Steven Spielberg and made possible by our new computerized culture. It also examines the new market in video games that the movie industry is developing as a result of interactive television technology.

Chapter 10, *Radio: A Wireless Wonder*, describes the three very different stages of radio's development: ship-to-shore communication; a popular home entertainment medium, and finally a specialized medium for music and talk. The chapter also focuses on the new political phenomenon of talk radio. Digital radio is also explored. Readers of this chapter will learn about the versatility of radio and its ability to influence our culture while at the same time making its own adaptations to our cultural changes.

Chapter 11, *Recorded Music: Powerful and Controversial*, explores the role of popular music and the recording industry in our culture and examines the controversies that have surrounded the mass medium since the jazz era of the 1920s. It also discusses the cyclical changes in the musical genre of rock and roll and the technological revolution being created by digital sound.

Chapter 12, *Television: From Soaps to Satellites*, concludes the electronic media section with a discussion of the evolution and cultural impacts of television, one of our most pervasive and influential mass media. It looks at this medium historically as well as from the viewpoint of its impact on our culture. Also discussed is the future of television as we develop high definition television, digital compression, virtual reality, holography, and the merger of computers and television which will give us a new era of interactive TV. The efforts of government to regulate TV content through such things as the V-Chip and the industry's reaction by adopting a controversial rating system are also explored.

The next section of this book, *Media Shapers, Ethics, and Consequences*, moves from individual looks at mass media to other industries that use the mass media to deliver their messages and shape our culture. It is also designed to bring the study of mass communication to a close by examining ethical issues involving the media, research on the cultural impacts of the media and the consequences of media practices on our culture.

Chapter 13, *Advertising: Selling the Message*, discusses the historical development of the advertising industry and the current-day trends. It examines various theories of advertising effectiveness and also looks at propaganda devices used in advertising, the area of motivational research, including values and lifestyle (VALS) research, and the controversy of subliminal imbeds in ads. The impacts of advertising on our culture are highlighted.

Chapter 14, *Public Relations: Creating an Image*, explores how public relations has evolved since the nineteenth century and how Freudian psychology has played a role in developing such controversial PR campaigns as making smoking acceptable for women. Modern professional PR practices are described and contrasted with early-day press agentry. The chapter also focuses on a number of current problems and the development of the importance of crisis management public relations.

Chapter 15, *Media Ethics*, deals with the growing concern of ethical decision making in the mass media. The chapter examines ethical decisions in reporting the news, the conflicts that often arise when economic interests interfere with media content, and ethical concerns in developing entertainment content. The controversies of entertainment content in television and the recording industry are highlighted in this chapter.

Chapter 16, *Media Research, Effects and Consequences*, concludes the book with a look at historical research on media effects and current studies and concerns. The raging debates about violence on television and in recorded music and in "gangsta" rap music videos are also discussed. The chapter concludes with a discussion of the cultural consequences of the mass media and how we as consumers of the media must be concerned about the content of the mass media as we move into the information age.

In addition to these chapters, the popular chapter *The Selling of American Politics* is available to students on the Internet. This chapter will be updated immediately following the presidential election of 2000.

ACKNOWLEDGMENTS

In developing this fifth edition of *Mass Media/Mass Culture*, we have become indebted to many people. Contributors Mary-Lou Galician, Walter Cronkite School of Journalism and Telecommunications, Arizona State University, Internet webmaster J. Gregory Wilson and long-time television newsman Dennis Hart are thanked for bringing their expertise to these pages in guest boxed inserts. Reviewers, Larry Foley, Walter J. Lemke Department of Journalism, University of Arkansas; Mary-Lou Galician, Walter Cronkite School of Journalism and Telecommunications, Arizona State University (also a contributor); Lynn Hinds, Perley Issac Reed School of Journalism, West Virginia University; Maria B. Marron, Southwest Texas State University; David C. Martin, California State University, Sacramento; Sarah Projansky, University of California, Davis; Thimios Zaharopoulos, Pittsburgh State University; Robert D. West, Kent State University; Frank Nevius, Western Oregon University; Judy House, College of the Sequoias; Elizabeth Jean Nelson, University of Minnesota, Duluth; William Tillinghast, San Jose State University; Maclyn McClary, Humbolt State University; John Fiske, University of Wisconsin, Madison; Ronald D. Gordon, University of Hawaii, Hilo; Jules d'Hemecourt, Louisiana State University; and Ralph Carmode, Jacksonville State University, are given special thanks for making many of the suggested changes that have gone into improving this edition.

And lastly, special thanks must go to the many students who have given us feedback on previous editions and encouragement and ideas to compile this revised edition. It is for them and those who follow that this book is written.

Jim Wilson
Roy Wilson

Brief Contents

Contents

Culture and Communication

Development of the Print Media

Chapter **6**
Books: The Permanent Medium 128

Chapter 7

Newspapers: Past, Present, and Future   156

Chapter 8
Magazines: The Specialized Medium   188

Development of Electronic Media

Chapter 10
Radio: A Wireless Wonder   250

Chapter 11
Recorded Music: Powerful and
Controversial   274

Chapter 12
Television: From Soaps to Satellites   306

*Media Shapers, Ethics,
and Consequences*

Chapter 14
Public Relations: Creating an Image 374

1

Culture and Communication

Culture and Communication

Basic Concepts

Communication is mankind's most important single act. When improperly performed it turns friends into enemies and plunges nations into wars.

—**Anonymous**

The tragic killings at Columbine High School and at other schools during the latter days of the 20th century created a great deal of discussion about violence in the media and the need for more media literacy (a term used to describe better understandings of the impacts of the media on our society). ● Were the media guilty of emphasizing violence and downplaying moral values? ● Was violence on TV and in the movies, along with violent lyrics in popular music and the killing themes of computer games causing some youngsters to grow up warped and insensitive to the value of human life? Was more teaching needed to help youngsters distinguish between reality and fantasy in the media? ● These and other questions generated by the shootings on school campuses across the nation led to much debate over the role of the media in our society. Are the media at fault, or are they merely scapegoats for something more fundamentally wrong with our society? This is just one reason that media literacy is so important in our society and why academic studies of the interrelationship between the media and our popular culture have become so important. ● But not all of the influences of the mass media in our society are alarming and causes for concern. Many of them are subtle influences that help determine who we are and what we do. Stop and ask yourself why you have a particular hairstyle or wear certain brands of clothing. Or ask yourself why the Super Bowl became one of the biggest mass-media events in our popular culture or how rock and roll became such an important form of music in our culture. The answers to these questions and many more may be found by studying American popular culture and its interrelationship with the mass media. Before we begin our study of this relationship, however, it is important for us to define some basic terms that will be used throughout this book.

CULTURE

First, let's consider the word *culture*. Some see culture as synonymous with fine art and other "highbrow" activities and interests. However, anthropologists define culture as everything that occurs in a society—all of the customs and practices handed down from generation to generation. These contributions usually come from formal institutions, such as churches, the government, and, increasingly, the media; mores, or standards of behavior; laws; and conventional practices and customs. In this book, we will use the anthropological definition of culture.

Elite Culture

In early times there were distinct differences between the culture of the elite (the rich and ruling classes) and the culture of the common person. The *elite culture* is sometimes referred to as "high culture." During the Middle Ages a caste system kept the culture of the elite separate from the folk culture of the peasants. The elite culture consisted of fine art, literature, and classical music. Folk culture consisted of street carnivals, tavern drinking, and folktales. People who participated in the elite culture could also enjoy the folk culture, but the reverse was not true. Although some elite culture exists today, ordinary people can at least observe some of it on TV shows featuring the "rich and famous" and in the supermarket tabloids, which often feature the British royal family and celebrities such as American developer Donald Trump.

Popular Culture

Popular culture, or pop culture, can be defined as the culture of everyone in a society. Pop culture scholar Ray B. Browne defined it as the cultural world around us, that is, our attitudes, habits, and actions: how we act and why we act; what we eat and wear; our buildings, roads, and means of travel; our entertainment and sports; our politics, religion, and medical practices; our beliefs and activities and what shapes and controls them. In other words, it is to us what water is to fish: It is the world we live in.[1]

As the fish analogy suggests, our popular culture can be so pervasive that we seldom notice it. To do so, we must step back and consciously observe all the objects in our society and ask ourselves why we idolize the things we do, why we buy the things we do, and why we believe in the things we do (see Box 1.1).

In the 19th century, the distinction between elite and folk culture began to blur following the development of political democracy, public education of the masses, and the Industrial Revolution, which ushered in the era of popular or *mass culture*. The term *popular culture* was developed in the 19th century to replace the term *folk culture*.

Throughout history, every society has had its own popular culture. Most of today's popular culture is mass-produced and is disseminated through the mass media. Popular music, cheap paperback novels, soap operas, videocassette movies, and a myriad of advertised products from designer jeans to disposable razors make up our everyday environment. Stephen King novels, Levi's jeans, and McDonald's golden arches are instantly recognizable symbols or icons of contemporary pop culture.*

---

*Even today, however, we can see the remnants of the elite culture. Going to the movies is participating in the popular culture, but attending the opera is deemed elite. A Pablo Picasso painting is part of the elite culture, whereas a poster of Brad Pitt is a pop culture artifact. Bowling is a leisure activity of the popular culture, while polo is definitely a part of the elite culture. Golf and tennis are now pop culture activities in areas with public courses and courts, but they were once exclusively elite. Television exposure of golf and tennis events helped to expand their popularity among the masses and soon there were demands for public facilities.

As we begin the 21st century, the study of popular culture on college and university campuses has continued to grow. Such topics as the messages found in MTV videos, television programs, movies, comic books, detective novels, and rock and roll music have been rigorously examined in many academic settings. Many additional courses explore the relationship of the mass media to popular culture.

It has been estimated that more than 2,000 students a year have been enrolling in popular culture classes. At Bowling Green State University in Ohio, students can earn degrees in popular culture. The study of MTV videos has been the subject of a course at California State University, Los Angeles. There are even professional organizations, such as the Popular Culture Association (PCA) and the American Culture Association (ACA), that attract some 3,000 members to annual conventions where such papers as "The Reconciliation of Archie and Meathead, *All in the Family's* Last Episode" and "The Tupperware Party and the American Dream" are presented.

In the early years, many academics looked down on pop culture, believing the study of everyday culture was not appropriate in a university setting where students examined Western civilization, philosophy, and the sciences. Supporters of the study of popular culture point out that it is part of our history and holds as much relevance as war, slavery, and revolutions. They note that by examining the themes and styles of a culture, we can better understand the values of the people.

Mass Culture

Because of the mass mediation of our popular culture, another term, *mass culture*, has evolved. This refers to the things in our popular culture that are mass-produced or shared through the mass media. In America today, that represents almost everything in our popular culture. It is so difficult to think of anything in our modern popular culture that isn't either mass-produced or promoted in the mass media that the terms *mass culture* and *popular culture* have come to be used almost interchangeably.

Media Literacy

Another important term in our studies is media literacy, which refers to the need for the consumer of media content to be aware of the impacts of the media on our culture. Studies have shown that Americans spend more time with the media than they do eating, sleeping, and participating in family activities. To be media literate a person should know who creates the content for the media, what the purpose of that content is, what effects the media have on our society, the **role of the consumer** in the mass-communication process, and, perhaps most importantly, how the media have evolved from their beginnings to their place in today's world culture.

role of consumer

THE EPS CYCLE

Throughout this book, we will refer to a concept known as the *media progression cycle* which describes how new mass media get adopted in our culture. The concept was developed by mass-communication scholars John Merrill and Ralph Lowenstein, who in 1971 first pointed out that media usually develop in three stages.[2] The definitions

Box 1.2
MEDIA WATCH
Is the EPS Cycle Heading Back to the Elite Stage?

Specialization, the third stage of the EPS cycle, is rapidly taking over the mass media in American culture. Futurist Alvin Toffler calls this phenomenon the "demassification of the mass media." But it can also be very expensive.

Along with this specialization has come increased costs to the consumer. A specialized magazine today costs many times more than the magazines of yesteryear, and their numbers are countless. The price of admission to a motion picture theater is also much higher today. How much will we pay to read a book if it becomes necessary to purchase a computer and compact disks to read one (see Chapter 6)? Television was a once free entertainment medium when it was limited to the popular stage of the EPS cycle. All you needed was a TV set and an antenna. Today the specialized programming available on television can be very costly. You must either purchase a satellite dish to pick up signals and then pay a descrambling fee or pay a cable company for programming that generally costs anywhere from $20 to $40 per month—more if you add the premium channels. These costs are expected to increase dramatically when we begin taking advantage of the many interactive-TV options available.

Interactive TV has tremendous potential to accelerate learning for youngsters and make adults much better informed and more knowledgeable citizens. Does this mean we may be headed back to a distinct caste system with definite economic and social differences between the elite and popular cultures? Will a tremendous knowledge gap separate rich and poor in the new information age? This appears to be the case as studies in this country and around the world indicate a divide between those who have computers and those who don't. One might argue that the EPS cycle is cyclical and that it might be better described as the EPSE cycle.

---

media progression cycle

of elite and popular culture discussed earlier will help you understand the three stages of the **media progression cycle** known as the elitist–popular–specialized (EPS) cycle.

A mass communication medium usually starts out in the elite stage. Here the media appeal to, and are consumed by, the affluent leaders in the culture. After a nation breaks through the barriers of poverty and illiteracy, its media enter the popular stage and are enjoyed by the mass culture. Eventually, as the elements of higher education, affluence, leisure time, and population growth coalesce, the mass media begin to enter a third stage of the EPS cycle: specialization. In this stage the media are consumed by highly fragmented segments of the population, each with its own interests and cultural activities. While media in the United States are entering the stage of **specialization**, in many underdeveloped nations the media are still in the elite stage of the EPS cycle (see Box 1.2).

specialization

The United States was the first nation in which all of the factors necessary for specialization converged. During the latter half of the 20th century, the American mass media have made great strides toward specialization. Futurist Alvin Toffler describes this trend as the "demassification of the mass media," and he believes it will continue as we complete our move from the industrial age to the information age.[3] Although all American media are beginning to specialize in one form or another, magazines have been the most specialized medium for the longest period of time (see Chapter 8). We will look at the EPS cycle again when we begin our examination of individual mass media.

@ **Practicing Media Literacy**

Do you think we're headed back to a distinct caste system with definite economic and social differences between the elite and popular cultures?

This painting by Renaissance artist Pieter Brueghel the Elder, The Peasant Dance, was intended for the elite culture but portrays some of the customs of the folk culture during that period.

THE COMMUNICATION PROCESS

Now that we have a common understanding of these terms, let's examine how the communication process, and mass communication in particular, works.

Communication can be defined simply as the process by which individuals share information, ideas, and attitudes. A key word in this definition is *share*, which means to give or receive a part of something or to enjoy or assume something in common. Some people use the term *send* rather than *share* when they discuss the communication process. However, sending merely implies transmitting a message with little concern for the person receiving it, whereas sharing implies that the source and the receiver are actively working together for common understanding.

You will also note that we call communication a process, because communication is ongoing and dynamic. The communication process encompasses various components that interact with one another, causing specific consequences. For example, what information, ideas, and attitudes are shared, how much is shared, when they are shared, and what tools are used to share them are all variables in the process.

Types of Communication

Various types of communication exist. Intrapersonal communication describes a person talking to himself or herself. In interpersonal communication, two or three people talk with one another in close physical proximity. In group communication, groups of people communicate with one another in face-to-face encounters. In mass communication, professional communicators use technological devices known as mass media to communicate over great distances to influence large audiences.

Several basic components make up the communication process. While these components can be presented in a variety of diagrams or models, our basic model includes the source, the message, the channel, and the **receiver** (see Figure 1.1).

Source

The source (sometimes called the sender, communicator, or encoder) is the person who shares information, ideas, or attitudes with another person. The writers of this textbook are sharing their ideas on the definition of the term *source* with you. The message is being disseminated to you through the process of mass communication—in this case, book publishing.

In mass communication, the source is usually a professional communicator who shapes the message to be shared. He or she might be a newspaper or television reporter or an entertainer who must gather material or ideas and then share them with the audience.

Message

The message is whatever the source attempts to share with someone else. It originates with an idea, which then must be encoded into symbols that will be used to express that idea.

symbols

Symbols are words, pictures, or objects that the source uses to elicit meaning in the mind of the receiver of the message. Words and pictures are the most common symbols used in communication. Words attempt to describe an object or a concept, while pictures actually show a representation of the object or idea. When giving some friends directions on how to find your home, you might use words to identify the directions they should follow and the various cross-streets they need to look for. Or, if you preferred, you could draw them a map.

Selecting symbols for an idea or an object is a very important step in the communication process because poorly selected symbols will result in a confusing or misunderstood message. Care must be taken to choose symbols that will elicit responses in the mind of the message receiver that are similar to those the source intended.

When communicators select symbols for their messages, they must keep in mind that each person has a different frame of reference and, as a result, certain symbols may mean different things to different people. A frame of reference (sometimes called field of experience) is the set of individual experiences each person possesses; no two people have exactly the same experiences.

Each experience or event in our lives leaves some sort of impression on us, and we use the accumulation of these experiences to give meaning and interpretation to symbols. For example, a person who was the victim of a crime will respond differently than a street gang member to the message "The police are coming." These

FIGURE 1.1

Communication model

different reactions are based on the meanings given to the word *police* that have developed as a result of the individual experiences.

Although we primarily use words and pictures to send our messages, we also communicate in other ways. Facial expressions, gestures, and body language can effectively send messages. For example, a television newscaster might report on the president's new deficit-reduction package by stating only the facts about the plan, while his facial expression or tone of voice reveals his biases against the plan.

Channel

The channel is the way we send our message. In interpersonal communication we use the senses of sight, sound, and touch to communicate messages. These are our channels. In mass communication such technological devices as books, newspapers, magazines, movies, radio, recordings, and television are our communication channels.

Mass communication differs from interpersonal communication in that its messages must be moved over greater distances. This movement is achieved through the use of technological devices. Radio and television messages are transmitted electronically, while newspaper and magazine messages are reproduced on high-speed presses and distributed through the mails or via carriers.

Today, however, even some print media messages are transmitted electronically. Wire services send news via satellite, and *USA Today* transmits the entire contents of the newspaper by satellite to printing plants around the country and to other parts of the world. By the mid-1990s, many newspapers, radio stations, and television stations across the nation were also making news available on the Internet.

Receiver

The receiver (sometimes called the destination, audience, or decoder) in the communication process is the person with whom the message is intended to be shared. Without a receiver, there is no communication. In fact, if any one of the above four communication components is missing, no communication will occur. To properly share your message, you must also be sure that the receiver is listening and is understanding what you have to communicate.

Just because a story is carried in a newspaper or broadcast over radio or television does not mean everyone has received the message. If some people do not read the story or pay attention to the broadcast, it has not been communicated to them.

The receiver in mass communication is usually a large audience that is often referred to as the masses. Because of the audience's size and diversity, mass communication requires careful choices of symbols that will elicit similar interpretations among receivers, each of whom has a different frame of reference.

Can you guess from Dan Rather's facial expression and clothing what type of news he is reporting?

Feedback

If the receiver or audience in the communication process transmits back to the source an observable response to the message, a component called feedback has been added. Feedback enables the source to determine if the message was correctly understood and, if it wasn't, to modify it (see Figure 1.2).

Feedback can take many forms. It can consist of words, gestures, facial expressions, or any other observable element. A person making a pass at an attractive member of the opposite sex, for example, might get a clear message to "get lost" without a word being spoken.

Feedback is absent, or at best very much delayed, in mass communication. This makes mass communication much more difficult than face-to-face communication. Messages in mass communication must be clearly constructed because there is seldom a chance to restate their meaning. It is true that if a newspaper story is erroneously interpreted or misunderstood, people will write letters to the editor, and if a broadcaster's statement is incorrectly perceived, the station may get irate telephone calls. However, such feedback comes too late to do much good.

Noise

Certain additional factors, called communication noise, can complicate the communication process. Three examples of this are channel noise, semantic noise, and psychological noise.

Channel noise refers to external interference in the communication process. The message doesn't make it through as sent. You might be listening to your car radio when, all of a sudden, a large blast of static blocks out your talk-show host's message or the lyrics of a song. This is a case of channel noise in mass communication. Other examples of channel noise are print that is too small, a voice that is too soft, or a picture that is blurred.

Semantic noise occurs when you clearly hear the message but can't understand it. For example, what if you heard on the radio that someone had just found a Polyphemus moth or that one of your civic leaders had a case of hyperbilirubinemia? Chances are you would not clearly interpret the message. This communication would suffer from semantic noise.

When semantic noise occurs, the message gets through as sent but you don't understand what it means. Symbols causing semantic noise do not have to be long, multisyllabic words such as those used above. If a receiver of the message does not have a background in electricity, for example, he or she may find *ohm* and *watt* just as confusing as *hyperbilirubinemia*.

Semantic noise can occur even when we know the other person is familiar with the symbol we have selected. We must remember that words evoke mental pictures in the minds of both the source and the receiver. For example, if a newspaper article mentions that a dog seriously injured a child, the reporter might have had a German shepherd in mind. However, the story can lead to misunderstanding if the receiver of the message, who has read numerous stories describing attacks on humans by pit bull terriers, automatically pictures a pit bull when reading the story. Or perhaps the reader owns a dachshund and pictures her pet when reading the word *dog*.

Semantic noise can also occur when a word takes on connotations or emotional meanings that are based on experiences rather than on the word's dictionary meaning. Take the words *liberal* and *conservative*. These words mean different things to different people, based on individual political points of view. In America, a

FIGURE 1.2

Communication process with feedback

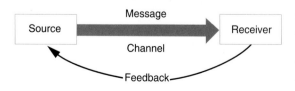

conservative is one who favors the status quo and resists change. Conservatives also have long been anticommunists. Thus, when the news media began referring to the hard-liners in the former Soviet Union who fought reform and wanted to preserve communism as "conservatives," many American conservatives squirmed.

The mass media also run into problems with semantic noise when reporters get caught up in the jargon of the beats they are covering. Government and education are two areas in which jargon is used extensively. When a reporter quotes the city manager as saying that the city has a "long-range strategic plan to interface the environmental negative declaration process with the private sector," the reader may quickly turn to the sports pages. Mass communicators must interpret ideas and information and select clearly understandable symbols to transmit that information to the masses. In other words, they must constantly guard against semantic noise.

Psychological noise refers to internal factors that lead to misunderstandings in the communication process. People try to protect themselves in three ways from information they might find offensive: selective exposure, selective perception, and selective retention. The concept of psychological noise comes from consistency theory research that found that people usually prefer to seek out information and ideas that are consistent with their beliefs, attitudes, and behavior and tend to avoid information that is inconsistent.

psychological noise

Selective exposure holds that, as a general rule, we expose ourselves to information that reinforces rather than contradicts our beliefs or opinions. For example, Republicans are far more likely than Democrats to watch a Republican candidate on television. Selective exposure also helps to explain why people with extreme political views have difficulty getting their ideas across to the general public: The audience just "tunes them out."

selective exposure

One of the most colorful episodes in American journalism in the 20th century, the flourishing of the underground press movement during the 1960s, clearly demonstrates this phenomenon. Various countercultural groups expressed a frustration that the establishment press was not telling people about their ideas, such as opposition to the war in Vietnam, "blissful" experiences with psychedelic drugs, and the joys of sexual freedom. So, in an effort to get their message out to the masses, many of these countercultural movements started up alternative, "underground" newspapers.

> **@ Practicing Media Literacy**
> Can you think of instances in your own life where psychological noise hindered communication?

After a few years, the messages were still failing to reach the masses, and the underground press movement started to decline. The reason was selective exposure: The only people reading the newspapers were those who already subscribed to the philosophy of the counterculture.

The second kind of psychological noise is **selective perception**: We tend to see, hear, and believe only what we want to see, hear, and believe. As the late Canadian philosopher Marshall McLuhan pointed out, "Everyone has his own set of goggles," and we all think that what we see with our set of goggles is what everyone else sees. The Swiss biologist and psychologist Jean Piaget, who was influential in 20th-century educational philosophy, called this phenomenon *autistic thinking* and defined *autism* as "thought in which truth is confused with desire."

selective perception

Many studies have demonstrated selective perception at work. One involved showing people an editorial cartoon from a northern newspaper ridiculing the Ku Klux Klan; the cartoon was repeatedly interpreted as pro-Klan when shown to southern Klan sympathizers.

A classic example of selective perception appeared in the early 1970s when television producer Norman Lear introduced the bigot Archie Bunker to American television audiences in the situation comedy *All in the Family*. Bunker's prejudices were reflected in a number of controversial topics, including sex, religion, and racism, that had previously been considered taboo on prime-time television. The character of Archie Bunker was designed to satirize American bigotry. But the result was Archie Bunker fan clubs and Archie Bunker T-shirts proclaiming America's number-one television bigot a folk hero. Many people thought what Archie said was true and thus failed to see the satire underlying the message.

selective retention

Selective retention is the third basic psychological defense. It means that we tend to remember those things that reinforce our beliefs better than those that oppose them. For example, try to remember some good things about someone you dislike, or try to come up with a list of faults for someone you really idolize. Chances are you will remember mostly bad things about your enemies and good things about your idols.

By now you should see that the communication process is more complicated than our initial simple definition indicated. Let's now consider a more comprehensive definition that attempts to recognize some of the complexities we have covered:

> @   **Practicing Media Literacy**
> Can you think of any leading television characters who might project a negative image to some people?

> **COMMUNICATION** is a process involving the sorting, selecting, and sharing of symbols to help a receiver elicit from his or her own mind a meaning similar to that in the mind of the communicator.

Television bigot Archie Bunker, as played by Carroll O'Connor (r), became a folk hero because of the controversial topics he frequently argued with his liberal son-in-law, Michael (the Meathead) as played by Rob Reiner. While the character of Archie was designed to satarize bigotry, many felt that he was speaking for them—even though by the end of the show, Archie was often the butt of the joke.

MASS COMMUNICATION

We also need to define the more complex process of mass communication. As previously noted, mass communication consists of (1) professional communicators shaping and sharing messages, then (2) transmitting them over great distances using technological devices called mass media to (3) influence large audiences.

The word **influence** in the third part of this process refers to the effect the mass-communicated message has on the audience. This effect can be as simple as increasing a person's knowledge or understanding of an issue or event, such as explaining how a hurricane destroyed a town. Or the effect might consist of making people feel good after they watch a movie or television show. However, media effects can also be far more significant, such as changing a person's cultural attitudes and behavior.

influence

This latter, more complex effect causes many people to be disturbed by the mass media and their influences on our culture. Concern about excessive sex and violence in the media and explicit rock-music lyrics has generated a great deal of mass-media criticism in recent years. These issues will be discussed in more depth later in this book.

If we translate these factors in the process of mass communication into an operational definition, we might say:

> **MASS COMMUNICATION** is a process whereby professional communicators use technological devices to share messages over great distances to influence large audiences.

Channels of Mass Communication

The technological devices or mass media used to send messages over great distances include books, pamphlets, magazines, newspapers, direct-mail circulars, newsletters, radio, compact disks, audiotapes, television, motion pictures, videotapes, and computer networks.

You will note that we have not included telephones, stage plays, or rock concerts. One could certainly argue that telephones transmit messages over great distances and that long-running plays or huge rock concerts are seen by large audiences. Then why aren't they considered mass media? Let's examine each of these in relation to our definition of mass communication.

The telephone does use technological devices to transmit messages across great distances, but it does not reach large audiences. Instead, it usually transmits a one-on-one conversation and is an electronic extension of interpersonal communication. Although new technologies such as videoconferencing expand the size of the audience, the result is still not sufficient to fit the concept of a large mass-media audience.

Although stage plays and rock concerts use some technological devices (e.g., lighting and sound systems) to reach large audiences, such shows are limited to a confined area and thus do not transmit those messages over great distances. If these events are broadcast or if audiotapes or videotapes are made, the broadcast medium or the tapes become the mass medium, not the stage play or concert itself. The annual Comic Relief benefits for the homeless, for example, make an impact on our popular culture largely because they are shown on cable TV and later on individual television stations.

We must keep in mind one more thing about the media: The American mass media are businesses, and their purpose is to make a profit. If they don't, they go out of business. Collectively, the mass media in the United States comprise one of the country's largest industries. By the end of the 20th century, the industry generated an estimated income of more than $150 billion and employed more than one million people.

INFORMATION PROCESSING BY THE MEDIA

The importance of mass communication increases as we develop from children into adults. After early childhood, we learn very little firsthand. Once we learn to talk and then read, we start gathering information from secondhand sources: other people and, eventually, the mass media.

In our early education, television and textbooks become important sources for our secondhand information. Other media, such as newspapers and magazines, join them as we grow older. For example, we might know that terrorists have bombed a crowded air terminal or that a tornado has devastated a community, but we probably didn't experience this information firsthand. We relied on the secondhand sources—usually the mass media—to inform us. Because we depend on secondhand sources for information, the mass media play a major role in determining the content of our culture.

Gatekeeping

gatekeeping

One way the media control our access to news, information, and entertainment is through **gatekeeping**. This sociological term was coined in 1947 by Kurt Lewin, who used it to describe the fact that news must travel through a series of checkpoints (or gates) before it reaches the public.

The television network gatekeepers were faced with a dilemma when jurors in the civil trial against O.J. Simpson returned their verdict at the same time President Clinton was delivering his State of the Union address to Congress and the nation. Both stories had to be reported at the same time, but decisions had to be made as to which story received the top coverage.

The fifth Simpson verdict is in.
The jury has found OJ Simpson
DID commit battery against
Nicole Brown Simpson.
abc

In the gatekeeping process, numerous people make decisions as to whether or not we will see or hear a story or be exposed to a new musical or entertainment performer or group. A story about the United States shifting its policy toward a Middle Eastern country may or may not reach the American people, depending on decisions made by the gatekeepers. A group of rock musicians may or may not make it to the top of the charts, depending on decisions made by gatekeepers.

Let's take a hypothetical example of a change in policy by the president of the United States regarding a Middle Eastern country. Whether the American people learn about this shift in policy is not necessarily in the hands of the president. Government officials may issue a news release or hold a news conference announcing the change. However, a number of news media personnel must determine that the announcement is important before it is reported as a news story.

Before it appears in a newspaper, the news item must pass to the reporter as a news release or through a news conference. He or she then decides whether the item is important enough to be covered and how much coverage it should receive. If the reporter decides the item is important, he or she may rewrite the news release or write a story about the news conference or perhaps dictate the item over a telephone to a rewrite person at the newspaper. The rewrite person then functions as the next gate in evaluating the story's importance. Next, a copy editor edits the item and judges its importance. The story may also appear before additional gates—the national or international editors and perhaps the entire editorial board of the newspaper—before a determination is made as to if and where the story will run in the next edition.

Before this same story appears on radio or television, it must go through a similar set of gates: Writers, editors, and tape editors all make judgments as to what portions of the news conference will be aired. (In the case of television, if no videotape footage accompanies the news item, it might be stopped at this gate because television depends on visuals to keep the news interesting.)

Similarly, a rock group that is the rage at a local college may never make it in the entertainment world because gatekeepers in the recording industry believe they have enough performers with a similar sound. In addition, once the group has made a recording, radio station programmers may think it doesn't fit their station's "sound" and therefore won't play it. A pilot program for a new television series may never make it on the air because network gatekeepers have decided it is not what the public wants. A potential best-selling book may never see print because a gatekeeper in the publishing industry makes a decision to reject the manuscript.

Agenda Setting

Another process whereby the mass media determine what we think and worry about is called agenda setting. The word *agenda* means a list, plan, outline, or the like of things to be considered. Mass-media agenda-setting theory contends that the mass media, not we, determine what will be news and what won't.

According to researchers Maxwell McCombs and Donald Shaw, "Here may lie the most important effect of mass communication, its ability to mentally order and organize our world for us. In short, the mass media may not be successful in telling us what to think, but they are stunningly successful in telling us what to think about.[4]

@   Practicing Media Literacy

What are some recent examples in which the mass media set an agenda for what you should be thinking?

The professional communicators working for the mass media set the news and information agenda for us. If they determine that something isn't important, it most likely won't be, because it will receive very little, if any, media attention. And, of course, the reverse is true. Often the media give stories far more extensive coverage than they actually deserve. Sensational murder cases, for example, sometimes get week after week of front-page coverage, even when very little new information has been uncovered. Such headlines as "No New Clues in Hillside Strangling" are common.

Most professional communicators, particularly those involved in processing the news, attempt to be objective and fair in their selection of news items. Very few purposely slant the news to fit their own particular biases. Yet there is far more news than space or time available to disseminate it. This means selections must be made as to what is news on any given day and how much space or time to devote to it. Stories of limited interest, such as activities of the local water district, church ladies' aid society, or Boy Scout troop, frequently go unreported.

Political candidates have a great deal of trouble with media agenda setting at election time. For example, in the year 2000, Republican presidential candidate George W. Bush wanted to focus on how he could bring a new spirit of morality to the White House and how he could serve as a positive role model for the nation, much like he had done in Texas as Governor. Instead, the media focused on whether or not in his youth Bush had used illegal drugs (something Bush would neither confirm nor deny).

It is important to understand that agenda setting can differ greatly from one news medium to another. The content of a suburban weekly newspaper will not be the same as that of a nearby metropolitan daily, for example. The suburban weekly may set as its primary agenda local activities in the community, whereas the metropolitan daily probably feels obligated to include more coverage of national and international news.

People absorb only a fraction of all the information available to them.

INFORMATION PROCESSING BY THE CONSUMER

Although the mass media determine what news and entertainment the public will see and hear, people will not absorb all the information they receive. Instead, people process information by condensing it, selecting aspects of interest to them, and integrating what they select into their own thinking.

People pay attention to only a small amount of the information available to them. To do otherwise would risk information overload. Can you imagine reading or remembering everything that has been printed or broadcast during your lifetime? As the years go by, most of us accumulate a substantial backlog of information. This allows us to filter new information into our memories to update and refresh previously developed perceptions and to reject information we deem unimportant.

No matter how hard candidates may try to deal with issues they consider important to their campaigns, intense coverage by the media quite often is responsible for political agenda-setting.

In a field study in Evanston, Illinois, communication researcher Doris Graber discovered that newspaper readers ignored two out of three stories, read no more than 18 percent of the stories in full, and looked at only the first and second paragraph of the rest.[5] (Reading only the beginning of a story is actually an efficient process because it takes advantage of the inverted-pyramid writing style, the most common style of news writing: The most important aspects of the story are summarized in the first paragraph, the next most important information follows, and the least important angles appear at the end.)

Graber also found that a similar screening process goes on for television news: Of all the stories on a typical half-hour newscast, only one is retained sufficiently to be recalled shortly afterward. Despite this haphazard news selection process, however, she found that people manage to stay on top of the most important stories. (Many television news directors believe the second most important story in a newscast, after the lead story, is the final story—the kicker—because that's the one the viewers will remember the most. They want the audience to associate humorous or heart-warming stories with the station on which they saw it.)

> @   **Practicing Media Literacy**
> How many stories do you remember from last night's television newscasts or from this morning's newspapers?

In addition to ignoring large numbers of stories, people reduce the amount of information they need to store by extracting only the essential points from the few news stories they do read or hear. An example of how this works could be seen in what the public remembered about the controversial 1999 federal budget. Although the budget contained thousands of pages of detailed information, the public knew only that the Republicans wanted a larger tax cut and President Clinton wanted to save social security.

As a result of her study, Graber concluded:

Average Americans are capable of extracting enough meaningful political information from the flood of news to which they are exposed to perform the moderate number of citizenship functions that American society expects of them. They keep informed to a limited extent about the majority of significant publicized events. They also learn enough about major political candidates to cast a thoughtful vote and make some judgments about post-election performances.[6]

These basic definitions and concepts are needed to assist your study of popular culture and mass media. In the next chapter, we will provide an overview of how popular culture and mass communication have been influencing each other since the 15th century.

SUMMARY

The term *culture* refers to everything that occurs in a society. It represents all of the customs and practices handed down from generation to generation. Popular culture is the culture of everyone in a society. It is so pervasive that we seldom see it. *Mass culture* is a term often used synonymously with *popular culture*. It refers to everything in our culture that is either mass produced or disseminated through the mass media.

Most mass media evolve through a media progression cycle called the elitist–popular–specialized (EPS) cycle. The media usually start out in the elitist stage, then progress to the popular stage, and finally settle into a stage of specialization.

Several basic components are important to the proper functioning of the com-munication process. These include the source, message, channel, and receiver. In addition, communication has such important elements as feedback, symbols, frames of reference, and a variety of noises that include channel, semantic, and psychological noise.

Mass communication is one of the more complex forms of communication. It is a process whereby professional communicators use technological devices to share messages over great distances to influence large audiences.

The mass media are the channels used in mass communication. In addition to providing information and entertainment, U.S. mass media are in the business of making money, earning more than $150 billion by the end of the 20th century.

Information processing by the media includes gatekeeping and agenda setting. People who work for the mass media serve as gatekeepers, determining what news, information, and entertainment reach us. Agenda setting is a process whereby the mass media help us decide what is important and what isn't.

Consumers also exercise information-processing techniques that help them prevent information overload. They very selectively filter information of interest to increase their knowledge about what they deem important while screening out a great deal of nonessential material.

Find a review of *Key People and Concepts*, a message board for *Practicing Media Literacy* questions, self tests, and more at: www.mhhe.com/wilson.

Thought Questions

1. What are some examples of elite culture not mentioned in this chapter?
2. Are there any popular cultural items or activities that are neither mass-produced nor shared through the mass media?
3. Make a list of instances in your own life where psychological noise hindered communication.
4. What are some recent examples in which the mass media set an agenda for what you should be thinking about?
5. After watching a TV newscast, make a list of five or more stories that you remember and list the reasons you remembered them.

Notes

1. Ray B. Browne, "Popular Culture—The World Around Us," in *The Popular Culture Reader*, ed. Jack Nachbar, Deborah Weiser, and John L. Wright (Bowling Green, OH: Bowling Green University Press, 1978), p. 12.

2. John C. Merrill and Ralph L. Lowenstein, *Media Messages and Men: New Perspectives in Communication* (New York: McKay, 1971), pp. 33–44.

3. Alvin Toffler, *The Third Wave* (Des Plaines, IL.: Bantam Books, 1980), pp. 155–167.

4. Maxwell E. McCombs and Donald L. Shaw, "The Agenda Setting Function of the Press," in *Enduring Issues in Mass Communication*, ed. Everette E. Dennis, Arnold H. Ismach, and Donald M. Gillmore (St. Paul, MN: West, 1978), p. 97.

5. Doris A. Graber, *Processing the News* (New York: Longman, 1984), pp. 201–216.

6. *Ibid.*, p. 204.

Culture and Mass Communication

How They Interact

In my opinion, we are in danger of developing a cult of the
Common Man, which means a cult of mediocrity.

—**Herbert Hoover,** 31st U.S. President

The death of Britain's Princess Diana in a Paris automobile accident stunned the world. In the United States, the major networks provided wall-to-wall coverage of the story. During the week between the accident and the funeral, the networks continued their coverage of the story on the various nightly news magazine programs. ● Ratings for that week listed 9 of the top 25 programs and 5 of the week's top 10 as being network news magazines. And those figures did not include the coverage of Diana's funeral, which was telecast live in this country at 8 A.M. eastern time, 5 A.M. Pacific time. Despite the early hour on a Saturday morning, the A. C. Nielsen Company estimated the viewing audience at 33 million people. Because a lot of people were tuning in and out and many watched the repeat broadcasts of the funeral later that day, the networks estimated the viewership to be as high as 50 million.[1] ● What surprised many people was the fact that the Internet, which became a bona fide news medium by the end of the 20th century, also proved to be a successful vehicle for covering the story of Diana's death. Using words, pictures, video, and sound, Internet news sites chronicled the events following the crash and retold the story of her life. ● Research also showed that hundreds of thousands of Internet users around the world turned to chat rooms and message boards to express their shock and share their grief. And the top Internet news sites managed to keep pace with the traditional news media. MSNBC's website (msnbc.com) and CNN Interactive (cnn.com) both reported the accident at the same time as their cable counterparts were breaking the story. Other websites, relying on news sources such as Reuters, also kept pace with the TV coverage.[2] ● By the next day, the Internet was offering far more comprehensive coverage than network television. *USA Today*'s web page (usatoday.com) had joined MSNBC and CNN Interactive and many other news sites in providing news updates and articles on nearly every aspect of Diana's life, her failed marriage to Prince Charles, and her charitable work.[3] And the American public was consuming as much of this information—whether from newspapers, radio, television, magazines, or the Internet—as they could possibly receive. • The mass media, media technology, and our culture all interact with one another. In this chapter, we'll see the origins of this interaction and how it's happening today now that the flow of information has become a flood. The people's "right to know" is much more easily fulfilled than it has ever been in the history of the world. We've come a long, long way—and the information revolution is continuing.

THE BEGINNINGS OF MASS COMMUNICATION

Gutenberg

In Western culture, mass communication began in the 15th century when the German printer Johannes **Gutenberg** (1398–1468) invented the process of movable type. Movable type allowed molds of alphabet characters to be rearranged to form any message. After the desired number of copies of a particular page were printed, the letter molds could be reused to form new words and pages.

Prior to that time, most books were handwritten and very time consuming to produce. Because of this, reading material was scarce and limited to those in the elite culture—the clergy and the nobility. Printing from carved wooden blocks was attempted in the 14th century but did not become a popular form of mass communication. Gutenberg's invention increased the number of books and made them available for an emerging middle class.

Cultural Changes

The development of printing, which led to the spread of literacy to the middle classes, and the emergence of trade and commerce caused major cultural changes in Western civilization. The medieval economy, particularly from the 8th to the 12th centuries, was very regional and agrarian. Except for religious pilgrimages, wars, and the Crusades, people did not travel, and they produced consumer goods only to meet local needs.

During the Middle Ages, society was highly stratified; people belonged to one of three groups—clergy, nobility, or peasants/artisans—and their social rank virtually never changed. Organizations such as guilds and monasteries, though established for different purposes, helped to preserve the stratification of social ranks. Moreover, a strict equality was enforced among peers. Guild masters, for example, had to follow closely a set of rules governing their output and their conduct; no master was allowed to produce more work than any other.

Life in medieval society was very stable. People were born into a social class and remained there throughout their lives. However, by the 14th century, Europeans had started to travel and explore the world beyond them. They began to discover different cultures and different types of consumer goods, and these discoveries led to the development of long-distance trade.

@ **Practicing Media Literacy**

Compare the spread of literacy after the development of printing to the spread of "media literacy" happening today.

Pictorial Prints

Printing became the first mass-produced and mass-distributed commodity in this new Western culture. Pictorial prints also had a special place in the early history of printing: They were the first form of mass-produced images for popular markets. Albrecht **Dürer** (1471–1528) was one of the most successful Renaissance artists to use the art forms of woodcuts and engravings to mass-produce pictorial prints. These prints became an early form of mass culture that helped to foster consumerism in the lower classes of society.[4]

Modern scholars do not consider works of mass-produced graphic art made before the 18th century examples of mass culture; their antiquity and their display in museums give them the status of fine art. But this view reflects a social redefinition that began in the late 17th century, when collectors in Holland and France started treating prints as works of art that could be enjoyed, such as paintings, both for their aesthetic merits and as investments. Before this time, printmaking primarily involved images for a popular audience.[5] (This same phenomenon can be found today as such popular cultural items as old comic books, baseball cards, posters, and magazines are collected and exhibited as art. The current value of such items far exceeds their original selling price.)

In addition to books and pictorial prints, maps were widely published and circulated. They not only facilitated trade and travel but were also used like pictorial prints as decorative wall hangings.

The Four Horsemen of the Apocalypse, one of 15 Woodcuts by Albrecht Dürer in the late 1490s.

Dürer

Early Books

Most books published during the first century of printing were reproductions of traditional religious works, such as the Bible, the Book of Hours (which contains the prescribed order of prayers, readings from the Scriptures, etc.), and the like. Although produced with movable type, they were made to look like their handwritten predecessors by using traditional layouts and typefaces designed to resemble handwriting. Woodcut illustrations were used in these books not so much to illustrate a scene as to decorate the pages.[6] As the accuracy of illustrations became more important in the latter half of the 15th century, woodcuts gave way to metal engravings, which were more reproducible.[7]

According to Canadian media theorist Marshall McLuhan, the development of printing had a profound impact on the thinking process in Western culture. In his popular books written in the 1960s, *The Gutenberg Galaxy* and *Understanding Media*, McLuhan contended that print restricts our thinking

> @ **Practicing Media Literacy**
> How does the Internet force a change from the pattern of linear thinking?

to **linear patterns**: One thought follows the next in an orderly fashion. Not until the advent of the electronic media was our culture given alternatives to linear thinking. Electronic media—particularly television—McLuhan said, give us an "all-at-onceness" that breaks down the logic of linear thought.[8]

THE PROTESTANT REFORMATION

Reformation

Although printing flourished during the 15th century, mass distribution of these first mass-produced products was not yet possible. Then, in the 16th century, as the Protestant **Reformation** spread across Europe, rulers began to fear printing because it permitted the wide distribution of pamphlets criticizing political and religious authorities. They attempted to control it by licensing printers and suppressing books. King Henry II of France, for example, vowed to stamp out all heretical books, and both books and printers were put to the torch during his reign.[9]

Mass Movement

The Reformation, led by German monk Martin Luther, was the first mass movement made possible by mass communication. Print was used to mobilize people of all social classes. Luther's main argument was that the pope and his agents should no longer be the sole authority for the interpretation of the Bible and that people should read and study the Bible on their own. He translated the Latin Bible into German, and through mass communication it was made available to the people.

Luther and his followers used mass-produced pamphlets to distribute the new religious thoughts to the masses. They communicated with the illiterate through pictorial prints, resembling present-day editorial cartoons, which carried propaganda messages against the Catholic Church and the pope.

Despite the efforts to censor these materials by rulers who remained faithful to the Catholic Church, the Reformation spread. In fact, censorship led to the development of international printing. Publishers in one country would print a book censored in another for distribution in the prohibited country. Protestant Geneva, Switzerland, for example, became a center for the publication of the works of French Protestants.

Also developing at this time were agents who worked as book distributors. Printing became firmly entrenched as the first successfully mass-produced and mass-distributed technology. Venice was the center of printing in this early period, and Italy had the most print shops, 50, followed by Germany, with 30.

DEVELOPMENT OF THE NOVEL

After mass communication developed, more and more people learned to read and write, especially among the middle classes. However, in those days, the elite did not think of literacy as merely the ability to read and write. Only those who could read critically and understand the Greek and Roman classics were considered truly literate.

Chapbooks

chapbooks

The new readers were not interested in the ancient classics, however. In addition to the Bible, they read small, inexpensive books called **chapbooks**, which contained folk stories and romances. People read chapbooks simply for enjoyment, not to engage in erudite literary analysis. Reading was a new way to enjoy the ancient art of storytelling, only now stories were told in printed version rather than orally.

The Novel

In the 18th century, middle-class readers also provided a market for a new form of book: the **novel**. No longer reliant on the patronage of the elite and obliged to satisfy their expectations of elevated, stilted language, writers began to use the everyday language of the masses.

A major characteristic of the novel was its realism. Each new novel was supposed to be different. Novels emphasized individual experience over collective experience. They were concerned with morality and attempted to present moral themes. To make the novels affordable and widely available, many—such as the works of Charles Dickens in the 19th century—

Novelist Charles Dickens was one of the authors to have some of his work published in serial form.

novel

were published in serial form (that is, a few chapters were published each week or month in pamphlet form). With the evolution of the novel, the language of the written word became descriptive rather than conceptual or abstract.

INDUSTRIALIZATION

Printing technology remained virtually unchanged during the first several centuries of mass communication. Movable type and hand-cranked presses were state of the art until the early 19th century, when a steam-powered cylinder press was perfected in England. This new development allowed for the rapid reproduction of printed materials. In 1846, a **rotary press** was developed that could produce about 20,000 copies of a newspaper per hour.

rotary press

The rotary press was just one tiny part of the great technological explosion known as the Industrial Revolution, which irreversibly changed Western culture and lifestyles. It opened up new jobs in the cities and caused a migration of people from family farms to urban areas. Immigrants and migrants left their traditional popular culture behind and moved into the cities, where their work was regimented, standardized, and homogenized.

Artisans and craftspeople were displaced by semiskilled workers who could operate machines. The use of these machines restructured society into one that focused on mass production and mass consumption. It also brought about the eventual shortening of the work week from 12-hour days, six days a week, to the current 40-hour (or shorter) week.

Sociologist Louis Wirth described the new urban culture as one that saw "the weakening of bonds of kinship, and the declining social significance of the family, the disappearance of the neighborhood, and the undermining of the traditional basis of social solidarity."[10] Set adrift from their familiar surroundings and the age-old rhythms of rural life, the new urban working class had new needs: a way to learn about their new environment and ideas for spending their leisure time. These needs helped to transform our culture.

Newspapers moved into the popular stage of the EPS cycle when The New York Sun *sold its daily editions for a penny.*

The Metropolitan Newspaper

One of the first things to develop to meet these needs in the new industrial society was the metropolitan newspaper—often called the penny press—which was aimed at common people in the city. The first such paper in the United States was the *New York Sun,* which was established in 1833, shortly after the invention of the steam-driven press.

Although newspapers had existed since the late 17th and early 18th centuries, they had been read by the educated elite, not the general public. The costs of printing were too high to reach a mass audience, and the content was not everyday news items but dated information from abroad, political reports, and essays.

Early issues of the *New York Sun* sold for a penny, rather than the usual 6 cents, and carried stories about ordinary people. Other penny-press newspapers followed, running news items about local events and common people's problems and interests. This new form of journalism helped to reduce anxiety and solitude by revealing to the lonely, displaced city dwellers their common humanity and their mutual pursuit of money as the common denominator of urban life.[11] According to sociologist Michael Schudson, the penny papers "expressed and built the culture of a democratic market society, a culture that had no place for social or intellectual difference."[12]

@ **Practicing Media Literacy**

Based on the role of mass communication in the development of our industrial society, what impact do you think the media will have as our culture moves down the global information highway?

Entertainment

Although not directly related to mass communication at that time, two other institutions developed during the latter part of the 19th century to meet the needs of the new urban dwellers: the **ballpark** and **vaudeville**. Both kinds of entertainment helped to fill the growing amount of leisure time workers enjoyed and later were transformed into mass-media activities.

ballpark
vaudeville

The first professional baseball team, the Cincinnati Red Stockings, was founded in 1869, and soon there were teams in all the major eastern and midwestern cities. The *ballpark* brought together crowds of strangers who could experience a sense of community within the big city as they watched a baseball game. Immigrants were able

Yankee Stadium, shown here on opening day, April 19, 1923, was one of the early ballparks which brought urban dwellers together as a community. The mass media opened the experience to a national audience.

to shake loose their ethnic ties and become absorbed in the new national game, which was becoming representative of the "American spirit." The green fields and fresh air of the ballpark were a welcome change from the sea of bricks, stone, and eventually asphalt that dominated the city scene.

Workers could temporarily escape the routine and dullness of their daily lives by vicariously participating in the competition and accomplishment that baseball games symbolized. Baseball reflected the competitiveness of the workplace and the capitalist ethic, as players were bought and sold and were regarded as property. The ballpark also provided a means for spectators to release their frustrations against authority figures: The umpire became a symbol of scorn, and cries of "kill the umpire," accompanied by tossed debris, were frequent.

Vaudeville entertainers, such as Drane and Alexander, took traditional forms of popular entertainment (or folk art) and made them part of the new mass culture. (1912 photo from the Bettmann Archive)

As professional baseball emerged as a popular pastime, it became an increasingly commercial enterprise. Stadiums were built to seat the spectators, and hawkers of beer, soda, hot dogs, peanuts, and Cracker Jacks soon appeared. Advertising on signboards, streetcar posters, handbills, and balloons and in newspapers helped to "sell" the ballpark to the public.[13] With the advent of the electronic media in the 20th century, baseball and other sports became a form of mass-media entertainment.

Vaudeville, the other popular form of entertainment in the 19th century, took the traditional forms of popular entertainment or folk art, such as ethnic humor, juggling, dancing, and clown acts, and made them part of the new mass culture. Vaudeville set the mold for entertainment programs on the electronic media that eventually displaced it in the 20th century. Radio incorporated the style and humor of vaudeville, and television in turn took over the entertainment format of radio when it developed in the late 1940s and 1950s. The quick cuts and action of modern-day television are ultimately based on the conventions of vaudeville entertainment.[14]

In the late 19th century, the ballpark and vaudeville were followed by the first two mechanized mass-communication media: the phonograph and motion pictures. These media and their cultural impact will be discussed in separate chapters.

MASS MEDIA IN MASS SOCIETY

In the 19th century, the role of mass communication was to supplement face-to-face communication and provide a means of disseminating—and creating—the new mass culture.

Cultural Niches

As new technologies developed in the industrial age, they had to find a way to serve the new society. Among the mass media, for example, the newspaper found its niche by becoming a medium from which the common person could learn about what was happening in his or her city.

The *telephone* was invented by a person working on the invention of a hearing aid and at first was considered as a possible device for broadcasting. However, its developers found a better use for it as an electronic extension of interpersonal communication.

Photography was invented in the 19th century as a quicker and less expensive alternative to family portraits produced by an artist. It later became an essential vehicle for covering events by metropolitan newspapers. Today photography is important in many fields of mass communication.

Radio was developed in the early 20th century for ship-to-shore communication and for military use; messages could now be transmitted without having to string wires between two points. However, radio's more important function was as a mass medium for news and entertainment. For the first time, people could hear news as it was happening and listen to a variety of free vaudeville entertainment in their own homes. Radio became a mass medium just before the Great Depression hit in 1929, and free entertainment was one of the few bright spots in the bleak 1930s.

The ethnic humor of Amos 'n' Andy (Freeman Gosden and Charles Correll) was a popular feature on network radio from the late 1920s to the early 1960s.

Besides providing free entertainment, radio allowed members of the newly mobile society to take their favorite entertainment with them when they moved from the family farms and small towns to the large cities. To be able to still hear such familiar voices as Amos 'n' Andy and Jack Benny when they left their homes in Iowa or Oklahoma for the impersonal cities or the agricultural lands of California was an enormous comfort to the migrants of this era.

Television was invented as a potential replacement for radio by adding a picture to the sound. When radio programs—

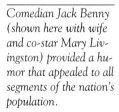

Comedian Jack Benny (shown here with wife and co-star Mary Livingston) provided a humor that appealed to all segments of the nation's population.

comedies, variety shows, and soap operas—moved to television, the format of radio changed to specialized music and news. Radio became a different medium, thus finding a new place for itself in mass society. This trend continues as new technologies come on the scene.

MASS MEDIATION OF LEISURE

As leisure became an important ingredient in the new mass culture, as a means of both stimulating consumerism and providing activities for the increased hours away from the workplace, the mass media started to promote leisure-time activities.

Sports

Pulitzer
Hearst

The metropolitan press began to cover the ballpark in the latter part of the 19th century. First came the sports page, pioneered by Joseph **Pulitzer** in his *New York World*, followed by the sports section, introduced by his rival, William Randolph **Hearst**, in the *New York Journal*. Sports magazines also developed during this period.

When radio became a mass communication medium in the 1920s, broadcasters soon found that sporting activities in the ballpark were ideal for programming. In addition, innovative radio sportscasters took their broadcasts one step further when they couldn't actually attend a game by broadcasting recreations of the games, with an announcer and a sound effects person sitting in a studio creating descriptions and sounds of the game from bits of information fed to them by Western Union.

As television developed, network executives eventually decided that baseball—the national pastime—was not as "visual" as football, so they turned professional football into TV's number-one electronic sports entertainment. (It is interesting to note that professional football was the first team sport to call time-outs for commercials.)

Prior to this time, professional football had not become a major sport because of the popularity of collegiate football and the long tradition of baseball as America's favorite professional sport. The National Football League (NFL) was barely holding its own, and the American Football League (AFL) was about to disappear when the television networks came to the rescue. If NBC hadn't put down money for the television rights to AFL games, the league would have folded long before it merged with the NFL.

A third professional football league, the United States Football League (USFL), began play in 1983. However, in 1986 the USFL had to suspend operations when it secured only $1 in damages in a lawsuit it had filed against the NFL. The USFL claimed that the NFL had kept the television networks from giving the USFL a broadcasting franchise—and a guaranteed source of income. The need for mass mediation for a professional sport to survive was made brutally clear.

In 1990, the NFL signed a record-breaking $3.6 billion, four-year contract with five broadcast and cable networks, including Turner Broadcasting System and ESPN. The contract added two more teams to the playoffs and, by the fall of 1992, two more weeks to the professional football season. To help the networks recoup some of their investment, the contract allowed for the addition of five 30-second commercial spots to each game. By 1990, time-outs for commercials had extended the average length of a professional football game from 2 hours, 57 minutes in 1978 to 3 hours, 11 minutes. This marriage for profit between television and the ballpark became very lucrative by the end of the 20th century.

One of the biggest popular cultural events in American society today comes, after months of media hype, at the conclusion of the professional football season: the Super Bowl. This media-created and media-promoted event, traditionally held on the third or fourth Sunday of January, has become a worldwide party–event, with many Europeans getting up in the middle of the night to view the game on television.

Super Bowl Sunday, like Monday night football, fulfills many of the socialization functions the early ballpark did. People come together for Super Bowl parties or Monday night football cocktail hours to share a common interest. Strangers with nothing else in common can talk about the electronic ballpark festival for days afterward. Those who attend a football game in person are happy to find the same features of the electronically broadcast version available to them: instant replays shown on a large TV screen on top of the scoreboard. This was particularly helpful for fans attending Super Bowl XIX held at Stanford Stadium in California in January 1985, because they

The Super Bowl has become a media event watched each January by millions of TV viewers around the world.

could watch with the rest of the television viewers around the world as the official coin toss at the start of the game was handled from more than 3,000 miles away by President Ronald Reagan at the White House.

Football, however, is not the only sport that television has changed. The World Series is played in chilly October temperatures at night on the East Coast and in late afternoon on the West Coast so that the games will be shown on television during prime time in the eastern and central time zones. Professional basketball playoffs now include 16 of the 27 NBA teams, and the season stretches into June so TV can have more high-rated games. The National Hockey League has expanded the pauses in play following certain penalties to more than 30 seconds to allow time for a commercial.

@ **Practicing Media Literacy**
Do you think television has too much influence over baseball and other major sports?

Sports has proven over the years to be a major money winner for television. Each year the baseball playoffs and World Series help the network carrying the games to top the ratings charts. Unlike sitcoms, which have to be promoted to build an audience, sports is a form of programming that comes with a built-in audience: the fans. During large-audience sports events, the networks can, in addition to making money on commercials, promote their own season's programming.

Consumer Goods

By covering a variety of other leisure-time activities, the mass media influence people to buy things so they can participate too. Recreational vehicles, boats, all-terrain scooters, ski outfits, and designer jeans are just some of the consumer goods that have become a part of our popular leisure culture through the mass media's establishment of a need. Advertisements and reflections of active lifestyles on TV and in the movies create these needs.

@ **Practicing Media Literacy**
What products have you recently purchased as the result of the media?

CRITICISM OF MASS SOCIETY

The new mass culture ushered in by the Industrial Revolution was not accepted without criticism. Intellectuals found the new society debased and believed it encroached on the elite or high culture. This critique by some European intellectuals, Germans in particular, led in the 19th century to the development of romanticism and the first real study of popular culture. Leaders of the romantic movement examined the traditional folk culture that was symbolic of the good old days. Such things as folk costumes, customs, foods, and history took on new importance. (Perhaps the most famous and enduring of these efforts was the collection of fairy tales by the Brothers Grimm.)

escapism

Other critics of mass culture believed that it had transformed our culture into just another commodity to be bought and sold and that it was intellectually destructive because it provided **escapism** and served a narcotic function in society. They saw the new mass culture consuming rather than preserving cultural objects that were being mass-produced to meet society's entertainment needs. These critics also detested the fact that the mass media conformed to average tastes and did nothing to elevate the cultural level of the masses.

Current Complaints

This criticism of mass culture still exists today (and in fact seems to be increasing), with a primary focus on the mass media and their influences on society in general.

low culture

Some intellectuals still believe television entertainment is "**low culture**" and is undermining the elite arts. Critics complain that most TV programming is nothing more than a mindless pacifier with no educational or artistic value. Sociologist Dwight MacDonald theorized that a significant part of the population is "chronically confronted with a choice of going to a concert or to the movies, of reading Tolstoy or a detective story, of looking at old masters or at a TV show."[15]

Defenders of high culture express concern that the proliferation of commercialized mass culture is blurring the distinction between elite and mass culture. They point out that this fusion of the two types of culture is not raising the level of mass culture but instead is corrupting high culture. MacDonald says, "There is nothing more

kitsch

vulgar than sophisticated **kitsch**" (a German term for mass culture).[16]

> @ **Practicing Media Literacy**
> What do you think is the major problem with each of the mass media today?

Critics contend that art in popular or mass culture is predigested so that spectators are spared the effort of understanding genuine art and given a shortcut to appreciating its pleasures. It is much easier to view a Norman Rockwell painting and instantly understand it than it is to quickly comprehend the meaning of an expressionistic Van Gogh.

This democratization of art, critics continue, leads to the homogenization of our culture, which is analogous to the homogenization of milk: The globules of cream are evenly distributed throughout the milk instead of floating separately on top.[17] In other words, the qualities of high and low culture have been blended together, and the demand for the "cream" has all but disappeared. Some have even suggested that the way we view ourselves and our expectations for romantic relationships are often shaped by our exposure to the mass media (see Box 2.1).

Another major criticism leveled at the mass media, particularly television, is that both news and entertainment are treated superficially. Critics charge that there seems to be a preoccupation with celebrity status, and the major focus is to entertain rather

Box 2.1
MEDIA LITERACY
Popular Culture and Mass Media Myths about Romantic Love by Dr. Mary-Lou Galician

Dr. FUN!'s Mass Media Love Quiz is based on the research of Dr. FUN!—otherwise known as Dr. Mary-Lou Galician of Arizona State University. This material is copyrighted and all rights are reserved. Test yourself: Answer True or False to each statement to indicate your own personal belief.

1. Your perfect partner is cosmically predestined for you and nothing/nobody can ultimately separate you.
2. There is such a thing as "love-at-first-sight."
3. Your true "soulmate" should KNOW what you're thinking or feeling (without your having to tell).
4. If your partner is truly meant for you, sex is easy and wonderful.
5. The man should NOT be shorter, weaker, younger, poorer, or less successful than the woman.
6. To attract and keep a man, a woman should look like a model or a centerfold.
7. The love of a good and faithful true woman can change a man from a "beast" to a "prince."
8. "All we really need is love," so it doesn't matter if you and your lover have very different values.
9. Fighting a lot shows that a man and a woman really are passionate about each other.
10. The right mate "completes you" by filling your needs and making your dreams come true.
11. In real life, actors are often very much like the romantic characters they portray.
12. Since mass media portrayals of romance aren't "real," they don't really affect us.

I hope you answered "FALSE" to ALL the above statements from my "Mass Media Love Quiz," based on my research examining what we learn about romantic love from the mass media and how these portrayals affect us.

The problem is that while most of us "know" the "right" responses to my quiz items, we still "believe" the unrealistic ones our popular culture presents to us!

Mass media are very powerful socialization agents. From the time we're very young, we're barraged with fairy-tale depictions of romantic love in the popular culture—movies and television, books and magazines,

recordings and the radio, advertising, and even the news—so we shouldn't feel too badly if we wind up with some unrealistic expectations. Remember: Mass media rely on simplification, distortions of reality, and dramatic symbols and stereotypes to communicate their messages.

Unfortunately, "false-love" images and scripts of coupleship put pressure on BOTH women and men—to measure up to *Playboy* centerfolds and Prince Charmings. Some media-constructed unrealistic expectations can even lead to depression and other dysfunctions, several can be downright dangerous. So it's smart to become aware and change our unhealthy views.

With this in mind, let's look more closely at the mass media myths in my quiz:

1. A partner who is "perfect" would be less than fully human, but media myths glorify the unrealistically ideal. While you're seeking your one-and-only Mr. Or Ms. "Right," your blinders prevent you from seeing a whole spectrum of candidates who could make an excellent match.
2. There's attraction-at-first-sight, but real love takes real time. Too many movies and TV shows give us the opposite idea. But they have only two hours to spin their tales. And advertisers have only 30 seconds.
3. Mind-readers function only in circuses—and romance novels, which feed our fantasy of having a perfect relationship without really working at it. Realistically, romantic partners learn about each other by daring to be open and honest about what they want.
4. As with all intimacy, genuinely good sex takes time, trust, and togetherness. In real life (unlike in the pages of *Playboy* or *Cosmo*), the essential element of love is NOT sex.
5. To fit the "Me-Tarzan, You-Jane" cultural stereotypes that the mass media perpetuate, many leading men in movies and TV shows have to stand on boxes to appear taller than their leading ladies. Even news anchor "couples" are usually an older male–younger female duo. These images reinforce

continued

sexual inequality and block many potentially wonderful relationships from ever getting started.

6. Real love doesn't superficially turn a person into an object. Nevertheless, even though they might not realize it, many males subconsciously use actresses, models, and centerfolds as a standard for their own real-life partners, who cannot help disappointing them (unless they, too, have had the surgical and photographic enhancements that pop culture icons get). What's worse is that even women's magazines reinforce unhealthy female body images.

7. Children who see *Beauty and the Beast* should be warned that Belle's attempts to reform her captor would be most unwise in real life. We cannot change others—especially not abusive "heroes" (or "heroines"!) who have some good inside if only their partner can be "good enough" to bring it out. This fallacy underlies domestic violence.

8. Opposites frequently attract—but they don't stay together very long except in mass media mythology. Can you imagine a real-life dinner party mixing the friends of "Pretty Woman" and her stockbroker boyfriend? Though rarely demonstrated by the mass media, shared values (not "interests") form the basis of lasting romantic relationships.

9. Invariably in mass media, a male and female who take an instant strong dislike to each other will (eventually) discover that they're made for each other—despite their continual bickering. Respectful disagreement is healthy, but these constant combatants need conflict-resolution training. Don't confuse fighting with passion: Love is about peace, not war.

10. Although "love" songs cultivate this *Snow White* syndrome (Her big Disney solo was "Someday My Prince Will Come"!), using your partner as a completer, fixer, or rescuer—someone from whom you "take" or "get"—is robbery, not romance. (And that goes for "incomplete" MEN like Jerry Maguire!) But where's the dramatic conflict in well-adjusted, self-sufficient individuals who choose to share their already-full lives?

11. Many men and women are less than satisfied with their real-life romantic partners because they aren't like their idealized image of a celebrity they think they know.

12. Though we might not be aware of the all-pervasive media culture, we subconsciously incorporate its messages and myths into our own lives. In my own studies of baby boomers and generation X-ers, I've found that heavier consumers of movies and fashion and fitness magazines tend to have more unrealistic and stereotypical expectations about coupleship, and, correspondingly, less satisfaction in their own real romantic relationships.

Does all this mean we should avoid romantic media entirely?

We can still enjoy the "escape" that romantic media myths offer us, but it's not wise to use them (or media celebrities) as models. It's much healthier and smarter to make yourself the hero or heroine of your own true romance.

My ultimate advice: "Get real!"

Source: Dr. Mary-Lou Galician is an associate professor in the Walter Cronkite School of Journalism and Telecommunication at Arizona State University in Tempe. She has written a book about romanticization of love in the mass media, and she and her husband—Dr. David Natharius—conduct Realistic Romance seminars and workshops.

than to inform or educate. Some felt that the extensive coverage of the death of John F. Kennedy Jr., his wife, and her sister in the summer of 1999 was too much. They charged that it was merely because of the Kennedy name that the networks provided almost continuous coverage of the story.

The rapid escalation of violence in our society has also brought about criticism that violence in the media is causing the problem. In 1993, television networks began carrying warning labels on programs that contain violence as their answer to the increasing criticism coming from the public and Congress. Even that wasn't enough, and Congress approved a new Telecommunications Act in 1996 that required the implementation of the V-chip to give parents more control over programs viewed in the home. Many believe young people in particular learn violent behavior from the media (see Box 2.2).

COMMERCIALIZATION OF CULTURE

The Industrial Revolution brought into our culture the concept of rapid production and consumption of goods and services. As our mass culture grows and expands and new forms of mass media develop, consumerism grows with it.

Individuals in our new mass society are still struggling to regain their identity, but many of them now seem to believe the best way to establish that identity is through the purchase of the "right" types of consumer goods. The automobiles they drive, the clothes they wear, and the type of houses they live in tell the world "who they are." The industrial-age American myth holds that the more material goods a person acquires, the better off he or she is. Since having more symbolizes being better, there is never enough, and the society of production and consumption continues to grow.

Product Images

The multibillion-dollar advertising industry in the United States is not the only vehicle through which consumer goods are sold in the mass media. The way products are displayed on television, in motion pictures, in magazines, and in music videos plays an important role in transmitting meaning and generating desire for products.

It was no accident that Ford Explorers were the vehicles of choice in Steven Spielberg's film *Jurassic Park*. In Michael Crichton's novel about the Mesozoic theme park, the vehicles described were Toyota Land Cruisers. But six Explorers were donated for the movie, in which they are chased, stomped, and flipped by *Tyrannosaurus rex*. Three studio dumpsters were filled with Explorer parts by the time the movie was completed. This is an example of **product placements**, a recent trend where products appear in films only because companies were willing to pay top dollar for the exposure or supply them free.

product placements

An entire profession, called "product brokerage," has developed around the need to portray consumer goods in the entertainment business. Product brokers represent companies willing to pay or donate products for movies and TV shows. For example, Mercedes-Benz of North America will lend its expensive automobiles to film producers free as long as they agree to let only the "good guys" drive them. When Mercedes-Benz executives agreed to let Clint Eastwood and Charlie Sheen drive a 500SL through a warehouse window and onto the roof of an adjoining building in the film *The Rookie*, they insisted that the car land intact and shiny side up, with no injury to the occupants and with its air bags and automatic roll bar visibly deployed. They also insisted that Eastwood utter their advertising slogan, "Engineered like no other car in the world."

Identification with a hero has been the motivation of many car manufacturers to get their vehicles driven by agent 007 in the James Bond movies. Although there are no quantitative measurements of the sales impact of such product placements, such companies as BMW and Aston Martin see value in the added exposure for their products. Computer manufacturers have also fought to have their particular brands on display in some of the more recent high-tech motion pictures.

Sometimes these product placement agreements can go astray. When the hit movie *Jerry Maguire* was presented on the Showtime premium cable channel in 1999, it was 47 seconds longer than it had been in the movie theaters. The change in the Tom Cruise movie was the addition of a fake, satirical commercial for Reebok that the writer-director of the film had edited out. Director Cameron Crowe felt it ruined his ending. No one would say why it was then added back in for cable television, but the action was taken following settlement of a Reebok product-placement lawsuit against Sony's TriStar Pictures. Reebok had provided $200,000 to help produce the fictional

Box 2.2
MEDIA LITERACY
Does the "Monkey See, Monkey Do" Concept Apply to the Media?

For most of the 20th century, from the early days of the motion pictures through the modern television era, there have been those who believed they could emulate what they've seen on the screen. Whether it was the way one smoked a cigarette in an attempt to look like a favorite movie hero or children putting a towel around their necks and jumping off a rooftop to see if they could fly like Superman, the media have had an enormous impact on our culture.

Studies have shown that certain individuals do tend to imitate what they see in the media. The rash of skyjackings that led to the necessity for metal detectors in airports, the escalation of carjackings in recent years, the placement of cyanide in Tylenol and Excedrin capsules, and the reported findings of syringes in Pepsi cans are all examples of how the copycat mentality affects the relationship of media content and our popular culture. This phenomenon is called the *information-imitation theory* (see Chapter 16).

The tendency to blame the media for society's woes seems to be escalating. The general public seems convinced that media influences are creating and fostering antisocial behavior and are the causes of all that is wrong with society. These arguments are supported by members of Congress who have tried to curtail the violence on television, blaming it for the increase in violence in our cities. The end result was the introduction of the V-chip in television sets to allow parents to control the types of programs their children watch. But no matter what controls have been attempted, the imitation continues.

Blaming the media for violence in our culture, however, is nothing new. Complaints about violence in the movies, from the gangster films of the 1930s to the westerns of the 1940s, have been around since action scenes began flickering on the silver screen. From the time they entered our popular culture in the late 1930s, comic books were blamed for causing youngsters to behave violently. By the 1950s, television had replaced comic books as the perceived cause of our violent behavior. Escalating depictions of violence in today's movies and in music videos have also come under attack.

The problem centers on the issue of free speech and artistic freedom versus the need to protect society from those who might have a copycat mentality. To date, the courts have ruled in favor of artistic and speech freedoms. Although the U.S. Supreme Court has not ruled on this issue, the lower courts have held that those who sue the media over content must be able to show that the program in question intended to incite the violent act.

@ Practicing Media Literacy

What examples can you list of current efforts to commercialize our leisure culture?

commercial for the film in exchange for "recognizable product visibility."

One of the most successful examples of product placement came in 1982 when the Hershey Foods Corporation got Steven Spielberg to use Reese's Pieces to cement a friendship between the extraterrestrial creature and the young boy, Elliot, in the film *E.T.* Sales of Reese's jumped 70 percent the month after the film was released, and within two months the candy was being sold at the refreshment counter of 800 theaters that previously had not carried it.[18]

Exporting Commercialized Pop Culture

The commercialization of our popular culture is not limited to the confines of the United States. For many years America has been exporting its popular culture, first as images in motion pictures, magazines, music, and television and finally as commercial enterprises. Coca-Cola and its logo and Levi's jeans have long been popular around the world. Even replicas of the ultimate American leisure playground, Disneyland, can now be found in France and Japan.

The opening of the first McDonald's restaurant in Moscow was a worldwide news event as more than 30,000 Russians stood in line almost two hours to get their first taste of Big Macs, french fries, and chocolate and strawberry "milk cocktails." Worldwide, McDonald's has more than 11,000 fast-food restaurants, 741 of them in Japan alone. Japan also has 875 KFC (formerly Kentucky Fried Chicken) outlets.

> **@   Practicing Media Literacy**
> What are some other examples of America exporting its popular culture?

CULTS IN POPULAR CULTURE

Many of the mass media we will study have already entered the specialized stage of the EPS cycle (see Chapter 1). As you will see, this move toward specialization has been assisted by a need that has existed in our mass culture since the early days of the Industrial Revolution: a need for individuals to stand apart from the masses while maintaining a sense of belonging to something, such as a subcultural group or "**cult**." Thus, it is important that we understand what a cult is and how it fits within our mass culture.

cult

The cyberpunk cult of the 1990s, racist groups such as skinheads and the Ku Klux Klan, Satan worshippers, and David Koresh's Branch Davidians often come to mind when we use the word *cult*. Cults, however, do not necessarily have to be bizarre or dangerous. Webster's *Third New International Dictionary* includes in its definition of cult: "a. great or excessive devotion or dedication to some person, idea or thing . . . such devotion regarded as a literary or intellectual fad or fetish; b. the object of such devotion; c. a body of persons characterized by such devotion." Under such a definition, cults can include a wide variety of devoted groups, including skateboard enthusiasts, baseball card collectors, and rockstar fan clubs.

Many cults are interrelated with the mass media. Some develop as a result of media attention given to a "person, idea or thing," while others are catered to by specialized media publications that help to perpetuate the interest in the cult or activity.

Rock Fans

One category of cults that has developed around the popular music industry is characterized by "great or excessive devotion" to rock stars. In the eyes of their followers, these superstars can do no wrong. Long after the Beatles split up and Elvis Presley died, cultlike followers have continued to worship these performers. Even though he died in the 1970s, Elvis Presley is still featured regularly in the mass media and appeared on magazine covers in the 1990s. Several radio stations have developed "all-Elvis" music formats, and the U.S. government helped to keep the cultlike devotion alive in the 1990s by issuing a postage stamp honoring Elvis.

Movie — TV Buffs.

A large, cultlike following developed around the movies *Star Wars*, *The Empire Strikes Back*, and *Return of the Jedi* and continued some 25 years later with the 1999 release of *Star Wars: Episode 1—The Phantom Menace*. Another cult sprang from the *Rocky Horror Picture Show*. Some people said they saw the movies hundreds of times, and box office receipts seemed to support these claims.

"Live long and prosper" is a universal greeting shared by "Trekkies," fans of the Star Trek series and its many spinoff programs.

Probably the largest and most interesting television-produced cult has been the "Trekkies," devoted followers of the *Star Trek* television series. The Trekkies have long outlasted the original series of the late 1960s. Each year thousands gather at conventions, many of them dressed in *Star Trek* costumes complete with pointed plastic ears. Exhibitors at these conventions sell a variety of *Star Trek* memorabilia.

subculture

In the 1990s, TV once again helped to form a **subculture**. Soon after the Fox network introduced the cartoon family *The Simpsons* to prime time, young people began wearing Bart Simpson T-shirts with such messages as "Underachiever and Proud of It" and "Don't Have a Cow, Man." Some schools reacted to the new youth subculture by banning the T-shirts.

Gang Members

Inner-city gangs provide still another subcultural identification for individuals attempting to establish their own identities in a mass society. Gangs have been glamorized in the mass media for years, particularly in motion pictures, from *The Blackboard Jungle* and *Rebel Without a Cause* in the 1950s to the more recent *Boyz N the Hood* and similar movies which followed. In recent years, however, gang activities have become much more violent, with random killings and drive-by shootings. Gangs such as the Bloods and the Crips have been killing one another for years over such seemingly unimportant issues as wandering into the wrong neighborhood or wearing the wrong color of shirt. Gang membership often provides a support group for youngsters from dysfunctional families.

Subcult Characteristics

It is important to examine subcultures to see how they fit into the larger cultural scene and how mass media affect them. Many of our subcultures, particularly those involving youth, are music oriented. Subcultures consist of the practices, fashions, and styles of subgroups in society. Members of some subcultures tend to stigmatize themselves and thus establish roles as social outcasts. They often use signs or badges of identification to accomplish this. Styles become a signal to the mass culture that the subculture wants to be "different."

Punk rockers, for example, gave hidden meanings to various objects, using safety pins, patches, earrings, spiked hair, and tattoos to set themselves apart from and ridicule mass society. Punks used their badges and style to symbolize anarchy, provoke people to dislike them, and oppose the usual practices of society.

Thus, the style of a subculture has two points: (1) to oppose everyday life and (2) to establish acceptance within the subculture. Contrary to popular myth, which portrays subcultures as lawless forms, "the internal structure of any particular subculture is characterized by an extreme orderliness: each part is organically related to other parts and it is through the fit between them that the subcultural member makes sense of the world."[19]

Although punk started in England as an effort by some people to reject mass society, it wasn't long before the mass media had transmitted their styles and customs throughout the world. People with spiked and dyed hair, tattoos, and safety pins in the cheek could soon be seen in such scattered locations as San Francisco, Vienna, and Tokyo.

Cultural Industries

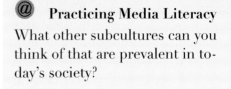

@   Practicing Media Literacy

What other subcultures can you think of that are prevalent in today's society?

Although subcultures attempt to reject the larger mass culture and establish their own identities, they are an important part of the mass culture industries. They are promoted and perpetuated by the mass media and mass industry—and not just the music industry, around which many of them develop.

Manufacturers of mass-produced consumer goods soon get on the bandwagon and merchandise the subculture. Even major chain drugstores carried washable colored hair spray for punk rockers. Sales of safety pins, earrings, and leather jackets multiplied after the punk movement began. In the 1990s the alternative rock subculture, known as grunge rock and roll, found itself co-opted into the mass culture when its funky clothing style became fashionable in major department stores.

Another subculture, the biker subculture, started out as youth oriented in the 1940s, but today its members are gray-haired, middle-aged men and women. This subculture grew dramatically after the motion picture *The Wild One,* starring Marlon Brando, was released for a youth-oriented audience in the 1950s. The movie, based on a true incident that took place in Hollister, California, depicted a motorcycle gang taking over a town and wreaking havoc. Brando played a tough-talking gang leader who was seen as an antiestablishment hero. As numerous biker cults developed, it became necessary for them to establish their own subcults within the larger subculture by adopting their own gang names and proudly displaying their own colors, which gave them individual identities.

The Harley-Davidson motorcycle company has made millions from this subculture. All kinds of paraphernalia imprinted with the now-famous Harley-Davidson wings have been marketed. Some of these products include Harley-Davidson blue jeans and Harley cigarettes catering to the macho smoker. The Harley insignia has become an icon as commonly worshipped as McDonald's golden arches and the Coca-Cola logo.

Although subculture members try to be different from and antagonistic toward the mass culture, they cannot escape from the commercialization of mass society. Each time a new subculture develops, the economy of the main mass culture benefits by providing products for the subculture, and the mass media also are right there to get a piece of the action, either through recorded music or special-interest magazines catering to the new subculture.

The takeover of a California town by Motorcycle gangs was glamorized in the 1954 Marlon Brando movie, The Wild One. *Today, that community holds an annual festival for bikers.*

Wherever possible, marketing efforts of subcultural products are designed to expand the market into the mass culture. The blue jeans of the youth subculture of the 1950s and 1960s, for example, eventually found their way into the mass culture as an acceptable form of dress. The mass culture also attempts to water down the subculture until it becomes acceptable to the masses. For example, the health-food movement was once a fringe subculture but now is big business in the mass culture.

We will further explore these interrelationships among our mass society, its subcultures, and the mass media when we examine the various media and how they function later in this book.

SUMMARY

Political democracy, public education, and the Industrial Revolution of the 19th century ushered in a new mass society that depended on mass production and mass consumption of goods and services. The mass media developed as an integral part of this new mass society and became the disseminators and creators of the new mass culture.

With the new culture came more leisure time. To fill people's leisure hours, new cultural industries were developed, which the mass media marketed. Among the first cultural institutions to develop in the new mass society were the metropolitan newspaper, the ballpark, and vaudeville. Each helped the new city dwellers to cope with their new lifestyle.

As new technologies developed, they had to find a niche in society. Some of the communication media that found a role in the new mass society were newspapers, telephones, photography, motion pictures, radio, and television.

Today's mass culture has been commercialized to the extent that our economy revolves around selling us consumer goods as cultural items. The mass media play an important role in this commercialization of culture and even help to export it.

Even the subcultures in our society that consciously reject mass culture are caught up in its commercialization. Members of these subcultures buy items that proclaim their identities. These items are produced by the mass society and often become fads in the mainstream culture.

Find a review of *Key People and Concepts*, a message board for *Practicing Media Literacy* questions, self tests, and more at: www.mhhe.com/wilson.

Thought Questions

1. What are some current complaints about the mass media in today's society?
2. What role did mass communication play in the development of our industrial society? Are there similar activities at work as our culture moves into the Internet's information age?
3. What examples can you list of current efforts to commercialize our leisure culture?
4. What are 10 major examples of America exporting its popular culture?
5. List several subcultures that are prevalent in today's mass culture.

Notes

1. "Nielsen Ratings Confirm Power of Diana Coverage." *Palm Springs Desert Sun*, September 11, 1997.

2. David Einstein, "Net News Sites Cover Tragic Death of Diana," *San Francisco Chronicle*, September 4, 1997, p. D1.

3. Ibid., p. D2.

4. Chandra Mukerji, *From Graven Images* (New York: Columbia University Press, 1983), p. 38.

5. *Ibid.*

6. *Ibid.*, p. 53.

7. William Ivins, *Prints and Visual Communication* (Cambridge, MA: MIT Press, 1953), pp. 47–49.

8. Marshall McLuhan, *Understanding Media: The Extensions of Man* (New York: Signet Books, 1964), pp. 84–90.

9. Mukerji, *From Graven Images*, p. 45.

10. Louis Wirth, "Urbanism As a Way of Life," *American Journal of Sociology*, July 1938, p. 21.

11. Gunther Barth, *City People* (Oxford: Oxford University Press, 1980), pp. 58–109.

12. Michael Schudson, *Discovering the News: A Social History of American Newspapers* (New York: Basic Books, 1978), p. 60.

13. Barth, *City People*, pp. 148–191.

14. *Ibid.*, pp. 192–228.

15. Dwight MacDonald, "A Theory of Mass Culture," in *Mass Media and Mass Man*, ed. Alan Casty (New York: Holt, Rinehart & Winston, 1968), pp. 13–14.

16. *Ibid.*, p. 17.

17. *Ibid.*

18. Joseph Winski, "Hershey Befriends Extra-Terrestrial," *Advertising Age*, July 19, 1982, pp. 1, 66.

19. Dick Hebdige, *Subculture: The Meaning of Style* (London: Methuen, 1979), p. 113.

Globalization of Information on the World Wide Web

The collapse of space, time and borders may be creating a global village, but not everyone can be a citizen.

> —1999 United Nations Human Development Report

There is no truth to the report that famed comedian Bob Hope died in June of 1998. ● This may be somewhat shocking to some people, because Hope's death was announced on the floor of the U. S. House of Representatives and the news was quickly spread around the world by legitimate news outlets. ● How could something like this happen? The Internet. ● It all started when the Associated Press, due to "human error," sent out a story over its website that the majority leader in the House of Representatives mistook for a death announcement. When the congressman saw the story, he took a printed copy of it to the floor and handed it to a fellow congressman, asking him to make a statement since he had authorized legislation making Hope an honorary veteran. ● Saying, "No man in uniform ever had a better friend. We're all going to miss him," the congressman broke the news to those in attendance. Others joined in their praise of Hope. Said one: "He was a great American. A great world figure. We thank him for the memories." ● Following the congressional tributes, the Reuters news service immediately sent out a news bulletin: "Entertainer Bob Hope is dead, lawmakers say." ● ABC news picked up the Reuters report and moments later interrupted broadcasts on hundreds of affiliated radio stations across the nation with news of the death. ● In California, the still-alive Hope was not listening to the radio when all nine telephone lines into his home began to ring. One of the first to call was Reuters, seeking confirmation of their report, but Hope's daughter told the news agency that the 95-year-old comedian was fine; he was eating breakfast—there was no truth to the report. ● A short time later, ABC News reported that the report of Hope's death had been denied by his agent; within minutes the entire story was retracted by the network.

In this age of instant news and electronic media, it doesn't take much for information to spread quickly around the world—whether it is accurate or not.

NEW TECHNOLOGY AND COMMUNICATION

@ **Practicing Media Literacy**

What do you think can be done to keep erroneous information from being spread on the Internet?

It's hard to believe that 100 years from now, as historians look back on the beginning of the 21st century, the names of Steve Jobs and Bill Gates may have as much significance to them in the field of global communication as past innovators Johann Gutenberg and Samuel F. B. Morse have to today's historians.

But the world of communication has changed drastically, primarily due to such computer innovators as Jobs and Gates. Any many of those changes came in just the final third of the 20th century.

For example, when the Apollo 11 spacecraft made the first manned landing on the surface of the moon in 1969, the on-board computer that helped Neil Armstrong and Buzz Aldrin to land and takeoff from the moon's surface was extremely limited when compared with home computers of the year 2000.

The fixed memory—what is now referred to as ROM—held about 72,000 bytes, which is only 1/20th of the storage capacity of a single 3.5-inch floppy disk used with today's computer systems. In addition, the Apollo 11's total random access memory, or RAM, was about 4K. Thirty years later, the average home computer could handle 8,000 times more memory.

But the new technology was not unlike the preceding forms of mass communication that were also involved in making the world a global village. And many of them faced the same types of problems: government control, censorship, privacy, universal operating languages, electronic commerce, information overloads, even online romances.

The Telegraph and the Web

Morse code

Because of its ability to link distant communities, the telegraph was hailed in the 1840s as a means to solve the world's problems and to assist in global understanding. Using the **Morse code**—a series of dots and dashes sent out over telegraph wires or over the airwaves—cities that were forced to wait days and even weeks for news of events from nearby communities were now able to receive instant information by telegraph.

So it is ironic that as the 20th century drew to a close, so did the legacy of Morse. On Monday, July 12, 1999, the last commercial telegraph transmission of the famed Morse code ended. The four North American commercial telegraph stations owned by Globe Wireless ceased operation—one of them using the same statement that Morse had used in his first telegraph message, sent from Washington, D.C., to Baltimore in 1844: "What hath God wrought?"[1]

The Morse code was no longer an official international language of distress for ships at sea. Now, anyone interested in tracking a ship's exact location (and even finding out about any problems the vessel may be having) can receive the information from the Internet.

But in its early days, the telegraph was faced with many of the same problems and complaints encountered by the Internet in the 1990s.

In his book *The Victorian Internet*, British journalist Tom Standage points out that the telegraph brought about social and business changes that were even deeper than those of today, with the same type of misunderstandings about the new technology.

He cites examples of governments trying to control the telegraph network (and failing). He notes that the development of online commerce through the telegraph was slowed by worries about the security of money transfers. There were also concerns in those days about privacy and 19th-century hackers.

And would you believe that author Ella Cheever Thayer's book *Wired Love*—dealing with "online" courtships and romances—was first published in 1879. It was quickly followed by other tales of "online" romances and marriages, including a magazine essay that warned of "The Dangers of Wired Love."

But Standage also maintains that when it comes to making the world a global village, the telegraph accomplished it long before the Internet came along.[2]

For centuries, news spread only as fast as a galloping horse could travel from one area to another. The telegraph brought cities, states, and even nations closer together with its form of instant communication.

For example, in the early 1800s, there was no need to keep military shipping information secret. The London *Times* regularly printed details of military troop deployments knowing that there was no way that such information could reach the ship's destination any faster than the ship itself.

By the second half of that century, reports of British troop movements could be lifted from the daily newspapers and telegraphed to its destination in a matter of minutes. The telegraph had changed the face of war, as well as the manner in which governments and businesses were run.

Long before satellites and the Internet, the world was considered much smaller due to the telegraph. As early as 1846, there were claims that this new technology would "bring all inhabitants of the earth into one intellectual neighborhood," and in 1858 it was labeled the "instantaneous highway of thoughts."

IMPACT OF THE WEB ON OTHER MEDIA

The development of the World Wide Web and its access to information from around the world has also had a strong impact on all forms of the more traditional media.

Television, Radio, and the Web

The introduction of radio during the early part of the 20th century helped to bring the world closer, as radio signals sent out on the airwaves do not observe international boundaries. However, most nations set limits on the power that their stations could use in order to avoid interfering with the radio signals in neighboring nations.

The last half of the 1900s was dominated by television, but it wasn't until the introduction of satellite technology in the 1960s that the next step in global shrinkage took place. **Satellites** orbiting the earth made it possible to send video images from one point to any other place in the world almost instantly.

satellites

The world had once again become smaller, thanks to the fast flow of television news pictures from around the world.

For example, when Queen Elizabeth assumed the throne of Great Britain in the early 1950s, all the networks had crews on hand to film the proceedings for viewing in the United States. Once the coronation was over, the camera hurried to the airport in London, where chartered planes were waiting. As the planes flew across the Atlantic, the network crews developed and edited the films so they would be ready for televising upon arrival. Motorcycle couriers picked up the finished products and rushed them to the network headquarters in New York City, where they were then televised to the American public—some 11 hours after the event had taken place.

Compare that with events 30 years later, when Queen Elizabeth's son, Prince Charles, married Lady Diana Spencer (Princess Di). The event was viewed worldwide as it happened, live. Then in 1997, the funeral for Princess Di was one of the most-watched television events around the world. Satellites had moved the news to instantaneous coverage from anywhere.

Today even local television stations are using satellites for their news coverage. Not only do many of them send reporters to national and international events (some stations had local reporters traveling with National Guard troops to the Middle East to report on what the "local boys" were doing during the Gulf war); satellites have also expanded their coverage of regional events. Satellite news gathering (SNG) has allowed television news to provide even more visual coverage of the news to viewers.

Computer users can now listen to or watch both live and recorded news and sports reports from such sources as ABC, CBS, ESPN, NBC, and even National Public Radio. Radio stations from around the nation and the world can be fed live into your computer speakers, and you can even hear the music of fledgling bands or tap into music from major recording companies. Fans can even access the sounds of the Super Bowl or World Series by calling up cbsradio.com on their computers.

When Peter Arnett, the Pulitzer Prize–winning reporter for CNN first left the Associated Press in the early 1970s to work for the 24-hour news cable channel, the idea was quite new, and many journalists questioned his move. After 18 years with CNN, Arnett announced that he was again going in a new direction—joining a new international video news service on the Internet, ForeignTV.com.

The Pageantry of Queen Elizabeth's Coronation was seen by American TV viewers, but not until many hours after the event. In contrast, the wedding of her son, Prince Charles, to Lady Diana Spencer some 30 years later was beamed by satellite around the world as it happened.

Many websites have been broadcasting live speeches and news conferences on the Internet for years, but they are now moving into new areas of information and entertainment.

Computer Aided Technologies of Sacramento, Calif., has tested the "televising" of minor league baseball games on the Internet. Events of this type had not been done much because the action moves too fast for most computer screens. However, officials at the company pointed out that advances in digital TV and faster modems have allowed the Internet and TV to begin melding. Such telecasts were expected to bring about a new digital age of video movies-on-demand, live Internet teleconferences, and same-day highlights of sporting events on the home pages of professional teams.

Another high-tech California company has developed the first **video search**   video search engine that lets online users type in a phrase or keyword and then view only video segments from news conferences or events associated with those words. If a subject you were interested in was among the many topics covered at a congressional hearing, you wouldn't have to sit through footage of the entire event to find what you want; you could call up a specific topic on demand.

And what was the first event to be placed online for such research? The video of the four-plus hours of grand jury testimony of President Bill Clinton in the Monica Lewinsky case in 1998 (video.altavista.com).

When Yahoo!—said to be the world's most popular website—paid $6.1 billion to acquire Broadcast.com, the leading distributor of sound and video programming on the web, it set the stage for the Internet to look more and more like television—including the commercials (See Box 3.1).

As a result of the merger, Yahoo! users would have direct access to hundreds of live and on-demand programs, from TV and radio broadcasts, as well as other sources. Yahoo! planned to make Broadcast.com's distribution network available for multimedia ads that could be viewed by anyone with high-speed access to the Internet. Many of these ads were expected to be similar to regular television commercials, a departure from the banners and text ads which have become a regular part of the Internet.

A 1999 study by the A.C. Nielsen Company showed that home use of the Internet has cut TV viewing, with wired homes watching an average of 13 percent less television. That amounts to about an hour a day less viewing time than homes without Internet hookups (See Box 3.2).

However, the networks and their shows now have websites of their own. These official sites, created and supervised by people directly related to the programs in question, must battle for the attention of web surfers with the websites created by fans of the programs, which are usually more informative and elaborate.

> @ **Practicing Media Literacy**
>
> Will the computer ever replace the television as the main entertainment activity in America's homes?

Fans of programs will even create websites for special occasions. When the *Seinfeld* show finished its run on NBC-TV in 1998, freejerry.com was created to allow fans the opportunity to sign an e-mail petition to free Jerry, George, Elaine, and Kramer from the jail cell where they landed on the season finale.

MCI Communications Corporation and a Seattle software company have teamed up to sell an Internet broadcasting service that could make television and radio programming available to computer users around the world. The joint operation was formed to sell the service to broadcasters, cable channels, and sports networks so that they could then offer it to home computer users. The move was said to be designed to make the Internet more capable of providing multimedia.

Box 3.1
MEDIA WATCH
The War for the Eyeballs of the Consumer

For many, the computer revolution during the latter part of the 20th century was a "war for consumer eyeballs." But the revolution was in danger of coming to a halt in the mid-1990s unless companies could win over those people who still spent their leisure time in front of the television screen instead of the computer screen.

During the early 1990s, personal computers and the microprocessors that drive them popularized the concept of multimedia entertainment by mixing sound, video, and graphics with the text. By 1996, the personal computer was no longer just a word processor; it was an important form of communication.

According to the CEO of Intel Corporation, Andrew Grove, however, personal computers would not be able to keep up their tremendous growth unless they could enhance and combine those features consumers were already receiving from their television sets.

According to Grove, the key was to recognize that the computer business was not just about building and selling PCs; it was also about the delivery of information and lifelike, interactive experiences. To prove his point, Grove demonstrated an Intel PC that provided what was described as "far better video and sound" of a scene from the 1996 movie box office hit *Twister*. The presentation was at Comdex, the computer industry's annual trade show in Las Vegas.

Since the computer was now being used extensively by the motion picture and television industries, those attending Comdex learned that consumers would have to be lured away from television by a computer industry that also provides "irresistible and compelling features." Only then will millions of couch potatoes be converted to mouse potatoes.

@   Practicing Media Literacy

Have you ever used your computer to listen to radio stations from other areas of the nation or world? If so, what did you think of what they were doing?

Thousands of radio stations around the world are already sending their programming out by way of the Internet, allowing people to tune in with the click of a mouse. A company that tracks web broadcasting, BRS Media of San Francisco, says that some 2,400 radio stations around the world were sending out some or all of their programming on the Internet by 1999 (you can find out if your local station is on the Internet by calling up the MIT List of Radio Stations at wmbr.mit.edu/stations/list.html).

And while radio broadcasters used to look at the Internet as a threat to their existence, they are now embracing the new technology as a way to boost their ranks of listeners and sell more advertising.

sound quality

Of course, there are technical problems with radio on the web. The **sound quality** through a computer is not the greatest, and occasional glitches may cause an interruption in the programming. But to many Internet listeners these are only minor inconveniences when weighed against the opportunity to listen to radio stations from all around the world. Among the biggest users are those who have had to move to other areas and can overcome homesickness by listening to the radio stations they grew up with.

Internet radio

The problem for many broadcasters is the growing move toward **Internet radio**—stations that broadcast only on the web and not over the airwaves. These stations are not subject to the same rules and regulations as regular government-licensed broadcasters. There is no FCC regulating the Internet; there are no restrictions as to what can or cannot be said on such stations.

While studies have shown that television viewing has decreased because people are spending more time online, the fascination with computers has apparently had little affect on other forms of entertainment.

As the 20th century drew to a close, a survey of 1,000 online users and 1,000 households about media preferences showed that going to a movie was preferred by 77 percent of all consumers over spending time on the Internet; movies were also the choice of 76 percent of online users. In fact, renting a movie to watch at home was preferred by 79 percent of all consumers and 68 percent of online users, while watching cable TV was the choice of 74 percent of all consumers and 65 percent of those online.

Reading was also highly regarded over the Internet by those polled by Fairfield Research of Lincoln, Nebraska. Some 72 percent of all consumers chose books over the web, while 61 percent of online users also preferred books. Reading magazines was the preference of 70 percent of all consumers, 61 percent of the online users.

According to Kate Delhagen of Forrester Research, people are still testing the Internet, trying to figure out what it's all about. "As an entertainment medium that you would substitute for a movie, it's obviously not there yet," she said.

While most Internet users still couldn't take advantage of the developing computer video and sound technology during the latter part of the 1990s, the future still holds the potential for the World Wide Web to become more like television.

As mentioned, several studies have already indicated that TV viewing was down because people were spending more time on line. The Fairfield study found that 47 percent of the online users would rather surf the Internet than watch network television. However, it was also found that many people eventually reverted to their previous patterns until something new came along on the web.

Source: USA Today, July 31, 1997, pg. D1

As to the listenership of such stations, Arbitron reported that only 6 percent of Americans had tuned into radio online in the summer of 1998. Six months later that figure had jumped to 13 percent, enough to draw the attention of potential advertisers.[3]

According to a study by Forrester Research, the core ingredients necessary to build and maintain a loyal online audience are strong content (cited by 75 percent of the respondents), easy use (66 percent), quick download time (58 percent), and frequent updating (54 percent).[4]

Producers, directors, and other creative people are working more and more with digital technology in an attempt to create programming they hope will be distributed around the world on the Internet. As the technology improves and high-speed modems become more prevalent, the World Wide Web is expected to become more of a multimedia source using streaming videos and fast sound downloads.

This type of programming has been available in crude form on the web for some time, but the interest increased during the late 1990s with such successful Internet video events as a Victoria's Secret fashion show, which drew more than 1.5 million viewers. The increased interest was stimulated by the billions of dollars being spent by America Online, Time Warner, AT&T, Microsoft, and other high-tech corporations

> **@ Practicing Media Literacy**
> What affect do you think the lack of FCC regulations will have on Internet-based radio stations?

seeking to increase the capability of transmitting wide data streams across the Internet to homes around the world equipped to receive the higher-quality feeds.

Newspapers, Magazines, and the Web

Many newspapers and magazines have taken note of the need for improved websites. Many are now increasing the amount of original material on their websites, part of a shift toward using the Internet as a separate news outlet. A survey in 1999 showed that 58 percent of the newspapers and magazines in this country had their own websites. Of those, 31 percent used original material for at least half of their website's content.[5]

One of the advantages of Internet journalism is the ability to get information out immediately. Two leading Internet search engines, Yahoo! and Infoseek, have introduced news services that stress the immediacy of news in cyberspace. The services provide a wide range of news, sports, entertainment, and business information that's updated around the clock. Computer users can choose the kinds of news they want to see and view it all through a single screen.

According to Hoag Levins, executive editor of the online news industry trade publication for *Editor & Publisher, Mediainfo.com*, "The Web makes every medium the same, whether you're a television network, a newspaper or a radio station."[6]

Editors working with cyberspace publications are trying hard to get as many web users to their sites as possible and often gear their Internet news accordingly. "On the web, the audience is in charge," says John Barth, vice president for news at America Online.[7] As an example, Barth notes that on the day Ginger Spice left the British pop rock group the Spice Girls, the *New York Times* splashed a picture of the singer across the front page of its Internet website (nytimes.com). That is not something you'd see in the print edition of the paper.

The Knight-Ridder newspaper chain announced that it was transforming its websites into a nationwide network of regional Internet portals, hoping to target advertising to people who use the sites as their first stop in cyberspace. The announcement followed similar actions taken by the *Washington Post* and the *New York Times*. A **portal** is a starting point for computer users when they surf the web, a place for them to go when they are seeking other things. If portals offer enough services in the one place, the theory is that the audience will grow and spend enough time on the site to persuade advertisers to buy more space there.

portal

> **@ Practicing Media Literacy**
> Would you read a newspaper more regularly if it were delivered to you on the Internet each day?

There are those who say that newspapers and magazines are becoming an endangered species in this digital age. But with more and more publications going online, the demise of the print media seems somewhat exaggerated. Even Internet-based news organizations have begun selling their content to newspapers and magazines in an attempt to attract more readers (and eventually more advertisers) to the Web.

Syndicated online content reaches 10 times more readers in print than on the web, even though some publications are hesitant to carry content from online rivals.[8] Though the syndication fees are not very high for newspapers, the potential payoff is quite high for the online news operations. Syndication in the print media helps the websites build brand-name recognition, reach a wider audience, and make some money at the same time.

The Music Industry and the Web

The development of MP3 technology is considered a major revolution in the recording industry. Basically, **MP3** is compression technology which squeezes music data into smaller files, allowing personal computer users to easily download music to their hard drives and play it back whenever they want. As a result, many musical groups have been bypassing the record companies and putting their work directly onto the Internet (see Chapter 11).

In addition, more and more live musical concerts are being made available on the Internet. For example, in 1996 the Lollapalooza rock festival, which had already been touring the nation each summer for six years, began broadcasting its performances on the Internet. Fans who visited the Lollapalooza website could download software that let them hear festival music immediately. In addition, the site hosted text-only online chats with rock stars from several of the bands taking part in the tour.

There are also several jazz clubs in New York City that regularly feature the performances of artist on the Internet directly from their clubs.

MP3

While many musical artists, such as Mary J. Blige, still rely on music videos to promote their recordings, MP3 technology allows them to sell their product directly to the consumers on the Internet.

> **@ Practicing Media Literacy**
> Do you think MP3 technology will eventually replace the major record companies or the music stores?

Movies and the Web

Many believe that a new art form of Internet movies is just around the corner. There are already several websites showing films made specifically for the Internet. The director of such films as *The Blue Lagoon* and *Grease*, Randall Kleiser, has directed his first drama for the new Digital Entertainment Network, an Internet hub of TV-type programming. Another website shows several made-for-the-net movies daily, but also features hundreds of short subjects from the heyday of the movie houses. In addition, you can find some regular feature films, including the camp classic *Reefer Madness*, on the Internet. These websites thrive on material that you can't see in theaters or on television.

This was true in 1997 when a long-lost film of Richard Burton's Tony-award winning Broadway performance of *Hamlet* in 1964 was found and restored. The film wasn't released to theaters; it was presented on the Internet in what many considered a first for the worldwide computer network. Alternative Entertainment Network (aeniv.com) also offered an early interview with Burton, who died in 1984. The print shown on the web was the only one remaining of the three-hour film.

> **@ Practicing Media Literacy**
> Will the high cost of movie theater tickets help in the development of movies on the Internet?

The motion picture industry has also found another way to make money from the Internet. With warehouses full of costumes and props from their movies, the studios are now going online with **auctions** of the memorabilia. While many studios and production companies have had online sites where fans could purchase mass-produced items related to current popular movies, Universal Studios and New Line films were

auctions

the first to use the Internet to auction off pieces of movie sets, one-of-a-kind wardrobe items, and even props from classic films.

Many have predicted that the rise of the Internet as a new medium would bring about the decline of traditional media, including the fall of traditional advertising companies. However, from the perspective of Madison Avenue, nothing could be farther from the truth.

Advertising and the Web

Advertising agencies have been reaping huge profits in recent years and are said to be thanking the Internet all the way to the bank. The rush among Internet companies to get the word out about their brands to the computer users has reaped heavy benefits for such traditional media as television, radio, newspapers, magazines, and even outdoor advertising.

> **@   Practicing Media Literacy**
>
> Have you ever purchased anything from a company on the Internet? Have you made a purchase of something because you saw it promoted on the web?

How strong has the growth for the traditional media from the online media been? Figures from Competitive Media Reporting show that while spending among all advertisers in traditional media during the first quarter of 1999 rose 4.6 percent from figures in the same period a year earlier, the largest gain by far came in the category of new media: up 183.1 percent to $284.2 million from $100.4 million the year before.[9]

Books and the Web

The book publishing industry is also being affected by the Internet. Many large bookstore chains have moved onto the web to handle sales. Some were forced into the move by Amazon.com, which started as merely an Internet source for purchasing books but has since expanded into an auction site as well. Of course, there are still many authors who bypass the publishers and sell their books directly over the Internet.

Shortly after author Tom Wolfe gave his first public reading of his novel *A Man in Full* at New York's Town Hall, it was on the Internet. Those who wanted to hear the famed writer's own interpretation of his work had only to log onto nytimes.com/books.

At many public libraries, the interest is not so much in the books anymore as it is in the computers. A librarian with the Brooklyn Public Library, Richard Suico, told the *New York Times* that computers are a big attraction to kids, many of whom don't have a computer at home. "They come in for the computers, but we hope to supplement it with books," he said.[10]

One book that recognizes the impact of the new technology is Merriam-Webster's Collegiate Dictionary, which added 100 new words to its 1999 edition. Many of those words, of course, relate to computers. Among the new words listed: *bit-map, html, chat room,* and **netiquette**.

netiquette

Mixed Media

As we've discussed, many forms of media have turned to the World Wide Web as an outlet for their material. Many television networks and individual stations have established web pages, as have most of the major newspapers. Magazines are also available on the Internet as well on the newsstands, and Microsoft has even created its own online magazine, *Slate.*

When established in 1996, Slate was edited by the former chief of *New Republic*, Michael Kinsley, and offered a theme song; panel discussions; thought-stimulating articles about politics and economics; public opinion polls; TV, movie, and book reviews; and even a weekly report on how the media cover the big stories of the week.

Also introduced in 1996 was a consumer magazine for the Internet. The first edition of the San Francisco-based monthly, called *The Web*, featured articles from film critic Roger Ebert ("Hangin' with the Movie Man Online") and sex therapist Dr. Ruth Westheimer ("In Defense of Online Sex"), as well as a cover photo of actress Sandra Bullock, who was promoted as discussing fans, friends, and online stalkers.

One of the major players in the computer wars, Microsoft, joined with the NBC television network to form a cable channel, MSNBC, an all-news outlet with an Internet connection. Designed to challenge the dominance of the Cable News Network (CNN) in the area of all-news programming, MSNBC provided a feature that allows viewers to see something on the news and then use their computers to seek out more information on the story. The system was even designed to let viewers set up their own menus for news preferences. That allowed them to routinely call up information on local weather, find out how their favorite stocks were doing, or even update specific types of stories that interested them.

As the 1990s drew to a close, companies were involved in the manufacture of computers that used the television set to connect to the Internet, complete with a remote control that allows users to zip through the Internet's World Wide Web, send or read electronic mail, and then return to regular TV viewing. The move came primarily because some 98 percent of American homes had television sets, but only 35 percent had computers, which, until then, were the only means of accessing the Internet. The web now became available for millions more.

Government Controls

Around the world, governments still try to maintain some sort of control over the media, including the Internet. In the People's Republic of China, for example, the owner of a software company that set up websites and offered other Internet-related services, was convicted of "inciting the overthrow of state power" because he supplied 30,000 e-mail addresses to a prodemocracy Internet magazine in the United States. In sentencing the man, the court said he deserved to be "punished harshly." It showed just how much the Chinese government feared "the ability of 20th century technology to spread the voice of independence and human rights world wide."[11] But how can the government exercise control?

There are millions of Internet users in the People's Republic of China—and these totals more than doubled between 1998 and 1999. The capital city of Beijing accounted for around 22 percent of the users, and a survey said most users around that nation spent 6 to 10 hours online each week.[12] While computer use is still in its early stages in that country of more than 1 billion people, it is expanding very quickly.

Meanwhile, countries in the Arab world are faced with the dilemma of embracing the Internet's potential for linking people and providing knowledge or blocking it entirely with censorship. Like the cellular phone, the Internet has increased the flow of information in some areas of the Middle East. In others, it is seen as a tool of Western cultural domination. According to a Human Rights Watch report in 1999, only about 1 million people were online in the Middle East. While Israel was reported to have 11 percent of its population connected to the Internet, no other country in the Middle East had more than 5 percent of its people with Internet access.[13]

GLOBAL PROBLEMS WITH THE INTERNET

With the new technology has come a new set of problems. One of the areas of most concern has to do with pornography on the Internet and the issue of freedom of speech. And because the Internet does not observe international boundaries, this has become a worldwide issue.

International Child Pornography and the Web

In 1999, the World Citizens' Movement to Protect Innocence in Danger, working under the auspices of the United Nations, announced that it was seeking to make cyberspace more free of online child pornography and sexual preying on minors. One of the organization's main areas of study was to be the discrepancies in national child protection laws around the world. The purpose was to see if such laws could be better coordinated among the nations of the world and to determine if tougher legislation was needed in some countries.

Homayra Sellier, the president of the group and a Switzerland-based child advocate who has also worked against child prostitution in East Asia, said "Before the Internet, child abusers were isolated and lonely. Today the Internet has made it possible for them to communicate with each other, from one continent to another and make them feel they are part of a 'normal group.'"[14]

Sellier adds that the group does not want to limit use of the Internet, but wants to eliminate its abuse with child pornography. The organization got started with chapters in nine countries in North and South America, Asia, and Europe, and was planning to expand to Africa.

U.S. Pornography and the Web

Of course, something of this nature can easily become a political issue, and that was the case in the United States. Members of Congress tried to ban indecent material on the Internet with the 1996 Communications Decency Act, which tried to prevent children from gaining access to sexually explicit material on the Internet.

However, in a unanimous decision, the Supreme Court of the United States struck down the measure in 1997, saying that in seeking to protect young visitors to the Internet, the law covered too much material and was so vaguely defined that it trampled on the constitutional rights of adults as well.

In writing the court's decision, Justice John Paul Stevens said "It is true that we have repeatedly recognized the governmental interest in protecting children from harmful materials. But that interest does not justify an unnecessarily broad suppression of speech addressed to adults."[15]

One of the groups pleased with the court ruling was the American Library Association, one of the plaintiffs in the case. An attorney for the organization said that future attempts to curb access to material on the Internet will have to meet the highest constitutional free speech standards. Given the breadth of the court's ruling, he said, "there are going to be very few ways in which Congress is going to be restricting" the Internet.[16]

His predictions came true two years later when a federal judge in Philadelphia blocked Congress's second attempt to protect children from Internet pornography. The new law, called the Child Online Protection Act (**COPA**), would have made it a

COPA

federal crime to operate a sexually explicit website considered
"harmful to minors," unless access was limited to adults. In his
ruling, the judge noted "we do
minors of this country harm if
First Amendment protections,
which they will with age inherit
fully, are chipped away in the
name of their protection."[17]

*Computers in class-
rooms and libraries
make the World Wide
Web available to young
people, but this also
creates the problem of
protecting them from
Online pornography.*

In this second attempt to
shield those younger than 17
from pornographic sites, Congress had sought to require operators to verify that they were
dealing with adults. This would
have been done by requiring use of a credit card or some form of registration.

Supporters of the second law noted that it was more narrowly drawn than the
1996 Communications Decency Act to stop only objectionable sex material. Critics
charged that the legislation would allow conservative groups to attack commercial
websites that dealt with issues ranging from gay rights and sex education to modern art.

The law had been challenged by the American Civil Liberties Union, the Electronic Frontier Foundation, and the Electronic Privacy Information Center, an organization opposed to what they described as "online censorship." The three represented
17 plaintiffs, among them the *New York Times* Online, *Playboy* magazine, *Time* Inc., a
chain of gay and lesbian bookstores, and an obstetrics and gynecology website.

The primary problem for lawmakers is the realization that the Internet is an international network. Laws of the United States have no impact on foreign-based websites. But that doesn't mean that other nations aren't trying to accomplish the same
thing. The Australian government approved the Broadcasting Services Amendment
(Online Services) Bill 1999 which would force Internet service providers in that nation to remove objectionable material from Australian sites and to block access to
similar sites oversees. The measure immediately came under fire from such organizations as Electronic Frontiers Australia, which said that as soon as it becomes obvious
that national governments are powerless to control a worldwide communication system, the bill would make the Australian government an "international laughing
stock."[18]

In the United States, one response to the problem was a
call for leading online companies to band together and form a
self-regulating organization. Such a proposal was made by
America Online CEO Steve Case, who proposed what he
called an Internet Alliance that would set standards for indecency, privacy, electronic commerce, and other issues. Said
Case: "We have to get our act together or we can be sure that
others will regulate us."[19]

The Clinton Administration announced that the government would work with Internet industry groups to use existing
laws and technology to help parents protect their children from

@   Practicing Media Literacy
Since the World Wide Web does
not recognize national or international boundaries, what do
you think should be done, if
anything, to keep Internet
pornography from children?

objectionable material available in cyberspace. The announcement came after a meeting the president had with representatives from Internet industries, child advocacy groups, and legislators.

Several months later, the administration announced that online industries had agreed to report child pornography to law enforcement officials. According to Vice President Al Gore, industry groups representing 95 percent of home Internet users would help enforce the laws against child pornography. Under the policy, Internet providers would remove child pornography from their bulletin boards and services, said Donna Rice Hughes, a spokeswoman for Enough is Enough, an advocacy group trying to get child pornography off of the World Wide Web.[20]

A little more than one year later, Donna Rice Hughes was giving a San Francisco newspaper reporter "a tour of some of the web's smuttiest sites, ones which are freely accessible to minors."[21] The problem still existed.

One of the reasons was shown in the first comprehensive poll of sexual habits on the Internet in which a team of psychologists concluded that "erotic pursuits" were among the most frequent uses of the web and that *sex* was the most searched word online.[22] Said one of the people who conducted the survey, "Sexuality is a big phenomenon in our society—and it's mirrored on the Internet. Males and females go online for arousal, entertainment, and information."[23]

Religion and Pornography

Leaders of the Roman Catholic Church have condemned the use of the Internet for the proliferation of obscene material and have even suggested that the church begin rating Internet sites. The president of the world's largest cable television company, Leo Hindery of TeleCommunications Inc., told church leaders that the Internet is "one of the greatest threats to morality and decency that we face today" and he urged the church to use it as an **"electronic pew"** to preach morality and family values.[24]

A leading expert on cyberspace and chairwoman of the Electronic Frontier Foundation, Edith Dyson, also urged the church to create a system for rating websites. However, other church leaders pointed out that there was no practical way for the church to rate websites, which often changed on a daily basis.

electronic pew

Libraries and Internet Pornography

In a related issue, free speech advocates and parents across the nation have been agonizing over what to do about library access to the Internet, where a wealth of important information and ideas mix indiscriminately with hard-core pornography.

In Loudoun County, Virginia, the public library's board voted 5 to 4 to install blocking software to deny public library patrons access to computer Internet sites that featured "child pornography," "hard-core pornography" and "material deemed harmful to juveniles" under Virginia law. The American Civil Liberties Union sued the board, charging that the policy violates the First Amendment rights of library patrons because the blocking device would not only deny access to pornographic material that have no constitutional protection but also sites that do have such protection, including sites maintained by the Yale University Biology Department and several newspapers. The Director of the Loudoun County Library said the policy puts librarians "in the position of being parents, and it makes second-class citizens out of those not affluent enough to have this technology in their home."[25]

Opponents of Internet censorship reported that many programs don't reliably censor smut and sometimes blocked educational information, such as disease prevention news and information about the National Organization for Women, as well as pornography. They noted that one program allowed adolescents to see the home page for *Hustler* magazine for several minutes before it shut down access, while another screening program did not permit access to material on poet Anne Sexton because of the first three letters of her last name.[26]

In California, the San Jose City Council rejected a plan to install similar blocking hardware on computers at city libraries. The proposal would have allowed minors to use only computers in the children's section of the libraries that would contain the blocking software.

Several council members pointed out that people generally don't look at sexually explicit material on library computers, which are located in open areas to discourage such use. Said Mayor Susan Hammer, "I can't think of anything worse than government and politicians getting into the role of censors."[27]

OTHER GLOBAL PROBLEMS

Other problems brought on by the new Internet technology include content of material available on the web, privacy, and control of intellectual property.

Speed vs. Accuracy

When the *Dallas Morning News* decided to go with a story that Timothy McVeigh told his lawyers that he alone drove the Ryder truck involved in the Oklahoma City bombing, it did not print the story in the next morning's edition. The newspaper made the story available on its website that afternoon.

For journalists around the world the question became whether the newspaper's decision to get the story out more quickly by releasing it on its website in advance of the next day's publication had started a new direction in the way newspapers delivered information to the consumer.

As mentioned earlier in this chapter, more than half of the newspapers and magazines in this country have their own websites and almost one-third of those publications use original material for at least half of their websites' content. This raises the question for all consumers as to whether this "new" material on the web had gone through the thorough editing process usually followed before stories are printed or, in the interests of speed, has just been put out on the web for all to see, whether it is accurate or not.

Freedom of the Press on the Web

This Constitutional right has come under fire in the way some high school newspapers have been using the Internet. Many such newspapers have been publishing online in order to keep in touch with alumni who would not normally see the printed publication, as well as to create more of a dialogue with the community.

However, some administrators have been putting restrictions on the Internet versions of high school papers by not allowing the use of the last names of students online. Other schools are requiring permission from parents before publishing a student's photo. The main area of concern appears to be the 1974 Federal Education Records Privacy Act, federal legislation that limits the information that schools can give out about students.

Many high school journalism teachers disagree with the different policies for Internet publications, saying it hinders their ability to teach students the true power of the medium. Said Mark Goodman, executive director of the Student Law Center in Arlington, Virginia, "We have to ask, is it wise for us to cut off one of the new potential avenues to let kids express what they are thinking and feeling. It seems a much wiser choice to channel kids into a school-sponsored publication."[28]

freedom of speech

In the area of **freedom of speech**, the Internet is a public forum similar in many ways to a soap box in London's Hyde Park, where anyone can espouse his or her beliefs and concerns. At first, these consisted of a lot of conspiracy theories about anything and everything from the assassination of President John Kennedy in 1963 to a government cover-up in the crash of TWA flight 800 in 1996.

The Internet is, in essence, a high-tech party line where people can eavesdrop on the conversations of others and then spread that information to others. There's a vast free flow of information on the World Wide Web, and anything sent to one or two people can be quickly forwarded to many others at the stroke of a button, and those recipients in turn can forward it on to many others.

Hate Groups and the Web

One of the newest trends on the Internet is the proliferation of messages of hate. The Ku Klux Klan, neo-Nazi organizations, and other groups have been increasing their use of the web to spread their messages of white supremacy and racism. Where it once was a major problem for a Klansman to even find anyone who would print his hate literature—and then it would be seen by only a handful of people—such literature can now be sent around the world and be received by a large audience of curious web surfers. According to Rabbi Abraham Cooper, associate dean of the Simon Wiesenthal Center in Los Angeles, "The Internet is best understood and still mostly used by young people, and a natural tendency of youngsters has nothing to do with the Net. It has to do with being a teenager and wanting to go where you think adults don't want you to even take a look."[29]

> @ **Practicing Media Literacy**
>
> Should there be laws to keep hate groups from using the World Wide Web to spread their messages?

Meanwhile, civil rights groups have also begun to exploit the power of the Internet in combating intolerance. "We're dragging these people out of the shadows," said David Goldman, the founder of a nonprofit organization called Hatewatch.org, which posts information about a variety of hate groups on its own site. "Let's bring them out where we can examine them and learn from them and make sure we can protect ourselves from their influence."[30]

But some of the hate groups are clever. Readers attempting to access a dozen major newspaper websites in October of 1998 did not find the news, weather, and sports that they were seeking. Instead, they accessed the hate messages of a former Ku Klux Klan leader. The online deception was not a form of hacking into those newspaper websites, but instead of legally registering web addresses that closely resembled the names of the newspapers.

false web site

For example, the website for the *Philadelphia Inquirer* is phillynews.com/inquirer. The **false web site** was registered as philadelphiainquirer.com. While many of the newspapers vowed legal action to stop the use of the "nearly correct" web addresses, they were confronted with the fact that there is no law banning individuals or companies from securing addresses that may appear affiliated with brand-name corporations.

So be alert when seeking a website. If you want to check what's going on at the White House in Washington, D.C., you should go to whitehouse.gov. If you go to whitehouse.com you'll only find pornographic material.

CULTURAL GLOBAL PROBLEMS

In 1999, those attending a conference on entertainment and media in Asia, sponsored by the Asia Society of California Center in Burbank, were told that Asia's heavy influx of American television programs, movies, and the Internet was creating what was described as a cultural storm on the Pacific.

One of the panelists, Christine Choy of New York University's Institute of Graduate Film and Television Studies, told the gathering to "face the reality about the images [with which Asia is] being bombarded by Hollywood, such as 'women need larger eyes and breasts.'"[31]

Commented the chairman and CEO of Phoenix Pictures, Mike Medavoy, "I'm painfully aware that our content needs to be international. After all, 60 percent of our income comes from the international market. We need to mirror more of society."[32]

Several years earlier, in 1995, television came to the South Pacific island of Fiji. Suddenly, in a culture where eating was thought of as a cultural norm and big was considered beautiful for women, the female population was now seeing the girls of *Melrose Place, The Bold and the Beautiful,* and *Seinfeld.*

A little more than three years later, studies in Fiji showed that teens at risk from eating disorders had more than doubled and the number of high school girls who vomited for weight control went up five times (See Box 3.3). The culture of Fiji was being changed by American television, and this was even before they started receiving images of Calista Flockhart in *Ally McBeal.*

Psychological Impact of the Web

There's no doubt that the Internet has had an impact on our society and our culture. And that doesn't mean that it has all been positive.

The Canadian Medical Association Journal reported that "Internet-addiction disorder" **(IAD)** had entered the medical lexicon and was considered by some to be as real as alcoholism. The article quoted a University of Pittsburgh researcher describing the social problems of IAD as paralleling other addictions, including loss of control, cravings and withdrawal symptoms, social isolation, marital discord, academic failure, excessive financial debt, and job termination.[33]

A study presented to the American Psychological Association in 1999 appeared to bolster the expanding acceptance of compulsive Internet usage

> @ **Practicing Media Literacy**
> Will the distribution of American culture through syndicated television programs have a negative or positive affect on other nations of the world?

IAD

The star of Ally McBeal, Calista Flockhart, has received worldwide Media attention because of her extremely thin figure.

Box 3.3
MEDIA WATCH
The Media Help Spread American Cultural Problems

When television was introduced to the Pacific island nation Fiji in 1995, only 3 percent of the girls living there reported the symptoms of bulimia—vomiting to control weight problems. Just three years later, 15 percent of the girls reported taking part in such behavior.

This was the finding presented to the American Psychiatric Association in 1999 by Anne Becker, head of the Harvard Eating Disorders Center and assistant professor of medical anthropology at Harvard Medical School. As was the case in America, young women looked to television characters as role models, she reported. What was different was that while this has been going for many years in America, "reshaping the body is a new concept to Fijians," she said.

The culture in Fiji has always accepted heaviness as the norm in the lifestyle of that nation. Any noticeable loss of weight was seen as an illness or a lack of resources. But once television arrived on the scene, the young girls of Fiji saw women who were tall and slim. "We want our bodies to become like that," one girl in the study told Becker, "so we try to lose a lot of weight."

Becker cautioned that the study does not establish a definite link between television and eating disorders, but she said that the increases were dramatic in a culture that traditionally has focused on the importance of eating well and looking robust.

"Television is part and parcel of this rapid change and exposure to global values and media images," she said. "In a community such as Fiji, adolescents are particularly vulnerable. They're trying to emulate a lifestyle: Western-style clothes, haircuts and slim bodies."

Those are the American images being spread around the world by television.

Source: Associated Press, May 20, 1999.

---

as a psychological disorder. According to the study, almost 6 percent of Internet users suffered from some sort of addiction to it, with marriages being disrupted, kids getting into trouble, people committing illegal acts as the result of it, and people just spending too much money on the web.[34]

Meanwhile, researchers at the Carnegie Mellon Institute conducted a study on the effects of Internet use at home and found that people who spend even a few hours a week online experience higher levels of depression and loneliness than they would have if they used the computer network less frequently. For some, this was quite a shock.

@   Practicing Media Literacy

Have you ever noted any signs of depression related to your own use of the Internet?

The Internet has been praised as superior to television and other so-called passive media because it allows users to choose the type of information they want to receive and often to correspond actively with others in the form of e-mail, chat rooms, auctions, and electronic bulletin board postings. Research on the effects of watching television have indicated that it tended to reduce social involvement. But the Carnegie Mellon study suggested that the interactive medium may be no more socially healthy than older mass media. It also raised troubling questions about the nature of "virtual" communication and the disembodied relationships that often are formed in the vacuum of cyberspace.[35]

But there are still those who can find humor on the Internet. One story started circulating shortly after world chess grand master Garry Kasparov had lost to an IBM computer known as Deep Blue. As the joke went, a reporter approached the computer to ask about its plans following the historic victory and the computer responded: "I'm going to http://www.disneyworld.com."

NEW DIRECTIONS

Microsoft Corporation says there are 14 million mainstream web users in the United States alone. A study by the Nielsen ratings organization found that some 42 percent of the Internet users are between the ages of 25 and 44, while 30 percent of the users are 24 years of age or younger and 28 percent are in the 45 and older category.[36]

As the 20th century drew to a close, studies showed that Internet usage was growing among women, baby boomers, and seniors who were mostly using it to get news and to communicate with friends. A survey conducted by America Online and the research company Roper Starch Worldwide showed that 44 percent of those questioned felt that being online had become a necessity.[37] But it is also a form of mass communication that is not available to everyone.

The chairman of the Federal Communications Commission, William Kennard, has proposed that schools and libraries be given nearly $1 billion dollars in additional money for a program to give them discounted hookups to the Internet. Supporters of the proposal say it would give students and others access to information from a wide range of worldwide sources that they wouldn't otherwise be able to receive.

But some consumer groups voiced concern that such a plan would also result in higher phone charges. The money for such a venture would have been collected through fees on phone bills.

Such a proposal shows how access to the Internet is becoming an important part of everyday life—in this country and around the world. Many other organizations are continually examining how they can take a more active role with this new technology, which has been described as the biggest revolution in communication since the publication of the Gutenberg Bible.

For example, Harcourt General announced that it wanted to be the first publishing house to offer accredited college degrees on the Internet. The company said it planned to apply for accreditation from the New England Association of Schools and Colleges, the same organization that certifies Harvard University. The cost to "attend"? Officials at Harcourt indicated that tuition would be in line with that of state colleges, at about $1,200 a course.

> **@ Practicing Media Literacy**
> List what you consider to be the advantages and disadvantages of taking a course on the Internet.

Meanwhile, UCLA and numerous other colleges and universities are already offering extension courses on the Internet. Students can complete their coursework, participate in class discussions, and interact with the instructors through their home computers.

While others have been talking about offering online degrees, there are some who oppose such a course of action—even by accredited universities. As a spokesman for the American Association of University Professors put it, these virtual universities are "prepackaged education."[38] There is a fear that students will lose much without the interaction with professors and other students found in the classrooms. Proponents, however, claim academic chat rooms provide more interaction than classroom discussions.

Meanwhile, the technology continues to expand. In July of 1999, Malaysia cut the ribbon on its version of California's famed Silicon Valley. It's a high-tech project expected to eventually cost $5.3 billion and push Malaysia into the information age. Unveiled by Malaysian Prime Minister Mahathir Mohamad, the futuristic city is named Cyberjaya. It is expected to be completed by 2011.

Many large corpora-tions from around the world plan to establish operations in Cyber-jaya, Malaysia's $5.3 billion answer to Cali-fornia's Silicon Valley.

In what was once a giant clearing occupied by wetlands and rubber trees, the city will sit in the center of the so-called Super Corridor, a suburb of Kuala Lumpur, with one end anchored by the world's tallest buildings, the Petronas Towers, and the other held down by the international airport. Wired with high-speed fiber optics, the city will span 300 square miles—an area roughly the size of New York City. Over 200 companies have applied to set up operations in Cyberjaya—jaya means success in Malay— and 78 of them are foreign corporations, including such giant firms as Microsoft, Fujitsu, Oracle, and Microsystems.[39]

GROWTH OF THE WEB

By the year 2000, area codes for telephone service in many states across the country had doubled. But the growth in the population of those states did not increase at the same rate. So why was it necessary to make these changes in telephone area codes? Simple: Americans were making a tremendous demand for more cellular phones, pagers, faxes, and computers. And most of this new communicating was not person to person. In 1996, for the first time, Pacific Bell in California had more minutes on its networks used by computers rather than people. More than 50 percent of telephone line usage was not human to human but computer to computer.[40]

The increased use of computers and the Internet also created a problem for web addresses. In recent years, an international committee agreed to create seven new "domain names." Representing Internet experts from business, government, and education, the International Ad Hoc Committee took action to greatly expand the number of web addresses available for commercial use. Domain names are the cyberspace equivalent of ZIP codes, and the new seven included *.firm* for general businesses; *.store* for online shopping services; *.web* for web-related activities; *.arts* for cultural and artistic institutions; *.rec* for recreation and entertainment sites; *.info* for information services; and *.nom* for individuals.[41]

In the 21st century, the new technology is providing citizens with even more ways to receive information from anywhere in the world.

Are you wondering what's going on with the president of the United States? No problem; just check the Internet web site for the White House (whitehouse.gov). Do you want to know the latest from the hierarchy of the Catholic Church? Then you can browse the Vatican's website (cwnews.com). What about the Swedish royal family? They have a website too: "The Kungawebben Page" is a venture of the state telephone company in Sweden and the Swedish royal household, with pages devoted to King Carl XVI Gustaf, Queen Silvia, and Crown Princess Victoria (lysator.liv.se/nordic/divlroyalfam.html).

But if you're not interested in politics, religion, or royalty, check your local newspaper—not for news, but for the online schedule for many of your favorite movie, television, or recording stars. Such schedules are offered daily in *USA Today*, for example.

During its coverage of the XXVI Olympiad in Atlanta in 1996, NBC was forced to temporarily restrict access to its Olympics website when it offered a live chat with gymnastics hero Kerri Strug. NBC Interactive Media said the move came when an estimated 50,000 people entered the online "auditorium" for the chat with the Olympic gold-medal gymnast.

And that's not all. Internet broadcasting has now overcome such technical obstacles as the limits on compressing multimedia data and the narrow bandwidth of telephone lines. According to *Byte* magazine, this has allowed real-time audio and video—radio and TV—to reach "modest desktop machines over ordinary phone lines. Not download-for-20-minutes-and-play-later clips, but audio and video streaming through the wires in real time."[42]

While many people may not be too thrilled about using a $2,000 computer to listen to the radio or receive low-end television images, several high-tech companies have provided a solution to that problem as well. Apple Computer, IBM, Netscape, Oracle, and Sun Microsystems were the first to announce they had reached agreement on the technical details for what are known as "network computers." These are less powerful and less versatile than personal computers but good enough for exchanging e-mail and surfing the Internet. Network computers sell for between $500 and $1,000, much less than the price of a personal computer.

ACCESS TO THE NEW TECHNOLOGY

Use of the Internet has been exploding around the world in recent years. Based on users per 1,000 population, the most-wired nations are 1) Iceland, 320 per 1,000; 2) Finland, 305 per 1,000; 3) Norway, 304 per 1,000; 4) Sweden, 290 per 1,000, and 5) the United States, 283 per 1,000.[43] But as was noted earlier in this chapter, there are many nations around the world that do not have the same type of access to this new technology.

In China, the Internet is reportedly taking off because the country is hungry for news and information. China's online population hit seven million by the year 2000, up from two million at the beginning of 1999, according to Internet consultant BDA Ltd.[44] China's Internet market is still in its infancy for many reasons, and there is a lack of a nationwide credit card network, which has slowed the development of e-commerce in that nation. There are also no laws governing the industry and no organizations to monitor site traffic, which has left open the possibility that companies are distorting data.

Meanwhile, the government in nearby Singapore has been working hard to wire its citizenry to the Internet. Singapore has been hoping to transform the island nation of about four million people with no natural resources from an economy built on trade and service to one built upon information technology. Singapore has undertaken one of the most far-reaching technology-promotion efforts in the world. "Our purpose is to prepare Singaporeans for a web life, so they become the **'netizens'** of tomorrow, super-connected, technologically savvy, civic-minded and knowledgeable," said Pam Oh, an official of the National Computer Board. However, some have expressed concern that the government has been pouring millions of dollars into developing a technology infrastructure with no people to use it. By the end of the 20th century, the Internet service Singapore One had only 30,000 paying customers.[45]

netizens

The Gap between the Rich and the Poor

A racial divide appears to be developing on the Internet. According to a 1999 Commerce Department's study of the Internet in the United States, whites and Asians are at least twice as likely as blacks and Latinos to have access to the net. Said Kelly Levy, director of the domestic policy office for the Commerce Department's National Telecommunications and Information Administration (NTIA):

> "These findings are meaningful because the Internet itself is meaningful. It is no longer simply a technological marvel. It is having a very significant impact on people's lives. The way things are now you can forget paying jobs if you don't know how to use it and you can't use it if you don't have access."[46]

However, according to the annual market survey published by Target Market News, "The Buying Power of Black America," African-American households nearly quadrupled the amount spent for computer hardware in 1998 compared to the prior year. The report says that the spending increase pushes African-American household computer-related spending to $1.3 billion. The president of Target Market News, Ken Smikle, attributed the increase to the lure of the Internet as an alternative to traditional media.[47]

But the gap between the haves and the have-nots is not a situation that is unique to the United States. A report released in 1999 by the United Nations shows that the spread of the Internet and the globalization of information are contributing to a gap between rich and poor nations. The U.N. Human Development Report points out that the United States has more computers than the rest of the countries in the world combined.

According to the report, the richest nations of the world have 20 percent of the population, but 91 percent of the Internet users and 86 percent of the income. The study also notes that while it may take one month's salary for a U.S. citizen to purchase a personal computer, it would take eight years' income for an average resident of Bangladesh to purchase that same computer.[48]

@ **Practicing Media Literacy**
What actions would you propose to help the less wealthy nations keep up with the Internet explosion?

The War in Kosovo

As was the case with the Voice of America radio broadcasts to Eastern Europe and Asia since the 1940s, the United States Information Agency (USIA) provided free Internet and e-mail access to refugees of the Kosovo conflict in 1999. Known as the Kosovar Refugee Internet and Technology Assistance Initiative, the project was expected to cost USIA less than $100,000, with equipment and services valued at more than $1.5 million donated by such organizations as Apple Computer Inc. and Bell Atlantic Corporation.[49]

Computers and the Internet helped Kosovo refugees search for loved ones and keep contact with family and friends.

Although most of the refugees had never surfed the web before, with some training they were soon watching Albanian newscasts, checking websites on Serbian war crimes, searching the International Red Cross's Kosovo Crisis website for loved ones, or keeping in touch with family and friends scattered around the world through e-mail.

The Internet also helped Americans find out what was happening in Kosovo. A 16-year-old reporter for Youth Radio in Berkeley, California, Finnegan Hamill, made news when he was receiving and broadcasting messages from a teenaged girl caught in that nation's violence. Hamill described the 16-year-old girl, known only as Adona, as a modern-day Anne Frank with a laptop. Her messages were like a diary, except in a real-time environment. Here is some of what she wrote:

> "Just from my balcony, I can see people running with suitcases and I can hear gunshots. A village just a few hundred meters from my home is all surrounded. As long as I have electricity, I will continue writing to you. Right now, I am trying to keep myself as calm as possible. My younger brother, who is 9, is sleeping now. I wish I will not have to stop his dreams."[50]

Her poignant messages, which were broadcast on National Public Radio, indicated that her bags were packed, but she had nowhere to go except into the snow-covered hills nearby. According to the news director of Youth Radio (youthradio.org), the response from teenagers from around the world was overwhelming.[51] The Internet has also shown that it has the power to move people emotionally.

Suppression of Information

Around the world, satellite technology and the web have caused some problems. During the 1989 demonstrations for democracy in Tiananmen Square in Beijing, China,

---

@ **Practicing Media Literacy**

Have you learned anything about other countries or cultures by using the Internet to correspond with citizens of those nations?

Originally criticized by World War II veterans because it turned life in a German prisoner of war camp into a situation comedy, reruns of Hogan's Heroes are still seen world wide, including in Germany.

the Chinese government became concerned about the image of that nation's authoritarian rule being spread around the world by satellite. When troops were called out to put down the demonstrators, television networks from around the world were ordered to shut down their satellite transmissions from that country.

When the 10th anniversary of the Tiananmen Square demonstrations came around in 1999, the Chinese Communist Party prohibited any commemorations of the bloody event. To make sure that this edict would be followed, dozens of cable companies were ordered to stop broadcasting foreign satellite programming. In addition, the Chinese government ordered all foreign television broadcasters, including the Cable News Network (CNN), to shut off their transmissions from Beijing until a week after the anniversary.[52]

Satellite reception in China is officially limited to foreign housing, luxury hotels, and companies that can demonstrate a business need for such service. But with some 15 approved foreign broadcasters beaming programming into China, unauthorized satellite dishes and decoder boxes are an important part of the black market. That's why popular foreign programs such as *Baywatch* are viewed by large audiences in China.

The syndication of American programs to foreign nations has provided a major source of income for the television networks. It is not unusual to see the 1960s program *Hogan's Heroes* in Berlin or Munich, with the dialogue dubbed into German, or to see your favorite soap opera characters from *All My Children* or *The Young and the Restless* speaking Norwegian, as those programs are shown in Scandinavia.

PRIVACY AND INTELLECTUAL PROPERTY RIGHTS

One of the main issues of the privacy debate has been anonymity on the Internet. Of major concern is the anonymity of those who put information out on the Internet with no way for the consumer to know how accurate that information might be. Websites with official sounding names may only be a project of a teenager who wants to spread gossip about others. It may be an actual Internet gossip, such as Matt Drudge, who freely admits that some of the information he puts out may not be correct. With more and more people turning to the Internet as a legitimate source of news and information, this can be a major problem in the worldwide dissemination process.

On the other side of the coin, the Clinton Administration has been pushing for an "Electronic Bill of Rights," federal laws to prevent companies from collecting personal information from those who use websites, chat rooms, and e-mail and then releasing it to others.

In 1999, employees of Raytheon discussed business issues, rumors of mergers, and finance problems on a Yahoo! website where anyone could read the comments. As a result, Raytheon claimed that its company secrets were being revealed to the world and got subpoenas demanding that Yahoo! identify the anonymous participants. Yahoo! complied and 2 Raytheon employees reportedly resigned, while 21 others were sued for publicly discussing company business.

Should Raytheon have been given access to such information? Organizations such as the Electronic Privacy Information Center are opposed to the release of any data about Internet users.

Privacy was also a concern in 1996 when thousands of e-mail users received an electronic chain letter warning that their names, social security numbers, addresses, birth dates, mothers' maiden names, and other personal information were available to anyone through the Lexis-Nexis database known as P-Trak. The anonymous message added that the information could be used to commit credit card fraud.

Lexis-Nexis is a legal information and news information service with 650,000 subscribers worldwide. The new program, which was available only to Lexis-Nexis subscribers, had been in operation just a few months when the message spread through e-mail circuits. Officials at Lexis explained that it was used to help subscribers track down others.

Lexis-Nexis

While P-Trak had some 300 million pieces of information in its database, the problem apparently was not as extensive as the anonymous e-mail message had stated. In addition, most of the data P-Trak contained were also available elsewhere. But when Lexis-Nexis set up special phone lines to handle inquiries about the accusations, the lines were quickly jammed with concerned computer users. As privacy experts explained, it is not irrational to fear that personal information could be spread across the Internet.

> @ **Practicing Media Literacy**
> Are you concerned about maintaining privacy when you access the Internet?

Computer users are warned that cyberspace is a public place. Just as you wouldn't want to reveal some of your most personal information to a stranger on the street, you should be wary of passing on such information over the Internet. The words sent onto the Internet when you hit the "send" button don't just disappear; an electronic record may be kept on the recipient's computer or on a backup system. And, as an extra precaution, remember that libel laws (see Chapter 4) may also apply to online communications.

Copyright Problems

In the area of control of intellectual property, many national news organizations, such as Reuters, Gannett, AP, UPI, *Sports Illustrated*, the *New York Times*, the *Los Angeles Times*, the *Boston Globe*, and the *Miami Herald*, have claimed the right to reproduce articles and photographs on the Internet. This comes even when the writers and photographers have sold only the rights to publish them in print.

The Second Circuit U.S. Court of Appeals may have made it harder to reproduce articles on the Internet in a 1999 ruling against several nationally known newspapers and magazines. In a widely watched copyright case, the court sided with six freelance writers who claimed that several major media organizations had infringed on their copyrights by making their articles available on commercial databases, such as Lexis-Nexis, without providing additional compensation.

The New York Times Company, Newsday, Inc. And The Time Incorporated Magazine Company had argued that they owned the copyright to the "collective works"—the entire periodical in which the stories were published. Under an obscure section of the Copyright Act of 1976, they claimed they were allowed to reproduce the individual works in a "revision" of the collective work, citing Lexis-Nexis as a "revision" of the original publications. The Circuit Court disagreed and ruled in favor of the writers.[53]

In 1998, the *Los Angeles Times* and the *Washington Post* launched what was considered a legal strike that could shape how copyright laws apply to the Internet. The action came in a jointly filed copyright-infringement suit that sought to bar a conservative website from copying and posting stories from the two newspapers.

online copying

In the development stages of the Internet, news organizations and other copyright holders had tended to overlook the pervasive practice of **online copying**, which occurs countless times daily on the global computer network. But now the two newspapers were claiming that such action was cutting into their online revenue.

The case was being watched carefully by legal scholars because the application of copyright protection on the Internet has generated great debate since the early days of the web, when "Information wants to be free" became a rallying cry of online activists.[54]

 Practicing Media Literacy

Who do you think should own the distribution rights of a person's work — the writer or the publisher?

Another form of copyright dispute arose as the 1999 baseball season was drawing to a close. Major League Baseball's legal office began requiring stations around the country to suspend Internet simulcasts of their individual coverage of the major league teams they broadcast throughout the season. The league office argued that the webcasts were a violation of copyright and other specific contractual clauses. Many television stations were more inclined to discontinue the webcast duplication of their telecasts, rather than pay for the costs of securing a second set of broadcast rights from the major league teams.

BUSINESS TRENDS

With a workforce of 1.2 million people, the Internet industry has been more productive than almost any other in recent years, generating more than $300 billion in revenues. Researchers from the University of Texas Graduate School of Business, who conducted a study, found that the Internet rivaled the automobile and telecommunications industries. In addition, the study found that e-commerce was the fastest growing component of the Internet, grossing over $100 billion in revenues.

e-commerce

Traffic on the Internet has been estimated to be doubling every 100 days, with business use growing the fastest. The Commerce Department estimates that 10 million people in the United States and Canada are using the Internet for **e-commerce**— from airline tickets to books, from automobiles to auction items.

Researchers at the University of California at Los Angeles have launched plans for a long-term study designed to track the social consequences of the Internet and its expanding role in the lives of consumers. The project was to involve periodic surveys of thousands of households in up to 18 nations.

Meanwhile, the Commerce Department study has estimated that by the year 2002, business-to-business purchases—such as office supplies—could reach $300 billion alone. This could routinely save many of America's largest corporations hundreds of millions of dollars by reducing costs and inventories.[55]

Among some of the other findings in the Commerce Department report were:

- In 1994, only 3 million people were connected to the Internet. By the end of 1997, more than 100 million worldwide, including 62 million in the United States, were using it.
- The Internet is growing faster than all other technologies that have preceded it. Radio existed for 38 years before it had 50 million listeners, and television took 13 years to reach that mark. The Internet took only four years.
- The information technology industry has been growing twice as fast as the nation's overall economy.
- Workers in the information technologies were earning an average of nearly $46,000 annually, compared to an average of $28,000 in the private sector.[56]

The Federal Communications Commission has decided to keep a hands-off policy to help foster further growth of the Internet, with only minimal regulatory action to deal with anticompetitive behavior. The action came as the FCC was avoiding one of the most contentious debates about the future of how the Internet would reach consumers, particularly whether cable businesses offering high-speed Internet service must share their lines with competitors.

The Commission has declined to force such line sharing. The Commission staff report also advised against the FCC imposing regulations developed for old technologies on new Internet based technologies. However, some critics charge that the debate over the sharing of high-speed lines was a prime example of where government guidance is needed.[57]

Still one other problem has been brought home dramatically in recent years as millions of computer users have learned that the new technology is not infallible. Computer failures in recent years have knocked several online services offline for great lengths of time. In addition to subscribers losing access to the Internet and many other computer services, businesses found that they couldn't place electronic orders or were forced to turn to fax machines and telephones to conduct normal business.

SUMMARY

The world of communication has changed drastically in recent years, primarily due to the development of computer technology and the World Wide Web. The world has become a global village with instant communication to any part of the planet.

The development of the Internet and its access to all types of information from around the globe has also had a strong impact on the more traditional media:

- Radio now provides coverage of major events over the Internet and there are many radio stations around the world which can only be heard on the web.
- Research shows that television viewing time has decreased in homes wired to the Internet.
- Newspapers are creating their own web sites and, in many cases, are getting stories out faster by breaking them first on the web.
- The recording industry is being revolutionized by MP3 compression technology which allows musical artists to offer their material directly to computer users.
- Movies are now being made for direct release on the Internet.
- The advertising world has now found a new source of income through the World Wide Web and e-commerce.

- Large bookstore chains have moved on to the Internet for increased sales and convenience.
- Several magazines are now published only online.

One of the major problems that has come with the new technology is the control of pornography. Because the Internet does not observe international boundaries, pornography has become a worldwide issue with no solution in sight.

Another area of concern is whether some newspapers will sacrifice accuracy for the speed of getting a story out over its website. In order to be first with a late-breaking story, some publications may bypass the normal editing process that a printed story would go through before reaching the consumer.

The Internet has also brought out numerous hate groups who use the web to spread their messages to computer users of all ages around the world. Some civil rights groups have begun a counteroffensive by using the Internet to combat intolerance by exposing the hate groups for what they are and what they stand for.

Studies have shown that there is a large divide between those who have computers and those who don't. In the United States, whites and Asians are at least twice as likely as blacks and Latinos to have access to the Internet. Studies conducted by the United Nations show that the spread of the Internet and the globalization of information are contributing to a widening gap between the rich and poor nations of the world.

In a related concern, the spread of American culture to other nations through movies, syndicated television programs, and the Internet is having a negative impact in many areas of the world.

The growth of the web has been phenomenal, with the majority of computer users in the United States said to be in the 25-to-44 age group and the second largest group being the under-25s. Many colleges and universities are now offering courses on the Internet.

But the concern still exists that private information about the consumer can be obtained by others when that person goes online. On the other hand, many are worried about those who are using the Internet anonymously to put out information that may or may not be accurate.

There is no doubt that the World Wide Web is a rapidly growing business enterprise, with a workforce of 1.2-million. The Internet industry has been generating more that $300 billion in revenues, and traffic on the Internet has been estimated to be doubling every 100 days.

However, there is now the additional problem of computer addiction, with a study showing that almost 6 percent of computer users have developed a form of addiction to it. In addition, another study has found that those who use computers for even a few hours a week online can experience high levels of depression and loneliness.

Find a review of *Key People and Concepts*, a message board for *Practicing Media Literacy* questions, self tests, and more at: www.mhhe.com/wilson.

Thought Questions

1. Do you think books, newspaper, magazines, movies, recordings, radio, and television will all someday be replaced by online versions?
2. If these media are *not* replaced by online versions, what impact do you think the Internet revolution will have on them?

3. How long do you think it will be before all nations will have a population that is computer oriented?

4. Do you consider privacy on the Internet to be a major issue? If so, why? If not, why not?

5. What type of impact do you think American culture will have on the rest of the world if it continues to spread through the Internet and other media?

Notes

1. Zachary Coile of the *San Francisco Examiner*, "Morse Tapped Out," in the *Fresno Bee*, July 14, 1999, pg. Al l.

2. Bruno Giussani, "Looking at the Net From a 19th Century View," *New York Times CyberTimes*, May 11, 1999.

3. Statement of reporter Ian Hunter on "The Wall Street Journal Report," syndicated show #874, broadcast June 27, 1999.

4. "Forrester Research; Strong Content Means a Loyal Audience," e-mail news release, www.forrester.com, February 1999.

5. Associated Press, "Media Put More Original Content on Internet," *Fresno Bee*, March 3, 1999, pg. C2.

6. Michael Stroh, "All That News Gives Fits Online," *Baltimore Sun*, August 8, 1998, pg. 9C.

7. *Ibid.*

8. Jon Swartz, "Web News Goes to Print; Online Ventures Peddle Content to Newspapers," *San Francisco Chronicle*, June 19, 1998, pg. El.

9. Stuart Elliott, "New Media Helps Old Media Hold Off Forecasts of Doom," *New York Times*, July 23, 1999, pg. C1.

10. Randal C. Archibold, "At Library, Computers Compete With Books for Pupils' Time," *New York Times*, July 20, 1999, pg. A18.

11. "Cracking Down on E-Mailers," *San Francisco Chronicle*, January 22, 1999, pg. A22.

12. Reuters Wire Service, "China Internet Users Double To 4 Million," *San Jose Mercury News SiliconValley.com*, July 15, 1999.

13. Howard Schneider, "In a Spin Over the Web," *Washington Post*, July 26, 1999, pg. A13.

14. Pamela Mendels, "International Effort to Fight Online Child Pornography," *New York Times CyberTimes*, June 16, 1999.

15. Harriet Chiang and Ramon G. McLeod, "Net Porn Law Voided: Decency act went too far, justices say," *San Francisco Chronicle*, June 27, 1997, pg. A1.

16. *Ibid.*

17. "Judge Cites Free-Speech Protections in Blocking Internet Porn Law," from *Newsday*, printed in the *Fresno Bee*, February 2, 1999, pg. A7.

18. Jamie Murphy, "Australia Passes Law on Limiting Internet," *New York Times CyberTimes*, June 30, 1999.

19. Jon Swartz, "AOL Chief Urges Online Firms To Form Self-Regulating Body," *San Francisco Chronicle*, May 30, 1998, pg. D1.

20. Jeannine Aversa of the Associated Press, "Gore Backs Online Police to Rid Net of Child Porn," *San Francisco Chronicle*, December 3, 1997, pg. D1.

21. Jon Swartz, "Donna Rice Says No Excuses for Net Porn; Gary Hart's Ex-Paramour Has Reinvented Herself," *San Francisco Chronicle*, November 9, 1998, pg. B1.

22. Jon Swartz, "Sex Called A Big Deal On Internet; Poll Says Women Talk, Men Look," *San Francisco Chronicle*, June 10, 1998, pg. A1.

23. *Ibid.*

24. Robert Weller of the Associated Press, "Catholics Plug Internet as 'Electronic Pew,'" *Fresno Bee*, March 28, 1998, pg. A14.

25. "Library's Decision to Block Porn Sites Triggers Lawsuit by ACLU," Hearst Newspapers, printed in *Fresno Bee*, July 14, 1998, pg. A6.

26. Jon Swartz, "The Problem With Software That Censors the Net; Parents Find It Hides Too Much or Too Little," *San Francisco Chronicle*, May 27, 1997, pg. A1.

27. Ken Hoover, "San Jose Upholds Net Porn Access; Rejects Plan to Screen Computers for Minors," *San Francisco Chronicle*, September 25, 1997, Pg. A15.

28. Lisa Napoli, "School's Online Publications Face Curbs of Their Own," *New York Times CyberTimes*.

29. Connie Lauerman, "WWW.IHATE," *Chicago Tribune*, Section 5, pg. 1.

30. Brandon Bailey and Pete Carey, "Net Spreads Hate, but Also Fights It," *San Jose Mercury News SiliconValley.com*, July 14, 1999.

31. Tom Plate of the *Los Angeles Times*, "Asians Bristle at Culture Invasion," in the *San Francisco Chronicle*, June 17, 1997, pg. A21.

32. *Ibid.*

33. "Ann Landers," *Fresno Bee*, March 19, 1997, pg. E5.

34. Jeff Donn, Associated Press, "5.7% of Net Users Addicted, Study Finds," in the *Fresno Bee*, August 23, 1999, pg. A1.

35. Amy Harmon, "Study Expected to Favor Internet Finds It Causes Depression; Project Determines That High Use Makes People Lonelier," *New York Times*, printed in the *Fresno Bee*, August 31, 1998, pg. A1.

36. "Who's On the Internet? Nearly a Third of Internet Users Are Middle Aged or Older," Neilson/NetRatings, *The Nation*, May 1999, pg. 4.

37. Aimee Picchi, "More Americans Going Online; Study Finds Internet Use Has Grown among Women, Baby Boomers and Seniors," *Bloomberg News*, printed in the *Fresno Bee*, December 4, 1998, pg. C1

38. John Hechinger, "Textbook Publisher Lays Plans for an Internet University," *Wall Street Journal*, pg. B1.

39. "Malaysian Cybercity," Associated Press, in the *San Jose Mercury News SiliconValley.com*, July 8, 1999.

40. Natalie Shore, "Phone Users Face Splitting Headache," *Long Beach Press-Telegram*, July 8, 1996, p. A1.

41. Jon Swartz and Julie Angwin, "Web Gets Wider With new Names; Supply of Internet Addresses to Increase," *San Francisco Chronicle*, May 2, 1997, pg. A1.

42. Edmund X. DeJesus, "Toss Your TV: How the Internet Will Replace Broadcasting," *Byte*, February 1996, p. 51.

43. "Five Most-Wired Nations," *Parade Magazine*, October 10, 1999, pg. 7.

44. Leslie Chang, "China's Web Boom Attracts Big Crowd of Entrepreneurs," *Wall Street Journal* October 27, 1999.

45. Michelle Leavander, "A Web-Savvy Singapore Seeks to Turn People Into E-Citizens", *Wall Street Journal*, October 27, 1999.

46. Ramon G. McLeod, "Internet Revolution Misses Blacks, Latinos; Rural Residents, Poor Also Left Behind, Government Survey Shows," *San Francisco Chronicle*, July 9, 1999, pg. A1.

47. "Blacks' Spending on Computers Surges-Survey," Reuters News Service, in the *San Jose Mercury*, October 26, 1999.

48. R. C. Longworth, "A 'Grotesque' Gap; The Global Economy's Winners and Losers Are So Far Apart That Balancing Efforts Are Needed to Avoid Disaster, According to a New UN Overview," *Chicago Tribune*, July 12, 1999, pg. 1.

49. Nathan Abse, "Keeping Kosovo Refugees Connected," *Washington Post*, July 8, 1999, pg. A23.

50. Charles Burress, "Kosovo Teen E-Mails Her Diary to the World; Messages Relayed Through Berkeley Youth Radio," *San Francisco Chronicle*, March 26, 1999, pg. A25.

51. *Ibid.*

52. "10th Anniversary News Coverage Forbidden by China's Rulers," *Chicago Tribune*, in the *Honolulu Advertiser*, June 3, 1999, pg. A6.

53. Mike McKee, "Appeals Court Sides with Writers in Copyright Fight," *Recorder/Cal Law*, September 28, 1999.

54. "Papers Target Site That Copies, Posts Stories," California Newspaper Publishers

Association *Bulletin,* October 26, 1998, pg. 164.

55. Ted Bridis, Associated Press, "Internet Use Explodes around World; Business Use Growing Fastest, with People Relaxed Enough with It to Make Credit-Card Purchases," in the *Fresno Bee,* April 16, 1998, pg. C1.

56. *Ibid*.

57. "FCC Study: Net Prospers without Heavy Regulation," Associated Press, in the *Reno Gazette-Journal,* July 20, 1999, pg. 4A.

Legal
Controls
on the Media

Congress shall make no law respecting an establishment of
religion, or prohibiting the free exercise thereof; or
abridging the freedom of speech, or of the press or the right
of the people peaceably to assemble, and to petition the
Government for a redress of grievances.

—First Amendment, U.S. Constitution

Key People and Concepts

Alien and Sedition Acts

Prior Restraint

Federal Communications Commission (FCC)

Section 315

Fairness Doctrine

Closed Hearings

Gag Orders

Canon 35

Meese Commission Report

Telecommunications Act of 1996

Libel

You've seen it on your local news; you've seen it on such reality-based programs as the Fox Network's COPS program: television cameras following law enforcement officers armed with warrants as they rush into someone's home to search for drugs or make an arrest. But you won't be seeing much of that anymore.   •   In May of 1999, the Supreme Court of the United States ruled that police violate the Fourth Amendment right to privacy when they allow the media into people's homes to document raids and arrests. The unanimous decision means that the police can be sued for inviting the TV camera crews and other journalists to cover such raids. Writing for the court, Chief Justice William Rehnquist held that such police actions violate "the right of residential privacy at the core of the Fourth Amendment."[1]   •   More than 20 news organizations sided with law enforcement officers in the case, citing First Amendment rights of the news media and arguing that ride-alongs provide a valuable public service by enabling the media to monitor police activity. However, a spokesman for the American Civil Liberties Union (ACLU), which brought one of the cases to the high court, scoffed at that argument. "We'd love the press to be more of a watchdog on police," said Arthur Spitzer, legal director for the ACLU's Washington office, "but this had nothing to do with being a watchdog. This was about wanting to be in on a juicy raid."[2]   •   Meanwhile, officials with the Fox Network said they would continue shooting COPS as a "pure ride-along show" because they had always received releases from anyone shown on camera, even people under arrest. This wouldn't be a problem, they said, because most of the material used happens on the streets or in cars. The court ruling will allow the media to accompany police on ride-alongs, as long as reporters stay outside when officers enter private homes.   •   The First Amendment has been the subject of many court cases during its more than 200 years of existence. But for the most part, free speech and freedom of the press have survived most of the challenges.   •   Some contend that the First Amendment was meant to be absolute, but the courts have disagreed on occasion. For example, Supreme Court Justice Oliver Wendell Holmes, Jr., said in 1919 that the First Amendment was not absolute and that under certain conditions Congress could prohibit free speech. This was when he stated his famous analogy, "The most stringent protection of free speech would not protect a man in falsely shouting fire in a crowded theater and causing panic," to support the Court's position that if free speech posed clear and present dangers, it could be abridged.   •   In this chapter, we will examine the various laws and regulations that exist to govern the mass media in American society. Although the government imposes the most stringent regulations on the broadcast media, the print media as well as videotapes, movies, recordings, and even the Internet have been the subjects of attempts to make laws governing their content.

GOVERNMENT REGULATION OF PRINT

Efforts by the government to restrain freedom of expression have been around almost as long as the First Amendment itself.

Early Efforts: Sedition and Advocacy of Violence

restrictions

The Alien and Sedition Acts represented the first efforts by the government to impose **restrictions** on the press and free speech in our new republic. After a decade of partisan attacks on the Federalists who were in power, these laws were passed in 1798, just seven years after the First Amendment became law, to suppress critics. (At the time, the reason given for passing these laws was to protect the United States in a war against France that was never declared.) Among other things, these acts outlawed false, scandalous, and malicious publications against the U.S. government, the president of the United States, and Congress. Fifteen people were prosecuted under these laws, some for making offhand, humorous remarks about President John Adams. Anti-Federalist Thomas Jefferson challenged President Adams in his reelection bid in 1800, and his supporters used the Alien and Sedition Acts as a campaign issue. After his victory, Jefferson pardoned everyone convicted under the laws, and the acts were allowed to expire.

The Espionage Act of 1917 and the Sedition Act of 1918 enacted similar First Amendment restrictions in the 20th century. These laws made it illegal for anyone to openly oppose the nation's involvement in World War I. Some 2,000 people were prosecuted, and major restrictions were placed on ethnic newspapers, particularly German-language papers. This time, however, the First Amendment restrictions were fought in the federal courts and, ultimately, in the Supreme Court. (This was not done in 1798, probably because the Supreme Court justices were Federalists and supporters of President John Adams.) The first challenge to these laws was *Schenck v. United States* (1919).[3] In this case a Socialist leader, Charles T. Schenck, was prosecuted for circulating antiwar leaflets to army recruits and draftees. Schenck contended that the First Amendment protected his right to express his opinions, but the Supreme Court upheld his conviction on the basis of wartime circumstances. It was in this case that Justice Holmes used his fire-in-a-crowded-theater analogy and formulated the clear and present danger doctrine.

After the Schenck decision, a number of other convictions of Socialists were upheld, including the conviction of Eugene V. Debs, who later received nearly a million votes for president of the United States while serving time in prison.

In 1940 the government passed the Smith Act, which made it unlawful to advocate the violent overthrow of "any government in the United States" or to conspire to advocate such violence. In 1957 the Supreme Court, in *Yates v. United States,* took a significant step toward expanding First Amendment **protections** by overturning the convictions of 14 persons who had been charged under the Smith Act with pro-Communist, subversive activities.[4] The Court said that teaching unpopular ideas was protected by the First Amendment.

protections

In 1969, in *Brandenburg v. Ohio,* the Supreme Court ruled that even advocacy of violence was protected by the First Amendment as long as there was no threat of imminent lawless action.[5] This case involved a Ku Klux Klan leader.

Prior Restraint

It has long been believed that the intent of the First Amendment was to prevent prior restraint. **Prior restraint** is the ability of the government to prevent something from being published or spoken. This differs from the ability to punish someone afterward. Support for First Amendment protection comes from the belief that the framers of the Bill of Rights intended the First Amendment to provide for a free marketplace of ideas and that no idea, including one that may be unpopular or repugnant, should be suppressed.

> **@ Practicing Media Literacy**
> Do you think government actions such as the Alien and Sedition Acts or the Smith Act will be possible in this country in the 21st century?

prior restraint

The Supreme Court affirmed this belief in 1931 in *Near v. Minnesota.*[6] The case stemmed from a Minnesota law that allowed courts to declare scandalous newspapers to be public nuisances and order them closed. When a court declared his newspaper, which had been critical of government officials in Minnesota, a public nuisance and ordered it closed, publisher J. M. Near appealed the ruling to the Supreme Court. The Court declared that the Minnesota action was a form of prior restraint and a violation of the First Amendment. (It did say, however, that Near could be sued for libel if his paper printed untrue defamations.)

In 1971, the executive branch of government challenged the First Amendment in the Pentagon Papers case. Several newspapers had begun printing the papers in serial form based on documents compiled by Rand Corporation, a California-based think tank. The papers were basically a critical history of the Vietnam war. The Nixon administration obtained a prior-restraint order barring the *New York Times, Washington Post,* and *Boston Globe* from continuing to print the series until the courts could rule on whether the material would endanger national security.

The case, *New York Times Co. v. United States,* quickly went to the U.S. Supreme Court, which ruled that the government could not prove that anything in the papers would harm national security.[7] The newspapers won the case and resumed printing the documents. Joining the newspapers was the book publishing industry, which released books carrying the Pentagon Papers immediately after the Court's decision. (Although many people supported the right of the media to print these documents, few bothered to read the newspaper series or books after the court-authorized publication.)

In 1979, *The Progressive* magazine was restrained by a court from printing an article entitled "The H-Bomb Secret: How We Got It and Why We Are Telling It," following action filed by the Carter administration. The article, which had been

Vietnam Archive: Pentagon Study Traces 3 Decades of Growing U. S. Involvement

By NEIL SHEEHAN

A massive study of how the United States went to war in Indochina, conducted by the Pentagon three years ago, demonstrates that four administrations progressively developed a sense of commitment to a non-Communist Vietnam, a readiness to fight the North to protect the South, and an ultimate frustration with this effort—to a much greater extent than their public statements acknowledged at the time.

The 3,000-page analysis, to which 4,000 pages of official documents are appended, was commissioned by Secretary of Defense Robert S. McNamara and covers the American involvement in Southeast Asia from World War II to mid-1968—the start of the peace talks in Paris after President Lyndon B. Johnson had set a limit on further military commitments and revealed his intention to retire. Most of the study and many of the appended documents have been obtained by The New York Times and will be described and presented in a series of articles beginning today.

> Three pages of documentary material from the Pentagon study begin on Page 35.

Though far from a complete history, even at 2.5 million words, the study forms a great archive of government decision-making on Indochina over three decades. The study led its 30 to 40 authors and researchers to many broad conclusions and specific findings, including the following:

¶That the Truman Administration's decision to give military aid to France in her colonial war against the Communist-led Vietminh "directly involved" the United States in Vietnam and "set" the course of American policy.

¶That the Eisenhower Administration's decision to rescue a fledgling South Vietnam from a Communist takeover and attempt to undermine the new Communist regime of North Vietnam gave the Administration a "direct role in the ultimate breakdown of the Geneva settlement" for Indochina in 1954.

¶That the Kennedy Administration, though ultimately spared from major escalation decisions by the death of its leader, transformed a policy of "limited-risk gamble," which it inherited, into a "broad commitment" that left President Johnson with a choice between more war and withdrawal.

¶That the Johnson Administration, though the President was reluctant and hesitant to take the final decisions, intensified the covert warfare against North Vietnam and began planning in the spring of 1964 to wage overt war, a full year before it publicly revealed the depth of its involvement and its fear of defeat.

¶That this campaign of growing clandestine military pressure through 1964 and the expanding program of bombing in 1965 were begun despite the judgment of the Government's intelligence community that the measures would not cause Hanoi to cease its support of the Vietcong insurgency in the South, and that the bombing was

Continued on Page 38, Col. 1

This introduction to the New York Times *publication of the Pentagon Papers shows why the federal government wanted to keep the information from being published.*

compiled from nonclassified public documents, told readers in accurate detail how to make a hydrogen bomb. Before the case reached the Supreme Court, an almost identical article appeared in the *Madison Press Connection*. The government eventually dropped its case against *The Progressive*, which then printed the story. A Supreme Court showdown between the government and the media regarding *The Progressive*'s right to publish the article versus the government's right of prior restraint was avoided.

CNN fought several court battles in its attempt to broadcast the jailhouse tapes of former Panama dictator Manuel Noriega.

In November 1990, the Supreme Court reversed this precedent by letting stand a federal judge's gag order forbidding CNN from broadcasting tapes of Manuel Noriega's jailhouse telephone conversations. The government had secretly recorded the tapes of the former Panamanian dictator while he was awaiting trial on drug charges. CNN had acquired the tapes and was broadcasting them when the judge implemented the prior-restraint order. The Supreme Court ruled 7–2 on its decision, with the dissenters expressing concern that prior restraint should not be allowed. (Later the federal judge lifted the prior-restraint order because the damaging tapes had already been aired.)

GOVERNMENT REGULATION OF BROADCASTING

In the 1920s, as the new medium of radio spread across the country, many stations tried to get on the air and jammed one another's frequencies with overlapping signals. At that time there were no regulations of radio broadcasting. Previous legislation had dealt only with ship-to-shore types of radio communication. In fact, the only laws on the books required the secretary of commerce to grant radio licenses when requested; he did not have the authority to reject any such requests or assign power and frequencies for radio operations.

Chaos on the airwaves resulted. Many broadcasters, as well as Secretary of Commerce Herbert Hoover, became concerned. As a result, Hoover held a series of four Radio Conferences during the 1920s to allow all interested parties to discuss the problem and suggest possible solutions. These conferences involved educators, legislators, labor officials, businesspeople, and religious leaders. Each time proposals were made and presented to Congress, but no action was taken until President Calvin Coolidge finally urged Congress to deal with the problem.

The result was the Radio Act of 1927, which established the Federal Radio Commission (**FRC**), a five-member board that was instructed to establish a system for **licensing** new radio stations and assigning frequencies and power to existing stations. Congress wanted the FRC to complete the project in one year and then disband; future enforcement of broadcast regulations and further licensing action were reserved for the secretary of commerce.

But the FRC was still operating seven years later when President Franklin Roosevelt asked Congress to update the act by bringing telephone and telegraph operations under the same communications blanket. The result was the Communications Act of 1934 which, in addition to including most of the regulatory legislation of the 1927 act, replaced the "temporary" FRC with a permanent Federal Communications Commission (**FCC**).

The FCC made it clear from the very beginning that broadcasters would have to operate under the congressional mandate and broadcast in the "public interest, convenience and necessity" if they were to keep their licenses. As did the FRC, the FCC and Congress have acted on the premise that the airwaves belong to the public, not to private broadcasters. The basis for decisions concerning broadcasters is thus determining how responsibly they serve the public interest.

When the commission's right to refuse to renew licenses of stations involved in questionable broadcast practices was first tested, the courts ruled that while the government cannot tell a station in advance not to broadcast something (which would be prior restraint), it can review past performance to determine if a station has been operating in the public interest. If it has not, the government can refuse **license renewal**.

Although clauses in both the 1927 Radio Act and the 1934 Communications Act stated clearly that "Nothing in this Act shall be understood or construed to give the licensing authority the power of censorship," the U.S. Criminal Code *does* prohibit the broadcasting of anything obscene, indecent, or profane. In addition, the FCC established rules regarding fraud and lottery information.

For many years the FCC also required broadcasters to air certain types of program content, noting that news, public affairs, educational, informational, and agricultural programs were in the public interest. Many of those requirements were lifted during the deregulation period of the 1980s, but Congress and the FCC still feel very strongly about requiring broadcasters to provide programming for children. In 1996, for example,

---

@ Practicing Media Literacy

Do you think there is ever a time other than during war, when censorship of the media is warranted?

FRC
licensing

FCC

@ Practicing Media Literacy

Do you think that Internet radio stations have an unfair advantage over regular radio stations in this country because they aren't regulated by the FCC? *Should* they be regulated by the FCC?

---

license renewal

broadcasters approved an FCC, White House, and congressional proposal to establish a guideline of three hours of children's programming per week to ensure license renewal for television stations. The action came despite the findings of the Annenberg Parents, Children and Television study, released by the Annenberg Public Policy Center of the University of Pennsylvania, that most parents don't think their children watch too much television and think television has done their kids more good than harm.

Section 315

Congress included Section 315 in both the 1927 and 1934 legislation to protect candidates for political office. It requires broadcasters to give bona fide political candidates equal opportunities for airtime on their stations. This requirement, which does not apply to any print medium, means that a station must grant all candidates for office the same opportunities other candidates receive on the station's airwaves. This applies not only to free time given to a candidate (in which case all of his or her opponents would receive the same free access on that station) but also to political commercials. If one candidate purchases a certain amount of time for commercials, the station must give all of his or her opponents an equal opportunity to purchase advertising in the same time periods at the same cost.

> **@   Practicing Media Literacy**
> Should candidates for political office be given free time on radio and television so that they don't have to raise so much money for political advertising?

This equal opportunity section has been modified to exempt certain types of programs, including newscasts and bona fide news interview programs, such as *Meet the Press*, *Face the Nation*, and *Nightline*. Candidate debates are also excluded.

Fairness Doctrine

fairness doctrine

The **fairness doctrine** was another important requirement of the FCC up until its abolition in 1987. Not written into the Communications Act, the doctrine evolved over the years from commission rulings on controversial issues.

In 1949, the FCC began encouraging broadcasters to take stands on controversial issues, provided that reasonable time was given to opposing viewpoints. Over the years, this fairness doctrine ruling required broadcasters to be aware of important community and national issues and devote broadcasting time to airing all sides of those issues.

The fairness doctrine was applied to advertising content in 1967, when the FCC ruled that because cigarette smoking was a controversial public issue, broadcasters carrying commercials for cigarette companies had to give free time to antismoking groups (such as the American Cancer Society and the American Lung Association). This ruling eventually led to congressional legislation banning all cigarette commercials from radio and television as of 1971 (see Chapter 13).

Red Lion decision

In the 1969 ***Red Lion*** **decision** (named after a five-year-old personal attack case involving Red Lion Broadcasting Company in Pennsylvania), the Supreme Court reaffirmed the fairness doctrine by declaring that the rights of the public, not the broadcaster, are paramount. In that decision, the Court ruled that Congress and the FCC were not violating the First Amendment when they required broadcasters to devote airtime to replies to personal attacks and editorials.

However, a federal court of appeals challenged this decision in the 1980s when it ordered the FCC to reconsider its position on the fairness doctrine, implying that it might not be constitutional. The case resulted from a suit filed by a Syracuse broadcasting company challenging the FCC's ruling that it had violated the fairness doctrine by not broadcasting anti–nuclear power plant ads after running advertisements in the plant's favor. The broadcaster argued that the rule violated his First Amendment rights.

The FCC did rethink its position and, in 1987, abandoned the fairness doctrine, saying that it wished to "extend to the electronic media the same First Amendment guarantees that the print media have enjoyed since our country's inception."[8] Anticipating this ruling from a deregulation-oriented FCC, both houses of Congress had passed legislation earlier in the year to codify the fairness doctrine. However, President Reagan vetoed the bill, stating it was "antagonistic to the freedom of expression."[9]

After President Clinton was elected in 1992, Congress revived its efforts to pass fairness doctrine legislation. However, proponents were strongly opposed by religious broadcasters who feared the law would require them to give equal time to gay, lesbian, and abortion rights supporters, whom they regularly attacked as sinful on their religious broadcasts, and by talk radio and television hosts, such as Rush Limbaugh, who had no desire to balance their attacks on the government and political opponents by granting reasonable exposure to contrasting viewpoints.

> **@ Practicing Media Literacy**
> Would radio talk show hosts such as Rush Limbaugh and G. Gordon Liddy be as successful if they had to operate under the fairness doctrine and give "reasonable exposure" to opposing viewpoints on their programs?

Censorship

FCC **censorship** of broadcasting stations is technically prohibited by the broadcasting acts of 1927 and 1934. However, the Supreme Court ruled in 1978 that the commission does have the right to ban the broadcast of indecent speech during hours when children might be in the audience. The case involved a New York radio station that played a cut from a George Carlin comedy recording, "Seven Words You Can Never Say on TV." Some listeners didn't think those words should be said on afternoon radio either.

censorship

A recording by comedian George Carlin had much to do with FCC rulings on what can be aired on radio and television and at what time.

Although the FCC has adopted a philosophy of deregulation and believes the marketplace should regulate the airwaves, it is not averse to punishing broadcasters that air objectionable material. In 1989, for example, the FCC levied fines on four radio stations for broadcasting "indecent" material in the daytime and threatened to fine four others who were sent letters of warning. Most of the fines and charges involved explicit language during talk shows and music with explicit lyrics. By the latter part of the 1990s, well over $1 million in fines had been levied by the FCC against radio stations that carried "shock jock" Howard Stern, who uses explicit language and sexual innuendos on the air (see Chapter 10).

@   Practicing Media Literacy

Do you think it's okay for network television programs such as *NYPD Blue* and *Chicago Hope* to use offensive language and nudity as long as the programs are on the air after 9 P.M.?

@   Practicing Media Literacy

Have you ever heard the Howard Stern show and, if so, do you think the FCC has been justified in fining him for "obscene" and "indecent" program content?

In 1990, the FCC launched an investigation into the well-known public broadcasting station WGBH-TV for showing examples of Robert Mapplethorpe's controversial photography on its 10 P.M. newscast. However, ABC's *Nightline* defended its showing of Madonna's MTV-banned video "Justify My Love" because the program aired at a late hour when children would not normally be watching.

In 1992, following congressional action, the FCC adopted rules that defined indecency as "language or material that, in context, depicts or describes, in terms patently offensive as measured by contemporary community standards for the broadcast medium, sexual or excretory activities or organs." It banned all such broadcasts between the hours of 6 A.M. and midnight and used the rule to issue fines to stations carrying Howard Stern's morning show. In 1993, a federal appeals court struck down the ban.

Other Agencies

In addition to the FCC, more than 80 government entities have regulations that affect broadcasters, including the Federal Aviation Administration, which regulates the placement of lights on broadcasting towers and antennas so that aviators can see them. A major federal agency involved in broadcasting is the Federal Trade Commission (FTC), which monitors advertising on radio and television as well as in the print media. Of particular concern to the FTC has been TV advertising directed at children, particularly on Saturday morning shows. The Food and Drug Administration, the U.S. Postal Service, and the Bureau of Alcohol, Tobacco and Firearms are also involved in regulating and monitoring mass-media advertising.

COURT REGULATIONS

The judicial branch of our government imposes a number of legal regulations on the media. For years the media and the courts have clashed over two sometimes conflicting constitutional provisions: the First Amendment right of a free press and the Sixth Amendment guarantee of a fair trial.

The free press versus fair trial conflict occurs most often when the press attempts to cover sensational or highly publicized trials. In 1954, for example, Dr. Sam Sheppard was tried in Ohio for the murder of his wife. The Cleveland press sensationalized the case and even pronounced Sheppard guilty before the jury did. In 1966 the Supreme Court overturned Sheppard's conviction, citing unfair publicity.

Closed Hearings

Many judges and attorneys believe efforts by the news media to cover every detail of a case before the trial is concluded prejudice the jury's ability to render an impartial verdict. As a result, many judges have barred the media and the public from pretrial hearings.

In 1986, however, the U.S. Supreme Court overturned a California Supreme Court decision that pretrial hearings could be closed. In the 7–2 decision, the Court

There was much media coverage of the 1954 murder trial of Dr. Sam Sheppard. Various aspects of the case were still receiving media coverage in the year 2000.

found in favor of the *Riverside Press-Enterprise*, ruling that "**public access** in criminal trials and the selection of jurors is essential to the proper functioning of the criminal justice system. California preliminary hearings are sufficiently like a trial to justify the same conclusion." The Court added, however, that judges may close pretrial proceedings in rare circumstances when there is no other way to protect the defendant's right to a fair trial.[10]

public access

Voluntary press–bar guidelines have been set up in some states in an effort to balance the needs of the news media, the bar, and the public. More than half of the states have adopted such guidelines. However, the guidelines have no legal force and are effective only as long as all involved parties act reasonably and responsibly.

Gag Orders

Courts can also restrain the media by issuing gag orders, which limit what attorneys and court officials can say to reporters and what the news media can print or broadcast. Journalists who have violated gag orders in the belief that the restrictions infringe on their First Amendment rights and the public's right to know have been found in contempt of court.

Disclosing Sources

The refusal to disclose sources or turn over personal materials such as notes, tapes, photographs, and film has also led courts to jail journalists for contempt of court. Although some states have shield laws, which allow journalists to protect the

@ **Practicing Media Literacy**

If the news media lose their ability to protect the identity of their sources, do you think those sources will be more hesitant to come forward with important information?

identities of their sources, no such protection exists at the federal level. In a 5–4 decision in 1972, the Supreme Court ruled that journalists have no absolute privilege to protect sources of information if they are subpoenaed to testify in court proceedings.

Canon 35

Other court regulations of news media conduct have been relaxed, however, particularly in regard to the long-standing rules known as Canon 35, banning cameras, tape recorders, and microphones from the courtroom. By the 1990s, these rules had been lifted in more than 40 states.

The rule against cameras was instituted in the 1930s, when loud, popping flash units were used. In 1935 cameras caused a major disturbance at the trial of Bruno Hauptmann (who was accused of kidnapping and murdering the young son of national hero Charles Lindbergh), and many members of the bar believed these cameras upset courtroom decorum. Two years after Hauptmann was convicted, the American Bar Association adopted Canon 35 as part of its Canons of Professional Ethics. In 1952 and 1963, the ban on photography was extended to include radio and television equipment.

Photography and broadcast equipment have since become miniaturized and less conspicuous, and journalists have been fighting to get the ban lifted. As noted above, these efforts have finally achieved some results in most states. However, the ban still exists in all federal courts.

Televising Trials

Televising trials has also been slowly gaining acceptance. In recent years, 39 states have experimented with televised trials. Opponents say televising trials turns attorneys and judges into actors and makes a mockery of justice. This was one of the main concerns expressed after the famed murder trial of former football star O.J. Simpson.

While the CNN and Court-TV cable channels joined with most Los Angeles television stations in providing continuous coverage of the Simpson trial, the major networks also provided extensive reports on the day-to-day proceedings. Very few people in the United States had not witnessed at least some portion of the trial.

When the verdict was in, talk was renewed about prohibiting cameras in the courtrooms, with California's governor Pete Wilson supporting such a ban. In 1996, a task force of the California State Judicial Council issued a proposal to impose new restrictions on what can be televised, including a ban on televising any proceedings that are not also seen by the jury.

That same year, the governing board of the state bar of California went on record as supporting a move to give judges the discretion to permit TV cameras in the courtroom. The action marked a reversal in the bar's long-standing opposition to the televising of trials. According to a California state bar official, there is one main reason to allow the televising of court proceedings: What goes on in the courtroom is the public's business.

> @ **Practicing Media Literacy**
>
> Do you think it is helpful or harmful to the public and the judicial system to allow the televising of criminal trials?

LAWS AGAINST OBSCENITY

Laws against obscenity or pornography have been constantly in conflict with First Amendment rights of free speech and artistic expression.

Attempts to Define Obscenity

Laws governing obscenity have undergone some clarification during the latter half of the 20th century. In 1957, in a case against Samuel Roth, a New York publisher of erotic books, the Supreme Court issued a decision that liberalized the definition of obscenity. The court said that the test for obscenity would be "whether to the average person, applying contemporary community standards, the dominant theme of the material taken as a whole appeals to prurient interest."[11] Although Roth went to jail, this decision was the first to liberalize the interpretation of obscenity. (Prior to that time, obscenity was defined as anything that tended to deprave or corrupt anyone's mind. Thus, if one page of a book contained a statement that

Protestors demonstrate outside a Minnesota convenience store which sold "adult" magazines, including Playboy.

could corrupt anyone—a child, for example—the book was judged to be obscene.) Then, in 1973, the Supreme Court tightened up the standards again, setting these new guidelines for defining obscenity (*Miller v. California*):[12]

- The work taken as a whole must appeal to the prurient interests of the average person applying contemporary community standards.
- The work must depict or describe, in a patently offensive way, sexual conduct specifically defined by the applicable law.
- The work taken as a whole must lack serious literary, scientific, political, or artistic value.

One problem resulting from these interpretations was the difficulty of measuring "contemporary community standards" and the inconsistencies that could exist in various regions of the country. What might be judged obscene in one part of the country might not be so judged in another.

In 1987, the Supreme Court (*Pope v. Illinois*) applied the "**reasonable person standard**" rather than the "contemporary community standard" in judging the third part of the *Miller* test. In this latest court interpretation of obscenity, the Court said:

reasonable person standard

> Only the first and second prongs of the Miller test—appeal to prurient interest and patent offensiveness—should be decided with reference to "contemporary community standards." The ideas that a work represents need not obtain majority approval to merit protection, and the value of that work does not vary from community to community based on the degree of local acceptance it has won. The proper inquiry is not whether an ordinary

@ **Practicing Media Literacy**

How do you personally decide what is obscene, indecent, or offensive when choosing what movies to see, what books or magazines to read, what radio programs to listen to and which television shows to watch?

member of any given community would find serious value in the allegedly obscene material, but whether a reasonable person would find such value in the material as a whole.[13]

Along with the liberalization of the definition of obscenity has been a gradual change in the culture toward acceptance of sexual discussions and representations heretofore considered taboo. Sexually explicit themes in books, magazines, compact disks, tapes, and movies have become acceptable to many in the popular culture; nevertheless, others still find them immoral and pornographic. As a result, numerous efforts have been made to curb the proliferation of this so-called pornography. In 1967, a presidential commission was set up and funded with $2 million to study the effects of pornography on our culture. The two-year study found no causal relationship between the dissemination of pornography and crime and other antisocial behavior. Government panels in Great Britain in 1979 and in Canada in 1984 came to similar conclusions.

Meese Commission Report

However, in 1986 an 11-member panel put together by U.S. Attorney General Edwin Meese released very different and controversial findings. The Meese commission, which had spent one year and $500,000 studying pornography, issued a 1,960-page report stating that it had found a causal relationship between exposure to sexually violent books, films, and magazines and aggressive behavior toward women. It called for stringent enforcement of the nation's antismut laws and the extension of those laws into new areas. Soon after, a new, harsh antiobscenity law was passed in North Carolina; supporters of the legislation hoped it would set a nationwide precedent.

The American Civil Liberties Union and other opponents of censorship in any form immediately criticized the commission's findings. Even two of the commissioners, both women, wrote dissenting opinions claiming that "no self-respecting investigators would accept conclusions based on such a study." However, the report was lauded by religious, conservative, and feminist groups that had been complaining about pornography for years.

Opponents claimed the report was not objective because the commission had been stacked with conservatives who supported the Reagan administration's position against pornography. Supporters said the report was the first step in "defense of decency and the sanctity of the family."*

The Internet and Regulation

The newest form of mass media, the Internet, has also been the subject of legislation attempting to control pornography. In the first-ever decision by a federal court that addressed the limits of free speech on the Internet, a federal court ruled in 1996 that a new law had gone too far in barring indecent material from the Internet and could

---

*Even before the report was issued, lawsuits had been filed alleging that the commission had intimidated major retail chains into removing such magazines as *Playboy* and *Penthouse* from their shelves. Letters signed by Alan Sears, executive director of the commission, had been sent to 23 major American companies, advising them that they had been identified in testimony before the commission as being "involved in the sale or distribution of pornography." Several of those companies, including the 7-Eleven chain, subsequently removed "adult" magazines from their inventory.

not be enforced because it was unconstitutionally vague and violated
First Amendment protections of free
speech.

Just a few months earlier, President
Clinton had signed the Telecommunications Act of 1996 into law, and many
people were happy that the legislation
contained a provision designed to stop
pornography from reaching people
younger than 18 through such means as
radio, television, telephones, and, most
recently, computers. The bill contained
two controversial sections. One pro-
hibited the use of "a telecommunications device" to transmit
"indecent" material; the other banned the use of "any interactive computer services" to display "patently offensive" material
in a manner available to a person under 18 years of age.

But critics had charged the bill went too far in that it was
making it illegal for users of the Internet to discuss abortions or
safe sex or to even display some works of art, such as Michel-
angelo's paintings on the ceiling of the Sistine Chapel at the
Vatican. The American Civil Liberties Union and some 19 other organizations went
to court shortly after the bill was signed into law, saying that the obscenity provisions
were so broad and vague as to bar material protected by the First Amendment.

Just four months after the bill became law, a three-judge panel for the U.S. district
court in Philadelphia ruled that the ban of indecent material from the Internet could
not be enforced because it was unconstitutionally vague and violated free speech protections. While stressing that current laws against obscenity and child pornography
would still apply to the Internet, the federal court called the Internet "a never-ending
worldwide conversation" that deserves more protection from government regulation
than radio, television, or almost any form of mass communication. The government,
the court stressed, has no right to interrupt this conversation.

United States district court judge Stewart Dalzell wrote that the Internet "is a far
more speech-enhancing medium than print, the village green or the mails."[14] Judge
Dalzell added that because the legislation "would necessarily affect the Internet itself,
the Communications Decency Act would necessarily reduce the speech available for
adults on the medium. This is a constitutionally intolerable result."[15] Congress has attempted to pass other bills to control indecency on the Internet, but these laws have
also been ruled unconstitutional by the courts (see Chapter 3).

*President Clinton signs
the 1996 Telecommu-
nications Act, the first
major revision in com-
munications law in
some 62 years.*

> **@ Practicing Media Literacy**
> Do you think there should be
> *ANY* form of regulation on the
> Internet?

LAWS TO PROTECT THE PUBLIC

In addition to court-imposed restrictions on the media, the laws of libel and invasion
of privacy give the public legal recourse when harmed by media abuses of power.

Libel Laws

The laws of **libel** are designed to protect people from uncalled-for attacks or careless
errors by members of the news media. Libel is the defamation of a person's character

libel

through the print or broadcast media. Defamation is any communication that exposes people to hatred, ridicule, or contempt; lowers their esteem in the community; causes them to be shunned; or injures their careers. The media have three major defenses against libel suits:

truth

1. **Truth** is an absolute defense against libel. If it can be proven that a report is true, the plaintiff has no case. For many years, the burden of proof rested with the media. However, in 1986, in the case of *Philadelphia Newspapers v. Hepps,* the Supreme Court ruled that the person suing the media must prove the statements are false.[16]

privileged statements

2. **Privileged statements,** those made at legislative, judicial, and other official public proceedings, are immune to libel suits. For example, if a witness makes a false (or libelous) statement at a trial, the news media can report it as long as the judge doesn't order it stricken from the record. If the witness made the same statement outside the courthouse, it would be libelous to print it and a suit could be filed.

fair comment and criticism

3. **Fair comment and criticism** is the defense that holds it is permissible to publish critical comments as long as they consist of opinion, rather than fact, about issues of public interest. This defense protects writers of editorials and critics of plays, books, movies, recordings, sporting events, and so on, as long as they are expressing opinions about the public performances of the people involved rather than their private lives. This defense was significantly weakened in 1990 when the Supreme Court ruled that a writer or speaker may be sued for statements that expressed "opinion." The ruling resulted from the writing of a sports columnist who had claimed that a Cleveland, Ohio, wrestling coach had "lied" his way out of a suspension.

absence of malice

Another defense against libel suits involving public officials is the **absence of malice.** A landmark Supreme Court decision in 1964, *New York Times v. Sullivan,* ruled that a public official must prove malice before she or he can win a libel suit;[17] others need to prove only carelessness. This landmark decision was based on an advertisement that had been placed in the *New York Times* by a group of Alabama African-American ministers claiming that police commissioners in that state were racists. The commissioners sued the ministers and the newspaper. Both lost in lower courts and in the Alabama supreme court. The ministers and the newspaper finally won the case before the U.S. Supreme Court, and the decision gave the news media much greater latitude in criticizing public officials than private citizens.

Some libel cases involving public figures have attempted to collect judgment for special considerations. In a 1988 case, *Falwell v. Hustler,* the Reverend Jerry Falwell, founder of the conservative Moral Majority organization, sued *Hustler* magazine for publishing a satirical pseudoadvertisement implying that the minister had had his first sexual experience with his mother in an outhouse.[18] A jury that couldn't find in favor of libel because malice couldn't be proven—the ad was clearly labeled as satire— awarded Falwell $200,000 for emotional distress. The Supreme Court overturned the verdict, citing the need for the media to have freedom to make satirical comments about public officials even if such statements might be stressful. It noted that satirical political cartoons were a long-standing American tradition.

punitive damages

Any person who believes he or she has been libeled by the mass media may bring a civil suit against those responsible and seek payment for damages. Because actual damages are hard to prove in a libel suit, the plaintiff can seek **punitive damages,** whose purpose is to punish the libeler. Some punitive damages have run into millions of dollars, especially in cases where actual malice was proven.

A 1993 study by the Libel Defense Resource Center reported that juries were awarding plaintiffs in libel trials an average of about $9 million each during the first part of the 1990s. This was six times higher than the average of $1.5 million during the 1980s. In 1990, the two largest libel verdicts in the history of the American news media were handed down. In *Sprague v. Walter,* a Pennsylvania jury awarded $34 million in damages, including $31.5 million in punitive damages, against the *Philadelphia Inquirer* for a 1973 story that questioned the handling of a homicide case by a local prosecutor. In *Srivastava v. Harte-Hankes Communications, Inc.,* a Texas jury awarded $29 million, including $17.5 million in punitive damages, as a result of a series of news broadcasts examining the activities of a local heart surgeon.[19]

Many other libel suits arise from **carelessness** in what *Editor and Publisher* calls "nickel and dime" stories. These are small stories in which reporters mix up the names and identify an innocent person as the accused or leave out the "not" in a not-guilty story. These stories are also actionable (see Box 4.1).

carelessness

A group of Texas cattlemen sued syndicated television talk show host Oprah Winfrey, claiming that when she falsely warned on a 1996 program that American beef could spread mad cow disease to people, the cattle industry suffered a collapse in prices. The lawsuit was expected to be the first major test of the "veggie libel" laws enacted in Texas and 12 other states to protect perishable agricultural products from false and disparaging remarks. The 1998 trial took five weeks, but it took the jury just seven hours to reject the suit against Winfrey. While the attorney for the cattlemen said the jury was swayed by Winfrey's star power, one juror said deliberations centered on a First Amendment issue. The cattlemen had been seeking $11 million in damages from Winfrey.[20]

> **@ Practicing Media Literacy**
>
> Should television talk show hosts be held accountable for things that are said or done on their programs which might hurt others?

Large awards of punitive damages in libel cases have had a chilling effect on the mass media, and some claim these awards, which seem to be getting larger each year, are responsible for weakening freedom of the press by discouraging investigative reporting and aggressive journalism (see Box 4.2).

Invasion of Privacy

Another form of legal action against the media comes when a clear invasion of a person's privacy has occurred. Citizens can recover damages from the media for any of the following reasons: (1) intrusion into a person's physical solitude, (2) public disclosure of embarrassing private facts, (3) placing the person before the public in a false light, and (4) commercial exploitation of a person's name or likeness.

Intrusion into a person's physical solitude involves trespassing on private property to interview or photograph a person. Most celebrities have had confrontations with paparazzi, freelance

"Free speech not only lives, it rocks," declared Oprah Winfrey after winning a libel suit against her. Two years later it was revealed that she requires all employees to sign an agreement not to talk or write about her for the rest of their lives.

intrusion

Box 4.1
MEDIA LITERACY
Libel Suits Can Come from Anywhere—About Anything

Libel suits are not limited to statements contained in news stories. Believe it or not, anything published or broadcast in the media in any form—from ads to comments made on talk shows—is subject to the laws of libel. Talk show hostess Oprah Winfrey was sued for libel when she commented that she'd stop eating hamburgers after hearing about some of the problems with diseased cattle. Here are some other examples of libel suits coming from outside the area of news.

A Chicago newspaper was sued for libel for running a map attempting to show the location of a house of prostitution. The newspaper contended that such illegal bordellos existed in the city and that the Chicago police were not doing anything about them. The only problem with the map was that the X locating the brothel was placed on the house next door, and its owners sued for defamation.

In another case, a professional wrestler sued a Chicago newspaper for running his photograph next to one of a gorilla. A sports editor had noted a similarity in features in the two photos and had run them side by side with a humorous caption suggesting that there was something to the theory of evolution.

Even advertisements can end up in the courts. The famous *New York Times v. Sullivan* case that expanded the rights of the media to criticize public officials resulted from an advertisement run in the *New York Times* by a group of African-American ministers from Alabama.

In another case resulting from an advertisement, a jury found *Soldier of Fortune* magazine liable for $9.4 million for publishing a classified ad that led to a contract killing. The case began when the son and mother of a slain Texas woman sued the publication because the woman's husband had hired the killer through a classified ad in the magazine. The ad read: "Ex-marine. '67–'69 Nam vet. Ex-DI, weapons specialist—jungle warfare. Pilot. ME. High-risk assignments U.S. or overseas."

Lawyers for the publication unsuccessfully argued that the publication should not be found liable for the slaying because the magazine's executives had no way of knowing the ad was for an illegal activity. The jury disagreed.

---

photographers who stalk them in order to get pictures that can be sold to the media. Paparazzi tactics came under criticism when there was speculation that the pursuit of Princess Diana's car by Paris photographers may have led to her fatal accident.

public disclosure

Public disclosure of embarrassing private facts deals with information that is considered so intimate that it should remain private. Such things as revealing that a person has had a sex-change operation or exposing the criminal record of a rehabilitated ex-convict have been found to be invasions of privacy.

false light

Placing a person before the public in a **false light** applies to instances where the media incorrectly place a person in a position or social status that embarrasses him or her. One such case involved a photograph of an office worker sitting on a park bench during a lunch break. The photo had been used to illustrate a story on the homeless and implied that he was one of them.

In Chicago, a doctor sued a television station because it had used file footage of her treating a patient while reporting a story of another doctor allegedly using AIDS-infected swabs on patients. She told the court that her reputation had been severely damaged.

Box 4.2
MEDIA WATCH
If You Don't Like What They Said, Sue 'em — Maybe They'll Settle

We live in a litigious society and when it comes to threats of legal action, the media have been a prime target during the final decade of the 20th century. But many of those legal actions never made it to court; they were settled out of court. And, in several cases, the media were not being sued for what they said, but rather how they got the story in the first place.

For example, Chiquita Brands International went after the *Cincinnati Enquirer* not for a story it was printing about the banana company, but for the reporting tactics, which included allegedly stolen telephone messages. Even though substantial parts of the story may have been true, the Gannett newspaper chain, which published the *Enquirer*, elected to avoid what has been described as a "morass of litigation" and settle with Chiquita for more than $10 million. The Gannett Co. also renounced the original story in the *Enquirer*.

Both CBS and ABC found themselves involved in threatened legal actions by the tobacco industry. The Brown and Williamson tobacco company was successful in pressuring CBS to cancel plans to broadcast a *60 Minutes* interview with an industry whistle-blower in 1995. Brown and Williamson was not planning a libel suit but was threatening to go after CBS for "interference with business relations" for persuading the former employee to reveal internal company practices in vio-

lation of a signed agreement he had with the tobacco company. When the *Wall Street Journal* published its own account of the whistle-blower's story a few months later, *60 Minutes* finally ran its interview. Neither the *Wall Street Journal* nor CBS were sued by Brown and Williamson. This story became the plot for the 1999 Al Pacino movie *The Insider*, which linked the acquiescence of CBS to the pending sale of the network to Metromedia.

In 1994, ABC broadcast a report indicating that cigarette makers were "spiking" the nicotine levels of their product during the manufacturing process. Philip Morris sued the network for $10 billion, alleging that the report was libelous. But with the pending merger with Walt Disney Co. moving closer to reality in 1995, ABC elected to settle the lawsuit by reimbursing Philip Morris for the cost of its legal fees, which were said to be in the area of $15 million. In addition, the network publicly apologized on one of its prime time newsmagazine programs.

In a book published in 1999, First Amendment Attorney Bruce W. Sanford looked at such legal threats and concludes that there's a growing canyon of distrust between the public and the media. He fears that the attempts to curtail the ability of the media to gather and report news will make us a less informed citizenry. His book is called *Don't Shoot the Messenger*.

When the FBI cleared security guard Richard Jewell in 1996 of any connection with the bombing at the Olympic games in Atlanta, Jewell threatened to sue NBC for libel because the network had reported that he was a principal focus of the FBI's investigation, which was true. But even though Jewell's case would have been weak, NBC settled with him reportedly for a half-million dollars. However, the network admitted no wrongdoing or editorial error and said that a major consideration in its decision to settle was to protect confidential sources.

Commercial exploitation of a person's name or likeness without permission involves using the pictures or names of famous people and others to advertise or promote commercial ventures. Photographs and names can be used in news stories without permission, but not in ads or commercial endeavors.

commercial exploitation

Although invasion of privacy laws are designed to protect people from general nuisances and intrusions into their privacy, recent court actions have blurred the line between invasion of privacy and legitimate news coverage. In 1989, the *Los Angeles*

Times settled an invasion of privacy case out of court for an undisclosed amount following a charge by a San Diego woman that she became a "walking target" after the *Times* named her as a witness in a murder case. The plaintiff had discovered the body of her roommate, who had been raped and murdered, while the intruder was still in the apartment. California's 4th District Court of Appeals ruled that a jury should decide whether publication of the woman's real name was newsworthy and necessary to the story.

In a well-publicized rape case, the woman who had accused William Kennedy Smith of sexually assaulting her at the Kennedy family compound in Florida was shown on television during her testimony at the trial with a blue bubble covering her face to maintain her anonymity. However, after the *National Enquirer* revealed her name, NBC's *Nightly News with Tom Brokaw* also began using her name, saying it was already public knowledge due to the tabloid's story. In this case, as with all rape cases, it is not against the law to reveal the names of people who have been sexually assaulted, but most media avoid doing so to protect the privacy of the victims.

The two basic defenses for the mass media in an invasion of privacy case are **newsworthiness** (or public interest) and consent. Any legitimate news story should qualify in the newsworthy category (although the *Los Angeles Times* case places a shadow of doubt over this defense). **Consent**, however, usually takes proof of a contractual agreement, such as a signed model release (a standard form permitting one's likeness to be published).

Truth is not always a defense for the media in invasion of privacy cases, although it is in libel suits. Newsworthiness, on the other hand, is not necessarily a libel defense. Something that is perfectly nonlibelous may be an invasion of privacy, and vice versa. As you can see from this discussion of legal controls on the media in the United States, free press and speech are somewhat tempered by our laws and regulations. However, the net effect of this seems to have been the creation of a climate that requires the media to operate with more social responsibility.

Access to Information

In addition to laws that protect the public from the press are laws that protect the public's right to know by giving the media, and citizens in general, access to public information.

The most important public access law on the national level is the Freedom of Information Act (**FOIA**), passed by Congress in 1966. This law requires agencies of the federal government to declassify and divulge certain information that is no longer considered sensitive or harmful to the national security. Although several categories of information are not affected by this legislation, the FOIA has enabled the press and the public to obtain significant data that have shed light on important government activities. The federal government also has a "sunshine act" that allows about 50 federal agencies to open their files to the public.

In addition to these federal laws, numerous states have sunshine laws giving the public and the press access to government agencies and requiring open meetings of governmental bodies. Many states also have public records acts that make public documents available to the news media and citizens.

@   Practicing Media Literacy

Do you feel the victims of crimes other than rape—such as robbery or burglary—should also have their privacy protected by the news media?

---

newsworthiness

consent

truth

@   Practicing Media Literacy

Do you think the identity of a person accused of committing rape should also be protected until that person has actually been convicted of the crime?

FOIA

SUMMARY

A variety of government and judicial statutes place legal controls on the media. Despite First Amendment protections, laws have been passed that restrict First Amendment provisions of free speech and the press. The first such laws were the Alien and Sedition Acts of 1798. Similar laws enacted during World War I were challenged but were upheld by the Supreme Court. In 1940 the government passed the Smith Act, which placed some restrictions on free speech during World War II.

Efforts to exercise prior restraint have been made in recent times, despite a Supreme Court ruling that such actions violate First Amendment provisions.

Since the 1920s, the federal government has had laws that restrict the operations of the broadcast media. Although originally established to protect broadcasting stations from overlapping one another's frequencies, these laws have been extended to content as well.

The courts also have legal restrictions on mass-media operations. These laws range from prohibitions on cameras and microphones in courtrooms to gag orders on the news media. Laws against obscenity restrict the content of the mass media. Although many believe such laws violate the First Amendment protections of free expression, prosecutions continue into the 21st century.

The people also have legal recourse, through civil suits for libel and invasion of privacy, against injuries inflicted by the media.

The right of the public to be well informed in a democracy is protected by a variety of state and federal laws giving the press and the public access to government information and meetings.

Find a review of *Key People and Concepts*, a message board for *Practicing Media Literacy* questions, self tests, and more at: www.mhhe.com/wilson.

Thought Questions

1. Did the U.S. district court do the right thing when it struck down a ban on indecent material on the Internet? Why or why not?

2. Do you support the FCC's position on a ban on broadcasting of indecent material? Why or why not? If you do not support the ban, how would you protect children from hearing such material?

3. Should musical recordings, books, magazines, videos, and movies be censored if they are considered pornographic by community standards? Why or why not?

4. Why should "truth" be a defense in libel cases but not in invasion of privacy cases? Do you think this inconsistency hinders freedom of the press?

5. How can we ensure that monetary judgments in libel and invasion of privacy cases do not inhibit freedom of the press?

Notes

1. Kenneth Howe, "Police Can't Bring Media into Private Homes; High Court Says Cops Can Be Sued but Press Liability Still Uncertain," *San Francisco Chronicle*, May 25, 1999, p. A3.

2. Linda Greenhouse, "Police Violate Privacy in Home Raids with Journalists," *New York Times*, May 25, 1999, p. A25.

3. *Schenck v. United States*, 249 U.S. 47 (1919).

4. *Yates v. United States*, 354 U.S. 298 (1957).

5. *Brandenburg v. Ohio*, 395 U.S. 444 (1969).

6. *Near v. Minnesota*, 283 U.S. 697 (1931).

7. *New York Times v. United States*, 403 U.S. 713 (1971).

8. Raymond L. Fischer, "The FCC and the Fairness Doctrine," *USA Today Magazine*, May 1988, p. 42.

9. *Ibid.*

10. *Press-Enterprise v. Superior Court of California for Riverside County*, 478 U.S. 1 (1986).

11. *Roth v. United States*, 354 U.S. 476 (1957).

12. Quoted in *Publishers Weekly*, May 22, 1987, p. 20.

13. *Ibid.*

14. Reynolds Holding and Ramon G. McLeod, "Free-Speech Ruling for Internet," *San Francisco Chronicle*, June 13, 1996, p. A1.

15. *Ibid.*

16. *Philadelphia Newspapers v. Hepps*, 105 S. Ct. 1558 (1986).

17. *New York Times v. Sullivan*, 376 U.S. 254 (1964).

18. *Falwell v. Hustler*, 485 U.S. 46 (1988).

19. Lee Levine and David L. Perry, "No Way to Celebrate the Bill of Rights," *Columbia Journalism Review*, July–August 1990, pp. 38–39.

20. "Oprah Winfrey Beats Beef against Her; Texas Cattle Industry Plans to Appeal," *Fresno Bee*, February 27, 1998, p. A1.

The News Media:

Keeping the Culture Informed

Were it left to me to decide whether we should have a government without newspapers, or newspapers without a government, I should not hesitate a moment to prefer the latter.

—**Thomas Jefferson**

The summer of 1998 was perhaps an excellent example of the changes taking place in all fields of journalism. And those changes had a tremendous impact on the accuracy of the information being received by people around the world. ● It all started in January of that year when an Internet gossip writer by the name of Matt Drudge posted on his Web site that *Newsweek* magazine had killed a story about an alleged affair between a White House intern and the president of the United States. *Newsweek* officials stated that they were not killing the story, merely holding it for a later publication while certain facts were being double-checked. But it was too late. The Drudge Report had broken the story that was to dominate the news media for the remainder of the year and into 1999. ● The Internet was now setting the tone for news coverage, and it involved the speed of getting the story out, not the accuracy necessary for the more traditional media. And that put pressure on those media, which later led to several newspaper reporters and well-known columnists around the country being fired for either making up facts for the stories, using erroneous information, or stooping to plagiarism for their columns (see Chapter 15). ● And, to top off that summer of media turmoil, the Cable News Network (CNN) was forced to retract a story that had charged the U.S. military with using nerve gas against American defectors during the Vietnam War. The story drew intense criticism and denials from the military. ● The news media were finding themselves involved in a major change—and the driving force behind much of that change is convergence. Computer technology and the Internet are converging with television, radio, and print journalism in ways that are making new forms of communication.

THE IMPORTANCE OF INFORMATION

A well-informed citizenry has always been an important ingredient for a democratic society. Even in nondemocratic societies, government takeovers by revolutionary groups have usually started with a takeover of the news media outlets in those nations. The general feeling has been that whoever controls the sources of information controls the people.

The need to inform the public has been important to our society, dating back to the development of movable type in the 15th century and the creation of the telegraph and the telephone in the 19th century. These developments made possible the major mass communication tools of the 20th century: newspapers, radio, television, and computers.

> ### @ Practicing Media Literacy
> What do you consider to be your main source of news and information?

Today the sources of information are almost limitless. Newspapers continue to serve almost all communities across the nation, while radio and television usually have at least as many outlets in each city. With the development of satellite communication, the continuing increase in the number of cable channels available to the average home, and the computer boom that has allowed citizens access to the world, some form of information is at the fingertips of almost anyone on the face of the earth.

We'll cover the history of the various mass communication media in later chapters. In this chapter, we will focus on the news media and the worldwide sources of information. From the early days of this nation, when our founders realized the importance of an informed citizenry and included provisions for a free press in the U.S. Constitution, we have come a long way in our ability to keep the people aware of local, national, and world events.

global village

Today we live in a **global village** where news and information from any part of the world can be instantly broadcast around the earth. This fact makes it very difficult for governments that wish to control and restrict the flow of information to their people. To better understand the problems global communication is creating in the high-tech information age, let's look at four theories of media operation: authoritarian, libertarian, Soviet communist, and social responsibility. These theories were categorized in Siebert, Peterson, and Schramm's classic book, *Four Theories of the Press*.[1]

AUTHORITARIAN THEORY

The *authoritarian theory* is the oldest theory of the press. When mass communication began expanding in the 16th century, this theory developed quickly throughout Europe to protect the autocratic monarchies and the church from heretical publications.

When the printing press was invented, authoritarian states saw it as an important tool. Many attempts were made to use printing to unify the people. This was done by printing only wisdom and truth, which, of course, were identified by the heads of the church and state.

Martin Luther

Thus, the early press, starting with Gutenberg, published mostly authorized religious materials and, as people became more literate, chapbooks, the forerunner to the romance novel. Only after **Martin Luther's** challenge to the Catholic Church in 1517 led to the Protestant Reformation did books begin to appear that threatened the authoritarian state or religious order. Attempts were immediately made to censor heretical books by burning them and their printers. In a less drastic action, to limit printing to those who would operate for the "good of the state," governments established a system of state licensing for printers.

American Colonies

England was one of the countries to require the licensing of printers, and this policy, as well as other aspects of the authoritarian theory, was carried over to her American colonies. Although the British Parliament allowed the Licensing Act to expire in 1694, colonial governors retained controls on the press. When John Campbell received permission to establish the first regularly published newspaper in the colonies in 1704, he agreed to permit the authorities to screen all material before it was published.

The official attitude toward printing in the American colonies was best summed up in a 1671 statement attributed to Sir William Berkeley, governor of the Virginia colony: "But, I thank God, we have no free schools nor printing; and I hope we shall not have [them] these hundred years. For learning has brought disobedience and heresy and sects into the world, and printing has divulged them and libels against the government. God keep us from them both."[2]

Authoritarian states that did not have licensing laws attempted to exercise prior censorship by requiring that all printed material be approved by an official government censor before it could be printed and distributed. As the number of presses and the volume of printed materials grew, however, this approach proved too cumbersome. In the 18th century, control by prior restraint was largely replaced by the threat of punishment after publication. The laws of **treason** (the act of intending to overthrow the government) and **sedition** (the act of showing disrespect for the government) were used to prosecute printers of materials that were considered dangerous to the state.

treason
sedition

Modern Examples

Although the authoritarian theory of the press waned in many Western cultures by the second half of the 18th century, versions of it are still manifested in authoritarian states today. With the advent of global communication, journalists accustomed to one form of press freedom can find themselves in trouble when reporting in a country with authoritarian control.

> **@   Practicing Media Literacy**
> Do you think there should be more government control over the media in this country?

As noted in Chapter 3, the owner of a software firm that set up websites and provided other Internet-related services in the People's Republic of China was convicted of "inciting the overthrow of state power" because he supplied 30,000 e-mail addresses to a prodemocracy Internet magazine in the United States. The Chinese courts said the man must be "punished harshly."

A Japanese journalist was arrested in South Korea in 1993 for reporting a story that South Korea was anticipating an attack from North Korea because of the collapsing economy in the North. The article, entitled "The 1995 Unification with Guns and Swords," told how North Korea's army had taken up the title of the article as a slogan and how South Korea was preparing for war by lowering the age of military recruits and strengthening its defense capabilities.

In the last decade of the 20th century, Turkey has 150 laws and rules governing the press. These laws have been implemented by the Turkish government since 1921; the result is that dozens of journalists are jailed at any given time for publishing political views unacceptable to the government.

The Chinese government put a clamp on all information coming into that country in 1999 for fear that some media outlets would attempt to commemorate the 10th anniversary of the events at **Tiananmen Square** (see Chapter 3). It was in 1989 that the world was shocked when the government of the People's Republic of China sent out a horrifically authoritarian message by massacring the Tiananmen Square demonstrators for democracy, then clamped down on foreign reporters and directed its own media to show the protesters as the aggressors.

The Chinese government had ordered all foreign television news reports from Beijing to be stopped, but soon found that stopping the television images would not stop the flow of information about the student protests to other points around the world. Amateur photographers allowed their home videos to be beamed by satellite to the awaiting news media in other countries. Faxes and telephone calls helped those in Beijing to tell their stories to friends and relatives around the world, who then relayed the information to the news media. New technology had allowed the story to be told, even though the Chinese government had done everything possible to halt the newspaper and electronic media coverage of the story within the country itself.

But the Chinese government took its form of authoritarian control even further. In 1993, the government banned private ownership of satellite dishes. Then, in 1995, Internet use began to spread, primarily among university students. In what was described as the most sweeping example of government censorship of the Internet, China announced in 1996 that it was blocking access to hundreds of politically sensitive websites, including those of foreign media outlets, human rights groups, and Hong Kong and Taiwanese democratic political organizations. The action was described as China taking another step backward in the information age.

LIBERTARIAN THEORY

In contrast to the authoritarian view that the media should be controlled so that they do not interfere with the mission of the government, the *libertarian theory* emerged from a premise that the government should exist solely to serve the interests of the individual. It holds that the media should serve the people rather than the government and that the best way to find the truth is to have as many opinions aired as possible. Media scholar Wilbur Schramm said that the libertarian movement was "foreshadowed in the sixteenth century, envisioned in the seventeenth, fought for in the eighteenth and finally brought into widespread use in the nineteenth."[3]

The **Age of Enlightenment**, during which the libertarian theory emerged, resulted from a number of developments in Europe during the early modern period (15th to 18th centuries). These developments included scientific and geographical discoveries; the rise of trade and consumerism; the rise of the merchant class, which led to the growth of a middle class; the Protestant Reformation, which freed the individual from established church dogmas; and political and social revolutions that challenged the authoritarian concept and championed individual rights and freedoms.

Libertarians

Many philosophers and writers contributed to the formation of the libertarian concept. Among them were John Milton (1608–1674), John Locke (1632–1704), Isaac Newton (1642–1727), Adam Smith (1723–1790), Benjamin Franklin (1706–1790), Thomas Jefferson (1743–1826), James Madison (1751–1836), and John Stuart Mill

(1806–1873). The philosophy behind the libertarian theory of the press is described in the following letter, which Thomas Jefferson wrote to a friend in 1787:

> I am persuaded that the good sense of the people will always be found to be the best army. They may be led astray for a moment, but will soon correct themselves. The people are the only censors of their governors; and even their errors will tend to keep these to the true principles of their institution. To punish these errors too severely would be to suppress the only safeguard of the public liberty. The way to prevent these irregular interpositions of the people, is to give them full information of their affairs through the public channel of the public [news]papers, and to contrive that those papers should penetrate the whole mass of the people. The basis of our government being the opinion of the people, the very first object should be to keep that right; and were it left to me to decide whether we should have a government without newspapers, or newspapers without a government, I should not hesitate a moment to prefer the latter.[4]

Thomas Jefferson, the man who wrote the Declaration of Independence and later became the third President of the United States, was an early champion of freedom of the press.

Jefferson, who also felt strongly about the need for a literate society, qualified his statement favoring a society with free newspapers by saying, "I should mean that every man should receive those papers, and be capable of reading them."

James Madison, another framer of our constitution, also expressed his views on the importance of a free press to our country's experiment in democracy:

> Nothing could be more irrational than to give the people power and to withhold from them information without which power is abused. A people who mean to be their own governors must arm themselves with power which knowledge gives. A popular government without popular information or means of acquiring it is but a prologue to a farce or a tragedy, or perhaps both.[5]

American Democracy

Because of such people as Jefferson, Madison, and others, the libertarian theory of the press was an inherent part of the American experiment in democracy. The First Amendment in the Bill of Rights guarantees not only free speech but a free press as well.

Under the libertarian theory, it is the press that keeps the individual informed about the operations of government. It is important to remember that the American experiment in democracy was based on a system of checks and balances. Three separate and independent branches of government were established: the judicial, legislative, and executive branches. In addition, the First Amendment provided that the press serve as a "watchdog" of government. This is why the press is often considered a fourth branch—the **"fourth estate"**—of the governmental power structure. Likewise, with the recent advent of the electronic press, those media have been referred to as the "fifth estate."

fourth estate

In the First Amendment, the founders of our country installed a mechanism to protect the public's right to be informed. Thus, the American press operates under the

@   Practicing Media Literacy

Do you think that today's news media are functioning in the manner envisioned by those who drafted the First Amendment?

libertarian premise that the people's right to know is an essential ingredient of a free society. This right prevails over the right of any government official to silence a critical press. (Read about the limited efforts to restrict this press freedom, such as the Alien and Sedition Acts, in Chapter 4.)

Modern Examples

Examples of the libertarian theory at work appear in American newspapers and on radio and television daily. The impeachment process against President Clinton and his relationship with White House intern Monica Lewinsky is a case in point. The 1997 scandal over the Chinese government's efforts to influence U.S. elections is just another example, along with the Whitewater investment case allegations against President Clinton and his wife. Every president since George Washington has had problems with the reporting of information that they would just as soon be kept quiet.

THE SOVIET COMMUNIST THEORY

Although the term *Soviet communist theory* seems out of date today following the demise of the Soviet Union, this theory still applies to press operations in the remaining communist nations, such as China and Cuba.

A modern offshoot of the authoritarian theory, Soviet communist theory was crafted after the Russian Revolution in 1917 and served the communist bloc countries well until global electronic communication created problems for the closed-society concept. Prior to the mid-1980s, when Soviet president Mikhail Gorbachev introduced *glasnost* (openness) as part of the restructuring of Soviet society to counteract growing unrest, the Soviet communist theory held that the media should be extensions of the state and should foster unity and social cohesiveness. The Soviets contended that theirs was a "people's press": the Communist party served the people, and the press helped the party carry out that function.

In the former Soviet Union, the mass media were owned and operated by the state. The mass communicators needed to be loyal party members so they could interpret all communications correctly from the party's point of view. Westerners criticized this control of the press, claiming the media cannot serve two masters; the press is either a publicist for the government or a voice of the people. This state-owned and state-operated press was even more regulated than the authoritarian press. Lenin, the founder of the Soviet state, explained why an unregulated press was seen as a threat to the Soviet society:

> Why should freedom of speech and freedom of the press be allowed? Why should a government which is doing what it believes to be right allow itself to be criticized? It would not allow opposition by lethal weapons. Ideas are much more fatal things than guns. Why should any man be allowed to buy a printing press and disseminate pernicious opinion calculated to embarrass the government?[6]

Although the authoritarian and Soviet communist theories are similar in their belief that the state must be protected from a free and unregulated press, only the latter system makes use of the media to communicate party and state doctrines to the masses. Governments adhering to the authoritarian theory merely exercise control to ensure that the media do not publish anything that might harm the state. The mass media in an authoritarian system can be private as long as they are subject to licensing, prior censorship, postpublication prosecution, government subsidization, or some other form of government control. Thus, the Soviet communist theory results in a **planned system,** whereas the authoritarian theory results in a **controlled system.**

planned system
controlled system

Glasnost *and New Global Technologies*

The Soviet communist theory of the media allowed for a closed society in which the government controlled what people knew and thought. Gorbachev's **glasnost,** allowing people and the media to express views in opposition to the official position, was diametrically opposed to this closed-society concept. Some say Gorbachev had no choice but to open up the society because modern mass communication technologies—TV, VCRs, camcorders, and satellites—were making it impossible to shield people within the society from other viewpoints.

glasnost

Impact of the New Technologies

These electronic technologies are given partial credit for the fall of the communist regimes in Eastern Europe and the demise of the Soviet Union. Although television in Eastern Europe was state owned and controlled, videocassette recorders gave people a choice over what they could watch. In Poland, the Solidarity movement used VCRs and video documentaries to sustain itself.

Satellite dishes were used behind the Iron Curtain to obtain news and information not provided on the official government television channels. The American Cable News Network (CNN) became one of the most heavily watched channels in Eastern Europe among those with access to satellite dishes. In Poland and Hungary, the manufacture and sale of satellite dishes were legal. The effect of this satellite technology was to force the official Polish and Hungarian television stations to become more open or to become irrelevant, and they chose the former.

Adding to the problem was the spillover of TV signals across **national boundaries.** People in East Germany could watch West German television; Hungarians could see Austrian TV; and the liberalized Polish television signals were seen in East Germany, Czechoslovakia, and parts of the Soviet Union. In Romania, where dictator Nicolae Ceausescu personally controlled the content of government television, people watched Bulgarian, Soviet, and liberalized Hungarian TV signals. In 1994, the People's Republic of China attempted to restrict the sale of satellite dishes by requiring licenses. The government feared what might happen in this communist country if the people were continually exposed to BBC and CNN broadcasts.

national boundaries

Personal satellite dishes around the world have broken down national boundaries to provide information that many governments have tried to suppress.

Since the collapse of the Soviet Union, freedom of the press has not been guaranteed. When Russian president Boris Yeltsin turned out the army to put down an attempted revolt by communist hard-liners unhappy with his new government, one of

@ Practicing Media Literacy

What role do you think media from other nations played in the dissolution of the Union of Soviet Socialist Republics?

his first acts was to close opposition newspapers, including *Pravda*, the once powerful Communist party newspaper. The 81-year-old paper was allowed to start up again after a 30-day closure.

However, the newspaper, which was founded in 1912 by Nicolai Lenin and whose name was the Russian word for *truth*, was shut down in 1996. The owners of *Pravda*, two Greek millionaires, noted that the number of readers had dropped from 11 million in the communist years to around 200,000 by the mid-1990s, most of them elderly. But the decline in revenue and the rising cost of publication weren't the only reason the owners cited for the closure. "The editors and reporters drink too much. They publish nothing worth reading. They say they are a paper of the opposition and we oppose them because we oppose their politics. This is nonsense. Even the papers that support the government are more aggressive critics than *Pravda*."[7] According to the *San Francisco Chronicle*, the Greek owners "will be sending *Pravda* readers a new weekly tabloid specializing in crime, sex, and death." But there was no word yet on when "*Pravda*'s titillating tidbits will be on the World Wide Web."[8] *Pravda* not only continues to publish in a limited manner, but it has indeed established a website—but it's printed in Russian (pravda.ru).

THE SOCIAL RESPONSIBILITY THEORY

As early as the late 19th century, critics began to identify flaws in the libertarian theory. The free press was evolving in a manner that fell short of the idealistic libertarian goals.

profit

As the metropolitan press developed, it became large and centralized. More and more media outlets became controlled by fewer and fewer owners as chain ownership of newspapers grew. The press also became **profit** oriented: Selling newspapers and advertising space took precedence over the need to keep the public fully and accurately informed.

Major criticism of how the press was functioning in the American society began to be heard, and by the 20th century, the voices for change were loud. The main areas of concern were the following:

1. The press has wielded its enormous power for its own ends. Its owners have propagated their own opinions, especially in matters of politics and economics, at the expense of opposing views.

2. The press has been subservient to big business and at times has let advertisers control editorial policies and content.

3. The press has resisted social change.

4. The press has often paid more attention to the superficial and sensational in its coverage of current happenings, and its entertainment has often been lacking in substance.

5. The press has endangered public morals.

6. The press has invaded the privacy of individuals without just cause.

7. The press is controlled by one socioeconomic class, loosely the "business class," and access to the industry is difficult for the newcomer; therefore, the free and open market of ideas is endangered.[9]

In 1947 an influential report issued by the Commission on Freedom of the Press, chaired by Robert Maynard Hutchins, then chancellor of the University of Chicago, called for a socially responsible press. The report made it clear that freedom and responsibility go hand in hand and that the press should be periodically reminded of its responsibility. Siebert, Peterson, and Schramm later expanded on this theory:

> Freedom carries concomitant obligations; and the press, which enjoys a privileged position under the Constitution, is obliged to be responsible to society for carrying out certain essential functions of mass communication in contemporary society. To the extent that the press recognizes its responsibilities and makes them the basis of its operational policies, the libertarian system will satisfy the needs of society. To the extent that the press does not assume its responsibilities, some other agency must see that the essential functions of mass communication are carried out.[10]

This concept of placing power in the hands of other agencies to ensure that the press acts responsibly has been applied to the broadcast media in the United States to the extent that they are licensed by the government. Although there have been recent efforts to deregulate the broadcast media, the Federal Communications Commission (FCC) has the authority to revoke a broadcaster's license if it is determined that he or she is not serving the public interest. This type of regulation does not apply to the print media in this country, although some other Western democracies do license their journalists. Thus, social responsibility for the print media in the United States is voluntary and is adhered to by some print media officials, but not by all.

> **@ Practicing Media Literacy**
>
> While newspapers have the op-ed page to present divergent viewpoints, what steps do you see the broadcast media taking to be socially responsible?

> **@ Practicing Media Literacy**
>
> Do you think there's a need for government regulation of the print media as well as the broadcast media?

Early Proponents

During the latter part of the 19th century, newspaper editors such as Horace Greeley of the *New York Tribune* and Henry J. Raymond of the *New York Times* recognized the need for some form of press responsibility and started to promote social good and community welfare. Then, at the turn of the century, Joseph Pulitzer, whose *New York World* had been embroiled in a war of sensationalism with William Randolph Hearst's *New York Journal*, began reflecting on the dangers of circulation at any cost and started speaking out for more press responsibility. He wrote, "Without high ethical ideals a newspaper not only is stripped of its splendid possibilities for public service, but may become a positive danger to the community."[11]

Shortly thereafter, journalism education programs began to be established in colleges and universities. These programs not only offered career training in journalism but also stressed higher ideals and professional standards consistent with the social responsibility concept.

Self-regulation within the industry also reflected the press's acceptance of social responsibility. The American Society of Newspaper Editors adopted its Canons of Journalism in 1923. These guidelines call for the press to serve the public with truthfulness, impartiality, a sense of fair play, decency, respect for individual privacy, and concern for the general welfare. Since then other professional journalism associations have stressed ethics and standards as a means of upgrading the profession.

self-regulation

Current Efforts

Today some American media organizations voluntarily adhere to the social responsibility theory; others do not. Those that do attempt to present all sides of issues and strive to see that minority views and issues, as well as those of the establishment, are covered. They may even open up editorial comments to dissenting opinions, usually on the "op-ed" (opposite editorial) page.

FUNCTIONS AND PROBLEMS OF JOURNALISM

The American press serves five basic functions (both print and electronic): (1) to inform, (2) to entertain, (3) to influence through editorials, (4) to present advertisements, and (5) to transmit the culture. Most of the criticism of the press focuses on how it carries out the first function: to inform. Reader, listener, or viewer biases account for much of this criticism.

Blaming the Messenger

For one thing, it is simply human nature to blame the messenger for bad tidings. (In an ancient Greek play by Sophocles, for example, a king beheads a messenger who has brought him some bad news.)

For instance, the total fascination by the media with the Clinton–Lewinsky escapades in the White House drew much criticism from the public. There were those who felt that the whole thing would've gone away and the president wouldn't have been impeached if the media had left the story alone. Just like the coverage of the O.J. Simpson murder trial, many complained that the media were giving too much exposure to the story. And yet, in both instances, newspaper sales increased while the ratings for news programs covering the stories on both radio and television increased dramatically. While the public said they didn't want it, their actions showed that they did.

> **@ Practicing Media Literacy**
>
> Are the media just giving the public what it wants or do the people want such news coverage because the media tell them that it's important?

When riots broke out on American streets and university campuses in the 1960s, many people blamed the press for causing the disturbances. They claimed that by publicizing riots in one place, the media were giving others the idea to riot elsewhere. Similarly, during the unraveling of the Watergate scandal in 1972–1974, many people criticized the press for "harping on Watergate" because they didn't want to hear about the highest government officials committing crimes.

This is one reason the press ranks near the top of most lists of the nation's controversial institutions. Researchers have found that criticism of the press rises in direct proportion to the amount of unpleasant news being reported.

Watchdog Function

Of course, under the libertarian theory, it is an essential function of the American press to serve as a watchdog of government. Keeping the citizenry informed about its government necessarily puts the press and the government in an adversarial relationship, at least some of the time. When the press reports on activities that do not reflect favorably on the government and its leaders, it often receives a great deal of criticism from the government.

The "Bad News Only" Myth ✓

Many people also suffer from a misconception that the media present "only bad news because that's what sells." In fact, the news media carry both good and bad news, but readers, viewers, and listeners often ignore the good. Stories about the Boy Scouts, PTA, and church socials tend to interest only Boy Scouts, PTA members, and people who attend church socials.

There is some disagreement on just what constitutes bad news. Although an obituary should be considered bad news, just ask your newspaper editor what happens if he or she leaves one out of the paper. Editors are bombarded with angry telephone calls from family and friends. And, for that matter, a story about a blizzard might be bad news for residents of a community but great news for people elsewhere who are planning a ski trip.

Myth of Media Truth ✓

Another problem the media have is the popular misconception that if something appears in print or is heard over the airwaves, it has to be true. How many times have you heard someone attempt to win an argument by saying "I read it in the newspaper" or "I saw it on television"? So when the media do make mistakes, as they inevitably will, people are bitterly critical.

> **@ Practicing Media Literacy**
> Would you watch a television newscast if you knew it was only going to report "good" news?

Biases ✓

Finally, many people blame the press for being biased. Certainly everyone has his or her own biases, and newspeople are no exception. Good journalists do try to keep their biases out of their stories and present all sides of the story fairly, objectively, and accurately. However, most readers and viewers forget that they too have biases. And often, when they read or hear a story that is trying to present several sides, they react negatively to those parts that conflict with their own biases.

Cultural bias has become another area where journalists strive to be sensitive. Journalism schools and news organizations are now providing training to make journalists more aware of cultural diversity and to emphasize the need to keep the news columns and airwaves "politically correct."

STYLES OF JOURNALISM

Over the years, many changes have occurred in the styles of journalism in this country, from the days of the penny press and yellow journalism to today's world of broadcast journalism and the Internet.

The most significant change in the way people get the news has been the introduction of electronic journalism—first radio and then television news. In the following discussion, we use the term *press* to include both print and electronic news gathering.

Of course, most of the news media follow the basic concept of striving for a fair and unbiased report of activities that are out of the norm or that are important to a large audience. The foundation of this type of reporting are the five Ws and the H: who, what, when, where, why, and how. But over the years, other journalistic styles have also gained a foothold in the news media.

Interpretive Reporting

Although *interpretive reporting* was first introduced in the 1930s, it has increased markedly during the past decade or so. These articles, often labeled "news analysis," appear alongside straight news stories and on the op-ed pages of many newspapers. They try to explain the implications and possible consequences of certain events and have become an important part of modern journalism.

For example, in recent years the Clinton–Lewinsky story has drawn much analysis in the media. Columnists from both the conservative and liberal sides of the political spectrum have put forth their "**spin**" on the entire story and its impact on the government.

Pick up any newspaper today and you're bound to find "news analysis" pieces dealing with everything from events in Bosnia to the lack of privacy on the Internet.

Investigative Reporting

Investigative reporting has a longer history; it dates back to the late 19th century, when muckraking reporters began exposing the corruption and abuses of the new industrial society (see Chapter 8).

Classic examples of investigative reporting are Edward R. Murrow's exposure of the tactics of Senator Joseph R. **McCarthy**, Seymour Hersh's revelations about the My Lai massacre during the Vietnam war, and Bob Woodward and Carl Bernstein's uncovering of the Watergate scandal in 1972–1974.

Murrow was the first to use the new medium of television to investigate stories and give a more in-depth report on the events affecting the lives of American citizens. He did it with his weekly news magazine program, *See It Now,* which usually devoted its entire 30 minutes to just one topic.

In 1954, that topic was the junior senator from Wisconsin, Joe McCarthy, who was at the height of his popularity in his four-year crusade to remove Communists from high places in our government. He had the support of the people in this Cold War mission against a takeover of our government by the Soviet Union, although many believed his campaign was merely a political witch hunt.

McCarthy had conducted many hearings and, through guilt by association and activities from out of the past, had ruined the careers of many people. But McCarthy's crusade had actually found no Communists working in high places in Washington. Thus, CBS news reporter Ed Murrow devoted his entire program to the subject of McCarthy to show the American public just what the senator was up to. He used little comment, mostly showing video of McCarthy at work.

spin

McCarthy

It was a bold move by Murrow, as many citizens who had tried to stand up to McCarthy in the past had become the object of public scorn. Many historians still consider the Murrow broadcast, along with the televised Army–McCarthy hearings that followed a few months later, as among the most important steps leading to McCarthy's downfall and censure by the U.S. Senate. In ranking the original Murrow telecast as 21st among television's 100 most memorable programs in TV history, *TV Guide* wrote in 1996,

> Murrow devoted an installment of his CBS investigative show, *See It Now*, to McCarthy, using the senator's own comments and speeches to reveal him as a blustering demagogue. McCarthy never recovered from the devastating exposé. It was an early and powerful testament to television's ability to influence public opinion.[12]

In 1969, journalist Seymour Hersh discovered that American soldiers had killed over 300 Vietnamese civilians in the village of **My Lai** the previous year. His reports led to congressional hearings and the indictment of military personnel involved in the episode. The incident shattered the myth that American soldiers were always the "good guys" who protected the innocent in times of war.

My Lai

Hersh's investigation resulted in several books, including *My Lai Four: A Report on the Massacre and Its Aftermath* and *Cover-Up: The Army's Secret Investigation of My Lai Four*. In the 1970s, he worked for the *New York Times*, winning numerous major journalism awards, including the 1970 Pulitzer Prize for International Reporting. Hersh's investigative reporting led to several more books in the years that followed.

As the 1990s drew to a close, Hersh published two more major works. *The Dark Side of Camelot* (1997) revealed a wealth of indiscretions and malfeasance by President John **Kennedy** during his years at the White House. Hersh's investigation charged

Kennedy

that these transgressions ranged from frequent dalliances with prostitutes and mistresses to the attempted assassination of Cuba's Fidel Castro to involvement with organized crime. While scandals in the White House were certainly nothing new, Hersh maintained that Kennedy's activities went beyond minor abuses of power and personal indulgences. He charged that they threatened the integrity of the office of president and the security of the nation, particularly in the area of foreign policy. Hersh's investigation was the basis for a two-hour ABC-TV news documentary in 1997, hosted by Peter Jennings.

In *Against All Enemies: Gulf War Syndrome: The War Between America's Ailing Veterans and Their Government* (1998), Hersh makes two important points: 1) military officials, either through a lack of knowledge or deliberate concealment, did not fully inform the government and, more importantly, their own troops about the risks of biochemical exposure during combat in Iraq; and 2) whatever the causes of the so-called **Gulf War Syndrome,** the government has done far too little to help the ailing U.S. veterans of that battle.

Gulf War Syndrome

For the *Washington Post*, the Watergate story began with a police report about a burglary at the Democratic national headquarters in a Washington, D.C. office and apartment complex called **Watergate.** *Post* reporters Bob Woodward and Carl Bernstein were teamed to find out what was behind the break-in. With the help of an anonymous source within the government, called "Deep Throat," they began uncovering a series of illegal activities that they traced to the White House. When President Richard Nixon himself was implicated in a cover-up, he resigned from office rather than face impeachment. This event shook the foundation of our American culture because it ran counter to the myth that we could trust our presidents to respect the laws of the land.

Watergate

Bernstein also caused much discussion in 1996 with his book *The Choice*, which examined the two candidates for president, incumbent Bill Clinton and challenger Robert Dole. The book revealed that the First Lady, Hillary Clinton, had been having conversations with a former First Lady, the late Eleanor Roosevelt. While Mrs. Clinton later explained that she liked to think out problems by having an imaginary discussion with Mrs. Roosevelt, the media, particularly television comedians, put their own slant on the story to make it appear that she was communing with the dead.

@   Practicing Media Literacy
Can you cite any examples of investigative journalism in today's media?

Bernstein's Watergate partner, Bob Woodward, caused a stir in 1999 when his book *Shadow* explored the impact of Watergate on the institutions of the presidency by tracing the scandals of each of the five presidents since Richard Nixon. As one observer described it, the book ranged from Watergate to Monicagate.

Washington Post *reporters Bob Woodward and Carl Bernstein led the way for all media in the investigation of the Watergate coverup story, which eventually led to the resignation of a president.*

In all of these investigative news events, many Americans blamed the media for revealing the information. Nevertheless, in a free society, the role of the press is to keep the people informed and reflect all of the culture, including its unpleasant secrets.

Advocacy, Subjective, or New Journalism

Not all journalists subscribe to the standard of strict objectivity. In the 1960s, some reporters began to practice what they called *advocacy journalism, subjective journalism,* or even *new journalism.* Believing they should report the truth "as they see it," these reporters became personally and emotionally involved in the events they covered. This type of reporting has not been welcomed by the establishment press, but it has found a home in certain specialized publications.

Although *new journalism* has had many meanings over the years, today the term refers to a 20th-century writing style that applies literary techniques to journalism. The result is a semiobjective, journalistic view of reality written from a subjective, first-person viewpoint. Some writers who have used this style are Tom Wolfe, Jimmy Breslin, Joe McGinniss, Norman Mailer, and Gay Talese.

NEWS WIRE SERVICES

Since the 19th century, the American news media's coverage of our popular culture has been greatly assisted by press wire services. Wire services were established as news-gathering and disseminating services for newspapers after the invention of the telegraph in the 1840s. Today wire services work for radio and television as well.

American Wire Services

The first wire service was the Associated Press (**AP**), which was established in New York in 1848. It remains the largest American wire service and has always been a non-profit organization; news media that use and pay for the service belong to the Associated Press. Thus, members share as well as receive news stories.

AP

United Press International (**UPI**), the second major American wire service, was founded as United Press by E. W. Scripps in 1907. It has operated like other businesses, with users subscribing to its service. Thus, AP has members, whereas UPI has clients or customers.

UPI

The third wire service formed in the United States was International News Service, which William Randolph Hearst established in 1909. In 1958, United Press merged with International News Service to become United Press International.

Foreign Wire Services

AP and UPI are not only the two major news services in the United States; they are dominant worldwide services as well. However, three others are equally influential in global news coverage: Agence France-Presse (**AFP**), headquartered in Paris; Reuters, in London; and the Telegrafnoie Agentsvo Sovetskovo Soyuza (**TASS**), in Moscow.

AFP

AFP, which was organized in 1945 at the end of World War II, has 100 foreign bureaus. Like AP, it is a nonprofit service. **Reuters** was founded in the 1850s and has more than 1,000 correspondents in 180 countries, including a half-dozen bureaus in the United States. In recent years its revenues have come to exceed AP's, thanks mostly to the addition of financial news and information retrieval services.

TASS

Reuters

Until 1991, TASS was the official voice of the former Soviet Union. Its foreign correspondents in more than 100 countries now gather and report local and international news for the Commonwealth of Independent States.

Although UPI was established as a profit-making wire service, it has been losing money since 1963. In 1982 it was sold by its co-owners, the E. W. Scripps Company and the Hearst Corporation, to the Media News Corporation. But the new owners were not able to turn the service around either, and in the summer of 1986, they sold UPI to Mexican newspaper magnate Mario Vazquez Rana, who owned Mexico's largest chain of newspapers. This alarmed American journalists, who were concerned about Vazquez Rana's ties to the Mexican government.

Foreign ownership of such an essential news source was unprecedented. Troubled by dwindling profits, UPI twice declared bankruptcy and was sold three times in a decade, including to a Saudi Arabian media company in 1993. Due to financial problems, employees were later forced to take a 35 percent pay cut and in recent years many of the wire service's European bureaus were closed down to save money.

By May of 2000, UPI changed hands once again as it was purchased by News World Communications Inc., which publishes the conservative *Washington Times*. News World is an affiliate of the Unification Church, founded by the Reverend Sun Myung Moon, a South Korean evangelist.

RADIO NEWS

With the development of radio as an entertainment medium in the 1920s, news was a limited part of the programming available to listeners. Quite often, a newscast was presented by a staff announcer who might later appear as the straightman for one of the network's top comedians. It wasn't until the 1930s that radio news began to develop as an important part of the broadcast operation.

In the early days, news was not heard on a regular basis; newscasts were offered only when there was news to report. But by the 1930s, the networks (and some local stations) began scheduling a few newscasts at regular times, perhaps one in the morning, one at midday, and one or two during the evening hours.

During this time, newspapers realized that the public was turning to this "instant" news reporting as a source of information. In addition, many advertisers were starting to put their revenue into this new medium. As a result, the newspapers put pressure on the wire services to stop servicing the radio networks. This battle, known as the Press–Radio War of 1933–1935, forced the networks to begin establishing their own news bureaus around the nation and the world to supply news for their broadcasts. It was probably the best thing to happen to radio news.

By 1937, reports of the military activities of German leader Adolph Hitler were reaching our shores, and Americans began debating whether the United States should get involved in a possible war on another continent.

During this period, CBS had sent a young man with little broadcast experience to Europe to handle the arrangements for a weekly panel discussion featuring world leaders. He was not to work on the air but merely serve as a program producer. His name was Edward R. Murrow.

Once on the scene in Europe, Murrow realized that a lot was going on that the American people needed to know. When Hitler's troops marched into Vienna, Austria, in 1938, Murrow was on the scene providing live shortwave radio reports to CBS and the American public as to what was happening. His regular reports from London during Germany's bombing attacks on the British capital also brought the sound and voices of a distant war into the homes of the American people. Many historians believe Murrow's broadcasts, as well as other radio news reports of the European war, helped to change attitudes about American involvement in the battle against Nazi Germany. Murrow's broadcasts during and after the war kept Americans informed as to what had been going on while their loved ones were fighting the Nazi regime (see Box 5.1). Historians also agree that radio news "came of age" with its coverage of World War II. Radio news now had credibility with the listening audience.

It was during World War II that network radio news adopted the schedule of providing five minutes of news every hour on the hour. The American people were anxious to hear about what was going on in Europe, especially since many of their loved ones were now fighting "over there." This format of news on the hour still exists today.

But radio news has changed quite a bit over the years. As television took many of the entertainment programs away from the radio networks in the 1950s, all that was left were the hourly newscasts and some news specials. Local radio stations relied on those programs to serve their communities with news from around the nation and the world.

Today four radio networks still provide news to those stations wishing to affiliate with them. However, it's not the same product offered during the past 50 years. For example, ABC now has some six separate news operations to fit the format of each type of station (a faster-paced newscast for rock-oriented stations, a more detailed newscast for news and talk stations, etc.). The NBC Radio Network is no longer affiliated with the NBC Television Network. When it purchased National Broadcasting Company, General Electric sold off its radio network to Westwood One, which also owns the Mutual Radio Network (in fact, many of the newscasts for those two networks are exactly the same, except for the short opening that mentions the specific network, using the same newscaster).

With the deregulation of radio in the 1980s (see Chapter 4), stations were no longer required to devote a portion of their daily programming to news and public affairs shows. As a result, many music stations decided to stop doing news completely, or at least cut back to just a few short news reports during the morning drive times—usually fluff, entertainment-type stories delivered by someone who also serves as a straight-man for the morning DJ's jokes.

> **@   Practicing Media Literacy**
>
> Does the radio station you listen to most regularly provide any newscasts? Do you wish that it did?

DEVELOPMENT OF TELEVISION NEWS

Networks began experimenting with television news as early as January 1940, when NBC began airing radio newscaster Lowell Thomas on its New York TV station. CBS's first television news broadcasts began in the spring of 1941. Since early television was unable to broadcast film of news events, newscasters simply read the news aloud to the audience. When President Roosevelt delivered his war message to Congress in December 1941, for example, CBS's New York station put an American flag in front of the camera and turned on an off-camera fan to make it wave while the station carried the president's voice.

Although World War II produced a number of top-notch radio journalists, such as Edward R. Murrow, William L. Shirer, Eric Sevareid, Walter Cronkite, Charles Collingwood, and Howard K. Smith, none of them wanted anything to do with television news after the war because they believed radio was the more serious medium.

CBS and NBC took the first major steps in network television journalism when they broadcast the Democratic and Republican national **conventions** in 1948. For the

conventions

Box 5.1

MEDIA WATCH

The Horrors of War, as Reported to America by Edward R. Murrow

From 1935 to 1961, Edward R. Murrow worked for the CBS network before resigning to become director of the United States Information Agency in the administration of President John Kennedy. Prior to and during World War II, Murrow's ability to calmly describe news events on radio in a manner that left no confusion in the minds of the audience helped to bring the realities and the horrors of the war home to Americans. The following is an excerpt of Murrow's April 15, 1945, broadcast describing what he found when he visited the German concentration camp at Buchenwald at the end of the war.

Permit me to tell you what you would have seen, and heard, had you been with me on Thursday. It will not be pleasant listening. If you are at lunch, or if you have no appetite to hear what Germans have done, now is a good time to switch off the radio, for I propose to tell you of Buchenwald. It is on a small hill about four miles outside Weimar, and it was one of the largest concentration camps in Germany, and it was built to last. As we approached it, we saw about a hundred men in civilian clothes with rifles advancing in open order across fields. There were a few shots; we stopped to inquire. We were told that some of the prisoners had a couple of SS men cornered in there. We drove on, reached the main gate. The prisoners crowded up behind the wire. We entered.

And now, let me tell this in the first person, for I was the least important person there, as you shall hear. There surged around me an evil-smelling horde. Men and boys reached out to touch me; they were in rags and remnants of uniform. Death had already marked many of them, but they were smiling with their eyes. I looked out over that mass of men to the green fields beyond where well-fed Germans were ploughing.

When I entered, men crowded around, tried to lift me to their shoulders. They were too weak. Many of them could not get out of bed. I was told that this building had once stabled eighty horses. There were twelve hundred men in it, five to a bunk. The stink was beyond all description.

I asked how many men had died in that building during the last month. They called the doctor; we inspected his records. There were only names in the little black book, nothing more—nothing of who these men were, what they had done, or hoped. Behind the names of those who had died there was a cross. I counted them. They totaled 242. Two hundred and forty-two out of twelve hundred in one month.

As I walked down to the end of the barracks, there was applause from the men too weak to get out of bed. It sounded like the hand clapping of babies; they were so weak. The doctor's name was Paul Heller. He had been there since 1938.

As we walked out into the courtyard, a man fell dead. Two others—they must have been over sixty—were crawling toward the latrine. I saw it but will not describe it.

In another part of the camp they showed me the children, hundreds of them. Some were only six. One rolled up his sleeve, showed me his number. It was tattooed on his arm. D-6030, it was. The others showed me their numbers; they will carry them till they die.

We proceeded to the small courtyard. The wall was about eight feet high; it adjoined what had been a stable or garage. We entered. There were two rows of bodies stacked up like cordwood. They were thin and very white. Some of the bodies were terribly bruised, though there seemed to be little flesh to bruise. Some had been shot through the head, but they bled but little. All except two were naked. I tried to count them as best I could and arrived at the conclusion that all that was mortal of more than five hundred men and boys lay there in two neat piles.

There was a German trailer which must have contained another fifty, but it wasn't possible to count them. The clothing was piled in a heap against the wall. It appeared that most of the men and boys had died of starvation; they had not been executed. But the manner of death seemed unimportant. Murder had been done at Buchenwald.

Source: From *In Search of Light: The Broadcasts of Edward R. Murrow, 1938–1961* edited by Edward Bliss, Jr. (New York: Knopf, 1967), pp. 91–92. Copyright © 1967 by the Estate of Edward R. Murrow. Reprinted by permission of Alfred A. Knopf, Inc.

In the early days of television, the networks provided gavel-to-gavel coverage of the daily sessions. Today, the political parties schedule their main convention events for prime time in order to get TV coverage.

first time, America's political process in the selection of candidates for president of the United States was brought into the homes of the voting public.

ABC did not launch a news show until the 1950s and did not become a ratings contender in news until the late 1970s, when Roone Arledge, the producer of ABC's *Wide World of Sports* and *Monday Night Football*, was appointed head of the news division. With the use of many of the visual graphics that he had used in his ABC sports broadcasts, Arledge was able to make ABC news number one in the ratings during the late 1980s and early 1990s.

Technical Limitations

Early-day television news could not begin to compare with radio news. Radio could go to the scene of events and broadcast live. TV news required motion picture cameras, and the film had to be processed after it was shot. Some early network newscasts relied on motion picture newsreel photographers to provide footage, but often this material was not available until several days after the event. In the meantime, the networks often used still photos, which the newscasters held up in front of them. However, portable cameras and videotape recorders made television a much more credible news medium by the 1960s because viewers saw pictures of the news events on the day they occurred. By the 1980s, many television stations had the capability of broadcasting live from the scenes of news events. Eventually TV provided more people with their news than newspapers and radio combined.

The Kennedy Assassination

The most profound demonstration of the power of television in bringing news to our popular culture came in November 1963, when President John F. Kennedy was assassinated in Dallas. The three networks provided continuous, 24-hour-a-day coverage from Friday through Monday, canceling all commercials at significant cost. TV cameras at the Dallas jail also captured live the murder of Lee Harvey Oswald, Kennedy's suspected killer, as he was about to be transferred from the Dallas jail to another location.

For four days Americans sat in front of their TV sets watching reruns of both assassinations, historical film of the Kennedy presidency, and the emotional burial of the

*Television's uninter-
rupted coverage of
President John
Kennedy's assassina-
tion, funeral and burial
helped bond this nation
together during a
national tragedy.*

president in Arlington National Cemetery. Television's ability to unite the entire nation in one common emotion demonstrated without doubt just how socially powerful
this new mass communication medium had become. It also demonstrated that television could hold a nation together in a time of national tragedy and potential danger.

The Vietnam War

As the nation's involvement in the Vietnam war escalated during the administration
of President Lyndon Johnson in the 1960s, television was there to bring the sights and
sounds of the war into America's living rooms every night. For the first time in history,
Americans could watch ordinary people being killed on foreign battlefields. People
could no longer ignore the horrors of war and soon began to question American involvement in Vietnam. Many blamed television news for turning the Vietnam war
into an unpopular effort.

The Debate over TV's Newsmaking Role

Television news differs profoundly from newspaper journalism. Readers of the print
media can be their own editors, selecting what they want to read. With television,
people have only two choices—leave the TV on or turn it off—and most people
choose to leave their sets on.

Eventually some critics started wondering whether television wasn't shaping the
news rather than merely reporting it. In the summer of 1968, after the assassinations
of Martin Luther King, Jr., and Senator Robert F. Kennedy, the widespread riots in urban ghettos, and the battle between Chicago police and antiwar demonstrators outside the Democratic national convention, many Americans became convinced that
TV news was the cause of the nation's troubles.

The newly elected Republican vice president, Spiro Agnew, articulated this concern in 1969:

The members of Congress or the Senate who follow their principles and philosophy quietly in a spirit of compromise are unknown to many Americans—while the loudest and most extreme dissenters on every issue are known to every man in the street. How many marches and demonstrations would we have if the marchers did not know that the ever-faithful TV cameras would be there to record their antics for the next TV show? . . . By way of conclusion, let me say that every elected leader in the United States depends on these men in the media. Whether what I have said tonight will be heard and seen at all by the nation is not my decision; it's not your decision; it's their decision.[13]

There are those today who feel that the media are setting the agenda for what has been going on in Washington. Matt Drudge and his Drudge Report on the Internet was the first to break the story of President Clinton and Monica Lewinsky. *Newsweek* magazine, which had been set to break the story was quick to follow, and then all media were on the story, covering it from every possible angle for well over a year. Critics feel this was overkill and a media attempt to make the news.

> **@ Practicing Media Literacy**
> Does television news spend too much time covering certain high-profile news events at expense of other stories?

TV Covers the Space Race

Television demonstrated what it could do best in July 1969, when it took the world live to the scene of Apollo XI's landing on the moon. Hundreds of millions of people saw the first human steps on the moon. The American dream of space conquest had been achieved, and television brought the event into the world's homes—live.

TV's coverage of the space program again influenced the popular culture in January 1986, when the space shuttle Challenger, carrying the first teacher into space, exploded on live TV seconds after liftoff. The nation was plunged into mourning. Many people interviewed at the time indicated they had not felt such an emotional loss since the assassination of President Kennedy 23 years earlier.

Watergate

Although the Watergate scandal was first exposed by newspaper reporters, TV played a crucial role in bringing the story to the masses. Millions of Americans were glued to their television sets as Congress conducted investigative hearings in 1973–1974. As a parade of top Nixon administration officials revealed the web of lies, burglaries, money laundering, and obstruction of justice committed on the president's behalf, a growing sentiment for impeachment developed. On August 8, 1974, these same Americans saw their president go on television to announce his resignation.

The Iran–Contra Hearings

Some 33 years after TV news demonstrated its influence on the culture by televising the Army–McCarthy hearings, it again set the national news

Hundreds of millions of television viewers worldwide saw man walk on the moon for the first time.

agenda by broadcasting live congressional hearings into the Reagan administration's sale of arms to Iran and the diversion of profits to the Contra freedom fighters in Nicaragua.

Whereas TV had earlier transformed Senator McCarthy from a hero into a villain, during the televised Iran–Contra hearings Lieutenant Colonel Oliver North, who had been fired by President Reagan for his illegal activities in the Iran–Contra scandal, was transformed into a folk hero with a cultlike following. Wearing his Marine Corps uniform decorated with ribbons, North, who had been one of President Reagan's national security advisers, convinced many Americans that he was a young, patriotic officer who was "just following orders from his superiors." North had previously been cast by the news media as a villain, or at best a scapegoat. Within days the American consumer culture was selling "Ollie North for President" bumper stickers and T-shirts. His popularity convinced him to run for a U.S. Senate seat in Virginia in 1994, but he lost.

Monicagate

Television news coverage of the special prosecutor's investigation into the White House activities of President Bill Clinton and intern Monica Lewinsky dominated the airwaves through all of 1998 and the early part of 1999. When the House of Representatives voted articles of impeachment against the president, the networks provided complete coverage of the impeachment trial in the Senate. Despite the fact that television reporters continued to bring out new and more damaging information about the president, Clinton's popularity continued to soar to astronomical heights.

TV News and Sensationalism

In recent years, regular television news has gotten more sensational to compete with tabloid TV shows such as *Inside Edition* and *Hard Copy*. Local newscasts as well as network news spend countless hours covering such stories as the O.J. Simpson murder trial, the deaths of Princess Diana and John Kennedy, Jr., and the Bill Clinton–Monica Lewinsky White House scandal. According to CBS anchor Dan Rather, all of the networks have sold out to sensationalism (see Box 5.2).

Proof of America's fascination with the sensational stories came on the morning the jury announced its verdict in the Simpson double murder trial. According to Pacific Gas and Electric Company, at 10:10 A.M. that day, the largest public utility in the country had a power surge of 160 megawatts. The company believes people had their TVs and radios tuned in all morning for the verdict in the case. When it was finally announced and the year-long trial was officially over, hundreds of thousands of people turned off the electricity to those appliances at exactly the same time, creating the sudden power surge. Utility companies across the country reported similar incidents. There's no doubt that America was watching and listening.

TV News, Sexism, and Ageism

Women more than men have been finding that an attractive appearance is essential for employment as a television anchorperson. In 1983 a jury awarded Christine Craft,

Box 5.2
MEDIA LITERACY
The Blurred Line between Journalism and Entertainment

One of the *Washington Post* investigative reporters who broke the Watergate story in the 1970s feels that cultural changes have dulled the distinctions between journalism and entertainment, with some reporters and editors disregarding truth, accuracy, and fairness in opting for sensationalism.

According to Carl Bernstein, "There is a voracious appetite out there for garbage and we are supplying it. What is changing is that people who years ago would not supply it now supply it."

Bernstein was part of a 1999 panel discussion, which also included reporter and Ronald Reagan biographer Lou Cannon, Washington First Amendment attorney Bruce W. Sanford, *New York Daily News* columnist Lars-Erik Nelson, former U.S. Representative Dan Rostenkowski, D-Illinois, and *Congressional Quarterly* publisher Robert Merry. They agreed that the celebrity culture and information deluge which has hit the nation from radio, television, newspapers, magazines, and the Internet has increased competition and brought about a tabloid mentality in many newsrooms.

"The role of profit has started to erode the basic standards of our craft," Bernstein said. "And it has ultimately to do with the question of what is news and the so-called 'dumbing down' of the news—sensationalism and gossip is the best example of it."

Bernstein says that since Watergate, journalism began to see a new kind of reporter focused on career advancement rather than doing the job the traditional way. "It's no longer based on traditional values related to truth, accuracy, and fairness," he said. "A cultural phenomenon overtook those values and, combined with careerism, in some ways has created a monster. . . ."

The biggest offender in all of this, he says, is television, with many shows from *Jerry Springer* to *Extra* to the local news blurring the viewer's distinction between news and entertainment. "The state of local television news all over America is a disgrace. It has nothing to do with what is going on in your city or town," he said. "'If it bleeds, it leads,' as they say in those newsrooms."

Congressional Quarterly publisher Robert Merry also wasn't very optimistic. "The bad news is it's going to get worse," he told the gathering.

Source: Jeff Wilson, Associated Press, Oct. 14, 1999.

---

a former Kansas City TV anchor, $500,000 in damages in a sex **discrimination** suit. She had been fired from KMBC-TV because a consulting firm found she was "too old, too unattractive, and not deferential enough to men." Although a United States district court judge threw out the verdict, a new jury awarded her $325,000 in a retrial in 1984. But that award was also overturned, and the Supreme Court refused to hear her final appeal.

discrimination

Because television needs attractive anchors and reporters to lure viewers, ageism is a problem in television news. While some male anchors can get away with showing gray hair and other signs of growing older, female anchors can run into problems at the first signs of aging.

However, in the final decade of the 20th century, the California court of appeals upheld a $514,449 award for a veteran San Francisco television reporter who had claimed he was illegally fired from his job because of his age. Reporter Steve Davis sued the station on the grounds of age discrimination because his contract had been canceled after 20 years with the station. California law forbids the firing of employees over age 40 because of their age. Davis was 53 at the time of his release. The station denied that Davis was let go because of his age, saying that his competence as a journalist was not up to the station's standards.

Meanwhile, the search for the perfect anchor continues. One Los Angeles television station faced with declining ratings even used galvanic skin response tests on randomly selected viewers to measure the perceived attractiveness of various anchors. By measuring the sweat produced by viewers, station management could determine who to keep and who to fire.

TV News as Big Business

Two cable news operations have been in the news in recent years, leading to a feud between two of the world's top media moguls, Rupert Murdoch and Ted Turner. When Time Warner merged with Turner's broadcasting properties in 1996 for a reported $6.7 billion, the cable company gained control of Turner's Cable News Network (CNN), along with his other cable properties. Later in the year, Murdoch launched his Fox News Channel (FNC) but faced the prospect of not having the new cable channel available in the nation's largest market. The cable system in New York City was owned by Time Warner, which elected not to carry the Fox channel but instead to continue carrying Turner's CNN.

New York mayor Rudolph Giuliani, who had received support from Murdoch and his *New York Post* during the mayoral campaign, tried to pressure Time Warner into carrying the Fox News Channel, but when that didn't work he sought to have FNC made available on one of the city's public access channels. Much name calling and legal action followed, as well as a monumental feud between Murdoch and Turner. At one point, Murdoch's *New York Post* even elected to stop carrying the listings for Turner's CNN on its daily television page. When multibillion-dollar corporations go to battle, anything can happen.

TV News Dominance

Today more Americans claim they get their news from television than from any other source. Since TV cannot begin to provide the variety of stories or the in-depth

Media mogul Rupert Murdoch began his empire with newspapers and later expanded into television, movies and cable (see Box 5.3).

Box 5.3
PROFILE
The World Wide Media Empire of Rupert Murdoch

As the 20th century drew to a close, Rupert Murdoch's News Corporation has continued to grow. While selling off one of its most popular print publications for some $7.6 billion in 1999, its acquisitions or expansions have been in the area of electronic media and computer technology, including Hong Kong–based STAR-TV, a pan-Asian TV service that reaches from Tokyo to Tel Aviv; Delphi Internet Services, with access to a worldwide Internet system that reaches 20 million computer users; and an expansion of his British Sky Broadcasting (BSkyB) satellite from 6 to 14 channels.

News Corporation also purchased the Los Angeles Dodgers baseball team and immediately created one of the highest payrolls in the major leagues by signing numerous high-priced free agents. The team finished third in its division that year, some 20 games out of first place.

All of these acquisitions were in addition to his various newspapers around the world and his ownership of Fox Corporation, including a television network and a major motion picture studio. But they also presented problems for the media mogul. In July of 1998, a court in India issued three arrest warrants against Murdoch for refusing to appear to face charges that his STAR-TV network was showing allegedly obscene movies in that nation. The warrants were sent to Murdoch's addresses in the United States and Australia, but had all been returned unserved because the media tycoon had refused to accept them.

Rupert Murdoch was born in Australia, where he inherited a small newspaper company from his father. He expanded the operation by starting up or taking over numerous sensation-mongering tabloids in Australia, Great Britain (*The Times of London*), and the United States (including the *New York Post*) and now has vast holdings in Australia, Britain, Europe, Asia, and the United States.

Murdoch became a U.S. citizen in 1986 in order to purchase a group of Metromedia television stations (U.S. law prohibits foreign ownership of broadcast media). In 1988 he paid $3 billion for Triangle Publications, which at the time published *TV Guide*, *Daily Racing Form*, *Premiere*, and *Seventeen*.

In October of 1999, Murdoch announced that Gemstar International Group had agreed to buy *TV Guide* for about $7.6 billion in stock. While *TV Guide*, with 11 million subscribers, ranks among the largest circulation magazines, Murdoch was apparently looking ahead, as this deal was motivated by "point-and-click" electronic program guides that will increasingly dominate how viewers select the programs they watch in the years ahead.

In addition to the Fox network, and the FX and Fox Movie cable channels, Murdoch's U.S. assets include the 20th Century Fox movie studio, numerous TV stations, more than 100 newspapers, and Harper-Collins Publishers. His Fox Television network—known for such shows as *The Simpsons*, *Beverly Hills 90210*, *Party of Five*, *Ally McBeal*, and *The X-Files*—has been rapidly expanding. Known for his flair for tabloid newspapers, he has successfully introduced this style of sensationalism into American television, and his direction has had a major impact on U.S. network TV.

In 1994, Murdoch started the FX and FXMovie cable channels in the United States to augment his Fox network offerings. In 1996 he introduced the Fox News cable channel, which challenged Ted Turner's cable news operations, CNN and CNN Headline News, now controlled by Time Warner, and NBC's cable news channels, MSNBC and CNBC.

In 1997 Murdoch—whose Fox network had given the world the risqué and controversial *Married—With Children*—agreed to pay $1.9 billion to acquire the former Christian Broadcasting Network cable channel from the Rev. Pat Robertson, the one-time presidential candidate of the religious right. Renaming it the Fox Family Channel, Murdoch has not made any moves with the network which would alienate the viewership that had turned the operation into the ninth-largest cable network in the United States, reaching 67 million homes. Robertson continued to host his *700 Club*, a Christian talk program which runs on the channel each weeknight.

In Europe Murdoch is working on digital video compression, which will allow his TV satellites to beam down 180 channels. He is also working in the field of cellular telephones and the development of a digital superhighway information system.

If, as futurist Alvin Toffler states, the control of information in the Information Age equates to power, Murdoch is rapidly becoming one of the most powerful men on earth.

coverage that newspapers do, this has serious implications for a democracy that needs a well-informed citizenry to function properly.

Although network TV news seems more serious and sophisticated, it too depends on ratings and its share of the audience. Often those ratings are dependent on the local news because in most cities, local news immediately precedes network news, and most viewers will watch their favorite local news show and stay tuned to whichever network news follows. The second and third reason people watch one network news show over another, according to an executive producer of *NBC Nightly News*, are the popularity of the anchor and the content.[14]

CNN Develops

24-hour news

Cable TV tycoon Ted Turner began giving the big three network news operations a run for their money in the 1980s with the introduction of two 24-hour-a-day satellite–cable news channels: Cable News Network (CNN) and Headline News (see Box 5.4). For the first time, the American people were able to watch worldwide TV news whenever they wanted rather than when the networks told them they could watch it. This type of independence from the network news "clock" appealed to many people who were ready to break away from old habits and try something new.

Adding to the network woes was the fact that Turner aggressively built a worldwide news operation that gained respect abroad as well as at home. During the uprisings in Eastern Europe and in China's Tiananmen Square during 1989, people throughout the world were using satellite dishes to learn the latest from the news-gathering forces of CNN. When the United States invaded Panama in December 1989, the Soviet foreign minister didn't call the U.S. embassy to protest but instead called the Moscow bureau of CNN to announce that he wanted to go on camera with a statement condemning the invasion.

Just before the Persian Gulf war began in 1991, many people believed this would be the first war to actually be witnessed live on television in American homes, but that was not the case. While viewers did see many missiles in the air behind reporters, much of the access to the actual battle activities was tightly controlled by the military, and viewers saw no more than the U.S. military leaders wanted them to see. One reason was that in addition to the American people and the other television networks relying heavily on CNN for war news coverage, the enemy, Iraqi leader Saddam Hussein and members of his military, were also watching the same news coverage thanks to satellites.

Citizen Camcorders

Gas masks were often necessary for reporters covering the Gulf War, but that was about as close as television coverage got to the actual battles.

King

The sale of home-use camcorders introduced another element into TV news. Citizens who happen to have their camcorders at the scenes of news events are able to sell their tapes to TV stations. The most famous example of this came in 1991 when a spectator videotaped the arrest and beating of an African-American, Rodney **King**, in Los Angeles. The tape, which showed white police

PROFILE
Philanthropist Ted Turner — Doing What He Enjoys

One billion dollars. That's what media mogul Ted Turner pledged in 1997 to create a new foundation to benefit United Nations causes, such as cleaning up land mines around the world, helping refugees in war-torn nations, and fighting disease and hunger. Turner's pledge was to donate $100 million in stock every year for 10 years.

In making the announcement, Turner expressed pride that the money was going to "the poorest people in the world, the people who need it the most." It was obvious that Turner didn't need it. When he made the announcement of the grant, Turner said his net worth at the start of 1997 was $2.2 billion, but added that a surge in his stock in Time Warner during the next nine months had boosted his worth to $3.2 billion.

While Rupert Murdoch may be one of the most powerful media moguls on earth, he certainly has competition from this Southern media baron who has developed his own media empire, making it one of the largest in the world with the 1996 merger with Time Warner. This competition has also developed into a very strong media rivalry. Sportsman and media mogul Ted Turner was the uncontested king of cable television during the latter part of the 20th century. The four-time Yachtsman of the Year and 1977 winner of the Americas Cup yacht race is the owner of the Atlanta Braves and the Atlanta Hawks, as well as Turner Broadcasting System, Inc., until its merger with Time Warner.

Turner's venture into cable television began when he purchased Atlanta television station WTBS and turned it into a superstation by expanding its range via satellite and cable TV. After Warner-Amex beat him to the punch to develop an all-music cable network (MTV) in 1980, he teamed up with a cable-programming developer and launched the Cable News Network (CNN), a 24-hour news station. The industry elite laughed at him and called his venture a "nitwork" instead of a network. But Turner was determined to succeed, and he did. During the 1980s, CNN developed into a credible news source. Its expansion worldwide positioned the network for the "news showdown" of the century when the United States entered the Persian Gulf war in 1991.

Months of sophisticated planning and lobbying efforts to gain special permission from Saddam Hussein

Cable tycoon Ted Turner is said to be worth billions and he's now becoming a philanthropist.

to broadcast via satellite from Baghdad, Iraq, primed the all-news network for the Gulf war. When war broke out and the United States began bombing Baghdad, CNN newsmen Bernard Shaw, John Holliman, and Peter Arnett were on hand to describe it live from the window of a Baghdad hotel.

Independent TV stations and even CBS, ABC, and NBC began carrying CNN reports and attributing their war news to Ted Turner's "nitwork." The number of CNN viewers skyrocketed, and the increased audience allowed the news network to raise its advertising rates from $3,800 for a 30-second spot to $138,000. Ted Turner wore that "I told you so" smile all the way to the bank.

In 1986, Turner decided he needed programming (software) for his cable ventures and decided to acquire a large collection of movies. To do this he made an offer to Kirk Kerkorian, owner of MGM/UA Entertainment, that Kerkorian couldn't refuse. Turner offered $1.5 billion to acquire the movie studio and its library holdings. Since Turner didn't have that much money in cash or assets, Kerkorian introduced him to his financial adviser, junk bond king Michael Milken, to put the deal together. He did, and Turner ended up making one of his worst business deals, encumbered with a huge junk bond debt.

continued

To bail himself out, Turner had to sell back much of MGM to Kerkorian (Turner did keep the library of films that he was originally after), and he had to sell some of his stock in Turner Broadcasting. This required him to give up some control over his company and curtailed his seat-of-the-pants management style. He now had to get board approval for any purchases in excess of $2 million, and in 1989 the board told him he couldn't buy the Financial News Network.

Turner's cable holdings prior to the merger with Time Warner included TBS, CNN, CNN Headline News, TNT, the Cartoon Network, and TMC (Turner Movie Classics). In 1993, Turner expanded his holdings in the movie industry with the purchases of Castle Rock Entertainment and New Line Cinema companies for $650 million. Turner had much to bring to the table when he began talking about the 1996 merger with Time Warner. The merger created one of the largest cable operations in the world and allowed Turner to become a philanthropist as well as a media mogul.

Speaking at the commencement exercises of Virginia Commonwealth University in 1998, Turner urged the graduates to choose a career they really enjoy, put family first, and continuously exercise their minds. "There are other things in life much more important than just making money," the billionaire cable giant said. "Having made a lot of it myself, I'm qualified to speak about it."

officers kicking and beating King, found its way onto TV airwaves around the world. When the officers were later acquitted by a jury, the memory of the videotape's reality sparked outrage and led to the worst rioting and violence in Los Angeles's history and violent outbreaks around the country. It also led to a federal trial against the officers on the grounds that they had violated King's civil rights, and two officers were convicted. In 1994, another amateur videotape caught an African-American police officer beating a 17-year-old Hispanic in Compton, California.

NEW TECHNOLOGY

The development of the Internet has opened up many more sources for information around the world. But that is also a major problem (see Chapter 3). With the emergence of such nontrained Internet journalists as Matt Drudge, information is spread quickly but is not always totally accurate. The more traditional media look at Drudge and other Internet reporters as online gossip columnists. But that doesn't mean they aren't popular—or successful.

Drudge reports that his website gets eight million "hits" each month and his fame also propelled him for a short time into a weekly job as a commentator on the Fox News Channel. He takes pride in the fact that no one edits what goes into The Drudge Report on the Internet. When he has something to say, it goes out instantly on the Internet.

But this new technology and lack of editing has created problems. Says Jack Nelson, the chief Washington correspondent for the *Los Angeles Times*:

> It's not just Drudge. There are others on the Internet, too. And they put this information out there, and a lot of it is bad information. But you can't ignore it. And sometimes because of the competitive pressures and other factors, it gets picked up by the mainstream media. The problem is that there are no editors, no filters on this information. And the situation is getting worse.[15]

Journalism students at many universities across the country are now learning to work in more than one medium. In addition to knowing how to work in print journalism or radio and television news, the students of tomorrow will also have to know how to work online.

SUMMARY

In the 21st century, communication will continue to rapidly change our society and our culture. Through the development and expansion of the World Wide Web during this past decade, any individual can be in instant contact with someone else anywhere around the world. To understand what is ahead, it is important to know the basic historical theories of mass communication: authoritarian, libertarian, Soviet communist, and social responsibility.

The authoritarian theory is the oldest and requires that the press be regulated so as not to hinder the state in any way. The libertarian theory offers the opposite viewpoint: that the press should function to serve the governed, not the governors. Each of these theories has an offshoot. The Soviet communist theory is an extension of the authoritarian theory and makes the press a planned, integral part of the state's efforts to govern the masses. The social responsibility theory expands on the libertarian theory by emphasizing that the media must be socially responsible as well as free from government control.

Individual biases and other problems contribute to the complexity of mass communication. Although the various functions of the media—to inform, entertain, influence, advertise, and transmit culture—have been criticized, the most severely criticized is the function to inform. The reasons are that people (1) tend to blame the messenger for unpleasant information, (2) fail to understand the watchdog function of the media, (3) believe the myth that the mass media dwell only on bad news, and (4) bring their own biases into the information-sharing process.

Journalism in the 20th century, for the most part, attempted to blend objectivity and social responsibility. This era also saw the development of electronic news media, interpretive reporting, investigative reporting, advocacy journalism, and "new journalism."

Wire services play an important role in gathering news and information for the mass media. The two largest American wire services are the Associated Press and United Press International. The other dominant worldwide news sources are AFP, Reuters, and TASS, headquartered in Paris, London, and Moscow, respectively.

Radio news became an important part of our culture during the Great Depression and World War II.

Television news was primitive in its developmental days, but it soon became a powerful force. Eventually it dominated the news scene, with more people reporting that they got their news from TV than from any other source. In the 1960s, when assassinations and riots received major coverage, people started blaming TV for shaping the news.

Local television news began changing in the 1970s to become more entertaining for the masses. Feature stories and humor were added to the evening newscast, and newscasters began to be hired for their looks and personalities rather than their news judgment. Networks, which have been a major source of news and information since the early days of television, found that by the 1990s new technologies, such as satellites, were making local news shows more competitive.

Today computer technology has opened the world to everyone seeking information. Books, magazines, recordings, and even interviews with celebrities are available through the Internet. Almost everyone, from the White House to the Vatican to perhaps your next-door neighbor, has a site on the World Wide Web. The problem with the new technology is that a lot of information is being put out on the Internet on a regular basis, but some of it is erroneous and there is no system of checks and balances to help the consumer determine what is correct and what is not.

Find a review of *Key People and Concepts*, a message board for *Practicing Media Literacy* questions, self tests, and more at: www.mhhe.com/wilson.

Thought **Questions**

1. Give some current examples (not mentioned in the chapter) of the application of authoritarian press theory principles.

2. What problems arise from the ability to communicate news instantaneously from around the world?

3. Does television news shape as well as reflect our popular culture? If yes, what are some examples? If no, explain why it does not.

4. What impact do you think the Internet will have on the news media and the way news stories are covered and reported?

5. Will the increasing development of and interest in the Internet bring about a decline in interest in traditional media news coverage?

Notes

1. Fred S. Siebert, Theodore B. Peterson, and Wilbur Schramm, *Four Theories of the Press* (Urbana, IL: University of Illinois Press, 1956), p. 33.

2. Frank Luther Mott, *American Journalism*, 3rd ed. (New York: Macmillan, 1962), p. 6.

3. Wilbur Schramm, *Responsibility in Mass Communication* (New York: Harper & Row, 1957), p. 72.

4. Quoted in Warren K. Agee, Phillip H. Ault, and Edwin Emery, *Introduction to Mass Communication*, 9th ed. (New York: Harper & Row, 1988), p. 60.

5. Quoted in *Speaking of a Free Press* (New York: ANPA Foundation, 1970), p. 15.

6. Speech in Moscow, 1920. From H. L. Mencken, *A News Dictionary of Quotations on Historical Principles from Ancient and Modern Sources* (New York: Alfred Knopf, 1966), p. 966.

7. "Pravda: Dead Again," *Fresno Bee*, August 2, 1996, p. B6.

8. "A Giant of Propaganda Falls," *San Francisco Chronicle*, August 1, 1996, p. A22.

9. Siebert, Peterson, and Schramm, *Four Theories of the Press*, pp. 78–79.

10. *Ibid.*, p. 74.

11. Joseph Pulitzer, "The College of Journalism," *North American Review*, May 1904, p. 667.

12. "The 100 Most Memorable Moments in TV History," *TV Guide*, June 29, 1996, p. 51.

13. Quoted in George McKenna, *Media Voices: Debating Critical Issues in Mass Media* (Guilford, CT: Dushkin, 1982), pp. 67–74.

14. David Shaw, "Future of Network News: Is the Signal Weakening?" *Los Angeles Times*, December 29, 1986, p. 17.

15. Edmund X. DeJesus, "Toss Your TV: How the Internet Will Replace Broadcasting," *Byte*, February 1996, p. 51.

2

Development of the Print Media

6 Books

The Permanent Medium

A book is the only place in which you can examine a fragile thought without breaking it, or explore an explosive idea without fear it will go off in your face. . . . It is one of the few havens remaining where a man's mind can get both provocation and privacy.

—**Edward P. Morgan**

Key People and Concepts

Johannes Gutenberg

The Reformation

Censorship

Poor Richard's Almanack

Charles Dickens

Harriet Beecher Stowe

Mark Twain

Public Library System

Desktop Publishing

Conglomerates

Online Booksellers

E-books

It has been described by one professor at the University of California as the "amazing shrinking collection." He was talking about the decrease in the number of books on the shelves at the University of California at Berkeley's Moffett undergraduate library, which saw the number of books available drop from 180,000 volumes to about 80,000 by the start of 1998. They had been replaced by computers, television sets, and VCRs. ● While there are many who welcome the new technology that allows students and faculty to look up information on the Internet, there are others who fear that in the rush to create a "virtual" library, books are being completely forgotten. But so far, attempts to replace the printed page with electronic books have not been totally successful. ● Less than a year after the first two portable "e-readers" were introduced in late 1998, sales were reported slow, funding for the projects was slow, and potential competitors were dropping out.[1] The American public just didn't seem to be enamored yet with the electronic book, which was about the same size as a regular book but could hold more than 10 conventional books, magazines, or newspapers at a time. New material could be downloaded and stories could be annotated and searched for key words or phrases. Pages were turned with the push of a button. ● Even authors and publishers were using the Internet to push new publications. Weeks before John Grisham's novel *The Partner* was released in 1997, several chapters of the book had been made available on the Internet at The Book Report on America Online. In addition to the introductory chapters, cyberspace readers could see an interview with the reclusive author, covering everything from his thoughts on critics to his coaching philosophy with Little League baseball teams. ● But not all authors are supportive of the new technology. Science fiction writer Ray Bradbury says "Stay away from it." Agreeing that the Internet is great for some practical things such as finding information, he told a gathering in California's Silicon Valley that it can't offer the intimate and aesthetic experience of books. "You've got to be able to take a book to bed with you," he said. "You can't do that on the Internet."[2] • Obviously, the comfort of reading a book from the printed page is firmly entrenched in our society. In this chapter, we'll examine the development of the printed word in book form, the changes in the way people have used books over the centuries, and their impact on our culture today.

THE ROLE OF BOOKS IN OUR CULTURE

Books are the oldest form of mass communication, and despite the rapid advancement of electronic mass media in the 20th century, the book publishing industry remains profitable. Even with the recession during the first half of the 1990s, the industry published approximately 50,000 titles a year and employed over 76,000 people.

Gross annual revenue from U.S. book sales has exceeded $20 billion in recent years. Sales of textbooks led the industry, with trade books and technical, scientific, and professional books tying for second place (the trade-book category includes adult and juvenile fiction, nonfiction, advice, and self-help/how-to books).

The two fastest areas of growth in book publishing are in electronic media. The market for audio books has grown at double-digit rates since the 1980s. By the beginning of the 21st century, audio-book clubs were as prominent as the record and CD clubs of the previous five decades. Publishers of textbooks and technical, scientific, and reference books expanded their sales to libraries and institutional markets with CD-ROMs.

bookless bookstore

The new technology has had its impact on the book business in recent years, creating what some might call the **bookless bookstore.** Many small independent bookstores have closed their doors due to the availability of books from online booksellers. One of the first to close up shop was a Silicon Valley bookstore in California's computer heartland where people would often express surprise when the store didn't have a particular book. They would usually point out that Amazon.com had it, one of the owners said. "It's a warning to consumers," explained co-owner Gerry Marsteller. "If they want bookstores that they can go into and browse and touch, I think that's at risk."[3]

Books play an important role in preserving the ideas, thoughts, and histories of civilizations. Since these records are handed down from generation to generation and are collected in libraries—a practice that has been going on for thousands of years—books have become the most permanent of all the mass media. For example, to learn about the Persian Wars of 500 B.C., one need only read *The History of the Persian Wars* by Herodotus, who lived at that time. To learn about early Greek literature and the Homeric age, which fell between the 13th and 9th centuries B.C., one can turn to Homer's *Iliad* and *Odyssey*, written around the 8th or 9th century B.C.

@   **Practicing Media Literacy**

When was the last time you went into a bookstore to browse? Would you miss such stores if the Internet took over the distribution of books?

Cultural History of **Books**

		Elitist	Popular	Specialized
c. 2500 b.c.	Sumerian clay tablets.	•		
c. 600 b.c.	Papyrus scrolls used in Egypt.	•		
c. 540 b.c.	First public library founded in Athens.	•		
1st century a.d.	Books regarded as household treasures by the elite.	•		
5th century	Great Library of Alexandria, Egypt, destroyed.	•		
5th–10th centuries	Books preserved in monasteries.	•		
9th century	Chinese invent printing.	•		
13th century	Rise of European universities.	•		
1456	Gutenberg Bible printed from movable type.	•		
16th century	Books become the first mass-produced and mass-distributed commodity.	•	•	
16th century	Books help spread the ideas of the Protestant Reformation; authorities invoke censorship to control printers.	•	•	
1640	*Bay Psalm Book* published at Harvard College.	•	•	
18th–19th centuries	Industrial Revolution.	•	•	
19th century	Rise of American novelists and publishing houses.		•	
1852	*Uncle Tom's Cabin* is published; sells 7 million copies, helps spark Civil War (1861-1865).		•	
1867	Horatio Alger, Jr., publishes his first "rags-to-riches" story, *Ragged Dick*.		•	
1873	Anthony Comstock founds the New York Society for the Suppression of Vice.		•	
1920s	Novelists use publicity from having their books "banned in Boston" to promote sales elsewhere.		•	
1945	Books begin serving a variety of specialized interests as post–World War II years change American culture.			•
1957	Supreme Court begins to liberalize its interpretation of obscenity in *Roth v. United States*.			•
1960s	Wide range of books published, reflecting new subcultures and protest movements.			•
1973	Supreme Court adopts stricter "contemporary community standards" test to define obscenity (*Miller v. California*).			•
1980s	Book publishers begin marketing audio books and CD-ROM books.			•
1990s	Consolidation of large publishing firms continues.			•
1990s	Censorship of books continues.			•
1994	"Downsizing" of book publishing industry causes layoffs of top editors at major firms.			•
1997	Bookstores, libraries, and publishers continue to use the World Wide Web to reach the book-reading public.			•
1998	Random House agrees to merger with German conglomerate Bertelsmann AG for $1.3 billion.			•
1999	Jeff Bezos, founder of the online bookstore Amazon.com, named *Time* magazine's Man of the Year.			•
2000	John Grisham joins Charles Dickens and Stephen King as a serial book author.			•

ORIGINS OF BOOKS

To understand how books influence our culture today, it is necessary to review how this mass communication medium developed and how it has been influencing and changing cultures for centuries.

Early Forms

clay tablets

We can trace books in one form or another back to Sumerian **clay tablets,** which were used 4,500 years ago to record various items of religious, legal, and medical interest, as well as narrative tales. These are the oldest written documents known to humankind.

papyrus scrolls

Next came **papyrus scrolls,** which were used throughout ancient Egypt, Greece, and Rome. These large rolls of papyrus were attached to two rods that permitted the book to be held and rolled from either end. Although the lengths of the manuscripts varied, some rolls contained entire books. Archeologists have unearthed ancient handwritten scrolls in Egyptian, Greek, Latin, Arabic, Hebrew, and Syrian. In addition to religious writings, these scrolls contained the philosophies, histories, oratories, drama, poetry, and anthologies of such ancient writers as Eustathius, Plato, Aristotle, Demosthenes, Homer, Sophocles, Euripides, Archilochus, and Ascepiades.

Public Libraries

The first public library was established in Athens in 540 B.C. Later, around 300 B.C., Ptolemy I founded the great library in Alexandria, Egypt. The library became the intellectual center of the Hellenistic Empire, and the most famous scholars, scientists, poets, philosophers, and artists of the day gathered there to study and work.

At its peak, the library contained between half a million and a million hand-copied papyrus volumes—almost all of Western civilization's recorded knowledge. Transcribers were often sent there to copy manuscripts for other libraries. This great repository of learning was burned and ravaged by Romans, civil warriors, and soldiers of the Christian emperor Theodosius I; by A.D. 400, the world's greatest intellectual treasury up to that time had been lost forever.

The selling and collecting of papyrus scrolls in ancient Rome peaked around the time of Christ, with some households reportedly having libraries containing thousands of volumes. As the Roman Empire began to decline and libraries were ravaged and burned during barbarian invasions, books found sanctuary in Christian monasteries, especially in Ireland.[4] Middle Eastern and Muslim scholars were also instrumental in saving Western literature during this period.

The Middle Ages

Although relatively little is known about the development and use of books during the Middle Ages (A.D. 5th through 14th centuries), there were some improvements in how knowledge was recorded. For example, in the fifth century the Saxons began using books made of animal skins; these more closely resembled paged books as we know them today. About this same time, the Romans were replacing the awkward scroll with the codex, a stack of folded leaves that was bound along one side and protected by wooden covers. The more durable animal parchment was replacing papyrus as the medium on which books were written.

paper

Also at about the same time, the Chinese were perfecting and using **paper** made from tree bark, old rags, hemp waste, and fishnets. The art of making paper slowly spread through Europe around the 12th century, although paper wasn't produced in England until the late 15th century or on the American continent until the late 17th century. The Chinese were also the first to develop printing, sometime during the ninth century. The oldest existing printed book is *The Diamond Sutra*, printed in China in A.D. 868 from carved wooden blocks and containing Buddhist wisdom.

However, printing did not spread from China to the Western world. Bookmaking and manuscript copying by cloistered clergy in monasteries remained a handcrafted process in Europe through the Middle Ages. Thus, most medieval codex production consisted of sacred works such as Bible texts and interpretations, liturgical manuscripts, and the works of those philosophers and classical authors whose thoughts were believed to contribute to Christian principles (see Box 6.1).

The Renaissance

Six centuries after the Chinese began to print books, printing technology was introduced into Western culture. Credit for bringing mass communication to the Western world belongs to the German inventor Johannes **Gutenberg**, who used movable type and a converted wine press to publish a 42-lines-per-page Bible in 1456. This large-size Bible, written in Latin, was a replica of existing hand-copied manuscripts. Gutenberg's Bible was a work of great precision and beauty, and the reproduction of 200 identical copies was astonishing in a world that was used to handwritten books.

Gutenberg

Although Gutenberg died a pauper shortly after his press was confiscated to pay his debts, by the end of the 15th century this new craft was established in every major capitol in Europe. The first printer in England was William Caxton, who published his first book in 1476.

EARLY BOOKS AND THE ELITE

From the days of clay tablets to well beyond the invention of mass communication, books were limited to the elite. Thousands of years passed before the medium began to enter the popular culture.

Even after Gutenberg's new technology spread throughout Western Europe, books remained in the elite phase of the elite–popular–specialized (EPS) cycle (see Chapter 1). Illiteracy among the poor was the main cause. Books were read primarily by the clergy, educators, scientists, professionals, and members of the aristocracy.

However, the Renaissance also saw a great expansion of trade and commerce and the creation of a new middle class. These prosperous merchants and bankers had a practical interest in secular learning and proved a ready market for books. Thus, the first mass communication medium began at last to reach beyond a tiny elite to mainstream society.

The Reformation

By the time of the Protestant Reformation, in the 16th century, printing had reached the developing middle class. In the 1520s, for example, Martin Luther became the first person to use this new mass-communication technology for propaganda purposes. He wrote a series of pamphlets in German attacking the doctrines of the Roman Catholic Church. Luther's revolt boosted the printing of books in Germany from 150 in 1518 to 990 in 1524. Four-fifths of these books favored the Reformation. Soon his works were being printed in other languages and were spreading throughout Western

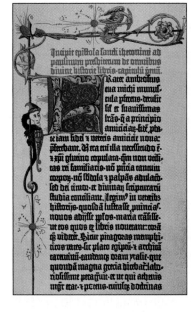

Some 200 copies of the Gutenberg Bible were printed in 1456. Although using movable type, they were made to resemble the handwritten Bibles done for centuries before by monks.

Europe. As one historian has written, "Printing was the Reformation; Gutenberg made Luther possible."[5]

Part of Luther's new religious doctrine was the idea that the people, not the Catholic Church, should be the interpreters of the Bible. To facilitate this premise, he translated both the Old and New Testaments of the Latin Bible into conversational German. During his lifetime, 100,000 copies of the New Testament were printed, and it became and has remained the best-selling book in Germany.[6]

Censorship

The practice of censorship developed at the time of the Protestant Reformation. It did not take long for those in authority—kings and popes—to realize that Gutenberg's new technology, which allowed ideas to be mass-produced and distributed, posed a threat to those in power. As previously noted in Chapter 2, King Henry II in Catholic France made it a practice to burn books and printers who attempted to distribute Protestant thought. In England, King Henry VIII established a list of prohibited books and by 1529 had developed a system of licensing printers. Even Martin Luther advocated the censorship of books written by Huldreich Zwingli and John Calvin, Protestants with views different from his own. This era of religious censorship and suppression lasted over 100 years, and many people were executed for expressing their beliefs. The voices of religious and political dissent were never completely stilled, however, as printers could always find a haven somewhere to publish "heretical" writings.

STAGES OF BOOK PUBLISHING IN THE UNITED STATES

England's policy of strict censorship of the press and the licensing of printers was transported to the new English colonies in America in the 17th century. Although this helped to curtail the early development and spread of books in the colonies, book publishing eventually grew and flourished. To better understand the development of book publishing in America, we will examine this industry as it evolved through each stage of the EPS cycle (see Chapter 1).

The Elitist Stage

Printing remained in the elite culture in the American colonies from the 17th to the 19th centuries. The conditions necessary for books to enter the popular culture (see Chapter 1) were slow to develop. Most colonists had few luxuries. Like all frontier people, they worked hard and had very little leisure time to cultivate aesthetic and intellectual values. With the exception of the elite and clergy, most colonists could not read or write.

Religion, which played a major role in the expansion of book publishing in 16th-century Europe, was also instrumental in launching this industry in the colonies. Many settlers belonged to strict religious sects, such as the Puritans who settled in the Massachusetts Bay colony. The Puritans were responsible for establishing the first printing press in North America in 1638 at Harvard College near Boston; two years later the Harvard press published the first book in the 13 colonies, the *Whole Booke of Psalmes*, better known as the *Bay Psalm Book*. Harvard controlled this press until 1662, when the Massachusetts legislature took it over. The early Harvard press was used to produce religious books, pamphlets, and sermons, as well as some government and educational materials.

One of the first successful secular contributors to the development of book publishing in the American colonies was Benjamin **Franklin**. He began publishing one of America's most famous early books, *Poor Richard's Almanack*, in 1733. It became successful—selling about 10,000 copies a year—by giving people something besides the Bible to read. The almanac contained a wide variety of useful and entertaining information, including poetry, short stories, mean temperatures in various parts of the country, lists of public officials, and public affairs articles. In 1744 Franklin published the first novel in America, *Pamela*, by English novelist Samuel Richardson. Franklin also established the first subscription library in the colonies.

Publishing developed slowly in the North American colonies. However, a number of important pamphlets produced by political dissenters around the time of the American Revolution stimulated an interest in reading. In 1774, three separate publications challenged the right of England's Parliament to govern the colonies: James

Franklin

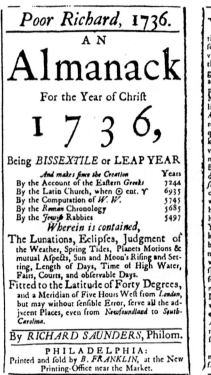

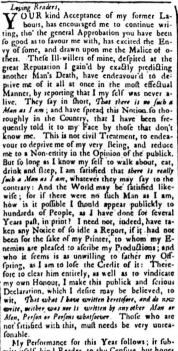

Poor Richard's Almanack—*published, printed and folded by Benjamin Franklin*—*provided a wide variety of useful and entertaining information for readers.*

Paine

Wilson's *Considerations on the Nature and Extent of the Legislative Authority of the British Parliament,* Thomas Jefferson's *A Summary View of the Rights of British America,* and John Adams's *Novanglus Papers.* In 1776 Englishman Thomas **Paine**, who had come to the colonies two years earlier, published *Common Sense.* In 47 pages it spelled out the meaning of the American revolutionary movement and made it clear that the Americans were not quibbling over the details of taxation but were standing up for their liberties as a nation. The pamphlet sold 120,000 copies in three months, a tremendous number when one considers that the colonial population at the time was only about 400,000.[7]

Following the Revolutionary War, book publishing centers were established in New York, Boston, and Philadelphia, and the new industry began to expand. According to historian Oscar Handlin, "The exciting current events of the Revolution fortified the desire for printed matter. Americans wished to learn what was going on in every part of the continent, and they were anxious to follow the political arguments provoked by the debate over their rights. The result was a steady rise in the volume of publications."[8]

A number of American novelists soon began publishing. Although some were writing in a style similar to that of their European counterparts, others were developing a uniquely American style of writing. Examples include Hugh Henry Brackenridge's *Modern Chivalry* (1792), a satire on the first few years of the politics of the new nation; Charles Brockden Brown's *Wieland* (1798), a romantic tragedy in a genre of horror and remorse that Edgar Allan Poe would later cultivate; and Washington Irving's *A History of New York, by Diedrich Knickerbocker* (1809), a humorous parody of an earlier work about New York City. Noah Webster helped to establish an American language by publishing a national dictionary.

The Popular Stage

As the new nation struggled with its destiny as a republic dedicated to the common wealth of all its people, its economy and culture began to change. The nation underwent an expansion to the West. To accommodate this vast new country, a transportation system of canals and, eventually, steam-engine railroads developed. The new methods of transportation furthered economic, political, and social unity by bringing the vast regions of the nation closer together. This growth stimulated trade and commerce, and the nation's cities grew.

Conditions in Europe—landlords were ousting tenants from their land to combine larger acreages for more profitable farming, and famine was sweeping across Ireland and Germany in the 1840s—caused hundreds of thousands of people to immigrate to the United States annually. This large, unskilled labor pool stimulated the growth of industries, and by the mid-19th century the agrarian American culture was being transformed into an industrial society as the Industrial Revolution swept the land.

The Industrial Revolution also brought new technology to printing. Cylinder and rotary presses and Ottmar Mergenthaler's Linotype machine greatly sped up book production. Large numbers of trees were also available, making wood-pulp paper abundant.

At the same time, the concept of compulsory **public education** was taking hold; only an educated citizenry, it was argued, could uphold and protect the new democracy from the threat of tyrannies. By the 1840s, universal public education had been established in most Northern cities, and a large literate population began to emerge. By the 1850s, all states had accepted the principle of tax-supported elementary schools. (In the South, however, blacks were barred from this education.) By 1861, the United States had the highest literacy rate in the world: 94 percent of the population in the North and 83 percent of whites in the South (58 percent of the total population). Industrialization and universal public education together created the conditions that moved book publishing from the elite into the popular culture.

| public education |

Books by such American writers as Ralph Waldo Emerson, James Fenimore Cooper, Henry David Thoreau, Catherine Sedgwick, Lydia Sigourney, and Edgar Allan Poe were finding their way into the popular culture. In addition, many Americans were enjoying the works of popular British authors such as Charles **Dickens** and William Wordsworth. By 1855, U.S. book sales far exceeded sales figures in England.

| Dickens |

Recognizing the immense market for books, entrepreneur Erastus Beadle decided to mass-produce a line of inexpensive books that appealed to common interests. He and his brother Irwin published huge printings of paperback books that followed a set formula of praising the spirit of individuality and the virtue of common people. A typical title was *Malaeska: Indian Wife of the White Hunter*, by Mrs. Ann S. Stephens. He sold these books, called Beadle's Dime Novels, for 10 cents each and began advertising them as "Dollar Books for a Dime!" Between 1860 and 1865, he sold more than 4 million copies.

> **@ Practicing Media Literacy**
>
> Can you think of any recent best-sellers which you think might someday be considered literary classics?

During this period a number of other individuals established major publishing houses, many of which are still prominent today. Among these entrepreneurs were the brothers James and John Harper, John Wiley, George Palmer Putnam, Dan Appleton, Charles Scribner, E. P. Dutton, Henry Oscar Houghton and George Harrison Mifflin (Houghton Mifflin), and Charles Little and James Brown (Little, Brown).

These publishing houses opened up opportunities for a newly developed crop of American authors to publish their works, and many outstanding literary works resulted. Nathaniel Hawthorne's *The Scarlet Letter* (1850) is said to be one of the greatest books ever written in the Western hemisphere. Herman Melville's *Moby Dick* (1851) is still considered one of the finest novels in American literature. Harriet Beecher **Stowe's** *Uncle Tom's Cabin* (1852), which helped to forge antislavery thinking before the Civil War, established the American novel as a powerful literary and social force. The story of a literate, kindly slave known as Uncle Tom, who was abused and finally killed by the evil Simon Legree, was published first in serial form in a magazine and later as a two-volume novel. Although banned from sale in the South, the book was an early success, selling about 1,000 copies a week; a total of 7 million copies were eventually sold. *Uncle Tom's Cabin* had a profound influence on public opinion and evoked sympathetic responses from various national leaders, including the future president of the United States, Abraham Lincoln.

By the end of the 19th century, a number of writers had large followings and fan clubs similar to those that idolize today's rock stars. They included Mark **Twain**, who wrote about Tom Sawyer and Huckleberry Finn growing up on the Mississippi River, and the English poets Robert Browning and Rudyard Kipling.

The most commercially successful author in this period was Horatio Alger, Jr., who wrote more than 120 books about growing up in the new industrial society. His books, which offered hope for the young in the new mass culture, were all rags-to-riches tales of the American dream: a pious, intelligent young boy makes his way to the top through hard work and virtue. The theme of upward mobility seemed to strike a responsive chord in the hearts of many.

This era also saw the development of a **free public library** system, which made books available to all segments of the public regardless of whether they could afford to purchase them. This library system helped to establish the concept of egalitarianism in the American culture.

As industrialization spread and the number of immigrants in the United States increased (there were 4 million foreign-born in 1860 but 9 million by 1890), worker exploitation through poor working conditions and low wages became common. To expose those conditions, a new kind of book emerged in the popular culture. Books such as Upton Sinclair's *The Jungle* (1906), which described intolerable working and sanitation conditions in Chicago's meatpacking plants, helped to raise the public's social consciousness during this era. This and similar books were instrumental in changing public attitudes about the benefits and dangers of unfettered free enterprise. Eventually laws were passed to protect consumers and employees, such as statutes requiring federal inspection of food products and child-labor laws aimed at preventing the exploitation of children in sweatshops.

Meanwhile, as book publishing became firmly entrenched in the popular culture, major efforts were still being made to censor books. One of the first such efforts in the new nation came in 1821 when the book *Fanny Hill,* published

Stowe

Twain

free public library

@ Practicing Media Literacy

Can you think of any recent best-sellers which could be considered investigative reports or exposes?

before the Revolution by the famed printer Isaiah Thomas, was found at a trial in Massachusetts to be obscene.

A major push came in 1873 when Anthony Comstock, a New York City dry-goods store employee, founded the nonprofit New York Society for the Suppression of Vice. Its stated purpose was to "clean the filth out of the wickedest city in the world." Comstock devoted 40 years to this effort and was successful in getting federal legislation passed making it illegal to send anything obscene through the mail. One result was that providing information about contraception was illegal in many states for almost 100 years (until a Supreme Court decision in 1965).

According to historian Paul Boyer, the vice society movement grew "in response to the deep-seated fears about the drift of urban life in post–Civil War years." As Boyer notes, the migration of Americans away from the familiar sources of guidance and support—family, church, and close-knit communities—and into the metropolitan areas made people such as Comstock believe there was a need to protect the nation's young from the "filth" found in some popular literature.[9]

Efforts at **censorship** continued well into the 20th century. It took court action before certain books, such as Erskine Caldwell's *God's Little Acre* and James Joyce's *Ulysses*, could be sold in the United States. (Both books were attacked by censors because they contained sexually explicit language.)

censorship

One of the most famous censoring efforts of this century was conducted in Boston. This community, which still had strong religious influences, established a book-censoring commission; books found objectionable by the commission were "banned in Boston." Some writers whose works were banned were John Dos Passos, Theodore Dreiser, Ernest Hemingway, Sinclair Lewis, Upton Sinclair, and H. G. Wells. Boston's strict censorship codes did not reflect national attitudes toward literature and conflicted with many people's desire for a wide range of reading material. As a result, the city's efforts seemed to do more to stimulate sales in other parts of the country than to suppress books in Boston. As Upton Sinclair once said, "We authors are using America as our sales territory and Boston as our advertising department."

> @ **Practicing Media Literacy**
>
> Do you feel that censorship publicity does more to help sell a book than to suppress sales?

Whatever impact censorship had on sales, there is no doubt that publishing houses flourished in the first half of the century as reading became one of the most popular leisure activities in both the elite and popular cultures. An example is the success story of Bennett Cerf and Donald S. Klopfer. In 1925 Cerf, a book salesman for Boni & Liveright, persuaded his wealthy friend Klopfer to invest $100,000 to purchase the Modern Library, Boni & Liveright's classical-book division. Two years later, the partners formed an additional company to print books other than classical reprints, "sort of at random," Cerf later noted. To suit their aim, they called this new publishing operation Random House. In 1966 they sold Random House to RCA for $40 million (RCA later sold Random House to Samuel I. Newhouse, Jr.).

The Specialized Stage

The period from 1945 to the present has seen a dramatic shift in the book publishing industry as the business has responded to new and changing audiences. For example, after World War II ended, many military personnel enrolled in college under the GI bill, which paid veterans' educational expenses. As a result, the textbook business boomed, and it wasn't long before textbook publishing led the list in revenue genera-tors for the book publishing industry.

In addition, people began to take up or renew other interests, such as their families and children; suburban living; and leisure activities such as hunting, fishing, bowling, tennis, golf, and spectator sports. The book publishing industry responded by bringing out more nonfiction "**lifestyle**" titles each year rather than relying so heavily on a few blockbuster popular novels. Child care manuals, books on how to landscape the back-yard or fix up the house, and tell-all biographies became hot sellers in the marketplace. With these expansions, book publishing began to enter the third stage of the EPS cy-cle: specialization. The ratio of literary works such as fiction, biography, poetry, and drama to nonliterary works such as textbooks, professional books, reference books, cookbooks, and self-help and do-it-yourself guides shifted dramatically. By the 1970s, new nonliterary works outnumbered new literary works by more than two to one.[10]

Self-help/how-to books came to represent one of the most successful categories of specialized book publishing. As people became absorbed with "who they were" and "self," the publishing industry started catering to their interests. Today many books are available about how to deal with life, such as *Life Preservers: Staying Afloat in Love and Life* and *How Could You Do That?! The Abdication of Character, Courage, and Con-science*. Many of the popular self-help books also deal with relationships, such as *Men Are from Mars, Women Are from Venus: A Practical Guide for Improving Communication and Getting What You Want in Your Relationship* and *The Complete Idiot's Guide to Dat-ing*. Among the how-to books are such popular topics as how to pan for gold, fix up your home, or make your garden beautiful. Many of these how-to books feed on the American myth that everyone in this country can succeed if he or she is determined and has the "inside scoop" on how to do it. At the start of the 21st century, book titles in this genre ranged from *The New Decorator's Handbook: Decorative Paint Techniques for Every Room* to *The Reader's Digest New Fix-It Yourself Manual*.

As the book publishing industry adapted to providing reading material for special interests, the promotion of these books helped to expand the special-interest area into larger segments of the culture. Specialized books on diets and exercise, for example, helped to form a new cultural belief that being thin means being healthy and "every-body should lose weight." It is interesting to note that with this new cultural attitude came an increase in reported cases of anorexia and bulimia in the late 20th century.

Instant books, another extremely successful form of specialization, put book pub-lishing in competition with news-oriented mass media by providing immediate, de-tailed coverage of news events. The instant book is a paperback about a current topic that is published immediately after the event. Within weeks after the deaths of Princess Diana and John F. Kennedy, Jr., books about their lives were on the shelves.

The same was true during the impeachment scandal involving President Clinton, but in that case, the Internet also played a role. Many Internet servers were jammed when the complete text of federal prosecutor Kenneth Starr's investigation of the president's relationship with White House intern Monica Lewinsky hit the web as many Americans wanted to read the detailed testimony.

The 445-page report accusing Clinton of 11 impeachable offenses was released in printed form a few days later by three different publishers and, with prices ranging from $5.99 to $10 (depending on the quality of the cover), they were quickly swept off the shelves by eager readers.

The release of the Starr Report was immediately followed by the Clinton admin-istration's first rebuttal, which sold for $10. The second rebuttal went for $7.95. Nei-ther one sold well, apparently because they weren't as lurid in the details.

lifestyle

When a special review board appointed by the president of the United States, known as the Tower Commission, released its report on the Reagan administration's involvement in the Iran–Contra scandal in 1987, paperback books containing the complete report were available for sale 47 hours and 29 minutes later. Copies were rushed to bookstores across the country, and large chain bookstores, such as B. Dalton, were selling them out as quickly as they were getting them in. When newspaper heiress Patty Hearst was kidnapped in 1974, several paperbacks about the kidnapping went on sale shortly thereafter. It was reported at the time that FBI investigators were buying the books in search of leads in the case. Within a week after O. J. Simpson was arrested in connection with the deaths of his former wife and her friend, an instant book on the topic was for sale. Many more followed.

Even previously released books can become instant books if publishers see that there is a need. The popularity of the movie *Titanic* saw the influx of many new and re-released books about the 1912 tragedy. At one point in 1998, the New York Times best-seller list contained nine titles connected to the sinking of the *Titanic*.

Nonfiction novels also compete with the news media by presenting more detailed interpretation of news events than the news itself. The pioneer in this category is Truman Capote's *In Cold Blood*, a nonfiction novel based on the true story of two men who killed a Midwestern farm family (it became a made-for-TV movie in 1996). Another major contributor in this category is Joe McGinnis, who wrote *Fatal Vision*, which details the murder of an army officer's family. The book became controversial after the imprisoned army officer, who professed his innocence, claimed McGinnis had betrayed his trust by concluding in the book that he was guilty. The release of the official biography of former President Ronald Reagan in 1999 created controversy, as the author of *Dutch*, Edmund Morris, wrote himself into the story as a fictional character who was with Reagan during many of the historic moments of the president's life.

@ Practicing Media Literacy
How do you feel about books based on fact which have been fictionalized? Do they have the potential of distorting history?

Personalized books have become possible as a result of new computer technology. These publications, composed and printed entirely by computer, are designed primarily for children. The computer stores a complete text of the book, with a few key items left blank. To purchase such a book, a person gives the publisher the name, address, and other personal data about the child who will be given the book. This information is fed into the computer, and out comes a book (obviously not a great literary work but something simple or mundane) that incorporates the specified data in the story. Thus, the recipient of the book becomes the hero of the story. CD-ROM technology is also helping children learn to read. Hot sellers include "living books," which

The popularity of the movie Titanic *brought about a renewed interest in the maritime tragedy. Many books on the subject were quickly published and became best-sellers.*

combine sound, text, and animation on computer screens via CD-ROMs to entertain and educate children at the same time.

Fotonovels are part printed text, part picture book, and part comic book. They usually develop as spinoffs of a popular movie or television program. "Star Trek" became one of the first successful topics for a fotonovel in this country. The books were a hit with the "Trekkies" (see Chapter 2). Although fotonovels have been popular in South America and Europe for more than 40 years, they are relatively new in the United States and seem to reflect the fact that specialized interests in our multimedia world tend to overlap from one medium to another (see Box 6.2).

Graphic novels are a spinoff of the comic books and have been gaining popularity since the 1980s. This book form consists of an original, self-contained story told in the comic book format, but with much higher quality paper and binding. Graphic-novel titles sell for about $13 to $17. The titles cover a wide range of action adventure–type stories, such as *The Return of Superman, Batman: The Last Arkham*, and *X-Men: The Mutant Massacre*. Many are based on popular movies, ranging from the *Star Wars* and *Indiana Jones* films of the 1970s and 1980s to the 1996 "live"-action cartoon movie, *Space Jam*, starring Bugs Bunny and Chicago Bulls star Michael Jordan. For those who didn't want to stand in line to see the 1999 movie *Star Wars: Episode I—The Phantom Menace*, a graphic novel was available at bookstores at $12.95—which was more than the cost for a theater ticket. The same story was also split into a four-part series at $2.95 an issue.

The graphic novel can also take on more serious subjects, such as 1995's *Timothy Leary: Surfin the Conscious Nets*. Even Fox's long-running TV series *Married . . . With Children* was depicted in the graphic-novel format. This genre of books is designed to appeal to visually oriented individuals who do not read much. Publishers hope the graphic novel will introduce these individuals to reading, and the experience will then lead them to try other types of books.

Novelization is a book genre that developed in recent years from the book industry's symbiotic relationship with motion pictures. Books and motion pictures have been linked since the early days of film. Many books have been made into movies through the years, and the ability to sell the movie rights to a best-seller means a great deal to publishers and authors. Recently a reverse trend, called novelization, has occurred, whereby book publishers print novels based on successful movies. One of the most recent was a novelization of George Lucas's 1999 *Star Wars* movie, published under the title *Phantom Menace*.

Mass-market paperback books, often sexy romance, western, or mystery novels, also account for large revenues in book publishing. Such high-volume books often have press runs that exceed a million copies. These paperbacks, which once sold for around 75 cents, now bring about $6 to $13 a copy and prove that despite the variety of other media for recreation and escape, the novel still appeals to the masses.

A new trend, based on one of the original concepts of book publishing, was the *serial form* novels. In the mid-1990s, Signet began issuing one of best-selling author Stephen King's ghoulish stories in serial form, that is, in a series of six inexpensive books. King's *The Green Mile* is a fictional memoir of a former death row prison guard. Each book sold for only $2.99 and, as one critic pointed out, at that price, if you hate the first installment, you don't have to buy the rest and you're not out very much money. Each volume of the six-part serial thriller was also

@ **Practicing Media Literacy**

How do you feel about the serialization of books? Would you read such a series or do you prefer to have the entire book in one volume?

Box 6.2
MEDIA LITERACY
The Evolution of the Comic Book in American Popular Culture

An American publishing genre that has become an international phenomenon, believe it or not, is the comic book. These colorful publications became popular in the late 1930s with the introduction of Detective Comics and Action Comics, publications that featured original stories rather than comic strip reprints.

Soon youngsters in the American popular culture were reading about the fantastic achievements of such superheroes as Superman and Batman and Robin. Following these flying crime fighters onto the comic book pages were animal characters developed by Terrytoons Comics and Walt Disney's comics and stories. In 1939, 60 different series of comic books were being published. This figure grew to 650 by 1954 (the year a strict self-censorship code was enforced) and included such comic characters as Airboy, Captain America, Captain Marvel, Little Lulu, The Phantom, Dick Tracy, Popeye, Flash Gordon, Donald Duck, Mickey Mouse, and Tarzan. There was even a series of classical literature tales told in the comic book format, such as *Huckleberry Finn, Robin Hood, Ivanhoe,* and *King Arthur and the Knights of the Roundtable.*

The development of the American comic book was influenced by other 20th-century mass media, particularly motion pictures, radio, and eventually television. The Western genre of the motion picture became a popular subject for comic books. Even such singing cowboy radio and movie stars as Gene Autry and Roy Rogers became comic book characters, as did fictitious action-adventure characters such as *The Lone Ranger, The Shadow, Sergeant Preston of the Yukon,* and *The Green Hornet.* In the 1950s, following television's entry into the popular culture, some comic books began featuring TV action-adventure themes such as *Have Gun, Will Travel, Gunsmoke, Lawman,* and *77 Sunset Strip.*

Although created in the United States, the modern comic book never really gained respectability here as an art or literary form. It was perceived as children's entertainment and as such became a target for concerned parents and others who feared the comic book would corrupt youth. Strong objections developed over the use of themes of sex and violence in comic books. The Comics Magazine Association of America (CMAA) attempted to establish a code of ethics in the 1940s.

The man of steel known as Superman was a comic book hero introduced in the 1930s.

Superman continued to gain popularity on radio, television and in the movies.

The government got into the act when the Kefauver Crime Committee began holding hearings on the effect of comics on children. The CMAA enforced a stringent code of conduct in 1954, and approved comics began carrying a seal indicating they contained only wholesome material. In 1955 the state of New York passed a law making it illegal to sell obscene,

continued

objectionable comics to minors or to carry such words as *crime, sex, horror,* or *terror* in the title of any comic book. Other states followed with similar legislation. The number of comic books in this country declined significantly after that. It wasn't long before those who had been concerned about sex and violence in comic books shifted their efforts toward the newer medium of television.

In Europe, Japan, and Central and South America, on the other hand, people of all ages read comic books. In France and Japan, for example, comic books represent a very large publishing market. In Japan, 20 percent of all publications sold in the late 1980s were comic books, called *mangas,* selling approximately 70 million copies a month. Some of the American superheroes, such as Superman, became popular speaking in foreign tongues. The American genre of the Western became very popular abroad. Other comic characters were developed that were unique to the foreign cultures. The themes or plots of these comic books range as widely as those of American popular novels and are aimed mostly at adults. Sex, violence, and even nudity are not uncommon in many foreign comic books.

There is new hope for the comic book genre in the United States, however. Numerous book publishers are bringing back a version of the American comic book with a new name and a new target audience: adults. These new comics are called *graphic novels.* Each graphic novel contains a complete story—as any other novel does—and the quality of writing is very high. Also, the graphics are more spectacular than in the old comic books, and the production quality is far superior to that of ordinary paperbacks.

Author Stephen King has gained popularity with his books, serialized novels, audio books, television dramas, and movies.

available on audiocassettes, but they were priced at $7.95 each—more than double the cost of the books. King modeled his serialization efforts after Charles Dickens and called his small, pocket-size novels "chapbooks" (see Chapter 2). In 1998, it was reported that novelist Jackie Collins had signed up with Pocket Books to do a four-part paperback novel entitled *L.A. Connection.* John Grisham serialized his novel *A Painted House* in the *Oxford American* magazine in the year 2000.

Audio books have become very lucrative. As more and more people found themselves on freeways for great lengths of time fighting traffic to and from work, the concept of listening to books on audio tapes became popular. By the 1990s, some businesses in southern California were establishing audio-book libraries for their employees as an incentive to ride-share. Today audio books can be rented at daily rates and audio-book clubs make current best-sellers, either fiction or nonfiction, available to members. The audio books are also very up-to-date; most of them are available to the public shortly after they come out in print.

It took over a decade for author Tom Wolfe to come out with a new work of fiction to follow his successful *The Bonfire of the Vanities* and *The Right Stuff.* But when he did in 1997, it was a book released exclusively on audio. *Ambush at Fort Bragg* was available on four cassettes or three CDs for a price of $21.95, about the price of most new novels.

@   **Practicing Media Literacy**

Do you feel an audio book can help a driver pass the time or does it become a distraction for the person behind the wheel?

Box 6.3
HOW IT WORKS
Book Publishing

A lot happens between the time a writer signs a contract to publish a book and the moment a finished product reaches a bookstore. The process can take 18 months or longer and involve many people. Although the process varies depending on the size and clout of the publishing house, here is what usually happens.

First, an *author* must contact an acquisitions editor. The author usually has an outline or overview of the book and some sample chapters. Sometimes an agent does the contacting and negotiates a contract.

The *acquisitions editor*'s job is to look for potential authors and work out contract agreements. Contracts usually call for an advance and a percentage of the book's sales to be paid to the author. The acquisitions editor also manages one or more "lists" of books in a particular discipline or area, overseeing projects and making sure books are proceeding as planned.

A *development editor* sometimes works with the author during the development of the manuscript. In the case of textbooks, the development editor sets up and handles the task of getting multiple reviews from instructors who are potential users of the book and uses that information to help shape the finished product. A development editor may also edit and help rewrite the manuscript and guide the selection and creation of artwork for the book.

The *production editor* manages the book during the various stages of production, which include copyediting, design, typesetting, proofreading, and printing. Usually the book is typeset and printed by outside firms.

The *marketing department* is responsible for advertising the book and getting reviews for promotional purposes. Marketing activities include writing advertising, catalog, and back-cover promotion copy; developing thematic promotion campaigns for books; and getting authors booked for lectures or guest appearances on television and radio talk shows.

The *fulfillment department* is responsible for getting the book to bookstores and making sure additional copies are printed when supplies run low. In the case of textbooks, sales representatives are responsible for visiting schools or college instructors and telling them about the book.

Advances in electronic and computerized technologies have prompted publishing firms to add a new division in the 1990s. Sometimes called the *new media* division, it handles the hardware and software for computerized books, CD-ROMs, and interactive media. This area is expected to continue expanding rapidly as more new technology is developed.

In 1991, Carol Publishing expanded this category by starting to publish audio books on compact disks. The development of CD books is seen as the next major growth area in the book publishing industry and many audio-book clubs now offer their books in either format.

Desktop Publishing

Since the mid-1980s, a new technology, computerized desktop publishing, has added to the ability of authors and publishers to enter the marketplace with specialized books via the self-publishing route.

Today many authors get their works published by first producing them on their personal computers using desktop publishing software. If successful, these books are then picked up by regular publishing houses, where they are given better marketing and larger distribution. An example of such a book is Richard Nelson Bolles's *What Color Is Your Parachute?*, which was first self-published and later printed by Ten Speed Press. The use of the Internet has been another way for authors to get their work circulated. The hope is that Internet users will get interested in the novel found on their computer screens and will then order a hard copy of the book directly from the author.

Another use of the Internet is in the actual creation of a book. Famed author John Updike wrote the beginning and the end of the book *Murder Makes the Magazine*, but the thousands of words in between were written online in 44 days by Internet surfers. They submitted their passages as part of a contest sponsored by Amazon.com, with the author of each winning passage added to the story receiving $1,000. The complete story was then made available to readers on the Internet.

CENSORSHIP

Efforts at censorship not only continued but increased during the period of specialization. In the late 1940s and 1950s, the book publishing industry was attacked for printing materials that critics believed to be pro-Communist or anti-American. Alleged obscenity also remained a popular target for censors. For example, in 1950 the Chicago Police Bureau of Censorship banned a novel called *A Diary of Love*, which had been written by Maude Hutchins, the estranged wife of the president of the University of Chicago.

The attacks on books increased during the 1980s and 1990s. For example, from 1980 to 1984, censorship complaints brought to the attention of the American Library Association increased from 300 to almost 1,000 cases a year. According to Judith Krug, director of the American Library Association's Office of Intellectual Freedom, the number of annual complaints took another jump above the 1,000 level by the start of the 1990s.[11] In recent years, efforts have been made to censor a variety of books for various reasons. Topics popular for attack included sex, race, politics, religion, and drugs. Some of the more popular works targeted because they contain references to one or more of these taboo topics include *The Adventures of Huckleberry Finn, 1984, Slaughterhouse Five, Go Ask Alice, The Diary of Anne Frank, Of Mice and Men, To Kill a Mockingbird,* and *The Catcher in the Rye.* In a northern California lumber community, there was even an effort to ban Dr. Seuss's *Lorax* because it tells a story about a fuzzy little creature losing its home in the forest because the greedy "Once-lers" cut down all the trees (see Box 6.4).

> **@   Practicing Media Literacy**
> How do you feel about attempts to censor books both in schools and for the public in general?

Censorship attacks in this decade seem to have focused on the schools. At one point, a group called People for the American Way found that 41 percent of the efforts to ban 347 books during one school year were successful. Alice Walker's Pulitzer Prize–winning novel *The Color Purple,* which contains profanity, and Lois Duncan's *Killing Mr. Griffin,* a book about students who kidnap and murder their teacher, were among the books removed from classrooms.

A study of 421 California school districts by a California State University, Fullerton, professor disclosed that 150 of the districts had been challenged by parents and organizations unhappy with the content of school materials during a two-year period. Of those challenges, 13 percent of the time the objectionable materials were removed. About half of the 300 reported challenges were based on religious grounds, including depictions of Satan or witchcraft in such classics as *Macbeth* and *Snow White.*

Although book banning is usually a tactic of conservative political and religious movements and tends to be criticized by liberals, no clear-cut political categories exist

Box 6.4

MEDIA WATCH
The Top 100 Books of the Millennium

As the 20th century drew to a close, lists of the top books, movie, events, and so on began popping up everywhere. One of the most controversial was the list of the top 100 English language novels of the century, selected by a panel of scholars and writers for Modern Library publications.

Heading the list was the story of one man's experiences during a single day of living in Dublin, Ireland: James Joyce's *Ulysses*. The book, which features such topics as adultery and religion and is written in a stream of consciousness prose with explicit language, was banned in many countries, including Ireland and the United States, when it was published in 1922. It has also been the bane of many students required to read it in later years. But the controversy over the list was not so much about the book selected at the top, but about which books made the list, which didn't, and who made the selections.

Since Modern Library, a division of Random House, released the list of classics and is also known for having published classic literature since 1917, many felt that the publisher was merely trying to hype its own product. But officials of the company said the novels were chosen regardless of their publisher. There was also concern that the panel consisted of only one woman and no African-Americans.

The author with the most books selected to the Top 100 list was Joseph Conrad with four. The works of only eight women authors were selected to the list. In addition to *Ulysses*, Joyce placed another novel, *A Portrait of the Artist as a Young Man*, in the top 10. Here are the top 10 books selected:

1. *Ulysses* by James Joyce
2. *The Great Gatsby* by F. Scott Fitzgerald
3. *A Portrait of the Artist as a Young Man* by James Joyce
4. *Lolita* by Vladimir Nabokov
5. *Brave New World* by Aldous Huxley
6. *The Sound and the Fury* by William Faulkner
7. *Catch-22* by Joseph Heller
8. *Darkness at Noon* by Arthur Koestler
9. *Sons and Lovers* by D. H. Lawrence
10. *The Grapes of Wrath* by John Steinbeck

How many of these books have YOU read? How many were read because they were required in a class you were taking? That was the question facing librarians and booksellers when they came up with their own lists of favorite novels of the 20th century. Both groups said their lists were based on books that people actually read rather than those others might feel they *should* have read. Surprisingly, both lists had the same two novels at the top of their separate lists: Harper Lee's *To Kill a Mockingbird* at number one and J. D. Salinger's often-banned *Catcher in the Rye* at number two. Other books making the top 10 on both lists included J. R. R. Tolkien's *Lord of the Rings*, Margaret Mitchell's *Gone With the Wind*, George Orwell's *1984*, Toni Morrison's *Beloved*, and Alice Walker's *The Color Purple*.

---

when it comes to reacting emotionally to the contents of books. A 1993 study found that 7 percent of efforts to remove books were attributed to liberal organizations. Twain's *Huckleberry Finn*, which describes the evils of racism in the 19th century, has been branded as racist by many who find the use of the word *nigger* offensive. Other books have been condemned by feminist groups that claim pornography degrades women. The National Organization for Women (NOW) boycotted the publisher of the novel *American Psycho* because of the book's "violent and women hating" content. The novel, by Bret Easton Ellis, dealt with a yuppie serial murderer who sexually mutilates women. On the more conservative side of the political spectrum, even the Reverend Jerry Falwell of the Moral Majority has condemned the censorship of conservative books.

According to historian John Tebbel, this "virtual epidemic of censorship" that has been sweeping the country in recent years is the result of a combination of cultural factors: (1) a militant advocacy of fundamentalist values by nearly 70 million evangelicals organized by radio and television evangelists; (2) a large number of traditionalists who found themselves unable to accept a changed world and longed for what they considered the peaceful days of repression and rigid traditional morals and manners; and (3) the Supreme Court's 1973 decision to leave the definition of obscenity to local community standards (*Miller v. California*).[12] Others say this trend is a reflection of cultural paranoia, and they cite Supreme Court Justice Potter Stewart's comment that "censorship reflects a society's lack of confidence in itself."

If we use history as a basis for predicting the future, it is safe to assume there will always be attempts to impose censorship as long as book publishing and other forms of mass communication play a major role in disseminating information and ideas in our society.

CURRENT BUSINESS TRENDS

As a major industry in the United States, book publishing has not been immune to the takeover fever that has been sweeping American businesses. Many small privately owned publishing houses, as well as medium- and large-size companies, have been taken over by large **conglomerates**.

conglomerates

The largest U.S. publisher, Random House (randomhouse.com), agreed to merge with German conglomerate Bertelsmann AG in 1998 at a price estimated by financial analysts at $1.3 billion—slightly more than Random House's annual book sales, which *Publisher's Weekly* had estimated at $1.1 billion. Bertelsmann was the world's third-largest media and entertainment company, with holdings that included Bantam Doubleday Dell, publisher of John Grisham's novels, while Random House published the books of John Updike, Norman Mailer, and Michael Crichton. Shortly after the merger was announced, a group of 26 prominent authors, including Erica Jong and Kurt Vonnegut, sent a letter to the Federal Trade Commission asking it to look into whether the deal would hurt the bargaining power of established authors and reduce the outlets available for aspiring writers to sell their works.

Several months after the Random House/Bertelsmann merger, the flow of American publishing firms into foreign hands continued with the announcement that Pearson PLC, the largest publisher in Britain, had agreed to purchase most of Simon and Schuster's operations from Viacom, Inc., for $4.6 billion in cash. Although takeovers by European firms were relatively new, mergers in the book publishing industry had been going on for some time.

@ Practicing Media Literacy
Do you think the takeover of American publishing firms by foreign corporations will affect the quality of books in this country?

In 1989 the publisher of this book, McGraw-Hill (mcgraw-hill.com), merged its school textbook division with Macmillan, and together they purchased Merrill Publishing Company to form the new Macmillan/McGraw-Hill School Publishing Company conglomerate, the nation's largest el–hi (elementary–high school) publisher. In 1993, McGraw-Hill paid $337.5 million to acquire its partner's interest in the venture.

In 1996, McGraw-Hill Companies' College Division acquired the companies comprising the Times Mirror Higher Education group and became the largest publishing company in the world. The new division publishes college textbooks under the names of McGraw-Hill, WCB, Irwin, and Brown & Benchmark.

By 1994, industry mergers were taking their toll on the book publishing business as large corporations began **downsizing** to make their newly structured operations profitable. Macmillan Inc. merged with Paramount, which was acquired by the cable television giant Viacom. The newly merged publishing firm began reducing the number of book titles and closed a number of imprints, the small houses-within-houses that bear the imprimaturs of their individual editors. Houghton Mifflin closed Ticknor & Fields, and Harcourt Brace began reducing its number of titles and fired many of its top editors.

In addition to the publishing of books, a lucrative and growing market is developing in the field of distribution. Chain bookstores are becoming commonplace and are forcing many smaller book dealers out of business. The three largest chain bookstores are Barnes & Noble, B. Dalton, which is operated by Barnes & Noble, and Waldenbooks, which is owned by Kmart Corporation.

Barnes & Noble (barnesandnoble.com), the nation's largest bookseller, came in for criticism in November of 1998 when it purchased the leading wholesaler, Ingram Book Group, for $600 million. The deal made two of Barnes & Noble's rivals, Borders Group Inc. and Amazon.com, Inc., its customers. The deal drew immediate criticism from a leading group of independent booksellers who called it "blatantly anticompetitive," while Amazon.com, the **online bookseller** that competes with Barnes & Noble for Internet business, said the deal raised "industrywide concerns."[13]

The battle between online booksellers intensified in 1999 when Amazon.com (amazon.com) announced that it was taking 50 percent off the price of all *New York Times* best-sellers. The announcement was quickly followed by similar actions by Barnesandnoble.com and Borders.com. Not only was the move seen as one that would leave the three competitors with little or no profit on such books, but would also cut deeper into the profits of traditional booksellers.

And while all of this competitive maneuvering was taking place, lawsuits were flying. For example, in 1998 Wal-Mart Stores, Inc., sued Amazon.com for hiring current and former employees who were familiar with Wal-Mart's computer system to obtain access to trade secrets of the world's largest retailer. That same year, a group of independent booksellers filed a federal suit charging Borders and Barnes & Noble with making backroom deals with publishers in an attempt to drive their competitors out of business. The suit accused the two large bookstore chains of using their clout to obtain discount prices and preferences in violation of antitrust and business practices

> **@ Practicing Media Literacy**
>
> Have you ever purchased a book on the Internet? If so, do you prefer that to going to the bookstore? Other than convenience, why?

law. And, as 1999 drew to a close, Amazon.com sued Barnes & Noble over alleged copycat use of its popular one-click feature, which simplifies the process of making online purchases.

Some 40,000 people were on hand for the 1998 BookExpo America, formerly the American Booksellers Association, convention in Chicago to look over the lineup of fall books and to get autographs from such authors as Tom Wolfe, Alice Walker, Anna Quindlen, and Richard North Patterson. But the main focus of the event was clouded by everyone still being in shock over the merger of Random House with a German conglomerate and the sale of Simon and Schuster to a British firm, by the mood of the independent booksellers who were suing chain bookstores, and by the publishers who were still upset because they had been sued by the American Booksellers Association

downsizing

online bookseller

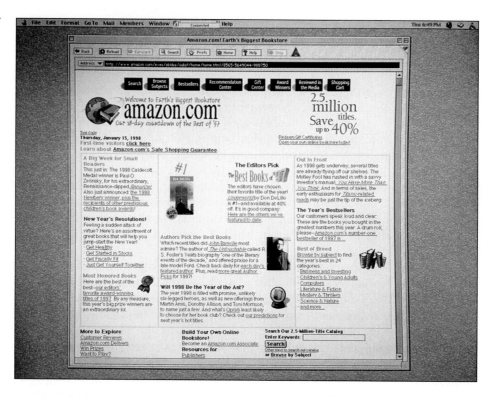

While many small, independent book-sellers have lost business to the large book store chains, those chains have also lost customers to the online book-sellers, such as amazon.com.

just a few years earlier. In fact, three major publishers, Random House (and its subsidiaries Knopf, Crown, Pantheon, Ballantine, Villard, Times, Vintage, and Fodor's), Penguin USA (including Viking, Dutton, and New American Library), and St. Martin's (and its imprints Picador and Griffin) were conspicuous by their absence at the 1996 ABA convention. These publishing houses elected not to be represented at the convention because of the association's lawsuit against them for allegedly favoring major bookstore chains over independent dealers.

The closing years of the 20th century were not the best for the book publishing industry. Book sales were down in 1997 and returns, the unsold copies booksellers can return to the publishers without penalty, were up. As a result, HarperCollins (harpercollins.com) downsized its future lists by canceling more than 100 titles it already had under contract. Final figures for 1997 showed that adult trade for hardcover mass-market bookselling was down 7.2 percent and mass-market paperbacks were down slightly more than 8 percent. The only bright spots were college and academic publishing, which posted healthy increases. As 1999 drew to a close figures for the previous year showed a slight turnaround as book sales rose 4 percent in 1998. The Book Industry Group then predicted that sales would rise 2 percent annually through 2003. But some of that strength had to be credited to the online retailers who were accounting for roughly 4 to 5 percent of sales. Said Random House Chief Executive Peter Olson, "I think the attention that Amazon.com and Barnesandnoble.com have generated has increased interest in books in general, and that has led to buying not just online, but in stores."[14]

The publishing industry is driven by the blockbuster books, but good public relations work can turn middle-level books into profitable ventures. The publishing industry turns out thousands of books each week, many of which are described as having literary merit, while most of the others will lose money. This is not good news for the conglomerates that are taking over the book publishing industry, according to Richard Turner of *New York* magazine:

> Viacom had taken a $140 million write-down at Simon & Schuster, sales were off, imprints were being closed. People wondered whether the book publishing business could avoid being crushed by its new media-conglomerate owners, not known for their sentimentality about literature. But the business survived, advances are still out there, lists haven't been cut, sales are up, books of literary merit are being published. There are myriad reasons: hardcover discounting, superstores, aging baby-boomers, better inventory control. And publishing has managed this even now that it shares corporate ownership with the movie, music, and television businesses.[15]

NEW TECHNOLOGY AND BOOKS

As noted earlier, the electronic revolution is having an impact on book publishing. Audio, CD, and CD-ROM books are accounting for major growth in book publishing sales. However, this may be just the tip of the iceberg when it comes to new technological changes in book publishing.

As we enter the new millennium, we will witness many changes in the way we communicate. Books such as this one will probably change from their 500-year-old format to exciting, "user-friendly" forms enhanced by the computer age. According to futurist Alvin Toffler, tomorrow's books will be read on book-size video screens. These electronic devices will be able to immediately translate foreign language editions, enlarge or reduce the size of the type, change type styles, adjust the degree of reading difficulty, and allow readers of novels to increase or decrease the levels of violence and sexual explicitness to fit individual tastes. All of these newer "user-friendly" options along with the content itself will be delivered on tiny microchips, floppy disks, or CD-ROMs. Personal computer owners can already access books electronically by connecting to the many online book stores provided on the Internet, such as hyperbole.com. One such company, Fatbrain.com, sold 10,000 short stories (generally less than 100 pages) on its website between November 1999 and February 2000. Among the works sold was an essay by famed science fiction writer, Arthur C. Clarke, which web browsers could purchase and download for a mere $2.

Computer technology has long been changing the book publishing industry. Some authors compose books on computers and e-mail their manuscripts to their publishers, who edit the material and then typeset it without additional keystroking. McGraw-Hill uses computer technology to offer college professors **customized textbooks**. Instructors can select from a variety of text materials and have a customized text printed for their students.

customized textbooks

There has been much talk about a book bank system for use in college bookstores. With this plan, students would be able to download up to 50 textbooks onto a two-square-inch computer disk. The disk would then be used in pocket-size or notebook-size computer readers. The computers would allow students to do automatic searches and other computer functions while reading text materials. However, concerns about violations of copyright laws have slowed the development of the system.

The future of textbook publishing is headed toward a multimedia approach in which teaching tools will consist of a process that integrates print, sound, and full-motion video into an interactive delivery system for educational materials for students.

As 1996 drew to a close, Internet users were offered what was described as the first "electronically published, original, novel-length literary fiction for general distribution." The book, *Arcadia Ego*, did not require going to a bookstore to obtain it, it had no pages to turn, and—best of all—there was no cost. Readers could log onto the Internet site and read as much of the book as they wanted. If they didn't have time, they could download the text for future reading. If the readers enjoyed it, they were invited to send a donation to the publisher, but they were under no obligation to do so. This example is still another indication that the Internet will in all likelihood become the primary source of information in our society.

e-books

By the end of the 20th century, developers of **e-books**, hand-held electronic book devices, were finding that the new technology was colliding with the publishing industry and its old traditions. While some publishers said they didn't fear losing out because readers will always savor the touch of real paper, others expressed fear for the future of publishing. The first e-books became available in the fall of 1998 and many schools expressed a desire to use the new technology to ease the burden of students having to carry heavy textbooks. In Davis, California, the school board applied for a $6 million federal grant to help purchase 3,000 e-books to be shared by 7,700 students. Meanwhile, authors were making the case that e-books would result in savings on paper costs, resulting in higher author royalties. However, publishers were pointing out that e-books would incur new expenses such as formatting manuscripts and privacy protection for digital material.[16]

Author Ken Auletta in a 1997 *New Yorker* article about hard times in the book publishing industry explored the possibility that literature may someday be "published" solely on computer screens. Author Scott Turow is quoted in the article as saying "I think the Internet or some other alternative technology could dramatically change publishing. If Stephen King or John Grisham posted a book on the Net, and came up with an appropriate technology that allowed him to be compensated, what the hell would he need a publisher for?"[17]

> @   **Practicing Media Literacy**
>
> How do you think new technology will have impacted the book publishing industry 10 years from now?

The traditional form of print publication received a boost at the 1998 BookExpo when IBM and Ingram, the nation's largest book wholesaler, introduced their Lightning Print Inc., a print-on-demand (POD) service for publishers, booksellers, and readers. Without the need for typesetting and printing plates, an operator cuts out the pages of an aging out-of-print book and in less than an hour can scan the pages, print them by laser on paper from another machine, cut and trim the pages and bring the laminated, full-color book cover into a final machine, the binder. Thanks to the new technology, a brand-new paperback edition of a classic is ready to be sold.[18]

Libraries use computers to catalog collections, retrieve data from around the world, and reduce the need for storage space. CD-ROMs provide library users with computer access to vast amounts of information from encyclopedias, periodicals, and dictionaries.

The Library of Congress (lcweb.loc.gov) is now putting texts and periodicals on indestructible 12-inch disks that many people can use at one time. At the time of publication of this book, printed materials were being stored in computerized memory banks.

Still another trend involving computers developed in the mid-1990s: online bookstores, such as Amazon.com, Barnesandnoble.com, and Borders.com. Instead of visiting or writing letters to bookstores, computer users can place orders through the

Internet. In addition, online bookstores offer helpful hints for finding hard-to-locate publications as well as discounts and, of course, convenience.

But even with all of this, the traditional book clubs—from the Literary Guild to the Book of the Month club—continue to flourish. However, many of them are now offering their customers the opportunity to place their orders through the clubs' online websites (booksonline.com, bomc.com, qpb.com). Convenience is still the key word.

SUMMARY

Books are the most permanent form of mass communication because they are durable, designed to be passed from person to person, and housed in libraries. Civilizations have been recording permanent messages in portable form since the Sumerians used clay tablets 4,500 years ago. Other ancient forms of books included papyrus scrolls and the codex; these were the predecessors of the handwritten book on paper made from wood pulp.

In the mid-15th century, Johannes Gutenberg's invention of movable type turned the ancient art of bookmaking into a mass communication medium. Soon after the development of mass communication, those in authority saw the medium as a threat to their rule and took steps to regulate it. Despite these efforts at censorship, books spread the ideas of the Protestant Reformation in the 16th century.

In the United States, book publishing has gone through three stages of development: the elitist, popular, and specialized stages. Specialized books outsell novels by two to one, and book publishing is a major cultural industry.

Throughout the history of book publishing, censorship and book banning have remained an integral part of society. Such efforts don't seem to be declining as we approach the 21st century.

Book publishing is a major industry in the United States, generating more than $20 billion in sales annually. In recent years many smaller firms have been taken over by huge conglomerates, and some of the major American publishing firms are "downsizing" their titles and workforces. There is also rapid growth in book distribution, with chain bookstores now accounting for a major share of book sales.

New electronic technologies will soon change the way we read books. CD-ROMs and audio books already account for large sales increases in the book publishing industry. It is predicted that many books of the future will be sold on microchips or CD-ROMs and read in personal computer-readers.

Find a review of *Key People and Concepts*, a message board for *Practicing Media Literacy* questions, self tests, and more at: www.mhhe.com/wilson.

Thought **Questions**

1. What cultural factors readied Western civilization for the printing of books in the 15th century?
2. What limitations or problems will likely develop from the change in books from paper form to computer-readers?
3. What kind of picture will today's mass-market paperbacks paint for future anthropologists who might use them to study our civilization thousands of years from now?

4. Should books be censored to protect certain classes of people and society in general from potential harm? If so, how should this be done? If not, how can we protect our culture from such potential abuses?

5. What potential dangers lie ahead if the trend of conglomerate takeovers and "downsizing" of titles and personnel continues?

Notes

1. Martha Mendoza (Associated Press), "Electronic-Books Concept off to a Dog-Eared Start," *Fresno Bee*, August 30, 1999, p. C1.

2. "Not an Internet Fan," *Fresno Bee*, January 31, 1998, p. A2.

3. Carolyne Zinko, "Internet Smashing Small Bookstores," *San Francisco Chronicle*, December 26, 1998, p. A17.

4. Edward Edwards, *Libraries and Founders of Libraries: From Ancient Times to the Beginning of the Nineteenth Century* (1865; reprint Amsterdam: Gerard Th. Van Heusden, 1986), p. 25.

5. Will Durant, *The Reformation: A History of European Civilization from Wyclif to Calvin: 1300–1564* (New York: Simon & Schuster, 1957), p. 368.

6. *Ibid.*, p. 369.

7. Oscar Handlin, *The History of the United States, vol. 1* (New York: Holt, Rinehart & Winston, 1967), p. 234.

8. *Ibid.*, p. 258.

9. Paul S. Boyer, *Purity in Print: The Vice Society Movement and Book Censorship in America* (New York: Scribner's, 1968).

10. Curtis G. Benjamin, "Book Publishing's Hidden Bonanza," in *Readings in Mass Communication: Concepts and Issues in the Mass Media*, ed. Michael C. Emery and Ted C. Smythe (Dubuque, IA: Brown, 1972), p. 182.

11. Alan Parachini and Dennis McDougal, "Censorship: A Decade of Tighter Controls of the Arts," *Los Angeles Times*, December 25, 1989, p. F-1.

12. John Tebbel, *Between Covers: The Rise and Transformation of Book Publishing in America* (New York: Oxford University Press, 1987), p. 460.

13. Brendan Intindola (Reuters News Service), "Bookseller Deal Gets Criticized; Barnes & Noble buys distributor," *San Francisco Chronicle*, November 7, 1998, p. D1.

14. Doreen Carvajal, "Book Sales Grew 4 Percent Last Year, Study Shows," *New York Times*, August 16, 1999, p. C1.

15. Richard Turner, "Hyping Type," *New York*, June 17, 1996, p. 21.

16. Doreen Carvajal, "Publishing Industry Contends With the Uncertainties of E-Books," *New York Times*, May 10, 1999, p. B1.

17. Leah Garchick Personals, "Will the Net Make Books Outdated?," *San Francisco Chronicle*, September 30, 1997, p. D8.

18. Patricia Holt, "Novel Way to Reprint Old Books," *San Francisco Chronicle*, June 2, 1998, p. D1.

Newspapers
Past, Present,
and Future

The decade of the nineties is going to be one in which the traditional newspaper may face a decline, extinction or at least complete internal self-reappraisal.

—**Anthony Smith,** *Goodbye Gutenberg,* 1980

Key People and Concepts

Publick Occurrences

Federalist Papers

The First Amendment

Alien and Sedition Acts

Penny Press

Yellow Journalism

Joseph Pulitzer

William Randolph Hearst

Edward W. Scripps

Adolph Ochs

Social Responsibility and the Press

Jazz Journalism

Specialization

Tabloids

Chain Ownership

Online News Association (ONA)

In 1965 it was estimated that 71 percent of all adults in the United States read a daily newspaper. By the end of the 20th century, that figure had dropped to 50 percent. In addition, some 75 percent of the people surveyed in 1999 didn't worry about not reading the daily newspaper because there were so many different news outlets available—including radio, television, cable news channels, and the Internet. In addition, many newspapers themselves were using the Internet to get information out to the public. Between 1997 and 1999, the number of daily newspaper websites had almost doubled, from 487 to nearly 1,000. In addition, the websites for weekly newspapers more than doubled from 505 to 1,271. These were the findings published in the 1999 *Editor & Publisher Year Book*, which also reported that while all this was going on, circulation for both daily and weekly newspapers had grown during the same period of time.[1] While the annual report didn't draw any conclusions from the figures, it suggested that online publishing was a complementary medium to the traditional form of newspaper publications. During the 20th century, newspapers faced competitive challenges from many different sources. But they have managed to survive. This chapter will take a look at the development of the newspaper, including its early origins, its growth and popularity, and its evolution to meet the competition of the Internet in the 21st century.

Cultural History of Newspapers

		Elitist	Popular	Specialized
1st century	Romans post news sheets in town squares.	•		
16th century	Italians sell printed news sheets for a coin called a *gazetta*.	•		
17th century	*Corantos* (newspaper forerunners) begin in Germany.	•		
1665	*Oxford Gazette* founded, first English-language newspaper.	•		
1690	First newspaper published in 13 colonies, *Publick Occurrences*; lasts one issue.	•		
1704	*Boston News-Letter* becomes first regularly published American newspaper.	•		
1735	John Peter Zenger tried in New York for libeling the governor.	•		
1765–83	American newspapers promote revolution.	•		
1791	Bill of Rights ratified; press is given protection from government censorship by First Amendment.	•		
1798	Alien and Sedition Acts passed, leading to prosecution of newspaper editors for criticizing government.	•		
1827	*Freedom's Journal* founded, first African-American newspaper in the United States.			•
1828	*Cherokee Phoenix* becomes first Native American newspaper.			•
1833	*New York Sun* founded, first penny press.		•	
1841	Horace Greeley begins *New York Tribune*; introduces the editorial page and attacks slavery.		•	
1848	Associated Press (AP), first news wire service, founded.		•	
1883	Joseph Pulitzer begins publishing *New York World*.		•	
1895	William Randolph Hearst buys *New York Journal*; circulation war with Pulitzer is branded "yellow journalism."		•	
1896	Adolph Ochs buys *New York Times* and ushers in objective journalism.		•	
1907	United Press (UP) becomes second news wire service.		•	
1909	Hearst starts third news wire service, International News Service (INS).		•	
1920s	Tabloids begin reflecting Roaring '20s lifestyles.		•	
1923	Society of Newspaper Editors adopts Canons of Journalism, stressing social responsibility.		•	
1958	United Press and International News Service merge to become United Press International (UPI).		•	
1965–1970	Underground newspapers reflect new American subcultural lifestyles.		•	•
1982	*USA Today* founded as a national daily, using satellite technology and innovative color graphics.		•	
1985	Desktop publishing, using computers, makes possible inexpensive publication of specialized newspapers.			•
1995	Many large newspapers, from the *Houston Post* to the *Baltimore Evening Sun*, go out of business.			•
1996	While the number of weekly newspapers continues to increase, daily newspaper publication continues to decline.			•
1997	California's McClatchy newspaper chain becomes eighth largest in nation with purchase of *Minneapolis Star Tribune's* parent company.			•
1999	*Los Angeles Times* creates all-new web site which offers more breaking news headlines, updated every two minutes, 24 hours a day.			•
2000	Most major American newspapers now have web sites for dissemination of news and information			•

MODERN CHALLENGES

In the early part of the 20th century, a new electronic gadget, radio, mounted the first major challenge to newspapers. For the first time, citizens could remain in their homes and hear the voices of newsmakers from around the world coming directly into their living rooms. While the newspaper realized the threat of this new electronic gadget in the early 1930s and tried to do something about it (see "Press-Radio War" in Chapter 5), radio news didn't come of age until World War II in the 1940s. For the first time, radio demonstrated effectively that it could keep the public informed about news events anywhere in the world.

The next challenge for newspapers came midway through this century when television became a dominant force. Although many of the early newscasts were still primitive—using still pictures held by the news anchors or film footage that was days or even weeks old—the 1960s saw two events that brought about a major change in the audience's perception of television news. The first was the **expansion** by the three television networks to a 30-minute newscast in 1963. It was also in 1963 that television news came of age in the eyes of viewers with its extensive coverage of the assassination and **funeral** of President John Kennedy.

expansion

Kennedy funeral

While radio could provide immediacy to the news (all a reporter needs is a telephone, and he or she can be on the air with the story right away), television provides the visual image—actual pictures of the news event, sometimes as it is actually taking place.

Through these challenges, newspapers continued to exist, providing the written history of events, as well as more details than most radio or television newscasts could ever hope to include. But along the way, newspapers have had to make some adjustments to remain competitive.

For example, in the 1960s, newspaper production speed increased with the advent of computerized typesetting and offset printing. Newspaper layout and design changed in the 1970s to compete with the visual appeal of television, and newspaper formats radically changed in the 1980s with the introduction of a national newspaper.

In 1982 Al Neuharth, then chairman and executive officer of Gannett Company, Inc., the largest newspaper chain in the United States, launched *USA Today* (usa today.com) as the newspaper industry's answer to television. Filled with short, "TV-style" news stories, many features, and ample **color** and graphics, the newspaper was distributed to Gannett-owned printing plants around the country by satellite.

color

Soon after *USA Today* was launched, other newspapers were utilizing computerized color graphics and condensing much of their news into brief summaries to allow more space for human-interest articles. Even the *New York Times* (nytimes.com), known as "the old gray lady" for most of its life for its bland, colorless layout, began using color pictures on its front pages. The look and content of newspapers, which had remained relatively unchanged during most of the century, underwent a transformation in an effort to adapt to TV-influenced popular culture.

This was not the first time that new electronic media had forced changes on newspapers, however. Radio's and television's more immediate coverage of news events toned down the use of sensationalism by many newspapers to sell more papers. Home delivery subscriptions replaced street hawkers screaming out lurid headlines in most communities. Nor will it be the last change. At a convention of the American Society of Newspaper Editors, the audience was told about a study showing that young Americans who have grown up with television do not read well enough to understand newspapers and they were abandoning them. The editors were told to simplify the writing in newspapers to accommodate the decline in literacy.

Now, in the 21st century, newspapers again face a challenge from an electronic medium: computers and the Internet (see Chapter 3). As more and more sources of information from around the world are becoming available to the public, newspapers are again looking for ways to survive. One approach has been for newspapers to subscribe to the old adage "if you can't beat them, join them." As a result, many newspapers across the nation and the world have established their own home pages, making information from their data banks available on the Internet.

> **@ Practicing Media Literacy**
>
> What do you consider to be your main source for news and information: radio, television, newspapers, or the Internet?

EARLY ORIGINS OF NEWSPAPERS

gazetta

Early attempts to disseminate printed information to the public can be traced back some 2,000 years to the official news sheets, called *acta diurna* (daily acts), posted by the Roman government in public places. However, it wasn't until the mid-16th century that efforts to sell printed news began. Leaders in Venice made news regularly available to the public on printed sheets that sold for a coin called a **gazetta.** Later many newspapers would adopt the name Gazette for their publications.

Corantos

Another forerunner of today's newspaper began appearing in Germany around 1609 and in London in 1621. Called *corantos,* they consisted of printed single sheets containing current news that was published at regular and frequent intervals, often once or twice a week.[2] Amsterdam, where *corantos* were published in Dutch, German, French, and English, became the first major newspaper center.

First English Papers

In 1665 the first real English-language newspaper, the *Oxford Gazette*, started publishing twice weekly under the authority of the English Crown. Later renamed the *London Gazette*, it continued publishing into the 20th century.

The first daily newspaper in English was the *Daily Courant,* which began publication in London on March 11, 1702. This high-quality, highly literate paper was aimed at the educated elite. Like newspapers of today, it relied on advertising for its revenue.

As was the case with all other publications, these early English newspapers were subject to censorship by the Crown, although censorship was rarely enforced after the late 17th century. In the American colonies, however, colonial governors continued to censor newspapers well into the 18th century.

THE COLONIAL AMERICAN PRESS ERA (1690–1820s)

Credit for the first effort to found a newspaper in the American colonies belongs to Benjamin Harris, a former London publisher. He brought out the first edition of *Publick Occurrences Both Foreign and Domestick* in Boston on September 25, 1690. Harris had fled to the colonies after being arrested in England for printing seditious material against the Crown.

The first issue of *Publick Occurrences* apparently didn't please those in authority any more than Harris's previous efforts in England. Among other things, the paper carried unfavorable comments about some Indians who were allies of the English and about the French king, who allegedly had seduced his daughter-in-law. The newspaper's first issue was therefore its last. The governor of Massachusetts Bay colony banned Harris's paper on the grounds that it had been published without authority and contained material not approved by the government.

In putting Harris out of business, the authorities reaffirmed their right to prior censorship: Publishers had to first secure permission from the government before publishing anything. A firmly established authoritarian principle dictated that the press be controlled to protect the interests of the Crown, and in the colonies the governors represented the Crown.

It was another 14 years before the *Boston News-Letter* became the first newspaper to be published regularly in the colonies in April 1704. Its publisher was the postmaster of Boston, John Campbell, and under its nameplate were the words "published by authority."

The post office connection was important for several reasons. First, the postmaster was the governor's appointee and in effect was "approved" by him. Second, the post office was an effective place for gathering news because people assembled there to read letters from England aloud to one another.

Because most colonists were English, it was not surprising that the *Boston News-Letter* was similar in appearance and content to the *London Gazette*. Two-thirds of the *News-Letter* consisted of news taken from London journals. Thus, most stories concerned English politics and European wars. The rest of the space was filled with very brief articles about ship arrivals, sermons, deaths, political appointments, court actions, the weather, and the activities of Indians and pirates.

When Campbell retired from his job as postmaster in 1718, his successor, William Brooker, seemed to consider newspaper publishing a part of the job. But when Campbell refused to relinquish the *News-Letter*, Brooker started a second paper, the *Boston Gazette*, in 1719. Unlike Campbell, when Brooker lost his job as postmaster a year later, he turned the paper over to his successor. Five postmasters, including Brooker, served as publisher of the *Gazette*.

The Spread of Newspapers

Philadelphia's first newspaper, *The American Weekly Mercury*, was founded by the William Bradford family in 1719. Although it too was an authorized publication, Bradford's son Tom, the publisher, soon got into trouble for writing that he hoped the General Assembly "will find some effectual remedy to revive the dying credit of the Province and restore to us our former happy circumstances."[3] Tom went to jail for the statement; he was later released and was allowed to continue publishing the paper until his death in 1742.

In 1721 James Franklin, the older half-brother of Benjamin Franklin, started the *New England Courant* in Boston. Unlike the two older Boston papers, the *Courant* was not "published by authority" and had no connection with the post office.

The *Courant* did not resemble the *London Gazette*, as its predecessors had, but modeled itself after such English literary essay papers as the *Spectator* and *Guardian*. Its content was thus more entertaining than informative. The *Courant* ran humorous literary essays, most of them satirically critical of the Puritans and the colonial government. Eventually James Franklin was thrown in jail for a month and

Starting his career as an apprentice in his brother's print shop, Benjamin Franklin went on to become one of Colonial America's leading newspapermen.

forbidden to publish the *Courant* or any paper "of like nature." Franklin circumvented that government order by naming his brother, Benjamin, an apprentice in his print shop, as publisher.

Ben Franklin, who had perfected his writing style by reading and rewriting Joseph Addison's essays in the *Spectator* which his brother kept in the print shop, started contributing satirical essays to the *Courant.* Appearing under the pseudonym of Silence Dogood, the articles soon became a popular feature.

In 1723, Benjamin Franklin left his apprenticeship to strike out on his own. He moved to Philadelphia, where he worked for Tom Bradford for several years. Then, in 1729, he bought an interest in an unsuccessful newspaper, *The Universal Instructor in all Arts and Sciences* and the *Pennsylvania Gazette.* He shortened the name to the Pennsylvania Gazette and turned it into a highly regarded newspaper, thus launching a successful publishing career that was to include a chain of newspapers as well as **Poor Richard's Almanack** and one of the first American magazines, *The General Magazine.*

Poor Richard's Almanack

New York became the third colony with a newspaper when William Bradford started the *New York Gazette* in 1725. Bradford had left Philadelphia to become the official printer for the New York colony. Although not a postmaster, he benefited from the status of being an agent of the government.

Struggle against Authority

Zenger

In 1733, a young German immigrant named John Peter **Zenger** began publishing the *New York Weekly Journal.* Zenger had the backing of a number of antiestablishment merchants who disliked the colonial governor, William Cosby. Zenger printed one attack after another on the governor and his council until he was arrested for seditious libel. During the nine months he was held in jail awaiting trial, Zenger continued to edit his newspaper, which was printed and distributed by his wife and friends.

The trial began ominously, as Zenger's two attorneys were disbarred for attempting to get the judge to disqualify himself (on the grounds that he had been appointed by Governor Cosby). Zenger's supporters then hired Andrew Hamilton, a Philadelphia attorney, to represent him. At that time truth was not a defense in a libel suit (it is today), and the jury needed only to decide whether or not Zenger had printed the papers in question. The judge would decide if the material was criminally libelous.

During the trial in 1735, Hamilton argued for truth as a defense of libel. He challenged the jury to ignore the technicalities

> **@   Practicing Media Literacy**
>
> Do you think there is any correlation between the development of colonial newspapers in Boston and Philadelphia and the seeds for the American Revolution movement in those same areas?

of the law and recognize the greater issues at stake: "The question before the court is not the cause of the poor printer . . . No! It may in its consequences affect every freeman on the main[land] of America. It is the best cause; it is the cause of Liberty, . . . the liberty both of exposing and opposing arbitrary power by speaking and writing Truth."[4]

The jury responded to Hamilton's oratory, ignored the letter of the law, and returned a verdict of not guilty. Although the Zenger decision set no legal precedent, it sent a clear signal that the people were no longer compliant toward government suppression of the press. The press was beginning to play an important role in shaping cultural attitudes in the colonies.

> @   **Practicing Media Literacy**
>
> Do you feel that over the years the courts have given the press too much freedom from libel suits?

Following the Zenger case, other newspapers started up in the colonies. By 1765 all but two colonies, Delaware and New Jersey, had newspapers. There were four papers in Boston, three each in New York and Philadelphia, and two each in Connecticut, Rhode Island, and North and South Carolina. The other four colonies had one paper each, published weekly at the seat of government.

With the exception of Benjamin Harris, John Campbell, and the various postmasters who published the *Boston Gazette,* most newspaper editors and publishers in colonial days were printers by trade. Besides publishing a newspaper, these printers usually had a for-hire printing business and also printed books and pamphlets. Sometimes the printer–publisher was the postmaster, a magistrate, and, in many cases, the official printer for the colony. Frequently they ran bookstores where they sold their own publications as well as books from London and, occasionally, general merchandise. Ben Franklin, for example, advertised coffee, soap, wines, patent medicines, eyeglasses, Rhode Island cheese, and lottery tickets for sale along with his books and stationery.[5]

The Press and the Revolution

Slowly the colonial culture, with its strong loyalty to England, was changing. This loyalty was severely strained in 1765, when the British Parliament passed the Stamp Act imposing a tax on all legal documents, official papers, books, and newspapers. To ensure that the tax was collected, all printing had to be done on taxed paper. This law was followed by the Townshend Acts, which placed taxes on tea, wine, oil, glass, lead, and paint.

Hostility toward this "taxation without representation" was building in the colonies, and colonial printer-publishers started speaking out boldly against second-class colonial citizenship. Soon many newspapers were at the center of the controversy. Samuel Adams's *Boston Gazette* and Isaiah Thomas's *Massachusetts Spy* were leaders in the patriotic movement that was sweeping the colonies. A number of prominent figures in the American Revolution were writers for the colonial press, including John Adams, John Dickinson, Benjamin Franklin, Thomas Jefferson, Richard Henry Lee, and Thomas Paine.

When the Revolution broke out in 1775, the press attempted to cover the war. However, there were no effective ways to gather the news, and papers often had to rely on hearsay and secondhand reports from the battlefield. Facts were not always a major element in some of the war reports, as the partisan press helped to sustain the spirit of the American people. Typical was the May 3, 1775, *Massachusetts Spy* report on the first battle of the war:

Americans! forever bear in mind the BATTLE OF LEXINGTON!—where British troops, unmolested and unprovoked, wantonly and in a most inhuman manner, fired upon and killed a number of our countrymen, then robbed, ransacked, and burnt their houses! Not could the tears of defenseless women, some of them were in the pains of childbirth, the cries of the helpless babes, not the prayers of old age confined to beds of sickness, appease their thirst for blood!—or divert them from their design of MURDER AND ROBBERY!

The Press in the New Republic

Neither the Articles of Confederation of 1781 nor the Constitution drawn up in 1787 included protection for the press. Nevertheless, the practice of prior censorship had died with the end of British rule, and newspapers participated vigorously in public debate. In particular, the New York newspapers played an important role in securing the ratification of the Constitution by publishing the **Federalist Papers,** a series of essays in defense of the new document. Finally, in 1791, the First Amendment, the constitutional foundation for freedom of the press in the United States, was ratified.

Federalist Papers

In the early days of the new republic, the press played a major role in American politics. The new nation split into two parties: the Federalists, led by Alexander Hamilton, and the Republicans, or anti-Federalists, led by Thomas Jefferson. Newspapers became partisan, lining up with one or the other party. Some even became party organs, directly subsidized by the party. The development of a highly partisan press has caused some historians to see the 1790s as the "dark ages" of American journalism.

Pro-Federalist papers included John Fenno's *Gazette of the United States*, William Coleman's *New York Evening Post,* Noah Webster's *American Minerva,* and William Cobbett's *Porcupine's Gazette*. Pro-Republican newspapers included Philip Freneau's *National Gazette,* Samuel Harrison Smith's *National Intelligencer,* and Benjamin Franklin's *Bache's Aurora* (Bache was a grandson of Ben Franklin).

@ **Practicing Media Literacy**

Do American newspapers of the 21st century exert much influence in the political campaigns?

The content of these postrevolution newspapers was not all political, however. Americans still placed a great deal of importance on foreign news, particularly from England. Even though the new nation had won its independence through a bloody war, the United States was still dependent on the "mother country" for many things, including cultural leadership, the models for newspapers and magazines, and news about English customs and thought.

However, the partisan postrevolutionary press differed in many ways from the tame colonial newspapers with their noncontroversial accounts of foreign and domestic news. Now the papers were run by strong-minded editors, who routinely expressed their political convictions and attacked those who held opposing points of view.

Alien and Sedition Acts

In 1798, just seven years after the First Amendment gave the press explicit constitutional protection from government interference, the Federalist-controlled Congress passed the Alien and Sedition Acts. The Sedition Act placed serious restrictions on a person's right to criticize the government, the president, or any members of the president's cabinet. Some Republican newspaper editors, at least one Republican congressman, and other critics of the government were tried under the new law. Those convicted were fined and sent to jail. Citizens became so angry at this government high-handedness that they voted Federalist president John Adams out of office in

1800 and elected Thomas Jefferson, who had campaigned against the acts. Jefferson pardoned those who had been imprisoned under the acts, and all fines were repaid with interest. The laws expired with the end of the Federalist reign.

Early 19th Century

The dark ages of American journalism continued into the 19th century as Thomas Jefferson, a long-time defender of a free press in a democratic society, suffered outrageous personal attacks from Federalist newspapers. Even President James Madison, the "Father of the Constitution" and the author of the First Amendment, was harshly criticized by certain elements of the press when he succeeded Jefferson to the presidency.

In the meantime, a new kind of paper, the **mercantile newspaper,** had emerged in the new nation. *The Courier, The Enquirer,* and the *Journal of Commerce* carried business news, shipping information, and advertisements. In the early 19th century, the mercantile press and the political press began to merge, forming the prototype of today's American newspaper.

As the American experiment in democracy unfolded in the years after independence, the press played an important role in shaping and reflecting political culture and values. Political leaders and thinkers differed on how the new democracy should function, and their lively war of ideas was amplified and disseminated through the mass medium of newspapers.

It is important to note, however, that in this period newspaper readers consisted primarily of a rather select, educated elite of politically aware citizens and merchants. Newspapers did not reach out to the general public until 1833.

mercantile newspaper

> @ **Practicing Media Literacy**
> Should the newspapers of today have more restrictions regarding criticism of the federal government and the administration?

THE PENNY-PRESS ERA (1833–1865)

By the 1830s, New York had emerged as the metropolitan center of America's emerging industrial culture. Its population quadrupled to over 800,000 people between 1830 and 1860 as immigrants from Europe and migrants from rural New England arrived daily.

Popular Culture Newspapers

On September 3, 1833, Benjamin Day, a printer, launched a daily newspaper called the **New York Sun.** This paper represented a major departure from previous newspapers in terms of its content, cost, and target audience. Instead of aiming the paper at the elite, who could afford to pay the customary 6 cents per copy, Day priced his paper at 1 cent, within reach of the new urban masses: the factory workers.

New York Sun

Day hired newsboys to sell the four-page newspaper on the streets. He borrowed this "London plan" of circulation from English newspapers. To capture the interest of the newly arrived city dwellers, Day concentrated on stories of crime, violence, murder, fires, trials, executions, and other sensational topics. Another popular feature in the *Sun* was a humorous column that summarized the daily police court activities in New York (see Box 7.1). Day's approach proved successful, and by the end of his first year the *Sun* had a circulation of 10,000.

With such a large audience, the *Sun* was very attractive to advertisers, and increasing advertising revenues meant new independence for the newspaper. Up to now,

Box 7.1

MEDIA LITERACY
The Crime Beat Is Nothing New to American Newspapers

One of the most popular items in the old New York Sun *was George W. Wisner's report of the police court news. The following example of his work appeared in the July 4, 1834, edition. Check your local newspaper and see if it runs similar information under such headings as "Local News in Brief." Have the times really changed?*

Margaret Thomas was drunk in the street—said she never would get drunk again "upon her honor." Committed, "upon honor."

William Luvoy got drunk because yesterday was so devilish warm. Drank 9 glasses of brandy and water and said he would be cursed if he wouldn't drink 9 more as quick as he could raise the money to buy it with. He would like to know what right the magistrate had to interfere with his private affairs. Fined $1—forgot his pocketbooks, and was sent over to Bridewell.

Bridget McMunn got drunk and threw a pitcher at Mr. Ellis, of 53 Ludlow St. Bridget said she was the mother of 3 orphans—God bless their dear souls—and if she went to prison they could choke to death for the want of something to eat. Committed.

Catharine McBride was brought in for stealing a frock. Catharine said she had just served out 6 months on Blackwell's Island, and she wouldn't be sent back again for the best glass of punch that ever was made. Her husband, when she last left the penitentiary, took her to a boarding house in Essex St., but the rascal got mad at her, pulled her hair, pinched her arm, and

kicked her out of bed. She was determined not to bear such treatment as this, and so got drunk and stole the frock out of pure spite. Committed.

Bill Doty got drunk because he had the horrors so bad he couldn't keep sober. Committed.

Patrick Ludwick was sent up by his wife, who testified that she had supported him for several years in idleness and drunkenness. Abandoning all hopes of a reformation in her husband, she bought him a suit of clothes a fortnight since and told him to go about his business, for she would not live with him any longer. Last night he came home in state of intoxication, broke into his wife's bedroom, pulled her out of bed, pulled her hair, and stamped on her. She called a watchman and sent him up. Pat exerted all his powers of eloquence in endeavoring to excite his wife's sympathy, but to no purpose. As every sensible woman ought to do who is cursed with a drunken husband, she refused to have anything to do with him hereafter—and he was sent to the penitentiary.

John Movich, of 220 Mott St., got drunk and disturbed his neighbors. Committed.

most papers had either served the business interests (the mercantile press) or been tied to political parties, which restricted editorial freedom. But with advertisers footing the bills instead, Day could take the editorial stands he believed in.

There were 11 competing newspapers in New York when Day started the *Sun*. After five years, the *Sun's* circulation was over 30,000, more than the combined circulation of all the other papers. Day had successfully launched the metropolitan newspaper as a mass medium of popular culture.

New York Herald

Others soon copied Day's innovations. In 1835 James Gordon Bennett founded the **New York Herald,** which refined and expanded the popular content of the penny press. He designed his paper to "cover the city" by sending reporters to Wall Street, churches, social events, and the courts.

Bennett's newspaper took a middle-of-the-road approach. Although it too featured crime news as an essential ingredient, it was more serious and responsible than the *Sun*. Just as important, it was more lively and entertaining than the mercantile, or Wall Street, papers, which quickly struck back. In an effort to discourage sophisticated New Yorkers from reading the *Herald*, the Wall Street press implied that Bennett's newspaper was "not suitable for ladies and gentle-men."[6] This was the first major struggle between the elite and popular press in the United States.

Many other penny-press newspapers followed Day's and Bennett's lead. One of the more significant was Horace Greeley's **New York Tribune,** which was founded in 1841. Greeley, whose exhortation to "Go West Young Man, Go West" is legendary, hired others to handle the business side of the newspaper and concentrated his efforts on editorial work. He introduced the idea of separating news and opinion and developed the editorial page as we know it today. Greeley became one of the most influential editorial writers in the 19th century. He even ran unsuccessfully for president of the United States in 1872 on the Republican ticket.

Ten years after Greeley established the *Tribune,* Henry J. Raymond founded the *New York Times.* Modeling his newspaper after the *Times* of London, Raymond concentrated on news interpretation and background reporting and developed a strong editorial policy. He personally accompanied presidential candidates so he could write campaign stories firsthand. He also hired European correspondents to cover foreign stories exclusively for the *Times.*

The first newspaper to use color was the New York Sun, *which ran this artist's sketch of the sinking of the Lexington in 1840.*

New York Tribune

New Technology.   The Industrial Revolution had a major impact on printing technology, which had been virtually unchanged since the mid-15th century. Newspapers began using the new rotary and cylinder presses, first driven by steam and later by electricity. It was now possible to print nearly 100,000 copies of a 12-page newspaper in an hour—a far cry from the early days of hand-fed presses.

The Associated Press

Soon after Samuel F. B. Morse invented the telegraph in 1844—the first glimmer of the electronic age—American newspapers started to take advantage of this new technology. By 1848, six New York newspapers had joined together to use the telegraph to pool their news-gathering resources. This first wire service was called the Associated Press of New York, later simply the Associated Press.

The debut of electronic technology affected the content of newspapers, just as television would in the second half of the 20th century. Because telegraph lines were sometimes cut and news transmissions were often interrupted for military use during the Civil War, journalists started to put a complete summary of the story in the first paragraph. All of the traditional elements—who, what, when, where, why, and how—were crowded into the lead paragraph so that the important information could be received before the transmission was interrupted. This style of news writing, called the **inverted pyramid,** is still used in a modified version today. Use of the telegraph also led to the demise of editorial comment in news stories. Because editorial opinions varied from newspaper to newspaper, a reporter writing for a number of newspapers could not come up with a slant that would fit them all. It was better to stick to the facts and let the individual newspapers editorialize as they wished.

inverted pyramid

Newspaper Syndicates

The first independent newspaper syndicate was founded in 1865 to supply feature materials to rural newspapers. Then, in 1884, Samuel S. McClure (who later published

McClure's Magazine) established the first large-scale newspaper syndicate to furnish non-news features and entertainment material to participating newspapers. McClure concentrated on women's features and the serialization of popular novels. Today's syndicated materials include comic strips, editorial cartoons, political columnists, humor material, and crossword puzzles.

THE NEW OR YELLOW JOURNALISM ERA (1865–1900)

Between 1865 and 1900, the United States was transformed into a major industrial state. According to Agee, Ault, and Emery,

> Industrialization, mechanization and urbanization brought extensive social, cultural and political changes: the rise of the city, improved transportation and communication, educational advances, political unrest and the rise of an extensive labor movement. The mass media could not fail to go through great changes along with the society they served.[7]

The 35-year period between the end of the Civil War and the turn of the century, the era of "new journalism," was a scandalous period better known as an era of "yellow journalism," or sensational reporting. It was a time when the metropolitan press took on a flamboyance that was characteristic of the new industrial age. Newspapers became a major force in disseminating the new mass culture.

During this period the population of the country doubled, the national wealth quadrupled, and manufacturing output increased sevenfold. The United States was completing its transformation from an agrarian to an industrial society. One-third of the population was urban, and by 1900, 62 percent of the labor force was engaged in nonagricultural work.

As the nation changed, so did its newspapers. Urban workers looked to the press for crusading reporting on corruption and editorial support for laws to ban the worst abuses in mines and factories. Among the many crusading journalists who led the effort to provide newspapers for the new mass audience, three stand out. Of these, two fought head to head in New York in one of the century's fiercest circulation battles: Joseph Pulitzer, who was later named by his colleagues as the leading American editor of this period, and William Randolph Hearst. The third was Edward W. Scripps.

Joseph Pulitzer

The new nation of immigrants was ready for one of its own to take a leading role in American journalism. Born in Hungary in 1847, Joseph Pulitzer came to the United States at age 17 to fight in the Civil War.

After his discharge in 1865, Pulitzer moved to St. Louis, where he studied law and worked as a newspaper reporter for a German-language newspaper. In 1878, he bought the *St. Louis Post-Dispatch* and soon turned it into the city's leading newspaper. In 1883, he left the *Post-Dispatch* in the hands of an editor to move to New York. There he bought the run-down *World,* with similar results. Within four years the *World* was New York's leading newspaper, with a record-breaking circulation of 250,000.

Although Pulitzer was not above using entertainment and sensationalism to capture readers' attention, he did not neglect the basic purpose of a newspaper. He believed in accuracy, an aggressive and crusading editorial policy, and good news judgment. One of his famous commands to his staff was "Accuracy! Accuracy!! Accuracy!!!" Another was. "Terseness! Intelligent, not stupid, condensation." Still another showed his concern for the lighter side of the news: He reminded reporters to look for both the significant news and the "original, distinctive, dramatic, romantic, thrilling, unique, curious, quaint, humorous, odd, apt to be talked about" news.[8]

Pulitzer constantly crusaded for just causes. He was particularly concerned about the plight of his fellow immigrants, who were the victims of discrimination, poverty, ignorance, and crowded slum conditions. Pulitzer believed his paper should

Despite his high journalistic ideals, Joseph Pulitzer was not above using sensationalism to gain readership.

> always fight for progress and reform, never tolerate injustice or corruption, always fight demagogues of all parties, always oppose privileged classes and public plunderers, never lack sympathy with the poor, always remain devoted to the public welfare, never be satisfied with merely printing news, always be drastically independent, never be afraid to attack wrong, whether by predatory plutocracy or predatory poverty.[9]

Despite his high ideals, Pulitzer allowed himself to be pulled into one of American journalism's most degrading circulation wars. His opponent was William Randolph Hearst, who had become a successful publisher by using some of Pulitzer's techniques of entertainment and sensationalism.

William Randolph Hearst

In marked contrast to Pulitzer, William Randolph Hearst was born into a wealthy San Francisco family. As part of his privileged upbringing, Hearst was sent to Harvard for an education. While there he served as business manager of Harvard's *Lampoon* and became familiar with Pulitzer's style of journalism by working briefly for Pulitzer's *World*. About this time Hearst's father, George, purchased the *San Francisco Examiner* so that he could manipulate the California legislature into appointing him to the U.S. Senate. (U.S. senators were appointed by state legislators until the adoption of the Seventeenth Amendment in 1913.)

When Hearst returned to San Francisco in 1887, he persuaded his father (now a senator) to turn the *Examiner* over to him rather than sell it. Then, employing some of the techniques he had learned from Pulitzer's *World,* he turned the *Examiner* into a mass-circulation newspaper that found a niche in San Francisco's popular culture.

Hearst, like Pulitzer, attempted to protect the public from abuses by the rich and powerful and from political corruption. He even crusaded against his father's friend Senator Leland Stanford, the millionaire owner of the Southern Pacific Railroad. Hearst opposed Stanford's efforts to get government subsidies for the railroads and made that crusade a major topic of his paper. He also fought corruption in San Francisco politics.

In 1895 Hearst, seeking new worlds to conquer, moved to New York. There he bought the *New York Journal* to compete head-to-head with

The era of "yellow journalism" involved publisher William Randolph Hearst. His career was fictionalized in the movie Citizen Kane.

Pulitzer's *World*, which at the time had the largest circulation of any paper in the country. Although Hearst had Pulitzer's crusading zeal and his flair for sensationalism, he did not share his rival's concern for accuracy and fairness. As one book has pointed out, "Hearst did not blink at coloring, stealing, or even faking the news; he did not hesitate to appeal to jingoism and a variety of other cheap emotions; and the tone of discourse in his papers often fell to mere abuse."[10]

@   **Practicing Media Literacy**

Why do you think we do not see such newspaper battles in the 21st century?

---

yellow journalism

In the circulation war, which reached a peak in 1898, both publishers resorted to journalistic excesses, including bold, misleading headlines, intensive coverage of crime, sex, and violence, sensationalistic photojournalism, and bizarre promotional stunts. Hearst was even accused of provoking the Spanish-American War through his sensational coverage of Spain's activities in Cuba.

Eventually people started calling these tactics **"yellow journalism."** The term came from "The Yellow Kid" comic strip, which was drawn for the *World* by Richard Outcault, one of the most popular comic strip cartoonists of the time. (Pulitzer had introduced color comic strips to American newspapers in 1894.)

The strip featured a bald, toothless, grinning boy dressed in a yellow sacklike garment. Because of the strip's popularity, Hearst offered Outcault a tremendous salary increase to quit the *World* and draw for the *Journal*, an offer Outcault couldn't refuse. But Pulitzer, claiming he had sole rights to the comic strip, angrily hired another cartoonist to draw it. For awhile New York had two "Yellow Kids."

Although the two newspapers together sometimes sold more than a million copies a day during the circulation war, Pulitzer eventually lost his appetite for the competition and withdrew from the contest, leaving the field of yellow journalism to Hearst and a few of his imitators.

Hearst went on to build a major publishing empire consisting of a nationwide chain of newspapers, four feature syndicates (which merged in 1931 to form the King Feature Syndicate), a wire service (International News Service, which he founded in 1909 when his papers were denied membership in the Associated Press), and numerous magazines, including *Cosmopolitan*, *Good Housekeeping*, and *Harper's Bazaar*.

One of Hearst's more significant contributions to the field of journalism was the introduction of women reporters into the newsrooms, mostly human-interest feature writers who became known as **"sob sisters."** He also hired promotion managers to increase readership and led the way in proving the importance of strong circulation departments.

sob sisters

Edward Wyllis Scripps

The third crusader during this flamboyant period of American journalism was Edward Wyllis Scripps (1854–1926). Scripps concentrated his efforts in the nation's smaller cities, building a chain of newspapers with headquarters at the *Cleveland Press* in Ohio.

Like Pulitzer and Hearst, Scripps used his papers to champion the people's rights, but he never stooped to sensationalistic abuses. Scripps's goal was to improve the position of the new industrialized masses through better education, labor union organization, collective bargaining, and a reasonable redistribution of wealth. In this way, he reasoned, the ideal of a peaceful and productive society could be realized.

Scripps started many newspapers by sending an editor and business manager into a community with $25,000 and instructions to establish a newspaper. If they succeeded,

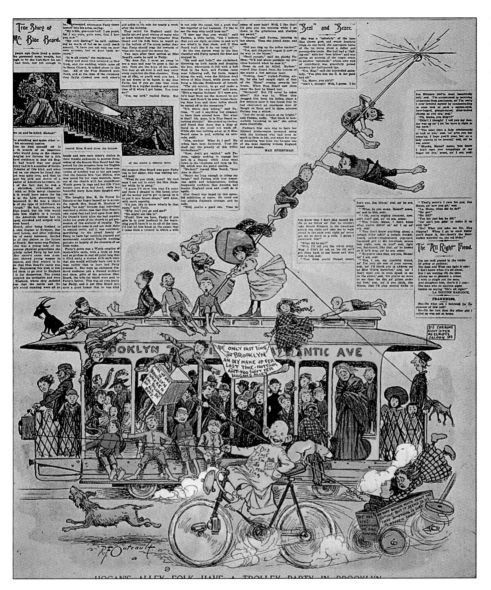

"The Yellow Kid," the cartoon character seen here on a bicycle, was a part of the circulation battle known as "yellow journalism." Note the colorful newspaper layout designed to attract readers.

they received 49 percent of the stock; if they ran out of money, they were replaced. If the paper did not show a profit within 10 years, it was shut down. In addition to his chain of 30 newspapers, Scripps founded the Newspaper Enterprise Association (NEA) syndicate in 1902 and the United Press wire service in 1907.

THE 20TH-CENTURY PRESS (1900–PRESENT)

By the late 1890s, many readers were looking for something better than what Hearst, Pulitzer, and others like them had to offer, and yellow journalism began to wane. Between 1900 and 1910, more than 2,600 newspapers were published in the United States, more than at any time before—or since.

Objectivity

What was lacking in New York and many other cities was a newspaper that was objective in its coverage of the news. Seeing an opportunity to improve the state of journalism in New York, Adolph **Ochs** purchased the near-bankrupt *New York Times* in 1896 and set out to make it the "newspaper of record." He introduced the slogan that still appears on the paper's front page today: "All the news that's fit to print."

Ochs guided the *Times* for 40 years and turned it into a paper that was respected worldwide for its comprehensive, accurate, and balanced news coverage. As Ochs hoped, the *Times* has become the newspaper of record, and today it can be found indexed in most scholarly libraries. The standards set by the *New York Times* became respected by readers and journalists alike, and soon other papers followed its lead.

> **@   Practicing Media Literacy**
>
> Do you feel that most newspapers in the United States today are "objective"?

Social Responsibility

The second trend at work at the beginning of the 20th century was an emphasis on the social responsibility of newspapers and journalists (see Chapter 5). Schools and departments of journalism were established in colleges and universities, and attempts were made to teach high standards. The Graduate School of Journalism, established at Columbia University in 1912 by a legacy from Joseph Pulitzer, took the lead in this field. (The school still administers the most prestigious awards in newspaper journalism, the Pulitzer Prizes.) Various professional newspaper organizations drew up codes of ethics during this period.

Many observers of the American press were convinced that the libertarian theory of the press, which forbade government interference with it, would not work if the mass media were not socially responsible. Some of the major newspapers in the country accepted this view and tried to make their publications more socially responsive by striving for fairness in news coverage and downplaying sensationalism.

Jazz Journalism

Although newspaper content was more responsible and objective during this period, sensationalism was not dead. Hearst publications continued to use bold headlines, sensationalized photography, and stunts to sell papers. Indeed, another wave of sensationalism spread during the Roaring '20s. This was called *jazz journalism*, and it reflected the jazz age of the time.

Helping to usher in this period of jazz journalism was Joseph Medill Patterson, copublisher of the *Chicago Tribune*. Patterson introduced a tabloid newspaper (half the size of a regular newspaper and similar in size to today's *National Enquirer*) to New York City. Patterson's *New York Illustrated Daily News* featured large photographs (sometimes one covered the entire front page), crime, violence, and sex stories, and sensational headlines to sell papers at newsstands. There was still a huge market for this type of journalism, and the *New York Daily News* (*Illustrated* was later dropped) soon became the nation's largest-selling daily newspaper, with a circulation that exceeded 2 million copies for many years. It finally surrendered first place in 1980 to the *Wall Street Journal* (a position the *Wall Street Journal* held until the last few months of 1999, when the Audit Bureau of Circulation announced that *USA Today* had inched ahead in circulation to become the nation's largest daily newspaper).

Soon Hearst and others started bringing out tabloid newspapers in New York City. It is interesting to note that the largest-selling weekly newspaper in the United States is also a sensational tabloid—the **National Enquirer** (natonalenquirer.com), which sells 4 million copies per week (see Box 7.2).

National Enquirer

THE EPS CYCLE

As our popular culture continues to fragment, American newspapers have remained in the popular stage of the EPS cycle longer than other media. Although newspapers do specialize in the sense that they serve a specific community or region, they generally attempt to appeal to almost everyone in that area.

However, in recent years there has been a major increase in newspapers that do cater to specialized audiences, particularly ethnic groups. For example, by the end of the 20th century it was estimated that there were some 60 publications in this country for Vietnamese readers and at least 20 aimed specifically at Russian immigrants. In Westminster, California, newspapers are printed in Vietnamese, Spanish, Cambodian, Laotian, and Farsi. Elsewhere in California newspapers can be found in Swahili, Korean, Armenian, Russian, German, and Italian. This trend has been spreading nationwide.

African-American Press

The first African-American newspaper, *Freedom's Journal*, was founded in 1827 by John B. Russwurm and the Reverend Samuel Cornish. The most important African-American pre–Civil War newspaper was Frederick Douglass's weekly, *North Star*. By the mid-1970s there were more than 325 African-American newspapers in the United States, with a total circulation of over 7 million (see Box 7.3).

Latino Press

The first Spanish-language newspaper in the United States was *El Misisipi*, started in New Orleans in 1808. More than 50 Spanish-language newspapers are currently published in the United States. Latinos represent the fastest-growing minority group in this country, including the Chicano or Mexican-American population of the Southwest and the Puerto Rican and Cuban concentrations on the East Coast. Some of the major newspapers catering to this specialized group include *El Diario-La Prensa* and *El Noticias del Mundo* of New York, *El Herald* and *Diario de las Americas* of Miami, *La Opinion* of Los Angeles, *El Mañana Daily News* of Chicago, and the *Laredo Times* of Texas.

Spanish language newspapers are one of the many specialized publications targeting the nation's various ethnic groups.

Native American Press

The first newspaper to be published by an American Indian nation was the

Cherokee Phoenix, started in northern Georgia in 1828. Since Native Americans had a spoken rather than a written language, a Cherokee named Sequoiah developed an 80-character alphabet for the Cherokee nation so they could communicate via the newspaper. The purpose of the newspaper was to use the "white man's" tools to try to bring logic and reason to the national leaders, including U.S. president Andrew Jackson, who were determined to force the Cherokees off their lands in northern Georgia and relocate them in Oklahoma. The newspaper failed in its endeavor, and the entire nation of civilized Indians was rounded up and marched on the infamous Trail of Tears to Oklahoma. Some 4,000 Cherokees, one-fourth of the entire nation, died in the endeavor. The Cherokees now publish a newspaper in Oklahoma, as do many other Native American tribes that have been relocated on reservation land. Some 325 Native American newspapers in 34 states are listed by the American Indian Press Association.

Alternative Press

Another type of newspaper specialization flourished in the 1960s to serve the alienated youth and political radicals of the period. Many people wanted an alternative source of news and information, and the underground press was born.

Although thousands of underground newspapers were established, few were successful. The primary problem was selective exposure: The only people who read the newspapers were those who already agreed with their radical points of view (see Chapter 1).

Some of the better-known underground newspapers during this period were the *Village Voice* and the *East Village Other* in New York, the *Los Angeles Free Press*, Chicago's *Seed*, Boston's *Avatar* and *Phoenix*, the *Berkeley Barb*, and San Francisco's *Rolling Stone*. The last publication is now an "establishment" rock music magazine.

NEWSPAPERS AS BUSINESSES

Although newspapers perform a crucial public service by keeping our society informed, we cannot forget that newspapers, like all mass media, are businesses that have to make a profit. If they don't, they die. Newspapers, in fact, generate the largest advertising revenue of all mass media: more than $48 billion estimated for 1996.[11]

The price of a newspaper does not begin to pay for the cost of producing it; the major source of newspaper revenue, 76 percent, is advertising. Of that figure, 52 percent is earned from retail advertising, 35 percent from classified, and 13 percent from national ads. The more circulation a newspaper has, the more it can charge for its advertising. Fatter newspapers do not necessarily have more news. They do, however, carry more advertising and are usually more financially successful.

Decline of Competition

The lack of competition among newspapers in recent years has caused some major changes in newspapers and their effectiveness. For example, when Americans started moving out of the cities to the suburbs in the mid-20th century, the number of newspapers serving many metropolitan areas steadily declined. Cities that once boasted many newspapers now had only one. Lack of competition within a city is always a cause for concern, since it can result in complacency and newspapers shirking their responsibility to keep their communities well informed.

Most Americans still have their newspapers delivered to their homes each day. A few buy them from newsstands scattered around town. But you'd be surprised at how many people think they're getting the latest news when they pick up a national newspaper strategically marketed at supermarket checkout counters. Here grocery shoppers are enticed with sensational headlines and teasers for unbelievable stories that supposedly will be found on the inside pages. (Admit it, *you* read those headlines as you stand in the checkout line, even if you *don't* actually purchase the publication. Right?)

The leader of these supermarket journals also happens to be the largest-circulating newspaper in the United States: the *National Enquirer*. This popular publication's success can be traced back to 1952, when Generoso (Gene) Pope purchased the *New York Enquirer*. He immediately began filling the newspaper with stories about crime, sex, and violence (topics that the *Enquirer* now downplays).

In 1958, Pope expanded it into a national publication and began selling it in supermarkets. He toned down the sex and violence to appeal to a broader audience and began focusing on stories about celebrity gossip, government waste, haunted houses, ghosts, psychic predictions, honest people who find and return money, life-threatening accidents, successful people who never went to college, heroic activities, overweight people who learned how to drop the pounds, ideas on saving money, and medical advice. In short, Pope had learned how to market our popular cultural interests through news columns.

The *National Enquirer* has been followed into the supermarket journalism field by such publications as the *Globe,* the *Sun,* and the *Weekly World News* (*WWN*). This last publication caters to the bizarre and ridiculous and doesn't even seem to blush when it runs such headlines as "UNBORN BABY HAS CANCER; ALIEN BACKS CLINTON; ELVIS IS ALIVE; BAT CHILD ESCAPES; I HAD BIGFOOT'S BABY"; and "MAN FROZEN IN 1936 REVIVED!"

Compared to *WWN*, the *National Enquirer* might be considered a credible newspaper. However, through the years it has been sued by numerous celebrities and has reached out-of-court settlements with many of

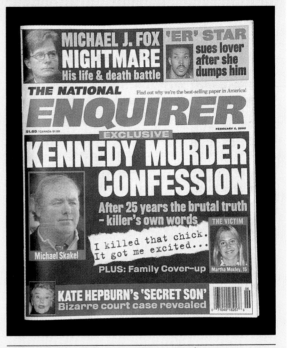

Bold tabloid headlines entice shoppers in the grocery checkout lines.

them. Lawsuits against the *Enquirer* have been filed by Carol Burnett, Cher, Johnny Carson, Frank Sinatra, Tom Selleck, Richard Pryor, and Shirley Jones, to name a few.

Despite large settlements to the plaintiffs, the *National Enquirer*'s flamboyant style has not changed. And sometimes it pays off. In 1996, a judge in Los Angeles ruled that Elizabeth Taylor and her ex-husband Larry Fortensky had to pay the *Enquirer* $432,600 to cover the legal costs resulting from their unsuccessful lawsuit against the tabloid. A spokesperson for the *Enquirer* thanked Taylor and Fortensky for their contribution, but added that the money would be turned over to the American Heart Association, the Arthritis Foundation, and Haven House, a shelter for battered women.

The *National Enquirer* does not represent anything new in American journalism. What it does represent is a continuation of the style of journalism that has

continued

existed since newspapers first began catering to the popular culture in this country in the early 19th century. The publications of Benjamin Day and James Gordon Bennett in the early days of the penny press, William Randolph Hearst and Joseph Pulitzer in the yellow journalism period, and the tabloids of New York in the jazz journalism age of the 1920s were not too much different in content from the *National Enquirer*. And they too were popular with the masses. Today this style of journalism is still the most popular form in the United Kingdom.

National Enquirer reporters are among the highest paid in the nation, and the paper covers major news events with teams of journalists and photographers. The *Enquirer* often rushes journalists to the scene of news events to sign up eyewitnesses to "exclusive stories." Because it has often been the first with information on major but controversial news stories, many other news media wait until something has been published in the *Enquirer* to justify reporting the same information. This was the case in a nationally prominent rape trial in Florida involving a member of the Kennedy family. The media had carefully protected the identity of the victim, even using a blue dot to cover her face during the televised court proceedings—until the *Enquirer* printed her name. The *NBC Evening News with Tom Brokaw* then began using her name as well, justifying its action by saying that the *Enquirer* had made the information public knowledge. The *New York Times* followed, citing the use of her name by NBC News . . . all because the *Enquirer* did it first.

At the conclusion of the O. J. Simpson murder trial in 1995, many news reporters across the nation begrudgingly conceded that the *Enquirer* had probably covered the story better than anyone else and had, in fact, broken more stories before the regular news media outlets. However, much of that credibility was lost in the final years of the 1990s as the *Enquirer*, as well as the other supermarket tabloids, continued to print weekly stories accusing numerous people of being responsible for the death of JonBenet Ramsey of Colorado. As the 21st century began, no one had yet been charged with the crime.

The *Enquirer* also found itself falling behind in reporting the latest rumors surrounding the White House escapades of president Bill Clinton and intern Monica Lewinsky. Just as the printed press had found during the years of the emergence of both radio and television, the people were turning to the media, which were reporting the news faster. In this case, the story was broken on the Internet by gossip writer Matt Drudge (drudge report.com), who continued to print the scandalous development, whether true or not, all the way through the Senate impeachment hearings and beyond.

Although highly criticized for its approach and style, the *National Enquirer* seems to be giving many people what they want: sensational stories about which, as its advertising has promoted, "enquiring minds want to know."

The *Los Angeles Herald Examiner* ended 118 years of service to the community by closing in 1989. Its major competitor, the *Los Angeles Times* (latimes.com), editorialized that its competitor would not be easily replaced and that its absence would "place an even greater responsibility on the *Times* to be fair, accurate and complete in its reporting and to be attentive to the views and concerns of all segments of this increasingly diverse community."[12]

@ **Practicing Media Literacy**

How many newspapers are published in your hometown? If there is a lack of competition, do you think this affects the way the one paper reports the news?

In 1995, the *Houston Post* folded, leaving the market to its longtime rival, the *Houston Chronicle*. That same year, the *Milwaukee Sentinel* and the *Milwaukee Journal* merged, leaving the market as a one-newspaper town and eliminating some 500 jobs. By the end of that year, the *Baltimore Evening Sun*, the *Greenville* (South Carolina) *Piedmont*, and the *Norfolk* (Virginia) *Ledger-Star* had ceased to exist, leaving some 13,000 newspaper employees in those cities without jobs.

For those newspapers remaining in operation at the end of the 20th century, there was an increase in layoffs of personnel. In Philadelphia, for example, Knight-Ridder Publications

Box 7.3
MEDIA WATCH
The African-American Press—One of the First Specialized Publications—and Its Early Leaders

As mentioned in this chapter, the first African-American newspaper, *Freedom's Journal*, was established March 26, 1827, to provide a voice for the black population. Wrote co-publishers Samuel Cornish and John Russwurm, "No longer shall others speak for us." These were not newspapermen. Cornish was a 32-year-old preacher, while the 28-year-old Russwurm was one of the first black graduates of an American university.

Although the paper lasted only two years, it paved the way for some 24 other African-American newspapers that began publication prior to the Civil War. One of the most influential of those was the *North Star*, which abolitionist Fredrick Douglass started December 3, 1847.

After the Civil War, African-American slaves who had not been allowed to learn how to read now discovered the power of the written word through newspapers. As a result, papers targeting this specialized audience began springing up in small towns across the nation. Such newspapers helped to pull the African-American community together nationwide after the end of slavery and during reconstruction.

Between the end of the Civil War and the start of the 20th century, more than 500 African-American newspapers began publishing in this country. Newspapers in the South, however, had difficulties during those post-war years as many of them were targeted for violence or were forced to close.

Ida B. Wells reported on the lynch-mob tactics and activities in the South, which resulted in the presses at her *Memphis Free Speech* being destroyed by an angry white mob in 1892. The threats against her life forced Wells to remain in New York for some 30 years, working for an African-American newspaper there.

Robert S. Abbott was trained as a printer in Georgia but couldn't find such work in Chicago because of discrimination. Although he then went on to get a law degree, racial prejudice forced him to leave that profession, and he returned to journalism by establishing the *Chicago Defender* on March 4, 1905.

Abbott created controversy when he began distributing his Northern newspaper in the South where he found an avid readership because his paper said

Charlotta Bass (UPI/Bettman)

things that Southern black newspapers couldn't for fear of violence and death. Abbott's presses were safe in Chicago.

The paper soon outsold every African-American newspaper in the nation, with each edition passing through several readers before being discarded. The *Chicago Defender* was also instrumental in the African-American migration to the North, as Abbott told of what was going on in the rest of the nation. He even printed one-way train schedules to Chicago.

When many Southern towns began banning the sale of the *Defender*, Abbott received help from those blacks who could travel safely anywhere in the nation—employees of the railroads. They took bundles of the *Defender* with them and threw them off the trains as they neared various Southern cities. The paper couldn't be stopped; Abbott became a millionaire.

In 1912 Charlotta Bass began her newspaper career at age 36 as a papergirl, selling and collecting subscriptions for an African-American newspaper in Los Angeles. She was soon promoted to an assistant to the publisher and was given a salary of $5 an hour. Two years later, while the newspaper was on the auction block, Bass's neighbor purchased the paper for $50 and turned it over to her to run. After changing the name of the paper from the *Advocate* to the *California Eagle*, Bass continued her long and distinguished 40-year journalism career as an African-American newspaper publisher.

continued

In 1914, she attempted to stop D. W. Griffith's making of *The Birth of a Nation* on the grounds that it glorified the Ku Klux Klan (see Chapter 9). During World War I, she fought for equal voting rights for African-Americans. By 1938, the *Eagle* had expanded to radio by taking its messages to the airwaves. On the eve of World War II, Bass crusaded against restrictive housing laws, known as the Jim Crow laws.

In 1951, at age 77, she sold her newspaper to pursue new challenges. She had already served as the first African-American on the Los Angeles County grand jury and had lost her first political campaign, a city council race. The following year she became the first African-American woman candidate for vice president of the United States on the Progressive Party ticket headed by San Francisco attorney Vincent Hallinan.

In 1964, when she was 90 years old, the *California Eagle* folded following the appointment of the new owner to a judgeship. Bass died in 1969 at age 95.

announced plans to cut some 250 positions at its two newspapers, the *Inquirer* and the *Daily News*. A tradition that had existed since its founding in 1764 was broken when the *Hartford Courant* announced that it was letting some employees go. Citing economic pressure from its parent company, Times Mirror, the *Courant* asked almost 200 staff members to accept voluntary buyouts.

Due to increased competition from television in recent years, many evening newspapers have been changing to morning publications, which tend to have higher circulations. Although daily newspaper circulations are larger, weekly newspapers far outnumber dailies: 7,654 weeklies and 1,537 dailies was the total in 1996,[13] a two-year increase of some 248 weeklies, while the daily publications had declined by 33 during the same period.

@   Practicing Media Literacy

Is the newspaper in your hometown a daily or a weekly? Is it a morning or afternoon edition?

Among the more recent changes, the *Seattle Times*, an afternoon newspaper that remained dominant while others struggled or failed, finally announced in 1999 that it would become a morning publication and go head-to-head with the Hearst Corporation's *Seattle Post-Intelligencer*. Hearst was also involved in a major change in the San Francisco newspaper scene when the company, owner of the afternoon *San Francisco Examiner* where William Randolph Hearst launched his empire some 100 years earlier, agreed to purchase the rival morning *San Francisco Chronicle* (sfgate.com) for an estimated $660 million. The two papers had been sharing certain facilities and printing and distribution costs while maintaining separate editorial staffs for many years under a joint operating agreement. It appeared that the sale would bring about the end of afternoon newspapers in San Francisco, where the *Chronicle* has dominated in the circulation battles for many years.

Another afternoon newspaper ended its 130 years of publication in 1999 when the *Indianapolis News*, once known as "The Great Hoosier Daily," ceased publication due to declining circulation. Between 1980 and 2000, the number of afternoon newspapers declined from 1,400 to fewer than 800—with most of the remaining afternoon papers located in small communities.

tabloids

Even the supermarket **tabloids** are not competing with each other as much as they have in years past. Near the end of 1999, American Media—the company that owns the *National Enquirer* and the *Star* tabloids—announced that it was acquiring Globe Communications Corporation, publisher of *The Globe* tabloid, for $105 million. The deal joins *The Globe*, a 40-year-old weekly tabloid and some 30 other titles owned by Globe Communications with American Media's *National Enquirer, Star, Weekly World*

News, and *Country Weekly*—assuring that almost half of the nation's supermarket tabloids are controlled by one corporation.

In the 1990s, newspapers suffered from very slow growth. Daily and Sunday circulations were stagnant for a good portion of the decade. Only weekly circulations were rising, and some of that circulation gain came from daily newspapers converting to weeklies. Some large national and metropolitan newspapers, such as the *Wall Street Journal* (wsj.com), the *Chicago Sun-Times* (suntimes.com), and the *Los Angeles Times*, were reporting decreases in circulation. By 1992 the *New York Times* had overtaken the *Los Angeles Times* as the largest metropolitan paper (see Table 7.1). The debt-ridden *New York Post* (nypostonline.com) briefly suspended publication in 1993. In 2000, the *Los Angeles Times* was sold to the *Chicago Tribune* organization.

> **@ Practicing Media Literacy**
> Would you read a newspaper if it were delivered to you in the afternoon or do you prefer to read the news in the morning before your day gets started?

TABLE 7.1

Top 25 Newspapers by Circulation (1997)

Rank is based on Monday–Friday circulation, except where noted. When papers report separate circulations for some weekdays, the number used is the weighted average.

Rank	Newspaper	Circulation	Sunday circulation
1	*Wall Street Journal*	1,774,880	None
2	*USA Today**	1,629,665	2,049,708
3	*New York Times*	1,074,741	1,658,718
4	*Los Angeles Times*	1,050,176	1,361,748
5	*Washington Post*	775,894	1,102,329
6	*New York Daily News*	721,256	807,788
7	*Chicago Tribune*	653,554	1,023,736
8	*Newsday*	568,914	644,988
9	*Houston Chronicle***	549,101	748,036
10	*Dallas Morning News****	506,202	789,004
11	*Chicago Sun Times*	484,379	423,685
12	*San Francisco Chronicle*	484,218	625,106
13	*Boston Globe*	476,966	758,843
14	*Phoenix Republic*	437,118	560,031
15	*New York Post*	436,226	326,087
16	*Philadelphia Inquirer*	428,233	878,660
17	*Newark (NJ) Star-Ledger*	406,010	606,007
18	*Detroit Free Press*	384,624	829,178
19	*Cleveland Plain Dealer***	383,586	508,787
20	*San Diego Union-Tribune***	375,598	454,085
21	*Minneapolis Star Tribune*	362,811	668,466
22	*Orange Co. (Calif.) Register***	356,520	415,638
23	*Portland Oregonian*	342,454	437,508
24	*Miami Herald***	338,643	463,702
25	*Denver Post*	337,372	471,180

*USA Today's Friday circulation is listed in Sunday column.
**Rank based on Monday–Saturday circulation.
***Figures adjusted by *Advertising Age* to indicate weekday circulation.
Source: Audit Bureau of Circulations, listed online by *Advertising Age*. Figures current through Sept. 1997.

One of the largest newspaper chains in the U.S. is Gannett, which owns papers in many cities across the country, as well as USA Today, which is circulated worldwide.

As the 20th century was drawing to a close, there was a lot of fluctuation in circulation figures. For example, in May of 1997, circulation figures showed that 6 of the nation's 10 largest newspapers were in decline. Only *USA Today*, the *Los Angeles Times*, *Newsday* (newsday.com), and the *San Francisco Chronicle* posted circulation gains.[14] But by November of that same year, the Audit Bureau of Circulation showed an increase at 9 of the nation's top 15 newspapers, partially attributable to a booming economy.[15] By the end of the 20th century, overall daily newspaper circulation was reported to have declined by .5 percent, and Sunday newspaper circulation had fallen by a full 1 percent. While the larger newspapers were still reporting slight gains in circulation, the smaller papers continued to struggle with declines. [16]

However, not all is gloom and doom in the newspaper business. As the 20th century was drawing to a close, it was estimated that newspapers were close to a $50 billion industry, up from $12 billion only 20 years earlier. But the rise of other outlets for news and advertising, from the Internet to all-news cable channels, has drastically altered the way one of this nation's oldest mass-communication media operates. The only reports of profit growth have been coming from the many newspaper *chains* that have been forming in recent years.

Chain Ownership

As with the other print media, newspaper ownership is being increasingly monopolized by a few media conglomerates, called *chains*. The four largest newspaper chains in the United States are Gannett, Knight-Ridder, Newhouse, and Times Mirror. By the mid-1990s, well over 130 companies owned two or more newspapers, and those chains controlled more than 75 percent of the daily newspapers and almost 80 percent of the daily circulation.

The trend of the 1990s has been for one group to own all of the newspapers in a particular region so that reporters and photographers can be shared. For example Liberty Group Publishing, based in Illinois, owns more than 300 newspapers—all acquired between 1997 and 1999. Between Minnesota and Louisiana, Liberty owns 225 community dailies, weeklies, and shopper newspapers. Investor-backed newspaper companies such as Liberty have been buying clusters of daily and weekly newspapers so that they could stake a claim for dominance in regional advertising buys. According to Owen Van Essen, president of the newspaper brokering firm of Dirks, Van Essen and Associates, we will soon be seeing "statewide clusters, with one company owning half the newspapers in a given state." To take it one step further, Dirks and Van Essen also forecasts that at the rate transactions were taking place at the start of the 21st century, half of the daily newspaper circulation in the United States will be a part of a cluster by 2015.[17]

One of the largest newspaper chains in the United States was formed in 1997 when California's McClatchy newspaper chain purchased the parent company of the *Minneapolis Star Tribune* for $1.4 billion. The acquisition made McClatchy the eighth-largest newspaper chain with greater geographic diversity.

The advantage of chain ownership is that a chain's local newspapers enjoy strong financial backing. The disadvantage is that as control of the nation's newspapers falls into fewer and fewer hands, local community interests may be subordinated to corporate interests. Where newspapers once acted as the voice of their communities, they now often serve as the mouthpiece of the corporations that own them. Some chains have been known to require that their corporate philosophy be reflected on news and editorial pages.

> **@ Practicing Media Literacy**
> What do you consider to be the biggest problem resulting from the concentration of control over newspapers into the hands of fewer owners?

And who controls the chain? Although most chains are media companies, there is nothing to stop a large oil company, for example, from buying newspapers. If this happened, would the newspapers remain impartial in reporting news about the oil business and the need for alternative sources of energy?

However, there are some who feel that large chains can have a favorable impact on the news. Robert Samuelson of the *Washington Post* Writers Group wrote in 1999: "For years, journalists and academics have criticized 'greedy media monopolies' for 'short-changing the news' to fatten profits. These attacks were exactly backward. As long as newspapers and broadcasters were highly profitable—and enjoyed market power and captive audiences—they provided a fair amount of space and freedom for news."[18]

There are still those who worry that foreign investors may buy up American newspapers. What is there to prevent political leaders of a wealthy country with a controlled press from buying a major interest in Gannett, for example? Would these newspapers—many of them the only paper in their communities—be unbiased in their coverage of the controlling country? This concern became a reality in the summer of 1986, when a Mexican newspaper magnate with reported close ties to the Mexican government purchased America's second-largest news service, United Press International (UPI). It occurred again in 1993, when UPI was sold to a Saudi Arabian media company.

Libel Suits

The recent rash of libel suits resulting in huge judgments against media companies (see Chapter 4) has created a chilling effect on many newspapers. Some newspapers have cut back on their investigative reporting to minimize their risk of being sued.[19] This trend could have serious implications for a democracy based on the premise that only a well-informed citizenry can determine its political destiny.

But the bottom line cannot become the only consideration in deciding what to publish. After all, as Tom Goldstein reminds us in his book *The News at Any Cost*, the press is not merely a business; newspapers were given constitutional protection "because the founding fathers felt a vigorous and independent press was essential to let people know what government was doing."[20] This conflict in roles was discussed further in Chapter 4.

Soft News

Another way newspapers have responded to the challenge of television is to expand the amount of space devoted to *soft* news, or *fluff* journalism. Designed to entertain readers, it includes such varied material as background stories that accompany news events; features on health and fitness, money management, and diet; and comics, crossword puzzles, and columns, such as "Dear Abby." Soft news is in contrast to **hard news:** straight, factual reports on current events.

hard news
_____

Efforts to Improve

In 1999, the Newspaper Association of America decided to do something to attract new readers and to stop current readers from switching to other sources for their news and information. The result was an $11.5 million marketing and advertising campaign known as Readership Initiative, designed to research what attracts or repels readers and to create a campaign for newspapers nationwide to bring readers back. But one of the main problems to overcome is public perception of the print media.

> **@   Practicing Media Literacy**
> Do you read the newspaper for the hard news or the features?

Future Challenges

The newspaper industry faces many changes in this decade. Experts predict that to survive, newspapers will have to enter more deeply the specialization stage of the EPS cycle. Forcing this specialization are major demographic changes in our culture: larger ethnic populations, a shift of the baby boomers into middle age, changing roles of women in our culture, increased time pressures on readers, a decline in reading ability among young people, and increasing elderly populations.

Meanwhile, the Newspaper Association of America asked the Federal Communications Commission to suspend the rule prohibiting ownership of a broadcast station and a daily newspaper in the same city. The action came in 1999 after the FCC relaxed ownership rules for broadcasters, allowing them to own more than one TV station in the same market and to own both radio and television stations in the same city. In its petition to the commission, the newspaper group asked for the rule suspension because the relaxation of the broadcast rules had put newspaper owners at a disadvantage.

> **@   Practicing Media Literacy**
> Are newspaper ads your main source for information about sales, new products, or where to buy certain items? If not, what is your main source?

Newspapers also face greater competition for advertising revenue from e-commerce on the Internet, direct mail, telemarketing, and home-shopping TV channels. Metropolitan newspapers are finding increased competition for readers coming from suburban daily and weekly newspapers and city magazines.

Environmental concerns will also play a role in future newspaper changes. Many states require newspapers to use recycled newsprint. Other environmental regulations controlling air pollution emissions from inks, solvents, and other newspaper products are in place. These tighter environmental regulations are forcing the industry into new, less polluting technologies, such as flexographic printing, a process that uses water-based ink and eliminates the need for traditional toxic ink and air-polluting cleaning solvents.

NEW TECHNOLOGY AND NEWSPAPERS

The newspaper as we know it will be changed by the electronic technological revolution that is under way. Predictions are that in the not-too-distant future we will be

able to get up, turn on the coffeemaker, and then turn on your computerized newspaper and have an electronic voice read the news to us as we prepare for the day ahead. Some people are already reading their newspapers on the Internet, and many journalists are using online computer services to research their stories.

Computers

The first electronic technology to affect the newspaper business was computers. Computers started making inroads in the newspaper industry in the 1960s as a tool to speed up and reduce the costs of typesetting. Although this made newspaper publishing much more profitable, it also led to the demise of one of the oldest unions in the United States, the International Typographical Union.

By the 1980s newspaper reporters and editors used computers to retrieve information, write and edit stories, and design pages. Computers were also being used to program the sorting equipment that sent specialized sections of newspapers to particular geographical areas. (Large metropolitan newspapers sell space at reduced rates to advertisers who want to run their ads in copies sold in a specific region.) Newspapers also computerized their accounting and record-keeping procedures.

Most major newspapers were using laser printers hooked up to inexpensive personal computers to produce graphics by the mid-1980s. This inexpensive equipment can also be used for typesetting. Small businesses and printing operations use computerized desktop publishing systems in place of more costly typesetting equipment.

specialization

Desktop publishing systems may make it possible for newspapers to enter the stage of **specialization** by allowing individuals with little capital, rather than large companies or chains, to start up small newspapers aimed at a selective market or interest. Computers and laser printers that will not only typeset but perform full pagination (display the layout and design of the entire newspaper page on screen) can be purchased for less than $2,500. This may bring back the era of small, individual voices transmitting specialized or regional culture.

Many newspapers have joined the computer age by establishing their own websites for the dissemination of news and information. In late 1999, the *Los Angeles Times* announced its all-new website (latimes.com), which offered more breaking news headlines, updated every two minutes, 24 hours a day. The site also had a split-screen display to make navigation easier, and its improved search feature provided easier access to the newspaper's more than 50,000 pages of information and news. Similar websites to make accessing news easier for Internet users were being established by newspapers across the nation. Now newspapers are not just competing with other media outlets in their own markets; they're competing with newspapers from around the world for the attention of the computer user. They're also competing with web-only news sites such as the Drudge Report, which provides access to other news sources including the Associated Press, TV news sites on the web, and search sites such as Yahoo and InfoSeek.

ONA

As a result, online journalists developed an organization in 1999 to help develop journalistic standards for the online world. The organization, the Online News Association (**ONA**), was styled after the long-established American Association of Newspaper Editors. ONA was also concerned about establishing online advertising guidelines.

For example, the rise of online classifieds is threatening one of the biggest revenue sources for newspapers. For the largest circulation papers, classified ads account for some 43 percent of the advertising revenues and more than one-third of a paper's total income. But media analysts are predicting a decline in revenue and profitability from the traditional newspaper classifieds due to online classifieds and auction sites, such as eBay.

Satellite Signals

The newspaper industry is currently taking advantage of satellite technology to distribute information in printed form. Satellites transmit wire stories for both the Associated Press and United Press International, and Gannett's national newspaper, *USA Today,* is made possible by satellite technology. In addition to national newspapers printed in regions around the country, Gannett publishes an international edition of *USA Today* by beaming its satellite signal to a printing plant in Switzerland.

SUMMARY

The history of American newspapers has paralleled the history of our culture. As our society has changed, so have its newspapers. Early colonial newspapers were designed for the elite—those who were interested in political and business information. With the new technology of the Industrial Revolution, compulsory education, and the major cultural changes brought about by industrialization and urbanization, newspapers moved into the popular culture with the advent of the penny press.

The significant changes that occurred as the United States was transformed into a truly industrial nation between the end of the Civil War and the turn of the century brought about many changes in American journalism, including the era of sensationalism, or yellow journalism. This was followed by an era of objectivity and social responsibility in the 20th century.

Despite the role news media play in our democratic society, they are still businesses, and business decisions play an important role in their operation. As a result, newspapers in small regions of the nation are being purchased by chain owners that seek to share costs among the papers. In addition, more and more dailies are closing down, leaving many major cities with only one newspaper.

Unlike other mass media, most newspapers have resisted the trend toward specialization (other than local or regional specialization). However, as competition has increased, more and more specialized newspapers, mostly religious and ethnic publications, have been launched.

The electronic technological revolution currently under way will bring about major changes in the way we receive our newspapers of the future. The new technologies of computers and satellites have already made major changes in the newspaper business.

Find a review of *Key People and Concepts*, a message board for *Practicing Media Literacy* questions, self tests, and more at: www.mhhe.com/wilson.

Thought Questions

1. In your opinion, what factors other than government restrictions inhibited the establishment of newspapers in the American colonies?

2. How did each of the four eras of American newspaper journalism differ from one another?

3. The underground press era of the 1960s failed as a serious movement to take newspapers into the stage of specialization. Do you think we will see another such movement again? If so, what social forces do you think will stimulate the movement?

4. If you were a newspaper publisher in a local community, what types of stories and issues would you cover to make the publication appealing to young people? Do you think the newspaper writing style should be simplified to be more accessible to young readers?

5. Will the electronic newspaper easily find a niche in our culture? If so, why? If not, why not?

Notes

1. Tim Jones, "As the On-Line World Grows, So Do Newspapers," *Chicago Tribune*, April 27, 1999.

2. Peter Burke, *Popular Culture in Early Modern Europe* (New York: Harper Torchbooks, 1978), p. 264.

3. George Henry Payne, *History of Journalism in the United States* (Westport, CT: Greenwood Press, 1970), p. 40.

4. Quoted in Warren K. Agee, Phillip H. Ault, and Edwin Emery, *Introduction to Mass Communications*, 9th ed. (New York: Harper & Row, 1988), p. 67.

5. Frank Luther Mott, *American Journalism: A History 1690–1960*, 3rd ed. (New York: Macmillan, 1962), p. 49.

6. Michael Schudson, *Discovering the News: A Social History of American Newspapers* (New York: Basic Books, 1978), pp. 50–56.

7. Agee, Ault, and Emery, *Introduction to Mass Communications*, p. 83.

8. *Ibid.*, p. 85.

9. Quoted in Edwin Emery, *The Press and America: An Interpretive History of the Mass Media*, 3rd ed. (Englewood Cliffs, NJ: Prentice Hall, 1972), p. 311.

10. W. Phillips Davison, James Boylan, and Frederick T. C. Yu, *Mass Media: Systems and Effects* (New York: Praeger, 1976), p. 15.

11. *Media Basic Analysis* (Standard & Poor's Industry Surveys), May 14, 1996, p. M-2.

12. "End of Herald Examiner," *Los Angeles Times*, November 2, 1989, p. B-4.

13. *Gale Directory of Publications and Broadcast Media*, 1996.

14. "Circulation Drops at the Majority of Big Newspapers," *San Francisco Chronicle*, May 6, 1997, p. C1.

15. "Circulation Climbs at Newspapers," *Fresno Bee*, November 4, 1997, p. C2.

16. "Slip in Daily Newspaper Circulation Reported," *Fresno Bee*, May 5, 1999, p. C2.

17. Tim Jones, "Big News—But Fewer Owners; Newspaper Chains Are Buying up Small Publications by the Fistful, Adding Muscle and, Some Say, Market Blandness," *Chicago Tribune*, September 30, 1999, Section 3, p. 1.

18. Robert Samuelson, "Can This Be the 'End of News'?" *Washington Post* Writers Group, *Chicago Tribune*, June 18, 1999, Section 1, p. 31.

19. Michael Massing, "The Libel Chill: How Cold Is It Out There?" *Columbia Journalism Review*, May–June 1985, pp. 31–43.

20. Tom Goldstein, *The News at Any Cost: How Journalists Compromise Their Ethics to Shape the News* (New York: Simon & Schuster, 1985), p. 83.

Magazines

The Specialized Medium

Literature is the thought of thinking Souls.

—Carlyle

The death of Princess Diana of Great Britain came at the worst possible time for America's two largest news magazines. The editors of both *Time* and *Newsweek* had already sent their publications to the press rooms by early Saturday evening, when word arrived from Paris that the popular princess had been involved in an automobile crash. ● With her condition still unknown, *Time* and *Newsweek* editors scrambled to pull the original cover stories (*Time* was dealing with religion; *Newsweek* was reporting on an outward-looking generation of young Americans) to switch to this late-breaking story of international interest. The report of the accident would have been enough for each magazine, but around midnight the editors received word that Diana had died. At *Time*, the initial 8-page story of the accident was expanded to a 21-page report on her death, with some 30 writers and editors on hand to help change more than half of the edition to cover the late-breaking story. The staff also expanded at *Newsweek* that night—many of them coming in on their own after hearing reports of the accident—helping to create a 24-page report on the tragedy for that publication. "This is the type of story that the country looks at the news magazines to do," said *Newsweek* national affairs editor John Meachum.[1] The fact that the story broke on the first day of a three-day Labor Day holiday weekend made the situation even worse. ● But both *Time* and *Newsweek* once again showed that while radio, television, the Internet and even newspapers may break a story faster than the other media, magazines were still fast at putting out detailed information on late-breaking stories—something they had been doing for centuries. In this chapter, we will examine the role of magazines—past, present, and future—in serving our mass culture.

Cultural History of **Magazines**

Date	Event	Elitist	Popular	Specialized
1704–14	First English-language magazines—*Review, Tatler,* and *Spectator*—published in London.	•		
1741	First two American magazines published within days of each other.	•		
1743	*Christian History* founded, America's first unit-specialization magazine.	•		•
1821	*Saturday Evening Post* founded.	•		
1830	*Godey's Lady's Book* becomes first women's magazine.	•		•
1865–1900	First magazine boom, following the end of the Civil War.		•	
1893	McClure and Munsey reduce prices of their magazines to make them truly affordable; *Saturday Evening Post* follows.		•	
1890s–1900s	Magazine muckrakers expose political corruption and unsafe working conditions.		•	
1920	Magazine advertising tops $129 million annually.		•	
1922	*Reader's Digest* is founded to serve the busy culture of the Roaring '20s.		•	
1923	Henry Luce starts *Time,* America's first newsmagazine.		•	
1936	Luce starts *Life* to fill the visual void created by radio.		•	
1947	*Reader's Digest,* with more than 9 million subscribers, becomes largest-selling publication in United States.		•	
1948	*TV Guide* begins in New York City; later expands nationally.		•	
1950s	General-interest magazines begin to decline in circulation as specialized publications develop.		•	
1952	*Mad* is founded; pokes fun at consumer culture.		•	
1953	Hugh Hefner's *Playboy* gives popular culture a sex life.		•	
1960s	Specialized publications take over circulation lead from general-interest magazines.		•	•
1972	*Life* ceases publication.		•	•
1972	*Ms.* becomes first magazine with a feminist viewpoint.		•	•
1974	Time Inc. introduces *People* as a smaller version of old movie fan magazines.		•	•
1978	*Life* resumes publication as a monthly.		•	•
1980s	More than 12,000 specialized magazines are available; new ones start daily. Computer, family, and lifestyle magazines are the latest to find a niche in the specialized culture.			•
1980s	The decade of major magazine expansion, with more than 2,500 new magazines founded during this period.			•
1990s	This decade began with an advertising revenue slump caused by many new publications competing for the same dollars and by a decline in tobacco and automobile ads. Video magazines make their appearance.			•
1996	Conglomerates continue to purchase publications, but advertising revenue continues to show an increase.			•
1997	The relationship between magazines and the World Wide Web continues to flourish.			•
1999	Stephen Brill's *Content* makes its debut; *Talk* magazine creates controversy with its debut interview with Hillary Rodham Clinton.			•
2000	*Life* magazine again announces that it will cease publication			•

HISTORY OF MAGAZINES

British Publications

The first English-language magazines were started in London in the early 18th century. The first such publication, the *Review*, was actually a cross between a newspaper and a magazine. It was published by Daniel Defoe (the author of *Robinson Crusoe* and *The Adventures of Moll Flanders*) in 1704. In 1709 Richard Steele began publishing the *Tatler*. He was soon joined by Joseph Addison, and together they published both the *Tatler* and its short-lived successor, the *Spectator*. These early magazines carried both literary and satirical essays about political figures. In 1731, the first British publication to carry the word *magazine* in its title began: Edward Cave's *Gentlemen's Magazine*. Cave later hired the famed scholar Dr. Samuel Johnson as one of his writers. Johnson then started his own magazine, *The Rambler*, in 1750. These magazines sought an audience among the elite—both men and women—by providing witty and stimulating reading in periodical form.

Early American Efforts

In 1741 two prominent printers in Philadelphia, Andrew Bradford and Benjamin Franklin, vied to publish the first magazine in the American colonies. Bradford was the victor, publishing his *American Magazine, or a Monthly View of the Political State of the British Colonies*, three days before Franklin's *General Magazine, and Historical Chronicle, for All the British Plantations in America*. Franklin was more successful, however, as his magazine lasted for six issues compared to Bradford's three. The content of these American magazines consisted mostly of material reprinted from British magazines; only about 10 percent of the material in the six issues of the *General Magazine* was original.[2]

These early American magazines were designed for the elite, the relatively few literate members of society. Thus, they carried essays and articles on religion, philosophy, natural science, political affairs, and literature.

In 1743, a publication that might be described as the first specialized magazine in America was printed. It was *The Christian History*, a religious magazine. Due to the low literacy rate in the 18th century and the slowness of the mails, the development of magazines during this period was less than spectacular. Indeed, prior to the 19th century, no American magazine lasted for more than 14 months.

Successful Expansion

By the 1820s, however, American magazine publishing began to develop into a lucrative and long-lasting enterprise. One of the more famous magazines of this era was the *Saturday Evening Post*, which was founded in 1821. It lasted as a weekly publication until 1969. It is now published on a less than monthly schedule. In 1825, there were fewer than 100 magazines in the United States. Twenty-five years later, there were 600.

This tremendous growth in magazine publishing resulted from advances in printing technology (steam power and cylinder and rotary presses), the eventual development of a literate society as a result of compulsory education, and major reform movements that generated topics for printed discussion. In 1820, for example, the first abolitionist magazine, *The Genius of Universal Emancipation*, was published in Ohio. As slavery became hotly debated and the nation moved toward the Civil War, magazines played an important role in informing and influencing the people. As mentioned in Chapter 6, Harriet Beecher Stowe's *Uncle Tom's Cabin* first appeared as a series of magazine articles before it was published in book form.

Nevertheless, before the Civil War, magazine readership was still drawn primarily from the elite. *The Saturday Evening Post* and other successful publications founded in this period—the *North American Review* (1815), *Harper's* (1850), and *Atlantic Monthly* (1857)—carried mostly short stories, novels, poems, scholarly essays, and political and social commentaries.

Expansion into Popular Culture

literacy

By the end of the Civil War (1865), compulsory education had helped give the United States the highest **literacy** level in the world, and the railroads had provided a means of transporting people and goods (including publications) across the continent. American magazines could now start to enter the popular culture. Numerous publications featuring both unit and internal specialization appeared. Two of the most popular genres of unit specialization were farming and women's magazines. *Godey's Lady's Book*, the forerunner of specialized women's publications, was first published in 1830, and some of the more popular publications of the late 19th century were *Ladies' Home Journal*, *McCall's*, and *Woman's Home Companion*.

The 1880s and 1890s saw the debut of a number of mass-circulation, general-interest magazines featuring fiction and nonfiction articles. The most important were *Collier's*, *Cosmopolitan*, and *McClure's*. Founded by newspaper magnate Samuel S. McClure, *McClure's* was the first inexpensive mass-circulation magazine, selling for 15 cents a copy. This prompted Frank Munsey to cut the price of his *Munsey's Magazine* to 10 cents. Soon the *Saturday Evening Post* was selling for a nickel. Now that they were very affordable, magazines became entrenched in the popular culture. The variety of their articles enabled these magazines to appeal to a wide range of Americans. Farmers in the Midwest could enjoy certain stories in the *Saturday Evening Post*, for example, while other articles appealed to merchants and bankers in New York. The magazine industry thrived. In 1865, there were about 700 magazines; by 1900, there were more than 5,000.

The Saturday Evening Post *was a popular magazine featuring short stories and articles. Because of its generalized content, it fell from popularity when specialized magazines began to flourish midway through the 20th century.*

The Muckrakers

The millions of Europeans who immigrated to the United States during the latter part of the 19th century provided a large labor force for the new industrial economy. Many workers were forced to live in deplorable slums and work long hours in sweatshops for abysmally low wages. Reformers turned to such magazines as *The Nation* and *Harper's Weekly* for support in their efforts to improve living and working conditions. In the 1890s, the populist movement attacked the great disparity between rich and poor and accused industrial capitalists of a greedy disregard for the common welfare. The medium for their crusading articles was magazines.

By the beginning of the 20th century, this new form of journalism, called muckraking, had become an important part of magazine content. **Muckraking** journalists sought out and exposed corruption and scandal. President Theodore Roosevelt coined the term muckraker to express his dislike for this negative form of journalism. To him, these journalists were like the "Man with the Muckrake" in the book *Pilgrim's Progress*, who would not look up from the filth on the floor even when he was offered a glittering crown. But the muckrakers themselves considered the term a compliment to their crusading efforts.

muckraking

Although *Harper's Weekly* had exposed political corruption in New York as early as the 1870s and the 19th-century magazine *The Arena* had attacked slums, sweatshops, and prostitution, it was not until the turn of the century that campaigns against corruption became commonplace in such mass-circulation magazines as *McClure's*, *Everybody's*, and *Collier's*. Soon both general-interest and opinion magazines were carrying muckraking articles exposing deplorable living conditions, corrupt business practices, exploitation of workers, and political corruption.

> **@ Practicing Media Literacy**
> Can you think of any magazines today which are noted for their investigative reporting? What types of stories do they investigate?

Among the more prominent muckrakers were Lincoln Steffens, Ida Tarbell, Ray Stannard Baker, David Graham Phillips, and Upton Sinclair. Steffens tackled the slums in his widely praised "Shame of the Cities" series; Tarbell exposed the corrupt business practices of John D. Rockefeller in the "History of the Standard Oil Company"; Baker wrote a series on the problems of corrupt labor unions entitled "The Right to Work"; Phillips attacked politicians who favored special interest groups in "Treason in the Senate"; and Sinclair wrote about worker exploitation and unsanitary conditions in Chicago's meat-packing houses in "The Condemned Meat Industry."

Muckrakers created popular sentiment for reform legislation, most notably for the Pure Food and Drug Act and the Meat Inspection Act, both sponsored by President Theodore Roosevelt.

World War I

As World War I approached, muckraking journalism declined; attention was increasingly focusing on the war in Europe. Magazines played a role in eventually getting the United States involved in the war. The British conducted an overt campaign to get propaganda for the Allies before the American people, some of

One of the most famous muckrakers in recent times was Jessica Mittford, who exposed excesses in the funeral industry.

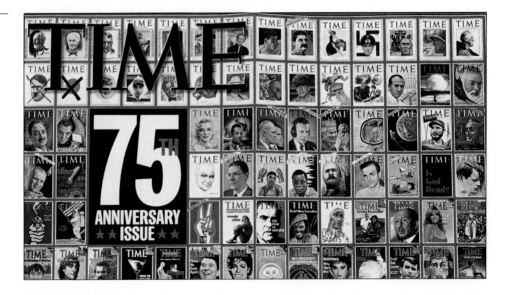

which made its way into American magazines. Numerous stories (many of them false) about German atrocities in Belgium circulated throughout the United States. Even President Woodrow Wilson was influenced by the British magazines that he read regularly.[3]

In more recent times, perhaps the most famous muckraker was Jessica Mittford, who died in 1996 at age 78. She is best remembered for her many articles and books exposing the excesses of the funeral industry. Her best-known book was *The American Way of Death*, a bestseller in 1963.

Postwar Trends

Although President Wilson overcame considerable domestic opposition to secure the entry of the United States into World War I in 1917, he was unsuccessful in persuading the nation to guarantee the peace. The U.S. Senate refused to ratify the treaty that would have made the United States a member of the new League of Nations. Many Americans believed peace and economic prosperity could best be achieved by isolating our nation from alliances and commitments with other countries. This isolationist attitude grew after the war. As the country turned inward, it began to focus on the **cultural changes** that were occurring in the 1920s. These included changes in the family structure, women's suffrage, prohibition, growth of urban life, a rising crime rate, the development of jazz music and dance halls, and more permissive moral attitudes, which many people blamed on the invention of the automobile (as it allowed young people to court one another away from home).

cultural changes

As the culture changed, so did magazine content (see Box 8.1). A variety of new magazines emerged. For example, the increasing pace of American life brought about by prohibition, popular music, and fast living during the Roaring '20s, set the stage for a magazine that would save the reader time by condensing articles from a variety of sources. In 1922, *Reader's Digest* (readersdigest.com) was founded by DeWitt and Lila Wallace; their idea was to take the best articles from other publications and reprint them in a condensed form. Their magazine became the largest selling one in the nation. As the 20th century was coming to a close, *Reader's Digest* began exploring the

Box 8.1
MEDIA WATCH
A Century of Our Culture Reflected in Magazines

Some 100 years ago, American popular culture was changing dramatically. As the culture changed, so did the content of the nation's magazines. One of the best ways to study the changing popular culture is to look at magazines over a period of time. Each new trend, fad, hobby, or subculture is reflected in our magazines. These changes are seen in general-interest as well as special-interest magazines.

One of the first studies of our changing culture as seen through the pages of magazines was published in *Radio Research* (edited by Paul F. Lazarsfeld) in 1942–1943. In this study, Leo Lowenthal compared the biographical articles in *Collier's* and the *Saturday Evening Post* for 1901 and 1940–1941; he found that in the 40-year interval the proportion of articles about business and professional people and political leaders had declined, while those about entertainers had gone up 50 percent.

The study showed how our culture had changed from the days of the Industrial Revolution—when workers played a paramount role in society—to a new age preoccupied with leisure pursuits and the popular rather than the elite arts. It confirmed too that our popular culture had moved from an interest in elite or high culture to mass-cultural interests: In 1901 the entertainers featured were mostly serious artists, such as opera singers, sculptors, or pianists, while the 1941 entertainers were all movie stars or baseball players.*

Probably more so than any other mass medium, magazines serve as a barometer for measuring our changing American culture. Obviously, magazine publishing has come a long way during the past 300 years.

*Alan Casty, *Mass Media and Mass Man* (New York: Holt, Rinehart, & Winston, 1968), p. 20.

possibility of branching into television. The magazine wanted to use its own articles and its strong name to create TV movies and miniseries, hoping that the TV exposure would bring in a new, and potentially younger, audience to the publication.

Because the United States did not have a strong system of nationally circulating newspapers, as England did, magazines filled the void. The first *newsmagazine*, a term coined by its founders, Henry R. Luce and Britton Hadden, was introduced in 1923 as *Time* (timeinc.com/time). It was followed in 1933 by *Newsweek* (newsweek-int.com), and in 1948 *U.S. News & World Report* (usnews.com) entered the field.

In 1998, *Time* celebrated 75 years of publication with an anniversary issue featuring reproductions of many historic cover pictures. But the issue became a collector's item for its recollections of American history and how many things were perceived at different times in our culture. From its depiction of the 1929 stock market crash as an event which would have only fleeting impact to its description of Ernest Hemingway as a "new U.S. writer" who "appears to have lived considerably . . . in unusual ways and places," *Time* had been there throughout most of the 20th century, reporting on the events that were shaping our world around us.

As the trend toward urbanization continued, metropolitan magazines featuring articles about lifestyles in the large, urban centers became popular. The first and most successful was the *New Yorker,* introduced in 1925 (see Box 8.2).

Specialization

Although it took books thousands of years to move through the EPS cycle to the specialized stage, and newspapers have yet to fully enter the stage of specialization, magazines evolved in one way or another since their birth in the 18th century.

unit specialization

According to mass-media scholars John Merrill and Ralph Lowenstein, all magazines have either **unit specialization** or internal specialization. Unit specialization occurs in magazines that target audiences with special interests—*Hot Rod Magazine*, *Surfer*, and *PC Magazine*, for example. Most magazines produced in the United States today fall into this category. Internal specialization magazines are general-interest publications that appeal to a larger audience and offer a wider variety of articles. Readers select the articles that interest them. Although many of these magazines have gone out of business during the past 30 years, some—such as the *Reader's Digest*—are still very successful.

Life

Henry Luce had another idea for making magazine history in 1936, when he brought out a large-size pictorial weekly called *Life*. By this time radio had become an important mass-communication medium and was taking listeners to the scenes of important news events. (It also competed with magazines for consumers' leisure time.) *Life* was able to fill the visual void radio created by providing pictures of major news events each week.

The new magazine was an almost instant success and soon was found in most households. Its excellent photojournalism is still admired today. Teams of *Life* photographers were sent out on news and feature stories, and only the very best of the photos were used.

Although *Life* (pathfinder.com/Life) became a very popular magazine, its development was not without controversy. A 1938 photo essay on the birth of a baby shocked many people, and the magazine was banned in 33 cities, to cite just one instance in which the content was too graphic or controversial for the conservative elements in the popular culture.

A year after *Life* began publishing, Gardner Cowles introduced *Look* magazine as an imitator. It too became a popular general-interest magazine. In 1945, John H. Johnson founded *Ebony* (ebony.com) as another version of *Life*, this time aimed at a burgeoning African-American audience.

Founded in 1945, Ebony magazine used pictures and articles to reach the African-American audience for more than a half-century.

TV Guide

When television started entering the popular culture in 1948, *TV Guide* (tvguide.com/tv) was established as a magazine catering to New York television owners. Sold soon after to Walter Annenberg's Triangle Publications, it became a national television guide, offering local area listings. In 1974 it replaced *Reader's Digest* as the largest-selling magazine in the country, and today its weekly circulation figures exceed 15 million. These two publications have been competing for first place ever since, with both publications topping 18 million circulation at

Box 8.2
PROFILE
The Impact of England's Tina Brown on American Magazines

When Tina Brown resigned as editor of *New Yorker* magazine in 1998, her six years as the head of the venerable publication received mixed reviews. A year later, she was drawing controversy once again with the introduction of a brand new magazine, *Talk.*

Since its beginnings in 1925 under the editorship of Harold Ross, the *New Yorker* had enjoyed an elite cultural following that admired its quiet, refined, intellectual writing style and conservative typographical look. The *New Yorker* seemed immune to the "trashy" pop culture that infiltrated other publications. The magazine had an aura of an elegant but musty institution known for its long and obscure articles. And its readers loved it.

All of this lasted until 1985 when the magazine was sold to S. I. Newhouse, Jr., for $168 million. Newhouse did not want the magazine to continue being a money loser, so he tried to find an editor who could turn things around. In 1992, he hired Tina Brown, pop culture editor of his *Vanity Fair,* to take over the editorship of the *New Yorker.* The elite culture went into shock as they feared the worst: radical change.

Brown had arrived in the United States in 1984 from her native Great Britain and had transformed Newhouse's *Vanity Fair* into a hot property by creating a shrewd mix of celebrity profiles, newsy features, and provocative photos. The most famous was the 1991 cover photo featuring a nude and very pregnant actress, Demi Moore.

Brown was born in Buckinghamshire, England, in 1954. Her father produced movies, including Agatha Christie mysteries, and her mother was Sir Laurence Olivier's personal assistant.

Brown received an M.A. in English from Oxford University, wrote for the campus magazine, and authored plays. In 1974, she wrote a series of articles for the *Times* of London on the women's movement in America. The editor of the *Times,* Harold Evans, took notice of Brown, and they were married in 1981. When Rupert Murdoch bought the *Times* in 1981 (see Chapter 3), he fired Evans. However, Evans went on to become the editorial director of *U.S. News & World Report* and then became president and publisher of Random House Books, another Newhouse property.

Actress Demi Moore (r), shown here with editor Tina Brown, helped Vanity Fair increase sales figures with two nude cover pictures—one taken while she was obviously pregnant and the other in which a tuxedo was painted on her naked body.

From 1979 to 1983, Tina Brown edited the British society magazine *The Tatler.* When Newhouse, owner of the Condé Nast publishing empire, decided to revive *Vanity Fair,* he hired Brown as an adviser. A year later, at age 30, she became its editor. Eight years later, she was heading up the *New Yorker.*

How did Brown do at the *New Yorker?* Critics blamed her for replacing the weekly's rich literary history with stories of glitz and celebrities. Admirers say she added some much needed pizzazz to the musty publication. Slang and obscenity were long-standing taboos at the *New Yorker* under editors Ross and Shawn. Under Ross, writers couldn't even use words like *sweat* and *deodorant.* Under Brown, even four-letter words could be found in almost every issue. Full-page cartoons and comic strips were also added.

Advertisements for Calvin Klein, including a spread showing shirtless rap singer Marky Mark lounging with a bare-breasted young woman, appeared in the magazine. Covers have included a college-like portrait of Malcolm X and an even more controversial Valentine's Day cover showing a Hasidic Jewish man and an African-American woman kissing. The anniversary issue in 1994 made history by replacing the traditional cover character, "Eustace Tilley," with his pimply

continued

grandson, "Elvis Tilley," reading a porno flyer in Times Square.

Although some of the staff of the *New Yorker* left when Brown took over, others who stayed saw her as having a positive influence. The magazine's 80-year-old grammarian and copy editor credited Brown for bringing back to life some of the magazine's "burned-out" writers. However, some critics were heard to murmur, "God protect the *New Yorker* from the British."

Was Newhouse happy with Brown's performance? Consider that in its first year under her editorship, the circulation of the *New Yorker* climbed by 100,000 to a total of 658,916. Readers were getting younger, and that was attracting advertisers. Despite all this, when Brown left the magazine in 1998 after six years of leadership, the now-800,000 circulation publication had lost millions of dollars each year. As one contributing writer commented, "If Newhouse could comfortably do it, he would probably fold the magazine. But nobody wants to be the person who killed the *New Yorker*."

A year later, Brown introduced a brand new magazine, *Talk*. The premiere issue in September of 1999 was headlined by an interview with first lady Hillary Rodham Clinton, entitled: "Hillary Opens Up," and the cover quoted her as saying "This was a sin of weakness . . ." The cover also featured an alluring picture of actress Gwyneth Paltrow in a leather bikini, with the headline "Gwyneth Goes Bad." Other articles touted on the cover dealt with Republican presidential candidate George W. Bush, an article on "The Unsolved Mysteries of Princess Diana," another called "Richard Butler's Iraq Bombshell," an article on actress Angelina Jolie ("The Once Grievous Angel"), and a picture spread featuring actor Ruper Everett portraying a "Bisexual 007."

Tina Brown was back.

*Quoted by Leah Garchik in the "Personals" column, *San Francisco Chronicle*, July 9, 1998, p. C16.

one time or another. In 1988, media baron Rupert Murdoch paid $3 billion for Triangle Publications, publishers of *TV Guide*, *Seventeen*, and *Racing Form*. As the 1990s came to an end, *TV Guide* was merged with Gemstar International Group, Ltd.—a producer of electronic guides for television—in a $9.2 billion stock transaction. The deal, which combined *TV Guide*'s access to programming information with Gemstar's technical ability to create interactive program guides, was expected to have an impact on the way Americans would select the programs they would view, how they would watch advertising campaigns, and even how they would purchase products.[4]

In recent years, *Modern Maturity*, a free publication for members of the American Association of Retired Persons, has jumped ahead of both *Reader's Digest* and *TV Guide* in annual circulation figures, but *TV Guide* still leads all publications in gross revenue (see Tables 8.1 and 8.2).

Mad

As the American culture became ever more obsessed with technology and conspicuous consumption, it was not surprising that a magazine developed to criticize these trends. In 1952 William Gaines established *Mad* (dccomics.com/mad), a satirical humor magazine that used a sophisticated comic book format. Much of *Mad*'s success seems to come from its ability to poke fun at the materialistic and commercialized American culture and the mass media's role in it. *Mad*'s willingness to satirize the very commercial products that other magazines rely on for advertising revenue has endeared it to many Americans. Until 1990, when *Ms.* magazine stopped running advertisements, *Mad* held the distinction of being the only major magazine to survive without accepting paid advertisements.

Playboy

A year after *Mad* began publishing, *Playboy* (playboy.com) appeared on the scene. It has since been credited by some and criticized by others for launching the sexual revolution in America. The first issue in 1953 was put together on a card table in the kitchen of founder Hugh Hefner, a former *Esquire* magazine employee.

Hefner enlisted the assistance of a freelance artist on the promise of some stock in his new company, and the first issue of *Playboy* was polished and released, featuring a nude centerfold of movie actress Marilyn Monroe. By 1954 *Playboy* was selling more than 100,000 copies a month, and this figure climbed to nearly 800,000 two years later. It now sells 3.5 million copies a month, down from its best year, when it sold more than 7 million.

Intent on building a sophisticated image for his nudie magazine, Hefner also ran articles by well-known and respected writers. At first he refused to accept advertising, but later he carefully added this form of revenue by accepting only "quality-image" advertising; he rejected more than 80 percent of the ads submitted for publication. His plan paid off, as in a few short years his magazine became accepted by many in the popular culture. John Brady, former editor of *Writer's Digest*, said that Hefner "gave popular culture a sex life."[5]

During the 1970s, Hugh Hefner's Playboy empire ran into financial difficulties and its presidency was turned over to Hefner's daughter Christie.

THE DECLINE OF GENERAL-INTEREST MAGAZINES

As many new special-interest magazines were launched in the 1950s, it soon became apparent that general-interest magazines were in trouble. In 1956, *Collier's* was the first modern mass-circulation general-interest magazine to go bankrupt and cease publication.

Demographic and Regional Breakouts

By 1967, *Look* had turned to alternative ways to survive. It began publishing demographic breakout editions, which allowed advertisers to pay less by placing their ads in editions of the magazine that went only to certain demographic categories. For example, an advertiser could place an ad in copies that would go only to people with incomes above $24,000. Despite these efforts, *Look* went out of business in 1971.

Another strategy magazines use is **regional breakouts.** Regional breakouts allow advertisers to purchase ads in copies circulated in particular geographic regions. Many surviving general-interest magazines and the successful national newsmagazines sell ads on a demographic or regional breakout basis.

regional breakouts

TABLE 8.1

The 25 Top Magazines in Circulation

Modern Maturity, *which is sent to every member of the American Association of Retired Persons, is the nation's leader in magazine circulation. The publication serves one of the largest and most politically powerful subcultural groups in our society and is mailed free to association members. In second place is* Reader's Digest, *which has long been this country's most successful internal-specialization publication, followed closely by* TV Guide, *a successful unit-specialization magazine. The rest of the top 25 is dominated by women's interest, travel, news, health, lifestyle, sports, science, and computer publications.*

Magazine	Circulation (millions)
1. *Modern Maturity*	20.3
2. *Reader's Digest*	13.4
3. *TV Guide*	11.8
4. *National Geographic*	8.6
5. *Better Homes & Gardens*	7.6
6. *Good Housekeeping*	5.1
7. *Family Circle*	4.6
8. *Ladies' Home Journal*	4.5
9. *McCall's*	4.2
10. *Woman's Day*	4.0
11. *Time*	4.0
12. *People*	3.6
13. *The Cable Guide*	3.4
14. *Sports Illustrated*	3.2
15. *Playboy*	3.2
16. *Home & Away*	3.2
17. *Newsweek*	3.1
18. *Prevention*	3.1
19. *React*	3.0
20. *Medizine*	2.9
21. *Cosmopolitan*	2.8
22. *Redbook*	2.8
23. *The American Legion Magazine*	2.6
24. *Southern Living*	2.5
25. *Seventeen*	2.3

Source: *Advertising Age* (adage.com), August 23, 1999, p. 21.

TABLE 8.2

The Top 25 U.S. Magazines in Gross Revenue

Circulation is not the only way to list America's leading magazines. For comparison purposes, the following lists the top 25 magazines according to their 1998 gross revenue. The total revenue is determined by both advertising and circulation income. Notice the difference in rankings between this list and the total circulation list of Table 8.1.

Magazine	Total Revenue
1. TV Guide	$1,170,810
2. People	1,078,027
3. Sports Illustrated	850,057
4. Time	814,300
5. Reader's Digest	563,105
6. Better Homes & Gardens	559,124
7. Newsweek	547,164
8. Parade	517,116
9. Business Week	416,922
10. PC Magazine	378,607
11. Good Housekeeping	344,829
12. U.S. News & World Report	329,431
13. Family Circle	320,316
14. Woman's Day	319,554
15. Forbes	315,752
16. Cosmopolitan	306,087
17. Fortune	305,916
18. Ladies' Home Journal	298,225
19. USA Weekend	274,551
20. Entertainment Weekly	253,544
21. National Geographic	225,397
22. Money	215,015
23. Southern Living	211,379
24. Glamour	205,612
25. Martha Stewart Living	202,828

Source: Advertising Age, June 14, 1999, p. 32.

Death of Life

The biggest shock for the millions of people who depended on general-interest magazines came in 1972, when *Life* announced that its December issue would be its last. Although American popular culture had changed greatly in the 36 years since *Life* was born, the magazine had reared more than a generation of Americans, and life without *Life* seemed too much for many of them to take.

A number of factors contributed to the demise of *Life* and other general-interest magazines. One was higher production costs and postal rates. Another was the competition for leisure time posed by the new medium of television. Television filled the same visual void for pictures of news events that *Life* did. It provided both pictures and sound—and did it daily. Still another factor was the fact that many readers were turning to more specialized magazines.

Specialization

Since advertising revenue is the "life's blood" of the magazine industry, the nail in the coffin for many general-interest magazines came when advertisers realized they could better target the specialized audiences they were seeking by using specialized publications. With the increase in the number and variety of special-interest magazines available, many advertisers no longer wanted to pay the higher cost of reaching the general-interest masses. The homogeneous interests of specialized magazine readers were superior to regional and demographic breakouts.

Despite *Life's* demise, 1972 was not all gloom for the magazine business. This was the year in which a new special-interest magazine, Ms., was founded. Devoted to women's issues in the face of the feminist movement, Ms. (Msmagazine.com) found a niche in American popular culture by recognizing that women should be something more than sex objects and housewives. The magazine was an overnight success. However, the magazine ceased publication twice in its history. The first time was in 1989 because it was losing money, but it returned in 1990 no longer carrying any advertising. Instead, Ms. cut its publishing schedule from monthly to bimonthly and raised subscription rates. Then in 1998, the magazine was sold to Liberty Media for Women, an investment group that included Ms. founder Gloria Steinem, and halted publication for three issues while the sale was being finalized. It returned with the April-May, 1999, issue and a cover price of $5.95 per copy.

In 1974 Time Inc. launched *People* magazine (pathfinder.com/people/), a smaller, livelier version of the old movie fan magazine. (Movie magazines had been popular

Hugh Hefner began publishing Playboy *in the 1950s to target the male audience by reflecting the changing attitudes toward sex and nudity in our society.*

during the heyday of the movies in the 1930s and 1940s, but their readership had declined after the motion picture industry was forced by television to move into the era of specialization in the 1950s.) Some believed *People* was an attempt to satisfy some of the diehard former *Life* readers with a more focused publication that was less expensive to produce.

It has become successful, with 85 percent of its sales coming from newsstands, particularly in supermarkets. It has even given birth to a youth-oriented version of the publication, *Teen People,* which was introduced in 1998 with Jennifer Love Hewitt on the cover. *People* also moved into the Hispanic field with a Latino edition of the magazine in the last decade of the 20th century.

> @ **Practicing Media Literacy**
> What do you think are the reasons for the success of such magazines as *People*?

Entertainment Weekly

In 1990, Time Inc. launched a new magazine that catered to the popular culture. *Entertainment Weekly* features the latest information on hot television shows, movies, books, music, and videos.

Life's *Rebirth—and Death*

Despite these new magazines, many who had grown up with *Life* still missed it. In response, Time Inc. began issuing a number of special editions of *Life*. Their success prompted Time to reintroduce the magazine as a monthly in 1978. The new *Life* featured quality photojournalism, but did not have the weekly news orientation it once had. In 2000, *Life* again ceased publication.

TYPES OF MAGAZINES

By the mid-1990s, it was estimated that more than 11,000 magazines were published in the United States. This figure has increased from 6,950 in 1950. Of these 11,000-plus

special interests

publications, only about 800 were general-interest magazines; the rest were devoted to **special interests.** (For a detailed look at the wide variety of magazines, consult the current edition of *Writer's Market*.)

These magazines can be broken down into three broad categories: consumer magazines, business publications, and farm magazines. However, within these categories are numerous subcategories reflecting a high level of specialization. Most of the new publications launched in recent years, for example, fit into the following narrowly focused special-interest categories: health and fitness, sports, travel and leisure, lifestyles, ethnic, regional, business, age-specific women's and men's magazines, and special-interest regional publications such as *Pacific Diver, Southern Bride, North Carolina Black Journal, South Florida Bride,* and *California Basketball.* Among the new business publications, subject areas include medicine, technology, business management, computers, and computer software, including *MacWorld* and *Windows Magazine.* We now turn to some of the narrow special-interest categories of magazines.

Family Magazines

One of the newest categories of magazines to become popular in the late 1980s was the family magazine. These publications reflected a revived interest in the family by a segment of the population that had previously been regarded as interested in self-fulfillment only—the yuppie generation. Following the lead of the successful checkout counter publication *Family Circle,* new magazines in this category included *Parenting, Fathers, Child, Children,* and *Grandparents. Child* now offers its subscribers age-specific editorial sections.

Magazine racks are now filled with many specialized magazines aimed at women, men, teenagers, sports fans, and even computer enthusiasts and motorcyclists.

Computer Magazines

Computer magazines constitute another successful new magazine category. As more and more people use computers at home and at work, they have created a market for such publications as *Wired, Byte, PC World, MacUser, PC/Computing Magazine, Portable Computing,* and *Publish* (see Box 8.3). In 1998, the Condé Nast unit of Advance Publications Inc. (publisher of *Vogue, Vanity Fair,* and the *New Yorker*) purchased *Wired* for an estimated $80 million. The seller, Wired Ventures Inc., said it would use the money from the sale to pay off debts and fund

Box 8.3

MEDIA LITERACY

The Computer Magazine—At Your Local Newsstand or on Your Home Computer

Three of the top 30 revenue-grossing magazines in the United States going into the 21st century were computer publications. In maintaining a high profile, computer magazines were among the first online. *PC Week, MacWeek, PC/Computing, MacUser,* and others have become outposts on the Internet for computer users, providing more detailed information regarding their published features as well as downloadable software archives.

One way they are able to differentiate their web content from their newsstand content is in the form of "online exclusives," a section of reviews, opinion, and in-depth analyses that often failed to make the editorial cut for the printed version. The web also allows for more instantaneous updates to the printed offering, which can be helpful considering that many of these magazines may be printed several weeks to a month in advance.

The Internet itself has spawned several periodicals dedicated to helping web surfers have a more productive and instructive time on the Internet. One of the more popular search engines on the Internet, Yahoo!, has spawned its own printed publication, dedicated primarily to hot sites on the web and new Internet tools.

Many popular magazines are now available through the various online computer services, and new titles are being added regularly. It's been estimated that well over 200 magazines are currently available online. The popularity of the online services grew dramatically in the 1990s, and now such services as America Online, Prodigy, and CompuServe offer subscribers full or partial texts of magazines ranging from *Time* to *Backpacker*. Subscribers can either read the stories online or download them to their computers to read at a later time.

Most of the online magazine services provide features that aren't available in the printed editions of the magazines. But according to the Standard & Poor's Industry Surveys, it is hard to predict the extent to which readers of a printed publication will switch to electronic versions of the same publication. The online magazine is not something you can take on a plane or train to read while traveling, but it does contain sound and video clips that provide something more than any print edition offers. Also, online magazines have the potential to attract new readers who might never look at the print version.

A key element in this new technology is that magazines have generally moved into cyberspace without the advertising carried in the print editions. The amount of time a user spends online reading an electronic publication usually determines the fee a publication receives from the online service provider. Publishers are still experimenting with different ways to bring advertisers online with them as they envision the online distribution mushrooming into a billion-dollar industry. For now, the profitability of online magazines is not a major concern. Magazine publishers are merely seeking to get in on the ground floor of this new market's technologies.

online ventures such as the HotBot search engine and online publications *HotWired* and *WiredNews* (wired.com), a daily news service "with an attitude."[6]

Erotica Magazines

Erotica or sex magazines began to reflect more permissive attitudes toward sex and nudity in the 1950s. Always controversial, this category came under renewed criticism in the 1986 report by the Meese Commission on Pornography (see Chapter 4). At the request of the commission's executive director, some companies, including 7-Eleven, removed these publications from their shelves. However, the report did not end the popularity of these publications. For example, in one recent year, some 584 new magazines were started, and 72 of them were sex magazines. Publications in this category include *Playboy, Penthouse, Playgirl, Screw, Oui,* and *Hustler* (hustler.com) (see Box 8.4.).

When the issue of freedom of the press comes up, most media giants band together in support of the First Amendment to the Constitution. But there are times when the *New York Times,* the *Washington Post,* the *Los Angeles Times,* and the ABC, CBS, and NBC television networks wish that the issue wasn't too controversial. This was not the case with magazine publisher Larry Flynt.

Flynt was in and out of the courtrooms during the final years of the 20th century, using the First Amendment to defend some of the shocking pictures, articles, and advertisements run in his *Hustler* magazine.

Many of Flynt's problems dealt with the issue of pornography in the city of Cincinnati, but he had one case involving the Reverend Jerry Falwell of the Moral Majority go all the way to the Supreme Court of the United States. That case involved a satirical ad run in *Hustler* which said that Falwell's first sexual experience was with his mother in an outhouse. The first jury found Flynt guilty of causing psychological damage to Falwell and awarded a substantial settlement to the conservative minister. But Flynt took the battle to the highest court in the nation and got the judgment overturned on the grounds of freedom of speech and press.

Flynt, who is confined to a wheelchair after being shot outside a courthouse by a sniper, has irritated judges by appearing in court wearing the U.S. flag as a diaper and by paying off fines of several thousand dollars in one dollar bills. He was also the subject of a major motion picture, *The People vs. Larry Flynt,* starring Woody Harrelson and Courtney Love.

In 1997, Flynt autographed copies of *Hustler* being sold in Cincinnati at the Hustler Books, News and Gifts store. It was the first time that the magazine had

Larry Flynt has spent a lot of time in court over First Amendment issues.

been sold in that city in 20 years, since Flynt had been convicted of pandering obscenity there in 1977. The conviction was later overturned.

Cincinnati's second obscenity trial for Flynt came to an end in 1999 when his corporation accepted a plea bargain that allowed the controversial publisher to continue selling *Hustler* magazine in that city but forever barred him from selling adult videos there. In exchange, Flynt's corporation entered a plea of guilty to two counts of pandering obscenity, which included a $10,000 fine. With the guilty plea, all other charges in the case were dismissed.

In most of his court cases, Flynt had the begrudging support of the major news media. As he himself once pointed out, the First Amendment wasn't created to protect the mainstream media; it was created to protect even the sleazy publishers, such as Larry Flynt.

Sports Magazines

A genre that caters exclusively to our culture's interest in leisure activities is the sports magazine. These publications range from magazines covering sports in general, such as *Sports Illustrated* (pathfinder.com/si/), *Inside Sports,* and *Sport,* to more specialized publications covering just one sport, such as *Runner's World, Boating, Backpacker, Flying, On Tour,* and *Skiing.* In addition, there is always an influx of magazines dedicated to college football and basketball, as well as to the National Football League, Major League Baseball, and the National Basketball Association as those seasons come around each year. Sports magazines, like erotica magazines, once seemed to be intended only for men. However, women now make up a large segment of the audience for general sports magazines, and some sports magazines are designed just for women. In recent years, a number of magazines have appeared dealing with exercise, health, and bodybuilding.

Each year, when the *Sports Illustrated* swimsuit edition comes out, the magazine comes in for much criticism from women. To help ease the situation, *Sports Illustrated* came out with a new magazine devoted to women athletes and the interests of their fans. *Women/Sport* was introduced in April of 1997, featuring a picture of pregnant basketball player Sheryl Swoopes on the cover, noting that both she and the new WNBA were due the following June.

Men's Magazines

Although men are the prime audience for most erotica and sports magazines, there are many other men's magazines, especially ones that focus on adventure and fashion. *Field & Stream* (fieldandstream.com), *Guns & Ammo, Esquire, GQ, Men, Men's Life, Details, M. Inc., FYI, Men's Journal,* and *Assets* are just a few publications in this field.

Women's-Interest Magazines

As discussed earlier, women's magazines have been popular since the 19th century and today include some of the highest-circulating magazines in the country, with at least a dozen selling between 1 million and 8 million each month. With more than 50 titles devoted to women's interests, there are actually subcategories within this one: women's general interest, health and fitness, parenting, style and fashion, and women's career magazines, to name a few. Some of the more popular women's publications are *Harper's Bazaar, Bridal Guide, Bride, Cosmopolitan, Good Housekeeping, Ms., Woman's Day, Woman's World, Complete Woman, Better Homes & Gardens, Modern Bride, McCall's, Redbook, Self, Shape, Elle, Glamour, Vogue, W., Savvy, Working Mother,* and *Working Woman.*

Youth Magazines

Magazines for young people, ranging from *Boy's Life* to *Seventeen* (seventeen.com), have been around a long time. As American youngsters mature earlier, their magazines have been tackling more adult topics. One such magazine, *Penny Power,* is designed to make young people consumer activists. In 1988, an Australian publishing firm began challenging *Seventeen* in the U.S. market by bringing out a sexier publication for teenage girls. Called *Sassy,* the magazine's first issue included articles on "How to Flirt" and "Losing Your Virginity." By the end of its second year, it had toned down its emphasis on sexuality. It has a circulation of more than 700,000, impressive but nowhere near *Seventeen's* 2.3 million. An

Teenaged girls are the target of many magazines which highlight articles about dating, clothing, makeup, teenaged boys, and romance.

important subcategory of youth magazines is the wide range of rock-and-roll fan magazines commonly referred to as teenzines.

Ethnic Magazines

Virtually all ethnic minorities have found magazines to be an effective way for members to communicate with one another. Some of the more successful ethnic publications are *Ebony, Jet, Black World, Tan, Lowrider, Upscale, Tafrija, Essence,* and *Identity.* In recent years, the American culture has also seen a growing number of Asian magazines.

Soap Opera Magazines

As the popularity of daytime television soap operas has expanded by gaining viewers among college students and businessmen, the publication of soap opera gossip magazines has also grown. Led by *Soap Opera Digest, Soap Opera Weekly,* and *Soap Opera Update,* these magazines are usually available to the target audience at grocery store checkout counters. The latest development in this area is the publication of magazines by ABC, CBS, and NBC that deal exclusively with the soap operas appearing on each of their television networks. These also are available at the grocery store checkout counter.

In addition to behind-the-scenes stories of the comings and goings of soap opera stars and characters, many of these magazines provide a regular synopsis of the story lines on the various programs. To top it off, there are even magazines that are not published on a regular weekly or monthly basis but provide a complete story line of each soap opera since the time it went on the air. This is to help new viewers find out how the plots developed before they begin purchasing the regular magazines to keep up to date.

> **@ Practicing Media Literacy**
>
> Have *you* ever purchased a soap opera magazine? If so, for what purpose?

Subcultural Magazines

Other subcultures, from motorcycle gangs to marijuana smokers, have magazines specializing in their interests. Such publications include *Easyrider* for bikers, *Advocate* for gay-rights supporters, and *High Times* for marijuana smokers.

Other magazine categories include newsmagazines, opinion, intellectual, quality, humor, city, regional, travel and leisure, hobbies, religions, romance, cars, gourmet foods, environmental, health and fitness, and lifestyles. During the magazine boom years of the 1980s, a publication for the affluent was launched with the appropriate title *Millionaire.* Among the many environmental magazines to join the original "mother" of them all, *Mother Jones,* was a publication launched in 1989 called *Garbage.*

> **@ Practicing Media Literacy**
>
> With such a small target audience for these subcultural magazines, what do you think are the chances for their success?

Even these subculture publications have their problems. In 1998, Jeffrey Klein, one of the cofounders of *Mother Jones* who had been the magazine's editor and president for six years, submitted his resignation, citing pressure from board members to toe a conventional left-wing line. Klein said he wanted to make the magazine "a useful journalistic force" in the 21st century. But some board members had questioned the editor's decisions, including the publication of an article that raised questions about affirmative action, an historically liberal cause. The fact that the magazine had run a $300,000 deficit the previous year may also have contributed to the conflict.[7]

Custom Publishing

In the past several years, a new type of magazine publishing has developed. Called custom publishing, this field calls for businesses to target a specific market and produce a magazine aimed at it. Some companies that have gotten into the custom-publishing field include Mary Kay Cosmetics, which has published *Beauty*; Jenny Craig International, publisher of *Body Health*; and Sony, which publishes *Sony Style* twice a year. Companies that are promoting custom publishing include Hachette Filipacchi Custom Publishing and NYT Custom Publishing.

Additional Periodicals

In addition to the 11,000 publications that are widely available are thousands of periodicals with limited circulation. The Standard Periodical Directory lists over 62,000 journals and magazines in this category, including academic publications, alumni magazines, trade journals, monthly reports from professional associations, industry magazines, free-circulation magazines (such as those produced by airlines), and business publications.

SPECIALIZATION AND POPULAR CULTURE

Many people have tried to explain the trend away from general-interest publications to highly specialized periodicals. The trend was slow at first, starting in 1945 at the end of World War II, but has rapidly accelerated in recent years.

In 1973 sociologist Richard Maisel suggested that the United States had moved from an industrial society to a **postindustrial society,** which is characterized by increased specialization and the growth of service industries. In such a society, he says, the populace tends to fragment into segments with various interests and concerns.[8]

postindustrial society

Jean-Louis Servan-Schreiber, a Frenchman, made the same point in his book *The Power to Inform:* "Americans today find that, as a result of an era of progress from which their country benefited before any of the other industrialized nations, their immense, reputedly homogeneous society of 200 million individuals is fragmenting."[9] In other words, the human resistance to the mass culture that developed during the Industrial Revolution has finally caused that culture to fragment into subcultures with individualistic interests.

Meeting Consumer Needs

This fragmentation has caused magazines to specialize. From their beginnings in the 18th century, magazines have had to give readers what they wanted in order to survive. As Americans had more money to spend and more leisure time to spend it in, people developed special interests to consume their time and money. Coupled with this has been the desire of individuals to find their own identities in our mass culture.

> **@ Practicing Media Literacy**
> What types of specialized magazines do you read on a regular basis and why do you choose those particular publications?

The need to break away from the mass identity created by the Industrial Revolution and find individuality through cults and other subcultural forms (see Chapter 2) has created an interesting paradox. It seems that in addition to our desire to be valued as individuals, we need to belong to some identifiable group—smaller, of course, than the masses as a whole. Thus, we seem to be seeking a compromise in the American popular culture between being faceless entities in mass society and individuals who belong to something. As mass-media scholar Don R. Pember puts it,

> We are young, middle-aged, or old. Many of us find an attachment to a racial or ethnic minority more important than a status as an American. We are Easterners or Southerners or Westerners or Texans or Californians—and proud of it. We are environmentalists, runners, women's liberationists, part of the counterculture, Jesus freaks, skiers, sports car enthusiasts, concerned parents, swinging singles; we collect stamps and coins and beer cans and model trains and antique cars and nostalgia items; we ski, surf, hike, climb mountains, scuba dive, sail, camp, fish, hunt, bowl, golf, ice skate, and swim.[10]

All consumer industries have tried to cater to at least some of these widely varying interests. Our mass media, particularly the magazines, have simply done so more visibly.

One policy of the Hearst Corporation, one of the more successful publishing firms, helped it move quickly into the age of specialization: "Find out what your readers want and give it to them."[11] By 1955 Hearst was already publishing mostly special-interest magazines, including *Motor, Motor Boating, American Druggist, Harper's Bazaar, House Beautiful, Town and Country, Good Housekeeping, Sports Afield,* and *Cosmopolitan*. And when *Cosmopolitan*, for example, started to show signs of decline, the old, rather conservative format was abandoned and a new format was developed by Helen Gurley Brown to appeal to a sophisticated, sexually liberated woman. Its circulation climbed as a result.

Advertising's Role

A magazine's success depends on its ability to attract advertising, and advertisers want magazines that can deliver readers. But not all readers are equally valuable to advertisers. As reader interests began to fragment, advertisers found they could reach their target audiences more effectively and at a lower cost by advertising in special-interest publications with smaller circulations. Magazine advertisers have changed their focus from a "shotgun blast" at the masses to a **rifle shot** at particular groups. From the start, the success or failure of any magazine has depended on its ability to predict reader interests and meet those interests with appropriate reading material. Specialization has made it easier to do so.

Magazine ad revenues continued to increase in the second half of the 1990s. One of the largest magazine advertisers in terms of spending was the automobile industry, for which advertising rose at a double-digit pace during the first half of 1995. Food advertising, the fifth largest category in terms of ad spending, showed signs of recovery from the recession and posted the strongest advance in magazine ad spending, up more than 40 percent. Spending was also reported to be on the increase for computers and apparel, as well as publishing and the media.

The revival in food advertising was credited for the strong growth in advertising revenues for food and women's service magazines. Other magazine ad categories reporting strong, double-digit increases included boating and yachting publications, computers, general interest, men's magazines, photography, and music–entertainment.

rifle shot

CONSUMER AND BUSINESS TRENDS

Despite the slump the magazine industry experienced in the first half of the 1990s, the 20th century as a whole has been a remarkable period of expansion for this mass-communication business (see Box 8.5).

Box 8.5
MEDIA LITERACY
And the Magazines Just Keep on Coming

The final years of the 20th century saw a number of new magazines make their debut, many aimed at the youth market and two magazines that made front-page news with their debuts.

One of the first publications targeting the youth audience in those final years came from the Time-Warner group and was a spinoff of one of its other successful magazines, *People*. When *Teen People* hit the newsstands in 1998, there was no doubt as to which audience it was trying to reach. The articles were about the young stars of movies and television, with Jennifer Love Hewitt on the cover of the first edition and Leonardo DiCaprio on the cover of the second edition.

Also making its debut in 1998 was *Gear*, a magazine aimed at males between 21 and 34. The publication was launched by Bob Guccione, Jr., the son of the founder of *Penthouse* magazine. The first issue featured actress Peta Wilson of the television series *La Femme Nikita* on the cover in her underwear. An interview and more photos were inside. The issue also featured an in-depth investigation of Saddam Hussein, interviews with actor Matt Damon and *Playboy* founder Hugh Hefner, as well as columns on the latest movies, fashions, and books.

At the end of June 1999, the publisher of 37 international editions of *Cosmopolitan* magazine introduced its new teen magazine, *Cosmo Girl*. Officials at Hearst Magazines said the publication and its related website (cosmogirl.com) were aimed at girls between the ages of 12 and 17.

Two other publications used hip-hop music to establish themselves as two of the fastest growing magazines in the nation. *The Source*, which started as a two-page newsletter written by a college radio disc jockey, was the nation's top music magazine in newsstand sales by the end of the 1990s. *Vibe* magazine was launched by music legend Quincy Jones and Time Inc. in 1993 and ended the decade as third in newsstand sales, behind second-place *Rolling Stone*. From the original newsletter, *The Source* grew to an overall monthly circulation of around 371,000, while *Vibe* has gone from a circulation of 100,000 to nearly 532,000 with strong subscription sales. While both magazines have relied on the music world, particularly hip-hop, for their audience, they have also proven successful with general audiences. By the end of the 1990s, *The Source* ranked fourth and *Vibe* was seventh in overall circulation growth, expanding faster than such publications as *PC World* and *Seventeen*.

Another magazine making its debut in the United States came to this country from Great Britain, where this type of publication was known as "laddie books." *Maxim* (maxim.com) is considered a man's magazine and, as one former *Penthouse* editor described it, we're seeing the mainstreaming of the flesh-peddling publications as we go into the 21st century. *Maxim* publisher Felix Dennis says he wants to "do for men what *Cosmo* has done for women . . . it's okay to be a guy."*

The two publications that generated the most headlines with their introductions were *Talk* and *Content*. Even before its first edition hit the newsstands, *Talk* had generated a lot of interest due to a well-publicized fight with the mayor of New York, a lot of hype from that city's tabloid newspapers, and a website that did a parody of the still-unpublished magazine. Steven Brill, who founded *The American Lawyer* magazine and the Court TV cable channel, launched *Content* with the idea of bringing media criticism to the masses. The first issue charged that reporters who had investigated abuses of power in the Watergate coverup of the 1970s had enabled the Clinton–Lewinsky story of the late 1990s to become a media-created scandal. What the magazine did not mention was that Brill had been a contributor to President Clinton's campaign fund, thus raising ethical issues and a lot of criticism from the media. The second issue of the magazine contained several articles defending Brill and the publication's first-edition criticism of how the media were covering independent counsel Kenneth Starr's investigation of the president. Other cover story headlines in several editions of *Content* included: "Lynched by 60 Minutes," "Inside the Boston Globe Fraud," "Dan Rather on How Fear Rules TV News," "*Time* Lynches a Dead Man," "Confessions of a 60 Minutes Producer," and "Who Owns Baseball's Announcers?" In February of 2000, Brill stepped down as editor-in-chief of *Content* while remaining as CEO of the parent company, Brill Media Holdings.

*Maureen Dowd, columnist with the *New York Times* Syndicate, "Beach Blanket Lingo: What Do American Men Really Want?" *Fresno Bee*, July 4, 1999, P. G1.

Box 8.6
HOW IT WORKS
Magazine Publishing

The business operation of a magazine usually has six divisions: administration, editorial, advertising sales, circulation sales, production, and distribution.

The *administration* department handles the business operation of the company. Duties range from paying the bills and keeping the books to ensuring that overhead expenses do not exceed the company's income. The cost of this area of the operation is about 10 percent of the total overhead.

The *editorial* department is in charge of gathering stories and photographs, editing the copy, and designing the pages. The size of this department will vary greatly depending on the type of publication. A newsmagazine, for example, may have many reporters and photographers. Other magazines have a very small editorial department because they rely on freelance writers and photographers to contribute materials. About 10 percent of the overhead goes to paying editorial costs.

The *advertising sales* department is responsible for keeping the magazine profitable. Without advertising revenue, most magazines would go out of business. The cost of advertising depends on the circulation. Magazines usually spend about 10 percent of their overhead on this department.

The *circulation sales* department has the responsibility of getting readers for the publication. The greater the circulation, the more advertisers will want to support a publication. There are two modes of circulation sales: single-copy sales on newsstands and mail-delivery copies to subscribers. Because of the large numbers of magazines available, getting the publication on newsstands is not easy. Obtaining mail subscribers involves numerous promotional activities, including media and direct-mail advertising. About 30 percent of the publication's overhead is spent on this activity.

Production of the magazine is the most expensive part of the process and usually runs about 32 percent of the entire cost of operation. Some magazines have their own typesetting and printing plants, while most rely on outside firms.

The *distribution* department of the magazine handles the transportation of the publication to numerous newsstands and to mailing houses for distribution to subscribers. Speed is an essential ingredient in handling the distribution of publications. Despite the importance of this activity, only about 8 percent of the overhead goes toward distribution.

As with other print media, the electronic age is opening up new areas for employment in the magazine industry. This is expected to increase rapidly as magazines move more fully into the use of videocassette and CD-ROM delivery systems.

---

conglomerate
takeover

As in the book publishing and newspaper industries, consolidation and **conglomerate takeovers** were the name of the game for the magazine industry during the 1980s and 1990s. This trend is expected to continue. According to *U.S. Industrial Outlook,* the Time-Warner merger in 1989 "added momentum to what is becoming a worldwide media consolidation trend."[12] Increased foreign ownership is anticipated, with major publishing firms throughout the world forming partnerships to ease the entry into less familiar markets. The United States is seen as an attractive magazine market for foreign firms because of its currency advantage, access to capital, and opportunities for media growth. U.S. companies are also purchasing foreign magazines. In 1993, Capital Cities/ABC purchased *Expansion,* the largest business magazine in Mexico. Ziff-Davis publishes all of its computer magazines in Europe.

Along with mergers and conglomerate takeovers has come controversy. Shortly after the merger of Time Inc. and Warner Communications, Time publications ran a 32-page advertising insert commemorating the 50th birthday of Warner Bros.' Bugs Bunny. The insert reached some 80 million people by appearing in *Time, Life, People, Fortune,* and *Entertainment Weekly.* Some media critics called the campaign "a prime example of intracompany back-scratching that is 'anticompetitive' and smacks of self-dealing by the giant media concern."[13] When Rupert Murdoch purchased *TV Guide* in 1988, critics complained it would give unfair advantage to his efforts to develop the Fox television network. Although increased coverage of the Fox network by *TV Guide* has not been blatant, it has been apparent.

While newsstand sales of magazines have seen some small increases, subscriptions are still the main choice for most readers. Subscriptions are not only less expensive than single copies but are often a more convenient way to receive the magazines. Studies have shown that single-copy purchases are usually impulse buys and quite often involve special issues. Among those in this category that sell well are the *Sports Illustrated* swimsuit edition and *Playboy*'s "Playmate of the Year" issue.

Although the outlook for magazine advertising remains favorable, rising paper costs and postal rates have put a squeeze on magazine publishers' margins. In recent years, the industry has seen the cost for the paper stock favored by most magazines increase as much as 20 percent over the comparable period a year earlier. At the same time, second- and third-class postage rates also increased more than had been expected. While revenue for newsstand and subscription circulation for more than half of the nation's 200 largest magazines was on the increase, analysts say the gains resulted largely from substantial hikes in cover prices. However, there may come a time when such price increases won't be able to offset the increasing costs of publication.

One area where magazines have found a new market is in **Russia.** Many magazines, from *Good Housekeeping* to *Playboy*, are thriving with Russian editions that target the wealthy and the want-to-be wealthy readers of this nation experimenting with capitalism. The glossy magazines serve as an escape—into fashion, art, music, film, and a better lifestyle. The Russian expansion is part of a trend as American and European publishers search to expand their markets. Before the Soviet Union collapsed in 1991, state-owned women's and general interest magazines carried drab stories and muddy printing. Today, newsstands in Russia supply everything from the women's fashion magazine *Elle* to the men's action publication *Soldier of Fortune*. The leader in circulation among American publications is *Cosmopolitan*, with 470,000, followed by *Good Housekeeping* (300,000), *Elle* (200,000) and *Playboy* (130,000).[14]

Russia

The magazine industry faces new challenges in the 21st century. Demographic changes brought on by aging baby boomers require more attention to such areas as the home, parenting, schooling, financial management, and careers. The industry has already begun focusing on these demographic changes and, with the move into cyberspace, will surely give increased attention to them during the remainder of this decade.

NEW TECHNOLOGY AND MAGAZINES

The electronic technology revolution is playing a role in changing the way we read magazines. Magazines, like newspapers, can now be read from computer screens through the World Wide Web. In addition, videocassette players and CD-ROMs are beginning to provide alternatives to traditional magazines.

Video Magazines

Video magazines for the VCR began making their appearance in the last part of the 20th century. Like print magazines, video magazines are published on a regular basis, with many sold at supermarket checkouts and other retail outlets for a cost of about

$5, not much more than the cost of a blank cassette. The cassettes can be reused for other recording purposes after the magazine has been viewed. Like the print versions, video magazines include advertising—about 20 minutes' worth in the two-hour program.

Compact Disks

Some magazines are currently looking at compact disks as new technologies for electronic delivery of magazines. These new technologies will allow magazines to join the book publishing and newspaper industries in the electronic delivery of print material to be viewed and listened to on the computer.

SUMMARY

Since the beginning of the 18th century, magazines have provided a wide variety of material for their readers. All magazines by their very nature specialize in some way. They either have unit specialization or internal specialization.

Magazines did not really begin to flourish until the 1820s, when new technologies, coupled with a newly literate society brought on by compulsory education, paved the way for their expansion. By the end of the 19th century, magazines had entered the popular culture with general-interest, special-interest, and low-cost publications.

The beginning of the 20th century was the heyday of muckraking articles in magazines, but by 1917 the public's attention had shifted to concern about World War I in Europe. In the 1920s, a new variety of magazines developed to meet the needs of the new, fast-paced American culture. After World War II, general-interest magazines started to decline, and the age of specialization was firmly established.

Magazines can be classified in a variety of ways, but clearly there seems to be a magazine for just about every interest and taste in both our popular and elite cultures. Individuals in our culture have gone from being faceless components of a mass society to being members of a variety of interest groups. Magazines, which must deliver readers to their advertisers, have changed to cater to these various special interests and, as a result, have become the first mass medium to effectively reflect these changes.

New electronic technologies, such as the World Wide Web, CD-ROMs, and videotapes, are changing the way magazines are delivered to readers. The computer age will make its impact on this print industry as it has on others.

Find a review of *Key People and Concepts*, a message board for *Practicing Media Literacy* questions, self tests, and more at: www.mhhe.com/wilson.

Thought Questions

1. What cultural factors contributed to the movement of magazines into the popular stage of the EPS cycle?
2. What impact on magazine popularity do you think new electronic delivery systems for magazines will have?
3. Will magazines in cyberspace ever replace the print versions? Explain.
4. Select a popular magazine that has been around for a long time and examine early copies on microfilm in your college library. What does such an examination tell you about changes in our culture?

5. Go to a major bookstore or newsstand that carries a wide variety of magazines. What does your examination of the types of magazines available tell you about our society's subcultural interests? How many different subcultures can you identify from these publications?

Notes

1. "Di's Death Challenged Magazines; *Time* and *Newsweek* Had to Scrap Their Editions over the Weekend and Start Over," Associated Press in the *Fresno Bee*, September 2, 1997, p. C2.

2. Frank Luther Mott, *History of American Magazines* 1741–1850 (New York: Macmillan, 1930), p. 232.

3. Oscar Handlin, *The History of the United States*, vol. 2 (New York: Holt, Rinehart & Winston, 1968), p. 322.

4. Alex Kuczynski, "TV Guide Sold for $9.2 Billion in Stock Deal," *New York Times*, October 5, 1999, p. C1.

5. John Brady, "The Nude Journalism," in Edward Jay Whetmore, ed., *Medi-America: Form, Content and Consequences of Mass Communication*, 5th ed. (Belmont, CA: Wadsworth, 1993), pp. 96–97.

6. Jon Swartz, "Wired Magazine to Stay in S.F.; No Culture Shock after $80 Million Sale," *San Francisco Chronicle*, May 9, 1998, p. D1.

7. Carol Emert, "Culture Clash; *Mother Jones* Magazine's Liberals at Odds," *San Francisco Chronicle*, August 29, 1998, p. D1.

8. Richard Maisel, "The Decline of Mass Media," *Public Opinion Quarterly*, Summer 1973, p. 161.

9. Jean-Louis Servan-Schreiber, *The Power to Inform* (New York: McGraw-Hill, 1974).

10. Don R. Pember, *Mass Media in America*, 4th ed. (Chicago: Science Research Associates, 1983), p. 89.

11. John Tebbel, *The American Magazine: A Compact History* (New York: Hawthorn, 1969), p. 211.

12. U.S. Industrial Outlook, 1990 (Washington, D.C.: U.S. Government Printing Office, 1990), p. 48–6.

13. Paul Farhi, "Time Warner Inc.'s 32-Page Ad Insert Bugs a Media Critic," *Los Angeles Times*, May 5, 1990, p. D-2.

14. Charles W. Holmes, "American Magazines Raise Spirits in Russia," Associated Press in the *Palm Springs Desert Sun*, November 28, 1997.

3

Development of
Electronic Media

Motion Pictures

Cultural Reflections

People tell me that the movies should be more like real life. I disagree. It is real life that should be more like the movies.

—Walter Winchell

Key People and Concepts

Thomas A. Edison

Persistence of Vision

Kinetoscope

Cinematographe

Vitascope

Nickelodeons

George Melies

Birth of a Nation

Keystone Kops

Charlies Chaplin

The Jazz Singer

Motion Picture Producers and Distributors of America (MPPDA)

Celebrities

The Red Scare

Cinerama

Ratings

Special Effects

Digital Video Disc (DVD)

Conglomerates

Virtual Reality

The much anticipated fourth release in the *Star Wars* series, *Episode 1: The Phantom Menace*, may not have been as big a hit as expected, but it still managed to gross almost $430 million during its run in the United States. That was enough to make it the largest grossing film of 1999. But it was a small-budget independent film that generated a lot of talk—particularly on the Internet; in fact, the Internet support and some clever promotion helped the film, *The Blair Witch Project*, to also crack the top-10 list of box-office hits during the final year of the 20th century (see Box 9.1). ● The success of the unusual film, which told the story of the final hours of three college students using their own hand-held cameras to make a documentary about the Blair Witch legend before they disappeared, was greatly hyped on the Internet. It had its own website. It encouraged discussion among those who had seen the film. It caused critics to charge that much of the buzz online was actually planted by people connected with the movie. The film ended up being featured on the covers of both *Time* and *Newsweek* during the same week. ● The directors removed their names from the opening of the film to make it seem more like a documentary. Another phony documentary was shown on the science fiction cable channel featuring interviews with the sheriff and the private detective who "investigated" the disappearance of the three students. (There were some who felt that this "documentary" was more realistic—and entertaining—than the actual film.) After the film had been released, several minutes of footage not used in the movie or the home video release were made available through Amazon.com on the Internet (amazon.com/blair witch.) A comic book telling the tale of the Blair Witch legend was released. Book clubs began advertising an illustrated companion to the film, featuring "interviews" with the townspeople, historians, and relatives of the "missing" students, as well as the students' "actual journals," police reports, and crime photos.

Called *The Blair Witch Project: A Dossier Compiled by D.A. Stern*, the book also promised an in-depth analysis of the disappearance of the three filmmakers.   •   It was a masterpiece of marketing and it may have opened a new area of promotion using the new media. It turned the movie industry on its ear, costing only $55,000 to make a small portion of the cost of the *Star Wars* epic, yet grossing $141 million, enough money to become a cultural phenomenon. The success also started talk of two sequels, *Blair Witch 2*, planned for release around Halloween of 2000 and *Blair Witch 3*, a prequel to tell the original story of the witch who lived in the 1780s, for release in the summer of 2001.   •   At the start of the 20th century, movies were still in their infancy—primarily featuring still shots of people and objects moving in front of the camera. As the 21st century began, the motion picture industry had become a multibillion dollar industry featuring flawless special effects through new computer technology and utilizing all other media to help promote its products. In this chapter, we'll look at this century-long development of a medium which has had a tremendous impact on our society and our culture.

EARLY HISTORY

In the late 19th century, as city dwellers were enjoying more leisure time, they began looking for new pastimes beyond reading, the ballpark, and vaudeville (see Chapter 2). This was the industrial age, and mechanical inventions of all kinds were dramatically changing the American way of life. It was only natural that some inventors turned their attention to developing mechanical devices for leisure use.

Thomas Edison

The leading American inventor of leisure technology was Thomas A. Edison, probably best known for inventing the light bulb. But he was also responsible for devising the phonograph in the 1870s, and by the late 1800s he was trying to come up with something similar for the eye. The concept behind motion pictures, however, actually dates back to the second century A.D., when the Greek astronomer Ptolemy discovered that the human eye retains an image on the retina for a moment after the image disappears. This is called *persistence of vision*. Over the years, many people theorized that a series of still pictures of similar but slightly different images could give the illusion of movement if flashed before the eye quickly, because persistence of vision would fill in the gaps.

Edison was not alone in experimenting with persistence of vision. Other early pioneers in the development of motion pictures were Etienne Jules Marey and Eadweard Muybridge, who conducted a number of experiments using multiple cameras to photograph the movements of animals.

Edison purchased some of Muybridge's pictures and met with Marey in Europe to examine his work. He then put his assistant, William Kennedy Dickson, to work on perfecting the process. Dickson developed a motion picture projection box that Edison called a *kinetoscope*, a four-foot-tall box that one person at a time could peer into to see a series of still photos "move" across a light source. In 1894, the first kinetoscope parlor opened in New York City. One of the first films Edison Company made for the kinetoscope was a 30-second strip called *Anabelle*. Sex and violence soon became the predominant themes for these early films.

Cultural History of Motion Pictures

		Elitist	Popular	Specialized
1888	First motion picture camera developed in Thomas A. Edison's lab.	•		
1895	Lumière brothers start projecting motion pictures in a Paris café.		•	
1896	Films shown in vaudeville theaters.		•	
1903	Edwin S. Porter's *The Great Train Robbery*, first American film to tell a complete story.		•	
1905–1910	Era of the nickelodeon, movie theaters charge a nickel.		•	
1912	Mack Sennett begins Keystone Company, which specialized in slapstick comedy.		•	
1915	D. W. Griffith releases *Birth of a Nation*, first full-length film to have an impact on the culture.		•	
1917	Charlie Chaplin becomes first entertainer to earn $1 million a year.		•	
1920s	Large, opera house-type theaters are built to lure the elite.	•		
1927	*The Jazz Singer* ushers in talking motion picture era.		•	
1930	Motion picture industry tightens its code of standards to avoid censorship.		•	
1930s–1940s	Golden Age of movies; movies provide an escape from the Depression and war.		•	
1939	*Gone With the Wind* breaks box office records.		•	
1941	Orson Welles's *Citizen Kane* is released.		•	
1941–1945	Hollywood promotes patriotism during World War II with propaganda films and rousing war movies.		•	
1946	Hollywood's biggest box office year—$1.7 billion gross income, 87 million Americans attending movies each week.		•	
1947	Red Scare leads to congressional investigation of Hollywood.		•	
1948	Supreme Court requires movie studios to sell their theaters.		•	
1949	Motion picture audiences decline with advent of TV.		•	
1950s	Hollywood experiments with 3-D, CinemaScope, and Cinerama to bring audiences back to the theaters.			•
1960s	Movie industry abandons self-censorship and adopts a movie-rating system.			•
1960s	Youth, sex, and violence help sell movies to new audiences.			•
1977	George Lucas's *Star Wars* is released; its computerized special effects give movies a new image and excitement.			•
1980s	Video movies expand industry revenues; multiplexes replace large-screen theaters.			•
1990s	Film industry gets into video game business.			•
1993	Special-effects film *Jurassic Park* breaks box office records.			•
1997	*Star Wars* trilogy reissued, setting new box office record. However, single film record is set by *Titanic*.			•
1999	*Star Wars* prequel, *Episode I: The Phantom Menace* is released. *Blair Witch Project* uses Internet to generate interest.			•
2000	Disney comes out with a new *Fantasia* for large screen IMax theaters.			

As the 20th century began, the makers of movies had little idea of this new media tool with which they were working. The normal procedure was to place a camera in a set spot and record all of the movement taking place in front of the camera, whether it was people leaving a factory after a day on the job, or people getting off of a train, or men knocking down a wall. That was it.

But a few innovative people began experimenting with editing to provide scene changes; then stories for movies began to develop, and soon we had short films that people would actually pay money to view. The industry was beginning to expand into a major entertainment force in our society.

Some 100 years later, the business was so large that marketing strategies were used to promote the latest releases; important decisions were made as to just which weekend was the right one to release the newest movies, and records were kept of box-office receipts each week, with television and newspapers running the weekly top 10 and final totals given out at the end of the year as to which movies made the most money.

At the end of the 20th century, the biggest film of the year had brought in almost $430 million in revenue in this country, with box-office figures from the release in other nations yet to be totaled. The 1999 movie season saw record box-office receipts, the best attendance in some four decades, and one of the most diverse lineups of hit movies as had ever been produced. Ticket sales in the United States for movies in 1999 hit $7.5 billion, a big jump from the 1998 figure of $6.95 billion.

However, taking inflation into account, the movie industry at the end of the 20th century fell well below Hollywood's golden years of the 1930s and 1940s. But that shouldn't take away from the fact that 1999 ticket sales of around 1.5 billion tickets was the highest in the last half of the century.

In all, 17 films made more than $100 million in 1999, compared with 11 movies reaching that level the previous year. When you consider that by the end of the century, the movie industry has had to compete with many home entertainment choices, such as television, video rentals, and the Internet, you would have to agree that it was a good year of getting people out to the movie theaters.

Perhaps the diversity of choices in quality movies to end the 20th century may have had something to do with good business. Here is the list of the top-10 box-office hits of 1999 (note the diversity, from science fiction to children's movies, to comedies, to love stories, to scary horror films.* How many did *you* put down money to see? (Remember, some of these films were still playing at the start of the year 2000, so the revenue will be even higher):

1. *Star Wars: Episode 1: The Phantom Menace,* $429.9 million
2. *The Sixth Sense,* $275.2 million
3. *Austin Powers: The Spy Who Shagged Me,* $205.4 million
4. *Toy Story 2,* $179.7 million
5. *The Matrix,* $171.4 million
6. *Tarzan,* $170.9 million
7. *Big Daddy,* $163.5 million
8. *The Mummy,* $155.3 million
9. *Runaway Bride,* $151.8 million
10. *The Blair Witch Project,* $140.5 million

*David Germain, "Diversity, Big Sales Give Movies Blockbuster Year," Associated Press; in *Fresno Bee,* December 28, 1999, p. C1.

Projection

In 1895, two brothers in France, Auguste and Louis Lumière, perfected Edison's invention by developing a projector called the *cinematographe,* which could project the film onto a large screen. They produced films and began showing them for an admission price in the basement of a Paris café.

In the United States, the novelty of Edison's kinetoscope began to wear off. In the meantime, two inventors of a movie projection system known as the *vitascope,*

Thomas Armat and Francis Jenkins, joined forces with Edison, and in April 1896 motion pictures began showing in penny arcades and vaudeville houses, supplementing the live entertainment. It is perhaps ironic that vaudeville houses were the location for the early development of motion pictures. Once the industry was fully developed, it played a major role in the decline of vaudeville.

The arcades, which charged a nickel to see the movies, sparked the development of storefront movie theaters that became known as nickelodeons, where admission cost a nickel. The average length of a motion picture was about 12 minutes, and most programs featured two films. By 1909 there were nearly 10,000 nickelodeons in the United States.

Early Classics

Another major innovator was the Frenchman George Méliès, who began producing films in 1896 and soon became an international distributor. He introduced the concept of special effects. Méliès most famous film, *A Trip to the Moon* (1902), showed a group of scientists and chorus girls launching a rocket to the moon. The rocket hit the "eye" of the man in the moon, and space travelers encountered moon men. The special effects in the film, although far from today's standards, were fascinating at the time and included the earth rising on the moon's horizon and moon people disappearing in smoke.

The founder of the story film was the American film producer Edwin S. Porter, an Edison Company cameraman. In his most famous film, *The Great Train Robbery* (1903), he developed new editing techniques to piece together different scenes to create a story line. The film, filled with gunfights, chases, and other action as a band of desperadoes robs a westbound train, was only 12 minutes long, but it set standards for drama and excitement that would become basic to American films for years to come. Incidentally, it also introduced the enduring Western theme into American filmmaking. The significance of *The Great American Train Robbery* has been summed up this way:

> For years *The Great American Train Robbery* was the nickelodeon's most widely exhibited picture and it is said to have insured the permanence of the movies. It became the bible for all film makers until Griffith's films further developed Porter's editing principle. The efforts of all movie makers to imitate its form and content stimulated the industry as nothing— not even Méliès' film—had ever done before.[1]

The next milestone in the development of American motion pictures was *Birth of a Nation*, directed by D. W. Griffith and released in 1915. Originally titled *The Clansmen,* the film was a masterpiece that lasted more than three hours. Although all early films were silent, Griffith's film was accompanied by a complete musical score performed by a symphony orchestra. The movie impressed the nation and led President Woodrow Wilson to say it was "like writing history with lightning."[2]

Griffith began his career in motion pictures in 1907 as an actor for Mutoscope and Biograph Company in New York. Because his acting skills were limited, he became a director a year later. He was the first to use close-ups and a variety of camera angles to add emotional impact to his films. Through new editing techniques, he showed how emotion and tension could be generated by the length of the scene, with shorter scenes creating greater excitement. An innovator who defied the conventions of moviemaking, Griffith insisted on hiring established stage actors and holding rehearsals. He was also among the first to shoot on location, at San Gabriel Mission outside Los Angeles in 1910.

Birth of a Nation, filmed in Los Angeles, used all of Griffith's innovations in shooting, lighting, and editing to capture the emotion of the Civil War. It was the first

D. W. Griffith's Civil War epic Birth of a Nation *revolutionized the way movies were made, but generated much controversy for its bigoted portrayal of African-Americans.*

motion picture to attempt to portray a part of U.S. history in dramatic terms, covering the period from pre-Civil War days through Reconstruction. Griffith, the son of a Confederate officer, had a flawed, sentimental attachment to the Old South. His sympathetic portrayal of the Ku Klux Klan and stereotyping of African-Americans offended many. The National Association for the Advancement of Colored People (NAACP), the president of Harvard University, and liberal politicians all condemned the work for its bigoted portrayal of African-Americans. Despite this, the movie was a box-office success, earning $18 million, and clearly demonstrated what a dramatic impact this new art form could have on popular culture. Its showing in major cities resulted in race riots and a rebirth of the Ku Klux Klan in the South.

Griffith was stung by the uproar his film created. He decided to invest some $2 million of the profits from the film to create a new movie, *Intolerance*, which preached against the evils of bigotry. He reportedly chose the name because he believed he himself had been a victim of intolerance. Despite high production costs and lavish sets, the film was a box-office flop.

MOVIES AND THE EPS CYCLE

Unlike the print media, motion pictures did not spend a long period in the elite culture before moving into the popular stage of the EPS cycle (see Chapter 1). In fact, there were more culturally elite films today than there were in the early days of motion pictures. A more realistic description of the media progression cycle for motion pictures would be the PEPS cycle.

Both social and economic factors explain why this new medium moved immediately into the popular culture. Silent movies appeared at a time when American cities sheltered large numbers of foreign workers. Even though many of these immigrants spoke no English, they could still enjoy the drama and comedy of silent films; **pantomime** is a universal language.

In addition to meeting a social need, movies were relatively inexpensive. The first movie houses, the nickelodeons, were inexpensive storefront theaters. Their 5-cent admission made the movies affordable for the immigrants and others in the popular culture. In fact, their admission price and melodramatic, slapstick acting actually discouraged the elite from attending. By the 1920s large, palace-like movie theaters were being built. They were modeled after the opera houses and concert halls of the 19th century. Between 1920 and 1930, 250 of these magnificent theaters were built. Among them were the Roxy Theater in New York City and Sid Grauman's Chinese Theater in Hollywood. Majestic theaters were opening at the rate of one per week during the latter part of the 1920's. Admission to these theaters usually cost 65 cents (35 cents before 6 P.M.), and the elite started attending films, often for the theater experience rather than for the movies being shown. Many of these ornate theaters still stand and are featured each week on the American Movie Classics cable channel.

Although most of today's movies are made for the mass audience, a few films are still released each year targeted at the more elite audience. These are quite often based on literary masterpieces and are displayed at art-movie houses and in major markets.

Unlike the print media, the motion picture industry moved almost immediately into the popular stage during the Industrial Revolution, bypassing the elite stage for the moment. It had come along at the right time to meet the recreational needs of a rapidly growing mass culture. The motion picture industry started out as a mechanical medium and later became electronically operated.

[margin note: pantomine]

THE RISE OF COMEDY

In the early days of the motion pictures, comedy came to play a special role in the socialization of immigrants and other workers who were often the victim of exploitation. It had a special appeal for this new workforce of the industrial society because it gave them an opportunity to laugh at the disappointments, frustrations, and confrontations of daily living.

Mack Sennett

One of the first to make a major contribution to motion picture comedy was Mack Sennett, who worked for Griffith in his early days in the film industry. The son of Irish immigrants, Sennett struck out on his own in the fledgling movie industry in 1912, founding the Keystone Film Company. Sennett fascinated his audiences by showing them the new 20th-century America. Typical scenes showed automobiles beginning to replace the horse and buggy, dusty roads, police officers in slapstick chase scenes, men with large mustaches, and women wearing full-length dresses and huge hats. Sennett's comedy effectively brought to the screen the visual and physical elements of burlesque, and his **Keystone Kops** became a Hollywood trademark.

[margin note: Keystone Kops]

Hal Roach

Another pioneer of early movie comedy was Hal Roach who at the age of 22 left employment as a gold miner and mule skinner to become a cowboy stuntman in silent films. This new career led him into motion picture production, where he did some directing and producing before developing the Hal Roach studios where he brought to the screen such outstanding movie comics as Laurel and Hardy, Charley Chase, and Harold Lloyd. But most people today remember Roach for the **Our Gang** comedies, which still turn up regularly on television and cable channels. Roach was honored with a special Oscar by the Academy of Motion Picture Arts and Sciences at the age of 91 and was again given a standing ovation at age 100 when he was recognized by master of ceremonies Billy Crystal at the Oscar awards in 1992. He died later that year.

Our Gang

Charlie Chaplin

An English stage comedian, Charlie Chaplin came to this country in 1913 to tour vaudeville stages with a music-hall act. Although leery of the new medium of film, he was enticed to start working for Sennett at Keystone for an attractive salary of $150 a week. One year later he signed a contract with Essanay Company of Chicago for $1,250 a week, plus a $10,000 bonus for signing and a guarantee of $75,000 for 1915 (a huge amount of money in those days). The contract allowed him to act, direct, and produce his comedies. By 1917 Chaplin was making more than $1 million a year, a figure that was almost incomprehensible at a time when many people earned less than $1,000 a year and new automobiles sold for several hundred dollars.

In 1915 Chaplin produced **The Tramp**, in which he played a vagabond in baggy pants who comes to the rescue of a pretty girl. The tramp and his girl were the heroes of many of the Chaplin movies that followed. While giving people an opportunity to laugh at the plight of the downtrodden in society, Chaplin also used comedy to make social commentary on good and evil in our culture. Only relatively few had prospered from the years of unfettered industrial expansion, while a vast and growing army of workers struggled to cope with low salaries and harsh working conditions. Chaplin's films depicted the dark and often cruel distances between the haves and have-nots.

But it was Chaplin's liberal, somewhat radical views that eventually ended his career in this country. During the years following World War II, when Americans were concerned that Communists were taking control of the motion picture industry to spread their propaganda, some people questioned Chaplin's beliefs. Rather than fight inquiries by the House Un-American Activities Committee, Chaplin returned to his native Great Britain to live. It was not until 1971, when he was asked by the

> **@   Practicing Media Literacy**
>
> Have you ever seen any of the old silent film comedies? If so, what did you think of it? Did it make you laugh, even though there was no dialogue?

The Tramp

The plight of Charlie Chaplin's Tramp also reflected many of the social ills of American culture.

Academy of Motion Picture Arts and Sciences to end his more than 20-year self-imposed exile, that he returned to Hollywood, the site of his many earlier movie successes, to receive an honorary Oscar—an award that had previously eluded him.

Chaplin was the first 20th-century superstar. Millions of fans rushed to novelty shops to purchase mechanical dolls and plaster tramp statuettes in his image, much as later generations have bought Mouseketeer, Beatles, *Star Wars*, and Teenage Mutant Ninja Turtle paraphernalia.[3]

"Another fine mess you've gotten us into!" The comedy team of Laurel and Hardy was also successful after moving into talking pictures.

Stan Laurel and Oliver Hardy

Other popular comedy stars in the silent film era were Stan Laurel and Oliver Hardy, who, in the Sennett and Chaplin style, portrayed the downtrodden against the world. Although they started out separately, they got together in 1926 and remained a popular movie comedy team well into the sound era. Indeed, of all the comedians from the silent film era, they were the most successful in making the switch to sound motion pictures.

Buster Keaton and Harold Lloyd

Although not a team, two other master comedians of the silent era were Buster Keaton and Harold Loyd. Keaton came close to rivaling Chaplin in his ability to provide funny and serious insights into human relationships and to dramatize the conflict between individuals and immense industrial society that surrounded them. Lloyd was an actor who was able to play a comedian for the Hal Roach production company. Like Chaplin, Lloyd was small in physical stature, which was portrayed as a disadvantage as his characters struggled against various misfortunes and dangerous predicaments in a hostile world.

WORLD WAR I AND THE MOVIES

The advent of World War I in 1914 helped the American film industry flourish. Moviemakers had moved their operations to Hollywood, California, where good weather and wide, open spaces allowed for year-round outdoor filmmaking. The European film industry was placed on hold when the war broke out. During the three years before the United States entered the war in 1917, the Hollywood film industry prospered. Many of the films during this period were propaganda films that promoted patriotism. Some 175 motion pictures about the war were produced between 1914 and 1918, with such titles as *Claws of the Hun* and *The Kaiser's Finish*. By the early 1920s, Hollywood was producing three-quarters of the world's films.

SOUND JOINS MOTION

By 1925, 46 million Americans were attending movies weekly. The American film industry had become big business. Movies made in Hollywood set standards of excellence throughout the world. This was the decade in which sound was synchronized with film and a new medium emerged.

Early Efforts

For 30 years, inventors had attempted to connect sound to motion pictures. William Dickson, Thomas Edison's assistant, claimed to have produced a rough synchronization of word and picture as early as 1889. Others experimented with synchronizing recording disks with motion pictures in France between 1896 and 1900. However, live sound was preferred during the nickelodeon days in the United States. Piano, organs, or trios of musicians provided musical accompaniment to many films. Actors sometimes recited the lines behind the screen. Sometimes narrators explained or commented on the scenes in the movies. (Oliver Hardy's first job in cinema, incidentally, was singing in a quartet behind the screen at an Atlanta nickelodeon.)

Serious problems continued to hamper efforts to put sound and motion together. Separate disk machines, such as the Vitaphone, could easily get out of sync with the film. After World War I, three German inventors discovered a way to put sound directly on film using light beams. In the United States, Dr. Lee De Forest developed a similar sound-on-film process. De Forest, whom many consider to be the founder of American radio (see Chapter 10), started demonstrating sound motion pictures in 1923.

The Jazz Singer

Not until mass audiences heard Al Jolson sing "Mammy" on screen in *The Jazz Singer* (1927) did people realize that sound motion pictures were really possible. Produced by Warner Bros., a small movie company, the film was an instant success and changed the movie business forever.

In 1930, the trade paper *Variety* summed up the impact of sound this way: "it didn't do any more to the industry than turn it upside down, shake the entire bag of tricks from its pocket and advance Warner Brothers from last place to first in the league."

The public's rapid acceptance of sound initially caught the film industry off guard, but soon all the studios were scrambling to produce "talkies." By 1930, the silent film era was history, and so was its universal language of pantomime. Also at an end were the careers of actors and actresses with unsuitable voices or accents. The problem of performers with unacceptable voices for the talkies was spoofed in the 1952 Gene Kelly musical classic *Singing in the Rain*.

Although it was called a talking picture, The Jazz Singer *actually had very little dialogue but lots of singing by star Al Jolson.*

Although Lon Chaney's 1925 silent classic *Phantom of the Opera* featured a masquerade ball filmed in Technicolor, the remainder of the film was shot in black and white. Several studios also experimented with Technicolor sequences in a few of their movies during those early years, but all-Technicolor films did not become common until the mid-1930s.

However, black and white was still the preferred format for most movies released through the 1940s.

Cultural Changes

The 1920s were a period of immense technological and social change in American culture. The automobile, radio, advertising, and the motion picture combined to change American lifestyles and help usher in an age of "New Morality." Many films glamorized the fast, loose life of the **Roaring '20s**. They showed men and women dancing, smoking, and drinking in public, activities previously considered unacceptable, particularly for women. The movies helped to break down these taboos and change cultural attitudes. Today movie critics note that since the 1920s there has been an increase in the number of cases of lung cancer and alcoholism among women.

Roaring '20s

A number of scandals in Hollywood during the 1920s led some to refer to the movie capital as a 20th-century Babylon.[4] A director named William Desmond Taylor was murdered; actor Wallace Reid, on the screen a symbol of virtuous young American manhood, died of a narcotics overdose; and comedian Fatty Arbuckle was charged with manslaughter in the death of a girl at a party in his San Francisco hotel suite.

Self-Censorship

In this era of Prohibition, when many people believed government should police public morals, it was not surprising that many cried out for some form of government censorship of the film industry. To forestall such an effort, the industry established its own organization to draw up a code of ethics. The Motion Picture Producers and Distributors of America (MPPDA) was founded in 1922. Its first president was Will H. Hays, who was a former postmaster general, the chairman of the Republican National Committee, and an elder in the Presbyterian Church. His credentials gave the office the political and moral stature needed to avert government censorship.

The MPPDA established a list of forbidden subjects that corresponded to the most frequent targets of critics. In 1927, this list was adopted as the Code of the Motion Picture Industry. Criticism continued, however, primarily from the Catholic Church. In 1930 the MPPDA, now commonly known as "the Hays Office," tightened the code to spell out more clearly what could not be shown in motion pictures. Depiction of immoral behavior and nudity was still permissible as long as it was made clear that such behavior was wrong and those who indulged in it were punished. According to film historian Arthur Knight, "The studios could present six reels of ticket-selling sinfulness if, in the seventh reel, all the sinners came to a bad end."[5]

The fast, loose life portrayed in movies eventually led to the Catholic Church's formation of a legion of decency, which advocated boycotts of motion pictures the Church deemed indecent.[6] Protestant and Jewish groups backed the legion's efforts, and Hollywood felt the impact of the boycotts on a national scale.

The Hays Office responded to this pressure in 1934 by issuing a stringent set of rules, the Code to Govern the Making of Motion and Talking Pictures, to be enforced by a new Production Code Administration (**PCA**). Movies released without PCA approval were fined $25,000. These self-imposed guidelines prohibited profanity, replaced skimpy-dress scenes with full-clothing scenes, and restricted bedroom scenes to married men and women only (and even they had to be shown in separate beds). Not only were such words as *God, hell,* and *sex* banned, but so were everyday slang terms such as *guts, nuts,* and *louse.* The Hays Office even got involved in timing the length

PCA

of screen kisses. The movies became so pristine during this period that a major national furor arose in 1939 when Clark Gable used the word *damn* in this now immortal line, "Frankly, my dear, I don't give a "damn," in *Gone With the Wind*.

Perhaps the first breaks in the Hays code came in the 1950s with two films directed by Otto Preminger. The first, *The Moon is Blue* (1953), did not receive code approval because it dealt with seduction and used the term *virgin*. Preminger decided to release the film, adapted by F. Hugh Herbert from his Broadway stage hit, without the approval of the Hays Office or the Catholic Church. Most people agree the film is quite tame compared to today's standards, but it caused much controversy in the early 1950s.

Another Preminger film, *The Man with the Golden Arm* (1955), also violated Hays Office standards because it dealt with drug addiction and actually showed the main character, played by Frank Sinatra, injecting heroin into his arm and later going through withdrawal as he tried to kick the habit. With the box-office success of these films and others, the Hays Office slowly lost its power.

> **@   Practicing Media Literacy**
>
> Do you think we would be better off today if there was a Hollywood office that set rules for the content of movies?

A Way of Life

In the 1930s and 1940s, moviegoing was not merely a form of entertainment but a way of life. People no longer went to see a particular picture; they "went to the movies," much as many people today sit down for an evening of TV watching.

Big Studios and Stars

To serve the rapidly growing audience, large film studios developed. MGM, Paramount, Warner Brothers (movies.warnerbros.com), 20th Century Fox, Universal (mca.com), and RKO all put actors and actresses under contract and made them into **movie stars.** Some of the all-time greats were Mary Pickford, Lillian Gish, Douglas Fairbanks, W.C. Fields, the Marx Brothers, Gary Cooper, Jimmy Stewart, Clark Gable, Clara Bow, Jean Harlow, Spencer Tracy, Katharine Hepburn, John Wayne, James Cagney, Fred Astaire, Ginger Rogers, Humphrey Bogart, Rita Hayworth, Joan Crawford, Edward G. Robinson, and Judy Garland.

movie stars

Studios started mass-producing motion pictures. Since each major studio owned its own chain of theaters across the country, it had to produce one feature film and one B movie (an inexpensive film for second billing) for each of the 52 weeks in a year. Cartoons and newsreels were also needed to round out the evening's entertainment.

The Great Depression

Offering a complete evening of entertainment for the price of one show became very important during the Great Depression of the 1930s. Although movie theater attendance declined in 1934, more than 60 percent of the American public found a way to afford to go to the movies during the Depression. The lavish spectaculars of this period helped people forget the dreary reality of daily living and escape into a make-believe world created by Hollywood.

Trends and Celebrities

Even in those lean years, movies played their role in keeping our consumer culture alive. For example, one of the top box-office stars of the decade was a curly-haired little girl named Shirley Temple. The star of 21 relentlessly upbeat films, she spurred the sale of Shirley temple dolls, books, and clothing.

The stars influenced everything in our popular culture, from what people wore to how they did their hair. Peroxide hair-rinse sales skyrocketed in the 1930s, thanks to Jean Harlow, Carole Lombard, and Mae West and such movies as *Platinum Blonde* (1931). In 1934, Clark Gable nearly destroyed the undershirt industry when he took off his shirt and exposed a bare chest in *It Happened One Night*. Soon men all over the nation were following suit and abandoning their long-standing habit of wearing undershirts. This impact on the viewing public has continued, from the clothes and the music of *Saturday Night Fever* (1977) to the sudden popularity of many of the products featured in the movies of today.

> **@ Practicing Media Literacy**
> Do you think that the movies of today have an impact on what we wear or how we act? In what way?

Motion picture stars, beginning with Charlie Chaplin, became the first **celebrities** of our popular culture. Celebrities have replaced political and military heroes as the objects of public adulation. Although heroes do things, celebrities tend to be passive objects whose popularity is created and maintained by the media. According to sociologist Daniel Boorstin, a celebrity is "a person who is well known for his well-knowness."[7]

celebrities

Film Genres

In addition to the traditional film genres—such as the Western, which began with *The Great Train Robbery*—a variety of new ones developed during the 1930s. One of the most popular was the gangster movie, which depicted the typical criminal activity of the Prohibition era (1920–1933). Since many normally law-abiding citizens violated the law and continued to drink, a large underground developed to supply their need. Gangsters got involved in the manufacture, distribution and sale of alcohol.

This world was graphically recreated in such films as *Little Caesar* (1930), *The Public Enemy* (1931), *City Streets* (1931), and *Scarface* (1932), the last based on the exploits of Chicago gangster Al Capone. These were followed by tough-talking-cop movies and prison fights. Although most of these movies depicted the gangster in an unfavorable light, some glamorized his get-rich-quick image.

As Hollywood exported its films, Western and gangster film genres created a distorted view of American culture. For example, until very recently many foreigners believed the United States was a land where gangsters ruled the cities and cowboys and Indians fought on the prairies. (These stereotypes changed to the perceptions of wealth and ruthlessness following the export of such TV shows as *Dallas* and *Dynasty*.)

Following the election of Franklin D. Roosevelt to the presidency in 1932 and the repeal of Prohibition the following year, the mood of the country seemed to improve. This upswing was reflected in a series of musical extravaganzas that were produced in Hollywood as alternatives to the gangster films. Three **Busby Berkeley** musicals, for example, were 1933 box-office successes: *42nd Street*, *Gold Diggers of 1933*, and *Footlight Parade*. These surrealistically choreographed fantasies allowed the audience to become absorbed in the singing, dancing, and comedy depictions of backstage show business life. For most people, they offered an escape form the woes of Depression years.

Busby Berkeley

Also popular during this period were a variety of comedies ranging from the slapstick of the Marx Brothers in *Duck Soup* (1933) to more sophisticated, fast-paced romantic comedies such as *It Happened One Night* (1934), starring Clark Gable and

Claudette Colbert; *Dinner at Eight* (1933), starring John Barrymore and Jean Harlow; and *Bringing Up Baby* (1938), with Katharine Hepburn and Cary Grant. *It Happened One Night*, about a journalist in professional and amorous pursuit of a runaway heiress, established the romantic comedy as a popular genre for the rest of the 1930s.

Hollywood also developed the film series, featuring continuing episodes much as modern television does. These included the Andy Hardy pictures, Charlie Chan films, and the Flash Gordon, Henry Aldrich, Thin Man, and Dr. Kildare series.

The fantasies depicted in the films of this period gave Americans hope and a way to cope with the harsh realities of the Depression. Many films had strong moral themes and showed that decent, honest people could overcome obstacles. All the films had a warm, happy ending. One of the masters of these films was Frank Capra, who directed *It Happened One Night* (1934), *Mr. Deeds Goes to Town* (1936), *You Can't Take It With You* (1938), and *Mr. Smith Goes to Washington* (1939). One of his all-time classics, *It's a Wonderful Life* (1946), starring Jimmy Stewart, is still shown on television each year during the Christmas season. Its heartwarming message is that everyone's life has value because of the other lives it touches.

When the United States entered World War II in December 1941, Hollywood was there to rouse patriotic enthusiasm. Numerous propaganda films were produced during the war, while entertainment movies showed the Americans triumphing over their Japanese and Nazi enemies. Such movies as *30 Seconds over Tokyo* helped to reassure Americans that they were winning the war and that the cultural myth of an indestructible American spirit was a reality.

Although Hollywood mass-produced many motion pictures during the Depression and war years, it managed to turn out a number of classics. Among the all-time greats were *Gone with the Wind*, which broke box-office records in 1939, and Orson Welles's *Citizen Kane* (1941), which did not do well at the box office at first, but has since been voted the best film of all time (see Box 9.2).

When it was released in 1939, Gone With the Wind set box office records. Now, more than 60 years later, it is considered a classic which has withstood the test of time.

Less than three years after convincing radio listeners that martians had landed on earth, a young Orson Welles created a movie which has since been declared the best film ever made, Citizen Kane.

Box 9.2
MEDIA WATCH
"AFI's 100 Years . . . 100 Movies"

When a decade or a century comes to an end, lists are always made of the top books, television shows, records, and movies of the period. Sometimes the lists are based on revenue generated by the particular medium. Other times, the lists are subjective choices of those involved with the medium. Some lists are accepted as gospel; others are questioned and challenged.

For the movie industry, the most talked-about list was prepared at the end of the 20th century by the American Film Institute (AFI) the result of an 18-month effort involving some 1,500 voters (including people involved in the film industry) to rank the top 100 movies of the previous 100 years. Box-office rankings merely reflect marketing efforts, rather than the actual artistic quality of the film, and the AFI list was designed to increase public interest in America's film heritage.

As soon as the list was presented on a two-hour CBS television special, the complaints started coming in—most of them concerned as to just where some of the movies finished on the list. Actress Meryl Streep led those who were critical of the fact that the list of voters was, like the film industry itself, heavy with males. Streep was questioning why only four of the top picks had a female protagonist, and one of those was the Disney cartoon *Snow White*. However, AFI officials insisted that women were well represented among those casting ballots. There were also complaints that too many older films made the list (people tend to be most impressed by movies they saw as youngsters and first became aware of the power of films) and not

enough of the more recent films were selected. While eight films from the 1990s made the list, only four from the 1980s were recognized.

AFI pointed out that its list was truly a 100 years of film list, rather than a 20th century list of films. Those considered were released between 1896 and 1996; *Titanic* was released too late to be considered.

Many of the films selected were past Academy Award winners, including *The Godfather* (#3), *All About Eve* (#16), *Annie Hall* (#31), *To Kill a Mockingbird* (#34), *Midnight Cowboy* (#36), *West Side Story* (#41), *The Sound of Music* (#55), *Ben-Hur* (#72), and Clint Eastwood's *Unforgiven* (#98). But the movie selected as the best of all time received only one Oscar after it was released over 60 years ago, and that was for best Screenplay: Orson Welles's *Citizen Kane*. Here are the top-10 movies from the AFI list of the 100 greatest American films:

1. *Citizen Kane* (1941)
2. *Casablanca* (1942)
3. *The Godfather* (1972)
4. *Gone With the Wind* (1939)
5. *Lawrence of Arabia* (1962)
6. *The Wizard of Oz* (1939)
7. *The Graduate* (1967)
8. *On the Waterfront* (1954)
9. *Schindler's List* (1993)
10. *Singin' in the Rain* (1952)

THE GIANT IS CRIPPLED

In 1946 the film industry was on top of the world, with 87 million Americans going to the movies each week (today about half as many go every month). The industry was putting out between 500 and 600 movies a year. This was the industry's peak box-office year during the golden era; the American film business grossed $1.7 billion domestically in 1946. However, during the next two years, three events rocked the industry and toppled it from its peak of success.

The Red Scare

In 1947, a subcommittee of the House Un-American Activities Committee (**HUAC**) alleged that members of the Communist party had infiltrated the movie industry and were using films to disseminate Communist propaganda.

HUAC

After World War II ended in 1945, a Cold War broke out between the United States and the Soviet Union. As Americans saw country after country in Eastern Europe fall to occupation by the Soviet army, rumors ran rampant that the Soviet Union was attempting to take over our country as well with the help of American Communists. The government responded by conducting congressional investigations to see whether national security had been breached, and the motion picture industry became one of the targets for the committee's inquiries.

The HUAC hearings, which began on October 20, 1947, led to the fining and imprisonment of 10 Hollywood writers and directors who refused to answer the committee's questions about their alleged Communist party affiliation. The writers and directors, who came to be known as the "Hollywood 10," were also blacklisted by motion picture executives, who feared that if they took no action the government, supported by public opinion, would take control and censor their industry. The blacklisting, which spread far beyond the original Hollywood 10, lasted for more than a decade. Many blacklisted entertainers and writers went without work for a dozen or more years.

The Hearst newspapers gave the hearings major coverage and called for restrictive laws: "The need is for FEDERAL CENSORSHIP OF THE MOTION PICTURES. The Constitution PERMITS it. The law SANCTIONS it. The safety and welfare of America DEMAND it.[8] Many Americans supported this point of view.

In fact, many Hollywood studios were more than willing to accommodate the new public mood. In the late 1940s, the industry turned out such anti-communist movies as *I Was a Communist for the FBI*, *I Led Three Lives*, *I Married a Communist*, and *The Red Menace*, films that only helped to fuel the anti-communist fervor that gripped the nation.

A few films, however, subtly criticized the witch hunting of this period. The most successful was *High Noon* (1952), a Western written under a pseudonym by the blacklisted Carl Foreman that offered an allegory on McCarthyism. The film, starring Gary Cooper, told the story of a courageous marshal whose own moral code tells him he must face the threat of attack from four gunmen even though his new bride, his friends, and fellow townfolk turn their backs on him. Like many people during the witch-hunting days, "they didn't want to place their own lives at risk by getting involved."[9]

Another film, to be produced long after that period, was *The Front* (1976), starring Woody Allen, which told the story of Hollywood writers who had to get their work accepted under another name because they had been blacklisted. Although Allen usually wrote and directed his own pictures, he appeared in this one only as an actor. The credits for *The Front* not only list Martin Ritt as the director but point out that he was blacklisted in 1951; writer Walter Bernstein is listed as being blacklisted in 1950; and costars Zero Mostel and Herschel Bernardi were blacklisted in 1950 and 1953, respectively. Several others involved in the production had also been blacklisted in the 1950s, and the dates of their blacklisting were also given in the film's closing credits. Although the subject of blacklisting was not often used in the movies, Robert DeNiro and Annette Bening starred in a 1991 film that dealt with the controversial topic, *Guilty By Suspicion*.

By the end of the 1990s, the Writers Guild of America announced that it was taking action to restore writing credits on 21 films released between 1950 and 1969 to recognize those blacklisted writers who had worked under fake names or had used fronts to sell their products to the motion picture industry. The first recognition of a blacklisted writer, however, came when actor Kirk Douglas formed his own production company and insisted that writer Dalton Trumbo be given onscreen credit for his screenplay for Douglas's film *Spartacus* (1960). Almost 40 years later, Douglas was honored in 1999 by the Screen Actors Guild (SAG) for that decision. "By giving . . . Trumbo credit, he helped end one of the darkest periods in Hollywood history," said SAG president Richard Masur.[10]

Antitrust

The next setback for the motion picture industry came in 1948, when the U.S. Supreme Court ruled that the major studios were operating an illegal monopoly on the production, distribution, and exhibition of films *(U.S. v. Paramount Pictures, Inc., et al)*. At this time, for example, Paramount owned 1,239 theaters, 20th Century Fox owned 517, and Warner Bros. owned 507. The five major studios owned 77 percent of the first-run movie houses in the 25 largest American metropolitan areas.

The Supreme Court decision forced the major studios to sell all their theaters. Warner Brothers sold its Stanley Warner Theaters, MGM got rid of its Loews Theaters, RKO divested itself of RKO Theaters, 20th Century Fox sold its National Theaters, and Paramount Pictures severed its connection with Paramount Theaters. No longer did the studios have guaranteed outlets for their movies; from now on they would have to compete in the marketplace to get theaters to show their films. This opened up movie production to many independent film producers and reduced the dominance of the large studios.

Television

But the greatest blow of all was yet to come. In 1948, two major radio networks began the process of transforming television from a toy for the rich to a new mass medium for the popular culture. At first, major studio executives ignored TV and told themselves it was a passing fad. They simply went with a national promotion campaign to tell the public that "Movies Are Better Than Ever." After all, they thought, no tiny television screen could compete with the larger-than-life silver screens in movie theaters. But they were quickly proven wrong, as more and more people chose the convenience of staying home to watch the free entertainment. One factor encouraging home viewing was a shift in demographics. After the war many Americans started moving from the cities to the suburbs, and most movie theaters were concentrated in the big urban centers. The baby boom following World War II also forced many young parents to stay home with their new families.

Television also hurt movie viewing indirectly by creating new interests in the popular culture. Telecasts of such team **sports** as baseball and football stimulated an interest in professional and collegiate sporting events. TV programs featuring such previously elite, individualistic sports as golf, tennis, and skiing helped to create an interest in these activities. Soon many more people were spending some of their leisure time enjoying these sports.

sports

Fight for Survival.   Movie attendance continued to decline in the 1950s. Weaker studios, such as Republic, Allied Artists, and Monogram, soon collapsed, and others followed. While the number of television sets in homes increased 400 times between 1948 and 1960, weekly theater attendance declined by 50 percent.

The motion picture industry fought back by introducing a variety of technical gimmicks to attract audiences. For example, studios begin experimenting with three-dimensional (**3-D**) films (which required special cardboard-framed glasses, given to people at the theater, to view them). Hollywood released such 3-D movies as *Bwana*

3-D films

Devil (the first commercial 3-D feature), *House of Wax* (which many consider to be one of the better 3-D attempts), *Creature from the Black Lagoon*, (now a cult horror classic), *The French Line* (seeing Jane Russell's bust in 3-D was the gimmick here), and the Cole Porter musical *Kiss Me Kate* (the film version of the Broadway show based on Shakespeare's *The Taming of the Shrew*). Audiences left their TV sets to experience the visual illusion of knives, arrows, avalanches, and chemicals being hurled at them, but they quickly tired of the novelty. The industry even experimented with "smell-o-vision," whereby odors were piped into theaters. But movie audiences continued to dwindle.

A second gimmick the industry tried was CinemaScope. It used a larger screen and was more successful because it required no special glasses. The first CinemaScope film was *The Robe* (1953), a biblical epic starring Richard Burton, Jean Simmons, and Victor Mature. It was followed by other large-scale, expensive films, such as *The Ten Commandments* (1956) and *Ben Hur* (1959), both starring Charlton Heston. Some CinemaScope features were successful; others flopped. *Ben Hur* held the record for the most Academy Awards in a year with 11, until it was tied in 1998 by *Titanic*.

Cinerama

Finally, the industry introduced **Cinerama,** a process of using three projectors and three screens to wrap around the audience. Whereas 3-D had attempted to bring the picture into the audience, Cinerama put the audience into the picture. Cinerama previously had been used for special-effect travelogues, but not by Hollywood to tell a story. An MGM film editor, Harold Kress, disputed the claim of Cinerama executives that this special-effects film could not be edited. After he proved a powerful story could be told with this new technology, Hollywood talent banded together and produced the first Cinerama story, *How the West Was Won* (1962), as a benefit for a Santa Monica, California, hospital. Many major Hollywood stars appeared gratis in the film. It was a box-office success in an era of low movie theatre attendance, and it won Kress his first Academy Award for film editing.

A second Cinerama production, *Brothers Grimm*, lost money, and Hollywood soon abandoned the new technology. Cinerama required larger screens as well as extra theater personnel to operate the three projectors and sophisticated sound equipment that gave the film its unique qualities. It was just too expensive to be practical.

The film industry's struggle to regain its audience from television was also partially responsible for the almost total conversion to color motion pictures in the 1950s. Although a few successful color films had been produced in the 1930s, including *Gone With the Wind* and *The Wizard of Oz* in 1939, color shooting was slow and expensive. Black-and-white films thus remained the rule rather than the exception until the more competitive years of the 1950s. Color television sets had not yet been developed.

Despite all of these efforts to win back its mass audiences, the motion picture industry was finding that the popular cultural interests had changed and the new medium of television was more than a gimmick; it had become a new way of life. By the mid-1950s, the film industry decided to end its boycott and permit old films to be shown on television. Some companies even rented out of their movie studios for TV productions.

YOUTH, SEX, VIOLENCE, AND SPECIAL EFFECTS

The motion picture industry now realized that to survive as a mass-communication medium in the age of television, it had to move from the popular stage of the EPS cycle to specialization. This change in focus began in the mid-1950s, when the industry discovered that although many adults were staying home to watch television, there was a potential audience among young people, who wanted to get out of the house and socialize.

Youth

Social-commentary films about young people, such as *The Blackboard Jungle* (1955) and *Rebel Without a Cause* (1955), appealed to the young and made box-office idols out of young actors. For example, James Dean, an unknown action from a small town in Indiana, became a teenage idol overnight after appearing in *Rebel Without a Cause*. Although he starred in only three hit movies before his death in a traffic accident in 1955, Dean remains a legend today. His memory has been kept alive in our popular culture in a number of ways: Television stations have continued to show his movies, video stores feature his films, and poster companies still sell blowups of publicity stills from his movies. The United States Postal Service issued a stamp with his picture on it in 1996.

The youth-oriented movies of the 1950s catered to a new American subculture: the **youth subculture.** These films portrayed the restlessness and rebellion of young people in a sympathetic way to which they could easily relate. Also developing at this time was a youth-oriented form of popular music, rock and roll (see Chapter 11). In fact, the theme song for *The Blackboard Jungle* was the first rock and roll hit of the 1950s, Bill Haley's "Rock Around the Clock."

The 1950s were also the years for such low-budget films as *I Was a Teenage Werewolf*, *I Was a Teenage Frankenstein*, *Joy Ride*, and *Riot in Juvenile Prison*. Then as now, horror and violence were popular genres in the youth subculture. Braving a horror movie become a rite of passage for young men, while their dates screamed in terror. (Surveys show that among dating couples, the male usually chooses the movie; among older married moviegoers, the choice generally falls to the wife.)

A string of beach movies followed, featuring teenagers enjoying life at the beach, including bikinis, surfing, volleyball, and romance. These films reflected the party flavor of the new youth subculture and featured similar plots, with such titles as *Beach Blanket Bingo* and *How to Stuff a Wild Bikini*. Movies featuring the rock and roll stars of the period, such as Bill Haley and the Comets, Jan and Dean, Chubby Checker, Elvis Presley, and the Beatles, were also box-office successes in the 1950s and 1960s.

By the latter part of the 1960s, the influence of the youth **counterculture** began to be felt. Some films were now featuring antiheroes—social misfits, deviates, or outlaws who usually lost out in the end but received sympathy from the audience. The youth subculture had become antiestablishment, opposing the war in Vietnam and defying the laws against drugs. Thus, when gangsters, such as the notorious bank-robbing team of *Bonnie and Clyde* (1967), were portrayed as heroes, the film was a hit with young people. Other films that glorified lawlessness were *The Dirty Dozen* (1967), *Cool Hand Luke* (1967), *Easy Rider* (1969), and *Butch Cassidy and the Sundance Kid* (1969). More sophisticated antiestablishment films that satirized the "hypocrisy" of middle-class values included *The Graduate* (1967), *Bob and Carol and Ted and Alice* (1969), and *Goodbye, Columbus* (1969).

Sex ✓

A major departure for the film industry in the 1960s was the explicit presentation of sexual themes, reflecting the new

youth subculture

counterculture

> **@ Practicing Media Literacy**
> Hollywood has targeted the youth audience for many years. Can you think of any recent films that were particularly aimed at the younger movie-going audience?

sexual permissiveness of the time. Since sexual themes were not allowed on television at the time, movie producers saw a golden opportunity. As the sexual genre developed during this period of specialization, a more explicit variety with actual nudity became commonplace as an effective tool to pull people away from their relatively sexless TV sets.

The sexual themes of such film as *Barbarella*, *Midnight Cowboy* (the only X-rated movie to win an Academy Award as best picture), and *Carnal Knowledge* helped to lure people to the box office. Three hard-core pornography films also become popular during this period: *Deep Throat*, *Behind the Green Door*, and *The Devil in Miss Jones*.

Obviously, the industry could make such films only by completely ignoring the standards of the Production Code Administration. By the late 1960s the industry had officially abandoned its former self-censorship by devising a **rating system** that placed the burden of censorship on the moviegoer. The ratings ranged from G, which designated wholesome movies for the entire family, to X (now NC-17), which prohibited anyone under 18 from attending and warned that anything might be found in the movie, from extreme violence to hard-core pornography. Although profanity and explicit themes and scenes were originally restricted to R- and X-rated movies, they now can be found in today's PG (parental guidance recommended) films.

rating system

At first, most movies received a rating of either G or M (later changed to PG), with 24 percent of the films rated G and 43 percent M or PG. However, within a decade, the movie industry found that moviegoers preferred more violent and sexually explicit films. By 1979, movies rated PG had content similar to that of earlier R-rated movies. The R category grew from 25 percent in 1969 to 45 percent in 1979; the G category fell from 25 to 6 percent.

In 1984 a storm of protest arose over two PG-rated films, *Gremlins* and *Indiana Jones and the Temple of Doom*. *Gremlins* caused a furor because many youngsters wanted to see the picture featuring the cute, cuddly creatures, which were also being promoted by a fast-food chain. However, the fuzzy creatures created much mayhem in the film, which many believed was too violent for preteenagers. *Indiana Jones* caused concern because it contained a scene in which a beating heart is ripped out of a man's chest. (The executive producer of *Gremlins* was Steven Spielberg, who also directed the Indiana Jones movies.) The industry responded to the controversy by adding a PG-13 category designating that children under 13 should not be allowed to see the film.

In 1990, when Hollywood released 10 mainstream movies with X ratings, a new category known as NC-17 was created to separate films with strong adult content from the pornographic films which considered themselves not just X-rated, but XXX-rated.

The violence created by the furry creatures in Gremlins was one of the reasons the PG-13 rating was created to protect younger theatergoers.

The problem for many film distributors is that many newspapers will not carry advertising for NC-17 rated films and, as a result, many theaters refuse to book them for showing.

The sudden increase in shootings at various schools across the United States in the final years of the 20th century spurred a strong response from legislators in Washington D.C. to violence in the movies, as well as on television and in video games (see Box 9.3). One of the main targets was the motion picture rating system, which gave an NC-17 rating in 1998 to the raunchy satire *Orgazmo* for its crude sight gags and sex jokes, but gave only an R rating to Mel Gibson's 1999 release *Payback*, which feature a number of graphic deaths before Gibson's character was captured and tortured. This raised the question of whether the code is tougher on movies with strong sexual content but more lenient regarding violence in movies. According to the man who created the rating system in the mid-1960s, Motion Picture Association of America (MPAA) President Jack Valenti, the system is imperfect and subjective but has consistently received support from parents. But there are those who still question the consistency of the voluntary film ratings. One instance often cited is the advertisement submitted to the MPAA by a studio, featuring a gun pointed at the reader. The MPAA rejected the ad, but later approved a resubmitted ad which had substituted a knife for the gun.

Valenti said in 1999 that while the rating system is designed to help parents evaluate content of the movies, the motion picture industry is also trying to tone itself down in light of the violent events taking place in American schools. As a result of this violence, President Clinton ordered the Federal Trade Commission to study the marketing of violent media to children. A short time later, theater owners announced that they were going to check photo IDs to be sure that no one under 17 was getting into R-rated films unless accompanied by an adult. The announcement was made by the president of the National Association of Theater Owners at a news conference with President Clinton. The trade group represents 65 percent of American theater owners. But a lot of the responsibility still fell upon the producers of the movies. Some questioned whether a movie with gratuitous violence should get a stricter rating than a movie with violence set in some sort of context in the film. Director Oliver Stone contends that violence in his movie *Natural Born Killers* was graphic not to glamorize it, as many critics had charged, but to show that violence is bad, while director Steven Spielberg's film *Saving Private Ryan* had to use violence to show that people are injured and killed in war.

Adding a twist to the ongoing battle over ratings was the report released in 1998 which said that G-rated movies make the most money. The study, commissioned by the nonprofit Dove Foundation, said that over a 10-year period from 1988 through 1997, the average G rated movie had a 31 percent greater rate of return on its investments than the average R-rated film. There was no sudden resurgence of G-rated films coming out of Hollywood in the years that followed.

Disasters and Violence

When television began toning down its depiction of violence in the 1970s to comply with consumer group complaints, the motion picture industry turned to disaster films and explicit violence as film genres. Disaster films became the big box-office draws of the 1970s. These films were filled with suspense as passengers scrambled for their lives in a sinking luxury ship (*The Poseidon Adventure*), summer vacationers were gobbled up by a giant shark (*Jaws*), air travelers faced various hazards (*Airport*), Los Angeles was shaken by destruction (*Earthquake*), and a giant skyscraper was consumed by flames (*The Towering Inferno*).

As people became accustomed to disaster movies, the films got more violent in an effort to keep the audience interested. Some of the more popular superviolent films were *The Wild Bunch* (which was less violent in its theatrical release than what director Sam Peckinpah had wanted, but was still quite violent) and *Dirty Harry*, starring Clint Eastwood as a tough San Francisco cop who doesn't let the law get in his way as he captures, tortures, and eventually kills a rooftop sniper. Although these films depicted people being gunned down in cold blood, it was still the "bad guys" who lost out in the end. However, as the 1970s drew to a close, many innocent people were being axed and mutilated in films such as *Halloween*, *The Texas Chain Saw Massacre*, *Nightmare on Elm Street*, and *Friday the 13th*. All of these films had sequels.

Of course, not everyone wanted to spend Saturday nights watching people being hacked to pieces. Some viewers, especially women, wanted good, clean, wholesome family entertainment, and movies were also made for this segment of the market. Some of the more successful included the musical about the life of the legendary singing Von Trapp family of Austria, *The Sound of Music* (1965); *Oliver!* (1968), the film of the Broadway hit based on the Charles Dickens classic, *Oliver Twist* (both movies won Oscars for Best Picture); and a long string of Walt Disney movies, including *Aladdin*, *The Lion King*, *Beauty and the Beast*, *Pocahontas*, *The Hunchback of Notre Dame*, *Hercules*, *Mulan*, *Tarzan*, and *Fantasia 2000*.

Cultural Impact

Legislators at both the state and federal levels have often expressed concern about the content of the movies. While violence has been the most talked-about area during the last half of the 20th century, another area of impact on our society came in for much discussion in the last years of the 1990s— smoking. In California, Democratic State Senator John Burton of San Francisco held hearings in which he warned Hollywood moviemakers to stop glamorizing the practice of smoking in their films. While smoking has been a part of movies from the days of Charles Chaplin's Little Tramp scrounging in the gutters for used cigarette butts, numerous movies in the 1990s featured smoking as glamorous, from the heroes of *Independence Day* lighting up cigars in celebration of their victory over alien invaders to Julia Roberts' character puffing away in frustration in a hotel hallway in *My Best Friend's Wedding*. Representatives of the American Cancer Society told Burton's Senate Judiciary Committee hearing that **on-screen smoking** was free publicity for the tobacco industry. A researcher from the University of California at San Francisco reported that while on-screen smoking had declined in the 1970s, there was a distinct reversal of the trend by the 1990s as 80 percent of the male leads and 27 percent of the female leads were shown smoking in movies between 1990 and 1996. And a UC–Irvine marketing professor told the committee that young people viewed smoking more favorably after watching movies featuring stars who were lighting up. In fact, 30 percent of the teens surveyed before watching the 1994 Generation X film *Reality Bites* said they approved of smoking. The figure increased to 44 percent after watching the film, which showed Winona Ryder and Ethan Hawke "looking cool" while smoking.[11].

Later that year, Vice President Al Gore blamed Hollywood for contributing to the "pediatric epidemic" of smoking among children. "We know that popular culture has an enormous impact on our children's habits and on America's values," Gore said after a meeting with Hollywood leaders. Citing a study by the American Lung Association of 1996 movies that found movie characters smoking in 77 percent of the 133 movies surveyed, Gore said, "Today, as more and more children start smoking, the fact is that smoking is way up as well.[12]

on-screen smoking

Box 9.3
MEDIA LITERACY
The Ongoing Struggle to Control Violence in the Movies—Who Wields the Most Power?

Starting in the fall of 1997, when a teenage boy killed his mother in Mississippi and then went to school where he fatally shot two students and wounded seven others, nine school shootings took place in various parts of the United States before the start of the year 2000. Three occurred in 1999—in Georgia, where a 15-year-old boy using a .357 magnum pistol and a rifle wounded six fellow students; in Oklahoma, where a 13-year-old middle school student opened fire with a semiautomatic pistol, wounding four classmates; and at Columbine High School in Colorado, where two students killed 12 students and one teacher before taking their own lives. Columbine provided images that have been burned into the consciousness of America.

In addition to these school shootings, there have been other incidents of violence, such as the wounding of five people when a white supremacist walked into a Jewish community center in Los Angles in the summer of 1999 and opened fire. It didn't take long for politicians to again begin expressing concern about violence in the movies and on television contributing to violence in our society. They may have been bolstered by Gallup polls in the spring of 1999 which showed that 81 percent of American adults believed that violent entertainment is a cause of increased violence, while 73 percent said that the government should restrict the access of minors to such material. But despite all of the shootings and the ensuing political talk in Washington, little had been done by the start of the year 2000. In fact, a bill that sought to ban the sale of extremely violent movies, video games, and books to minors was overwhelmingly defeated in the House of Representatives by a vote of 282 to 146. Lobbying against the measure was the head of the Motion Picture Association of America, Jack Valenti, who pointed out "This isn't cigarettes or alcohol. This is creative work that is protected by the First Amendment."*

Many politicians agreed. Said Senator Charles Schumer (D-NY), "If I could wave a magic wand and stop violence in the media, I would wave it. But it is impossible without the heavy hand of government starting to censor, and when the government starts censoring or giving a seal of approval, it has the potential to do more bad than good."**

However, other legislators warned Hollywood that while they did not want to resort to regulation, they would be forced to do so if the motion picture industry didn't do something to change its methods of entertainment. Several lawmakers, led by Senators Joe Lieberman (D-CT) and John McCain (R-AZ), even began a petition campaign focusing on putting pressure on Hollywood to clean up its act. The "Appeal to Hollywood" Initiative campaign was carried out through a website (media-appeal.org) and had the support of such entertainers as Naomi Judd and Steve Allen, former presidents Gerald Ford and Jimmy Carter, Army generals Colin Powell and Norman Schwartzkopf, and former New York governor Mario Cuomo.

The end result was a call by many, including President Clinton, for the motion picture industry to re-evaluate the way it portrays killings on both the large and small screens. It should be noted that the entertainment industry is a large contributor to political campaigns, and Clinton made his appeal at a dinner in Hollywood that raised an estimated $2 million for the Democratic Party.

There were early signs that the moviemakers were listening. Producers of one film which was to feature a motorcycle chase that would leave the streets of San Francisco cluttered with bullet-ridden bodies announced that the scene would not be filmed. But Hollywood was receiving mixed messages from the American public. While many complained about the violence in the media, they still put out large amounts of money to see the films containing such violence. For example, the violent cyber-thriller *The Matrix* opened shortly before the Columbine High School shootings and went on to make $171 million at the box office in this country alone. The frustration of those in Hollywood was voiced by the Oscar-winning scriptwriter for the film *Thelma and Louise*, Callie Khouri, who said: "When I first viewed my own movie with an audience, and they cheered when a man was shot, I was shocked because I had expected a completely different reaction. I had hoped for a stunned reaction—a realization that the character had just sealed her fate in a very powerful way. When the audiences burst into applause, I was terrified to realize that I couldn't control how my work was received."***

continued

Prior to going on their shooting rampage at Columbine High School, the two teenagers responsible for the shootings made a videotape in which they predicted that their actions would have Hollywood movie directors fighting over the story, even discussing whether Steven Spielberg or Quentin Tarantino would do best with such a script. Although two teenage cousins said they were inspired to kill one of their mothers by the horror movie *Scream*, they were both convicted of murder, with one sentenced to life without parole and the other sent to prison for 25 years to life.

There are those who feel that the only way changes can be made in decreasing the violence portrayed in the movie is for the public to stop supporting such films. Hollywood responds to dollars, and when people are willing to spend anywhere from $7 to $10 for a ticket to see one of the many variations of *Nightmare on Elm Street* or the extremely violent *Natural Born Killers*, and films of this type continue to gross millions of dollars, Hollywood will continue to make them.

*Jeffrey Taylor, "House Rejects Curbs on Sales of Violent Film," *Wall Street Journal*, p. B12.

**David Rosenbaum, "Politicians Speak Out but are Wary of Restricting Film Violence," *New York Times*, October 13, 1999, p. B1.

***Gary Dretzka, "Screenwriters Can't Script Audience's Reaction; Film Representatives Debate Responsibility for Violence in Society," *Chicago Tribune* syndication in *Fresno Bee*, June 15, 1999, p. E4.

The Office of National Drug Control Policy and the Department of Health and Human Services joined the battle in 1999, releasing a report about the frequency and nature of substance abuse in the entertainment media. The $400,000 study looked at 200 movies available on videotape and found that in 98 percent of the top movie rentals, people were depicted using drugs, drinking, or smoking, with fewer than half of the movies mentioning the downside of such activity. "We do not suggest that we want to dictate the message. Drugs, alcohol and tobacco are a reality of American life," said Barry McGaffrey, drug control policy director for the Clinton administration. "But we are suggesting they need to be tied to the consequences that are realistic, given our experiences in American life."[13]

There are many who are concerned that on-screen smoking by important characters and big name stars will influence young people to take up the habit.

Special Effects

As space-age technology and space exploration became part of our culture, the movies began to use this technology and depict these themes. With the help of such directors as Steven Spielberg and George Lucas, films started featuring amazing, computer-generated special effects. These special effects created graphic depictions of everything from interplanetary war to extraterrestrial beings. The first to dazzle audiences was Lucas's *Star Wars* (1977), which broke box-office records. It was followed by *Close Encounters of the Third Kind*, *The Empire Strikes Back*, *Return of the Jedi*, *Poltergeist*, *Raiders of the Lost Ark*, *E.T.*, *Poltergeist II*, *Aliens*, *Indiana Jones and the Temple of Doom*, and *The Fly*.

In 1993 the special effects surrounding ferocious dinosaurs helped *Jurassic Park* to replace another special-effects movie, *E.T.*, as the highest-grossing motion picture of all time. During its first year, *Jurassic Park* grossed $704.5 million in box office receipts, edging out *E.T.*, which had collected $701.4 at the box office. However, a summer 1996 release, *Independence Day*, was to surpass even *Jurassic Park* at the box office, racking up more than $200 million in ticket sales during its first three weeks alone and over $300 million before its theatrical run ended in this country. Special effects continued to improve throughout the 1990s, allowing audiences to experience mountain-climbing dangers (*Cliffhanger*), out-of-control buses (*Speed*), an almost deadly trip to the moon (*Apollo 13*), a terrorist takeover of Alcatraz (*The Rock*), the invasion of the world by outer-space aliens (*Independence Day*), and tornadoes blasting their way through Oklahoma (*Twister*), and tales of the future (*Matrix* and *End of Days*). Action films using computerized special effects dominate the box office every summer.

> @ **Practicing Media Literacy**
>
> Can you tell when the real action stops and the computer effects begin in the movies of today?

ETHNIC FILMS OF THE 1990S

In the early years of motion pictures, African-Americans had difficulty getting starring roles. However, by the early 1990s, many young minority filmmakers were finding success at the box office. Spike Lee, director of *Malcolm X* (1992), had a number of hits in the 1980s and 1990s, including *She's Gotta Have It* (1986), *Do the Right Thing* (1989), *Mo' Better Blues* (1990), *Clockers* (1995), and *Get on the Bus* (1996).

One of the top films in 1992 was *Boyz N the Hood*, written and directed by John Singleton, a 23-year-old African-American filmmaker. The film told a powerful story about three young African-Americans growing up in south central Los Angeles. "The Hood" is a place where drug dealers, drive-by shootings, and unemployment run rampant.

The realities depicted in these films, such as the violence in south-central Los Angeles, elicit concerns from parents and religious groups who believe violence, promiscuity, alcohol, and drug abuse shown in films

How Stella Got Her Groove Back *is an example of the many films now being created by and for African-Americans.*

encourage such behavior among young people. Gang shootings at showings of such films as *Colors* and *Boyz N the Hood* have fueled this argument. But there have also been love stories involving African-American characters, such as *Jungle Fever* and *Waiting to Exhale*.

BUSINESS TRENDS

Ever since the motion picture industry got over its initial shock from the invasion of television and began taking advantage of new market opportunities television created, profits and business opportunities have improved.

Estimated box-office revenue by the middle of the 1990s was $5.5 billion, with more than 25,000 theater screens in the United States producing annual ticket sales of more than 1.5 billion tickets. The leading studios at the domestic box office were Disney, Warner Bros., Universal, Columbia/TriStar, Paramount, 20th Century Fox, (fox.com) New Line, and MGM/UA (mgmua.com).

Foreign movie receipts for U.S. films were more than $4 billion, and some 80 percent of what those distributors' films grossed at home. Standard and Poor's estimated that for new movies, on average, 25 to 30 percent of the distributors' total revenues came from domestic theater rentals and another 15 to 20 percent from foreign distribution. Worldwide home video reportedly brought in another 35 to 40 percent, and television accounted for another 10 to 15 percent. The *S&P Industry Survey* reported, "Although theaters provide a substantially smaller portion of new movies' total revenue than they did before the arrival of pay television and home video, box office performance still has a major bearing on a film's ultimate profitability. Theatrical success influences a film's future reception and value in the ancillary markets, as do other factors."[14]

But to make money, you must spend money, and this is a well-known fact in the motion picture industry. Promotion budgets for movies can be astronomical, but that's the price that must be paid to lure consumers out of their homes and into the theaters. However, an expensive promotion campaign does not always guarantee a hit at the box office. Quite often, large amounts of money are spent to promote a new motion picture only to have viewers reject the movie at the box office.

As the 20th century came to a close, the industry came in for some criticism from a few of its own. Walt Disney Studios chairman Joe Roth complained that profit-driven Hollywood was turning out movies that wouldn't stand the test of time. Roth, who was in charge of production, marketing, and distribution of Touchstone, Walt Disney, Hollywood Pictures, and Miramax Films (miramax.com), charged that the industry was shortsighted; nobody was seeing movies as an art form, as a way to tell good stories. According to Roth, companies were too busy trying to capture the largest possible audience at the box office at the expense of producing films that had the potential to become classics. "It's always been a balancing act," said Roth, "but what's happening now tends to take the balance and shift it toward quarterly profits as opposed to a movie that will stand the test of time."[15] Film Director John Frankenheimer also charged that the quality of movies had declined because marketing executives call the shots on most productions. Said Frankenheimer, director of *Manchurian Candidate*, *Seven Days in May*, and *Ronin*, "The people that initiate scripts are the studio heads, and more and more, these studio heads are being guided by their marketing departments. You don't make good pictures by listening to marketing people, because they are always living in the past."[16]

Video Movies

Although the industry was cranking out more than 500 films a year by the 1990s, 8 out of 10 did not recover their investment in box-office receipts. However, the advent of video rental businesses gave all films, including the less successful ones, another opportunity to generate revenue.

The introduction of home video equipment in the late 1970s created a profitable market for the movie industry. Movies found a whole new audience as many people who had not been to a theater in years began watching films on videocassettes.

As videocassette recorders (VCRs) and the business of video rentals and sales spread throughout the country in the 1980s, Hollywood began recording old films onto videotape. Now new movies are also released on video after their run at the box office, generating considerable extra income. Although motion picture producers receive a percentage of the box-office receipts from theaters, they receive no such share from video rentals. However, the many rental outlets are a prime market for videocassette sales.

New Technology

By the end of the 1990s, new technology had also made inroads in the movie industry. Blockbuster Corporation announced that it was launching a program whereby videos would be rented by customers using the Internet instead of coming in to the store. However, the Internet is only capable of so much. Once the video has been reserved on the Blockbuster website, the customer would still have to drive to the store to pick it up and return it—unless the company develops a delivery service.

It is already possible for computer users with fast Internet connections to receive rental movies by way of the Internet, although the films have to be viewed on the computer screen. In 1999, the science fiction movie *Pi* was made available on the Internet for $2.95 per viewing, and later offerings included *Fait Accompli* starring Rosanna Arquette and a B movie, *Toxic Avenger*. The prospect of having movies "a mouse click away" had its impact on the entertainment industry. At the Cannes Film Festival, movie distributors were joined by web company executives looking for product. It's believed that the initial demand for Internet movies will come from college students, whose schools have broadband Internet connections that can download a feature length movie in about 20 minutes. The next step will be **high-speed hookups** in the average American home.[17]

high-speed hookups

The motion picture studios are also using the Internet to help get people out to theaters. Sneak previews of films that may still be months away from reaching the big screens are now being previewed online. The studios are using the Internet to give fans information about eagerly anticipated films, such as the *Star Wars* prequel, *Episode 1: The Phantom Menace* (starwars.com), as well as featuring the theatrical trailers on their websites. The *Star Wars* website was created almost two years before the film was released and initially featured still shots of director George Lucas working on phase one of filming.[18]

> **@ Practicing Media Literacy**
> Would you be satisfied watching new film releases on your computer screen or do you prefer the big theater screens?

But perhaps the most talked about development in video technology was the digital video disk (DVD), which is the size of a normal compact disc (CD) but can hold a complete movie and provide visual quality far superior to the laser disk. And, like the laser disk, the DVD can also provide additional material, including the director's narration about various shots, outtakes, and documentaries on the making of the films. When the DVD machines were first introduced to the public in 1997, prices ranged from $600 to $1,000, but by the start of the year 2000, some DVD players were priced at under $200, with more than 4.9 million of them having been sold in those two years—more than four times the number of CD players and VCRs sold in their first years, according to research done by an Arlington, Virginia, trade group.[19]

Conglomerates

Like the print media, the motion picture industry is not immune to conglomerate takeovers. Takeover and merger activity towards the end of the 20th century included Matsushita's $6.1 billion purchase of MCA; Sony's $3.4 billion purchase of Columbia; Pathé's acquisition of MGM/UA; and Time Inc.'s merger with Warner Communications, owner of Warner Bros.

In 1996, Disney Corporation purchased the ABC television network. The company soon began using its television network to promote the releases of its films, including special programs on how such films as *The Hunchback of Notre Dame*, *Tarzan*, and *Fantasia 2000* were made. In addition, entertainment specials were created for the network to help generate interest in Disney movies, including Olympic skater Michelle Kwan performing to the songs from Disney's *Mulan* (see Box 9.4).

Paramount (paramount.com), which until 1989 had been a subsidiary of Gulf and Western, became Paramount Communications Inc., with extensive holdings in the entertainment and publishing fields. After a five-month, $10 billion takeover battle with QVC Network Inc., Viacom Inc., owners of MTV, acquired Paramount Communications in February 1994 to form one of the world's largest communication conglomerates, which also includes Blockbuster Entertainment Corporation, the video rental chain, which had also merged with Viacom Inc. By the end of the 20th century, Viacom had become involved in another merger, this one with the CBS television network for an estimated $36 billion. This brought both a television and a radio network, as well as television and radio stations, a motion picture studio, a book publishing firm, and outdoor advertising all under one corporate ownership, allowing for each division to utilize the unique services of the others in the areas of development and marketing.

One year earlier, the owner of Universal Studios, Seagram Co., announced that it was purchasing PolyGram NV, the world's largest music company for $10.6 billion. At the same time, Seagram sold off its Tropicana fruit juice division, making entertainment the main focus of the company best known for its liquor products.

And in 1999, Sony Pictures Entertainment announced that it was combining Columbia Pictures and TriStar Pictures into one studio, in an attempt to unify film production under one studio name. TriStar, which had produced such hits as *Jerry Maguire* and *As Good As It Gets*, became a part of Columbia in the restructuring move, with the merger including the business, legal and story departments of the studios. Moves of this type have not been unexpected in Hollywood during the 1990s. Films have become so expensive to produce that profit margins have all but disappeared. The Motion Picture Association of America (MPAA) estimated that the average cost of a movie being made at the end of the 20th century was $78.1 million. As a result, the number of films released had decreased by about 8 percent from 1996.[20]

> @   **Practicing Media Literacy**
>
> Have you seen any significant changes in motion pictures as a result of the media mergers in recent years?

Box 9.4
MEDIA LITERACY
Is It REALLY the Wonderful World of Disney?

While the Disney organization has continued to release its cartoon features for the family, its expansion into a media conglomerate has led to other problems for the corporation. Perhaps the biggest blow came in June of 1997 when delegates attending the Southern Baptist convention in Dallas voted overwhelmingly to boycott all things Disney, including the ABC television network and both Disneyland and Disney World, saying the Disney was immoral and "gay-friendly" because of its same-sex employee benefits program and the featuring of a lesbian character on the ABC-TV sitcom *Ellen*.

The resolution, approved by a show of hands by the convention's 12,000 delegates, also urged the 15 million members of the nation's largest Protestant denomination to take action against Disney's "anti-Christian and anti-family direction." Also coming under fire were Disney movie companies, which had released films featuring sex and violence, such as *Kids* and *Pulp Fiction*.

The measure, which was not binding on church members, urged them to "take the stewardship of their time, money and resources so seriously that they refrain from patronizing the Disney Co. and any of its related entities."*

One month later, the American–Arab Anti-Discrimination Committee was protesting the release by Disney of the movies *Operation Condor* and *G.I. Jane*. The committee charged that the *Condor* film, an action movie starring Jackie Chan, used "the lazy movie cliché of violent, unscrupulous and irrational Arabs."** The organization added that Disney seemed to have launched "a holy war against Arabs" because of the way Arab characters were portrayed in *G.I. Jane*, in which star Demi Moore and her Navy Seal team members go on a "rampage of killing Arabs."***

In an unrelated protest, a Catholic antidefamation group demanded that the ABC-TV drama *Nothing Sacred* be taken off the air because of the way it portrayed priests. The program, which was praised by television critics, didn't last longer than one season. Meanwhile, the National Federation of the Blind called on Disney to cease production of the movie *Mr. Magoo* because it revived the cartoon character who gets into trouble because of poor eyesight.

In 1998, the Texas State Board of Education voted to sell its $46.4 million in Disney stock because of the sex, drugs, and violence contained in movies released by Disney subsidiaries. The corporation responded by saying that while it releases movies for all ages, it is still the leading producer of family entertainment, and others criticized the school board for joining the moralistic attacks on Disney at the expense of good investment decisions for the school children of Texas.

But not all of Disney's problems were in the United States. Authorities in China refused to allow Disney to show the animated *Mulan* in that country. It wasn't because of the movie itself, but because Chinese officials were not happy with the Disney film *Kundun*, Martin Scorcese's movie that was sympathetic to the Dalai Lama, the exiled spiritual leader of Chinese-controlled Tibet. Getting *Mulan* into some 100 cities in China, a nation of 1.3 billion residents, was essential to Disney's business plan, since China allows only 10 foreign films a year to protect its own movie industry. The film was based on a Chinese legend and the story was as familiar to the children of China as Cinderella is to American children, so Disney launched an aggressive lobbying campaign with Chinese leaders. The ban was finally lifted and the movie was allowed to open in the homeland of the cartoon heroine, to the delight of the young audience.

It *IS* a small world afterall.

*"Southern Baptists Vote For Boycott of Disney," *San Francisco Chronicle*, June 19, 1997, p. A1.

**"Disney's 'Condor' Draws Ire of Arab Americans," *San Francisco Chronicle*, July 19, 1997, p. E3.

***"Arabs, Catholics Protest How Disney Depicts Them," *San Francisco Chronicle*, August 21, 1997, p. E2.

OTHER TECHNOLOGY AND MOVIES

The use of cartoon and film characters in video games for kids started in the 1980s when video game makers agreed to pay Hollywood movie studios 5 to 10 percent to

The production of motion pictures today differs greatly from the "golden age" when large studios did everything. Current practices usually involve four groups of people: (1) moviemakers or producers, (2) investors, (3) distributors, and (4) exhibitors.

Production is a highly collaborative process involving many people. Major players in production can include an executive producer, producer, writer, director, composer, editor, director of photography, and the actors and actresses. Production people are supported by a crew of hundreds of other workers, usually unionized, who handle specific details ranging from building the sets to applying makeup to catering meals on location.

Investors are the venture capitalists who put up the money to fund the production. There is high risk in investing in movies, as many become box office flops. However, when a picture is successful, these venture capitalists stand to make a good return on their investments.

Distributors are responsible for making prints of the film and getting them delivered on time. The method of producing multiple prints and distributing them to each theater dates back to the early days of the industry. It is envisioned that the use of satellite technology will soon modernize this process.

Exhibitors are the theater owners who make showing of the movies possible. One of the biggest competitors of exhibitors today is video rental outlets. Movie theaters have changed greatly during the past century, from nickelodeons to grand theatrical palaces to the current multi-screen operations featuring 10 to 12 film showings at a time. Some predict a return to the large movie palaces when large-screen, high-definition television arrives, to provide an experience competitive with that offered by the home VCR. In addition to making their money on admission tickets, exhibitors make about 10 to 20 percent of their income from the refreshment counters.

A new division in the motion picture business, the interactive division, is expanding the industry into video games and virtual-reality technologies. People with computer expertise will find many opportunities available in this growing area of the industry.

use such characters as Peanuts, Mickey Mouse, E.T., and the Muppets in their video games.

As the video game business began to explode in the 1990s, Hollywood moviemakers couldn't help but notice that their 10 percent royalty checks were getting larger and larger. It wasn't long before major movie studios were either buying video game companies or developing their own divisions of interactive entertainment.

Movie studios are now involved in designing video games. At Sony Interactive, every movie script Columbia buys is screened by the video game department for its game potential. If it looks promising, a separate scriptwriting team develops the game version. When film crews go out to the set, the video game crews accompany them. In some cases, extra footage is shot on location to provide additional material for the games. Sony used footage from *Cliffhanger* and *Dracula* to create the backdrops for the CD versions of those games.

This is just the latest phase of the motion picture industry's efforts to find profitable markets in the specialized stage of the EPS cycle. It has been in the specialization stage since television moved into the popular culture in the late 1940s and robbed the movie industry of its popular-culture audiences.

It is predicted that the development of interactive television will radically alter the motion picture industry as well as our lifestyles. The motion picture industry will have an expanded market for increased profits as this computerized technology develops and superhighways carrying myriad information and entertainment into American homes become a reality. In addition, new technology is now making it possible to create home movies on personal computers.

Another electronic advance in television also has implications for the movie industry. High-definition television **(HDTV)** may eventually change the way motion pictures are delivered to theaters. Because the transmission of HDTV signals will have the quality of a 35mm motion picture film, satellite transmission of movies to theaters or fiber-optic transmission over the "superhighway" could replace the costly method of making and shipping thousands of prints to theaters. Studios could transmit the movies via satellite, and theaters could downlink the films by paying a descrambling fee.

HDTV

Virtual Reality

A new technology that was developed to assist pilots and astronauts in flight training is now entering the entertainment field. Known as *virtual reality* or *VR*, this technology uses computer technology to simulate experiences and give people a sense of being in a different place or time zone. Much like Edison's kinetoscope that introduced the popular culture to movies in arcades, VR booths are now becoming popular in video game arcades. They may soon expand into homes. Major motion picture studios are already involved in providing entertainment for VR booths, including Sony, Paramount Communications, and Time Warner.

The rapid expansion of electronic technology will continue to have a major impact on a wide variety of entertainment forms.

SUMMARY

The motion picture industry has had a major impact on our popular culture, and our popular culture has in turn affected the industry as new media, cultural attitudes, and changing lifestyles have forced it to change.

Soon after the invention of motion pictures in Thomas Edison's laboratory, film found its way to mass audiences. It was first used as a moving peep show in kinetoscope parlors and penny arcades. Then it was projected in vaudeville theaters and nickelodeons. By the 1920s, movies were providing grand experiences in large, palace-like theaters.

Films such as Edwin Porter's *The Great Train Robbery* and D. W. Griffith's *Birth of a Nation* proved the motion picture could be a powerful storytelling medium. Film moved quickly into the popular culture because it was invented at a time when immigrants in our industrialized urban society needed an entertainment medium with no language barrier. The international language of the silent film's pantomime and comedy provided that medium. Soon the likes of Mack Sennett, Hal Roach, Charlie Chaplin, Stan Laurel, Oliver Hardy, Buster Keaton, and Harold Lloyd were silently communicating to the masses.

During World War I, the movie industry in Hollywood flourished. It also was instrumental in producing propaganda movies to promote patriotism during wartime. This practice would again be repeated during World War II.

Although experimental sound pictures were made in the early days of the industry, it wasn't until Warner Bros. brought out *The Jazz Singer* in 1927, with Al Jolson singing on screen, that the full potential of "talking" pictures was realized. The success of the early talkies changed the industry and helped make Warner Bros. into a major studio.

In the 1930s and 1940s, going to the movies became a way of life in the United States. The major movie studios turned out hundreds of films a year and created movie stars who became as familiar to American audiences as members of their own families. These films also provided an effective escape from reality during a time of depression and war.

In 1947 and 1948, three events rocked the industry and toppled it from its peak of economic success. First came the congressional hearings into alleged Communist infiltration of the motion picture industry. The second was a Supreme Court ruling that forced major studios to sell their theaters. The final blow was the entrance of television into our popular culture.

The motion picture business changed from a big-studio-dominated industry that owned most of the stars and the distribution outlets to one of independent producers and theaters. The industry experimented with a variety of films and technology, such as three-dimensional pictures and large screens, but it could not win back its mass audience.

Soon Hollywood discovered that films aimed at specialized audiences helped to revive low box-office receipts. Finding popularity at the box office were films aimed at youth and films that contained sex, violence, and special effects.

Today the motion picture industry is thriving. Its acceptance of the new video technology has provided it with a significant additional source of revenue. The future looks bright as the movie industry attempts to capitalize on new interactive computerized television technologies and virtual-reality entertainment.

Find a review of *Key People and Concepts*, a message board for *Practicing Media Literacy* questions, self tests, and more at: www.mhhe.com/wilson.

Thought **Questions**

1. What problems do you see in a motion picture company using the television network it owns to promote its theatrical releases, as is the case with Disney using ABC to promote its new releases?

2. What similarities exist between comedy of the silent film era and today's humor? Are these similarities driven by cultural needs?

3. Why are topics such as sex and violence popular in motion pictures? Is this a case of Hollywood giving us what we want or our acceptance of what we are given?

4. If you were a movie producer, what changes would you make to create box-office hits for the 21st century?

5. What do you think will be the effect of such new technologies as interactive television, virtual reality, and DVD on the motion picture industry?

Notes

1. Lewis Jacobs, *The Emergence of Film Art*, 2nd ed. (New York: Norton, 1979), p. 27

2. Gerald Mast, *A Short History of the Movies*, 4th ed. (New York: Macmillian, 1986), p. 63.

3. *Ibid.*, p. 93.

4. David Robinson, *The History of World Cinema* (New York: Stein and Day, 1973), p. 104.

5. Arthur Knight, *The Livelist Art: A Panaramic History of the Movies* (New York: New American Library, 1957), pp. 112–113.

6. Robinson, *The History of World Cinema*, p. 190.

7. Deborah Weiser, and John Wright, eds., *The Popular Culture Reader* (Bowling Green, OH: Bowlling Green University Popular Press, 1978), pp. 211–212.

8. Walter Goodman, *The Committee: The Extraordinary Career of the House Committee on Un-American Activities* (New York: Farrar, Straus & Giroux, 1964), p. 218.

9. Robinson, *The History of World Cinema*, p. 253.

10. *TV Guide*, March 6–12, 1999, p. 35.

11. Sabin Russell, "Studios Asked to Deglamorize Smoking," *San Francisco Chronicle*, October 28, 1997, p. A1.

12. Elizabeth Shogren, "Gore Urges Hollywood to Cut Glamour Smoking," *Los Angeles Times* syndicate, in *Fresno Bee*, December 4, 1997, p. B9l.

13. "Entertainment Media Taken to Task by Study," *Chicago Tribune*, April 29, 1999, Sec. 1, p. 15.

14. *Standard and Poor's Industry Survey*, April 6, 1995, p. L25.

15. *Viewing Positions: Ways of Seeing Film*, (New Brunswick, NJ: Rutgers University Press, 1995).

16. "Director Blames Marketing Execs," *Fresno Bee*, November 10, 1999, p. A2.

17. Michael Fleeman, "Web Movie Video Rentals May Be Just around Corner," Associated Press, in *Los Angeles Times*, May 28, 1999. p. D1.

18. Mike Snider, "Studio Web Sites Offer Even Earlier Peeks at Films," *USA Today*, October 8, 1997, p. D1.

19. "Digital Video Disc Player Sets Record Sales Pace," *Salt Lake City Tribune* distribution, in *Fresno Bee*, December 6, 1999, P. C3.

20. "Walter Scott's Personality Parade," *Parade Magazine*, June 20, 1999, p. 2.

RADIO

A Wireless Wonder

*Radio was really a do it yourself television. Instead of a big
ugly glass picture tube, you saw the performers in your
own mind. You were not restricted by the boundaries of a
21-inch tube, but instead painted your own big as life
version of each moment with that loving creative brush we
call imagination.*

—**Jack Benny**

Key People and Concepts

Telegraph

Telephone

Guglielmo Marconi

Lee De Forest

Reginald A. Fessenden

David Sarnoff

Network

Radio Act of 1927

Federal Communications Commission (FCC)

Sitcoms

Soap Operas

"War of the Worlds"

Formats

Disk Jockey

Talk Radio

National Public Radio (NPR)

Frequency Modulation (FM)

Satellite Telecommunication Technology

Digital Radio Broadcasting

There have been newspaper stories and magazine articles about people being away from home who have managed to keep in contact with their hometown by tuning in the local radio station on the Internet. Thousands of radio stations around the world have begun to send out their music, news, talk programs, public service announcements, and even commercials through the Internet, allowing people to hear what's happening back home just with the click of a mouse. ● However, studies done shortly before the year 2000 showed that the radio industry in the United States has been slow in getting its material onto the Internet. For example, one study showed that while about 25 percent of the nation's 12,000 radio stations have established websites, only about 15 percent were running significant, local-oriented news. ● Another study showed that 64 percent of the people surveyed said they wanted radio stations to offer detailed, local community information on the Internet; 63 percent wanted information about concerts in the community, while 58 percent wanted the websites to provide information about the artists and song titles of the music played on the station, and 48 percent were looking for contests. ● Although 53 percent of those surveyed wanted the radio stations to put their broadcast programming on the Internet, a 1999 survey of radio stations found that only 20 percent were actually webcasting, while contests were being overloaded. At radio conferences, broadcasters were being told that stations need to give web users the materials they desire because there is advertising revenue available and untapped audiences that can be reached. ● For radio broadcasters, the need to use the new medium of the World Wide Web is very important (see Box 10.1). Radio has survived the challenges of newspapers, magazines, movies and television. But now the challenge is coming from the Internet itself. There are those who are now creating Internet radio stations, which are not subject to the rules and regulations of the Federal Communications Commission and are able to provide programming for a growing mass audience that is worldwide.   •   Despite more than a half-century of talk that the radio industry was doomed, it has continued to prove an enduring medium. In this chapter, we'll see how radio has undergone many changes and has successfully functioned in three separate niches in our culture during its relatively short history of less than a century.

HARNESSING SOUND WAVES

The invention of radio was the culmination of 70 years of technological advances in communicating messages. The need for instant communication first arose in the 1830s as the great era of railroad building got under way. The efficiency and safety of the railroads required a system that could send messages to distant stations faster than the trains traveled. Experimentation soon began on harnessing sound waves to meet this need.

The Telegraph

In 1844, a portrait painter and experimental photographer named Samuel F. B. Morse invented a system of sending coded sound waves over long distances on telegraph wires. To demonstrate his discovery, he strung 40 miles of telegraph lines between Washington, D.C., and Baltimore, Maryland, and transmitted in code his now famous message, "What hath God wrought?"

Soon telegraph lines were crisscrossing the country; by 1861 a transcontinental line was in place. This electronic communication system was adequate for the railroads' needs, but it was unsuitable for public use, since telegraph messages were limited to coded signals of dots and dashes, the well-known Morse code. However, the telegraph was not a tool of mass communication; rather, it was used only for point-to-point communication—from one sender to one receiver.

The Telephone

Many scientists went to work to find a way to send the human voice over telegraph lines. Although some claim that an Italian-American inventor named Antonio Meucci first laid out the plans for a voice transmitter and converter, credit for developing a workable system in 1876 goes to Alexander Graham Bell. His telephone consisted of a microphone, which converted sound into electrical energy, and a receiver, which changed it back into sound. Again, this was point-to-point communication and did not involve a mass audience to receive the message.

Three years earlier, the Scottish physicist James Clerk Maxwell predicted that someday it would be possible to generate electronic signals that could be sent through space at the speed of light without the use of wires. The German physicist Heinrich Hertz proved Maxwell's theory correct in 1888 when he sent a wireless signal from one point to another in his laboratory. (The unit of frequency called *hertz* is named in his honor.)

	Elitist	Popular	Specialized
1888	Heinrich Hertz transmits wireless sound waves.	•		
1901	Guglielmo Marconi sends wireless sound across the Atlantic.	•		
1906	Lee De Forest adds grid to vacuum tube, making voice transmission possible.	•		
1917	U.S. enters World War I; U.S. navy takes over broadcasting from American Marconi Company.	•		
1919	Radio Corporation of America (RCA) founded; Frank Conrad transmits music over the airwaves in Pittsburgh.	•		
1920	KDKA (Pittsburgh) goes on the air for Westinghouse; first fully licensed station with continuous broadcasting.	•		
1922	WEAF (New York) begins commercial broadcasting.	•		
1926	AT&T gives up effort to build a radio network; NBC (an RCA subsidiary) starts two networks.	•	•	
1927	UIB/Columbia network begins (later becomes CBS).	•	•	
1927	Federal Radio Act sets up commission to regulate the airwaves.	•	•	
1930s	Radio soap operas offer escape from the Great Depression.		•	
1933–1945	President Franklin Roosevelt uses radio for fireside chats with the nation.		•	
1934	Federal Communications Commission (FCC) established.		•	
1934	Mutual Broadcasting System goes on the air as fourth radio network.		•	
1938	Orson Welles's "War of the Worlds" broadcast panics nation.		•	
1939	First FM radio station goes on the air in New Jersey.		•	
1940–1945	Radio news "comes of age" and gains the respect of listeners as a legitimate news service with broadcasts of the war in Europe for American audiences.		•	
1943	Federal government forces NBC to sell one of its two networks; it eventually becomes ABC.		•	
1948	Network radio revenues reach a peak.		•	
1950s	Radio loses its programs and stars to television.			•
1950s	Radio begins to specialize with individual musical formats and disk jockeys; promotes rock and roll.			•
1959	Payola scandal rocks radio industry.			•
1960s	FM begins to increase in popularity, becoming more listened to than AM during the 1970s.			•
1970s	Country-western music and all-talk shows grow in popularity on radio.			•
1981	FCC begins deregulating radio during the Reagan administration.			•
1980s	AM radio adds stereo broadcasting to fight growing popularity of FM stations.			•
1992	FCC approves allocations of frequencies for digital radio signals delivered from satellites.			•
1996	More deregulation with the Telecommunications Act of 1996, which lifts limits on ownership of radio stations, bringing a dramatic increase in mergers and takeovers.			•
1999	A merger involving the two top owners of radio stations creates a conglomerate with more than 800 stations.			•
2000	Webcasting on the Internet takes radio into the 21st century			•

Box 10.1
MEDIA WATCH
The Internet: A Challenge to Radio or an Ally

Radio has fought many battles to survive in its more than 80 years of existence—against such competition as newspapers, movies, and television. But as the medium entered the 21st century, it was facing a new challenge: the Internet. While many radio station owners are concerned about the threat of competition from international radio stations on the Internet, others argued that the Internet should not be looked at as an opponent, but as an ally.

This was brought home clearly at the final meeting of the National Association of Broadcasters (NAB) Radio Show of the 20th century, where broadcasters and webcasters came together to discuss the future. The webcasters are those who are devoted to the Internet, which they think will change the world of radio broadcasting. However, there are also a lot of broadcasters—even some who have already put their stations on the Internet—who are not yet convinced of the web's value to their industry.

During the convention, radio broadcasters attended sessions with such titles as "Radio Will Survive the Next Audio World War" and "Broadcast Financing for the Future: The Internet Factor." They were told that the Internet appeals primarily to the core of radio's listening audience, the 16-to-24-year-olds who are not loyal to television but have been loyal to radio. In fact, of the 68,000 people in the United States alone who are said to access the Internet for the first time each day, 75 percent fall into that age range.*

But some broadcasters remained skeptical. There were those who said that stations were rushing too fast and should wait to see where the new technology was taking them. Others stressed that the Internet wasn't going to replace local radio stations, but would only help them. Some broadcasters pointed out that websites are valuable only when they add to a station's cash flow—rather than costing stations too much to set them up.

The head of the Radio Advertising Bureau (RAB) warned broadcasters that they need to learn about and capture consumers on the Internet, to help advertisers reach these consumers in new and exciting ways. However, RAB president Gary Fries also pointed out that radio is already benefiting in a big way from the heavy influx of "dot.com" advertising in recent years. Fried added that radio gets between 60 and 70 percent of the advertising budgets of Internet companies.**

A key point made at the conference for all broadcasters and webcasters tied right in with a lesson that most broadcasters have learned in their daily ratings fights with other stations in their communities—if your programming isn't any good, it won't make any difference whether your signal is just going out over the airwaves or on the Internet, nobody will listen to you.

*Elizabeth A Rathbun, "Clash of the 'Casters," *Broadcasting & Cable*, September 6, 1999, p. 38.

**Elizabeth A. Rathbun, "Log on or Lose, Fries Warns," *Broadcasting & Cable*, September 6, 1999, p. 38.

Development of the Wireless

Marconi

A wealthy young Italian, Guglielmo **Marconi,** experimented with Hertz's theories in Bologna, Italy, where he successfully sent signals across the hillside near his family home. Unable to interest the Italian government in his invention, Marconi and his mother traveled to England, where his mother's family had important social contacts. There he demonstrated his invention and obtained support from the British post office department. Marconi received his first patent on radiotelegraphy equipment in England in 1896, when he was 22 years old. The following year he formed the British Marconi Company, which continued to experiment with radio signal transmission over greater distances.

Marconi made history in 1901 when he set up a radio receiver in Newfoundland and picked up three dots (Morse code for the letter *s*) that had been sent through the air across the Atlantic by a colleague in England. He then developed a number of companies that expanded the ability of Morse code communication to mobile points. Wireless radio had found its first use in the culture, transmitting coded messages ship to ship and ship to shore.

Meanwhile, scientists were still struggling to find a way to send voices through the air. They were looking for a wireless telephone. The essential step came in 1906, when an American, Dr. Lee **De Forest,** perfected the vacuum tube by inventing a grid that became an amplifier when inserted into the tube. This improved vacuum tube, called an Audion, enabled radio receivers to pick up voice and music sounds. The vacuum tube remained a fundamental component of radio receivers until the transistor was invented in 1947. Although De Forest is generally credited for being the "father of radio," his patent rights to the Audion were disputed by J. Ambrose Fleming, who had patented a vacuum tube called the Fleming valve in 1904. De Forest's invention had been an improvement on Fleming's vacuum tube rather than a completely new invention.

De Forest

On Christmas Eve, 1906, University of Pittsburgh professor Reginald A. **Fessenden,** working with General Electric engineers, used wireless technology to broadcast music to ships at sea. They were providing entertainment for a mass audience. Since it was no longer point-to-point communication but the sending of a signal to anyone who had a radio to receive it, the process would be known as *broad*casting. Although a new era of wireless transmission had arrived, few people at the time had any idea that they were experimenting with a future mass-communication technology that would transform the culture.

Fessenden

THE BEGINNING OF RADIO AS A MASS MEDIUM

One person who did foresee radio's future as a mass-communication medium, and later became a force making it so, began his radio career as a wireless operator for American Marconi Company. At age 21, he was on duty when the *Titanic* hit an iceberg in the North Atlantic on April 14, 1912. The young radio operator who received the distress messages that would shock the world was David **Sarnoff.** The *Titanic*, which was considered unsinkable, had been on its maiden voyage from Europe to the United States and was carrying many socially prominent passengers. Sarnoff later became an executive with American Marconi Company, then went to work for Radio Corporation of America (RCA) and earned his place in radio history as the head of RCA's subsidiary, National Broadcasting Company (NBC).

Sarnoff

One of the driving forces in the development of radio was David Sarnoff, whose proposal for a radio music box was rejected by the Marconi Company.

Voice transmission continued in the experimental stages for a number of years. During the 1916 presidential election, De Forest sent out an experimental transmission of the Wilson–Hughes election returns, which is now considered to be the first radio news broadcast.

That same year, Sarnoff sent the following memo to his boss at American Marconi Company:

> I have in mind a plan of development that would make radio a "household utility" in the same sense as the piano or phonograph. The idea is to bring music into the house by wireless. . . . The receiver can be designed in the form of a simple "Radio Music Box" . . . supplied with amplifying tubes and a loud speaking telephone, all of which can be neatly mounted in one box. . . . Aside from the profit derived from this proposition, the possibilities for advertising for the company are tremendous for its name would ultimately be brought into the household, and wireless would receive national and universal attention.[1]

Like most such memos, this "music box memo" was largely ignored. However, in 1919 a Westinghouse engineer, Dr. Frank Conrad, started broadcasting music at an experimental station in Pittsburgh. A department store started running newspaper ads suggesting that people could hear "Dr. Conrad's magical music" come out of thin air by purchasing a crystal set (a small, tubeless radio receiver that used a crystal detector) at their department store.

Also in 1919, General Electric purchased the equipment and patents held by American Marconi Company and joined forces with Westinghouse, American Telephone & Telegraph (AT&T), Western Electric Company, and United Fruit Company to pool electronic patents and form RCA. Each company owned a percentage of RCA, and Sarnoff became RCA's general manager in 1921 at age 30. The decision to form an American radio distribution firm was prompted by the nation's involvement in World War I in 1917–1918 and the realization that Marconi, the major company in the field of radio at that time, was foreign owned. During the war, the U.S. Navy took over all U.S. commercial and amateur wireless stations, dismantling some and operating others as part of its own facilities. (Marconi, incidentally, served in both the Italian army and navy during the war.)

The rapid sale of crystal sets to hear Dr. Conrad's music proved Sarnoff had made a good suggestion in his 1916 music box memo. The next year, on November 2, 1920, Westinghouse went on the air in Pittsburgh with station KDKA, the first fully licensed commercial broadcasting station to have continuous programming. Its opening broadcast featured returns from the Harding–Cox presidential election, along with a request for people to write the station if they heard the broadcast. Officials at the company reasoned that people would purchase Westinghouse radio receivers if they had some programs to which they could listen.

Early Commercial Broadcasting

The success of Westinghouse's KDKA led other electrical companies to open their own stations. RCA went on the air with WDY in New York City; AT&T began WEAF in New York City; and General Electric started WGY in Schenectady, New York. Westinghouse later added stations in Massachusetts, New Jersey, and Illinois. The motivation for these electrical companies to start commercial radio stations was financial. While the sale of radio transmitters and receivers for ship-to-shore broadcasting was limited, by expanding radio to the masses the entire population became a potential market.

WEAF went on the air in 1922 as a toll station; that is, it sold air time to advertisers, the first commercial being a 10-minute message promoting a Long Island real estate development. The print media resented the competition and criticized the idea of radio advertising, calling it offensive. Even broadcasters disagreed as to whether commercials belonged on the airwaves.

The Beginning of the Networks

As more and more stations were founded around the country, AT&T started linking them together in 1923 using its telephone lines. This "chain broadcasting," which allowed stations to share programming, was the forerunner of **network broadcasting.** In 1926, AT&T bailed out of the broadcast distribution business and began leasing the wires to RCA's subsidiary, NBC. This launched the era of network broadcasting, with NBC establishing and operating two radio networks, NBC Red and NBC Blue. The company operated both networks until the Federal Communications Commission (fcc.gov) forced the sale of the Blue network in 1943. The Blue network became American Broadcasting Company (ABC).

network broadcasting

One year later, another broadcasting system was organized by the United Independent Broadcasters (a group of rival stations not affiliated with NBC), with the help

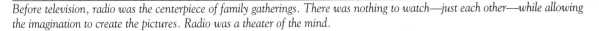

Before television, radio was the centerpiece of family gatherings. There was nothing to watch—just each other—while allowing the imagination to create the pictures. Radio was a theater of the mind.

of Columbia Phonograph Record Company. First called UIB/Columbia, it was re-named the Columbia Broadcasting System (CBS) after it was reorganized and pur-chased in 1928 by a 27-year-old cigar-company heir named William S. Paley. Paley, who chaired the board of CBS into the 1980s, had been impressed with the success of radio advertisements in boosting the sale of his family's cigars.

> **@ Practicing Media Literacy**
> Do you know how many radio stations in your city are affiliated with broadcast networks?

A fourth radio network, the Mutual Broadcasting System, was started in 1934 by four non-network-affiliated stations that joined together for their "mutual" benefit to carry a program from radio station WXYZ in Detroit, "The Lone Ranger." By 1935 Mutual had 60 affiliates and, in more recent years, has had more affiliates than any of the other major radio networks, but mostly in smaller cities. Mutual was the only major net-work to remain exclusively in radio after the other three ex-panded into television, and it is still in operation today.

The Need for Government Regulations

During the 1920s, the expanding radio industry found itself in need of stricter regula-tions to allocate radio frequencies and keep stations from jamming one another's sig-nals. It turned to the federal government for help and, after several unsuccessful attempts during the previous seven years, the Radio Act of 1927 was finally passed, es-tablishing the Federal Radio Commission (FRC). Soon the number of radio stations in the country was reduced to avoid interference in reception. The FRC was expanded and renamed the Federal Communications Commission (**FCC**) by the Communica-tions Act of 1934, which also gave the FCC authority over the telephone and tele-graph industries.

FCC

Radio Meets Cultural Needs

President Franklin D. Roosevelt assisted radio in becoming a major information source. After his election in 1932, Roosevelt started using the new medium to com-municate directly with the people through broadcasts that were called "fireside chats." Many Americans were in a panic over their financial troubles during the Depression years. Their only hope, they believed, was the leadership of the new president. For the first time in history, average people had the opportunity to sit in their homes and lis-ten directly to the reassuring voice of their president. (In the 1980s and 1990s presi-dents Ronald Reagan, George Bush, and Bill Clinton used radio to talk directly to the people, but these short Saturday morning reports were not carried by all stations. Rea-gan's programs often carried the first announcements of major policy decisions. Clin-ton's broadcasts, however, were not too popular, and some radio stations in major markets, such as Los Angeles, declined to air them.)

THE DEVELOPMENT OF RADIO ENTERTAINMENT

Shortly after radio entered the popular culture, the nation experienced the most seri-ous economic depression in its history. Many wealthy families lost their fortunes in the stock market crash; large numbers of poor and middle-class families lost their sources of income as their breadwinners were laid off; and many people lost their life savings as banks collapsed across the country.

President Franklin Roosevelt spoke directly to the American people by radio. Because these talks were more conversational than his political oratory, they came to be known as Fireside Chats—as if he were sitting in your living room speaking directly to you.

Radio had come along at just the right time. It provided free entertainment in the comfort of the home. Families that could no longer afford to go out for entertainment gathered together in their living rooms to escape reality by laughing, fantasizing, and dreaming of happier times.

Electronic Vaudeville

Radio had become a first-class entertainment medium after the networks were established in 1927. Variety shows, dramatic productions, and comedy series soon dominated the airwaves. Most comedy programs consisted of a series of jokes, gags, and short skits that were a form of burlesque comedy borrowed from vaudeville. Many vaudeville stars found jobs in this new entertainment medium, and eventually radio, coupled with motion pictures, led to the death of vaudeville.

Situation Comedy

After a few years, radio comedy shows evolved into a new form of comedy: situation comedy, or sitcom. Early radio sitcoms were 15 minutes long and ran five days a week. Episodes were in serial form, with the average plot or story line lasting for most of the week. This format was later changed to the 30-minute, once-a-week, self-contained situation comedy that we now have on television.

The first successful situation comedy, which started in the 15-minute format and then converted to 30 minutes, debuted on a Chicago radio station in 1928 as *Sam and Henry*; it later changed its name to *The Amos 'n' Andy Show*. It soon became the nation's most popular radio program—so popular, in fact, that some movie theaters announced to the public that they would stop their shows and pipe "Amos 'n' Andy" through the theater speakers to lure customers away from their home radios.

The stars of this series, Freeman Gosden and Charles Correll (both white men), played four to five characters each, all African-American men (it was common for one radio actor or actress to play more than one part on the same show). Although not as racist as D. W. Griffith's *Birth of a Nation,* the show did perpetuate the negative stereotypes of African-Americans that were common at the time.

Other popular situation comedy shows were Fred Allen and his *Allen's Alley,* which featured conversations between Allen and a cross-section of ethnic Americans, and *The Jack Benny Show,* which focused on Benny's famed stinginess. A number of other shows featured husband-and-wife teams in which one spouse handled the straight lines and the other, usually the dimwit, provided the comedy. Popular among these shows were the *Burns and Allen Show* and *Fibber McGee and Molly.*

Many of these early radio entertainers had started their show business careers in vaudeville. Eddie Cantor, Don Ameche, Nelson Eddy, Bing Crosby, Phil Harris, Alice Faye, and Bob Hope were just a few of the entertainers who became as well known as members of the family. Fictional heroes such as the Lone Ranger, the Green Hornet, and the Shadow added suspense to the lives of millions. Good radio drama, which required the audience to use its powers of imagination to visualize what was happening, was provided by such weekly shows as *Lux Radio Theater* and the *Mercury Theater on the Air.*

Imagination played a key role in the success of comedian–ventriloquist Edgar Bergen on radio because the star of his highly popular program was a wooden dummy, Charlie McCarthy. People envisioned the mischievous Charlie as a real-life little boy. Today the Charlie McCarthy dummy is on display at the Smithsonian Institution in Washington, D.C., while Edgar Bergen is known as the father of Candace Bergen, television's Murphy Brown.

The Soap Opera

Radio introduced another entertainment genre that is still with us today: the soap opera. Radio soap operas (named after the early sponsors of the shows, which were mostly soap companies) were similar to the daytime soaps on television today, with a couple of exceptions. First, radio soaps were only 15 minutes long, and their characters had "romances" (such as "The Romance of Helen Trent") rather than affairs. Today's TV soap opera characters also tend to be younger and sexier than their radio counterparts.

Early radio soap operas, particularly during the Depression, provided listeners with an escape from their troubles; they were often comforted to find that the radio characters had worse problems than their own. Up to 80 soap operas a day were broadcast on the three networks during radio's golden years (1930s and 1940s). Although many made the transition to television, only one, *The Guiding Light,* was still on the air in the 21st century.

A Mobile and Credible Medium

Radio has always been a mobile form of entertainment. The Great Depression forced many Americans to leave their homes in search of jobs, but their favorite programs

Radio is one of the most portable of the mass media—you can take it with you anywhere, even jogging (try reading a newspaper or magazine or watching television or a movie while jogging around the block). It's small, compact, and easily used by people of all ages.

were always waiting for them when they reached their destinations. And when the transistor made radio portable by eliminating the need for bulky vacuum tubes, people could take radios with them anywhere. Sony Walkmans, headsets, and other portable radios are now constant companions for sunbathers, joggers, bicyclists, and other people on the go.

Radio's credibility as a news medium also affected the culture. As radio news bureaus developed in the 1930s, regular programs were frequently interrupted for special news bulletins. An ear-witness account in 1937 of the fiery crash of the German dirigible *Hindenberg*, which killed 36 people in New Jersey, helped to establish radio's credibility. In addition, reports were now being heard from Europe about Hitler's invasions of other countries and the imminence of war. As more and more people came to depend on radio to take their ears to the scenes of major news events, the stage was set for one of the most famous hoaxes ever played on the American public.

On the eve of Halloween in 1938, a 23-year-old radio producer and actor named Orson **Welles** broadcast his rendition of H. G. Wells's short novel ***War of the Worlds*** on *The Mercury Theater on the Air.*

All week the cast had been struggling to adapt the story to radio and was finding it difficult to make the drama believable. So Welles decided to present the story as an interruption of a regular music broadcast, with news reporters breathlessly cutting in to describe the landing of creatures from Mars.

Although the broadcast included four announcements that the attack was just a dramatization, many people were listening to the more popular Edgar Bergen and Charlie McCarthy show on another network when "War of the Worlds" began. During the first commercial on the McCarthy program, many people turned the dial to see

@ **Practicing Media Literacy**

What type of radio do you listen to the most—a portable radio, a clock radio, a kitchen or bathroom radio, or a car radio?

Welles
War of the Worlds

what else was on. They tuned in to an announcer describing a strange creature climbing out of a vessel in Grovers Mill, New Jersey. Then they heard the announcer and a crowd of people being annihilated by the creature's ray gun. National panic set in as people telephoned friends and relatives to warn them of the impending disaster.

By the end of the hour-long broadcast, people had attempted suicide, jammed long-distance telephone lines, and caused national pandemonium. Military personnel were called back to their bases. In Concrete, Washington, a power failure during the broadcast caused a traffic jam as most of the town's residents fled in their automobiles to escape the invading Martians.

To understand how so many people could be fooled by a radio drama, one must remember that times were tense. The nation was in its eighth year of economic depression, Hitler had overrun Czechoslovakia and sent Nazi troops into Austria, and world war was imminent. Radio was a new and believable news medium. Psychologists and sociologists spent years afterward studying the national panic Welles had instigated. An estimated 6 million people heard the Welles broadcast, and 1 million of them believed it. It's not known how many others were caught up in the mass hysteria. As a result, the FCC quickly stepped in and banned fictional news bulletins from the airwaves.

RADIO AND THE EPS CYCLE

Radio prospered in the popular stage of the EPS cycle during World War II and the years right after the war, but soon the cloud of television began to cast its shadow over the medium.

The radio networks were turning their attention to TV, and numerous station owners were applying for TV licenses. Many people saw television as an improvement on radio, since it provided pictures as well as sound.

The CBS Raid

Television's breakthrough year was 1948, when radio network advertising revenue reached an all-time high of $210 million. This was also the year CBS made its famous raid on NBC radio personalities, signing such stars as Jack Benny, Freeman Gosden and Charles Correll (Amos 'n' Andy), Burns and Allen, Edgar Bergen, and Bing Crosby to CBS contracts.

According to broadcast historian Erik Barnouw, CBS's coup was made possible by the American income tax laws. CBS convinced these radio stars that they would reduce their taxes by selling their shows to CBS, since money from the sales would be taxed at the lower capital gains rate. CBS succeeded in buying all of NBC's highly rated Sunday night entertainment and gained control of important talent for the new television age.[2]

NBC's Recovery Efforts

NBC responded by signing for its TV network the popular vaudeville comedian Milton Berle. To ensure that he wouldn't be stolen away by CBS, they offered him a 33-year contract. It seemed like a wise investment, as Berle became **"Mr. Television"** and gave NBC several years of high ratings. He used many vaudeville and burlesque routines on television, such as dressing in outlandish costumes (many times in drag or in gorilla suits), and he featured lots of slapstick. However, TV shows proved not to have

Mr. Television

the staying power of their radio predecessors. After eight years, people began to tire of Berle, ratings declined, and the show was taken off the air. Milton Berle was forced to retire from series television, but on full salary for another 25 years.

The Specialization Stage

As the networks focused their attention on television, radio ratings and earnings steadily declined. However, radio did not die as some had predicted. Television had stolen radio's programming format and left it with a choice: change or die. It chose the former. After a period of transition, it entered the specialized stage of the EPS cycle.

Music and News

Gradually radio eliminated its programming of ballroom music, quiz shows, soap operas, sitcoms, dramas, and action–adventure shows from the networks and replaced them with a locally produced format of music and news. Network-affiliated stations, which had formerly all sounded alike, now took on their own identities. One station in an area might play top-40 music, while others featured rhythm-and-blues, country-and-western, jazz, or classical music. Born with the new era of radio was the **disk jockey** (DJ), an announcer who developed a following for his or her on-the-air personality and choices of music.

disk jockey

   The development of the disk jockey era was not without controversy, however. In 1959, the radio industry was rocked by the "payola scandal." A number of disk jockeys, including Alan Freed, the man who coined the term rock and roll, were charged with taking money and gifts from the recording industry to plug certain records. Many disk jockeys lost their jobs, and stations now hired program directors to select the music to be played on the air. Radio station employees must still sign a form acknowledging awareness of the FCC payola rules and promising to report to management any record company gift worth more than $25.

   The new era of specialization of radio and its popular music formats coincided with the development of rock and roll as the most successful form of popular music. Ever since the 1950s, the success of radio and that of popular recordings have been dependent on each other.

All-News and All-Talk

Not all radio stations feature music, however. Some markets have DJs who don't play much music but are known for their "shock" form of humor (see Box 10.2). Among them, Howard Stern and Don Imus are now syndicated by satellite around the nation. All-news stations broadcast a complete news show every 20 minutes or so—20 minutes is the average driving time for an all-news listener.

   All-talk shows feature a host with guests and telephone call-ins. Topics range from personal and sexual problems to politics and sports. **Talk radio** went through a boom period during the final years of the 20th century. In 1983, for example, there were 59 full-time talk radio stations in the United States. By the year 2000, there were more than 1,200 stations formatted for all talk. Host Rush Limbaugh, along with sports talk stations, are given much credit for saving AM radio in its battle with the better-sounding FM stations. The conservative message that Limbaugh provided on a daily basis resulted in many right-wing imitators, including convicted Watergate felon G. Gordon Liddy; former Marine officer Oliver North, who was involved in the Iran–Contra activities during the Reagan administration, and the former president's

talk radio

Despite her heavy accent, Dr. Ruth Westheimer gained national fame by giving advice on sexual matters on her radio talk show.

son Michael Reagan. Other noted talk show hosts heard nationwide included sex therapist Dr. Ruth Westheimer and moralist Dr. Laura Schlessinger. Even CNN interviewer Larry King first gained national prominence with his all-night talk show on the Mutual radio network.

Some hosts, such as Liddy and Limbaugh, have used their shows to advance their own political agendas. In fact, many attributed the Republican takeover of Congress in 1994 to the many conservative radio talk show hosts across the nation. However, their power was not enough to defeat Democrat Bill Clinton in his bid for reelection as president in 1996.

Sports

Radio still plays a major role in broadcasting sports events, despite television's inroads in this field. Credit for this must be given to radio's mobility. Radios can be taken to work, on picnics, and so forth. Some people even take their radios to the sporting event to be able to "hear" as well as "see" the activities. Some radio stations now feature all-sports formats with a combination of **sports talk** and call-in shows as well as the broadcasting of sports events. Most major markets have at least one radio station that carries only sports talk programming, allowing local listeners to call in to discuss the fate of their favorite teams. There are also several satellite networks, including ESPN Radio, which provide programming for such stations.

sports talk

Of course, the latest development in this type of programming is the Internet, where many sports stations are webcasting their programs—especially the play-by-play broadcasts of major league baseball games, so the fans in other parts of the nation and the world can tune in to hear broadcasts of their favorite teams. The San Francisco Giants, Baltimore Orioles, and Chicago White Sox have been the leaders in getting their play-by-play broadcasts on the Internet through their flagship stations. Other teams, such as Houston, Kansas City, Philadelphia, and Seattle, make their games available for free on AudioNet. One team, the Oakland Athletics, is believed to be the first to offer broadcasts of its games on the Internet with a crew of announcers who are not the regular team of daily broadcasters. Broadcasts of other sports, from football to hockey, can also be found online. But baseball is everywhere, as minor league and college games can also be found on the Internet.

> **@   Practicing Media Literacy**
> What type of radio programming to you listen to the most—music, news, talk, or sports?

Programming Potpourri

According to the *Gale Directory of Publications and Broadcasting Media*, radio stations are now categorized under almost 30 programming formats (see Table 10.1). The advantages of this new "formula radio" are many. Not only do radio stations now focus on specialized listening needs, they can also deliver well-defined target audiences to advertisers. And, as mentioned earlier in this chapter, many radio stations have expanded their audience base by providing programming on the Internet (see Box 10.3).

Box 10.2
MEDIA LITERACY
Today's Radio Personalities: Do They Go Too Far for Ratings?

Those who are familiar with shock jocks know that they'll say anything, no matter how outrageous or offensive, to build their audience. People will then talk about them at the office later that day ("Did you hear what he said this morning?") and they'll tune in again the next day to see if the shock jock will be even more outrageous.

During the 1990s, shock jock Howard Stern was not only generating ratings in his home-base city of New York, but was doing the same thing for radio stations across the country through the syndicated satellite broadcasts of his program. But at the same time, he was also generating millions of dollars in fines from the Federal Communications Commission for many of his comments.

The FCC generally investigates a shock jock only after receiving complaints from listeners. And the agency received plenty of complaints about Stern. He was fined for a broadcast in which a lesbian was supposedly hypnotized to have an orgasm every time Stern scratched his own ear, which he did often on the broadcast. He was fined for a holiday broadcast in which a guest was brought in to play a Christmas carol on the piano with his erect penis. Another complaint was filed against him when he examined three women for breast cancer on the air and then cautioned them to get a second opinion. The New York State Education Department's Office of Professional Discipline was asked to investigate whether Stern was practicing medicine without a license.

In the 1990s, Stern drew criticism and boycotts from the Latino population because of a comment he made after the death of singer Selena. During his program, he played a short segment of one of the Tejano singer's records, then dumped out of it saying it was no wonder that she'd been shot to death.

In California, commuters were given three days of toll-free travel on the San Francisco–Oakland Bay Bridge under a court-sanctioned settlement paid by a radio station because of a stunt pulled by one of its personalities. As a part of the settlement, KSOL-FM had to pay a half-million dollars to cover the tolls the motorists were spared and also had to pay $480,000 to help spruce up the bridge's toll plaza.

The self-proclaimed "King of All Media," Howard Stern is a successful radio shock jock, a best-selling author, a movie star, and a television personality—despite the many fines levied against him by the FCC.

It all came about as the result of a class action lawsuit filed four years earlier when morning commute traffic was tied up for more than an hour as disc jockey Erich "Mancow" Muller conducted his stunt. Muller was doing a parody of an incident a week earlier where flights at Los Angeles International Airport had reportedly been delayed while President Clinton received a haircut on Air Force One.

Muller's response was to park a radio station vehicle across the San Francisco-bound traffic lanes of the bridge to broadcast the haircut being given to one of his on-air sidekicks. In a separate court decision not related to the class action suit, Muller was fined $500 and ordered to do 100 hours of community service. He later left San Francisco to work for a Chicago radio station.

Even the mild-mannered host of public radio's *Prairie Home Companion* program, Garrison Keillor, created some controversy in 1999 when he began using his weekly variety program to deliver insults toward the new governor of his home state of Minnesota, former wrestler Jesse Ventura. Among the broadcast attacks: "You have the IQ of a salad bar" and "You couldn't pour water out of a boot if the instructions were printed on the heel." Ventura threatened to cut off state funding for Minnesota Public Radio, which produces Keillor's program.

And then there was the case of the Washington, D.C., shock jock known as "The Greaseman," who

continued

certainly is no stranger to controversy. But that controversy also delivered high ratings for "The Greaseman," Doug Tracht. However, a comment made on the air in February of 1999 finally cost him his job.

Over the years, Tracht had offended many listeners in Washington, particularly African-Americans. But he went too far in 1999 when he played a portion of a song by Grammy-winning African-American hip-hop artist Lauryn Hill and then commented "No wonder people drag them behind trucks." His remark was in reference to the murder of an African-American who had been dragged to his death behind a truck in Texas the previous year.

After the broadcast, WARW suspended Tracht without pay and later released a statement saying that the station had fired him: "While we will always strongly support the right of our on-air artists to express a wide range of opinions, even those that are unpopular or offensive to some, WARW cannot be associated with the trivialization of an unspeakable act of violence now at the heart of the national debate on race."*

Some 13 years earlier, "The Greaseman" had managed to keep his radio job in Washington despite another comment which stirred much debate in Washington as well as canceled advertising, picketing, bomb threats, and calls for his firing. In that case, Tracht had made a reference to the Martin Luther King holiday, adding "Kill four more and we can take a whole week off."

*Frank Ahrens, "Washington Disc Jockey Fired over Racist Remark," *Washington Post* syndicate, in *Fresno Bee*, February 26, 1999, p. A8.

TV has mounted a new challenge to radio as TV itself enters the specialization stage. Cable channels such as MTV and VH-1 are competing with contemporary hit radio stations by showing music videos, while other channels have country music videos, all-news or all-sports formats, and talk shows featuring radio personalities such as Dr. Ruth, Larry King, and Dr. Laura.

Public Radio

Another avenue for specialization in radio is provided by noncommercial educational radio stations. Many of these stations are owned and supported by educational institutions, others by private foundations.

NPR

Two networks serve these noncommercial stations, National Public Radio (**NPR**) and Public Radio International (**PRI**). NPR, founded in 1970, receives its funding through the Corporation for Public Broadcasting, which was established by the Public Broadcasting Act of 1967. The sources of funding are the federal government, private donations, and station membership fees.

NPR provides about 50 hours of programming each week for some 300 affiliates. Its two in-depth news programs, *Morning Edition* and *All Things Considered*, are highly regarded. Another popular show produced by NPR has been *Car Talk*, featuring Tom and Ray Magliozzi. In 1979, NPR became the first radio network to use satellites to transmit its programming.

Unlike NPR, PRI does not produce programs but instead distributes programming produced by its member stations. It uses some of NPR's satellite distribution facilities to accomplish this. Originally known as American Public Radio, the network was launched in 1981 and changed its name to PRI in 1994. PRI carries the popular *Prairie Home Companion*, starring Garrison Keillor.

Both PRI and NPR have cooperated effectively in the development of America One, a network formed in the early 1990s to broadcast public radio programming throughout Europe. Meanwhile, there has been ongoing talk of a merger of NPR and PRI due to the high cost of operations and the declining support of federal funds.

NEW TECHNOLOGY AND RADIO

A number of technological improvements have also helped radio to find its new niche in the stage of specialization.

FM Radio

In 1925, electrical engineer Edwin H. Armstrong began working on the problem of static in radio, the result being the development of frequency modulation (**FM**). This new technology enhanced radio reception quality. Armstrong set up the first FM station in 1937, and by 1953 he had introduced his multiplex technique, which led to FM stereo broadcasting.

FM operates on a higher frequency than AM and sends its signals in a straight line. Thus, it avoids the atmospheric distortion that is common in AM (amplitude modulation) broadcasting, which bounces its signal off the ionosphere. FM has less static and higher quality and was the first to broadcast in stereo.

Although FM was introduced before World War II, it did not become a successful alternative to AM broadcasting at first. However, in the 1960s the FCC made several decisions that assisted the development of FM radio. One was a freeze on the allocation of new AM licenses, leaving FM as the only avenue for new radio stations. The second was an FCC ruling that allowed FM to broadcast in stereo. The third was the 1967 "nonduplication rule," which required AM–FM combination stations to limit the duplication of their programming on both frequencies.

Until that time, most companies that owned both AM and FM stations in the same market merely carried the AM programming on the FM station so they wouldn't have to employ a separate staff of announcers. This nonduplication regulation was abandoned in the mid-1980s, but the result was AM stations carrying the programming of their FM sister stations, a reversal of the pattern of earlier years. The FCC's dropping of the regulation was taken as an attempt to save AM radio.

In 1945, only 50 FM stations were on the air. In 1960, there were 688. By 1990, more than 5,600 FM stations were reaching 95 percent of American households.[3] The enhanced quality of FM signals, particularly in delivering music, forced a large number of AM stations to turn to all-talk formats.

Computerization

In the 1980s, some radio stations started using computers to operate their broadcast studios. The station's entire daily operation could now be programmed into a computer. At the appropriate second, the computer could call up a cartridge tape of an announcer's voice giving the time, introducing a record, or reading a commercial. The next computer cue would turn on a tape machine to play a preselected song.

As a result, some disk jockeys and radio announcers found themselves replaced by computers. However, some audiences were not ready for this new technology, and a number of stations found that the rather impersonal computers were no substitute for the disk jockey, who could respond personally to telephone requests and had the gift

TABLE 10.1

Radio Station Formats
Adult Contemporary
Agricultural
Album-Oriented Rock
Alternative/Progressive/Independent
Big Band/Nostalgia
Blue Grass
Classic Rock
Classical
Contemporary Country
Contemporary Hit Radio
Country
Easy Listening
Eclectic
Ethnic
Folk
Full Service
Gospel
Hispanic
Jazz
Middle-of-the-Road
News
Oldies
Public
Religious
Soft Rock
Sports
Talk
Top 40
Urban Contemporary

Source: Gale Directory of Publications and Broadcasting Media, Vol. 3 (Detroit: Gale Research 1994), pp. 3321–3457.

FM

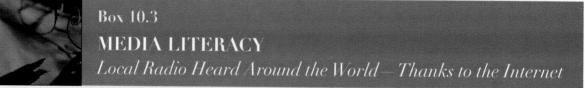

Radio stations on the Internet are more than just "voices from home" for those who are traveling or have moved to other cities permanently. It is a way for people from all over the world to learn about the music and cultures of other nations. For example, listeners in Europe can find out about what's going on in the United States by listening to numerous American news, talk, and sport stations webcasting on the Internet. These include WCBS-AM and WOR-AM in New York, WBAL in Baltimore, and XTRA in Tijuana, Mexico, which tells Internet fans that it provides play-by-play broadcasts of the San Diego Chargers professional football team, the Los Angeles Kings of the National Hockey League, and the UCLA Bruins.

KING-FM in Seattle promotes itself as the first radio station in the world to broadcast classical music live on the Internet 24 hours a day, seven days a week. Classical music is also available on the web from radio stations in Minneapolis and Dallas. Dallas also has KDGE—The Edge—featuring alternative and underground rock music for listeners worldwide. YesterdayUSA, based in Richardson, Texas, specializes in broadcasting vintage radio and music programs.

You can find adult contemporary Christian music on WHJT-FM, Alive 93.5, in central Mississippi. If that type of music is not to your liking, how about live rock, country, and blues? That's available on the Internet from KICK-AM in Sydney, Australia. Easy-listening music is available from Citylite 88.3 in Manila, the Philippines, while Radio Bandit broadcasts rock music from Sweden.

But there's more: Fun Radio presents live rock music from Paris; Radio Padova broadcasts a variety of music, along with news and sports programs from Italy; live news from Taiwan in Chinese is offered by the Broadcast Corporation of China; and stations in Greece, Colombia, Switzerland, Mexico, and even Ipanema are available on the Internet.

One of the most rapidly developing radio services on the Internet in recent years has been alternative radio, primarily college radio stations. But one station, CRUX Radio, advertises itself to Internet browsers as an alternative radio and music site with no commercials, no talk, and no FCC—just material not heard on mainstream radio.

of gab. By the end of the decade, some radio stations had returned to the old way of doing things.

Satellite Transmission

The new satellite telecommunication technology ushered in by the space age has affected radio as well as other media. The satellite is an electronic relay system that operates from outer space. United States communication satellites are placed in orbit some 22,300 miles above the equator so that they will rotate at the same speed as the earth (appearing to be stationary) and look down on the continental United States. Satellites are either launched into space by rockets or placed in orbit by space shuttles. They carry transponders that pick up and retransmit signals sent from the ground. Most satellites have 24 transponders, but in the future satellites are expected to carry up to 40. The more transponders, the more complicated and valuable the satellite becomes.

Satellites are used extensively to provide syndicated and network programming to radio stations across the country. Since computerized signals make it possible for local stations to insert commercials and station identifications, the average listener has no idea that the programming they are listening to is being beamed simultaneously to radio stations across the country. For example, syndicated programs such as *Country*

Box 10.4

HOW IT WORKS
Radio

Experience is important when it comes to getting a job in radio. Most people start at small stations and work their way up the ladder. Getting that first job at a small station often requires working for very low wages. However, this is necessary because larger stations usually won't hire a person without experience.

Departments within a radio station depend on the size of the station. Usually there are seven divisions that offer employment. These include management, programming, sales, news, promotion, traffic, and engineering.

The *management* of a radio station is essential to ensure that profits are made; the station's FCC license is not jeopardized; departments operate efficiently; and bills, paperwork, personnel, and payroll are handled. Depending on the size of the station, there is a general manager and perhaps a station manager. These positions can be combined at smaller stations. The general manager is in charge of the overall operation of the company. The station manager handles the day-to-day operations.

The *programming department* consists of the program director, who is responsible for the station's on-air content, the announcers, and the disk jockeys. The content of the station depends on the format management has selected. It might be a specialized type of music, all-talk, or news. Some stations today rely on satellite-fed programming made available through syndicated services. Others use computerized equipment to cut down on the need for music selection and announcers.

The *sales department* is responsible for generating the revenue to keep the station on the air and make a profit. This department has a sales manager and a sales force that usually works on a commission, selling air time to clients who wish to advertise. Each station has a rate card that gives the costs for commercials. The rate card is usually dependent on the station's share of the audience in the market: The bigger the audience at given times, the more the station can charge for commercials.

The *news department* is composed of a news director, on-the-air newscasters, reporters, and writers. Some stations have large news staffs that gather news from the community, while others rely on announcers to "rip and read" stories from the wire services and local newspapers. All-news operations have larger news staffs than music-oriented stations.

As the fight for survival in the battle for an audience continues, the *promotion department* is becoming more prominent in various-size markets. This department is responsible for setting up concerts for the station to sponsor and contests to involve the audience and lure listeners away from other radio stations in the market. Keeping the station in the public eye is important in today's competitive radio market.

The *traffic department* is in charge of the daily program log that shows when programs and commercials are aired. Today this log is usually computerized. The log is the official blueprint for all on-the-air talent to follow and becomes the station's permanent record for billing purposes.

The *engineering department* is responsible for keeping the station on the air and maintaining the equipment. The chief engineer is trained in electronics and must not only keep the station's transmitter and other equipment in good repair but also be up-to-date on new equipment and technologies to keep the station state-of-the-art. At large stations, the engineering department is responsible for operating the mixing boards. At smaller stations, this task is handled by the disk jockeys and announcers.

Coast-to-Coast, Stardust, and *Contemporary Top 40,* all produced by Satellite Music Network, radio talk shows featuring G. Gordon Liddy and Rush Limbaugh, and the morning shows of New York shock jocks Howard Stern and Don Imus and Los Angeles DJs Mark and Brian are sent to stations throughout the United States by satellite.

While the satellite technology has improved the quality of radio programming in rural areas, it has assimilated these rural listeners into the sounds and message of a national mass audience. In many areas, programs that reflect regional cultures are no longer broadcast.

Digital Radio

The next breakthrough in radio broadcasting technology will be digital radio broadcasting from satellites. In 1992, the FCC gave its approval for the allocation of frequencies for satellites to deliver digital radio signals to special digital audio radios. The quality of the signal is comparable to that of compact discs.

The digital signals are made up of the ones and zeros of computer codes rather than the traditional wavelike signals. The satellite signal will be received on an antenna about the size and shape of a credit card. The broadcast signal will be able to reach any digital radio in the country.

The National Association of Broadcasters (intervox.com/nab.htm) has been fighting the development of this new technology. Broadcasters fear that a system of some 40 national digital channels could destroy the local broadcasting market and have been working to develop a local broadcasting system of digital signals.

CURRENT TRENDS

Today FM stations are very profitable, while AM stations are seeing a decline of revenue. The cost to purchase an AM station today is much lower than it was 10 years ago.

The future of radio continues to look bright, however. By the start of the 21st century, more than 12,000 radio stations were operating in the United States: almost 5,000 AMs, over 5,000 commercial FMs, and some 1,800 noncommercial FMs.[4] The commercial stations were generating more than $12 billion in advertising revenue.[5]

There is more than one radio for every person in the United States: 91.1 million homes have radios, and 95 percent of all automobiles in this country are equipped with them, many of them now provided as standard equipment by the automobile manufacturers. Radio has a larger audience than television does for a sizable part of the day, usually around the "drive times" of 6 to 10 A.M. and 3 to 7 P.M. According to statistics compiled by the Radio Advertising Bureau, on average high school and college students spend more hours a day listening to radio than they do watching television.

But the current trend is for a takeover of radio stations by large conglomerates (see Table 10.2). The 1996 Telecommunications Act allowed single owners to possess more than one AM and one FM in each market, and many stations soon found themselves under the same ownership as five or six other stations in the same market.

One of the first big mergers occurred just four months after President Clinton signed the new Telecommunications Act into law, when the owner of CBS, Westinghouse Electric, agreed to purchase Infinity Broadcasting for $3.9 billion. The merger of the two companies created a single owner for 83 radio stations with a total revenue at the time of $1 billion per year. Westinghouse had found itself owning radio stations in 16 markets, but, more importantly, it now controlled 69 stations in the nation's top 10 markets, including

> **@   Practicing Media Literacy**
>
> When do you listen to radio the most? For what reason do you listen to the radio?

7 stations in New York, 6 in Los Angeles, and 10 in Chicago. A year later, Westinghouse added to its total by purchasing American Radio Systems, the nation's fifth largest radio company, for $1.6 billion. With the purchase, Westinghouse picked up an additional 98 stations from American Radio.

Also in 1997, in a deal said to be worth more than $2.5 billion, Evergreen Media swapped stock with Chancellor Broadcasting to form a new company known as Chancellor Media. The merged company then purchased 10 more radio stations from Viacom, giving it a total of 103 stations—becoming the second largest radio conglomerate behind Westinghouse–CBS. That ranking wouldn't last to the end of the 20th century.

The movement toward consolidation in the radio industry was underscored in 1999 when Clear Channel Communications, the nation's largest owner of radio stations, announced that it was purchasing the second largest owner, AMFM Inc., for $17.4 billion in stock and $6.1 billion in assumed debt. The deal was projected to create the largest radio company in the world in terms of revenue and number of stations, with the additional potential of reaching a weekly audience of approximately 100 million listeners.[6] Even though Clear Channel was expected to sell off some 125 stations under FCC rules, the new conglomerate would still end up owning some 830 radio stations—a lot more than what previous FCC rules allowed any one owner, which was a nationwide total of seven AM stations, seven FM stations, and seven TV stations. Under the old rule, no company could own more than one of each type of station in any given market. How the times had changed.

In fact, with so many stations in each city now being owned by large national conglomerates, one California radio station, located in a market served by some 30 signals, was promoting itself as the only "locally owned" station in its market.

TABLE 10.2

Radio's Top 25 Group Owners

This information was compiled by Broadcasting & Cable *magazine for publication in August of 1999, just as the FCC was again altering ownership rules which resulted in several large broadcasting mergers in the final months of the century. The groups are ranked by the amount of revenue they generated during 1998, a total of $7.6 billion. A group's prior-year ranking is shown in parentheses.*

Rank	Owner
1.	AMFM Inc. (1)
2.	Infinity Broadcasting Corp. (2)
3.	Clear Channel Communications Inc. (3)
4.	ABC Radio Inc. (4)
5.	Entercom Communications Corp. (6)
6.	Cox Radio Inc. (5)
7.	Hispanic Broadcasting Corp. (7)
8.	Cumulus Media Inc. (9)
9.	Citadel Communications Corp. (12)
10.	Susquehanna Radio Corp. (10)
11.	Emmis Communications Corp. (8)
12.	Bonneville International Corp. (13)
13.	Jefferson-Pilot Communications (15)
14.	Greater Media Inc. (14)
15.	Spanish Broadcasting System (17)
16.	Radio One Inc. (21)
17.	Beasley Broadcast Group (16)
18.	Saga Communications Inc. (18)
19.	Journal Broadcast Group Inc. (19)
20.	Tribune Broadcasting Co. (20)
21.	Sandusky Radio (23)
22.	Hearst-Argyle Television (not on list in 1998)
23.	Dick Broadcasting Co. (22)
24.	BP Holdings LP (not on list in 1998)
25.	Buckley Broadcasting Corp. (24)

@   **Practicing Media Literacy**

Have you noticed whether radio stations in your city are a part of a conglomerate ownership? If so, have you detected any differences in the way the stations are programmed?

Since they couldn't be seen by the listeners, radio actors could play many different roles—on the same program and on other shows. It was not unusual to see actors rushing from a network studio to a competing network to appear on another "live" broadcast. Some of those old radio programs are rebroadcast today in many cities on nostalgia programs.

SUMMARY

Although radio is a 20th-century mass-communication medium, its beginnings date to the 19th century, when scientists were attempting to discover ways to convert sound waves into electrical energy. Samuel Morse's invention of the telegraph, Alexander Graham Bell's discovery of the telephone, Guglielmo Marconi's wireless telegraphy, and Dr. Lee De Forest's amplifier vacuum tube all contributed to the development of radio.

Radio became a mass-communication medium in the 1920s, when stations started broadcasting music and news bulletins. Companies such as Westinghouse, General Electric, RCA, and AT&T played major roles in converting radio from a maritime communication system to a mass medium. They did so to sell more radio receivers.

The development of the networks in the late 1920s launched radio into its golden age as a news and entertainment medium. American lifestyles were drastically changed as people were able to hear major news events live from the scene and enjoy entertainment free in their homes.

During the Great Depression, many people escaped their troubles by listening to radio. They were also able to take their entertainment with them when they migrated to find new jobs in distant places.

After television adopted radio's programming in the 1950s, radio entered the specialization stage. Stations learned to cater to distinct segments of the listening audience and adopted music and news as the basis of their programming. Two national public radio networks, National Public Radio and Public Radio International, service noncommercial educational stations.

There have been a number of new technological developments in radio broadcasting. FM radio has improved radio broadcasting signals and has developed into a popular commercial and noncommercial delivery system. The quality of music on FM has diminished the popularity of AM radio and has caused AM radio to turn more to talk shows. Radio stations have also started using computers and satellites to improve their broadcasting services. On the horizon is the development of satellite-delivered digital radio signals with the quality of compact disks.

The future of radio broadcasting looks bright as radio continues to have more listeners than television has viewers during certain parts of the day. Most homes and automobiles have radio receivers. And now, more radio stations are beginning to offer their programming on the Internet.

However, the ownership of radio stations has shifted from local to out-of-town media conglomerates. The 1996 Telecommunications Act removed the ban prohibiting one owner from having several stations in the same market.

Find a review of *Key People and Concepts*, a message board for *Practicing Media Literacy* questions, self-tests, and more at: www.mhhe.com/wilson.

Thought **Questions**

1. What cultural factors were at work to create the need for the development of wireless communication?

2. What social and economic forces contributed to the conversion of radio into a mass communication medium?

3. Why did so many Americans believe the "War of the Worlds" broadcast was real? Could something similar happen today? Why or why not?

4. What are some social and economic problems that may develop with the advent of national digital radio broadcasting?

5. What problems have been created by the 1996 Telecommunications Act, which allows major companies to now own more than one radio station in a community?

Notes

1. Quoted in Archer Gleason, *History of Radio to 1926* (New York: American Historical Society, 1938), p. 85.

2. Erik Barnouw, *The Golden Web: A History of Broadcasting in the United States* (New York: Oxford University Press, 1968), p. 245.

3. *The Broadcasting Yearbook 1994* (Washington, D.C., Broadcasting Publications, Inc., 1994), p. A–3.

4. "By the Numbers," *Broadcasting & Cable*, July 29, 1996, p. 75.

5. "Media Current Analysis," *Standard & Poor's Industrial Surveys*, March 14, 1996.

6. Bill Carter, "The Leader in U.S. Radio to Buy No. 2," *New York Times*, October 5, 1999, p. C1.

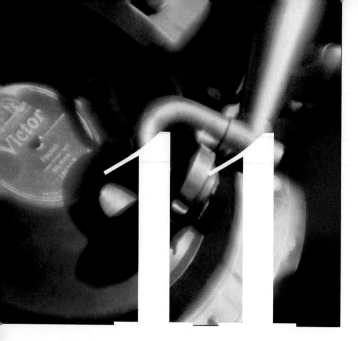

Recorded Music

Powerful and Controversial

Musick and women I cannot but give way to, whatever my business is.

—**Samuel Pepys, 1666**

Key People and Concepts

Sheet Music

Graphophone

Gramophone

African-American Music

Spirituals

Gospel

Blues

Ragtime

Jazz

White Swing

Jukebox

Rhythm and Blues

Rock and Roll

Generation Gap

The Beatles

British Invasion

Interactive Video

Subliminal Embeds

Backmasking

During the 100 years of the 20th century, popular music in the United States went through many evolutions. But perhaps the most dominant form, the most long-lasting type of music, has been rock and roll and its many variations.   When it came time to list the top 100 rock songs of the century, a poll of 700 people in the music industry selected as the top song a piece of music that represents many changes in rock music. It was recorded by a British group that invaded this country shortly after the success of the Beatles. It was a group that has lasted longer than any other rock group, now in its fifth decade of performing and still selling tickets for all its concerts. And the song deals with one of the most common themes in rock music since the 1950s, sex. The greatest rock song of the 20th century was judged to be "(I Can't Get No) Satisfaction" as recorded in 1965 by The Rolling Stones (see Table 11.1).   The list of top rock songs of the century presents a cross section of popular music in America during the last half of the century, but it also includes many songs recorded by international groups. For example, the Beatles placed nine songs on the list. Apparently because they had so many hit songs, the vote became divided and, although they outsold almost all recording artists during the century with numerous hits, their highest finishing song on this list was "Hey Jude" at number 9. The Rolling Stones placed five songs on the list, while Elvis Presley and Led Zeppelin had four.   The oldest song on the list was 1955's "Rock Around the Clock" as recorded by Bill Haley and the Comets. The most recent was from 1991—the only song from the 1990s to make the list—Nirvana's "Smells Like Teen Spirit." And the Stones not only had the top song, some might say they were also represented in the final song on the Top 100 list, the Temptations' recording of "Papa Was a Rolling Stone."   From the very start, rock music has been another form of youth rebellion. Throughout the evolution of popular music in this country, young people have enjoyed the fact that their parents "just don't understand" their music. Although other forms of music continued to exist during the 20th century, the music industry would not be the lucrative media business it is today if it hadn't been for the young and the rebellious who use the ever-evolving world of popular music as their vehicle for expression and protest. In this chapter, we'll examine the evolution of recorded music in America and its impact on our culture.

HOW IT ALL BEGAN

The influence and significance of music in our culture have long been recognized. More than 2,000 years ago, Plato called for strict censorship of popular music in *The Republic*, a book about his concept of an ideal society. He feared citizens might be corrupted by "weak and voluptuous" music and led to indulge in demoralizing emotions. Over the centuries, many philosophers and scientists have expressed this fear of music's power to corrupt. However, it wasn't until the 19th century that music began to be mass communicated and the criticism began to grow. This criticism of popular music intensified in the 1990s.

Sheet Music

The pervasiveness of recorded music in today's American popular culture sometimes makes us forget that recordings weren't the first form in which music was mass communicated in our society. In the 19th century, music started being transmitted in print: Sheet music was printed and distributed, first in the elite culture and then, in the late 19th and early 20th centuries, in the popular culture. A variety of popular folk songs were widely distributed, and people used the sheet music to play pianos or other instruments at family sing-alongs or social gatherings.

The Talking Machine

Although sheet music was popular, it did not have the cultural impact of recorded music. Thus, when Thomas A. Edison first heard his own words, "Mary had a little lamb," repeated back to him from his talking machine in 1877, the stage was set for the development of a powerful mass-communication medium. Edison called his invention a phonograph. He recognized the potential for the phonograph and by the following year had formed the Edison Speaking Phonograph Company.

Edison's early phonograph used a tinfoil cylinder to record and play back the sound. Two technicians working for Alexander Graham Bell improved on Edison's invention by developing the **graphophone,** which used a wax cylinder instead of tinfoil for longer wear and better sound. The new talking machines were first played publicly for vaudeville audiences; later they were leased to saloons, where people could "hear them talk" for a nickel.

graphophone

The American Graphophone Company and the Columbia Phonograph Company began leasing the talking machines to record dictation in offices during this period. Columbia did well because it had the Washington, D.C., franchise to lease the machines to government offices. When American Graphophone failed, Columbia obtained its patent rights and became known as Columbia–Graphophone.

Cultural History of Recorded Music

		Elitist	Popular	Specialized
1877	Thomas A. Edison invents the "talking machine."	•		
1902	Enrico Caruso begins recording opera.	•		
1905	Columbia introduces two-sided disks.	•		
1920s	African-American music helps recording industry expand its sales.		•	
1920s	Jazz music evokes charges that music is corrupting young people.		•	
1920s	Covering (white musicians playing African-American music) leads to development of "white swing."		•	
1925	Electric phonograph replaces hand-cranked machines.		•	
1927	Jukebox becomes popular.		•	
1930s	Recording industry declines due to Great Depression and radio's free music.		•	
1930s	Big band era keeps recording industry alive.		•	
1940s	Frank Sinatra gains fame appealing to youthful bobby-soxers.		•	
1950s	Specialization of radio introduces African-American rhythm and blues to white audiences.		•	
1954	Sam Phillips of Sun Records discovers Elvis Presley, who becomes the king of rock and roll.			•
1955	The motion picture industry, reaching out for a youth audience, uses Bill Haley and the Comets' "Rock Around the Clock" as the theme song for *The Blackboard Jungle*.			•
1955–1963	Rock and roll becomes firmly entrenched in the new youth subculture.			•
1960s	Led by the Beatles and the "British Invasion," rock music begins carrying less innocent messages that reflect changing American subcultures.			•
1970	The Beatles disband.			•
1970s	Disco palaces invade American culture.		•	•
1976	Punk rock emerges in Britain.			•
1981	Warner-Amex introduces MTV cable channel; popularizes music videos.			•
1985	U.S. Senate committee holds hearings on rock music lyrics; suggests a rating system to warn listeners of explicit lyrics.			•
1986	Michael Jackson pays a reported $40 million to $50 million for the rights to Beatles' music.			•
1988	CDs replace LPs as most popular format of recorded music.			•
1990	Jury finds Florida music store owner guilty of obscenity for selling rap music.			•
1990	Court finds Judas Priest innocent of causing the suicides of two Nevada youths by placing subliminal messages in their music.			•
1990s	Alternative or grunge rock provides popular protest to the show-biz glitz of the music industry.			•
1996	Gangsta rap star Tupac Shakur is gunned down in Las Vegas; his first posthumous album jumps to number one of the charts			•
1999	MP3 digital audio file format for computers causes concern for recording industry			•
2000	Time Warner announces plans to combine its music operations with Britain's EMI Records, creating a joint operation valued at $20 billion from almost 25 percent of global music sales.			•

gramophone

The next improvement on the early talking machines was the **gramophone.** It changed the way the stylus recorded sound and used a disk instead of a cylinder. The inventor of the gramophone, German immigrant Emile Berliner, joined forces with a New Jersey machinist, Eldridge Johnson, to found the Victor Talking Machine Company. They were the first to market the gramophones for use in the home.

World-famous opera star Enrico Caruso gave people something worthwhile to listen to on their gramophones when he began making recordings in 1902. Other opera stars followed suit, and the recording industry was on its way. Columbia introduced the two-sided disk in 1905. However, the new talking-machine industry was very much a communication medium for the elite, as only wealthier homes could afford a gramophone and records, which cost 65 cents apiece at a time when $5 a week was a good salary.

RECORDED MUSIC ENTERS THE POPULAR CULTURE

American culture has two distinct forms of folk music, both rooted in American subcultures: African-American music and hillbilly music, now better known as country-western. African-American music was the first to be transmitted throughout the popular culture through sheet and recorded music. Hillbilly music remained primarily in the southern region of its origin until the second half of the 20th century.

African-American Music

spirituals
gospel
blues

Early African-American music—**spirituals, gospel,** and **blues**—reflected the poverty and oppression of slaves in the South. The only thing the slaves were able to bring with them to this country was their culture, and that culture was expressed through their music.

ragtime

African-American music became popular in the 19th century after the Civil War as musicians of color were hired to play in saloons and brothels along the Mississippi River. A popular form known as **ragtime** made the transition from these establishments to the popular culture in the late 19th century through the distribution of sheet music.

jazz

As ragtime's popularity waned in the early 20th century, a new form of African-American music known as Dixieland **jazz** took its place. The 1920s were known as the Roaring '20s or the Jazz Age. In this decade, Prohibition was in effect and illegal drinking was promoted in speakeasies, which played music and allowed people to enjoy themselves by dancing the Charleston.

Until 1925, most phonographs were mechanical and hand cranked. In that year the industry started selling electric phonographs, and the recording industry moved rapidly from the elite culture into the popular. In 1927, 987,000 phonographs were sold, along with 104 million records.

As jazz entered the popular culture, it provoked a great deal of criticism—similar to what we hear today about popular music—that it was destroying the morals of youth. The themes of popular music in the 1920s were very similar to those in today's recorded music.

As early as the 1920s, blues songs on such labels as Okeh and Bluebird carried a variety of sexually suggestive titles. The music, which reflected the emotions and struggles of the poorer segments of the African-American community, often referred to the earthy conditions of everyday life and occasionally included four-letter words. The music was criticized by blacks as well as whites, as the following passage from an

African-American leader indicates: "To respectable, middle class, church-going Negroes, blues is often considered evil music; the devil's music that beguiles the listener and leads him to damnation."[1]

Such charges against recorded music were prevalent during the Jazz Age. The culture was changing during this period as new music, new dances, new styles of dress, the entrance of the automobile into the popular culture, and new moral codes began altering people's behavior. Women began smoking, drinking, and listening to jazz in speakeasies. They wore short "flapper" dresses and did the Charleston and other "shimmy dances." Men and women were displaying a new, carefree attitude in a culture that had previously been guided by Victorian morality. Cole Porter's suggestive song "Let's Do It" from the musical *Paris* was a smash hit in 1928, and Billie Holiday sang about "Love for Sale," another Porter song, released in 1930. Because of the lyrics, the song was banned by most radio stations during that time.

Leaders of such groups as the National Education Association, the Federation of Women's Clubs, and various religious organizations took up the antijazz cry. The following article in William Randolph Hearst's *New York American* reflected a common view:

Jazz Ruining Girls, Declares Reformer

Chicago, Jan. 21—Moral disaster is coming to hundreds of American girls through the pathological, nerve irritating, sex-exciting music of jazz orchestras, according to the Illinois Vigilance Association.

In Chicago alone the association's representatives have traced the fall of 1,000 girls in the last two years to jazz music.

TABLE 11.1

The Top Rock Songs of the 20th Century

Here are the Top 40 of the 100 greatest rock-n-roll songs of the 20th century as determined by a panel of 700 music industry voters, assembled by the cable music network VH1.

Rank	Song
1.	(I Can't Get No) Satisfaction—The Rolling Stones
2.	Respect—Aretha Franklin
3.	Stairway to Heaven—Led Zeppelin
4.	Like a Rolling Stone—Bob Dylan
5.	Born to Run—Bruce Springsteen
6.	Hotel California—The Eagles
7.	Light My Fire—The Doors
8.	Good Vibrations—The Beach Boys
9.	Hey Jude—The Beatles
10.	Imagine—John Lennon
11.	Louie Louie—The Kingsmen
12.	Yesterday—The Beatles
13.	My Generation—The Who
14.	What's Going On—Marvin Gaye
15.	Johnny B. Goode—Chuck Berry
16.	Layla—Derek and the Dominos
17.	Won't Get Fooled Again—The Who
18.	Jailhouse Rock—Elvis Presley
19.	American Pie—Don McLean
20.	A Day in the Life—The Beatles
21.	I Got You (I Feel Good)—James Brown
22.	Superstition—Stevie Wonder
23.	I Want to Hold Your Hand—The Beatles
24.	Brown Sugar—The Rolling Stones
25.	Purple Haze—Prince
26.	Sympathy for the Devil—The Rolling Stones
27.	Bohemian Rhapsody—Queen
28.	You Really Got Me—The Kinks
29.	Oh, Pretty Woman—Roy Orbison
30.	Bridge Over Troubled Water—Simon & Garfunkel
31.	Hound Dog—Elvis Presley
32.	Let It Be—The Beatles
33.	(Sittin' On) The Dock of the Bay—Otis Redding
34.	All along the Watchtower—The Jimi Hendrix Experience
35.	Walk This Way—Aerosmith
36.	My Girl—The Temptations
37.	Rock Around the Clock—Bill Haley and the Comets
38.	I Heard It Through the Grapevine—Marvin Gaye
39.	Proud Mary—Creedence Clearwater Revival
40.	Born to Be Wild—Steppenwolf

Source: "Stones Get Some Satisfaction: VH1 Ranks Hit No. 1 of All Time," Associated Press, *Fresno Bee,* January 7, 2000, p. A1.

The music of the 1920s and '30s was a break from the more Victorian morality of America's popular culture. Songs written by such composers as Cole Porter and sung by such artists as Billie Holiday (shown here) were considered by many to be very suggestive and some were banned from the radio.

Girls in small towns, as well as the big cities, in poor homes and rich homes, are victims of the weird, insidious, neurotic music that accompanies modern dancing.

The degrading music is common not only to disorderly places, but often to high-school affairs, to expensive hotels and so-called society circles, declares Rev. Richard Yarrow, superintendent of the Vigilance Association.

The report says that the vigilance society has no desire to abolish dancing, but seeks to awaken the public conscience to the present danger and future consequences of jazz music.[2]

Despite this and similar criticism, the popularity of jazz continued to grow.

Covering

Attempts by the recording industry to sell blues and jazz to the popular culture ran into some difficulties, however. In particular, many whites were reluctant to buy records by African-American artists. To overcome this, the process of covering was developed: White artists were hired to record black music.

White Swing

swing

Benny Goodman, for example, rode to fame playing the music of African-American songwriter–arranger Fletcher Henderson. From blues and jazz came white swing. **Swing** was a milder, watered-down version of African-American music that did not reflect the raw emotions of the black experience. Swing became a popular style of music that mainstream tastes could accept. This was established when the Goodman band was the first jazz group to appear at New York City's esteemed Carnegie Hall in 1938.

Is life reflecting art or is art reflecting life.

Jukeboxes and Sales

The recording industry grew and flourished during the last half of the 1920s. The jukebox became popular in 1927 and added another market for the sales of records as well as providing a new promotional device for home sales of records.

In the 1930s, however, the industry nearly collapsed as the Great Depression seriously curtailed people's ability to spend money on leisure pursuits and radio now offered music free. The end of Prohibition in 1933 helped record sales, though, by bringing back taverns, which had jukeboxes playing the latest records.

Radio and Sales

Radio networks also began to see a future in the recording industry, with CBS purchasing the Columbia Phonograph Company and starting to promot its recording stars on network

@ **Practicing Media Literacy**

Lyrics in many of the popular songs of today are more blatantly sexy than they were back in the 1920s and '30s. Do you think this is because radio has changed our acceptance of such things or has our culture changed, making it easier for radio to play such songs?

radio. RCA, the parent company of NBC, made phonographs and records. People were encouraged to go out and buy records featured on the network radio stations.

In the late 1930s, a young singer named Francis Albert Sinatra was discovered. Backed by the popular Harry James and Tommy Dorsey bands, he became the idol of many young "bobby-soxers" throughout the country. Teenage girls would scream and faint when they saw him in concert or heard his voice on records or radio. Many other popular vocalists, such as Peggy Lee, from the big-band era of the 1930s became successful as recording artists during the 1940s and early 1950s. Among them were Frankie Laine, Vaughn Monroe, Mel Tormé, Perry Como, Vic Damone, Dinah Shore, and Doris Day.

Rhythm and Blues

Rhythm and blues music (R & B) featured on African-American radio stations became very popular with young people during the early 1950s. Recording industry executives realized that if they could find white performers to sing rhythm and blues, they might capitalize on the expanding audience of young people for this new sound. One such "find" was a young, clean-cut Columbia University graduate, Pat Boone, who gained fame by recording covers of such songs as Little Richard's R&B hit "Tutti Frutti" and Fats Domino's "Blueberry Hill." In 1951 Cleveland disk jockey Alan Freed, who later coined the term *rock and roll*, started playing rhythm and blues records for a young, white radio audience. The station where he worked received many complaints about this "sinful" music with its erotic beat.

Rock and Roll

Sam Phillips, a Memphis, Tennessee, record promoter who formed Sun Records in the early 1950s, combed the South for a white country singer who could handle the beat of rhythm and blues. "What I need," he said unabashedly, "is a white boy who can sing colored."[3]

In 1954, he found country-western singer Elvis Presley and turned him into the "king" of rock and roll. Presley's first hit record was "That's All Right (Mama)" in 1954. By 1956, Presley had five songs at the top of the charts after being introduced to a mass audience on Tommy and Jimmy Dorsey's summer replacement television program. Later television appearances for Presley would be more controversial, when Ed Sullivan ordered that the cameras could not show him from the waist down because of previous protests about his hip gyrations. After a hitch in the army, Presley became a motion picture star as well. Although his recording career faded in the 1970s, he remains a living legend years after his death in 1977.

In a career that spanned almost 25 years, Elvis Presley blended country-western and rhythm and blues with a strong beat and some body gyrations to become the "king" of rock and roll.

@ Practicing Media Literacy

Do you think Elvis Presley could be a successful recording artist today? How has rock music changed since the 1950s and '60s when he was King?

Rock and roll was a new form of American music that evolved from a blend of rhythm and blues and country-western. The motion picture industry, which was attempting to recover from the television-caused box-office slump by focusing on the youth audience, helped promote rock and roll in some of its movies. For example, Bill Haley and the Comets' rock and roll song "Rock Around the Clock" was the theme for *The Blackboard Jungle*, a film about juvenile delinquency in the schools. The song became one of the best-selling records of 1955, even though it had been out several years before being used in the film. Other movies featured rock recording artists performing their songs, even though the music had little to do with the films' plots. Television featured rock and roll shows too, most notably Dick Clark's *American Bandstand*, which played the latest songs each weekday afternoon. The program showed rock stars lip-synching their hits and teenagers dancing to the music.

The American youth of the 1950s were forming their own subculture with its own fads, clothing styles, and music. Rock and roll filled the bill. America's white youth were being introduced to the African-American culture through music. Indeed, rock and roll was instrumental in breaking down the **color barrier** in music once and for all. The young were less prejudiced than their parents and enjoyed the music without caring about its ethnic origins. Many African-American entertainers became popular with white as well as black audiences. Among them were Chuck Berry, Fats Domino, Little Richard, Chubby Checker, Little Anthony and the Imperials, The Chantels, Bo Diddley, the Platters, the Shirelles, and the Coasters.

color barrier

The local music store became a gathering spot for teenagers in the 1950s as they formed a subculture around the new rock and roll music that was sweeping the country—much to the annoyance of their parents.

However, this new youth music was controversial among some adults. Because of this controversy—some racially prejudiced adults criticized the fact that young people were enjoying "colored" music, and others found Elvis's hip gyrations too sexually explicit (these critics referred to him as Elvis the Pelvis)—the record industry began to introduce a new breed of recording star to rock music. The period of 1959 to 1963 became known as the Age of Innocence, when wholesome, clean-cut, white, middle-class youngsters were recruited to be rock stars. Top-40 radio stations began featuring these performers to avoid the controversies. Such singers as Ricky Nelson, Frankie Avalon, Fabian, Paul Anka, Bobby Darin, and Bobby Rydell became teen idols. They sang largely about teenage romances. Also popular were female singers such as Lesley Gore, Annette Funicello, and Connie Francis. These performers helped take rock and roll into the mainstream and boost the audiences of Top-40 radio stations.

The merging of country-western music with rhythm and blues also helped to move country music into our mainstream popular culture. Many of the early rock and roll singers were former country stars, and this trend of crossing over from country to popular music helped to spark country music's acceptance in the popular culture. The 1970s saw the emergence of such popular country-western crossover artists as Kenny Rogers, Dolly Parton, Johnny Cash, and Willie Nelson. The trend continues today with such crossover artists as Garth Brooks, Reba McEntire, and k. d. Lang.

ROCK MUSIC CHANGES

Rock and roll was fun, innocent music for the young, despite the fact that the older generation didn't like it. Even parents who didn't mind their children listening to African-American music complained that the new music sounded awful and described it as a clattering of pots and pans. To keep it out of earshot, they sent their children to their rooms to listen to it. This helped set the stage for what was termed the *generation gap* between parents and adolescents in the late 1960s.

Cultural Changes

Following the assassination of President Kennedy in 1963, rock and roll music became more sophisticated, and its lyrics reflected the troubled and changing times. The counterculture, with its "flower children," "hippies," and psychedelic drug users, had arrived. The slogan of the day was "Make Love, Not War," as the counterculture preached free sex and opposition to U.S. involvement in the Vietnam war. This agenda was expressed in the rock music of the mid- and late 1960s. Such songs as the Rolling Stones' "(I Can't Get No) Satisfaction" and Bob Dylan's "Blowin' in the Wind," "A Hard Rain's Gonna Fall," and "Talkin' World War III Blues" presented ideas and viewpoints far removed from those of mainstream, middle-class America.

Many parents were shocked to find their children were developing values different from their own. They started to blame the schools for teaching such things to their children, unaware that much of the education was going on at home through the music they had banished to their children's rooms.

The Beatles

One of the most popular recording groups of all time was the Beatles, an English quartet that had a profound impact on

> **@ Practicing Media Literacy**
>
> Can you think of any current popular songs that will someday be remembered as a reflection of the times?

American popular culture and middle-class culture worldwide during the 1960s. Although the group disbanded in 1970, their cultural influence was so strong that their popularity endures as we close out the 1990s.

The Beatles, from Liverpool, England, consisted of John Lennon, Paul McCartney, George Harrison, and Ringo Starr. In 1964 they led the "British invasion" of rock stars who became household names in the American popular culture. These British performers had grown up with America's Elvis Presley and had popularized American rock and roll for British youth. Then, in 1964, the Beatles brought their British version of American rock and roll home to the United States, thus launching an invasion of British performers. The Beatles and other British groups also triggered a youth fashion revolution in the United States, which consisted of long hair and "Beatle" boots for boys and miniskirts and long, straight hair for girls.

The Beatles' early hits were simple, innocent songs such as "I Want to Hold Your Hand" and "She Loves You." Their music changed with the times, however, and began to rely on advanced recording techniques. In 1967 the Beatles released *Sgt. Pepper's Lonely Hearts Club Band*. The album took more than 400 hours to record and was highly sophisticated, with many hidden messages and meanings in the lyrics, sound track, and album cover. Some claimed four-letter words and other messages were embedded at a level where they could be heard only by the subconscious mind.

One song in particular, "Lucy in the Sky with Diamonds," was believed by some observers to be about the use of LSD. They pointed out that the key words in the title start with the letters of this hallucinogenic drug and that the lyrics describe a psychedelic acid trip with such phrases as "tangerine trees and marmalade skies." The Beatles, of course, denied any connection. *Sgt. Pepper* was so successful that 20 years later, in 1987, it was voted by rock critics around the world as the greatest rock album of all time.[4]

Some people also zeroed in on the Beatles' top-selling single "Hey Jude" (1968), saying it too was about the use of drugs. The word *her* was said to refer to heroin in such lyrics as "let her into your heart" and "the minute you let her under your skin then you begin to make it better." However, Beatles business associate and biographer Peter Brown says that Paul McCartney wrote the song to ease the pain of John Lennon's young son, Julian, during his father's divorce from his mother, Cynthia, and new involvement with Yoko Ono.[5]

Brown does confirm that the group was one of many that got heavily involved in drugs. Although the Beatles had been taking amphetamines to help them through concerts since their early days of performing in Hamburg, Germany, it was not until their first American tour in 1964 that they were turned on to marijuana. According to Brown, "On August 28 a small but auspicious event occurred at the Delmonico Hotel in New York that would grow to affect the consciousness of the world: Bob Dylan turned the Beatles on to marijuana for the first time in their lives.[6] Brown also confirms the Beatles' experimentation with LSD and admits that John Lennon became dependent on heroin.[7]

The change in the Beatles and their music was what kept them so popular. They led the British invasion with a new sound that the youth of America seemed to be waiting for as **Beatlemania** swept over the United States in 1964. In April 1964, the top five singles in this country were all recordings by the Beatles. Other British groups, including the Dave Clark Five, Herman's Hermits, and Peter and Gordon, had top-10 hits that year, but only the Beatles became a cultural legend because they were willing to change as rock music "grew up" in the troubled decade of the 1960s.

Beatlemania

Although they disbanded over 30 years ago, the Beatles (Paul McCartney, Ringo Starr, John Lennon, and George Harrison) are still considered to be one of the most dominant influences in popular music during the 20th century.

Even though the Beatles broke up in 1970, their impact on our popular culture remains profound. Paul, George, and Ringo have all maintained their own individual careers. Paul has dabbled in other forms of music, including the composing of his "Liverpool Oratorio" and "Standing Stone," recorded with symphony orchestras and choruses, while George has also spent time producing records and Ringo has pursued an acting career, including commercials. When John Lennon was murdered outside his New York apartment in December 1980, the event became one of the biggest news stories of the year. Hundreds of radio and TV stations throughout the United States honored his wife Yoko Ono's request for 10 minutes of silence. Magazines and newspapers ran extensive stories on the shooting and ordinary people's reaction to his death. An unsuccessful attempt on the life of George Harrison in his home outside London just as the year 2000 was about to begin also gained worldwide news coverage, although competing with "new millennium" ceremonies.

In 1986, singer Michael Jackson paid between $40 million and $50 million to purchase the rights to almost all of the songs written by the Beatles. Today many radio stations are still regularly playing the Beatles' music.

Second Wave of the British Invasion

The second wave of the British invasion brought the Rolling Stones, a group that sang about alienation and social discontent. Reflecting the hostility of the times, the Stones challenged the Beatles as the most popular group in the United States. However, feminist groups greatly criticized the Stones for the hostility toward women evident in such songs as "Under My Thumb," about a girl who does just as she is told, and "Time Is on My Side," about a dependent woman who keeps running back to her man. In the 1970s, feminists protested a billboard advertisement for the Rolling Stones' album *Black and Blue*. It showed a woman beaten and tied up with a caption reading "I'm black and blue from the Rolling Stones, and I love it."

However, the Rolling Stones have endured this criticism and have continued to perform for over 35 years. Now with members in their 50s, this group (called the

Songs of alienation and discontent helped launch the Rolling Stones (featuring Mick Jagger and Keith Richards) in the mid-1960s. Despite their age, the Stones continue to perform before sold-out audiences.

@ **Practicing Media Literacy**

Why do you think the Rolling Stones are almost as popular now as they were in the mid-1960s? Are they only popular with older people who were the young fans then or are they also reaching today's young listeners?

"geezers" by *Time*) has outlasted, outperformed, and outsold all other rock stars of the 1960s generation. According to the Recording Industry Association of America, the Stones have been awarded five platinum singles (representing sales of 1 million copies each) and 28 gold albums (500,000 copies each). In addition, they have had two albums go multi-platinum: *Tattoo You*, with 3 million copies sold, and *Some Girls*, with 4 million. Their 1999 tour played to sold-out audiences.

When it comes to setting records in sales, the British win out again. In 1997, England's Elton John rewrote the lyrics to his "Candle in the Wind" to make it a tribute to Princess Diana, which he performed at her funeral seen around the world. In the first week of its release, John's new recording of the song set a new record by selling 3.4 million copies. Just 37 days after its release, "Candle in the Wind '97" was declared the best-selling single of all time, with 31.8 million copies sold worldwide. It surpassed Bing Crosby's recording of "White Christmas," which has sold around 30 million copies in its 55 years on the market.

Meanwhile, the Beatles were declared the best-selling act of the 20th century by the Recording Industry Association of America (RIAA). The trade group's list of the top artists of the century credited the Beatles with selling more than 106 million albums in the United States alone, more than any other artist in the previous 100 years. The RIAA reported that the Beatles were the only act in history to register five diamond albums, signifying U.S. sales of 10 million copies or more of each. America did manage to register top sellers in the male and female single artists category, according to the RIAA: country star Garth Brooks was the 20th century's most successful male artist, selling 89 million albums in the United States, which was second only to the Beatles. The top female artist of the century was Barbra Streisand, with album sales of nearly 62 million.[8]

Other Favorites

Another popular kind of music in the 1960s was the Motown sound, danceable African-American soul music that originated in Detroit. This music featured the sounds of Diana Ross and the Supremes, the Temptations, and Stevie Wonder. By the early 1970s, these groups were singing such socially conscious songs as "Love Child" and "Ball of Confusion."

Other groups reflecting the new age of social protest and the culture during this period were the Doors and Jefferson Airplane. In a quieter, subtler way, Simon and Garfunkel also sang about alienation, social protest, and bitterness.

ROCK SPECIALIZES

From its beginnings in the 1950s, rock music has learned to specialize. Over the years, a variety of rock forms—pop rock, hard rock, acid rock, punk rock, bubblegum rock, glitter rock, new wave, heavy metal, reggae, rap, hip hop, Christian rock, and alternative rock—have evolved. Musicians who have been able to change with the music have endured.

Disco

In the 1970s, as the Vietnam war came to an end and people began to tire of protest music, they began searching for a new sound. The discotheque, a cabaret where patrons could dance to a DJ playing popular music, began to grow in popularity. Disco music, like rock, had its roots in the beat of rhythm and blues. It created a new cultural industry of disco palaces, such as the celebrity haven Studio 54 in New York. Even radio stations were adopting formats of all-disco music. This new form of heavy-beat dance music introduced a new group of stars, from soloists such as Donna Summer and Gloria Gaynor to such groups as the Village People, which consisted of six men dressed as a cowboy, a construction worker, an Indian, a policeman, a biker, and a soldier. One of the hottest disco groups, thanks to the music they provided for the John Travolta disco-themed movie *Saturday Night Fever* (1977), was the Bee Gees.

The record industry went into a financial slump in the late 1970s similar to the one it had experienced in the 1930s. Part of the problem was an increase in record prices due to the rise in petroleum prices (the vinyl used in records was a petroleum by-product). But some people, such as record producer Richard Perry, blamed disco for the decline in record sales: "Everybody spent their money dancing at discos, not on albums. Disco also was limited to 128 beats per minute, which gave it pulse but no solid melody. All disco began to sound alike. It became totally uninspiring to dance to. It got people out of the habit of buying records. It really hurt the whole music industry."[9]

Punk Rock

Also contributing to the decline of record sales was the recording industry itself, which tried to limit the expenses of promotion by restricting the number of new rock groups allowed to record during the 1970s. (This is a classic form of gatekeeping, which was discussed in Chapter 1.) Rock and roll had evolved from a youth subcultural movement of the 1950s to an establishment medium that was still providing groups from the 1960s, such as the Rolling Stones, Diana Ross, and the Who. Establishment control of the recording industry led in 1976 to the **punk-rock rebellion** in England. A youth subculture, known as punks, began developing a new antiestablishment music. Some of the first punk-rock bands, such as the Sex Pistols and the Clash, denounced the establishment's control of mass culture and spoke out against our consumer society. The punk movement spread throughout the world, but it did not become as much of a rage in the United States as it did in Britain. Eventually it was watered down and became popular as new-wave music. Punk and new wave both had an impact on American fashion. While some people bought fashionable new-wave clothing promoted by the establishment consumer culture, others spiked and colored their hair green or purple or attached safety pins to their faces to imitate the British punk look.

punk-rock rebellion

The alternative rock band Nirvana was one of the most popular until the death of its leader, Kurt Cobain (center). The group has since disbanded but the music of Nirvana is still played on many radio stations.

New Wave

Disco's popularity had declined by the 1980s as punk and new-wave music emerged. Among the new groups rising to popularity were the B-52s, Devo, Blondie, Elvis Costello, the Cars, the Motels, the Talking Heads, the Police, Duran Duran, and Boy George and the Culture Club. The new music plus the development of music videos and the debut of MTV in 1981 helped to restore the financial health of the recording industry.

Alternative Rock

Much like the folk–hippie music of the 1960s and the punk-rock movement of the 1970s, alternative rock (often called "grunge rock" or the "Seattle sound") is a musical genre that rejects the commercial values of mainstream popular music. Its main source of exposure comes from the student-run radio stations on college campuses across the nation. Alternative has no strict definition, but it does have a feel. Its musicians attempt to reject show-biz glitz, and they support progressive social causes. The music is usually guitar driven, with experimental touches. While pop songs are usually about love, alternative lyrics deal with tougher feelings such as despair, lust, and confusion. Alternative seems to be a reaction, especially among the "twenty-something" generation, to the years of being subjected to the commercialized efforts of Madonna and George Michael. Some of the more popular alternative groups include Nirvana (led by the late Kurt Cobain), Smashing Pumpkins, Soul Asylum, Stone Temple Pilots, and Pearl Jam.

THE MUSIC VIDEO PHENOMENON (MTV)

While alternative rock music was getting its first exposure on college radio stations that were trying to feature music not heard on the commercial stations, the cable television industry's partial answer to specialized radio, Music Television (MTV), also helped to promote the new alternative sound. Owned by Viacom, MTV was created in 1981 as an all-music channel targeted at 12-to-23-year-olds. It has had a phenomenal impact on the American popular culture.

Similar to home-shopping networks, MTV is one continuous commercial promoting rock music sales. Seventy percent of America's rock enthusiasts indicate that MTV is important in determining their musical purchases. Eventually music videos became another consumer product in music stores. This presented a new problem for recording artists; not only did they have to worry about how a new song would sound; they had to worry about how it would look on video. Today the international demand for the MTV cable network is profound, and the influence of America's youth culture music is global.

Other cable music channels are VH-1, featuring soft rock aimed at an older audience, and The Nashville Network for country-western fans. When Viacom, one of the largest cable companies in America, merged with Paramount Communications and Blockbuster Entertainment Corporation, it took over ownership of both MTV and VH-1.

Impact on Education

Some educators complained that students were spending too much time watching MTV and not enough on homework. Although many teenagers had been studying with rock music in the background since the 1950s, videos required visual as well as aural attention.

Other educators recognized the significance of MTV and began studying it. For example, California State University at Los Angeles began offering a course called Music Video 454 after the MTV phenomenon developed. Students studied the contents of music videos, listened to guest speakers from the video industry, and visited sets where some of the videos were produced.

> **@ Practicing Media Literacy**
>
> How many hours per week do you watch MTV? Do you actually watch it or do you use it as some use a radio—as background music?

MTV's Early Impact on Other Media

The influence of music videos has not been limited to the recording industry. The pace, style, and sound of rock videos have influenced many of the television commercials we see today. They are no longer 30-second minidramas about such social problems as bad breath or dandruff but are fast-moving, quick-cutting images used to convey an aura of energy about the products.

The former head of programming for NBC-TV, Brandon Tartikoff, is said to have been doodling while trying to come up with new programming ideas and wrote down the words "MTV cops." From that came the hit television series "Miami Vice," which featured MTV-worthy fast-moving video images with many of the current songs of the day on the soundtrack. Rock artists whose music is featured on the soundtracks of current movies often use scenes from those movies in their videos so MTV can plug the films as well as the recordings.

The impact of popular music on television was even more prominent by the start of the 21st century when several youth-oriented television shows starting with *Dawson's Creek*, began using current songs to help drive the stories along. The programs then credited the artists and the albums used at the end of each episode.

Some feared that the advent of MTV would force radio to specialize further if people turned from radio to television's music videos. However, the development of MTV actually helped radio stations featuring rock music. MTV was more willing to take a chance and air new releases than were radio stations. The radio programmers could measure the success of new releases by the MTV audience reaction and determine what new selections should be added to the station's playlist. When not in front of the TV, young people are listening to radio in large numbers.

Beavis and Butt-head

An MTV cartoon series about two raunchy 15-year-olds named Beavis and Butt-head became controversial in 1993 when a fatal blaze set by a five-year-old was blamed on the show. The youngster set fire to his bed with a cigarette lighter, killing his two-year-old sister, after allegedly watching a Beavis and Butt-head program on which the cartoon characters proclaimed that "fire is cool." In another instance, the program was blamed for a fire set by three girls.

MTV responded to the charges by moving the series from a 7:00 P.M. time slot to 10:30 P.M. and also announced it was removing all references to fire from the program. In addition, the network began developing a series of socially responsible cartoon programs that included Daria, The Dangwoods, The Grunt Brothers, and Aeon Flux.

New Directions for Music Videos

With the new technology exploding on the scene in the 1990s, music videos became a part of the new technology. In 1998, Internet websites began offering interactive music videos. One of the first to hit the World Wide Web was ShockRave (<u>shockrave.com</u>) which initially offered "Sexy Boy" by the French electronic band Air. As voices sang the song, a cartoon of a monkey could rise over skyscrapers with the nudge of a computer mouse and words would appear on the screen "Help! Jessica Lange! Fay Wray! Anybody!"[10]

interactive videos

The **interactive videos** allowed the viewers to bring up different animations, colors, figures, or text in a video box that took up about a quarter of the computer screen.

By the end of the 1990s, MTV itself had expanded to the Internet, introducing sites to help both couch and mouse potatoes to access the day's top music, as well as news and information about the music world. A short time later, MTV Europe began broadcasts of the new M2 Europe channel—first on the Internet (<u>m2europe.com</u>), then on television. Claiming it was the first time a European TV station had put a 24-hour video stream on the Internet, MTV introduced its second music channel in Europe.

> @   **Practicing Media Literacy**
>
> Do you watch music videos on your computer or do you prefer the larger television screen?

CONTROVERSIES SURROUNDING ROCK MUSIC

As previously mentioned, criticism and controversy have surrounded recorded music ever since its entrance into the popular culture. With the development of rock and roll music in the 1950s, many religious leaders and conservative politicians condemned this new sound as the devil's work and urged parents to destroy these recordings. Most of the criticism has focused around the songs themselves and, in particular, the lyrics.

Editorial Statements

We usually think of newspapers as the medium in which editorials are most effectively used. However, in reality, the most effective editorial statements are carried in recorded music because the messages are combined with music's ability to interact with our emotions.

Each CD or tape contains an editorial statement. It might be an innocent expression of the joys of love or a socially powerful statement about the need to feed starving people. Instrumental music contains melodies or beats that stir up some type of emotion, whether it be sadness, joy, relaxation, or an impulse to dance. Whatever the type of music, it directs some form of persuasion toward the listener.

Subliminal Messages?

A great deal of criticism has been leveled against the recording industry for releasing music with hidden messages designed to appeal to the subconscious rather than the conscious mind. Two types of hidden messages have been singled out in particular: subliminal embeds and backmasking.

Retail stores have used **subliminal embeds** in their background music for some time. Many department stores and supermarkets now play music that includes a voice, just below the level at which it can be consciously heard, that continuously repeats messages such as "You are an honest person; you will not steal." Studies indicate that shoplifting has been reduced when this music is played. The music itself has been found to influence what shoppers buy. An article in the British journal *Nature* reported that researchers tested music's power of persuasion and found that people reacted to what they were hearing without even realizing it. According to the study, conducted by a team of psychologists from the University of Leicester in the United Kingdom, when French music was played in a store's wine section, French wine sales increased. On alternate days, when German music was being featured, the German wine sales went up.[11]

	subliminal embeds

People can now buy subliminal tapes that claim to program their minds with various messages that will help them lose weight, stop smoking, think positively, and so on.

Many rock music critics charge that subliminal messages are also found in popular music—and often the messages embedded are quite different from the lyrics.

Backmasking, sometimes called backward masking, is even more controversial. People debate not only whether it can affect the listener but whether it exists at all.

	backmasking

Religious leaders have played records backward for congressional leaders to point out what they say are satanic messages. For example, in Led Zeppelin's all-time favorite "Stairway to Heaven," phrases that sound very much like "I live with Satan" and "Here's to my sweet Satan" can be heard when the recording is played backward.

In 1990, the British rock group Judas Priest spent nearly a month in court defending against charges that a subliminally embedded phrase "Do it" and a variety of backmasking suggestions promoting self-destruction in their 1988 album *Stained Class* had caused two Nevada youths to commit suicide. Although the judge ruled that these messages were contained in the album, he said the plaintiffs failed to prove that Judas Priest and CBS Records had intentionally planted them.

Also in the 1990s, the parents of a teenage girl who had been raped, tortured, and stabbed to death filed a lawsuit accusing the rock band Slayer for inspiring the killing. In the suit, the parents charged that lyrics to Slayer songs prompted three teenage boys to commit the crime. The parents of the victim said they didn't believe the band was protected by the First Amendment.

> **@   Practicing Media Literacy**
> Are musicians responsible for the impact of their music on the listeners or should they have the freedom to express themselves in any way they please?

Rap and Heavy-Metal Lyrics

Today the criticism of popular music is focused on lyrics. In recent years, some rock artists have gone to extremes in explicit language and antisocial sentiments. Topics dealt with in song lyrics include suicide, incest, homosexuality, bisexuality, illegal drug use, police brutality, murder of family members, cop killing, and explicit sex and bondage. By most cultural standards, these lyrics are raunchy and vulgar.

The controversial messages delivered by Ozzy Osbourne in his music and on stage performances have raised the ire of prosecutors and religious leaders across the country.

The performer formerly known as Prince has sung about sexual activities that would make almost anyone blush, Luther Campbell and 2 Live Crew rap about ghetto sexual activity that rivals animals in heat, and Ozzy Osbourne has boasted that he has made a living doing things most people get arrested for. (Osbourne also was repeatedly finding himself sued by parents of teenage suicide victims who claimed their children had been listening to his "Suicide Solution" at the time of their death. Although a California judge threw out the first such suit in 1986, similar charges brought Osbourne back into a Georgia court to face wrongful death charges in two suicide cases in the 1990s.)

rap lyrics

The biggest controversy surrounding popular music in this decade has centered around **rap lyrics.** When courts in Florida and Texas ruled in 1990 that 2 Live Crew's album *As Nasty As They Wanna Be* was obscene and could not be sold or performed in those states, many in the music industry were outraged. The outrage turned to shock in the fall of 1990 when an African-American music store owner was found guilty of selling obscenity by an all-white jury in Florida.

Other rap groups, such as N.W.A. (Niggers with Attitude) and Ice-T, have been criticized for their antisocial and sometimes explicit lyrics (see Box 11.1). The African-American community is divided on the issue. Some believe certain rap groups reflect negatively on their race, while others believe these groups are being singled out because they are African-American. Advocates of the latter point of view note that such white groups as Guns N'Roses have gotten away with obnoxious and obscene lyrics. Others maintained that the antipolice lyrics of so-called **gangsta rap** were an actual reflection of the feelings toward law enforcement in many minority communities. In fact, some sociologists maintained that the jury in the O. J. Simpson murder case reflected this sentiment in believing that Los Angeles police officers actually were racist, as portrayed in many of the popular rap songs of the day.

gangsta rap

In 1996, one of the leading producers of rap albums, Dr. Dre (formerly of N.W.A.), announced he was moving away from gangsta rap with his first solo album. Dre, who had produced a Snoop Doggy Dogg album that sold more than 5 million copies, said his new album would be about 55 percent R&B and 45 percent rap, but with no gangsta flavor—just hard-core hip hop. By the end of the decade, his album "Dr. Dre 2001" was being criticized as having offensive lyrics "without being notably imaginative, provocative or funny."[12] Old habits are hard to break.

But the controversy surrounding rap music continued. During the 1990s, a group including former Reagan administration education secretary William Bennett and the

Box 11.1
MEDIA WATCH
A Troubled, Plagued Music Genre — but Still Popular

During the last years of the 20th century, rap music maintained its popularity, despite the murders of several rap singers and the fact that many others were involved in brushes with the law. The music was a form of protest, full of rage and anger while dealing with the ills of society. The way many of these artists lived often reflected those same problems and frustrations.

The music industry was stunned in September 1996 when gangsta rap artist Tupac Shakur was fatally shot in Las Vegas. He died six days later. At the time, Shakur was out on bail while awaiting a decision on his appeal of his 1995 conviction for the sexual abuse of a 19-year-old woman in a hotel room.

The following year, Notorious B.I.G. (Christopher Wallace, also known as Biggie Smalls) was fatally shot in Los Angeles. It was not immediately known if his death was a retaliation for the murder of Shakur or if it was just another act of random violence.

But even with this type of negative publicity, gangsta rap was still a marketable commodity. Two months after Shakur's death, his posthumous album, *The Don Killuminati: The 7 Day Theory,* entered the pop charts as number one in its first week of release, generating the second-highest debut week sales total of any album released in 1996. The first-week total of 664,000 copies was just 16,000 behind the year's highest-selling album, Metallica's *Load.*

As for B.I.G., his ironically titled album *Life After Death* was released just two weeks after his death and sold 685,000 copies during its first week and remained on the top of the *Billboard* magazine charts for several weeks after that.

Meanwhile, two of Shakur's associates, rapper Snoop Doggy Dogg and Marion "Suge" Knight, the owner of the recording company for which both Shakur and Dogg worked—Death Row Records—had some problems with the law. Dogg and his bodyguard had been acquitted of murder charges in the shooting death of a young man, but Knight was sent back to jail for nine years after a judge ruled he had violated his probation by getting involved in a brawl in a Las Vegas casino just hours before Shakur was fatally shot. The record company president had been placed on probation in 1995 after pleading no contest to assaulting two

Gangsta rap artist Tupac Shakur was fatally shot at the height of his popularity.

rappers in a Hollywood recording studio. One year after his return to prison, he was given an additional 18 months sentence for violation terms of a federal firearms trafficking conviction.

Time Warner, which had stopped releasing albums by Shakur and other Death Row recording artists amid the 1995 political controversy over rap lyrics, announced it had agreed to make a television movie about Shakur's life. The movie, *Rebel for the Hell of It: The Life of Tupac Shakur,* was made by Time Warner's HBO Pictures. Several others, including Columbia Pictures, TriStar, and producer Quincy Jones, had previously expressed interest in making films of Shakur's life.

At one point, MTV reported that the most popular video being shown on the cable channel was B.I.G.'s "Mo' Money Mo' Problems," which was filmed shortly after his murder. The third most shown video was done by Sublime, featuring the late Brad Nowell, which was put together after Nowell's death by using performance footage of him. The last video done by B.I.G., "Hypnotize," a video tribute to him, "Missing You," and the Sublime video were all nominated for MTV video awards.

So what made this form of music maintain its popularity despite the controversy and negative images? Simply put, the music speaks strongly to an active record-buying public. There's no doubt that rap projects much that is troubling and ugly, both in the lifestyles of those involved and in the music itself,

continued

which often presents violent and misogynist messages. But many feel that the most powerful and purposeful rap music, like most great art, tells us something about the times and the society in which we live.

Rap music has been described as the sound of souls in distress, the clamour of children neglected. The public outcry against rap music started when law enforcement officers protested the antipolice messages of such artists as Ice-T, who gave us "Cop Killer" in 1992, and Ice Cube, who was responsible for "[expletive] the Police" in 1989. And yet the reaction of the jury in the O. J. Simpson murder case demonstrated that the antipolice sentiment does exist in many communities.

Rebellious music has been a part of the recording industry for years. From the rock and roll of Elvis Presley in the 1950s and the antiwar protest songs of Bob Dylan and Joan Baez in the 1960s to the grunge music of Pearl Jam and the rap music of Tupac Shakur, Notorious B.I.G., and Ice Cube in the 1990s, the music documented the experience of youth growing up in worlds they didn't create. Their music tells their story as they try to make sense of these worlds, define themselves against them, and find their way in them. And, it's profitable.

chair of the National Political Congress of Black Women, C. DeLores Tucker, charged that music industry giant MCA should be ashamed of profiting from lewd and violent lyrics by pushing what were described as X-rated albums for Christmas. Said Democratic senator Joseph Lieberman of Connecticut, "They're marketing death and degradation as a twisted form of holiday cheer."[13] The group charged that MCA had violated a pledge not to distribute violent and vulgar music. However, a spokesperson for MCA said the company had a review process for all of its releases and, in fact, had already chosen not to release some albums. However, he went on to point out that it was a subjective process with which not everyone would always agree. MCA had purchased a 50 percent share of Interscope Records, the label of several gangsta rappers, from Time Warner, which got out of the rap music business in 1995 due to the protests over the profane and controversial lyrics in rap music. Tucker also took on Time Warner two years after the sale of Interscope, attending the annual meeting of the media giant to read lyrics from the songs of rapper Lil' Kim to the gathered stockholders and company chairman Gerald Levin. While Tucker labeled the music "gangsta porno rap," Levin said he felt they were implicitly personal.[14] Tucker was also joined by Gloria Steinem and other feminist leaders to protest outside Time Warner's corporate headquarters in New York, this time in an attempt to stop distribution of Prodigy's "Smack My B——Up." The protesters presented a demand which said, "Women and girls must no longer be subject to the slander and humiliation that would not be directed at . . . any other group that includes men." A Warner Bros. statement said the company "and its partner, Maverick Records, believe that artists should be afforded every opportunity to express themselves through their work." Because the music video for the song showed women being hit and injected with drugs, MTV stopped airing it.[15]

Heavy-metal groups continue to face their own controversies, mainly that they sing about satanic worship, and their music is being blamed for the increase in satanic cults in a number of communities. Critics have linked bizarre killings, such as those committed by the Night Stalker in California, as well as sexual abuse of preschool children, to heavy-metal music. Such linkage is not new, however. The Manson family killings in Los Angeles during the late 1960s had been linked to the Beatles' popular hit "Helter Skelter" because the killers had scribbled the phrase in blood on the walls at the murder scenes. In fact, Guns N'Roses was criticized in 1993 for releasing a song originally written by Charles Manson on their *Spaghetti Incident* album. Lyrics about marijuana and cocaine continued to draw criticism in the 1980s and 1990s despite the fact that these themes have been around since the Roaring '20s.

Rating Systems

One of the most powerful lobbying groups against rock music lyrics has been the Parents Music Resource Center (**PMRC**), a Washington, D.C.–based organization formed by Tipper Gore, wife of Vice President Al Gore, when he was a U.S. senator, and Susan Baker, wife of James Baker, the former secretary of state in the Reagan administration. They began pressuring the recording industry to voluntarily label all explicit records so that parents would know what the music contained. They called for either a rating system similar to that used by the motion picture industry or the printing of lyrics on album covers. They were instrumental in getting a U.S. Senate subcommittee to hold a hearing on the issue in 1985. Opponents of the PMRC proposal argued that the job of censoring children's listening habits belonged in the home, not with government. Some also feared that warning labels on albums might have a reverse effect and *increase* sales among young people.

Although no federal laws were passed requiring the labeling, by 1990 more than 25 states had introduced legislation to require either labeling or printed lyrics or bans on selling and displaying "obscene" music, and the industry was making efforts to voluntarily comply with the request.

Another form of censorship has been occurring in certain chain stores. K mart and Wal-Mart, for example, have refused to carry certain albums they think are objectionable (see Box 11.2). One of the first to be banned by the stores was the Nirvana album *In Utero*, which had a questionable cover. Wal-Mart has also refused to carry Guns N'Roses' multiplatinum *Use Your Illusion I* and *II*.

Wal-Mart also stunned the music industry by banning the sale in its stores of an album by Grammy winner Sheryl Crow that contained lyrics suggesting that the store chain sold guns to children. A spokesperson for Wal-Mart said the attack was unfair because the chain has strict policies prohibiting the sale of guns to minors. Record industry spokespersons estimated that the ban on sales of the Crow album in Wal-Mart stores resulted in a loss of some 400,000 album sales.

Even MTV played the role of gatekeeper when it deemed that the Madonna video "Justify My Love" had gone too far in its explicit sexual images and refused to show it.

The Beat, Not the Lyrics

Despite the controversy over explicit lyrics, research has shown that lyrics about sex, drugs, violence, and satanism have little impact on the vast majority of teenagers.

At California State University in Fullerton, Lorraine Prinsky, a sociology professor, and Jill Rosenbaum, a criminal justice professor, wanted to know what teenagers thought about rock lyrics. They used a 40-page questionnaire to get teens to describe their favorite songs. They found that only about 7 percent of the respondents perceived that the 662 songs listed were about sex, violence, drugs, or satanism. The study concluded that specific lyrics seem to be of little consequence to most teens, who are far more interested in the beat or overall sound of a recording. (Perhaps what was often said on the old *American Bandstand* program was true. When rating new records, a young audience member would often give it a favorable review by saying, "It's got a good beat; you can dance to it.")

The PMRC pushed the music industry to place this warning label on recordings with explicit lyrics.

PMRC

Box 11.2

MEDIA LITERACY

Some "Gatekeepers" for Today's Music

When it comes to protecting the public from offensive music, there have been many "gatekeepers"—from public groups to retail stores to the owners of the record companies themselves. But in Washington, legislators have been vocal but inactive.

The Parents Music Resource Center (PMRC) was formed by Tipper Gore in the 1980s to get recording companies to label the albums being released so that parents would be forewarned if they contained offensive lyrics. However, others were opposed to such labeling, fearing it would make offensive albums even more desirable for the young record-buying public.

While the warning labels may be helpful to parents who supervise the purchase of music, some stores have gone one step further. For example, at some 2,300 Wal-Mart stores across the nation, the CD racks are filled with albums marked "cleaned," "edited," and "sanitized for your protection." The nation's largest seller of pop music, accounting for one out of every dozen CDs sold in this country, Wal-Mart has refused to stock albums with lyrics or cover art that it finds objectionable. As a result, record labels and recording artists have designed new covers to replace questionable artwork, dropped unacceptable songs from their albums, electronically masked objectionable words, or even changed the lyrics of songs to get their products on the racks at Wal-Mart.

Some believe this is a form of censorship; others are concerned that many people who purchase altered CDs are not even aware that changes have been made. And one newspaper editorialized that Wal-Mart's editing practices should not be mistaken for moral courage because the issue is really about market share. As the *San Francisco Chronicle* editorialized, "If Wal-Mart wants to take a stand—a *real* stand—against artists who offend, it should simply refuse to carry their work. But the chain is not willing to take the risk that shoppers might go elsewhere if they cannot find Nirvana, White Zombie or other groups whose albums have been sanitized for Wal-Mart's aisles."*

Wal-Mart has also pulled numerous CDs from its racks because of content, including Prodigy's *Fat of the Land,* because of the objectionable lyrics in the group's single "Smack My B——Up." But Wal-Mart isn't the only retail chain serving as a gatekeeper to protect the young from much of the popular but controversial music of the day. Family-oriented retail chains such as K mart and Blockbuster have also been having a strong influence on popular culture. K mart pulled the Prodigy album from its 2,100 stores nationwide.

MTV showed the "Smack My B——Up" video following an unprecedented warning to viewers that it contained drug use, full frontal nudity, and violence. MTV warned viewers who might be offended to turn off their TV sets. The video was later banned from any further showings on the music video channel.

When it comes to the record companies themselves, some have exercised controls because of their corporate image. Time Warner sold off its rap music label following complaints about the messages being delivered. The Walt Disney Company pulled 100,000 copies of an obscenity-laced rock album from retail stores just hours after its release. A statement released by the company said the Insane Clown Posse album *The Great Malenko,* contained lyrics that were inappropriate for a product released under any of the company's record label names.

In our nation's capital, many lawmakers have expressed concern about the obscenities, violence, and sexual content of records being released. However, when it comes to taking legislative action, nothing has been done. The main concern in Washington has been the First Amendment to the U.S. Constitution. No one wants to infringe upon the recordings artists' right to free speech.

*"Discounting Lyrics to Maximize Sales," *San Francisco Chronicle,* November 18, 1996, p. A24.

However, the stigma of drug involvement was still closely tied to the rock music world. Following the drug-related deaths of several musicians in the 1990s, including Kurt Cobain of Nirvana and Shannon Hoon of Blind Melon, the Recording Industry

Association of America (RIAA) gave $2 million over a three-year period to the Musicians' Assistance Program, which ran drug treatment centers and halfway houses. The grant was seen as a move to counter the criticism that the music industry was popularizing drug use by condoning it among musicians.

If the music themes of the 1990s were really not much different from those of the 1920s, why all the fuss? One answer is that the language used in the 1990s is no longer "cute" or suggestive, as was the case with Cole Porter's lyrics of years gone by; it was often outright explicit.

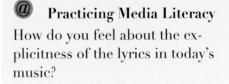

Practicing Media Literacy

How do you feel about the explicitness of the lyrics in today's music?

Another is that the age of the audience for recordings has changed. In the 1920s, the people who listened to recorded music were mostly in their 20s or, at the very youngest, in their late teens. In the 21st century, the audience consists of many impressionable preteenagers who worship such recording stars as N Sync, the Backstreet Boys, and Britney Spears with cultlike devotion. In addition, radio, television, and home audio and video recordings have made popular music a far more pervasive element in our mass-mediated popular culture than it was in the 1920s.

But there's no denying that the lyrics of today's music have a message. In the late 1990s, the University of California at Berkeley offered a class on the poetry of rapper Tupac Shakur, who died at the age of 25 after being shot on the Las Vegas strip. More than 100 students signed up for the course, with one saying that Shakur was "the Bob Dylan of our day."[16]

Some music critics today point to the fact that when it wants to, the recording industry can do a lot of good for society. They point to the Live Aid concert and MTV's "Rock Against Drugs" and "Rock the Vote" campaigns as examples. Some have suggested that the industry recognize its powerful influence over the young and introduce more "Rock Against" campaigns: Why not "Rock Against Alcoholism," "Rock Against Teenage Pregnancies," "Rock Against Gang Violence," and so on?

OTHER FORMS OF RECORDED MUSIC

Although rock and roll remains in its various specialized forms the undisputed champion of popular music, three other genres of recorded music deserve mention. They are Latino, country-western, and classical.

Latino Music

As the 1990s drew to a close, Latino music had become one of the most popular of the nonrock music formats. The Latino influence on music had been around for decades, from the Afro-Cuban experimentation in jazz of the late 1940s and '50s to the bossa nova craze of the 1960s.

Some pop music artists of the 1960s and '70s had their roots in Latino music, but preferred to perform for the mass pop-music audience, such as Ritchie Valens ("La Bamba") and Freddie Fender ("Wasted Days and Wasted Nights"). Singer Vikki Carr registered several pop hits in the 1960s, but later began recording all of her music in Spanish, reaching new heights of popularity in Central and South America as well as in the United States. When performing concerts in the 1990s, she was finding large crowds, some Latino, others nostalgic, expecting both types of music to be performed.

By the end of the 1990s, a new generation of artists had moved to the forefront in the music world. Among those leading the way for Latino artists to cross over to the pop-music area were Linda Ronstadt, Selena, Marc Anthony, Enrique Iglesias, Ricky Martin, and Christina Aguilera.

Country-Western

Toward the end of the 1950s and into the early 1960s, an alternative to rock and roll found its place on the pop music charts. This was folk music, which had been around for many years but had suddenly found a new voice with such artists as the Kingston Trio; the Limelighters; and Peter, Paul, and Mary. The popularity of folk music helped to bridge the gap between the twangier country-western music of Lefty Frizzell and Hank Williams to the more modern country music of recent years. In 1973 there were about 700 country music radio stations in the United States; by the beginning of the 21st century there were more than 1,600, many of them rated among the top stations in their individual markets.

Hollywood has assisted country-western's move into mainstream America with such movies as *Coal Miner's Daughter* (1980) and *Sweet Dreams* (1985), about the lives of country singers Loretta Lynn and Patsy Cline, respectively. In the late 1970s, *Urban Cowboy*, starring John Travolta, popularized country-western bars and music. In addition, such country stars as Kenny Rogers, Reba McIntire, and Randy Travis have forged new careers for themselves as motion picture and television actors.

Country-western music has been called many things over the years, including *hillbilly music* (it originated in the mountains of the South), *cowboy music*, and *Okie music* (it was brought west by migrants, called Okies, who left the dust-bowl regions around Oklahoma during the Great Depression). In reality, it might best be called "white soul music;" country songs are about the simpler things in life and the struggles of rural and small-town working people.

Like rock and roll, country-western has changed over the years. Some of it has adopted the beat of rock—country rock—and the industry is using more sophisticated recording techniques. Efforts to take the "twang" out of country-western music also have contributed to its increase in popularity. Today more songs are recorded in the home of country music—Nashville, Tennessee—than in any other American city, and for a while it was the home base for many mainstream recording artists, such as Perry Como, who were seeking the "Nashville Sound" for their music.

The popularity—and sex appeal—of country-western singer Shania Twain was so universal that she was hired to do a series of television commercials for a cosmetics company.

Classical Music

Although classical music was the first successful form of recorded music, with such opera stars as Enrico Caruso making records, it has remained primarily in the elite culture. Classical record sales remain steady but modest. Commercial classical music radio stations have actually declined over the years, from 50 in 1965 to only 25 in 1995. New York City, for example, had two classical stations until the 1990s, when one of the stations switched to hard rock. Most fans turn to noncommercial radio and television stations for classical music and other forms of "high cultural" programming.

However, some classical artists, such as opera star Luciano Pavarotti, have gained popular attention due to the mass media's informing the popular culture of "high cultural" participants and activities. The lines separating the elite from the popular cultures are less clearly defined than they once were.

BUSINESS TRENDS

Despite the controversies threatening to squelch the success of the recording industry, it has emerged as a multibillion-dollar-per-year enterprise. By the mid-1990s, revenue estimates for the recording industry were approaching $12 billion from the sale of more than 1 billion units of recorded music. This figure increased from $4.7 billion in 1987.

Changes in listening tastes and in the demographic profile of music buyers in recent years have altered the makeup of recorded music. According to surveys by the Recording Industry Association of America (RIAA), the popularity of rock music in album sales has been declining, while country music has been the fastest-growing genre.

The United States accounts for close to one-third of the estimated $30 billion in annual worldwide prerecorded music sales, with Japan ranking second, followed by Germany, the United Kingdom, and France. Six companies account for most of the music industry revenues: Sony, Inc. (based in Japan), Time Warner (U.S.), Philips N.V. (Netherlands), Thorne/EMI (United Kingdom), Bertelsmann A.G. (Germany), and Matsushita Electric Industrial, Ltd. (Japan). All of these companies are large conglomerates with various interests in the entertainment media.

By January of 2000, two of those companies had merged to create a joint operation valued at $20 billion. Together, Time Warner of the United States and Britain's EMI would account for almost 25 percent of all global music sales. With each controlling one half of the new Warner EMI music, Time Warner brought to the deal such recording artists as Madonna, Cher, the Eagles, Led Zeppelin and Eric Clapton, while EMI's catalogue included the Beatles, the Rolling Stones, the Beach Boys, Frank Sinatra, Janet Jackson and Garth Brooks.

When Seagram-owned Universal Music purchased Polygram Music in 1998 in what was then the biggest merger in music history, Seagram's officials said they were interested in "product." With the Time Warner/EMI merger, the key word was "content." According to *New York Times* writer Neil Strauss, the difference is that product is something physical that can be packed in a box and shipped to stores. Content is something intangible, converted into digital code and posted on an Internet site. Strauss wrote that the Time Warner/EMI deal could hasten the public's acceptance of the music computer file as an alternative to the compact disc.[17]

The recording business is dependent on young people for its sales, with buyers under age 30 accounting for 66 percent of all recordings purchased. Young people are also heavy users of the Internet.

NEW TECHNOLOGY AND RECORDINGS

Digital sound technology made its breakthrough in the entertainment world in 1983, when Sony introduced the first compact disk player in the United States. At first it was thought that CDs would remain a novelty for the elite for some time. However, their superior sound reproduction quickly moved them into the popular culture. Because

CDs were originally targeted for the elite, most of the early recordings were classical and jazz selections, and CD players sold for around $1,000. By 1986, though, CD players were priced at $200 to $300 and such popular recording artists as Bruce Springsteen and Dire Straits were releasing CDs. In 1988, CD sales surpassed sales of long-playing albums (LPs) for the first time. Radio stations faced the need to replace their turntables with CD players. By the end of the 1990s, it was almost impossible to find LPs in most record stores. CDs and cassettes had taken over and made LPs and 45-rpm single records a thing of the past, although some rock groups are insisting that their new works be released on LPs as well as CDs because records have a more lifelike sound.

DATs

Digital audiotapes (**DATs**), which are about the size of miniature cassette tapes but can record up to 120 minutes, reproduce the same high-quality sound CDs do. Sony originally announced the development of DAT technology in 1987, but digital audiotape players were delayed from entering the U.S. market until 1990 because recording companies feared that people would use the tape players to reproduce and illegally distribute CD-quality recordings. To settle the dispute and avert a possible ban on the product by Congress, Japanese makers agreed to equip DAT decks with copy-limiting circuitry. The circuitry allows owners to make unlimited numbers of copies of CDs, but they cannot make copies of the copies. In 1991, Sony introduced a DAT Walkman that would both play and record. It is expected that DATs will replace the standard audio cassettes, although consumer acceptance has been slow.

The music industry has also been affected by the Internet. It started with events such as Webstock '96 (Woodstock without mud), put together a large online music festival to cybercast rock concerts nationwide. The goal was to raise $1 million for a nonprofit organization that encourages young people to do good works in their communities. The money came from sponsors of the event, who were also involved in the new computer technology.

Also in 1996, rock star David Bowie released his latest single, "Telling Lies," exclusively on the Internet. The single was not sold in stores or heard on the radio. Fans could hear it for free only through their computers by downloading three versions of the song from Bowie's official Internet website. The music was said to be of compact disc quality.

Bowie was a big supporter of the World Wide Web. In 1998, he launched his own Internet service provider—BowieNet (davidbowie.com)—which offered high-speed Internet service around the world for $19.95 a month. "I wanted to create an environment where not just my fans but all music lovers could be a part of the same community—a single place where the vast archives of music information could be accessed, views stated and ideas exchanged," Bowie said.[18] By the end of the 20th century, Bowie was a CD-ROM game that featured the singer transformed into a video game character known as Boz. Bowie worked with game developers to create the original music for the game, "Omikron," including eight songs that were exclusive and wouldn't appear on any of his CD releases.

But he was not alone in turning to the Internet for music releases. The rap group Public Enemy was the first major group to release a full studio album online in 1999. The group signed with online record label Atomic Pop for exclusive Internet distribution of its album *There's a Poison Goin' On*. While the album could be downloaded directly online, fans of the group could also order the CD by mail or pick up a copy at their local record store.

A number of small record labels had begun offering complete catalogs on the Internet, thus bypassing traditional retail outlets. This also allowed for instantaneous access to rare recordings, including downloadable music clips.

Some controversy arose when hackers began distributing two unreleased songs by U2 on the Internet. The songs, "Wake Up Dead Man" and "Discotheque," appeared on Internet sites in at least four countries. The songs were to appear on an album scheduled for release in the spring of 1997, and it was speculated that the hackers had somehow managed to tap into computers at the Irish rock group's recording studio. Since their illicit appearance on the World Wide Web, the songs were also copied onto compact disks that were bootlegged for $10 at street markets in Ireland and Britain.

Other artists have expressed concern that their material is being made available without their consent. Pearl Jam fans were able to sample more than half of one of the group's albums before it was released because the material had been pirated and offered on the Internet. It raised the issue of whether record companies would be able to combat bootlegging in the age of the computer. Country singer Johnny Cash went to Congress to testify for adequate legislation to protect the works of recording artists when it is digitized and put on the Internet. Cash had learned that a website in Slovenia had made his songs available for downloading.

MP3

One of the newest technological developments at the start of the 21st century was the MP3 digital audio file format for computers. MP3 (MP3.com) allows for the compression of a CD-quality music file to about one-tenth of its size. The technology makes digital music available to computer users in their homes. With the development of home CD writers, the material downloaded from MP3 can be written onto a CD for use in your home, car, or portable CD players (see Box 11.3).

The Future of Music

As record labels begin to understand digital distribution, as well as the promotional power of the Internet, they want to monopolize the moneymaking aspect of the World Wide Web. Artists are realizing that they can make a larger profit through bypassing the record labels and offering their music directly for purchase on the Internet. And new online marketing networks, such as Electric Artists ARTISTdirect, are encouraging musicians to go for the profits themselves. But the question remains: Who owns the digitial rights to websites and online merchandising?

Universal Music, a subsidiary of the Seagram Company, announced that it would invest in technology to sell music over the Internet, seeking to deliver the music to computers embedded with a code which would prevent someone from playing the music without first paying for it. The decision came as the Recording Industry Association of America had been strugggling to agree on a standard for selling recordings as data on the Internet. And in Japan, Sony Corporation announced that it would start selling a 2.4 ounce Walkman that would not only fit into the palm of a hand, but would download music from the Internet while protecting copyrights. Users of the Walkman would pay for Internet music made compatible with Sony's encryption system, but would not be able to download songs from free music websites.

Whatever the case, more and more music is now showing up on the Internet, particularly with the advent of radio stations programming strictly for the World Wide Web. In addition, more and more regular broadcast stations are providing their signal over the Internet for computer users. For example, WebRadio (webradio.com) calls itself "the ultimate provider of streaming media programming on the Internet today."[19] The company provides stations with a specially equipped encoding computer which

Box 11.3
MEDIA LITERACY
The Newest Source of Music—Your Computer

Every day, millions of people seek out information on the World Wide Web. And what do you think would be the most sought-after websites? Several major search engines have reported that the most requested topic is sex. The second most requested is MP3.

So what is MP3, and why have so few people over 30 ever heard of it? In short, it is simply a method for encoding and compressing audio for playback on your computer. MP3 is an acronym for Moving Pictures Experts Group 1 (MPEG), Audio Layer 3. MPEG was initially devised as a standard to compress video data, while MP3 focuses more specifically on audio translation to a digital stream, and compression to make such files easier and faster to transmit.

So why is MP3 considered a revolution, and why is the recording industry scrambling to clamp controls on it? This revolution, as many others before it, began as a direct result of the exponentially growing popularity of the Internet and the convenience it provides. The Internet has transformed many "traditional" business models, and the recording industry has been slower than others to adapt.

The recording industry widely adopted the compact disc format in the early 1980s for delivery of music and spoken word product, primarily because of its clarity, low cost of manufacture, and relative indestructibility. The conversion of analog waves to digital bits was applauded first by classical music fans, who appreciated the tonal range of CD, and then by the general population as more and more titles were released. Recording companies soon found another revenue stream by digitally remastering and re-releasing material originally available on vinyl, which was soon left to die of attrition by an industry which had found a less expensive way to generate more revenue.

The technology curve and the Internet soon made audio editing on personal computers a reality. Today software to create and manipulate audio content and hardware capable of writing directly to compact disc have become affordable to the general population. The Internet (and the sharing culture often attributed to its participants) helped the home user by posting multimedia files for download. Soon any student with a computer and an Internet connection could download speeches, live concert segments—and copyrighted music. With a compression ratio of as much as 12 to 1, the MP3 format made such files faster to transmit and download. Responding to the growing popularity of the new file format and distribution medium, companies soon began to manufacture portable MP3 playback units, which could store these downloaded files for playback at any time.

The "ideal" of MP3 as an Internet concept was to create another distribution medium for struggling musicians who had been ignored by the recording industry, and to provide another channel for established artists to market directly to their fans by cutting out the record companies and distributors. But the reality of MP3 has often been more spotty: fly-by-night "pirate" sites offering downloads of copyrighted material available in the corner music shop; legally and illegally recorded live performances of major label acts, and occasionally "stolen" recordings not yet available for purchase. The recording industry responded with litigation, most notably in its unsuccessful suit to stop the distribution of MP3 playback units. While they still police and punish "pirate download sites," the attention of record companies is now more focused on how to generate a profit from this new medium they had previously reviled.

Now, major label artists such as Alanis Morissette are recording and offering free-to-download audio clips of live performances in hopes of generating interest in their upcoming tours. Groups such as the Beastie Boys have offered a wealth of live material for download to site visitors, and even the venerable Grateful Dead, long known for smiling upon live tape trading, have officially sanctioned sites that allow downloads of their live tracks and concerts, so long as there is no possibility of the site generating a profit for doing so. But these are the acts of the artists themselves, using live material not copyrighted by record companies, thus outside of recording industry conventions.

Major labels have begun investing in and partnering with technology companies and content providers, in hopes of generating new and profitable distribution channels. While the recording industry legitimately fears unauthorized duplication and mass availability of copyrighted material, the general focus has finally begun to shift from the probability of piracy to the possibilities for profit. In the new Internet economy, where six months is an eternity, it is yet to be determined whether they have responded too late.

Source: By J. Gregory Wilson, Webmaster AccuSubmit
http://accusubmit.com

Box 11.4
HOW IT WORKS
The Music Industry

Popular music is a multibillion-dollar-a-year business that has skyrocketed many to stardom and kept other talented performers out of the limelight.

How does a musical group make it in the recording industry? The best way is to be discovered by an *A&R* person—an artist-and-repertoire representative. These are the people who discover talent, sign them to the record label they work for, budget the album, and then do whatever is necessary to facilitate its production (including finding songs and producers as well as massaging the performers' egos). When the record is pressed, the A&R reps become in-house cheerleaders, pushing the company to mount a campaign to win radio station airplay.

There are fewer than 100 A&R jobs in American record companies. Many such positions are filled by former musicians, record company employees, or radio and entertainment managers.

Some A&R reps double as producers, recording the acts they sign and earning royalties on each album, tape, or compact disk. A&R rep salaries usually start around $50,000 and go much higher. These reps have liberal expense accounts. Record companies that hire reps look for people with musical expertise and a knowledge of what is current.

What do A&R reps look for when seeking new talent? According to John Milward, writing for the *Philadelphia Enquirer*, A&R executives offer the following advice to undiscovered musicians:

Don't go broke making a slick demo; they're used to hearing things in the raw.

Don't include more than three or four songs, and make sure the first is a killer.

Develop as much of a buzz about your live shows as possible, and expand beyond your hometown.

Don't quit your day job.*

Other jobs in the music industry are in *marketing and promotion*, *distribution*, and *administration*. The marketing and promotion people are in charge of finding the best way to promote and sell musical units. The distribution people are responsible for getting the musical units to the stores. As in all of the media business, the administration people handle the bills, contracts, and other day-to-day activities.

*John Milward, "Giving Their All for the Record," *Philadelphia Enquirer*, January 10, 1988.

---

allows the stations to provide programming for 85 percent of all web browsers without the need for special plug-ins. As a result, stations that participate can broadcast live seven days a week, 24 hours a day with unlimited bandwidth and streams. Some music publications, including the *College Music Journal (CMJ)* now chart the songs being played on internet broadcasts (cmj.com) as well as Internet retail sales.

SUMMARY

The ability to produce recorded music dates to the invention of the phonograph by Thomas A. Edison in 1877. By the beginning of the 20th century, opera stars were recording records for home sale in the elite culture.

In the 1920s the recording industry brought African-American music, such as blues and jazz, into the popular culture. However, the color barrier in our society at the time created the need for white performers to "cover" such music. The color barrier was not eliminated until the recording industry targeted the youth of America as its major market in the 1950s.

The expansion of the youth market led to the development of rock and roll and contributed to the emergence of the "generation gap" of the 1960s. Parents refused to listen to the new music, while their children grew up with it. As the editorial statements in this new music changed to reflect the changing culture during the 1960s, only youth were listening. While these young people were relishing the new rock and roll, the British invasion, featuring the Beatles and the Rolling Stones, was taking place. A new youth subculture developed.

Rock was also instrumental in helping the recording industry move into the specialization stage of media development. A wide variety of forms and styles of rock music have evolved through the years.

Recorded music is both powerful and controversial. Each CD or tape produced contains an editorial statement that has the ability to persuade. Some of the editorial messages are simple, while others are complex and profound. Many adults fear the lyrics in many popular songs will corrupt youth.

Many groups have criticized the lyrics of popular music, and the reported use of subliminal messages and backmasking has generated a great deal of controversy. Eliciting the most furor are heavy-metal and rap lyrics. Although rock and roll in its various forms remains the favorite popular music in the American culture, country-western and classical music also play an important role in keeping the recording industry healthy.

The recording industry is a rapidly growing commercial enterprise, with sales figures approaching $12 billion. The standard LPs and 45-rpm records have been replaced by CDs, and digital audiotape recorders (DATs) are expected to replace standard cassettes. The music industry has also been finding a variety of ways to use the Internet to reach the music consumer, from providing music from live concerts on the World Wide Web to offering instantaneous access to rare recordings from independent labels.

The development of MP3 technology, which can compress music files for downloading on home computers, has the record industry looking for ways to protect its material from being made available at no profit to the companies. Some artists also started offering their material directly to the consumer through their websites.

Find a review of *Key People and Concepts*, a message board for *Practicing Media Literacy* questions, self tests, and more at: www.mhhe.com.wilson.

Thought Questions

1. What musical fads have you experienced in listening to pop or rock music in recent years?

2. Do you think musical lyrics that discuss deviant behavior cause listeners to experiment with such behavior?

3. Are rappers getting a "bum rap" when it comes to court and police efforts to censor them?   Do white groups experience similar censorship efforts?

4. What influence on the youth culture has MTV had? Do you think MTV will continue to be popular among young people? Why or why not?

5. If you were appointed the "Music Czar of America," what would you do to eliminate the controversy surrounding popular rock music?

Notes

1. Paul Oliver, *The Blues Tradition* (New York: Oak Publications, 1970), p. 23.

2. *New York American*, January 22, 1922.

3. Quoted in Edward Jay Whetmore, *Mediamerica, Mediaworld: Form, Content, and Consequences of Mass Communication*, 5th ed. (Belmont, CA: Wadsworth, 1993), p. 157.

4. Paul Gambaccini, *The Top 100 Rock 'n' Roll Albums of All Time* (London: Harmony Books, 1987).

5. Peter Brown and Steven Gaines, *The Love You Make: An Insider's Story of the Beatles* (New York: McGraw-Hill, 1983), pp. 301–303.

6. Ibid., p. 155.

7. Ibid., pp. 250–251, 416.

8. Marc Pollack, "Beatles Still Hold Sales Records," from *The Hollywood Reporter*, in the *Fresno Bee*, November 21, 1999, p. H3.

9. Quoted in Don R. Pember, *Mass Media in America*, 4th ed. (Chicago: Science Research Associates, 1983), p. 162.

10. Laura Evenson, "A New Dimension in Music Videos; MTV Gets a Run for Its Money with Interactive Videos," *San Francisco Chronicle*, July 20, 1998, p. E1.

11. Lidia Wasowicz of United Press International, "Research Shows Music Influences Shoppers without Them Knowing," *The Daily Collegian*, November 13, 1997, p. 3.

12. Chuck Campbell, Scripps Howard News Service, "Good Sound Lost in Dr. Dre's Offensive Lyrics," *Fresno Bee*, December 24, 1999, p. E14.

13. Bob Dart, "MCA Blasted for Selling Lewd Rock Songs," *San Francisco Chronicle*, December 11, 1996, p. E3.

14. "Critic Slams Time Warner over Rap," *Fresno Bee*, May 15, 1997, p. C2.

15. "Women Protest at Time Warner against Prodigy's 'Smack' Lyrics," *San Francisco Chronicle*, December 10, 1997, p. C6.

16. "Tupac's Poetry Goes to Head of the Class," Knight-Ridder/Tribune News Service, *The Daily Collegian*, September 18, 1997, p. 1.

17. Neil Strauss, "Music Mergers Herald a Shift to the Internet," *New York Times*, January 26, 2000, p. B1.

18. "David Bowie Opens Internet Service," *Fresno Bee*, July 22, 1998, p. A2.

19. Bill Konig, "Web Site of the Week," *College Music Journal*, July 5, 1999, p. 24.

Television:

From Soaps to Satellites

Children will watch anything, and when a broadcaster uses crime and violence and other shoddy devices to monopolize a child's attention, it's worse than taking candy from a baby. It is taking precious time from the process of growing up.

—Newton Minow, former chair, Federal
Communications Commission

Key People and Concepts

Vladimir Zworykin

Philo Farnsworth

Live Drama

Quiz Show Scandal

Westerns

Variety Shows

Sitcoms

Miniseries

TV Sports

Prime Time Soaps

Hybrid TV

Televangelism

Public Broadcasting

Home Shopping

Cable Television

High-Definition Television (HDTV)

Fiber Optics

Virtual Reality (VR)

Digital Compression

On a Sunday in January of 2000, American Online registered more than 21 domain names, all of them related to AOL's merger with Time Warner earlier that month. The $160 billion deal was described as the largest corporate merger ever, bringing together the biggest name in traditional media with the biggest name in the world of new media. At a time when traditional media companies were trying to reinvent their Internet strategies, the merger gave Time Warner a huge and powerful outlet for reaching people through AOL and its 20 million subscribers. Among the Time Warner media properties are the CNN, TNT, HBO and Cartoon cable networks, the fledgling WB television network, and the Warner Bros. movie studio and record company, as well as *Time*, *People*, and *Sports Illustrated* magazines.   A short time later, AOL announced that it planned to launch an ambitious new interactive service, known as AOL TV.[1] Among the new features, subscribers would be able to execute stock trades while watching Time Warner's CNNfn (a financial news cable channel) or chat with friends while they're watching the latest film release on HBO. This was just another step in the way the media have been changing how people watch television in this country. And the television industry has also been changing drastically—through mergers.   The final years of the 20th century saw numerous corporations joining together, with AT&T being one of the busiest, buying into millions of homes with the purchase of cable giant Tele-Communications International, Inc. (TCI) for $48 billion. Ironically, AT&T had also made a deal with Time Warner to use that company's cable TV wires to provide customers with one-stop shopping for TV, Internet, and telephone service.   Microsoft got involved by investing $5 billion in AT&T in a deal that ensured that the computer software company would not be left out of the telephone giant's plan to use cable TV wires for Internet access. Meanwhile, the third largest cable company, Comcast Corporation, bought the fourth largest, MediaOne Group Inc., with a $44.3 billion exchange of stock. The merger allowed Comcast to double its subscribers, with 11 million in 33 states.   •   While the cable television companies were merging rapidly with computer companies, Viacom wrapped up the action of the late 1990s with the purchase of CBS and all of its properties for $37.3 billion. The acquisition provided the newly formed company with a major conglomerate of media properties, including a television network, a radio network, ownership of individual radio and television stations in major markets across the country, a motion picture studio, a book publishing firm, and an outdoor advertising company. The deal also meant that all three of the original television networks were now part of larger conglomerates—NBC is owned by General Electric, and ABC is under the ownership of the Disney Corporation.   •   As television got started midway through the 20th century, there were three major television networks and a lot of owners of small stations across the nation. Today, there are four major networks, three fledgling networks, numerous cable channels, and a few large corporations that own the networks, the cable networks, the program suppliers, the movie studios that help to produce the programming, and numerous other media to help promote the product.   •   There is no denying that television has transformed our culture and remains the major American pastime. In this chapter, we'll look at how this medium that is now controlled by just a handful of companies has become such an important part of our lives.

HOW IT BEGAN

Early Experimentation

The story of electronic television began in 1923 when Vladimir Zworykin, a Russian immigrant working for RCA, developed the iconoscope, which was the first practical electronic tube for a television camera.

In 1927 Philo Farnsworth applied for a patent on an electronic television system, and by 1928 General Electric was experimenting with telecasting. RCA and its NBC network followed with experimental telecasting in 1930, and by 1939 their station in New York was offering regularly scheduled programs. In Great Britain, the BBC began regular television broadcasting in 1936. However, it wasn't until the 1939 New York World's Fair that a large number of Americans saw television demonstrated for the first time.

Early TV Stations

The FCC authorized commercial television broadcasting in 1941. However, the nation's entry into World War II in December of that year put TV's development on hold, since all electronic research and development was diverted to the war effort. However, six stations remained on the air during the war: two in New York City and one each in Schenectady (New York), Philadelphia, Chicago, and San Francisco.

Cultural History of Television

Year	Event	Elitist	Popular	Specialized
1923	Vladimir Zworykin develops a television camera tube for RCA.	•		
1927	Philo Farnsworth applies for electronic television patents.	•		
1936	Great Britain is the first country to begin regular television broadcasting.	•		
1939	Large numbers of Americans see television for the first time at New York's World's Fair.	•		
1941	FCC authorizes commercial television broadcasting in the U.S.	•		
1946	Color television demonstrated by CBS and NBC.	•		
1948	Television's breakthrough year; CBS and NBC begin offering regular news and entertainment on TV.	•	•	
1951	A nationwide telephone cable connection allows coast-to-coast television broadcasts.		•	
1952	Edward R. Murrow changes radio's "Hear It Now" to TV's "See It Now."		•	
1952	FCC lifts the freeze on new stations that it had imposed in 1948.		•	
1954	Army–McCarthy hearings are televised; Murrow risks career to challenge McCarthy on "See It Now."		•	
1959	Quiz show scandal rocks TV industry.		•	
1963	Television's coverage of Kennedy assassination demonstrates its power to unite nation in one emotion.		•	
1967	Congress establishes Corporation for Public Broadcasting.		•	
1968	Riots outside the Democratic Convention televised; TV blamed for nation's unrest.		•	
1969	World watches humans landing on the moon live on television.		•	
1971	"All in the Family" brings Archie Bunker and controversy to TV.		•	
1973–1974	Watergate hearings and impeachment proceedings televised; Nixon resigns.		•	
1977	"Roots" becomes most popular miniseries; this program format becomes an effective way to increase ratings.		•	
1980s	Cable television and VCRs change American viewing habits.		•	•
1982	Home Shopping Network debuts; advertising becomes programming.	•		
1987	Iran–Contra hearings televised; Oliver North becomes a folk hero.	•		
1994	Fifth and sixth TV networks launched by Warner Bros. and United Paramount.	•		
1996	Telecommunications Act of 1996 is approved by Congress and signed into law; contains provision for the V-chip to allow parents to block programs with too much violence.			•
1996	Broadcasters meet with President Clinton and agree to provide three hours per week of educational programming for children to ensure license renewals.			•
1999	TV stations in top 30 markets begin offering programs in High Definition (HDTV) digital format on alternative channels.			•
2000	The success of ABC's "Who Wants to be a Millionaire" causes other networks to introduce more quiz shows, including NBC's "Twenty One," one of the programs involved in the 1959 quiz show scandals.			

Early Programming

Before 1948, only a small number of elite Americans could afford this expensive novelty. In 1946, there were approximately 7,000 television sets in American households. Programming was limited, but it included sporting events, such as football, baseball, tennis, boxing, wrestling, and hockey; news; studio productions of plays; dance recitals; musical shows; and old movies.

In the fall of 1947, TV began to generate interest in the popular culture. An estimated 3.5 million people watched the World Series on television that year, most of them in neighborhood taverns. Now they wanted TV sets in their own homes.

Breakthrough Year

Television's breakthrough year was 1948, the year the CBS and NBC radio networks turned their attention toward the new medium. Since television was offering radio programming with the added novelty of pictures, interest in network radio began declining and so did radio network advertising revenues. In this year CBS made its famous raid of NBC's radio stars, signing them for the new CBS television network; Milton Berle went on television for NBC, becoming "Mr. Television"; and New York newspaper columnist Ed Sullivan began his long-running variety show, *Toast of the Town*, on CBS.

In the fall of 1948 the FCC, recognizing that this new medium was going to grow rapidly, placed a freeze on TV station authorizations, restricting the number to the already approved 124 (although only 108 stations actually got on the air). During the freeze, which lasted until 1952, the FCC developed a comprehensive plan to allocate television frequencies to all parts of the United States. The plan authorized 2,000 channels in 1,300 communities. The FCC also worked on a proposal to standardize color television systems and allocate educational television frequencies.

Despite the freeze, television expanded as a mass medium during the period 1948 to 1952. A nationwide telephone cable connection was completed in 1951, allowing networks to broadcast coast to coast for the first time. The number of TV sets in American homes rose from 172,000 to 17 million during this period.

Lifting the Freeze

After the freeze was lifted, television expanded even more rapidly. NBC and CBS were far along in their efforts to shift their interests from radio to television. A third network, DuMont, was struggling to compete. ABC merged with Paramount Theaters and followed the other three networks into television. Mutual remained a radio-only network. DuMont was unable to compete with the three former radio networks and went out of business in 1955. However, DuMont earned its place in television history by producing *The Honeymooners*, with Jackie Gleason, and using kinescopes to preserve early television on motion picture film. Some 30 years later, Americans were enjoying *The Honeymooners* in syndicated reruns on cable TV.

THE EVOLUTION OF TELEVISION ENTERTAINMENT

TV entertainment started out as nothing more than a novelty. The shows consisted of pointing a camera at some action and letting it be transmitted. The early programs included variety shows, puppet-comedy shows, stand-up comedians, domestic comedies, and game shows. Many of these programs were carbon copies of radio shows, but with pictures. In fact, popular radio personality Arthur Godfrey merely brought television cameras into his studio to televise his daily radio program on CBS. Godfrey and the performers on the program wore headphones, had large microphones blocking part of their faces, and tended to ignore the cameras while concentrating on the radio broadcast. But people watching early television were dazzled to be able to see action and watch their long-time radio stars present familiar sitcoms in their living rooms.

Early Entertainers

Some of the leading entertainers during the beginning years of television were Milton Berle, Ed Sullivan, Sid Caesar, Imogene Coca, Lucille Ball, Art Carney, Jackie Gleason, Art Linkletter, Arthur Godfrey, Jack Benny, Amos 'n' Andy, ventriloquist Edgar Bergen and his dummy Charlie McCarthy, Bob Hope, Bing Crosby, Red Skelton, the witty comedy team of George Burns and Gracie Allen, and the puppets Cecil the Seasick Sea Serpent, Howdy Doody, and Kukla, Fran, and Ollie.

Most of these entertainers had started their careers in **vaudeville** and made the transition to radio. Now they were transmitting recreations of the early days of vaudeville into the living rooms of the United States. The content of popular cultural entertainment had changed little since the 19th century. Only the delivery system had changed.

vaudeville

Red Scare

During the early 1950s, House and Senate committees that investigated the alleged infiltration of Communists into the movie industry (see Chapter 9) also scrutinized television and radio. Their search was greatly aided in June 1950 by the right-wing publication *Red Channels*, which listed the names of some 150 radio and television industry personnel who were accused of being either sympathetic to or associated with the Communist movement. Many people on the list found themselves suddenly out of work and their careers destroyed as a fearful industry took the easy way out to avoid controversy. Many network executives referred to the list to see if certain performers, writers, and directors were "acceptable" for use in their programs. **Blacklisting** was now a fact of life in the broadcasting industry. Some of the better-known names cited were actors Orson Welles, Howard Duff, and Edward G. Robinson; composer Aaron Copland; musicians Leonard Bernstein, Burl Ives, and Lena Horne; and radio–television newsmen William L. Shirer and Howard K. Smith. Smith was listed because a Communist newspaper had praised his reporting of a particular news event. While many feel that broadcasters have an impact on society, this was a case of society having an impact on the way the broadcast industry was run.

blacklisting

Live Drama

Some of the best dramas ever shown on television were the plays broadcast live from New York studios in the 1950s. The major Hollywood movie studios, fearing competition from the new medium, refused to allow their facilities to be used to produce television programs. Four of the best-known live dramas of this golden age of television were Rod Serling's *Requiem for a Heavyweight,* starring Jack Palance; J. P. Miller's *Days of Wine and Roses,* starring Cliff Robertson and Piper Laurie; Reginald Rose's *12 Angry Men*; and Paddy Chayefsky's *Marty.* All four were later made into movies, with *Marty* receiving the Academy Award as best picture of the year. Because they were done live and were confined to the studio sets, these high-quality dramas focused on character development and analysis rather than on car chases and elaborate scenery.

Quiz-Show Scandal

Quiz shows, which had been popular on radio, offered greater rewards when transferred to television. Radio's *$64 Question* became TV's *$64,000 Question*, for example. The popularity of these shows grew as people could vicariously share in the delight of winning big money by knowing the right answers to questions.

However, in 1959 television was rocked by its first major scandal when it was revealed that certain quiz-show contestants had been given the questions prior to the broadcasts. This was done to ensure that the most popular contestants would win and return the next week. Until this time, TV programs had been produced by advertising agencies and the shows' sponsors. As a result of the scandal, the FCC required quiz shows to issue disclosures whenever assistance was given to contestants, and the networks were forced to take over production of the programs to ensure compliance with ethical standards.

It took almost 40 years for the quiz shows to return to the network prime time schedules, but they returned with a bang in 1999 when ABC introduced *Who Wants to Be a Millionaire*. The program, aired almost nightly for several weeks, scored well for the network in the ratings, resulting in it being given a regular slot three times a week in 2000. The other networks, as is usually the case, figured that if one quiz show could be successful, so could four—one on each network. Fox was quick to follow with its show, *Greed*, while CBS introduced *Winning Lines* and NBC went back into its past to resurrect *Twenty-One*, one of the programs first exposed as giving answers to the contestants in the 1959 quiz-show scandals. CBS also announced plans to bring back *$64,000 Question*, and there was talk that it might be renamed *$1,064,000 Question*.

The Westerns

By the late 1950s, TV entertainment had moved from live quiz and variety shows, domestic comedies, and drama to prerecorded dramatic series. One of the first genres to develop was the Western, which had long been popular in movies and on radio.

Such shows as *Gunsmoke* and *Have Gun, Will Travel* (which had been popular on radio), *Wyatt Earp*, *Rawhide* (with a very young Clint Eastwood), *The Rifleman*, and *The Virginian* (television's first 90-minute prime-time series) occupied the TV screen. By 1959, there were 30 Westerns on prime time each week.

Also in 1959, *Bonanza* began airing on NBC to sell color television sets for its parent company, RCA. It was the

The small money questions are usually easy on ABC's Who Wants to Be a Millionaire, *but they get tougher when they're worth more and host Regis Philbin asks: "Is that your final answer?"*

only color show on TV, and its time slot was important because department stores were open at the time, and color sets could be demonstrated by showing *Bonanza*.

Bonanza transmitted the American myth that the rugged rural life of the "good old days" was a glamorous and comfortable time. The program revolved around three grown sons, at least two of them in their 30s, still at home and subject to the authority of their father. Some sociologists believed the show appealed to people who missed the parental authority and support they had given up to leave home and marry.[2] Whatever the reason, *Bonanza* was one of the most popular shows on the air for 15 years.

@ Practicing Media Literacy
Why do you think Western adventure programs are no longer popular with the television viewing audience? Would you watch?

Urban Westerns

Other genres that became popular during this period included doctor, police, detective, and courtroom shows, in which—as in the Westerns—good always prevailed over evil. These adventure stories were sometimes referred to as "urban Westerns" because the moral themes were the same as in the Westerns; only the location and time period were changed. Some of the urban Westerns were *Dragnet, Highway Patrol, Racket Squad, The Lineup, Perry Mason*, and *The Defenders*. A few years later several series, *The Man from U.N.C.L.E., I Spy*, and *Mission: Impossible*, dealing with international intrigue and spy chasing, also reflected these themes (and the Cold War mentality) as the "good guys" pursued the forces of evil around the world.

Variety Shows

Variety shows, hosted by such performers as Carol Burnett, Bob Hope, Dean Martin, Flip Wilson, and Sonny and Cher, provided cheerful escape during the 1960s. However, by the late 1960s one variety show, *The Smothers Brothers Comedy Hour*, was introducing realism and social commentary into evening entertainment. In keeping with the cultural unrest and growing displeasure with the Vietnam war that was sweeping the country, the show ridiculed the war and other social ills and soon was canceled by CBS in a dispute over censorship. Audiences, the network executives believed, did not want controversy and realism mixed with their entertainment.

@ Practicing Media Literacy
What changes have taken place in our culture that would cause the decline in popularity of the television variety programs?

Another variety show that made its debut in 1968, *Rowan and Martin's Laugh-In*, became popular with younger audiences by dealing with sexual and political themes, topics that reflected the new openness that had swept the nation during the 1960s. Its hosts, Dan Rowan and Dick Martin, were able to touch on these topics without irritating network executives the way the Smothers Brothers did. This type of programming survived in the 1990s on such shows as *Saturday Night Live*. However, the more traditional variety shows had all but disappeared by the mid-1970s, except for an occasional special.

Sitcoms

From the beginning, the most popular of all TV entertainment genres has been the situation comedy. Other forms of television entertainment, such as the Western and the variety show, have come and gone, but the sitcoms have endured (although there was talk in the early 1980s that the sitcom was dead).

In an effort to appeal to middle-class America, early TV continued to produce the family sitcoms that had been popular on radio. The settings were always the same: a happy, white, middle-class home with humorous but bland family problems to cope with and solve by the end of each 30-minute show. *Father Knows Best, Make Room for Daddy, Leave It to Beaver, I Love Lucy, The Adventures of Ozzie and Harriet*, and *My Three Sons* were a few of the more popular shows in this category. *I Love Lucy* introduced to the American culture one of the greatest comediennes of all time, Lucille Ball, and the technique of filming sitcoms in front of a live audience (see Box 12.1). There were also such sitcoms as *Bewitched, I Dream of Jeannie, The Addams Family, My Favorite Martian*, and *The Munsters*, which featured supernatural characters trying to act like ordinary, middle-class folks.

As the American culture passed through the turbulent 1960s and entered the 1970s, TV sitcoms reflected changing cultural attitudes. One of the most **innovative** departures was *All in the Family*, a new kind of sitcom produced by Norman Lear, which debuted on January 12, 1971, with a warning label telling viewers that the program's contents were controversial. For the first time, a TV sitcom was dealing with, and joking about, the culture's social issues that had been taboo on television: sex, politics, and racial prejudice. The show starred Carroll O'Connor as Archie Bunker, who was characterized as a classic bigot. Archie unexpectedly became a folk hero in American popular culture. Many people apparently did not recognize the satire in the program and believed Archie's bigotry reflected their own latent or not-so-latent feelings. (*All in the Family* was based on a similar sitcom in England entitled *Till Death Us Do Part*.)

innovative

The show was so successful that it generated a number of spinoffs. Archie's wife, Edith, had a cousin named *Maude*, who eventually got a show of her own, as did Maude's maid, Florida (*Good Times*), and the Bunkers' next-door African-American neighbors, *The Jeffersons*. *All in the Family* and its spinoffs opened up the sitcom format to allow for biting social commentary in a humorous framework.

By the mid-1980s, there was talk that the situation comedy was dying. The networks were concentrating more on the one-hour dramas and action–adventure series. But that all turned around when NBC introduced *The Cosby Show* and made Thursday night its "must see" night of television. *The Cosby Show* soared to the top of the weekly ratings and helped NBC move from number three in the seasonal ratings to number one, a position it held through much of the 1990s. Bill Cosby's return to weekly television presented a look at the "nuclear" family of the period, both mother and father worked, the children had the same types of problems that kids were having across the nation. Many people saw the program as being not about a black family but about a family who happened to be black.

One of the most popular sitcoms of the 1990s was NBC's Seinfeld, *featuring Michael Richards (L) as Cosmo Kramer and standup comic Jerry Seinfeld as—standup comic Jerry Seinfeld.*

When *The Cosby Show* went off the air, NBC scrambled for a strong show to bolster its Thursday night lineup. It decided on *Seinfeld*, a program which had been bouncing around the schedule for a while (and had even lost a head-to-head ratings battle to

Box 12.1

MEDIA WATCH

The Top Five Television Programs of the 20th Century

As the 20th century drew to a close, *TV Guide* listed what it considered to be the five most important television series since the development of the medium in the late 1940s. The selections, made by the magazine's senior editors, include four situation comedies and one drama:

1. *I Love Lucy* which "invented TV comedy, in terms of the sitcom style. Along with *The Honeymooners*, it was one of the first shows to invent and define the great second bananas."

2. *All in the Family,* which the editors credited with "reinventing TV comedy. It actually reflected reality—a socially conscious show that wasn't afraid to attack what had previously been seen as taboo subjects."

3. *M*A*S*H,* which "reinvented comedy in another way, in that it incorporates drama with comedy. It came out at the end of Vietnam, and maybe

helped to heal a nation's wounds at the same time the doctors were healing people on the show."

4. *Hill Street Blues,* which the editors of *TV Guide* felt "totally reinvented the television drama: the vocabulary, the look, the feel, the tone. When you look at all 10 o'clock dramas, they really go back to *Hill Street*. It was the turning point in that it really made dramas very adult."

5. *The Cosby Show,* a crossover hit where "race was almost inconsequential. Everybody could relate to the show."

Receiving honorable mentions from the *TV Guide* senior editors were *The Mary Tyler Moore Show* and *Star Trek.**

*"*TV Guide*'s Top Five of All Time," *Fresno Bee,* January 4, 2000, p. A2.

Tim Allen's *Home Improvement* on Tuesday nights). But once settled into the Thursday night lineup, Jerry Seinfeld's weekly "show about nothing" quickly became a dominant ratings winner and a major contributor to our popular culture with such expressions as "master of your domain" and "yadda, yadda, yadda."

When *Seinfeld* ended its successful nine-year run on NBC, the final episode drew more than 76 million viewers, making it the third most watched finale in television history (*M*A*S*H* holds the number one spot with 105 million tuning in for the final program in its 11-year run, while *Cheers* drew 80 million for its finale). Three other high-profile TV shows went off the air the same year as *Seinfeld*, but they didn't come close to drawing the same size audience for their final episodes. *Murphy Brown* had 17 million, *Ellen* (see Box 12.2) had just under 10 million (down from its average weekly viewership of almost 12 million), and *The Larry Sanders Show* on the HBO premium cable channel drew more than 2 million. As for Jerry Seinfeld, *Forbes* magazine reported in 1998 that the comedian was the wealthiest of the 40 highest paid entertainers in the nation with an income estimated at $225 million. The cocreator of *Seinfeld*, Larry David, was number two on the list with $200 million.

As *Seinfeld* went off the air, even programs on other networks paid tribute to its success. For example, ABC's *Dharma and Greg* featured an episode in which the married couple decided to take part in some public lovemaking on the streets of San Francisco. Of course, the time they chose was 9 o'clock on the Thursday night of the *Seinfeld* finale because they knew no

@   **Practicing Media Literacy**

Do you prefer sitcoms to dramas or action–adventure programs on television? If so, why? If not, why not?

Box 12.2

MEDIA WATCH

The "Coming-Out" Party for Ellen

For months there had been all kinds of hype: would she or wouldn't she come out of the closet. They were talking about the TV character Ellen Morgan on the ABC-TV sitcom *Ellen.* They were also talking about the star of the show, Ellen DeGeneres. There had been hints on the program. There had been speculation in the media. Finally, DeGeneres appeared on the cover of *Time* magazine to proclaim that she was indeed a lesbian, with the inside story revealing that she was involved with actress Anne Heche. That set the stage for the TV character of Ellen Morgan to do the same thing, and ABC played it for all it was worth.

The coming-out episode was expanded to an hour, there were guest stars, led by actress Laura Dern, there were protests from religious leaders, and there were problems with advertisers. For example, a month before the telecast, ABC announced that it was rejecting an ad about discrimination against gays and lesbians in the workplace. The decision came when a Washington-based gay rights group, the Human Rights Campaign (HRC), sought to purchase 30 seconds of national air-time in the episode. ABC said the commercial violated network policy against airing controversial-issues advertising. The group ended up purchasing time during the program on individual stations in more than 30 markets across the country.

The head of the Moral Majority, the Reverend Jerry Falwell, urged sponsors of the program to withdraw their commercials in the coming-out episode. One of them, Chrysler, did just that. There were reports that the cost for a 30-second spot had jumped from $170,000 at the start of the season to $300,000 for the one-hour show. Despite the pullout of some of the regular advertisers, the episode was sold out.

Even calls for viewers to boycott the show didn't work—the episode was viewed by 42 million people, well above its normal weekly viewership of 13.6 million. The impressive ratings ensured that the program would be renewed for another season, but now that the leading character of the show was an announced lesbian things began to change.

The first problem came at the start of the 1997–98 season when ABC announced that it was going to place a disclaimer advisory, similar to the one used at the start of *NYPD Blue*, at the beginning of certain *Ellen* episodes. Although the network had already given

Women's themes dominated Ellen DeGeneres' program after she and her TV character came out of the closet.

the series a TV-14 rating, it was adding an advisory stating "Due to adult content, parental discretion is advised." DeGeneres was furious, saying the show didn't merit such a warning and saying that it represented an inequity relative to sitcoms with heterosexual characters. She said it amounted to censorship.

DeGeneres later threatened to quit the show over a dispute involving a script in which Ellen Morgan and her new girlfriend headed toward the bedroom, implying a sexual encounter. The network initially objected to the script, but finally allowed it to be shot as written. Despite such problems, the program received vocal support from Vice President Al Gore, who praised Hollywood for producing a program featuring an openly lesbian character. According to Gore, the program was forcing Americans to "look at sexual orientation in a more open light."*

The show finished the remainder of the season but was then canceled by ABC. DeGeneres says the program ended because she was gay. The network said it was because the show had become politicized and issue oriented, losing its edge and becoming less funny. The ratings showed that viewership had declined significantly from the high of the coming-out episode the previous year.

*"Gore Praises *Ellen* Show," *Fresno Bee,* October 17, 1997, p. A3.

one would see them. Everyone would be home saying good-bye to Jerry, George, Elaine, and Kramer. "Hey, San Francisco!" shouted Dharma as she stood on the steps of the courthouse and flashed the empty streets of the City by the Bay, "Must See This!"

The Miniseries

In the mid-1970s, the networks tried to break down traditional viewing habits by introducing a new format, the miniseries. The idea was to get people hooked on the series in the first episode, usually broadcast on Sunday night, so they would tune in again the next several evenings. Miniseries have proven very popular, and they are often scheduled during "**sweeps** periods," when TV stations are monitored to determine audience sizes. (Sweeps are conducted four times a year—November, February, May, and July—and are used to set advertising rates. High ratings mean higher advertising rates for the local stations and networks.)

sweeps

The miniseries concept actually came from public broadcasting, which began showing BBC-produced serials such as *The Forsyte Saga* and *Upstairs Downstairs*.

In 1977 ABC introduced *Roots*, a miniseries based on Alex Haley's book of the same name, which kept millions of viewers glued to the TV set for eight nights. The series, which traced Haley's ancestors from Africa through American slavery and into the 20th century, set ratings records and helped keep Haley's book at the top of the best-seller lists for months. Part of the popularity of *Roots* was its powerful portrayal of one of the darker aspects of American history.

By the 1990s, the miniseries was usually limited to a two-part movie because of the diminishing level of audience attention. Only a quality miniseries such as *Lonesome Dove* could sustain viewer interest over several evenings. America's television watchers had too many choices available to tie themselves down with one long story spread out over a week.

TV Sports

Sports, which have played an important role in providing leisure enjoyment for the masses since the 19th century, have become an important part of television programming. The popularity of electronically mediated athletics grew rapidly after the development in the 1960s of such new technology as instant-replay videotape recorders. Television permanently took over as the "electronic ballpark" (see Chapter 2).

Last-place network ABC led the way with its innovative *Wide World of Sports*, which cut between live, taped, and filmed sports events, some of which had taken place days before in various places around the world. In 1970, ABC paid $9 million for the rights to *Monday Night Football*. Eventually ABC found itself number one in the ratings thanks to its expanded sports coverage and a new lineup of such popular sitcoms as *Happy Days*, *Laverne and Shirley*, *Soap*, and *Three's Company*.

Daytime TV

Despite the fact that prime-time television has the largest audience and highest advertising rates, over the years daytime TV has been the biggest moneymaker. Soap operas and game shows have always been extremely popular and are much cheaper to produce, even though the game shows give away money and prizes. As we have seen, soap operas have been an important part of the American culture since the early days of

> **@ Practicing Media Literacy**
>
> Do you watch any soap operas? If so, are you hesitant to tell anyone that you watch them? If not, why not?

radio. Today they appeal to a wide range of viewers, from homemakers to business executives.

In the 1980s, as our culture became more tolerant of open media discussions of such controversial topics as AIDS, child molestation, gay rights, date rape, spousal abuse, alcoholism, and drug abuse, the popularity of daytime talk shows increased. By the mid-1990s, talk-show hosts such as Jenny Jones, Jerry Springer, Geraldo Rivera, and even Phil Donahue were paying large sums of money to guests to get them to reveal lurid details of bizarre behavior and sex practices. In 1998, auto mechanic Joey Buttafuoco launched his own half-hour talk show on a cable access channel. This came after had had served four months in jail after pleading guilty to having a sexual affair with 16-year-old Long Island high school student Amy Fisher. She was sent to prison after confessing to shooting Buttafuoco's wife in the face. Mrs. Buttafuoco was one of her husband's first guests.

In 1996, a trial began for a man accused of murder in the fatal shooting of another man. The incident came following a taping of *The Jenny Jones Show* in 1995 in which guests were to meet their "secret admirers." During the program, Jonathan Schmitz thought he was going to meet the girl of his dreams. Instead, the "secret admirer" turned out to be another man, Scott Amedure. Several days after the taping of the program, Amedure was found shot to death and Schmitz was accused of first-degree murder. Schmitz's father later charged that *The Jenny Jones Show* was responsible for the whole thing because his son was caught off guard as the cameras were rolling—all for the "entertainment" value of his situation. While that particular episode of *The Jenny Jones Show* was never broadcast, the Schmitz trial was carried live by the Court TV cable channel. Schmitz was convicted of second-degree murder.

However, the Michigan Court of Appeals overturned the conviction in 1998, saying that the trial judge should have allowed defense attorneys to remove a juror before the trial began. Schmitz was again found guilty in a second trial in 1999, but in a separate court action, the family of shooting victim Scott Amedure sued *The Jenny Jones Show* and its producer, Warner Bros., for $50 million, saying the program was responsible for his death because of the ambush tactics of the program. Jones herself was not a target of the legal action, but defended the program in her 12 hours of testimony. In 1999, a jury of five women and four men awarded $25 million to the Amedure family. While one of the jurors said there was little disagreement among members of the jury, Warner Bros. said it would appeal, and First Amendment scholars predicted that the verdict would be overturned on the grounds of freedom of speech (see Box 12.3).

> **@   Practicing Media Literacy**
>
> Do you feel that television programs—entertainment programs as well as talk shows—should be held accountable if people commit crimes based on what they saw on these shows?

Many of the television talk shows of the late 1990s were a form of tabloid television, seeking out topics and guests to titillate the viewer. On one typical day, the *Long Beach Press-Telegram* listed the following programs and topics for daytime TV talk shows: *Leeza*—Children who have been kidnapped; *Sally Jesse Raphael*—Adulterous parents are confronted; *Maury Povich*—Desperate ways to gain custody; *Ricki Lake*—Bickering loved ones return; and *Jerry Springer*—Family striptease acts.[3]

One of the most controversial, and popular, talk shows of the 1990s was hosted by Jerry Springer (see Box 12.4). His program regularly featured guests hurling obscenities or chairs at each other and numerous fights. The program managed to pull ahead of Oprah Winfrey's program in the ratings, becoming the most watched talk show on daytime TV. However, many viewers and some stations complained about the

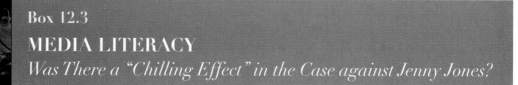

Box 12.3

MEDIA LITERACY
Was There a "Chilling Effect" in the Case against Jenny Jones?

When a jury ruled that *The Jenny Jones Show* and its producer, Warner Bros., were at least partially responsible for the death of former guest Scott Amedure, it sent a chilling message to all television talk shows. Do such daily exercises in tabloid entertainment have the right to discuss any and all topics, or will their freedom of speech be challenged by multimillion-dollar legal judgments?

There are those who feel that the First Amendment was designed to protect everyone, even irresponsible people and irresponsible statements. In the case of *The Jenny Jones Show,* Jonathan Schmitz had signed a waiver acknowledging that his secret admirer might be a male or a female. During her three days of testimony, host Jenny Jones said that Schmitz was an adult who had made an informed choice to appear on the program. The Amedure family was seeking $50 million on the grounds that the program was liable for Scott's death because of the humiliation suffered by Schmitz, which drove him to commit murder. During the trial, the jury heard a 911 tape of Schmitz in which he repeatedly mentioned the Jones program as he sobbingly told the dispatcher that he had killed Amedure. The defense maintained that it would be impossible for the producers of the program to know that Schmitz was apparently unstable enough to react so violently.

The jury also watched the episode in which Amedure made his revelation, a program that was never aired. In it, Schmitz appeared to be handling the situation like a good sport, laughing, clapping, but saying he was heterosexual and not interested.

While the defense attorney in his closing argument had told the jurors that they should not enter deliberations in the lawsuit with the idea of cleaning up the television talk-show business, many later saw the

Jenny Jones was called to testify about the role her TV talk show played in a murder case.

verdict as just such an action. Other studios that also produce daily talk shows declined comment, but others in the media saw it as a statement of public outrage against such shows as *Jerry Springer* and *Jenny Jones.*

Did the verdict have a chilling impact on these types of programs? Did television talk shows tone down the content and guests of their shows? Did the viewers show their disgust by refusing to watch such programs? If there is a public revulsion over television's tabloid talk shows, why are they still successful in the ratings? When was the last time *YOU* watched such a program without turning it off in disgust?

fights among guests, the "bleeping" of words, and the salacious topics, so the Springer producers announced that they were going to clean up the show and eliminated the more offensive guests and topics. The show began to drop in the ratings, and it wasn't long before the Jerry Springer program returned to its original, more successful format.

At one point, television programmers attempted to offer "clean" talk shows throughout the day. Going on the air to offer "clean, positive, and good-news topics" were Betrice Berry, Les Brown, and Ricki Lake. Berry, who held a doctorate in sociology,

Box 12.4

MEDIA WATCH
A Man Surrounded by Controversy: Jerry Springer

Following complaints from the media and, more importantly, from some of the stations carrying the program, it was announced in 1998 that *The Jerry Springer Show* would edit out the fist fights, the chair throwing, and other violence that had propelled the program to the top of the ratings among daytime talk shows. The decision came after a two-hour meeting between producers of the show and an activist group in Chicago, which had staged a boycott of the program and denounced it as a pornographic slugfest. Even NBC-owned WMAQ in Chicago, where the program was taped, had announced that it wanted to drop the show. Fox affiliate WFLD quickly agreed to carry it in that market.

For years, the Springer show had featured warped behavior on the part of the guests, with a raucous mix of screaming, obscenities, and fist fights, finished off by a closing comment from Springer who attempted to show that there was some sort of socially redeeming value to what had just taken place on the program. But representatives of the producer and distributor of the Springer show, Studios USA, agreed to completely eliminate the violence and even to go back and edit out any fights in programs that had been taped but not yet aired. It didn't take long for the public to register its position in the controversy—the ratings for *The Jerry Springer Show* began to decline. A short time later, Springer announced that the fights would be back.

Just a year earlier Springer was involved in another controversy in Chicago, this one coming when WMAQ announced that he had been hired to do a daily news commentary on its nightly newscasts. Springer, of course, had been mayor of Cincinnati before going into television and had also served as a political reporter and anchor in Ohio. But for some, his role as host of a tabloid television talk show that dealt with such topics as "My Boyfriend Is a Girl" disqualified him from being a news commentator. WMAQ anchor Carol Marin showed her disgust for the move by quitting her job after 19 years at the station, calling

Springer "the poster child for the worst television has to offer." She told *TV Guide* that she didn't want to appear on the same program with Springer and "validate what he does."* (Marin had already appeared on a WMAQ newscast where Chicago Bull Dennis Rodman had done a sports report wearing a velvet dress.)

Shortly after taping his talk show dealing with the topic of "Pregnant Women Who Work in the Sex Industry," Springer delivered his first commentary dealing with the criticism of his hiring and defending his right to free speech. It was also his last commentary for the station. By the end of that first week, Springer had sent a note to station management saying that it wasn't worth it; the controversy had gotten too personal.

As the 20th century was drawing to a close, England was the site of the next controversy for Springer as talk show host Oprah Winfrey singled him out to express her feeling that daytime television was becoming a "vulgarity circus." Said Winfrey: "Unless you are going to kill people on the air, and not just hit them on the head with chairs, and unless you are going to have sexual intercourse . . . then there comes a point when you have oversaturated yourself."** A month later, Springer appeared in England at a debate at Oxford University and defended his program by telling the audience that Britain's beloved Princess Diana had spoken publicly about the same topics featured on his program. "She talked about not being faithful in her marriage, she talked about bulimia and she talked about even contemplating suicide," he explained.***

But he didn't say whether she had ever hit someone over the head with a chair.

*"Tabloid Host on the Hot Seat in Chicago," *TV Guide*, May 10, 1997, p. 49.

**"Springer Show a 'Vulgarity Circus,'" *Fresno Bee*, February 10, 1999, p. A2.

***"Jerry Springer Defends His Show," *Fresno Bee*, March 4, 1999, p. A2.

was a comedian, while Brown had a background as a motivational speaker. Lake was an actress who targeted the twenty-something audience with "relationship-oriented" subjects. Of the three, only Lake was successful. But as shows were canceled, replacements sprang up, from Carnie Wilson (of the pop music group Wilson Phillips) and Tempest

Bledsoe (of *The Cosby Show*) to actress/comedian Rosie O'Donnell. Of that group, only O'Donnell was successful because she offered something different. Her program was a throwback to the afternoon variety–talk shows of the 1960s and 1970s as practiced by Merv Griffin and Mike Douglas. In fact, her programs were very similar to the late-night talk shows of Jay Leno and David Letterman, featuring celebrity interviews, musical guests, and comedy.

But even O'Donnell has generated some controversy on her show. Following the 1999 shootings at Columbine High School in Colorado, O'Donnell began speaking out for gun control during her program. When actor Tom Selleck, a member of the National Rifle Association, appeared on her show to plug his newest movie, Rosie began questioning him about his involvement with the NRA, asking why he would appear in a TV commercial for the organization, and why his name was used in an NRA newspaper ad quoting him as saying "I Am the NRA." Although Selleck reportedly knew that this subject would be discussed, he apparently wasn't prepared for the passion with which O'Donnell would discuss it. Halfway through this segment of the interview, Selleck quietly said, "I didn't come on your show to have a debate. I came on your show to plug a movie."[4]

Prime-Time Soaps

In 1964 ABC premiered the first prime time soap opera, *Peyton Place*, based loosely on a steamy best-seller by Grace Metalious. First shown two and then three nights a week, it launched the careers of Mia Farrow and Ryan O'Neal and demonstrated yet again the durability and versatility of the genre. Other networks were slow to follow ABC's lead, but in 1978 CBS launched *Dallas* as a weekly serial. During the 1980s *Dallas* and its imitators, *Dynasty, Knots Landing,* and *Falcon Crest,* topped the evening ratings by bringing the continuing stories and daytime troubles of TV families to nighttime viewers.

These shows appealed to the average person's interest in the rich and elite, and all seemed to revolve around one central theme: that rich families are plagued with turmoil and strife, and the American cultural myth that money can't always buy happiness is true. (It is worth noting that *Dallas* and *Dynasty* became the most popular American TV shows in Canada, Australia, Chile, Japan, and many western European countries during the 1980s. In Japan, the conniving J.R. Ewing became a hero.)

In the 1990s, the Fox Television Network (foxworld.com) successfully launched three prime time continuing dramas: *Beverly Hills 90210, Melrose Place,* and *Party of Five.* Attempts by the other networks to revive the genre were unsuccessful, as evidenced by the ratings failure of CBS's *Central Park West* (later called simply "CPW") in 1995.

Hybrid TV

As our culture evolves, so do the entertainment genres on television. In the 1980s, a new TV format developed that was a combination of a number of others. It borrowed the ongoing story line from the soap operas; character development of early-day TV dramas; action–adventure from the Western, police, and lawyer shows; comedy from sitcoms; and fast-paced action from vaudeville and TV variety shows. The genre was pioneered by Steven Bochco in 1981 with *Hill Street Blues.* Other shows, such as *St. Elsewhere, Miami Vice, L.A. Law, The Wonder Years,* and *thirtysomething,* were soon utilizing these same techniques as the trend continued its popularity throughout the 1980s and well into the 1990s. When NBC programming chief Brandon Tartikoff said

TV producer Steven Bochco broke new ground when he created network television's first weekly R-rated program, NYPD Blue. *The program, featuring Dennis Franz (L) and Rick Schroeder, often has explicit language and partial nudity.*

he wanted an MTV cop show, he got *Miami Vice*, known for its rock music background.

In 1990, Bochco added a new dimension to the MTV cop shows when he launched *Cop Rock*. Unlike *Miami Vice*, in which rock music was in the background, *Cop Rock* was a musical that featured cops and criminals who actually sang and danced. The departure from regular action–adventure proved to be too radical, and the series was canceled shortly after it began.

Bochco again broke new barriers in 1993 when he used this hybrid format to launch *NYPD Blue*, another police action–adventure show. However, this time he added nudity and explicit language to the show. This prompted the Reverend Donald Wildmon, a fundamentalist preacher from Mississippi, to run full-page ads in newspapers across the country denouncing ABC for running R-rated shows that included "nudity, more extreme violence and more profanity." Despite the fact that 33 ABC affiliates refused to carry the show, the controversy and its publicity helped the show earn high ratings. It also received praise from New York police officers for being the most realistic cop show on the air. Many of the affiliates that had declined to show the program during its first season later lifted the ban and began airing it.

Docudramas

Another development of the 1980s was the docudrama, which portrays a real-life situation in fictional form. While the shows take liberties with the facts to heighten the dramatic effect, the impression left in the viewer's mind is that the televised version is the way it actually happened. Although docudramas sometimes bring historical topics as well as current events into the popular culture through the medium of entertainment, they cause some concern because they often blend **truth with fiction.**

truth with fiction

One such docudrama was the 1997 showing of *George Wallace* on the Turner Network Television (TNT) cable channel, which drew both praise and criticism. The praise came from the way director John Frankenheimer recreated many actual scenes from Wallace's life, including the former Alabama governor's confrontation with representatives of the federal government as he tried to block the university entrance of several African-American students and the assassination attempt on Wallace's life as he campaigned for president in 1972. The criticism came from the creation of a fictional scene in which a composite, fabricated character—a black valet—considered killing Wallace with an ice pick.

In 1993, the three major networks each broadcast a docudrama (some critics called them "schlockudramas") about 16-year-old Amy Fisher, known in the tabloid press as the "Long Island Lolita." Each network had a different version of how and why the teenaged Fisher had been sent to prison for shooting the wife of her alleged lover, Joey Buttafuoco. All three programs, broadcast within a week of one another, did very well in the ratings.

In 1989 a controversial historical docudrama was challenged by former president Richard Nixon, who fought unsuccessfully to stop the production of a three-hour docudrama on the Watergate scandal, which led to his resignation in 1974. Based on the Woodward and Bernstein book *The Final Days,* the ABC production, according to Nixon's lawyers, was filled with inaccuracies and was an invasion of privacy.

But a docudrama can strive for accuracy and still be entertaining. The 1988 ABC miniseries *Baby* M carefully followed the sequence of events and court records of a famous surrogate motherhood case. Winning high ratings, this docudrama brought a complex social issue into focus for the masses.

As Americans became more concerned about social issues during the 1980s, some made-for-TV movies began providing information on such topics as alcoholism, AIDS, incest, child kidnapping, and spousal abuse. These educationally oriented movies were very helpful in disseminating important social information in the context of leisure entertainment.

> @ **Practicing Media Literacy**
> Do you feel television producers are distorting history by fictionalizing story elements and characters for the sake of making an entertaining docudrama?

Tabloid TV

By the 1990s, a television version of the titillating sensationalism of tabloid newspapers had emerged as a new genre of television programming. Leading the way was Rupert **Murdoch,** the "king" of tabloid newspapers in Australia, Britain, and the United States. Murdoch's Fox Broadcasting Company was using sex, murder, and mayhem in its efforts to establish a fourth TV network made up of independent stations.

Murdoch

One of the first newsmagazine shows, *A Current Affair,* featured bloody murder scenes, titillating sex crimes, and gore. A popular Fox show, *America's Most Wanted,* gained invaluable publicity when more than 400 suspects wanted for crimes (which are reenacted on the show) were captured as a result of the weekly broadcasts. However, one problem the program faced was that some of the actors portraying the wanted criminals in the reenactments were often stopped later for questioning by police.

When the Fox network elected not to renew *America's Most Wanted* for the 1996 season because of low ratings, law enforcement organizations across the country asked the network to reconsider its decision. Concern about the program's cancellation even prompted the head of the Drug Enforcement Administration (DEA), Thomas Constantine, to write a letter to the chairperson of NewsCorp, Fox's parent corporation. In his plea to Rupert Murdoch, Constantine said that the loss of the program would be "devastating to American law-enforcement efforts and the safety of our communities."[5] The governors of 35 states also wrote Murdoch, but Fox announced that while the program was off the air as a weekly series, it would still be seen as occasional specials. Two weeks into the 1996 television season, Fox announced that *America's Most Wanted* was being revived. "The audience spoke to us loudly," said the new head of entertainment at Fox, Peter Roth.[6]

Fox was not the only one getting into the tabloid business. The networks were keen to add real-life crime shows to their lineups, since they are so cheap and easy to produce. NBC began broadcasting *Unsolved Mysteries* as a weekly series, and CBS added *Rescue 911.* ABC aired a special by Geraldo Rivera, *Murder: Lives from Death*

Row, which included actual film footage of the murder of a convenience store customer as well as interviews with several convicted murderers, including notorious cult leader Charles Manson, talking about their crimes. *Hard Copy* and *Inside Edition* soon joined *A Current Affair* among the top syndicated programs.

Still another questionable form of tabloid entertainment was aired by ABC, a show featuring what were termed America's funniest home videos. Spawned by the popularity of the camcorder, the show invited people to send in their funniest home videos. The 30-minute program then featured what were considered to be the best of the week's entries. It soon became obvious that people were staging the videos and that many of the scenes could be dangerous—particularly for children or animals—if replicated. Ironically, these seemed to be the themes that succeeded in getting on the air and winning the cash prizes. After several months, ABC had to ask the producers of the show to issue warnings when soliciting videos that viewers should not tape anything that could be harmful to the persons or animals involved. But the success of the program spawned other such **"reality" shows,** both on networks and in syndication. These ranged from *Real TV* to such ratings winners as *When Wild Animals Attack* and *The World's Wildest Police Chases.*

"reality" shows

THE CULTURAL IMPACT OF TELEVISION

Television's impact on our society has been profound. It has changed the lifestyles of most Americans and become a major influence in our culture. Unlike printing, which took hundreds of years to influence the culture, TV's impact was almost instantaneous. During television's breakthrough year, fewer than 20 television stations were on the air. This figure grew to more than 1,500 by the mid-1990s.[7]

The number of television sets in homes also grew rapidly. From 172,000 sets in 1948, the sale of TV sets increased at a rate of a quarter million per month for the next two years. The sales figures climbed to 5 million sets per year during the 1950s and today exceed 22 million. By 1962, more than 90 percent of all households had at least one television set and 13 percent had more than one set. By the late 1980s, there were 125 million television sets in homes, representing nearly 98 percent of American households (a greater percentage than had indoor toilets).[8]

A. C. Nielsen Company reports that most American families today own a minimum of two television sets (1.83 is the national average), and most of these sets (87.3 million) are color. These sets are located in vital living areas, such as the living room, family room, bedroom, and kitchen. Because they own multiple sets, many families no longer watch television together, and parents often do not know what their children are viewing.[9]

As the final decade of the 20th century began, Nielsen also reported that the average television usage in U.S. households is more than seven hours per day, which translates into more than 2,400 hours per year—the most time-consuming activity besides sleeping.[10]

@ Practicing Media Literacy

How much time do you spend watching television each day? What about other members of your family?

Socialization Effects

TV's dominance as a household activity often reduces the level of communication among family members and, as a result, much of the culture being disseminated to youngsters today comes from the tube rather than the family. Television usage in homes with children is the highest, and it is believed that the average child has watched more than 18,000 hours of TV by the time he or she reaches age 15. This compares with 11,000 hours of schooling and 3,000 hours of church attendance. Television has become the most powerful tool for socialization that civilization has ever devised.

What has made television's significance even more profound is the fact that it took very little time for it to become pervasive in the culture. Unlike many media, TV spent relatively little time in the elite culture. The rich and middle classes were not the only ones to rush to purchase television sets. Many lower-class households went into debt to own this luxury item. However, to most Americans, television was not a luxury but a psychological necessity; it provided comfort to a lonely mass culture whose members sought both entertainment and solitude in their homes. Sociologists have been puzzled as to how something previously nonexistent could become a psychological necessity the moment it arrived in the popular culture. The answer seems to be that television found a niche by bringing the world to individuals isolated from the dominant culture. However, by bringing the world into the home, TV replaced many cherished activities, such as after-dinner conversations among family members and parents reading bedtime stories to children, with TV sitcoms, variety shows, and action–adventures.

> **@ Practicing Media Literacy**
> Can you think of anything you learned from television that helped you to fit in better as a student or member of society?

Reflecting Cultural Changes

Television programming has played an important role in reflecting for the masses the cultural changes that have been occurring in American society. When the civil rights movement calling for equality for all Americans gained momentum in the 1960s, TV started reflecting these changes. Women and African-Americans began to be portrayed in other than stereotyped roles for the first time. Such sitcoms as *That Girl*, starring Marlo Thomas, who portrayed a young woman making it on her own in the world, and *Julia*, featuring Diahann Carroll as an African-American nurse and mother, became popular. *The Mary Tyler Moore Show* of the early 1970s reflected the feminist movement of the time by allowing a single woman to have a career without worrying about whether she would find a husband. Prior to that time, women characters were limited to housewives (*The Donna Reed Show*) or schoolteachers (*Our Miss Brooks*).

In the 1950s, singer Nat "King" Cole had been the only African-American to host a network variety show (it was canceled for lack of advertisers), and in the 1960s, Bill Cosby became the first African-American to have a costarring role in a weekly drama series, *I Spy*.

These trends were significant in that they demonstrated that TV was culturally responsive. Besides merely reflecting these cultural changes, television helped transmit them to the masses and by doing so accelerated their acceptance into the mainstream popular culture. However, the development of new networks in the 1980s and 1990s to challenge the big three networks—ABC (abc.com), CBS

Bill Cosby, the first African-American to star in a weekly TV dramatic series in the 1960s, is also credited with reviving the TV sitcom genre in the 1980s.

(cbs.com), and NBC (nbc.com)—has also brought about a change in the way television programmers target audiences (see Box 12.5).

In action–adventure shows, women began playing previously male-only roles of cops, detectives, and lawyers. Shows such as *Cagney & Lacey*, *L.A. Law*, *The Mary Tyler Moore Show*, and *Murphy Brown* all showed women in professional rather than subservient roles. However, early versions, such as *Charlie's Angels*, were highly criticized for making the female stars more sexy than professional.

Resistance to TV's Cultural Takeover

Despite television's rapid takeover in the American popular culture, it did meet some resistance. In the early years, many academics and urban intellectuals resisted TV and viewed it as a "low cultural form" unworthy of serious attention from the "refined and thinking" members of our society.

At first, *not* owning a television set was a status symbol among the "cultured" because the new medium appealed to low cultural interests and was aimed at delivering the largest audiences. But quality live-drama productions of the 1950s, such as *Playhouse 90* and *Studio One*, and important news presentations such as the Army–McCarthy hearings, made it difficult for intellectuals to resist this new mass medium. It wasn't long before people in intellectual circles could be heard saying rather sheepishly that "We own one, but we never turn it on."

In 1964, only 16 years after television first started to make inroads into the popular culture, a survey of the 1939 graduating class of Harvard University revealed that 92.5 percent owned at least one TV set and 13 percent had three or more sets in their homes. By the 1960s, television had become nearly everyone's mass medium.

Despite this universal acceptance, criticism of television continued, with critics regularly expressing alarm that TV content was aimed at the masses and had little, if any, educational value. Many were calling television an "electronic **mind pacifier**" that had a narcotic effect on our culture. This was the theme of former television writer Paddy Chayefsky's movie *Network* in the mid-1970s. (Ironically, the movie ended up being a movie of the week on network television.) When one of the film's characters, Howard Beale, a TV newscaster suffering a nervous breakdown on the air, preached the following lines on his "news-entertainment hour," many TV network executives cringed:

mind pacifier

> Television is not the truth . . . We lie like hell . . . We deal in illusions, man. None of it is true. But you people sit there day after day, night after night. . . . We're all you know. You're beginning to believe the illusions we're spinning here. You're beginning to think that the tube is reality and that your own lives are like the tube, you eat like the tube, you raise your children like the tube. This is mass madness, you maniacs. In God's name, you people are the real thing: we're the illusions.[11]

Today, after entire generations have grown up with the pacifying effects of television and the medium is firmly entrenched in the culture, critics are still making satirical social commentary about its shortcomings. Members of a California group who called themselves the Couch Potatoes picked up on the theme that TV was turning people into mental vegetables. Their goal was to bring to the attention of the masses their belief that television is a passive, anti-intellectual medium. When asked by a reporter to comment on interactive television that allowed viewers to participate in quiz shows and electronic polling by talking back to their TV sets, a Couch Potato spokesperson said, "Why watch TV if you have to think and respond? As far as I'm

Television has always been considered a medium for mass audiences—trying to be all things to all people. But studies done during the 1990s showed that this wasn't the case. Viewers noted that while ABC, CBS, and NBC presented a mostly white world, the newcomer networks of Fox, Warner Bros. (WB), and the United Paramount Network (UPN) presented a mostly black world.

Of course, these divisions aren't absolute, but there are certainly clear patterns. For example, a study conducted by A. C. Nielsen Company showed that *Seinfeld,* the second most popular show among white viewers in the 1990s, was 89th among blacks. *Friends* was number three among white viewers, but was 111th among blacks. On the other hand, Fox's *New York Undercover* was the top-rated show among blacks but was ranked at 122 among white viewers. By 1999, the number-one show among black viewers was the WB's *Steve Harvey Show* (number 127 among whites) followed by *The Jamie Foxx Show* on the WB (ranked 120th in white homes).

The number one program of the 1990s, NBC's *ER,* demonstrated some cross-viewer appeal, ranking 1st among whites and 15th among blacks by the end of the decade. But only one network program ranked among the top 10 for both races: ABC's *Monday Night Football.*

This separation in viewing habits may also have something to do with the casts of the programs. The issue came to a head near the end of the 1990s as the National Association for the Advancement of Colored People (NAACP) threatened to sue the four major television networks and boycott their advertisers unless they began to feature minorities more prominently in leading roles on their shows. Looking at the 1999–2000 television season schedule, NAACP President Kweisi Mfume called it a "virtual whitewash," charging network executives of being either clueless, careless, or both. "We intend to make it clear that the frontier of television must reflect the multiethnic landscape of today's modern society," Mfume told the NAACP's 90th annual convention.*

Shortly thereafter, Latino and Asian groups began proposing boycotts of the networks (or, in the case of the National Council of La Raza, a "brownout"). The networks were quick to respond, citing the minorities appearing in major roles on their programs, but it was obvious that it wouldn't be enough; most of the leading minority roles were supporting characters, and none of the new shows featured recognizable minorities. Executives from each of the networks began meeting with representatives of the minority groups to see what changes could be made in the seasons ahead. In January of 2000, NBC announced that it had reached an agreement with the NAACP intended to generate jobs for minorities both at the network and on the programs it broadcast. The arrangement provided for internships, scholarships, and a guarantee that the network would increase its purchases from minority-owned suppliers. In addition, NBC agreed to pay for a minority writer to be added to the staff of every new network program that was renewed for a second year. Shortly thereafter, ABC signed a similar agreement and in February of 2000, CBS and Fox signed agreements to make television more ethnically diverse.

How did the networks find themselves in such a position? It's really quite simply a matter of economics: The big networks with the big ratings and big bucks on the line broadcast programs that reach the widest (or whitest) audience to make the most money. The young, just-getting-started networks (Fox in its formative years, the WB, and UPN) have gone after the segments of the audience that are left (ethnic minorities) to develop an urban niche. Once they've established themselves, they join the others in trying to reach the larger number of viewers to deliver an audience to the advertisers. In doing so, the minority viewers are left to watch those programs which they feel more accurately reflect their culture, and the networks continue to develop programs for what they consider to be the masses.

*V. Dion Hayes, "Bashing TV 'Whitewash.' NAACP Threatens to Sue," *Chicago Tribune,* July 13, 1999, p. 1.

concerned, the main point of watching TV is that it lets you avoid having to do that. To put it another way, if you're going to have to respond to your TV, you might as well go out and cultivate friendships or read a book or something."[12]

The cultural impact of TV during the last half of the 20th century generated a great deal of discussion and concern in several specific areas, including the effects of violence on TV and television's influence on children. These topics and research related to their effects on our culture are discussed in Chapter 16. The end result was the establishment of a television ratings system to help parents determine the content of programs before allowing their children to watch them (see Box 12.6).

Television and Religion

Even the way many people participate in religion has been affected by television and the development of **televangelism.** Fundamentalist Protestant revivalism has been part of American culture since the religious movement known as the Great Awakening swept the 13 colonies in the 1730s and 1740s. Preaching to mass rallies in the open air (and later in tents), ministers from Billy Sunday to Billy Graham have urged listeners to repent and start a new life.

One of the first to utilize the new medium of television to reach a mass audience with a regular weekly religious message was Catholic bishop Fulton J. Sheen in the 1950s. But it was also in the 1950s, as tent revival audiences started to dwindle due to the competition from television, that such tent evangelists as Oral Roberts started taking their messages to the home via the TV set. Televangelism was born. Television stations began selling air time to evangelical preachers, and the electronic church became a successful part of TV programming.

As the cost of airtime climbed and the new technology of cable became available, religious broadcasters started turning to this new delivery system. The Christian Broadcasting Network (CBN) built up a cable network that supplemented its own three TV stations. TBN (Trinity Broadcasting Network) and PTL (Praise the Lord or People That Love) followed with their own religious cable networks. Of course, it still costs money to produce telecasts, so pitches for donations are a regular feature of many of these religious programs.

A Nielsen survey found that 61 million people, representing more than 40 percent of the nation's households, watched one or more of the top 10 syndicated religious broadcasts during a February sweeps period. The most popular program was the Reverend Pat Robertson's *700 Club*, with 28.7 million viewers. The electronic church has become a multibillion-dollar-a-year enterprise and a significant part of TV programming in our popular culture.

Several scandals involving televangelists Jim Bakker and Jimmy Swaggart in the 1980s created problems for the other television preachers. With donations from the viewers dropping drastically due to a loss of faith in television ministries in general, many televangelists saw their programs being canceled by stations across the country for lack of payment. A new way to reach religious viewers had to be found.

By the 1990s one TV ministry, Paul F. Crouch's Trinity Broadcasting Network, was the largest single owner of television stations in the United States, and it used satellite technology to broadcast around the world. The ministry owned 14 full-powered commercial UHF stations, three full-powered educational noncommercial outlets, and 125 low-powered TV stations. Its annual revenue in viewer pledges exceeded $40 million. In addition, Robertson's Christian Broadcasting Network on cable systems nationwide became well established and changed its name to The Family Channel, which was later sold to Rupert Murdoch's News Corporation and was renamed The Fox Family Channel. The effects of televangelism have been both spiritual and economical and demonstrate still another area where television delivers audiences to commercial enterprises.

Box 12.6
MEDIA LITERACY
TV Ratings: What Do They Mean?

With the approval of the Telecommunications Act of 1996, the television networks knew they would have to provide the viewers with more information about programming content if the V-chip proposal was to work. The initial ratings were TV-Y (recommended for youths of all ages); TV-Y7 (recommended for youths 7 and older); TV-G (recommended for general audiences); TV-PG (parental guidance suggested); TV-14 (recommended for audiences 14 and older) and TV-M (recommended for mature audiences). News and sports programs were exempt from the ratings.

During its early stages, many were critical of the ratings, questioning why *The Tonight Show with Jay Leno* would be rated TV-14, while *The Late Show* with David Letterman would be given a TV-PG. Then a $3.3 million study done by scholars from four universities was released that recommended that the fledgling rating code be scrapped in favor of one that would label programs according to their content.

Under pressure from the Clinton administration, most of the networks agreed to add a code to the ratings to give parents more specific information regarding program content. Now, when that small box appears in the upper left-hand corner of your television screen for a 15-second period at the start of each program, you're alerted to the rating for the show and given the codes of V, S, L, and D. At first glance, there appeared to be only two problems with the new system: (1) many people didn't even notice the little ratings box in the cor-

ner, and (2) the majority of those who did see it had no idea what the four letters meant. Of course, the V and the S are obvious (violence and sexual content), but what were L and D? (L is for coarse language that could be offensive, and D is for suggestive dialogue that implies sexual innuendo.) All of the television networks agreed to the additional labeling except for NBC, which rejected the proposed content ratings while accusing the other networks of giving in to "political and special interest pressure" without regard to the constitutional implication of federal intrusion into program content. Said then-NBC Entertainment president Warren Littlefield, "It's no longer about a label, it's about controlling content."*

While many were praising the new labels as giving parents more information regarding program content, the Parents Television Council reported in 1998 that the system wasn't even coming close to informing parents as to whether or not a program was suitable for children. For example, the study of several weeks of network programming found that 65 percent of the shows containing at least one obscenity failed to carry an L rating for coarse language.

But the big concern for many parents was the fear the producers would feel that they could make their programs even more violent or more sexual in nature just because they now had a warning label at the start.

*John Carman, "'Be Afraid. Be Very Afraid' of the New TV Ratings," *San Francisco Chronicle*, July 23, 1997, p. E1.

TELEVISION SPECIALIZES

Television, like many other mass media, has entered the stage of specialization. A variety of specialized programming is now available to meet particular interests.

Public Broadcasting

A noncommercial form of broadcasting, servicing primarily the elite or high culture, is provided through the joint efforts of the Corporation for Public Broadcasting (CPB) and the Public Broadcasting Service (**PBS**). Efforts to provide noncommercial educational television (ETV) began in the 1950s. These activities were not very successful but did lead to the passage of the Public Broadcasting Act of 1967, which provided the first interconnected network of ETV stations and federal assistance.

PBS

PBS programming ranges from in-depth news and Wall Street analysis to opera, classical music, and sophisticated British Broadcasting Corporation (BBC) drama and comedy productions. Among the BBC shows that have been popular on PBS over the years are *Civilisation, Masterpiece Theater, Upstairs Downstairs, Are You Being Served?* and *Yes, Minister.* PBS also broadcasts programs developed by the Children's Television Workshop (CTW), such as *Sesame Street.*

PBS programs are carried on noncommercial television stations and are usually transmitted by satellite. The biggest source of revenue for public broadcasting is corporate sponsorship; the second largest source is local station membership dues, auctions, and other fund-raisers; and the rest is made up by revenues from federal funds through the Corporation for Public Broadcasting and other federal agencies, such as the National Endowment for the Arts.

However, the increase in specialized cable networks such as the Learning Channel, the History channel, the Arts and Entertainment channel, and the Discovery channel has created competition for PBS stations. Some wonder whether government-funded public broadcasting will succumb to cable specialization.

Home Shopping

In the mid-1980s, home shopping developed as another method of selling consumer goods in the American culture. Unlike regular broadcast commercials that attempt to create an interest in a product or company, home shopping is designed to stimulate interest in instant sales. Products are shown on the screen with a discount price, and viewers are urged to call in their credit card numbers immediately, before the limited number of items are sold. These programs, many of them broadcasting 24 hours a day, sell everything from cubic zirconia diamonds to fur coats and computers. Some viewers admit to watching these marketing channels more than 12 hours a day. All a viewer needs is a TV set, a telephone, and a credit card to make numerous purchases.

Major improvements in the way a buyer makes a purchase are developing for home-shopping network fans as we enter the era of interactive TV (see the new technology section). For many years, the home-shopping channel leaders were the Home

A popular television fad has been home shopping, where viewers purchase the displayed merchandise using a telephone and a credit card.

Shopping Network and QVC. The demographic makeup for home shopping was changed somewhat in 1998 when the Shop at Home network began, targeting a male audience in the 35 to 55 age range.

TV started out as a mass medium to provide entertaining programming that would deliver large audiences to advertisers. Today, in the stage of specialization, advertising often becomes the programming.

Other Specialization

By the 1990s, cable television was going the way of radio in the 1950s: targeting specific audiences. For those who wanted sports, there were ESPN, ESPN2, and Fox Sports as well as many regional sports networks; seekers of news and information could tune to CNN, CNN Headline News, MSNBC, or the Fox News Channel (FNC); music lovers had MTV, VH1, and The Nashville Network (TNN); children had Nickelodeon, the Cartoon Channel and the Disney Channel; and lovers of old-time movies had the American Movie Classics channel (AMC), the Fox Movie Channel (FMC), and The Movie Channel (TMC).

> **@ Practicing Media Literacy**
> Do you know of anyone who has ever made a purchase from a home shopping television program? Were they happy with the product received? Are they addicted to such programs?

NEW TECHNOLOGY AND TELEVISION

The technology revolution has had a dramatic impact on the development of television. Yet we have seen nothing compared to what the future holds. What is occurring has been described as follows: "All modes of communication we humans have devised since the beginning of humanity are coming together into a single electronic system, driven by computers."[13] We are experiencing rapid advances in electronic technology that include a merging of television as we now know it with computer and telephone technologies. This merger is providing us with interactive television and a wide array of information and entertainment options.

Finding a Niche

How rapidly the new technologies will become commonplace depends on numerous factors. Just as the mass-media technologies introduced in the 19th century had to find a niche in our culture, so must today's electronic inventions struggle to find their place.

Of all the new communication technologies developed in recent years, cable television, fiber optics, satellite communication, and computers have had the most significant impact on our culture. In this 21st century, we will continue to be affected by the development of interactive TV, virtual reality, holography, high-definition television, and digital compression.

Cable Television

Cable television developed in the 1950s as a way to relay television signals to remote communities that could not receive them over the airwaves. However, following the 1975 launching of RCA's communication satellite SATCOM I, the cable industry found a new market: serving metropolitan areas as well as rural communities with expanded TV programming.

Today cable and telephone companies are merging in preparation for a new era of electronic delivery of signals that will blur the lines between information, entertainment, and traditional telephone services. Electronic superhighways carrying vast amounts of information and entertainment possibilities are just around the corner, and major cable and telephone companies, such as Tele-Communications International, Inc. (TCI) and Bell Atlantic, are merging to position themselves for this new era of the information age. AT&T and Viacom International are already test-marketing an interactive consumer video system.

Cable and telephone companies continue to expand their services beyond regular phone services, cable networks, pay-TV, pay-per-view, and public access to new areas such as video malls, where viewers can visit retail stores and make purchases through their cable systems; home banking and reservation services; airline ticket purchases; video visiting with friends and relatives across the country; educational courses from video universities; and a wide range of information and entertainment.

High-Definition Television (HDTV)

picture elements

Television viewers in America will soon be seeing television in a completely different way. It's known as HDTV, which relies on an improvement in the process of sending television signals. For more than half a century, TV broadcasts in the United States have consisted of a series of dots, called **picture elements,** arranged in horizontal lines. The United States has been using a system consisting of 525 lines. The TV screen exhibits 30 of these 525-line still pictures every second, giving the illusion of motion. (Many foreign countries and most western European nations use a 625-line standard, which gives a higher-quality picture.)

In 1981, a coalition of Japanese companies unveiled an HDTV system that broadcasts a 1,125-line television picture. The system uses a wider screen, has better color reproduction, features stereo sound, and provides a dramatic improvement in picture resolution and clarity. Projected onto a large screen, the HDTV system produces a picture with clarity and sharpness similar to that found in a motion picture theater.

To accomplish the conversion to digital television in the United States, stations will be operating for a period of time on two separate channels: their regular one, for those who still have the older-model TV sets, and a digital channel for those who have made the conversion. In the year 2000, television stations in the top 30 markets were providing both analog and HDTV signals, with the FCC's plan calling for all stations in the nation to be broadcasting HDTV signals by the year 2006. However, the general public is still not ready for the conversion. The price at the start of the 21st century was still in the range of $3,000 for "cheap" HDTV sets. In addition, those who do a lot of videotaping would have to purchase new digital VCRs to handle the higher quality signal, and they were priced at around $1,000.

> **@   Practicing Media Literacy**
>
> Have you ever seen an HDTV picture? Are you eager for the conversion to HDTV to be completed in the United States?

By 2000, the television networks had begun providing a portion of their programs in digital form (with an alert to viewers that this was the case so that they might become curious about getting the proper TV set to receive the high-definition pictures). However, many cable companies were declining to carry the digital programming to their subscribers.[14]

Box 12.7
HOW IT WORKS
Television

Most entry-level jobs in television are with local TV stations. These stations usually have seven departments in which a person might find employment: sales, programming, production, engineering, traffic, promotion, and administration.

The *sales department* sells the commercials that bring revenue to the station. These commercials are divided into national and local ads. National ads are usually placed by advertising agencies, while local ads require direct contact with the local businesses. Salespeople often work on a commission basis.

The *programming department* selects and schedules the programs that will be shown. These programs are usually divided into two categories: news and entertainment. There are three types of TV stations, and each has different responsibilities for the programming department. Independent stations must buy and program all of the shows that are aired. "O and O" stations, stations that are owned and operated by the networks, air the network programming available to them. Affiliates are independently owned stations that carry network programming. They may also carry their own programs and purchase syndicated programs from other sources. Generally, affiliates carry a limited number of locally produced shows (usually news programs) and rely most heavily on the networks.

The *production department* creates the locally produced programs and all of the local commercials. It usually has entry-level job opportunities ranging from cue card holders and camera operators to master controllers who insert commercials into programs.

The *engineering department* is responsible for ensuring that all broadcast operations are working. These include the transmitter, antennas, cameras, and other production and broadcasting equipment.

The *traffic department* is in charge of monitoring the production schedule to make sure all advertising sold is aired at the required time. In addition to ensuring that the ads are aired, this department is in charge of the billing operation.

The *promotion department* is in charge of publicizing the station and the programs it carries. Such activities might include on-the-air promos of upcoming shows and advertising on local radio, in newspapers, and on billboards. It also handles special promotional activities such as giveaways and contests.

The *administrative department* handles the business operations of the station and is usually headed by the station manager. Activities range from clerical operations, payroll, and personnel to major management decisions.

A new department that deals with interactive TV programming and web pages on the Internet has also developed in the television industry. The scope and responsibilities of this new division are still being defined.

Fiber Optics

The installation of fiber-optic cable systems has made the expansion of cable television and electronic superhighways possible. Developed by Western Electric, fiber optics is an engineering breakthrough that makes it possible to carry 100,000 phone calls or more than 100 broadcast signals on a flexible glass strand the size of a human hair. The strand consists of tiny glass fibers that are spliced together by an intricate honeycomb crystal device, which holds them in perfect alignment so that no two are more than 1/8,000th of an inch out of line.

Unlike wire transmission lines, fiber optics transmits signals on light beams rather than radio waves. These light beams can even go around corners. The possible uses of fiber optics are limitless.

Satellite Communication

The communication satellite is an electronic relay system that operates from outer space. U.S. communication satellites are placed in orbit some 22,300 miles above the equator so that they will rotate at the same speed the earth does (appearing to be stationary) and look down on the continental United States.

Satellites are either launched into space by rockets or placed in orbit by space shuttles. They carry **transponders** that pick up and retransmit signals sent from the ground. Each transponder can carry one television signal or 1,000 telephone messages at a time. Most satellites have 24 transponders, but in the future satellites are expected to carry up to 40. The more transponders, the more complicated and valuable the satellite becomes.

Prior to satellites, TV signals were sent across the nation by microwave relay stations. In many respects, satellite transmission is much like microwave transmission. Each satellite receives messages on its transponders, amplifies them, and transmits them back to earth. However, instead of manipulating microwave signals over and around mountains and into valleys, the satellite avoids ground interference by providing a direct signal into space and back to earth. Satellites are also capable of sending signals many thousands of miles, thus providing a low-cost, long-distance means of telecommunication.

The advent of satellite television transmission has made it possible for people living in the most remote regions of the nation or world to join the telecommunications age. Both local network television affiliates and cable operators can now get their programming signals from space. The first television network to change from microwave to satellite transmission was the Public Broadcasting Service (PBS) in 1978. NBC converted in 1985, and ABC and CBS began making the switch in 1986. By the 1990s, local television stations had numerous sources of worldwide news available to them by satellite, thus freeing them from dependence on network affiliation.

The latest use of satellites has been in the development of direct broadcast satellites (DBS). Unlike the original satellite systems, which relayed programming primarily to cable systems, broadcast stations, and individuals who could afford large, expensive satellite dishes, DBS is designed to relay TV programming directly to inexpensive home satellite dishes. The system uses a new generation of high-powered satellites to send the television signals to small, pizza-size dishes. Hughes Communications began the first such system, DirecTV, in the United States in 1994. DirecTV delivers 150 channels of programming and is now competing with other DBS companies for customers.

The DBS business got a shot in the arm as the 1990s drew to a close when President Clinton signed an omnibus spending plan approved by Congress. Attached to the bill was the Satellite Television Home Viewers Act, which for the first time enabled companies such as DirecTV and EchoStar Communications to compete with cable television providers on an equal footing by allowing the DBS outlets to also carry local TV stations to subscriber homes. Until then, subscribers paid for the satellite dishes and the service, but also had to have a regular television antenna to receive the local news, sports, weather, and advertising from local stations.[15]

Computers

Computer technology has rapidly altered American culture. Personal computers not only have revolutionized many homes, schools, and businesses but have also

transponders

profoundly affected mass communication and are revolutionizing the way we use our television sets.

In the early days of computer development, television stations, cable companies, and satellite relay systems began using computer technology in their day-to-day operations. Today the merger of computer, telephone, and television technologies, assisted by the development of digital compression, is giving us an entirely new medium: interactive TV. And, of course, the World Wide Web has opened up new areas for promotion and profit for television stations.

Interactive TV

The development of interactive TV will allow viewers to select a wide range of programming from a menu, select instant replays of their choice during football games, play interactive TV games, and even participate in game shows. It holds great promise for home-shopping networks because people will be able to select the types of merchandise they want to see and make purchases instantly.

The variety of services available with interactive TV includes traditional network and cable programming on demand, access to movie libraries, interactive video games, recorded music videos, long-distance video phone service, interactive shopping channels, television archives, libraries and databases, news and information services, financial services, classified ads, and video catalogs. No longer will you have to make space on your bookshelf for the variety of catalogs you will find, from L.L. Bean to JCPenney to Land's End.

Virtual Reality (VR)

Virtual reality (VR) is the latest computer–sensory interfacing that significantly deepens a person's immersion in computer-generated simulation. It began as a way to assist pilots and astronauts with flight training by simulating the experience of flying without leaving the ground. It has since expanded into the entertainment world and someday may be a substitute for television programming.

Our consumer culture is already exploring the prospects of using VR to replace home-shopping channels on TV by simulating shopping trips through department stores and allowing the "traveler" to make purchases by pushing an interactive button.

Holography

Another form of television programming of the future may be the use of three-dimensional images delivered through a process called *holography*. These images will give the illusion of actual objects or persons and can be delivered right into the home. The application of holography to television was suggested to the masses in the 1993 television miniseries *Wild Palms*.

Digital Compression

Digital compression converts the analog signals that were originally used to broadcast video into digital signals. The signals are then compressed so that up to 10 channels can be transmitted on cable space that previously handled only one signal. The technology allows cable companies to deliver many more channels than previously possible and also allows for the transmission of interactive-TV and HDTV signals.

BUSINESS TRENDS

The television industry is the second largest of all the mass media. Advertising revenue for television is second only to that of newspapers and amounts to more than $30 billion a year.[16]

While the major networks have seen a decline in audiences, which translates into a loss of advertising revenue, there was tremendous growth in cable programming during the last decade of the 20th century as TV became entrenched in the specialized stage of the EPS cycle.

Television has been very successful in expanding the American consumer culture into the mass culture by providing new outlets for selling American products. Television delivers audiences to advertisers. The larger an audience watching a show, the more stations and networks can charge for commercials on that show. The average 30-second, prime-time network television announcement costs $100,000. (Spots on a top-rated series generally cost $200,000, although at the height of its popularity in 1996, *Seinfeld* was getting more than $550,000 for each 30-second commercial; low-rated programs averaged about $80,000 per spot.) An estimated 120 million people watch the Super Bowl telecast, for example, and because of this the networks are able to sell 30-second spots on that broadcast for more than $1 million apiece.

As more and more corporations get involved in network television there is always the possibility that business interests will enter into the programming decisions (see Table 12.1). For example, in 1996, Disney Corporation announced it would break from its own tradition to assist the television network it owned, ABC, in the ratings. It had decided to broadcast its highest-grossing animated feature ever, The *Lion King*, during the network's November ratings sweeps. Previously the Disney strategy was to keep its animated movies off the networks, tightly controlling home video sales, and occasionally re-releasing the films to theaters. Prior to 1996, only *Dumbo* and *Alice in Wonderland* had ever had network exposure. It was estimated that Disney might have made up to $20 million if it had sold the movie to another network. But a Disney spokesperson said that because the company owned ABC, it was in its best interest to help the network during the ratings period.

Two years later, Disney again came in for criticism when it opened its new theme park, Animal Kingdom. The event was a valid news story, but the Disney organization drew upon

TABLE 12.1

The Top 25 Television Ownership Groups

This list was prepared by Broadcasting & Cable *magazine in April of 1999. These 25 groups owned or controlled 471 stations—nearly 40 percent of the 1,200 commercial stations on the air in 1999. By the end of that year, the rankings had changed drastically due to the flurry of corporate mergers as the 20th century came to an end.*

Rank	Group	Position Previous Year
1	Fox	(2)
2	CBS	(4)
3	Paxson	(1)
4	Tribune	(3)
5	NBC	(6)
6	ABC	(10)
7	United TV	(11)
8	Gannett	(14)
9	Hearst-Argyle	(13)
10	USA	(5)
11	Sinclair	(9)
12	Paramount	(8)
13	Univision	(7)
14	Belo	(16)
15	Telemundo	(12)
16	Cox	(19)
17	Young	(20)
18	Scripps	(18)
19	Hicks Muse	(17)
20	Shop at Home	(15)
21	Post-Newsweek	(23)
22	Raycom	(21)
23	Meredith	(22)
24	Media General	(25)
25	Clear Channel	(24)

Source: Broadcasting & Cable, April 19, 1999, p. 38.

many of its television properties to promote the event. First, an episode of its Friday night ABC television show *Sabrina, the Teenage Witch* was set in Animal Kingdom. Then the syndicated *Live with Regis and Kathie Lee* program, produced and distributed by Disney subsidiary Buena Vista Television, did two shows from the wildlife park. Then ABC-TV star Drew Carey hosted a one-hour puff piece about the park on ABC's *Wonderful World of Disney*. And to top it off, Disney chairman and CEO Michael Eisner was interviewed on ABC's *Good Morning, America* by hostess Lisa McRee, who referred to him as "my liege" and "the supreme boss," while comparing the Animal Kingdom project to the Bible's Book of Genesis.[17] Anyone watching ABC programming was certainly made aware of Disney's new theme park.

> **@   Practicing Media Literacy**
> Are you concerned that large corporations are using their networks to promote the activities of other corporate divisions?

The trend toward a few conglomerates controlling the television networks, stations, program producers, and cable outlets was started with congressional approval of the 1996 Telecommunications Act, which lifted the restrictions on the number of stations that a company could own. Since it doesn't appear that the action will be reversed, we can look for more mergers of media corporations in the years ahead.

SUMMARY

Originally a novelty, television has become the most important entertainment medium in American culture. Although TV was invented in the 1920s, it didn't enter the popular culture until 1948, following a short period of serving the elite culture. By the 1960s, it was playing a major role in reflecting and shaping the culture.

Television borrowed most of its programming genres from radio. Its early days of programming also featured visual comedy, especially slapstick comedians reflecting the earlier era of vaudeville and burlesque, such as Milton Berle; variety shows, such as Ed Sullivan's *Toast of the Town* and *The Carol Burnett Show*, and shows starring puppets such as Cecil the Seasick Sea Serpent and Howdy Doody. One of the finest forms of TV entertainment in the 1950s was live drama, which presented character studies rather than action–adventure. Quiz shows, Westerns, and prerecorded action–adventure shows followed these early TV programs.

Television entertainment has changed during the past 50 years to reflect the ever-changing culture. Sitcoms, talk shows, and made-for-TV movies now deal with controversial and socially relevant topics. New ground in commercial television was broken in the 1990s with *NYPD Blue*, a realistic police action–adventure show, which sparked controversy because it included nudity and profanity.

Television's impact on our culture has been staggering. Ninety-eight percent of American homes have at least one TV set. TV has become one of the most powerful socializing agents in our culture. Many children spend more hours watching TV than they spend in school. The average American home has the TV set on nearly seven hours a day. Despite the widespread acceptance of television into our culture, however, it remains a controversial enterprise.

By the 1980s, television had entered the specialization stage of the EPS cycle. Public broadcasting was providing noncommercial programming for the high or elite culture, while cable and satellite channels offered a large variety of specialized programs to meet particular interests. And, perhaps inevitably, television, which from the beginning had been a vehicle to deliver large audiences to advertisers, now offers home-shopping channels that run nothing but ads 24 hours a day.

Television is currently undergoing major changes with a wide variety of technological developments, including advances in cable television; fiber optics; satellite communication; digital compression; and the merger of television, computer, and telephone technologies. Interactive TV, virtual reality, and holography may be new forms of television entertainment in store for us.

Business trends in television have built this relatively new mass-communication medium into the second-largest generator of advertising revenue, with more than $30 billion spent each year on commercials.

Find a review of *Key People and Concepts,* a message board for *Practicing Media Literacy* questions, self tests, and more at: www.mhhe.com/wilson.

Thought Questions

1. Why do you think television became such a pervasive mass-communication medium in our culture? Why did it catch on in the popular culture so rapidly?

2. What are the implications of television shows such as *NYPD Blue?* Does an increase in nudity and profanity during prime time degrade our culture or merely reflect reality?

3. Does television news shape as well as reflect our popular culture? If so, what are some current examples of this phenomenon? If not, give some examples to refute this argument.

4. Is television becoming too violent in its content? Do warning labels help or hurt?

5. What do you think our culture will be like when interactive-TV, digital compression, high-definition television, and other new technologies find their niche?

Notes

1. Nick Wingfield, "America OnLine Plans Campaign to See Interactive TV to Masses," *Wall Street Journal,* January 21, 2000, p. B6.

2. James H. Myers and William H. Reynolds, *Consumer Behavior and Marketing Management* (Boston: Houghton Mifflin, 1967), p. 239.

3. Leah Garchik, "Where the Watching Is Good," *San Francisco Chronicle,* April 23, 1997, p. D8.

4. Howard Rosenberg, "Rosie Upsets a Plugmeister's Paradise," *Los Angeles Times,* reprinted in the *Fresno Bee,* May 25, 1999, p. E4.

5. "Law Enforcement Pleads for 'Wanted'," *San Francisco Chronicle,* September 9, 1996, p. E3.

6. Peter Johnson, "'Wanted' Again," *USA Today,* September 25, 1996, p. 3D.

7. "By the Numbers," *Broadcasting,* July 29, 1996, p. 75.

8. *International Television Almanac,* 35th ed. (New York: Quigley Publishing, 1990), p. 26-A.

9. Ibid.

10. Ibid.

11. *Network,* Paddy Chayefsky, MGM, 1976.

12. B. A. Krier, "Practitioners of the Art of Zen TV Watching," *Los Angeles Times,* June 6, 1982, pp. 1, 14.

13. *International Television Almanac,* 35th ed. (New York: Quigley Publishing, 1990) p. 26 A.

14. Rob Pegoraro, "High-Definition Television Faces a Fuzzy Future," *Washington Post*, January 7, 2000, p. E10.

15. Jeri Clausing, "Satellite TV Industry Shoots for the Moon," *New York Times*, News Service.

16. *Standard & Poor's Industry Surveys*, March 14, 1996, p. M2.

17. "Cheers and Jeers," *TV Guide*, May 9, 1998, p. 13.

4

Media Shapers, Ethics, and Consequences

Advertising

Selling the Message

You can tell the ideals of a nation by its advertisements.

—**Norman Douglas,** *South Wind*

When the U.S. Women's Soccer Team won the World Cup in the summer of 1999, the story made the front page of sports sections across the nation and around the world. It also made the front page of many business sections. Immediately following the victory, there was a downpour of marketing interest in the team, as advertisers began seeking team members to endorse their products. ● Representatives of Wheaties began negotiations to feature the team's picture on the breakfast cereal box. The Walt Disney organization was ready to tape its commercials immediately following the game, and it wasn't very long before television viewers were seeing the ads with the team members shouting "We're going to Disneyland" and "We're going to Disney World." ● But one thing that drew a lot of media attention was the action of team member Brandi Chastain, who—following her match-winning kick—spontaneously pulled off her jersey and exposed her sports bra. It was a Nike bra. The speculation began that it was a publicity stunt for Nike. The 30-year-old Chastain said it was just a moment of "temporary insanity." A spokesman for Nike insisted that it was not a scripted moment to gain publicity for the Nike sports bra. A few weeks later, the new Nike Inner Actives sports bra, as worn by Brandi Chastain, went on sale for $40. ● Whether it was planned or not, Nike immediately began looking for ways to capitalize on the picture seen by millions around the world. The company began using a photo of Chastain in her sports bra for displays in stores and considered having her make extra personal appearances to promote the product. The picture of Chastain drew a large cheer at a rally staged by Nike in midtown Manhattan. *Sports Illustrated* used a shot of her kneeling on the field in celebration for its cover. Newspaper columnists wrote numerous articles questioning whether Chastain's action was a publicity stunt, mentioning Nike in every story. Nike was getting more publicity from that one act than it could possibly have imagined.   •   But as is often the case with celebrity endorsements, they last only as long as the fame of the celebrity. By the start of the year 2000, Wheaties had moved on to other sports, Disney was getting ready to tape the Super Bowl victory celebrations for its ads, and the U.S. Women's Soccer Team was out of the limelight. In a highly competitive world with all kinds of media outlets available to carry advertising messages, agencies must find unique ways to get those messages across. With the media competing for those advertising dollars that are the driving force of their operations, advertisers want to be sure they have the right celebrities for their products.   •   Advertising is a message business on the cutting edge of change in our culture. It not only reflects that change but is usually in position to take advantage of change. The industry's impact on our society is enormous. For example, by the time a person reaches age 21 in the United States he or she has been exposed to between 1 million and 2 million advertising messages, all of them designed to socialize and sell the consumer.[1]   •   The average American adult is exposed to approximately 500 advertisements each day. Advertising helps us determine our social identity, defines our gender roles, and shapes our attitudes on health, success, and lifestyles. It influences our choice to wear Reebok running shoes, brush our teeth with Crest, and feed our cats Fancy Feast. We are taught not so much by logic and dialogue as by advertising images. These images are used to sell the American popular culture both here and abroad. Images are used to create a desire for the products.   •   Obviously, advertising is an important element of our culture because it reflects and attempts to change our lifestyles. New cultural trends and fashions are first transmitted to the mass culture through advertisements. Advertising also plays an important role in shaping the kinds of mass media that predominate in our culture. Advertisers pay the mass media to disseminate their messages, and without advertising, newspapers, magazines, radio, television, and even the Internet would be far different from what they are. We would not have the number or variety of media and programming, and the cost to the consumer to access these media would be much higher. In this chapter, we'll present the evolution of advertising that has led to its role today as the foundation of almost all mass media in this country.

HOW ADVERTISING DEVELOPED

Mass advertising as we know it today began in the 19th century and developed with industrialization and mass production. It became the vehicle to sell mass consumption in our new, consumer-oriented society.

Early Advertising

barkers

The concept of advertising, however, dates back to early civilization. In 3000 B.C., Babylonian merchants hired **barkers** to hawk their wares to prospective customers and placed signs over their doorways to indicate what they sold. This practice continued in ancient Greece and Rome: advertisements were found on walls in the streets of the excavated Roman city of Pompeii. The use of handbills, posters, and newspaper advertisements emerged after Gutenberg developed movable type in the 15th century.

When Benjamin Franklin established the *Philadelphia Gazette* in 1729, it soon became a favorite medium for advertisers. When the weekly *Pennsylvania Packet and General Advertiser* became a daily in 1784, it featured an entire front page of advertisements for such things as dry goods, food, wine, and tobacco products. When the United States developed into an industrial nation in the 19th century and American newspapers and magazines entered the popular culture, advertising in print media expanded.

The First Ad Agency

Credit for organizing the first advertising agency goes to Volney Palmer, who started an

When the U.S. Women's Soccer Team won The World Cup in 1999, team member Brandi Chastain pulled off her jersey in celebration. The action, in which the Nike sports bra she was wearing, was seen by millions of TV viewers around the world. The sale of sports bras increased.

agency in Philadelphia in 1841. On his heels in this new business was another pioneer, John Hooper. Both these entrepreneurs perceived a need for someone to help publishers sell space to advertisers. (This new industry developed just four years after William Procter and James Gamble joined forces to make soap and candles. Today their company, Procter & Gamble (P&G), is one of the biggest advertisers in the world. In the 43 years between 1955 and 1997, P&G was the top advertising spender 31 years; General Motors was on top 9 years, and the Philip Morris Companies topped the list three times.)[2] Since they represented publishers rather than advertisers, these early agencies worked quite differently from the way agencies do today. By the 1870s, however, N. W. Ayer, the nation's oldest ad agency operating today, began representing advertisers, helping them get the best results for their advertising dollars. Using diversified advertising outlets, from newspapers to radio and television to cable TV and magazines, is the way all agencies operate today (see Table 13.1).

Expanding advertising from newspapers to magazines was the brainchild of a young ad man named J. Walter Thompson, who at the turn of the century saw the potential of literary magazines for advertising. He put together the so-called List of Thirty important women's and general-interest magazines that would be the best vehicles for advertisers. The list included *Harper's*, *Ladies' Home Journal*, and *Cosmopolitan*.[3]

Government Regulations

A lot of early advertising was deceptive and exaggerated. This was the era of patent medicines that claimed to cure everything from cancer to baldness. These heavily

TABLE 13.1

Where Advertisers Directed Their Media Spending at the End of the 20th Century

	Rank	Total Measured Ad Spending*
1.	Network TV	$16,272
2.	Newspapers	16,131
3.	Spot TV	15,487
4.	Magazines	13,780
5.	Cable TV networks	6,672
6.	Syndicated TV	2,692
7.	National newspapers	2,658
8.	National spot radio	2,040
9.	Outdoor	1,727
10.	Sunday magazine	1,029
11.	Network radio	824

*Dollars are in millions.
Source: "Competitive Media Reporting," *Advertising Age,* July 12, 1999, p. S1.

Advertising has been around for centuries. The use of women in advertising has been around for almost as long.

truth-in-advertising

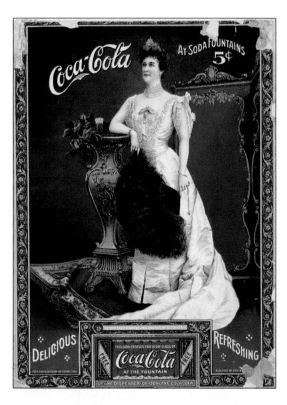

advertised products sold to millions but cured very few. Some of the potions gave relief because their high alcohol content deadened pain; some even contained pain-relieving cocaine and morphine. In 1906 Congress passed the Pure Food and Drug Act to control such advertising, and in 1913 the Federal Trade Commission (FTC) was formed to regulate untruthful claims in advertising. Some states adopted **"truth-in-advertising"** laws, and advertising organizations drew up codes of behavior. Today a number of federal agencies enforce truth in advertising, including the FTC, the Federal Communications Commission (FCC), the Food and Drug Administration (FDA), and the U.S. Postal Service.

@   Practicing Media Literacy

Knowing that there are federal agencies enforcing truth in advertising, do you believe what you see in today's television commericals?

Electronic Advertising

Although radio first began to function as a mass-communication medium in 1920, it was not until 1922 that station WEAF in New York began selling airtime to advertisers—$100 for 10 minutes. When network broadcasting entered the picture in 1926–1927 with the formation of NBC and CBS, the new medium's potential to carry advertisements was fully realized. Ad agencies began producing programs for advertisers. The ad business had become show business. A New York ad agency, Blackett-Sample-Hummert, developed a new type of daytime drama for Procter & Gamble's soap products. The daily serial became known as the soap opera.

Although the first television commercial was aired by the J. Walter Thompson agency (jwtworld.com) in 1930, TV's potential as an advertising medium wasn't realized until 1948. Many early programs carried the advertiser's name, such as Milton Berle's popular *Texaco Star Theater*, the *Camel News Caravan*, and the *Hallmark Hall of Fame* (which is still on the air today), because there was only one sponsor for the entire program. Soon television became the preferred advertising medium to reach the masses in the United States.

In the 1980s, with the development of cable and satellite TV, a new form of electronic advertising developed: direct-response home shopping services. These cable networks (HSN, QVC, etc.) sell discounted goods directly to consumers, who telephone in their orders to banks of operators. Instead of purchasing airtime from cable operators, home-shopping networks pay cable operators a percentage of the profits from sales generated in their viewing area. This form of **direct selling** is expected to

direct selling

take on new dimensions when interactive-TV and virtual-reality technologies find their niche in the marketplace (see Chapter 12).

The rapidly expanding world of computers during the 1990s also introduced a new arena for advertising: the World Wide Web (see Box 13.1). The final decade of the 20th century saw this new form of media communication turn advertising and marketing concepts upside down. Wrote Randall Rothenberg in *Advertising Age*:

> A mere eight decades after Claude Hopkins prematurely assured that advertising was a science, the Internet at last promises precise accountability. But it also destroys the hegemony of broadcast networks and other communications oligopolies that could reliably deliver mass audiences. . . . The boundary-blurring Internet has placed renewed emphasis on the importance of brands, now deemed the only forces powerful enough to draw the audience's eye and income through the chaos off the World Wide Web. That's why, only three years after its founding, Amazon.com is considered to have such a powerful marque that the market has valued it at close to $29 billion.[4]

One major U.S. cereal company began dabbling in this new technology when Kellogg Company launched what was described as the world's largest test of interactive television advertising. It ran commercials in London for Frosties cereal that allowed viewers to electronically surf along with Tony the Tiger. The fast-paced commercial encouraged viewers to use their remote controls to regulate the sequence of events. By touching one of the four color-coded buttons on the remote, a viewer could control such things as which way to turn the surfboard, what type of wave to ride, and so on. In all, the 90-second commercial offered almost 850 sequence combinations to choose from. The spots ran on Videotron's Interactive TV Channel in the United Kingdom, which featured interactive programming for children between 5:00 and 9:30 P.M. each weekday and between 10:00 a.m. and 4:00 P.M. on weekends.

THEORIES ON ADVERTISING EFFECTIVENESS

Despite the dominant role advertising plays in our society, people disagree as to whether advertising is as effective as it is thought to be. There seems to be universal agreement that certain types of price advertising (such as supermarket ads in the local newspaper and home-shopping networks) are effective in generating sales. However, when it comes to national advertising of consumer product images (most ads we see on television and in magazines), the agreement stops.

Minimal-Effects Theory

While some believe advertising makes our mass production–consumption culture possible, others contend that advertising has almost no effect on consumer buying habits.

The effectiveness of television advertising in particular has come under close scrutiny in recent years. Advertising researchers have found that while people may have a television on in their homes much of the time, they pay far less attention to it than previously believed. A study conducted by Gerard Tellis, a University of Iowa professor, found that an examination of products purchased by a study group of 250 people showed very little correlation with the advertisements they saw on television. A greater correlation was found between lower prices and the availability of coupons.[5]

Earlier research by sociologist Michael Schudson led him to conclude that, contrary to the common belief that advertising brings an increase in sales, the reverse is true: An increase in sales leads to increases in advertising.[6] This theory was supported

Box 13.1

MEDIA LITERACY
Advertisers Use the Web to Reach Consumers

Early media coverage of the Internet seemed charmed by the notion of a "geek network" visited by few. Four years later, the media appetite for anything "dot com" was insatiable: online mergers, stock IPOs, cyber-stalkers, and e-fortunes are all part of the coverage, and the public can't seem to get enough. "The Internet sells better than sex or crime," says John Huey, managing editor of *Fortune* magazine.*

Perhaps the most important development in Internet commerce is that the web is now selling itself . . . off-line. While the number of new persons online has been said to double every hundred days, web storefronts and portal sites are scrambling for name recognition and branding in the traditional media. Internet upstarts are spending billions of dollars on billboard advertising (in key markets), television, print, and even radio. According to the Radio Advertising Bureau, 1999 ad revenues from web companies alone were expected to triple the 1998 figures.** Super Bowl telecasts are now partially measured in the media by the percentage of "dot com" advertising sold.

Meanwhile, the web remains a buyers' market for advertising. Banner advertising is usually sold on a model of cost per thousand impressions, and volume advertising blocks are still generally considered a bargain for advertisers. A more costly but generally effective method is a pay-for-performance model, where the advertiser pays for generated leads or unique visitors derived from banner clicks. Much of today's web advertising purchases are based on a combination of both

models. The web's capacity for near instantaneous feedback on an ad campaign can produce joy or ulcers for purchasers, however, and many companies still struggle with the issue of how to effectively translate a successful traditional media campaign to the web. Many "brick and mortar" companies less likely to sell product online have not seen the potential of online "branding," or helping to build brand awareness, rather than attempting direct sales online.

Finally, Internet companies are finding new and inventive ways to get consumers to view more advertising. One company gave away free Compaq PCs with Internet access in exchange for an agreement from the recipient to view targeted advertising while browsing the web at least 10 hours per month for three years. Several companies built specially designed browsers that fed advertising, then gave away free Internet access with the additional advertising built in to cover costs. And more and more companies are paying web surfers to view ads and to refer others to enroll and do the same. It is yet to be determined how effective this form of direct advertising will be, considering that persons wishing to be paid to view ads may not be the most desirable consumer demographic for advertisers.

*Howard Kurtz, "All Aboard the E-Train," *Washington Post*, October 21, 1999, p. C1.
**Suein L. Hwang, "Old Media Get a Web Windfall," *Wall Street Journal*, September 17, 1999, p. B1.

---

by a study conducted by Richard Schmalensee, who found a closer correlation between consumption in a given quarter and advertising in the next quarter than between consumption in the given quarter and advertising in the previous quarter.[7]

Schudson cited numerous examples to support his contention that advertising doesn't automatically increase sales. He noted that heavy advertising by Ford Motor Company to promote the **Edsel** resulted in failure. The Edsel appeared on the market in 1957 as the most heavily promoted consumer product in history. The company expected to sell 200,000 cars the first year, but when it took the product off the market two years later, only 109,000 had been sold. The car was ugly, and no amount of advertising was able to get people to buy it. Conversely, he noted that Hershey Foods Corporation has been a chocolate industry leader since the turn of the century, even though it didn't start advertising until 1970. Schudson also noted that the two largest-selling products in the American popular culture, marijuana and cocaine, are never advertised.[8]

Edsel

In his comprehensive history of American advertising, *The Mirror Makers*, Stephen Fox supports the idea that, despite increased advertising expenditures, the industry's influence has declined during the 20th century:

> From its peak as an independent force in American life in the 1920s, advertising has been caught in a tightening vise between two contrary forces. Regulation by the government and (finally) by the industry itself has gradually limited Madison Avenue's freedom to lie. When restricted, more or less, to the truth, advertising lost some of its most powerful, frightening devices. Yet even as advertising grew less deceptive, the public grew ever more sophisticated and skeptical.[9]

Cutting-Edge Theory

Advertising's role in influencing our attitudes, lifestyles, and culture is beyond dispute. The advertising industry is often on the cutting edge of new cultural developments and trends in our society (see Box 13.2).

For example, when cigarette smoking by women started to become fashionable and suggestive of naughtiness during the Jazz Age of the 1920s, the advertising industry was there to reflect the new trend. One of the first smoking ads directed toward women was for Chesterfield cigarettes in 1926. It showed a romantic couple at night, with the man smoking and the woman sitting next to him. The caption read, "Blow Some My Way." When the women's liberation movement first got rolling in the second half of this century, ads began to depict women in previously stereotypically male roles. Often these women were smoking a "women's cigarette," such as Virginia Slims. When jogging, aerobic exercise, and tennis became popular recreational activities in the 1980s, magazines spent heavy sums on advertisements for fashionable clothing for these activities.

Another trend in advertising was the use of ethnically diverse models. Instead of exclusively featuring blond, Caucasian male and female models, as had been the case for decades, a variety of ads began appearing in magazines, newspapers, and on television featuring African-Americans, Asians, and Hispanics. One of the first advertisers to embrace the "rainbow look" was the Italian knitwear maker Benetton, which launched its "United Colors of Benetton" ad campaign featuring youth of diverse nationalities standing arm in arm. The advertising industry was again on the cutting edge, reflecting our ethnically diverse culture.

Although some critics blame advertising for creating new cultural trends to sell more goods and services, others argue that the message industry merely reflects cultural changes. One advertiser that does not fit that mold is the aforementioned Benetton,

Cutting edge advertising reflecting an ethnically diverse culture is exemplified by the "United Colors of Benetton" campaign.

Box 13.2
MEDIA WATCH
The World of Advertising: Finding New Media for the Message

As people escaped from commercial television by renting videos, many were surprised, if not outraged, to find that advertisements preceded many of the movies. The advertising industry does not miss a trick in finding ways to bring advertisements to audiences. So it is no surprise that by the end of the 20th century, advertising was keeping pace with the information-age explosion of new media technologies.

Electronic Newsstand, an online computer information subscription service on the Internet, began adding advertisements to its service in 1994. Called "business information," subscribers could access the service for more information about the businesses being featured. Since then, advertisers have been placing their ads on websites all over the Internet. Browsers of the World Wide Web were only a click away from the merchants seeking their business.

In 1993, the Japanese advertising agency Dentsu introduced Japan's first advertisement video game, called "Wonder Kitchen," to promote Ajinomoto mayonnaise. In 1994, the agency began developing interactive games for the new Matsushita REAL 3DO interactive multiplayer. The Japanese weren't the only ones getting into video game advertising. Launched for the 1993 Christmas season were two games featuring Ronald McDonald and Chester Cheetah. "McDonald's Treasure Island Adventure" was a successful advertising tool for McDonald's Corporation, while Frito-Lay's Chester Cheetah sold "Chester Looks for Hip City USA."

Other companies expanding into the video game advertising business by the mid-1990s included PepsiCo and Ford Motor Company. Other video games, such as Mortal Kombat, have tried advertising as part of their content. This game featured a 10-second video commercial for a limited-edition "Mortal Kombat" comic book. The ad generated tremendous response.

The trend of advertising in video games prompted the leading advertising industry publication, *Advertising Age*, to begin sponsoring an Interactive Advertising Awards Program.

@ **Practicing Media Literacy**

Do you think advertising is a cultural trendsetter or is it just following the trends that already exist?

---

which came in for criticism in early 2000 when it launched a year-long $20 million global campaign that provided a sympathetic portrayal of American murderers on death row awaiting execution. Explained Mark Major, Benetton's director of communications, "Once again, it's hard for people to see what we're doing and understand that it's not advertising . . . it's a way to get people to think." However, *Advertising Age* columnist Bob Garfield said he was repulsed by the campaign, saying "There is no brand—not a single one—that has the right to increase sales on the backs, on the misery, on the fates of condemned men and women, much less their slaughtered victims." The Benetton ads first started appearing in such magazines as *Rolling Stone, Vanity Fair,* and the *New Yorker.* Billboards and posters for the campaign also began appearing around the United States, in some cases not far from the communities where the inmates were imprisoned or where they had committed the murders.[10]

A-T-R Model

Getting a person to buy a product involves far more than simply running an ad in a newspaper or a commercial on television. To best describe the complexities of advertising, we will use the A-T-R model, which shows that there are three main stages in the selling process: awareness, trial, and reinforcement.

Awareness is the easiest step. Through repetition and other advertising techniques, consumers are made aware that a product exists. Usually the bigger the advertising campaign, the more awareness generated.

Trial, the second step, is much more difficult to induce. Merely advertising a product will not necessarily make someone try it. As a result, many companies use other techniques to get people to try the product, including sending free samples through the mail or giving them out in stores, giving away discount coupons, and offering price reductions.

Reinforcement is the necessary third step to get users to buy the product again. Studies have shown that after people try a new brand, they usually go back to their regular brand unless they are constantly reminded about the new brand by effective advertising. Of course, the new brand must be at least comparable in quality to the old brand. If the product does not please the customer, he or she will probably never purchase it again.

Thus, according to the A-T-R theory, increasing the advertising budget after a product is established will not necessarily increase new sales. However, cutting the budget will likely reduce repeat sales because some reinforcement will be lost (see Table 13.2).

Consumers' Information Environment

Advertising is not the only factor in our decision to make a purchase. As Schudson points out, the average adult consumer brings a lifetime of informational resources to any new advertisement. These resources, which Schudson calls the consumer's *informational environment,* include the following:

1. The consumer's own information from personal experience with the product or related products.
2. Word-of-mouth information about the product or related products from family, friends, or acquaintances.
3. Information in the media about the product or related products that is not paid advertising. Some of this information will be planted by the public relations efforts of commercial companies; some will be independently generated by government reports, consumer groups, journalists, and other noncommercial agencies.
4. Information available through formal channels of consumer education, especially the school system, credit institutions, and other agencies.
5. Advertisements for rival products and advertisements for unrelated products—the "clutter" of advertising in general.
6. Skepticism concerning the credibility of the medium in which the ad is placed.
7. Skepticism concerning the credibility of advertising in general.

TABLE 13.2

Top 10 National Companies by Ad Spending

Rank	Advertiser	Total U.S. spending*
1	General Motors Company	$2,125.5
2	Procter & Gamble Company	1,725.0
3	Daimler Chrysler	1,411.1
4	Philip Morris Companies	1,264.4
5	Ford Motor Company	1,066.4
6	Time Warner	830.6
7	Walt Disney Company	809.7
8	Sears, Roebuck & Co.	721.7
9	Unilever	691.2
10	Diageo	670.6

*In millions of dollars.
Source: *Advertising Age,* July 12, 1999, p. S1.

8. Information from nonadvertising channels of marketing.

9. Price. This is a special case, and an especially important one, of a nonadvertising channel of marketing.[11]

Selective Perception

Another factor in determining an advertisement's effectiveness is *selective perception* (see Chapter 1). Advertisers may bombard consumers with television and magazine advertising, sales–promotion discounts and premiums, point-of-purchase displays, and other promotional devices only to find little change in sales figures. Follow-up research will often show that the promotional activities never got through consumers' perceptual filters.[12] In other words, if the public is convinced the product is worthless, no amount of advertising will change that perception.

Thus, it is important to remember that even though a great deal of money is spent on advertising, the success or failure of ads to persuade us to buy things is far more complex than one might believe.

PROPAGANDA DEVICES

Although the industry might frown on a discussion of propaganda techniques in a chapter on advertising, there is an important relationship between the two. Webster's dictionary defines *propaganda* as "a systematic effort to promote a particular cause or point of view."

Thus, by definition, propaganda is not evil or deceptive. However, ever since the British used propaganda to solicit U.S. support for the Allies' war effort against Germany in World War I, the word has taken on undesirable connotations. But even though the goals of propaganda may not be evil, some of the techniques used are questionable because they appeal primarily to our emotions rather than to our intellect.

Propaganda was probably used most destructively in the 1930s, when Adolf Hitler used it to take control of Germany and neighboring lands. One of Hitler's first acts when he came to power was to name Joseph Goebbels minister of propaganda. Goebbels immediately took over the German mass media and turned them into propaganda outlets that endorsed Hitler and his reign of terror. While Hitler waged his propaganda campaign, the rest of the world sat back and watched. Yet years earlier, in his 1925 book, *Mein Kampf,* which he wrote in prison, Hitler had spelled out the importance of propaganda and how he planned to use it:

> The great masses' receptive ability is only very limited, their understanding is small, but their forgetfulness is great. As a consequence of these facts, all effective propaganda has to limit itself only to a very few points and to use them like slogans until even the very last man is able to imagine what is intended by such a word. As soon as one sacrifices this basic principle and tries to become versatile, the effect will fritter away, as the masses are neither able to digest the material offered nor to retain it. Thus the result is weakened and finally eliminated.[13]

If this philosophy sounds as though it is alive and well in American advertising today, it is because propaganda techniques are still very much in use. But fortunately the American advertising industry aims only to sell us consumer goods and political candidates, not the bigotry and totalitarianism of Adolf Hitler.

Propaganda is a daily feature of our popular culture. It is a prime ingredient in political rhetoric and is used extensively in advertising campaigns. For these reasons, it is important for all of us to be familiar with the basic propaganda devices so that we can detect them, ward off their emotional appeal, and analyze the messages intellectually. Following are some of the more common forms of propaganda devices used today.

Slogans ✓

The slogan is equally effective in advertising and political campaigns. In the latter, it usually takes the form of a chant that can unite large crowds into one common emotion. An example of a political slogan is "Four More Years," chanted by delegates to the 1996 Democratic National Convention. Product slogans include Nike's "Just Do It," "Always Coca-Cola," "It's Miller Time," The U.S. Army's "Be All That You Can Be," and Hallmark's "When You Care Enough to Send the Very Best."

> **@ Practicing Media Literacy**
> What do you think of when someone uses the term "Must See TV?" Would you say that was an effective slogan?

Name Calling

Name calling is a device used widely in political and ideological battles as well as in commercial advertising campaigns. It tries to make us form a judgment without examining the evidence on which it should be based. Propagandists appeal to our instincts of hate and fear. They do this by giving bad names to those individuals, groups, nations, races, or consumer products that they would like us to condemn or reject. Such names as *Communist, capitalist, imperialist, pervert,* and *egghead* are just a few that have been used to discredit the opposition.

Not all name calling is so blatant. Often it can work by inference or association. Presidential candidate Al Smith once used indirect name calling against President Franklin D. Roosevelt by stating, "There can be only one capital, Washington or Moscow." He was indirectly calling the incumbent president a Communist.

Most name calling in advertising uses this indirect approach: "Our painkiller doesn't give you an upset stomach"—implying, of course, that the competition does. Some advertisers actually name a competing brand and charge it with being inferior.

Glittering Generalities

Glittering generalities are broad, widely accepted ideals and virtuous words that are used to sell a point of view. Like name calling, glittering generalities urge us to accept and approve something without examination. Many ads declare the product to be "the best," or "the greatest," or "preferred by more people." Such expressions as "the American way," "it's in the public interest," and "taste America's favorite bran flake cereal" are examples. Words such as *America, truth, freedom, honor, liberty, justice, loyalty, progress, democracy,* and *America's favorite* are all common glittering generalities.

Transfer

Some advertisements use symbols of authority, prestige, and respect that arouse emotions to sell a cause, a candidate, or a consumer product through the process of subconscious transfer or association. Typical examples are a political candidate photographed next to the American flag ("She's a good American") and a cigarette smoker relaxing by a peaceful lake ("Enjoy the natural taste of this brand of cigarette and you too will feel healthy and calm").

Many ads for automobiles feature a physically attractive person in the passenger seat or at the wheel. The point, of course, is to transfer the sexuality of the person to

Advertising is used not only to sell products, but also to sell ideas. Newspapers, magazines, radio, television, and outdoor advertising have been used in the campaign against drug abuse.

the brand of vehicle. Designer jeans and perfume ads are also effective in transferring sexuality to their products.

And who can forget the cough syrup television commercial in which a soap opera actor established his authority as an official spokesperson for the product by looking directly into the camera and declaring "I'm not a doctor, but I play one on TV?"

Testimonial

A testimonial is an endorsement of a product or an individual by celebrities or other well-respected persons. When a movie star endorses a particular savings and loan institution, for example, thousands of people may invest there solely on the rationale that if it is good enough for their idol, it's good enough for them (see Box 13.3). How many sports fans have selected a certain brand of athletic shoe, shaving cream, or deodorant because their favorite professional athlete has endorsed it?

Plain Folks

The plain-folks device creates the impression that the advertisers or political candidates are just ordinary folks like you and me. In every presidential election, we see candidates doing things such as visiting a coal mine wearing hard hats. They don't actually go down into the coal mine, so obviously they don't wear the hard hats for protection. Instead, the hats are used to give the impression that they are just ordinary folks like the rest of the workers. Similarly, many laundry detergent ads show "ordinary housewives" rather than attractive models promoting the product.

Card Stacking

Card stacking is the technique by which facts, illustrations, and statements are carefully selected to make the maximum impact and sometimes give misleading

Box 13.3

MEDIA LITERACY

Celebrity Endorsements Can Mean a Lot for Advertisers

S ports fans were saddened when Michael Jordan announced that he was retiring from professional basketball after 13 years, but many advertisers were even more sad. They were concerned that once out of the limelight, his value to them in endorsing their products would also decline.

At the time of his departure from the National Basketball Association, Jordan was receiving between $42 million and $47 million a year in endorsement deals with such companies as MCI WorldCom phone service, Hanes underwear, Gatorade, and Nike. In fact, his contract with Nike runs until 2020. Jordan's fame and popularity was strong enough that his commercial work continued for years after his retirement.

No matter what the product might be, the message can be stronger with a celebrity endorsement. And the person being paid for the endorsement may not be just a sports celebrity or a movie star. Politicians have been used (former Kansas senator and 1996 Republican presidential candidate Robert Dole appeared in a commercial for Viagra) as was a world leader (Pizza Hut reportedly paid close to $1 million to have former Soviet Union president Mikhail Gorbachev appear in its TV commercial). Sometimes the commercial will feature someone who's been dead for years (the image of John Wayne has been digitally inserted into commercials for beer, dancer Fred Astaire was featured long after his death in commercials for the Dustbuster, and TV variety show host Ed Sullivan was used in a commercial for Mercedes-Benz).

Sometimes the endorsements are accidental, but still get results. Following the acquittal of former football star O. J. Simpson in a double murder trial, some items prominently mentioned during the court proceedings (Ford Broncos, Isotoner gloves, and Bruno Magli Italian shoes) reported increases in sales.

The person giving the endorsement of a product may not even be a real person. By the start of the year 2000, Procter & Gamble had brought back its most famous spokesperson, who had been featured in more than 500 commercials between 1964 and 1985. Grocer George Whipple was again warning people not to "squeeze the Charmin." The first campaign had been so successful, a 1978 poll named the fictional Mr. Whipple the third most-recognized figure in the United

One of the most successful athletes of the 20th century— including the area of celebrity endorsements—has been NBA star Michael Jordan.

States, behind only former President Richard Nixon and the Reverend Billy Graham.

Nixon himself was featured in a commercial at the turn of this century, which caused some problems for the manufacturers of Tracfone prepaid cellular service. The agency handling the account received a sternly worded message from the White House which pointed out a "longstanding policy" which prohibited the use of the name of the president, his likeness, his words, or his activities in any advertising commercial or promotion. The agency was asked to refrain from airing its ad, which opened with Nixon, in the thick of the Watergate investigation, assuring the American people "I am not a crook." This was followed by a clip of former President George Bush proclaiming "Read my lips . . . no new taxes!" And then, the clip that troubled the White House, showed President Bill Clinton uttering his famous denial, "I did not have sexual relations with that woman—Miss Lewinsky." The commercial then displayed the Tracfone logo with the message, "Talk is Cheap."*

*Bob Garfield, "Talk May Be Cheap, but Satire Is Priceless," *Advertising Age*, February 8, 1999, p. 77.

impressions. The cliché that "statistics don't lie, but you can lie with statistics" applies to this technique. For example, a politician may tell his constituents that he votes only for bills that help his district, while neglecting to mention that when special-interest groups have opposed such a bill, he has ducked the issue by not showing up for the vote.

An advertisement claiming that "Four out of five dentists surveyed recommend Chewy chewing gum" may certainly be true, but it may also omit the fact that only five dentists were contacted and four of them were paid to give an anonymous endorsement.

Bandwagon

The bandwagon device is based on the idea that "if everybody else is doing it, so should you." "Jump on the bandwagon," "follow the crowd," "be the first in your neighborhood," and "don't throw your vote away by voting for a loser" are clichés associated with this device. The psychology behind this technique makes political polling important at election time. The fact that each candidate needs to project the image that he or she is a winner often leads to some conflicting polling results. (Pollsters can skew their results by carefully selecting their samples or using loaded wording in their questions.) Advertisements telling you to join the Pepsi Generation ("Generation X") or to have a good time with the crowd when it's "Miller time" are examples of bandwagon appeal.

Sex Appeal

We don't ordinarily think of sex as a propaganda device, but it sells products in many ways. In recent years, emotional appeals based on sex have been used more and more in product advertising. How about beer commercials or the after-shave lotion ad that features a sexy female voice crooning, "My men wear English Leather or they wear nothing at all?" Or the billboard for Canadian Black Velvet whiskey showing a sexy blonde in a black velvet dress with the words "Feel the Velvet Canadian?" And don't forget the Calvin Klein ads that feature partially clad and sometimes nude men and women. When it comes to beer commercials, many people believe that you can only drink the product while playing volleyball on the beach with beautiful, bikini-clad women. Sex appeal is used to stimulate emotions and sell consumer products to both sexes.

Music

The last device in our list is also seldom thought of as a propaganda device, yet it is one of the most effective techniques in radio and television commercials. Music is an excellent tool for creating specific moods, and it can be used effectively for product identification. Often people will think of a certain product when they hear a tune that has been associated with the product in ads. In past years, songs used in commercials have gone on to become popular songs on the radio and in record sales (e.g., Coca-Cola's "I'd Like to Teach the World to Sing"), and popular songs have been used in commercials (e.g., the Beatles' "Revolution," used in Nike commercials). Other songs have been catchy enough to just run through your mind ("Give Me a Break, Give Me a Break, Break Me Off a Piece of That Kit Kat Bar").

 Practicing Media Literacy

Have you ever been doing something when you suddenly realize your mind is repeating some commercial jingle, even one you don't particularly like? Does that mean the advertising campaign was successful?

In politics, music is used to stir the crowds, and the president of the United States uses it effectively to generate a mood of respect when making a grand entrance to the strains of "Hail to the Chief," "Happy Days Are Here Again," or catchy political campaign theme songs.

CONTROVERSIES SURROUNDING ADVERTISING

By its very nature, advertising is controversial. In the early 20th century people clamored for the regulation of advertising, believing that much of it was exaggerated and untruthful. As we have seen, government regulations have succeeded in eliminating outright falsehoods from advertising, but many people are still critical. According to Agee, Ault, and Emery, most criticism of advertising centers on the following complaints:

1. Advertising persuades us to buy goods and services we cannot afford.
2. Advertising appeals primarily to our emotions, rather than to our intellect.
3. Advertising is biased.
4. Advertising involves conflicting competitive claims.
5. Advertising is unduly repetitious.
6. Much advertising is vulgar, obtrusive, and irritating.[14]

The advertising industry has answers for most of these charges. It points out that such criticism merely indicates that advertisers use natural selling techniques to make customers aware of their products. After all, aren't the above comments true of most types of selling? Also, keep in mind that advertising plays a very important role in informing the masses about the many goods and services available.

Subliminal Advertising

Since the 1950s, some criticism has been far more severe. One of the first critics to lash out was Vance Packard, who pointed out in *The Hidden Persuaders* that advertisers were using motivational research and other techniques to sell consumer goods. Packard charged that advertisers were using "depth manipulation," which causes us to do things that are irrational and illogical. Often, he said, ad messages were trying to invade the privacy of our minds through hidden **subliminal embeds.**[15]

subliminal embeds

In 1957, researcher James Vicary inserted one-frame Coca-Cola and popcorn ads among the 26 frames that are projected on a movie screen every second. Just as the frames around each still photo in motion picture film cannot be perceived by the eye, the advertisements went unnoticed. However, Vicary claimed that people's subconscious minds perceived the ads: His research found that Coca-Cola sales increased 18 percent and popcorn sales 57.8 percent after the subliminally embedded films were shown.[16]

When Vicary was asked to replicate his study under controlled conditions, the new test produced no increase in the sales of either Coke or popcorn.[17] But even though Vicary's claim was invalidated, it had long been known that subliminal stimuli can produce certain behavioral effects under laboratory conditions.[18] What was not known was whether consumers can be motivated to purchase a product by subliminal advertising. In the 1970s Wilson Bryan Key, a mass-communication researcher from Canada, took up Packard's and Vicary's charges. Key advanced the theory that advertisers were using hidden, sexually explicit messages, called *subliminal embeds,* to sell products. According to Key, the messages, primarily those in magazine ads, were designed to appeal to our subconscious instincts surrounding sex, death, and fear.

By the early 1980s, Key had written three popular books on the subject: *Subliminal Seduction, Media Sexploitation,* and *Clam Plate Orgy.* In 1992, he added two more: *Subliminal Ad-Ventures in Sensual Art* and *The Age of Manipulation: The Con in Confidence, the Sin in Sincere.* Key claims to have seen such hidden details as castrated penises in Parkay margarine ads, death masks and skulls in the ice cubes in liquor ads, and the word *cancer* in cigarette ads.

Although he couldn't explain how these embeds worked, Key was convinced they triggered a subconscious emotional response, thus ensuring that people would remember the ad and the brand when it came time to buy the product. He has not, however, been able to prove the ads actually sell more than other ads.

The advertising industry at first ignored Key's charges, claiming he was nothing more than a "dirty old man" who could see perverted symbols in cloud formations. Some in the industry claimed the images he saw were mere coincidences and were not intended to have any conscious or subconscious effect on consumers.

However, such discoveries led the U.S. Bureau of Alcohol, Tobacco and Firearms to propose rules in 1980 to outlaw subliminal advertising in liquor ads. Although the proposed regulations were distributed for comment and hearings were held, the regulations were never adopted. The executive vice president of the American Association of Advertising Agencies argued at the hearings that you cannot forbid the use of something that doesn't exist.

Finally, in 1984, articles in the industry's trade magazine, *Advertising Age,* urged the industry to challenge the lack of evidence for Key's assertions and prove him wrong once and for all. In one article, Virginia Commonwealth University professor Jack Haberstroh published the results of his own survey of 100 randomly selected advertising art directors: Of 47 usable responses, only 2 indicated that they had ever deliberately embedded a subliminal message.

By 1989, several big advertisers were running parody ads on the subliminal controversy. Schweppes inserted a 90-second commercial spoofing subliminal ads prior to the beginning of the home video of the movie *A Fish Called Wanda.* The commercial featured a man expressing concern about subliminal ads while the word *Schweppes* flashed constantly on the screen. In 1990, the House of Seagram introduced a print ad campaign featuring a "hidden pleasure": a woman swimming in a glass of Seagram's Extra Dry Gin. The image of the barely perceptible woman was enhanced by an arrow pointing to her. The headline on the ad read, "Have you found the hidden pleasure in refreshing Seagram's Gin?"

Nevertheless, some support for Key's contentions has come from other researchers. Warren Breed of the Institute for Scientific Analysis in Berkeley calls embeds UPOs, or "unidentified printed objects." A study by Breed and James R. DeFoe found hidden images in 45.5 percent of the alcoholic-beverage advertisements they examined, a percentage much higher than those in ads for other products.[19]

Pepsi-Cola was criticized by some consumers who claimed the word *sex* seemed to be subtly printed on the exterior of a newly released Pepsi "Cool Can." A Pepsi spokesperson said it was merely an "odd coincidence" and the design was selected only because consumers preferred it over hundreds of other designs. Another ongoing controversy surrounds the cartoon camel once used in Camel cigarette ads, which critics said was sexually suggestive and appealed to youngsters.

The jury is still out on whether there is something to the subliminal embedding theory. Whatever the outcome, more research needs to be done to determine whether or not the embeds actually help to sell consumer goods.

TELEVISION ADVERTISING

The advent of television dramatically changed American advertising. Today the annual expenditure on TV advertising exceeds $30 billion. These ads are creatively produced and have been instrumental in changing American attitudes and lifestyles as well as selling products.

What television ads don't do, according to some consumer organizations, is give the viewer much information. Commercials, they claim, are a slick attempt to get viewers to "feel good" about the product through effective emotional appeals, often directed at sexual instincts.

High Cost

Often more money is spent to produce a 30-second commercial than to make the hour-long program in which it is inserted. And the cost of buying TV time is equally high. In 1986 the top-rated television program, NBC's *The Cosby Show*, began charging $400,000 for each 30-second commercial. When *The Cosby Show* went off the air in 1992, it was replaced by *Murphy Brown* as the most expensive sitcom on which to advertise. By 1996, the asking price for a 30-second commercial in the weekly programs *Seinfeld* and *ER* on NBC was a whopping $550,000; that's $1.1 million for one minute of advertising time during the two hottest programs in NBC's Thursday night lineup! While *ER* continues to draw top dollar for it's advertising time, no other programs have come along in recent years that have the popularity to charge such large numbers (See Box 13.4). When NBC announced it would broadcast the final episode of *Cheers* during the May sweeps period in 1993, it sold out all of its commercial time in one day at $650,000 per spot. Only the Super Bowl, which gets over $1 million for a 30-second spot, has been able to command higher fees.

15-Second Spots

In 1986 all three television networks started running 15-second ads, which allowed them to reduce the cost per ad, double the number of ads run, and maintain revenue levels. The 15-second advertisements (called "15s") posed a new creative challenge to the industry: packaging a powerful message in half the time and still selling the product to the consumer. By the early 1990s, the popularity of 15s started to decline, and they represented only 32 percent of the market, but they have continued in use as part of "piggyback" advertising campaigns. In these instances, a corporation may purchase 30 seconds of time and then use each 15-second segment to advertise two separate products.

TV Ad Techniques

Many television advertisements have a tripartite structure: the problem, the advice, and the resolution. All three messages must be delivered in 15, 30, or 60 seconds. Let's take a mouthwash commercial as an example. First, you establish the problem: Some-

Box 13.4

MEDIA LITERACY

The High Cost of Television Programs Means More Commercials

In 1998, the NBC television network agreed to pay a record $13 million per episode to continue airing its top-rated drama *ER*. Prior to that, the typical license fee a network paid for two showings of a one-hour drama had ranged from $1 million to $1.5 million, with the exception of *ER*, which had been receiving $2 million per episode.

At the same time NBC was shocking the industry with its new contract for *ER*, four other networks (ABC, CBS, Fox, and ESPN) were agreeing to pay $17.6 billion for eight years of National Football League television rights, in several cases doubling the previous rights fees. So what do these high costs mean to you, the television viewer? Simple. More commercials.

Many television producers were soon complaining that the total content of their programs was being cut by as much as 15 and 20 minutes in order to make room for more advertising. In fact, two years before the astronomical fees were agreed upon, the Association of American Advertising Agencies (commercepark.com/AAAA/index.html) reported that the average time devoted to commercials and nonprogram material during a typical hour of network prime time shows was 15 minutes and 19 seconds. While the number of interruptions was not increased by much, each break was running two to three minutes longer.

In addition, the cost of the ads themselves went up. At the start of the 1998–99 television season, *ER* was still commanding the most for a 30-second spot, $575,000. The next highest shows were also NBC programs, *Frasier* ($475,000) and *Friends* ($425,000). Rounding out the top five were ABC's *Drew Carey Show* and *Monday Night Football* (both priced at $375,000). Two Fox network programs were also among the top 10 most expensive buys for the season, *The X-Files* was seventh ($330,000) and *Ally McBeal* was 10th ($265,000). CBS had only one show in the top 10, *Touched By an Angel*, which was ninth ($275,000).*

*Source: Advertising Age, September 21, 1998, p. 1.

one has bad breath. Then you suggest that the person try the advertised mouthwash. Finally, you show the person being chased by attractive members of the opposite sex—an obvious resolution of the problem. Quick as a flash, the person has gone from disaster to success.

In addition to delivering a message quickly, TV advertising uses imaginative techniques to make the advertised products attractive. For example, food stylists are hired to make advertised food look appealing. According to TV food stylist Lloyd Davis, Elmer's Glue is added to milk in television ads to make it look white and creamy, roasted chickens are spray-painted a delicious golden brown, and Ivory Soap is added to give coffee a fresh-brewed appearance.[20]

Infomercials

One of the fastest growth areas of TV advertising is infomercials. These are 30-minute television commercials that feature celebrities and resemble news or information broadcasts but in reality are promotional vehicles for such moneymaking items as kitchenware products, cosmetics, exercise equipment and weight-loss programs. Even *Wheel of Fortune's* Vanna White successfully advertised a tooth whitener on a 30-minute infomercial.

The infomercial industry has grown from a $350 million business in 1988 to over $4.5 billion. Palm Desert (California)–based Guthy-Renker Corporation, for example, grossed more than $100 million on the Tony Robbins *Personal Power Tapes* infomercial. Guthy-Renker is one of six major companies specializing in the production of infomercials.

Criticism of TV Ads

Because of its impact on our culture, television advertising has become the focus of considerable criticism in recent years. Probably the longest ongoing controversy concerns advertising directed toward children (see Box 13.5).

Children's advertising on television is a $200-million-a-year enterprise. Research reports that the average child sees 20,000 television ads a year—about three hours of commercials a week.

According to psychologist Patricia Greenfield, young children equate all of television except cartoons with reality. Youngsters under age seven usually cannot distinguish between a commercial and the program, and they learn a great deal from commercials.[21] That's one reason the FCC requires programs aimed at young people to distinguish between the programs and the commercials by providing such spoken messages as "We'll return after these messages" and "Now, back to our program."

Groups such as Action for Children's Television (ACT) began campaigning to get regulatory agencies to limit commercials aimed at children. A request for an FCC ban on children's advertising was denied. Opponents of such a ban pointed out that it would have meant the end of commercial television programming for children.

For years, concern has been expressed over the number of ads for sugar-coated breakfast cereals and unrealistic toys.

Parents have also complained about TV ads that entice children to call 900-prefix telephone numbers to hear such messages as "Santa's Christmas stories." Unlike the toll-free 1-800 numbers, 900 telephone prefixes incur charges. Some parents have been shocked to find hundreds of dollars in 900 charges on their monthly bills.

Beer and wine commercials have been the subject of controversy in recent years. Groups such as the National Institute on Alcohol Abuse and Alcoholism (NIAAA), Mothers Against Drunk Driving (MADD), and Students Against Drunk Driving (SADD) have been pressuring members of Congress to ban beer and wine advertising on television, claiming it contributes to alcoholism and drunk-driving-related deaths. Many people have also objected to depictions of television characters enjoying libations at the local tavern, thus encouraging viewers to emulate their favorite TV people.

The beer, wine, and broadcast industries counter that no causal relationship exists between alcohol-related problems and the commercials. Industry officials say their ads do not cause people to drink more or entice nondrinkers to drink; they aim only to increase a brand's share of the existing market. Opponents of liquor advertising are skeptical, however; they contend the ads do attempt to attract new drinkers, particularly young people, with their themes of good times, adventure, and sex.[22] In a move to show it was serious about helping to curb underage drinking, Anheuser-Busch, the maker of top-selling Budweiser beer, removed its beer advertising from teen-oriented MTV in 1996. The commercials were moved to the more adult-oriented music video channel VH-1, which is owned by MTV.

For years the National Association of Broadcasting (NAB) enforced restrictions on liquor advertising. First, no hard liquor could be advertised on radio or television. Second, broadcasters were prohibited from showing anyone drinking beer or wine in

---

@ Practicing Media Literacy

Do you think television advertising for beer and wine promotes drinking in our society? Do the "safe drinking" and "designated driver" commercials have any impact? How do you think the issue should be handled?

Box 13.5
MEDIA WATCH
A Big Spending Target Audience for Advertisers: Children

According to a study done by *Consumer Reports*, American children are allowed to choose how to spend $15 billion each year, and they also have a say in how their parents spend another $160 billion. While allowances for children have increased in recent years, most of this spending involved school clothes, requesting specific products for Christmas or birthday presents, or asking to be taken to fast-food restaurants to eat.

As a result, advertisers are targeting children to be sure that their products are the ones chosen by the young people of America. Of course, marketing to the younger audience is not new; it's been going on for decades. Many mothers and fathers, as well as grandmothers and grandfathers, probably remember wanting products which tied in with their favorite movie stars, their radio favorites, or such television heroes as Hopalong Cassidy or Superman.

Television programs feature many characters who may be tied in with products for children, from the Smurfs to the Mighty Morphin Power Rangers. But television isn't the only medium being used by advertisers to reach out to young people. The Internet offers websites where kids can connect with Ronald McDonald or other commercial characters. Children's clothing, as is the case with many adult lines, features corporate logos and brand names prominently displayed.

But by the end of the 20th century, a group of 60 psychologists and other professionals was calling on the American Psychological Association (APA) to restrict the use of psychological research by advertisers who are pushing toys, video games, and snack foods. The group was charging that a large gap had arisen between the mission of the APA and the move of the profession "into helping corporations influence children for the purpose of selling products to them."*

Meanwhile, others were expressing concern about the content of commercials being seen by kids in non-children's programs. For example, a physician in Minnesota reported that a child watching just one World Series game on television would see 14 overtly violent commercials, primarily promotional commercials for movies and television programs. The study was reported in the *Journal of the American Medical Association* and was noticed by Senator Joseph Lieberman (D, Conn.), who wrote a strongly worded letter to the National Association of Broadcasters and the advertising community, saying that while he didn't want the government to be restricting what's on television, he did want "to protect children."**

*Constance L. Hayes, "Selling to Children, or Manipulating Them?" *New York Times*, October 22, 1999, p. C6.

**Nora Fitzgerald, "Advertising Violence," *Ad Week* (adweek.com), November 17, 1997, p. 27–28.

---

a commercial; glasses could be hoisted, but no sipping was allowed. (It was permissible, however, to show characters in regular programs drinking like fish.) Third, currently active sports figures cannot appear in beer or wine commercials. Although the NAB's code stipulating these rules was ruled unconstitutional by a federal judge, most stations continued to follow it on their own. Alcoholic beverage companies are now running "safe drinking" and "designated driver" messages in their television commercials.

voluntary ban

The liquor makers and broadcasters had voluntarily agreed not to advertise hard liquor products on radio after Prohibition ended in the 1930s. The **voluntary ban** against such advertising on television came in television's formative year of 1948. However, as the 20th century was drawing to a close a major liquor company, Seagram, began running a series of 30-second commercials for Crown Royal whiskey on a TV station in Corpus Christi, Texas. Surprisingly, little adverse reaction occurred initially. The owner of the station had tested the waters years earlier by having local liquor stores include brand names and prices in their commercials. This was done during a Baptist convention in the city, and the spots were run at various times of the day and night. The station received fewer than 20 phone calls, most of which were not complaints but questions as to whether such advertising was legal. The Seagram ad was run only between 9 and 10 P.M.

Shortly thereafter, Seagram began advertising on television stations in New Hampshire, Connecticut, New York, and New Jersey. In addition, Seagram Company broke the more than 60-year-old voluntary ban against advertising hard liquor on the radio by launching a campaign for its Lime Twisted Gin on radio stations in San Francisco and other cities across the country. However, it didn't take long for opposition to such advertising to develop. Democratic congressman Joseph Kennedy of Massachusetts and Mothers Against Drunk Driving attempted to have the Federal Communications Commission look into Seagram's challenge to the self-imposed industry ban on the broadcast advertising of hard liquor. One concern expressed was that the 30-second advertisement for Seagram's Crown Royal whiskey featured pet dogs, which they felt might have an impact on children who viewed the commercial. President Clinton also added his voice of opposition to the lifting of the voluntary ban on hard-liquor advertising on radio and television (see Box 13.6).

Broadcasters found themselves caught in a bind. They were looking at the advertising of hard liquor as possibly a new source of revenue, but many feared that defying the ban would backfire and prompt lawmakers to prohibit all alcohol advertising, including the highly lucrative beer and wine advertising. Despite the restrictions and activities, commercials for beer and wine—rather than the program content—continued to be the center of controversy surrounding the issue of booze and the media.

Cigarette advertising on television and radio was caught in a similar controversy in the 1960s. The first result of this debate was a requirement that broadcast stations running cigarette advertising air counterads from such organizations as the American Cancer Society and the American Lung Association telling of the harmful effects of smoking. These ads began appearing in 1968, and cigarette smoking started to decline. In 1971, an alarmed tobacco industry accepted congressional legislation bringing about a total ban on cigarette advertising in the electronic media. When the advertising stopped, so did most of the antismoking ads, and soon sales of cigarettes (which could still be advertised in the print media) began to climb.

If the case of cigarette advertising can be used as a guide, banning beer and wine commercials will not help to solve this nation's alcohol problem, but increasing the frequency of counterads may help.

Cigarette advertising in the print media has also had its share of criticism in recent years, with antismoking groups charging that much of the advertising was aimed at young people. One of the biggest targets of such criticism was the symbol of Camel cigarettes, the cartoon character of Joe Camel. In California, 12 counties and one city expressed interest in joining a lawsuit accusing the R.J. Reynolds Tobacco Co. (RJR) and its advertising agencies of using Joe Camel to market cigarettes to children. The California State Assembly approved a resolution on a vote of 53 to 9 to urge the company to drop Joe Camel from its advertising campaigns. And the staff of the Federal Trade Commission in Washington, D.C., urged the agency to lodge an unfair advertising complaint against the company because Joe Camel was designed to lure children into smoking. A few months later, RJR announced that the familiar cartoon character, often pictured in sunglasses and surrounded by beautiful women, would be dropped in favor of the more lifelike illustration of a camel that appears on the cigarette

Cigarette advertising has been banned from both radio and TV since 1971, but the Congressional action did not ban such advertising in the print media or on billboards. However, the tobacco industry has now agreed to discontinue outdoor advertising, such as this New York City billboard using Joe Camel. In addition, use of such cartoon characters was discontinued, as was cigarette advertising on the Internet.

package. Joe would no longer appear in newspapers, magazines, billboards, or store displays that children might see.

Zipping and Zapping

Another headache for television advertisers is technology that permits viewers to eliminate commercials entirely: the double Zs. First, viewers can now sit in their easy chairs and change channels during commercials by remote control; in the industry, this is called zipping. Second, the VCR (videocassette recorder) allows people to zap commercials out of recorded programs by fast-forwarding right through them. There are now VCRs on the market that can be programmed to automatically skip the commercials.

The threats of zipping and zapping can be credited with continual improvements in the quality of TV commercials. The industry must make television ads extremely entertaining and compelling if they are to compete for viewers against the temptations of zipping and zapping. This, unfortunately, largely precludes providing any product information in commercials.

Box 13.6
MEDIA WATCH
Knowing When to Say When? Hard-Liquor Advertising Returns to the Airwaves

For most of the 20th century, the distilled spirits industry lived by its own code of not advertising its products on radio or television. While beer and wine advertising was abundant on both media, listeners and viewers were not bombarded with messages for scotch, gin, or bourbon. But that all changed in 1996.

Seagram was the first to begin advertising hard liquor on television—first in Texas, then in other parts of the country. It wasn't long before the Distilled Spirits Council of the United States gave its support to the move by lifting its self-imposed restrictions on such broadcast advertising. The council said it was updating its advertising and marketing codes.

The reaction was quick and certainly not unexpected. President Clinton, with no force of law behind him to stop the action, denounced the industry for its decision. According to Clinton, the lifting of the ban would expose children to the advertising before they knew how to handle alcohol or, for that matter, were even old enough to legally use it. That, said the president, is irresponsible.

Reed Hundt, then-chairman of the Federal Communications Commission, called for the commission to consider regulatory action on the issue. However, another member of the FCC, Commissioner James Quello, said that any action to halt advertising of hard liquor on radio and television should be taken by Congress, not the FCC. As Quello pointed out, the FCC has no legal authority to intervene. Democratic congressman Joseph Kennedy of Massachusetts was one of the first to promise legislative action.

But perhaps the biggest opposition to the move came from the beer industry and the broadcasters themselves. Both feared the action by the distilled spirits industry would jeopardize the more than $500 million beer and wine advertisers had been spending on television commercials each year. Their basic concern was that Congress would react to the lifting of the hard-liquor advertising ban by passing legislation prohibiting the advertising of *all* alcoholic products on radio and TV. Meanwhile, the distilled spirits industry was claiming "discrimination" because beer and wine advertising was accepted on radio and television but hard-liquor advertising was not.

While the four major television networks—ABC, CBS, NBC, and Fox—declined to carry advertising for hard-liquor products, two cable companies quickly invited the industry to advertise with them. A spokesperson for BET Holdings, Inc., whose Black Entertainment Television channel reached an audience of some 47 million households, said that if approached by a marketer that wanted to showcase its product responsibly, the channel would carry the advertising immediately. Meanwhile, one of the nation's largest cable operators, Continental Cablevision Inc., announced it had informed the managers of its five regions that they could carry liquor ads during local cutaways on the various cable networks.

Others supported the advertising of hard liquor on the airwaves. Some said that such advertising during the dinner hour would be more acceptable than commercials for hemorrhoid or feminine hygiene products. Others said the broadcasters should be defending the hard-liquor industry on the issue of freedom of speech guaranteed by the First Amendment. But the main argument of most proponents was that if it is legal to sell a product, it should be legal to advertise that product.

John (handwritten margin note)

MOTIVATIONAL RESEARCH

Psychological Advertising

From its inception in the 19th century, the advertising industry has relied on creative endeavors to sell goods and services. However, by the mid-20th century, creativity was no longer enough. What was needed were more sophisticated techniques that would persuade people to buy more to keep the wheels of our mass-production, mass-

subconscious desires

consumption economy turning. To develop these techniques, the ad industry turned to consumer research, which could provide insights into the personalities and **subconscious desires** of the public.

According to Vance Packard, who began writing about this research with alarm in the 1950s, the advertising industry started tailoring its ads to meet the needs of the id. (In Freudian psychology, the id is that part of our mind that generates our most basic animal urges and impulses.)[23]

Motivational research, or *MR*, was the name given to this new area of consumer analysis. Millions of dollars were targeted for MR, and social scientists soon found an industry ready and willing to fund this type of psychological exploration.

MR looked for the hidden "whys" of consumer behavior. It replaced the older statistical research approaches by borrowing from the disciplines of psychology and psychoanalysis. Instead of treating consumers as rational beings who knew what they wanted and why they wanted it, MR examined the subconscious, nonrational levels of motivation and suggested where and how ads should be aimed. The researchers used in-depth interviews, Rorschach (inkblot) tests, stress tests that measured eye-blinking frequencies in stores via hidden cameras and lie detectors, word association tests, and group interviews to compile their data.[24]

One of the leaders in this research was Dr. Ernest Dichter, head of the Institute for Motivational Research. By probing the subconscious, Dichter was able to discover unsuspected areas of tension and guilt that were important to sales psychology. He learned why certain ads had failed in the past and suggested ways to put together advertising campaigns to take advantage of these formerly unknown areas.

> **@ Practicing Media Literacy**
>
> When receiving advertising messages, whether through print or over the airwaves, do you ever feel that you're being psychologically manipulated?

"Sex sells" was an idea that had been around a long time. However, it wasn't until MR came along that researchers discovered just how subtle and complex sexual fantasies are in influencing consumer buying patterns. One study found that men were lured into automobile dealerships by ads and window displays of convertibles because the convertible was associated with youth and adventure and it was symbolic of a mistress. However, men usually ended up buying a sedan, which symbolized the girl they would marry because she would make a good wife and mother. What the industry needed in the 1950s was a new car that had the attractions of both a mistress and a wife. Dichter's organization took credit for suggesting the solution: the hardtop convertible.[25]

Another sex-related discovery was made when an ad agency ordered an in-depth study to find out why a campaign for the Cigar Institute of America had failed. The ads had shown a smiling woman offering cigars to a group of men. The study revealed that subconsciously men smoke cigars because they know the smell is offensive to women. Thus, the smiling woman enticing them to smoke a cigar was a turnoff.

Conflicts between MR and creativity developed over this new orientation in developing advertising campaigns. Copywriters and art directors regarded advertising as an art, or at least a craft, and resented the new emphasis on psychological research. As Les Pearl of Batten, Barton, Durstine & Osborn (bbdo.com) put it, "Merchandising men and research men are statistic-ing the creative man to death."[26]

Since earlier consumer research had dealt only with demographics (statistical information on ages, marital status, incomes, educational levels, etc.) a new name was coined for motivation-oriented research: *psychographics*.

The field of advertising offers numerous job opportunities. They include working for the mass media, for major companies that advertise, and in a variety of departments in advertising agencies. Women play a major role in advertising, filling about 50 percent of the available jobs.

There are about 6,000 advertising agencies in the United States, although only about 500 of them are considered large (with revenues in excess of $1 million). Most agencies usually have five major departments: market research, creative, account management, media selection, and administration.

Market research gathers information on the product: who will buy it and where to promote it. Depending on the size of the agency, this activity can be accomplished in-house or under contract by market research companies.

The *creative department* writes the copy, develops the graphics, and often produces the commercials or print ads.

Account management is in charge of working with the client to ensure that the ad campaign reflects the client's desires. The person in charge of an account is usually called an account executive.

Media selection is the department in charge of picking the right mass media for the client. Media selections range from radio, TV, newspapers, and magazines to billboards and direct mail.

Administration handles the day-to-day business activities. These include billing clients and paying the bills.

In addition to these departments, some agencies offer public relations services for clients that do not have their own PR departments.

VALS Research

In the 1960s, MR and Freudian psychoanalytical theories were challenged by a revival of creative, nonresearch-oriented ads. However, psychographic research continued. The Stanford Research Institute (now known as SRI International) began working on psychographic research in the 1950s, concentrating on VALS (values and lifestyles). In 1960, SRI issued its first report on the interrelationship of social values and consumer buying habits. The report, called *Consumer Values and Demands*, suggested that a neglected area of market research involved how people's values influence their spending patterns. This report, which was ahead of its time, had very little immediate influence on advertising research. One of the early pioneers of this research was Arnold Mitchell, a marketing analyst at SRI. Mitchell and his colleagues continued their "values-oriented" research through the 1960s and into the 1970s to determine how the children of the turbulent 1960s would affect the marketplace. What would happen when a generation that seemed to have rejected consumption and capitalism came of age? Business needed a marketing strategy to reach these people, and the SRI studies helped advertisers to determine the needs of the baby boomers.[27]

One finding of this research was an observation that by 1985 some of these consumers were blending the liberal values of the 1960s with more traditional values. This trend, called **neotraditionalism,** found consumers buying sports utility vehicles such as the Jeep Grand Cherokee and Isuzu Trooper and using them like the station wagons their parents owned.

neotraditionalism

This quest to learn what motivates consumer buying habits has seen a growing number of companies turning to psychographic research. Users of VALS data range from Christian church groups to Citibank. The growing use of this data coincides with the movement of the mass media into the specialization stage of the EPS cycle. Targeting professional women with children or suburban teenagers requires more detailed information than demographics, and the psychological profiles found in VALS data provide that detail.

The Carnation Company, for example, used lifestyle data to introduce its Contadina line of fresh pasta. The product is targeted at two-income couples who like freshly prepared foods that do not take long to cook.

The Mission of VALS

In 1978, the VALS project became a separate program at SRI, with a staff of four and 37 clients. By 1984, it had developed into a $2 million operation with a staff of 19 and 151 clients.

The VALS program has become more than a market research project. Its developers see it as a social agent for changing American culture. At its headquarters in Menlo Park, California, the following credo was placed on the wall of each staff member's office:

> The mission of the VALS program is to exert a positive and creative force in the evolution of the American culture. VALS aims to do this by acquiring, disseminating, and applying insights into how values can aid institutions and individuals to operate in a more humane, productive and ethical way. Specifically, VALS intends:
> - To become a significant part of American business thinking.
> - To enhance public awareness of the role of values in social change.
> - To contribute to SRI research, remain financially healthy and operate for the enjoyment and personal growth of the staff.[28]

VALS Users

At first, VALS research was treated rather secretively; only lately has it been fashionable to discuss it. Many ad agencies now boast about their "psychographic capabilities." The mass media now use VALS to sell advertising space. *Reader's Digest* used VALS data to persuade reluctant advertisers that its readers were the right type of people to be targeted for the advertisers' products. *The National Geographic* ran a full-page ad in the *New York Times* telling how it uses VALS to help advertisers. The ad was headlined "The National Psychographic."

Advertisers can use VALS data to determine which media to use to reach specific market segments. Product developers can use the data to project trends and future consumer needs.

The advertising of consumer goods has become a sophisticated, well-researched industry. The marketing community probably knows at least as much about our American popular culture and its future trends as most sociologists, psychologists, and futurists do. Whether we like it or not, the advertising industry may know more about us and why we do things than we do ourselves.

But this doesn't mean mistakes aren't made. For example, Just for Feet, Inc., a shoe retailer, dropped its plans to keep running its 1999 Super Bowl commercial after complaints were received for the ad, which showed a barefoot African marathon runner being tracked down like an animal by members of a "search and rescue" team in a humvee, who then tricked him into wearing shoes. While the company had intended the ad to celebrate the retailer's passion for protecting feet, many viewers protested the manner in which the runner was treated in the commercial, with some saying it was racist and condescending. The spot ran only the one time in the Super Bowl telecast.

A 30-second commercial for Long John Silver's restaurant chain came in for criticism from law enforcement organizations across the country for showing a police officer stealing a sandwich from a motorist. The ad was meant to be a lighthearted attempt at promoting the chain's "Grab and Go" chicken and fish sandwiches, but there was no humor in it for the police.

TWA issued an apology for running an advertisement that many believed was both sexist and racist. The ad, which ran in newspapers across the country, listed fares to warm-weather spots such as the Caribbean and Florida. It featured a picture of a woman's dress blowing up above her knees, similar to the famous shot of Marilyn Monroe in the move *The Seven-Year Itch*. The caption for the ad read, "Check out these fares. Your pasty white thighs will thank you."

Within the next 24 hours, the airline received over 140 complaints from women and minority groups charging the ad was saying that African-Americans, Asian-Americans, and Hispanics don't go to the beach. The use of a female pair of legs was considered sexist. The ad, created by the D'Arcy Masius Benton & Bowles advertising agency, did not run a second time.

THE FUTURE OF ADVERTISING

For many decades, the newspaper, magazine, radio, and television media have been the main sources for manufacturers to advertise their products. But that began changing in the 1980s and 1990s.

For example, the untapped audience of moviegoers is now being targeted by such advertisers as Coca-Cola, which began running commercials in theaters before the coming-attraction trailers were shown. The initial reaction of patrons was not too favorable. In an early survey, one-third of the audiences stated they were opposed to the advertising in movie theaters, one-third favored it, and one-third didn't care. Eight year later, a similar survey found that between two-thirds and three-quarters of moviegoers liked the commercials and only 2 to 3 percent objected. The next step was to follow the lead of European nations by increasing the advertising time. England has been showing around 7 minutes of commercials in movie houses, while theater patrons in France could expect to see an average of 20 minutes of advertising before the movies started.

The world of sports has found new ways to use advertising space to raise money. For years, stock-car racers have been covered with dozens of logos on the vehicles, as well as on the uniforms and hats of the drivers. Tennis and golf stars have advertised their sponsors on their clothing. Even Major League Baseball considered selling advertising space on the sleeves of the players' uniforms.

When the Food and Drug Administration (FDA) eased restrictions on the advertising of prescription drugs, there were soon numerous commercials on radio and television

Product placement has become big business for advertisers, from having a product displayed in a movie to having the company name placed on everything from clothing to race cars.

touting the benefits of such medications. For the first time, these prescription drugs could actually say what they did instead of just advertising the name, with little other information about the product. However, the FDA's ruling also required drug makers to provide information in their commercials to alert consumers about the products' possible side effects. This meant that listeners and viewers were soon hearing about the potential for intestinal gas with oily or uncontrolled discharge or diarrhea, as well as such dire problems as liver failure, heart damage, birth defects, and even addiction. Two years after the FDA eased the restrictions, a study found that the average television viewer was seeing nine commercials a day for various prescription drugs and, as consumers, they weren't happy about them. Most of the negative reactions were based on the side effects information, which was apparently confusing or alarming viewers. But the FDA insisted the information was necessary so that vulnerable patients would be aware of potential risks and would not be deluded into hoping for miracle cures. But the influx of this new advertising money was a boon to the media.

However, during the 1990s, the traditional media became concerned about a possible loss of advertising revenue as many large department store chains began turning to the Internet to not only advertise their products but also to sell those products using the Internet for mail orders. Cybershopping has become a multimillion-dollar industry, with the companies dealing directly with consumers just as they would with catalog shoppers. But the Internet was faster, as shoppers could browse the store's merchandise, order online with a credit card, and have the goods delivered within two days.

This latest example of advertising and the consumer industries availing themselves of the Internet is just one more instance of advertising remaining on the cutting edge of our culture.

SUMMARY

Advertising is a message industry that plays a major role in shaping the content and operation of the mass media. Although advertising has existed since ancient times, mass advertising as we know it today began growing up with the mass media in the late 19th century.

Advertising plays an important role in our popular culture because it shapes and reflects our lifestyles. It is one step ahead of other elements in our culture and is usually the first to reflect social trends. The average adult is exposed to approximately 500 advertisements each day. More than $161 billion was spent on advertising in the United States in 1995, with a worldwide expenditure in excess of $351 billion.

The first ad agency was established in 1841; since then advertising has developed into an important but controversial message business. Experts debate whether or not advertising is an effective tool for selling consumer goods. Some contend that advertising does not change consumer buying habits. Others say its effectiveness cannot be measured because too many other consumer information variables are involved. One study suggested that advertisers use sales records as indicators of whether or not to increase advertising. If sales go up, so does the amount spent on advertising.

Another controversy surrounds the use of propaganda devices in advertising to appeal to our emotions rather than to our intellect. Propaganda devices from slogans to sex appeal are used constantly in advertising.

Other advertising controversies include the charge that messages are often subliminally embedded in advertisements to appeal to our subconscious mind. Hidden appeals to the basic instincts of sex, death, and fear are said to be used to sell products.

Researchers have found that more of these hidden images lurk in liquor ads than in any other type of product advertising, but evidence that proves whether these embeds have any effect on our buying habits is lacking.

As American industrial society grew in the mid-20th century, the production of consumer goods reached a level that required new, sophisticated techniques to help mass-distribute the mass-produced goods. In the 1950s, the advertising industry turned to motivational research to help stimulate sales.

An outgrowth of motivational research was the study of lifestyles and how they affect consumer buying patterns. Begun in the 1950s, lifestyle research has been undergoing continual research and development. The VALS studies have led to a wealth of data that is now used on a regular basis to target the appropriate audience for a product, determine what media will best reach the target group, explain why the people in the target audience buy what they do, and help the ad agency develop an effective campaign to sell the product. VALS research is also used to help businesses determine what types of products will be marketable in the future.

Advertisers continue to search for new ways to promote their products with the public, from commercials in movie theaters to advertising—and selling—through the Internet.

Find a review of *Key People and Concepts*, a message board for *Practicing Media Literacy* questions, self tests, and more at: www.mhhe.com/wilson.

Thought **Questions**

1. What cultural factors were responsible for the development of the advertising industry as we know it today? Reflect on the 19th-century factors, mid-20th-century needs, and current forces shaping the advertising industry.

2. List all of the factors that contributed to a decision you recently made regarding a major purchase.

3. Do you think advertising is effective? List some examples of where it did or didn't play a major role in selling a product.

4. Reflecting on the 10 categories of propaganda devices discussed in this chapter, make a current list of examples for each category used in advertising today.

5. Do you think the use of motivational research by the advertising industry is ethical? Why or why not?

Notes

1. Harold Berkman and Christopher Gilson, *Advertising: Concepts and Strategies,* 2nd ed. (New York: Random House, 1987), p. 4.

2. "Marketing Elite; P&G Dominates Leaders," *Advertising Age,* 1999 Special Issue *The Advertising Century,* p. 128.

3. Berkman and Gilson, p. 34

4. Randall Rothenberg, "The Advertising Century," *Advertising Age,* 1999 Special Issue, p. 133.

5. William F. Allman, "Science 1, Advertisers 0," *U.S. News & World Report,* May 1, 1989, pp. 60–61.

6. Michael Schudson, *Advertising, The Uneasy Persuasion: Its Dubious Impact on American Society* (New York: Basic Books, 1984), pp. 18–19.

7. Richard Schmalensee, *The Economics of Advertising* (Amsterdam: North Holland, 1972), p. 43.

8. Schudson, *Advertising,* p. 33.

9. Stephen Fox, *The Mirror Makers: A History of American Advertising and Its Creators* (New York: Morrow, 1984), p. 328.

10. Hank Stuever, "Radical Chic: Benetton Takes on the Death Penalty," *Washington Post*, January 25, 2000, p. C1.

11. Schudson, *Advertising*, pp. 90–91.

12. James H. Meyers and William H. Reynolds, *Consumer Behavior and Marketing Management* (Boston: Houghton Mifflin, 1967), p. 138.

13. Adolf Hitler, *Mein Kampf* [English language edition] (New York: Reynal & Hitchcock, 1939), p. 234.

14. Warren K. Agee, Phillip H. Ault, and Edwin Emery, *Introduction to Mass Communications*, 11th ed. (New York: HarperCollins, 1994), pp. 418–419.

15. Vance O. Packard, *The Hidden Persuaders* (New York: Pocket Books, 1957).

16. Walter Weir, "Another Look at Subliminal 'Facts,'" *Advertising Age*, October 19, 1984, p. 46.

17. Ibid.

18. R. S. Lazarus and R. A. McCleary, "Automatic Discrimination without Awareness: A Study of Subception," *Psychological Review* 58 (1951): pp. 113–122.

19. Warren Breed and James R. DeFoe, "Themes in Magazine Alcohol Advertisements: A Critique," *Journal of Drug Issues*, Fall 1979, p. 46.

20. "30-Second Seduction," *Consumer Reports* television special, HBO Home Video, 1985.

21. Patricia Marks Greenfield, *Mind and Media: The Effects of Television, Video Games and Computers* (Cambridge, MA: Harvard University Press, 1984), pp. 51–53.

22. Michael Jacobson, Robert Atkins, and George Hacker, *The Booze Merchants: The Inebriating of America* (Washington, DC: Center for Science in the Public Interest, 1983), pp. 44–82, 103–130.

23. Vance O. Packard, "The Ad and the Id," in *Mass Media and the Popular Arts*, eds. Fredric Rissover and David C. Birch (New York: McGraw-Hill, 1971), p. 9.

24. Ibid., p. 10.

25. Fox, *The Mirror Makers*, p. 183.

26. Quoted in Fox, *The Mirror Makers*, p. 182.

27. James Atlas, "Beyond Demographics: How Madison Avenue Knows Who You Are and What You Want," *The Atlantic*, October 1984, p. 51.

28. Arnold Mitchell, *The Nine American Lifestyles* (New York: Macmillan, 1983), pp. 3–37.

Public Relations

Creating an Image

The media is an animal which needs to be fed every day . . . or it will eat what it wants.

—**Pat Riley,** NBA Coach

Key People and Concepts

Policymaking

Press Agents

Spin Doctor

Promotion

Public Affairs

Publicity

Paid Advertising

Ivy Ledbetter Lee

Edward L. Bernays

Harold Burson

Issues Management

Crisis Management

Flacks

Public Relations Society of America (PRSA)

Polaris Industries is a relatively small company. It competes with Suzuki, Yamaha, Kawasaki, and Honda. It was also involved in the recent trend of "manufactured hype," which some believe could shift the balance between what companies spend on advertising as opposed to what they spend on public relations. ● To get "free" publicity, Polaris and the Minnesota public relations firm of Shandwick International provided the company's latest personal watercraft for Minnesota Governor Jesse Ventura and his wife to take for a ride on a lake in the northern part of that state. The watery excursion by Ventura, a former professional wrestler who made headlines with his gubernatorial election, received much publicity. The Polaris craft was mentioned by name on radio and television newscasts and was pictured in newspapers because of its connection with the governor. ● "It didn't cost us a whole lot of money," said Polaris CEO Tom Tiller, "and there's a whole lot of media attention there."[1] But while clients save money with the use of public relations (PR) media events instead of advertising, there are no guarantees that they'll get the free publicity they're seeking. Advertising campaigns lock in ad placement and content, but a PR promotion depends on factors that can't be controlled. If there had been more news events taking place on the day of Governor Ventura's water trip, the story exposure might have been much less. If the governor had been called away at the last minute, there might have been no story at all. ● This upswing in public relations activities has caused several major advertising agencies to develop their own PR divisions. They have noticed that public relations "events" are generally treated as more credible than advertising because the public's perception is that it's being filtered through a third party—a broadcaster or an editor. But this also creates a problem for the media in being able to distinguish between meaningful news events and events that have been set up merely to get publicity for a product.[2] •   The public relations practitioners of the 21st century play an important role in our society, and they often make the difference between corporate successes and failures. Public relations is a profession that has developed into one of the most important message businesses in our culture.

WHAT IS PUBLIC RELATIONS?

The *Random House College Dictionary* defines public relations rather simply: "1. the efforts of a corporation to promote good will between itself and the public. 2. the methods used to promote such good will." In the *Public Relations Handbook* (1971), Philip Lesly expanded on this definition by noting that PR enables institutions and people to learn what others think of them, determine what they must do to earn the goodwill of others, devise ways to win that goodwill, and carry on programs designed to secure goodwill.[3]

For many years, confusion existed as to what PR is all about. In 1975, the Foundation for Public Relations Research and Education commissioned a panel of 65 public relations leaders to study 472 different definitions and come up with one single statement that reflected the profession. The outcome was the following 88-word sentence:

> Public relations is a distinctive management function which helps establish and maintain mutual lines of communications, understanding, acceptance, and cooperation between an organization and its publics; involves the management of problems or issues; helps management to keep informed on and responsive to public opinion; defines and emphasizes the responsibility of management to serve the public interest; helps management keep abreast of and effectively utilize change, serving as an early warning system to help anticipate trends; and uses research and sound and ethical communication techniques as its principal tools.[4]

In 1978, an attempt was made to develop a shorter, yet comprehensive definition of PR:

> Public relations practice is the art and social science of analyzing trends, predicting their consequences, counseling organization leaders, and implementing planned programs of action which will serve both the organization's and the public's interest.[5]

In 1980, a task force chartered by the Public Relations Society of America came up with two new and even shorter definitions:

1. Public relations helps an organization and its publics adapt mutually to each other.
2. Public relations is an organization's efforts to win the cooperation of groups of people.[6]

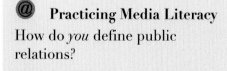

@   Practicing Media Literacy

How do *you* define public relations?

The many attempts to define public relations seem to indicate that it is a complex field with a variety of functions and activities. Central to all the definitions is that PR is an organized effort to handle relationships with the public. Some people confuse PR and advertising. Advertising involves the paid use of time and space in the mass media, usually to sell goods and services. Public relations, on the other hand, often uses free space and time in the media to sell corporate images, individuals, and goodwill. These two practices sometimes overlap when paid advertising is used to sell a corporate image or create goodwill, and, in fact, advertising often becomes an important part of the PR practitioner's total campaign. Thus, the confusion over these two fields is understandable.

Unfortunately, public relations still means different things to different people. Some who call themselves public relations practitioners engage in only a narrow aspect of the field. In its broadest sense, PR includes such activities as policymaking, press agentry, spin doctoring, promotion, public affairs, publicity, and, as previously noted, paid advertisements. All of these activities play a major role in shaping the content of the mass media and disseminating cultural information throughout our society. To distinguish among these activities, let's look at each separately.

Policymaking

A PR practitioner is a liaison between an institution and the public. He or she is responsible for setting a public relations policy to represent the corporation or agency to the public and for conducting research to provide adequate feedback from the public to the institution. Usually a PR practitioner works closely with top-level management and is instrumental in influencing management's policy changes. The PR person can be described as a strategist who plans and executes large-scale public relations efforts.

Press Agentry

Public relations had its origins in press agentry, and today some people still think the terms are synonymous. Press agentry consists of planning and staging events that will attract favorable attention for an institution, a person, an idea, or a product and placing positive news items in the media about the client. Although early press agents sometimes used fraud and deception to achieve their goals, today's practitioners are more honest and professional. Most personalities in the world of show business utilize the services of a press agent to keep their names in the media and to help offset any bad publicity.

Spin Doctoring

Related to press agentry is an activity that has become rather prevalent in recent years. It is known as spin doctoring. The term *spin doctor* is used to describe a person who is able to place a favorable "spin" on media coverage for companies or political causes. For example, when the United States decided to send troops to Somalia in 1992, the White House placed a spin on the story that American troops were necessary to facilitate the flow of food to starving children. Critics of the action could not overcome the humanitarian spin on the story even though they firmly believed the invasion was motivated by the need to end the civil war in the African nation so that U.S. oil companies could implement their oil-drilling contracts.

In 1996, as Bill Clinton was about to accept the Democratic party's nomination for president of the United States, the media broke a story that one of Clinton's top White House advisers, Dick Morris, had been carrying on with a $200-an-hour prostitute and had shared confidential government information with her. Even before Clinton delivered his acceptance speech, spin doctors for the Democratic National Committee were already telling reporters that Morris really wasn't as influential in the White House as many had thought and he definitely had nothing to do with Clinton's speech supporting strong family values.

> @ **Practicing Media Literacy**
> Can you think of any examples of spin doctoring by politicians or government agencies?

When special prosecutor Kenneth Starr revealed his findings that President Bill Clinton had been involved in a relationship with an intern at the White House, presidential spin doctors began their work. But instead of trying to make something positive out of the tremendous negative publicity the president was receiving, they took a different approach. In fact, they put their spin in two separate areas: 1) attacking Starr as being on a vendetta against the president and for spending millions of dollars on the investigation and 2) stressing how the majority of the people still supported the president because of the state of the economy and what Clinton had accomplished during his years in office.

Spin doctors are quite prominent during presidential election years, particularly around candidate debates. They listen carefully to what their man is saying to be sure that something isn't misstated. As soon as the debates are over, the spin doctors talk with the media to be sure that the proper interpretation is given to any statements that might be misinterpreted by reporters and the electorate.

But spin doctors don't just work trying to correct mistakes. They're often called upon to make something negative appear more positive. As the 2000 presidential campaign was getting underway, it was revealed that former Democratic Senator Bill Bradley of New Jersey suffered repeated episodes of irregular heartbeats. His spin doctors were quick to point out that this was not a serious condition; that such things as stress, fatigue, heavy amounts of caffeine, over-the-counter decongestants and even inhaling other people's cigarette smoke could trigger such attacks. They also pointed out that Bradley was under a doctor's care and was taking medication for the condition. By the time the first primary vote rolled around, the majority of the people were back to thinking about the issues of the campaign rather than the health of the candidates.

Public relations agencies represent a wide variety of clients, from politicians to community service organizations. This promotional campaign was developed for The Episcopal Church.

Promotion

Promotional activities go beyond getting publicity and involve generating support or endorsements for a client. Clients range from churches and charities to political candidates and causes and a variety of social concerns, such as the "Save the Whales" and "Right to Life" movements. Promotional activities often involve fund-raising campaigns. Public television stations, for example, promote some of their best programming of the season during their promotional campaigns. They then cut from the programs to a fund-raising telethon format to solicit money from viewers.

Commercial radio and television stations are regularly

involved in promotional activities to enhance their image with the listening and viewing public. These activities range from sponsoring a local concert by a top recording artist to sponsoring such community activities as blood drives, children's toy and clothing collections at Christmas time, and sponsorship of events at the local museum.

Public Affairs

The term *public affairs* is misleading because some corporations and government agencies use it to describe their entire PR effort. (Many institutions now call their directors of public relations "directors of public affairs," for example.) However, properly speaking, the term refers to a narrower public relations activity: direct institutional involvement with community and government relations.

Publicity

Publicity involves placing news and information in the mass media. People who work in this field are skilled in writing publicity in a news format; in government and military agencies they often carry the title of public information officer. Good public information officers need to have some of the skills and training of professional PR practitioners to handle the occasions when the mass media seek unfavorable news and information.

Advertising

Occasionally PR practitioners need to use paid advertising. For example, they may decide to mount an ad campaign to clarify a client's institutional policy, correct an unfavorable image, or provide assistance with a promotional or press agentry campaign. Public relations personnel who do not have experience in advertising usually call in a professional for assistance. However, many PR agencies today have expanded their operations to include advertising.

THE HISTORY OF PUBLIC RELATIONS

The concept of public relations can be traced back to the Roman Empire when Caesar Augustus erected statues of himself to enhance his public image and Julius Caesar promoted his military successes to gain personal political support. In America, the use of public relations dates back to the events leading up to the Revolutionary War. The **Boston Tea Party,** for example, was a staged event to bring attention to the growing dissatisfaction with British taxation of the colonies.

Boston Tea Party

Early Press Agentry

In the 19th century, following the advent of the penny press in the 1830s, it became common for press agents to invent stories to promote their clients in newspapers.

One of the early users of press agentry was P. T. Barnum, who successfully promoted the midget Tom Thumb and a singer known as the "Swedish Nightingale," Jenny Lind; they became popular sideshow attractions for the circus owned by Barnum, who coined the often-quoted phrase "There's a sucker born every minute." Other press agents promoted the Wild West touring shows of Buffalo Bill and Annie Oakley.

muckrakers

However, public relations as we now know it developed to help big businesses combat the negative images that were developing in the late 19th century from unfavorable articles written by muckrakers (see Chapter 8). The works of such **muckrakers** as Ida Tarbell, Lincoln Steffens, and Upton Sinclair painted grim pictures of big-business practices. Stories of huge profits and employee exploitation became common. Companies found they needed to improve their image with the public.

Corporate PR

Simple press agentry wasn't enough to overcome suspicions about big business. In fact, the lies and distortions associated with press agentry at the time were the last thing companies needed.

One of the first to try to change this negative corporate image was former newspaperman Ivy Ledbetter Lee, considered by many to be the first real PR practitioner. Lee started as a political publicist in 1904, but soon he was working for industrial giants. Lee began distributing press releases explaining business's side of labor disputes; he told city editors at the local newspapers that he was a "press agent who dealt in the truth."

Government PR

Government became involved in public relations when the United States entered World War I in 1917. President Woodrow Wilson established the Creel Committee, headed by newspaperman George Creel, to promote the sale of liberty bonds to finance the war, censor news about the war, and convince the American people of the necessity of the nation's participation in the war.

After the war, a member of the committee, Edward L. Bernays, emerged as a leader in the development of the PR profession, setting up his own firm in 1921 and becoming the first person to call himself a public relations counselor. Two years later he wrote the first book on the subject, *Crystallizing Public Opinion*.[7] He also taught the first course in public relations, at New York University. Bernays eventually earned the title of "father of modern public relations." As his reputation in PR grew worldwide, he found himself rejecting an offer by Adolf Hitler to help propagate Nazism (see Box 14.1).

The U.S. government again turned to public relations for help when it became involved in World War II in 1941. It established the Office of War Information (**OWI**), headed by radio commentator Elmer Davis. After the war ended, the OWI became the U.S. Information Agency.

OWI

The U.S. government used public relations to generate support for its efforts during World War II. Similar messages were presented on radio and in movie theaters.

YOU BUY WAR BONDS — I'LL FIGHT!

SIGN YOUR PLEDGE WHEN THE MINUTE MAN CALLS!

EVERYBODY · EVERY PAY DAY · 10%

The Great Depression

The PR industry's road to success as a respected profession was not without setbacks. When the Great Depression hit in 1929, the public was quick to blame big business for the nation's financial woes. A real need existed for corporate public relations people to respond to the critics. Although

Box 14.1
PROFILE
Edward L. Bernays: The Father of Spin

Edward L. Bernays, whom *PR Week* magazine has called the Father of Spin, has been one of the top names in 20th-century public relations work. The nephew of the famed psychoanalyst and psychopathologist Sigmund Freud, Bernays was born in Vienna in 1892. His family moved to America when he was less than a year old but maintained close ties with the Freuds in Vienna.

When Bernays was 22 years old, he traveled to Europe to visit with his famed uncle, and, according to Bernays, the two got along "like two contemporaries." They stayed in contact with each other.

During World War I, Bernays became a member of the Creel Committee, which was charged with promoting the war effort for the U.S. government. Following the war, Bernays voluntarily began promoting his uncle's work in the United States. He arranged for the translation of his uncle's book *Introductory Lectures on Psychoanalysis*. At his uncle's invitation, Bernays became the public relations counsel for the International Psychoanalytic Press of London and Vienna. Bernays continued to promote his uncle's work, arranging banquets in New York for Freud's 75th and 80th birthdays.

Bernays began applying Freud's psychoanalytical principles to public relations in 1929 when he was hired by American Tobacco Company to design a campaign to induce women to smoke in public places. Bernays consulted a psychoanalyst (Brill) who was an early follower of Freud to assist him. Bernays wrote in *Biography of an Idea* that "Brill explained to me: 'Some women regard cigarettes as symbolic of freedom. . . . Smoking is a sublimation for oral eroticism; holding a cigarette in the mouth excites the oral zone . . . [T]he first woman who smoked probably had an excess of masculine components and adopted the habit as a masculine act. But today the emancipation of women has suppressed many of their feminine desires . . . Feminine traits are masked. Cigarettes, which are equated with men, become torches of freedom.'"

Bernays staged a demonstration of women smoking in public on New York's Fifth Avenue during an Easter parade. He reported that an age-old taboo had been broken "by a dramatic appeal, disseminated by the network of media."

Bernays applied Freudian principles of persuasion to other campaigns by appealing to basic instincts. After World War II, the advertising industry, led by psychoanalyst Ernest Dichter (see Chapter 13), adopted principles of Freudian psychology in its campaigns.

Thus, the long and distinguished career of the "father of modern public relations" was enhanced by his kinship with Sigmund Freud.

---

some firms developed in-house public relations staffs, others ignored the need for public relations as they went about the task of cutting employees and scaling down their operations.

Post–World War II

After the Great Depression and World War II, however, public relations prospered. Industry and government both began to recognize the need to present their activities favorably to the public. By the mid-1990s, more than 200,000 people were engaged in PR activities in the United States. In addition to several hundred public relations firms, every sizable organization, whether public or private, had one or more employees working in the PR field. Today's public relations professional requires a broad range of skills, including listening, counseling, planning, and communicating. Public relations counselors Carl Byoir & Associates describe their business this way:

> *Analysis*—of policies and objectives of client . . . of relationships with various publics, including employees, customers, dealers, shareholders, the financial community, government and the press. Continuing research keeps the analysis of these relationships up-to-date.

Planning and programming—of specific undertakings and projects in which public relations techniques can be employed to help attain the objectives through effective communication between the client and its publics.

Implementation—of the programs and projects by maximum and effective use of all avenues of communication, internal and external, to create understanding and stimulate action.[8]

OPPORTUNITIES AND DUTIES OF PR PRACTITIONERS

The field of public relations is growing rapidly. According to the U.S. Department of Labor, public relations jobs during the last half of the 1990s continued to increase faster than the average for all occupations. This is because major companies have realized how important their image is in selling their products. Employment opportunities are numerous. Some 1,600 PR agencies exist; corporations employ thousands of PR practitioners, many of them at top management level; and most government and educational institutions have public relations offices (see Box 14.2).

Diverse Responsibilities

Since the field is so broad, it might be helpful to describe what public relations practitioners actually do. Frank Wylie, a public relations practitioner and an educator, points out that there are major differences between the job duties of an entry-level PR employee and those of an experienced executive. He says the average entry-level employee spends 50 percent of his or her time on techniques, 5 percent on judgment, and 45 percent on "running like hell." The experienced executive, on the other hand, spends 10 percent on techniques, 40 percent on administration, and 50 percent on analysis and judgment.[9]

Herb Schmertz, former vice president of public affairs for Mobil Oil, described his wide-ranging duties this way:

> Sometimes I describe myself as a lobbyist who tries to raise certain issues and arguments before the public, the government and the press. But I am also a publisher—of books, pamphlets, reports, and issue-oriented advertisements. In addition, I am a patron of the arts and culture. I am also a corporate spokesman who explains and defends Mobil's point of view. From time to time, I am an advocate who confronts individuals and institutions whose positions are, in our view, wrong or misinformed. And I am a media critic who refuses to allow inaccurate or damaging stories to go unanswered.
>
> In addition to all of this, I am responsible for administering a large department and a hefty budget. As a member of Mobil's board of directors, I participate in corporate investment decisions and other policy issues. When evening rolls around, I often represent the corporation at an art or cultural event, or at a political dinner, or as a guest on a TV interview show.[10]

Campaign Development

Public relations practitioners use a systematic approach to developing their campaigns. One such approach, developed by Bernays, is called "the engineering of consent" and consists of the following eight steps:

1. Define goals or objectives.
2. Research publics to find out whether goals are realistic and attainable, and how.
3. Modify goals if research finds them unrealistic.

The public relations field offers numerous opportunities. Entry-level jobs exist in charitable organizations, hospitals, government agencies, colleges and universities, chambers of commerce, trade organizations, entertainment groups, sports organizations, and small business firms.

In addition, large corporations provide opportunities to work in public relations, both internally and externally. These include positions as a public relations executive or staff member of a large corporation or representing the corporation as a staff member of a public relations agency.

A large number of job opportunities exist with big corporations, which often have hundreds of people working in various public relations activities. Approximately 85 percent of the 1,500 largest corporations in America have public relations departments. Although the organizational structure may vary from company to company, the director of public relations (who often carries the title of vice president) usually reports directly to the president of the company (or chief executive officer). Usually three divisions fall under the director of public relations: press relations, corporate communications, and community relations.

In addition, about a third of these corporations retain external public relations agencies. These firms can range from a one-person operation to 2,000 or more employees. They usually charge clients on a fee-plus-expenses basis. Typically a large public relations agency has five divisions: creative services, research, publicity and marketing, account executives, and administration.

PR practitioners are usually college graduates trained in the profession. More than 160 colleges and universities in the United States offer formal education in PR, usually in schools and departments of journalism and mass communication. In recent years, the advertising and public relations sequences in these schools have been the fastest growing and often represent the largest area within the school.

4. Determine a strategy to reach goals.
5. Plan actions, themes, and appeals to publics.
6. Plan the organization to meet goals.
7. Time and plan tactics to meet goals.
8. Set up a budget.[11]

As you can see, PR practitioners are skilled professionals who do much more than issue press releases and plant publicity in the media. They are planners who set goals, research needs, establish systematic campaigns, and select and work with the media. One of the leading firms in the United States, Burson-Marsteller, now labels itself a "global perception management firm." According to its website,

> At Burson-Marsteller we believe that communications is far more critical in business than simply generating awareness, disseminating information or enhancing reputation.
>
> We believe that through a Perception Management (TM) approach to communications it can motivate behaviors that create positive business results.
>
> We are totally focused on this idea as our mission, and we believe it assures that our disciplines create value for our clients.[12]

At the end of 1999, *PR Week* magazine (prweek.net) named Harold Burson, the chairman of Burson-Marsteller, the most influential PR figure of the past 100 years. The publication ranked him ahead of such well-known figures as Ed Bernays and Ivy Ledbetter Lee in its list of the 100 most influential PR people of the 20th century.

ISSUES AND CRISIS MANAGEMENT

publics

Issues management attempts to identify and correctly interpret problems before they become a crisis; *crisis management* attempts to react to crises, such as disasters, in as favorable a climate as possible and to rebuild the corporate image as quickly as possible.

Public relations practitioners who deal in issues management must assess events, trends, attitudes, and issues outside the organization to determine how they might affect the institution and its image with its **publics.** They then advise the organization's management as to what steps need to be taken to preserve or maintain a favorable public image or advance the corporate cause.

The bad publicity aimed at the tobacco industry during the final years of the 20th century caused one company to launch a PR campaign stressing that it is more than just a tobacco company. Philip Morris International Inc. also owns Kraft, the largest food company in the United States, and the Miller Brewing Company. To offset the negative publicity surrounding Philip Morris, Marlboro, and its other brands of cigarettes, the company began running advertising campaigns pointing out that Miller brewing plants in areas hit by floods stopped bottling beer and started bottling and distributing drinking water in beer bottles. In addition, the advertising pointed out that Philip Morris annually donated millions of dollars' worth of goods to food pantries for the needy and supported numerous shelters, facilities, and programs to help battered women. The company also worked hard to let the public know that it spends millions of dollars each year on programs to encourage people to drink in moderation ("Think When You Drink") as well as to educate children about the dangers of smoking.

In another example, during the government's push for approval of the North American Free Trade Agreement (NAFTA) in 1993, major companies that had a financial stake in the passage of the agreement assessed the political climate and developed public relations campaigns to solicit public and congressional support.

When the United States went into battle against Saddam Hussein in 1991, the U.S. government had the support of the people behind it. Hussein had the image of a Middle Eastern Hitler, and Americans were outraged by the atrocities allegedly committed against the Kuwaiti people after that tiny, oil-rich country was invaded by Hussein's troops.

While the tobacco industry struggles to improve its image, many states, such as New Jersey, have launched public relations campaigns to educate young people about the hazards of smoking.

Box 14.3
MEDIA LITERACY
Some Problems in Public Relations

Public relations is for everyone. Once thought of as the tool for large corporate America, public relations is now regarded as an essential element in our popular culture. So it wasn't a surprise when the U.S. Conference of Catholic Bishops awarded a $1 million-a-year contract for one to five years to one of America's largest public relations firms.

In hiring Hill & Knowlton, the church wanted to launch an anti-abortion campaign. The new campaign, however, brought the firm more than it bargained for. About a third of its staff signed a letter protesting the decision to promote anti-abortion. Other employees complained individually, and one person resigned. In addition, the company lost several accounts over the issue.

The 1999 MCI WorldCom outage that stopped Internet service for 10 days also disabled many ATMs across the nation. But when service was finally restored, there was still a lot of criticism aimed at the telecommunications giant for keeping its customers uninformed as to what was happening and playing down the seriousness of the situation. A spokesperson for MCI WorldCom explained that the company wanted to be sure that the information released was accurate, but critics pointed out that when AT&T had a shorter but more widespread outage earlier in 1999, the company gave daily updates. With organizations such as Powerline Internet Service posting on its web page that it was getting a "runaround" from MCI WorldCom whose "explanations are lame, to say the least," it was obvious that MCI needed someone to do some image building for the company.[*]

Without professional PR people in charge, there can be problems. Microsoft Corporation, hit hard by the public relations fallout from its antitrust court battle with the Justice Department, considered a massive media campaign designed to create the appearance of a groundswell of public support for the company. However, Microsoft came in for criticism when it was revealed that the plan hinged on a number of unusual, and possibly unethical, tactics. Among them were the planting of articles in the media, as well as letters to the editor and opinion pieces to be commissioned by Microsoft's top media handlers but presented by local firms as spontaneous testimonials.[**]

[*]Del Jones, "MCI WorldCom Service Restored, but Many Users Still Angry," *USA Today*, August 16, 1999, p. 2B.

[**]"Microsoft Plans Scheme to Polish Image," *Los Angeles Times* News Service, in the *San Francisco Chronicle*, April 11, 1998, p. D1.

How did the American people form such an image of the enemy? How did stories about Iraqi soldiers taking babies out of incubators in hospitals and throwing them into the streets reach an angry American public? For starters, the government of Kuwait hired the American public relations firm Hill & Knowlton (hillandknowlton.com) to develop an issues-management PR campaign to encourage anti-Iraq sentiment (see Box 14.3). The firm distributed "Free Kuwait" T-shirts and bumper stickers and held news conferences to show evidence of torture and other human rights violations by Iraqi troops in Kuwait. It also issued video news releases and orchestrated a "National Free Kuwait Day" and a "National Prayer Day" for Kuwait. Some $3 million was spent on issues management to gain American support for U.S. involvement in Kuwait.

Crisis management, on the other hand, is a **reaction** to an event or a disaster that has focused unfavorable publicity on the organization. Crisis-management public relations requires immediate attention, and the success of the effort is sometimes determined by how quickly the organization responds.

reaction

The first success in crisis management public relations is attributed to Ivy Ledbetter Lee, who represented the Pennsylvania Railroad in the early 20th century.

When one of the railroad's trains derailed in 1906, killing and injuring several people, Lee resisted company efforts to hush up the accident (a typical approach to crises at the time). Instead, he provided the media with full and accurate accounts of the accident and even ran special trains, at company expense, to take journalists to the scene. He also persuaded the company to conduct a systemwide survey of railroad beds to avoid future derailments and announced the company would provide financial aid to the families of those killed or injured. As a result, the Pennsylvania Railroad and the railroad industry received their first favorable press coverage in years.[13]

Johnson & Johnson (J&J) became involved in crisis-management PR after seven people in the Chicago area died from taking cyanide-tainted Tylenol capsules. The company immediately took all Tylenol capsules off the market and reissued the product in tamper-resistant containers, an effort that cost J&J millions of dollars. Many believed negative publicity about the Tylenol-related deaths would spell the end of the popular pain reliever, but it rapidly recovered its number-one position in market sales. The Public Relations Society of America's Honor and Awards Committee presented its Silver Anvil Award to Johnson & Johnson and its PR firm, Burson-Marsteller (bm.com), for their handling of the crisis.

Johnson & Johnson's success was due in part to a company philosophy of social responsibility. Lawrence G. Foster, vice president of public relations for Johnson & Johnson at the time, described the company's approach: "During the crisis phases of the Tylenol tragedy, virtually every public relations decision was based on sound, socially responsible business principles, which is when public relations is most effective."[14]

Johnson & Johnson again used this same management style and philosophy when the tamper-resistant containers proved fallible and another woman died from a cyanide-tainted Tylenol capsule. This time the company permanently ceased manufacturing all capsule medication.

The chairman of the board of Johnson & Johnson, James Burke, demonstrates the new safety cap designed for Tylenol. This was part of Johnson & Johnson's crisis-management PR campaign following several cyanide tampering incidents.

When the oil tanker Exxon *Valdez* ran aground in Alaska, spilling nearly 11 million gallons of oil in Prince William Sound, the public turned on the large oil firm, boycotting its gasoline and conjuring up images of a major polluter whenever the name Exxon was encountered. Exxon at first shrugged off responsibility for the oil spill and was slow to begin cleanup operations. As one public relations practitioner commented, Exxon should have had the president of the company on the shore cleaning the rocks within 24 hours.

Source Perrier, the maker of a popular French bottled mineral water product, found itself in crisis when the news media reported that the product had been contaminated with traces of a cancer-causing agent, benzene. Source Perrier bungled its crisis-management challenge by first trying to ignore the benzene contamination and then trying to minimize its extent. The public lost confidence in the company and its product. It wasn't until Perrier hired the PR firm that had handled the Tylenol crisis, Burson-Marsteller, that it began to recover from

@ Practicing Media Literacy
Can you think of any examples of large companies having to deal with crisis management?

the crisis. The solution included removing all of the bottled water from the shelves and reporting to the public the cause of the contamination and the successful efforts to eliminate it.

Perhaps one of the best examples of crisis management in recent years when PepsiCo faced a rapidly spreading rumor that needles and syringes were turning up in sealed Pepsi cans. It all began when an 82-year-old man in Tacoma, Washington, reported such a find. Two days later, a similar incident of this type was reported in the state of Washington. Then similar reports were made from coast to coast, with discoveries being reported in some 23 states and in such dissimilar cities as Bakersfield and New York City. Bad publicity for PepsiCo was rampant, and the fascination of the media and the public with the reports was described as a "feeding frenzy." What made

When reports began circulating of syringe needles being found in sealed Pepsi cans, the company quickly released a video showing it was virtually impossible for anything of this type to be placed in the cans during the canning process.

the case so attention grabbing was the grotesque image of syringes in Pepsi cans, particularly in the era of AIDS.

PepsiCo put together a crisis management public relations team of 12 executives and quickly went on the offensive. One of the first things they did was produce a video news release that showed the process of canning that the company used. In that process, the cans are upside down and are turned upright for only a second before being filled and sealed. They put out stories that the reports were a hoax and urged the Federal Food and Drug Administration (FDA) to immediately investigate the claims. In less than two weeks, the FDA issued a report that there was no evidence that syringes had been found in any Pepsi cans. Information was released indicating that making false reports to federal officials carried a five-year prison term and a $250,000 fine. The federal government started making arrests of people issuing false reports. Pepsi ran large ads in newspapers across the country stating, "As America now knows, those stories about Diet Pepsi were a hoax. Plain and simple, not true." The plan worked, and confidence in Pepsi products returned.

What had apparently happened was a mistaken report issued by the 82-year-old Tacoma man and a series of "copycat" reports from others around the country. The man found a needle, which apparently had been placed there by a diabetic relative, in an empty can of Pepsi he had been drinking the night before. He assumed it had been in the can when he drank the beverage. Had it not been for the fast action of the PepsiCo crisis management public relations team, that summer's sales season for Pepsi might have turned into a disaster.

Crisis management is an increasingly important function in corporate public relations as our society becomes more complex and news and information are more rapidly and thoroughly circulated (see Box 14.4). Public relations, like advertising, is a **message business** that in recent years has become highly sophisticated and respected. However, it is still surrounded by some of the controversies that have plagued it from its early days. Most of the controversy comes from the great deal of confusion that still exists regarding exactly what public relations is all about.

message business

CONTROVERSIES SURROUNDING PR PRACTICES

The fact that PR practitioners are involved in creating positive images for their clients often causes public concern and criticism. PR efforts determine much of the content of our mass media, and news consumers seldom know the difference between a story written by a news reporter and a public relations **news release.** When they find out that what they believed to be an unbiased account by a reporter is actually a press release, they become angry.

news release

Wall Street Journal Study

A study of a typical issue of the *Wall Street Journal* found that 53 news stories were based on PR releases and 32 of them were reprinted almost verbatim or in paraphrase. Curiously, 20 of these 53 stories, including some taken nearly verbatim from a press release, were listed as having been written by a *Journal* staffer.[15]

These findings are reflective of media content throughout the country. There would be no problem with the fact that PR practitioners generate a large amount of media content if the

Box 14.4

MEDIA WATCH

Using All the Media to Try to Improve an Image

No matter how strong a public relations effort may be, it doesn't always solve the problem. For example, when an outbreak of E. *coli* bacterial poisoning killed one person and sickened at least 66 others, federal health officials determined that the apparent cause was an unpasteurized fruit beverage sold in several western states.

As more cases were reported in Washington, Colorado (where a baby died), and California (where at least 10 children were believed to be stricken by the bacteria, including a two-year-old who was hospitalized in critical condition with kidney damage), the stock of the fruit juice manufacturer, Odwalla, Inc., quickly dropped 34 percent.

Of course, the company immediately pulled its product from the shelves of stores in the western states and Canada, but that only took care of the immediate situation. The damage to the company's image was longer range and necessitated a public relations campaign.

A crisis team was put together and a crisis communications center was established so that all information would be disseminated out of one place. Three people handled all media calls, including the company's chairman and its CEO. They reportedly fielded nearly 60 calls daily from reporters around the world.

The next step was to set up a site on the Internet to deal with public concerns about the recall. The website told customers that possibly tainted products had been removed from 4,600 retail outlets and outlined Odwalla's plant sanitation procedures. The website also offered a step-by-step description of how the company made its juice products.

Within days, Odwalla's chair and founder, Greg Steltenpohl, made a swing through the Northwest, meeting with the news media and the families of victims, to publicly apologize for the outbreak linked to his company. At the same time, Steltenpohl offered to pay outbreak-related medical costs for the affected families and assured the public that the company would not make any more of the juice until it could be sure the product was free of bacteria.

Odwalla then did something it rarely did before: It bought advertising in newspapers. The two nearly full-page ads were placed in some 25 to 30 targeted markets in Washington, California, and Colorado. The first ad expressed the company's shock and sorrow over the outbreak, but also outlined the company's quick recall response and its devotion to new safety research. The second ad was a message of gratitude for the company's supporters.

Public relations experts who later analyzed the manner in which Odwalla handled the crisis pointed out that the company had learned from previous situations, the Exxon *Valdez* and the Tylenol scare among them, that confronting a problem quickly is essential. But most also agreed that Odwalla might need more than just good PR; it would need money.

The end result was that Odwalla agreed to pay $1.5 million in criminal penalties for the bacterial outbreak. Odwalla also reportedly paid up to $15 million to settle lawsuits by the families of those sickened by the outbreak. To top it off, Odwalla had to sue its insurance company for refusing to pay more than $21 million in claims. Despite the critically acclaimed PR effort, the incident is said to have cost Odwalla millions of dollars in lost business income and millions more in the product recall and in the investigation and restoration of its production facility.

---

sources of that content were identified. People could then evaluate the information on the basis of its source, rather than blindly accepting it as unbiased "news."

Positive Aspects of PR News

Public relations practitioners argue that they actually help the free flow of information in our society. Our nation has grown very large since its founding more than 200 years ago. For the concept of a democracy dependent on a well-informed citizenry to work today, journalists must have help in gathering news and information. Public relations assists in this process.

Modern PR may also be an important ingredient in our culture because it provides a broader and sometimes more accurate flow of information. According to Herb Schmertz, former vice president of public affairs for Mobil Oil Company, most news reporters, particularly television reporters, don't understand business. As a result, they often distort business stories to the detriment of corporations. The job of corporate public relations departments, according to Schmertz, is to reflect accurately for the public the truth about business activities.[16]

"Flacks"

Despite the media's dependence on public relations for content and the fact that many PR practitioners have been trained as journalists, a rather cool and distant relationship often exists between journalists working for the media and public relations personnel (see Box 14.5). Since the early days of press agentry, journalists have called PR people *flacks*. For example, the *Associated Press Managing Editors* (APME) *Guidelines* had the following to say about flacks:

> A flack is a person who makes all or part of his income by obtaining space in newspapers without cost to himself or his clients. Usually a professional. The term also includes those persons who seek free space for causes which they deem beneficial to the country, to the nation, or to God. Mostly amateurs. Of the two categories, the pros are easier to handle. They are known formally as public relations men . . . A flack is a flack. His job is to say kind things about his client. He will not lie very often, but much of the time he tells less than the whole story. You do not owe the PR man anything. The owner of the newspaper, not the flack, pays your salary. Your immediate job is to serve the reader, not the man who would raid your columns.[17]

> @ **Practicing Media Literacy**
> Are media journalists justified in being skeptical of public relations people?

Lingering Negative Image

Criticism and distrust of public relations linger on, years after the profession has "grown up." This is one reason some large companies have renamed their public relations departments "public affairs" or "corporate communication" divisions. Changing the name, however, doesn't necessarily change the image, which, by and large, is created not by the true PR practitioners but by some not-so-professional individuals who call themselves public relations people.

One reason PR retains a poor image is the lingering practice by some companies of attempting to deceive the news media. According to Robert L. Dilenschneider, former president of Hill & Knowlton, the largest public relations firm in the United States, too many businesses have damaged their **credibility** by lying to the media. "If you look at American business over the past 25 years, there's been a lot of deception," he says. "But there's no substitute for telling the truth, no matter how tough that might be."[18]

credibility

On a more positive note, many strides have been made to improve the industry's image. The most effective efforts have been made by the Public Relations Society of America (PRSA) (prsa.org), which has adopted a stringent code of ethics and mandatory accreditation procedures for all members (see Box 14.6). It has more than 14,000 members, which represents fewer than 8 percent of all the people who claim to be working in public relations. Ironically, although the primary function of the public relations industry is the creation of positive public images, the industry has failed to create goodwill for itself.

Box 14.5
MEDIA WATCH
The Ethics of Public Relations vs. the Ethics of the Media

There is a distrust of public relations people on the part of the news media, even though those in the media often rely on PR people for information, sources, and news leads.

For example, when a respected journalist announced that she was leaving the world of television news to work in the field of public relations, she was quickly attacked by many of her former colleagues in the industry for "selling out" and "going to the other side." Television news people from across the country accused her of joining a profession that was "dishonest" and "despicable."

Of course, PR practitioners immediately came to her defense. Many pointed out that public relations people assist corporate and government officials in fulfilling their responsibility in letting various groups of people know what they are doing. But they also stressed that you don't give up your ethical principles just because you work in public relations. As one family man explained it, you can't tell your children they need to always tell the truth and then go out and lie for a client.

But many PR people took it one step further in their defense of the profession by pointing to the tar-

nished image of the news media. One noted that it wasn't PR people who wrote a Pulitzer Prize story for the *Washington Post* on child heroin addicts, only to have the paper return the Pulitzer when the author admitted that the subject of her article was fictitious. Nor was it a PR person who staged dogfights in Colorado to get good video for a local television news story. It also was not PR people who attached rockets to the underside of a pickup truck to get it to burst into flames for a report on the fuel tank hazards of the vehicle aired on NBC's *Dateline* newsmagazine series.

Many reporters with 10 to 20 years of experience have moved into the public relations field not because their clients want to "manipulate the media," as so many journalists fear. Instead, they say, the clients want to know how to avoid being manipulated *by* the media. As some explained, members of the public are worried about being misquoted, having their statements taken out of context, and not being given a fair chance to explain themselves. With the image of the news media now being as low as that of politicians, perhaps journalists would be better off hiring their own PR staffs rather than complaining about what a PR person does.

The PRSA also administers a voluntary accreditation program for public relations professionals. The purpose of the accreditation program is to unify and advance the profession by identifying those who have demonstrated broad knowledge, experience, and professional judgment in the field. The Universal Accreditation Program was formed in 1998 and during its early years, over 2,000 candidates took the examination, with an average of 65 percent of them passing. According to the PRSA, the designation Accredited in Public Relations (APR) signifies a high professional level of experience and competence.

SUMMARY

Public relations, like advertising, is a message business designed to promote and maintain goodwill for clients. PR depends on the mass media to promote this goodwill, and the media depend on PR practitioners for much of their content.

Public relations now involves a variety of activities, including policymaking, legitimate press agentry, spin doctoring, promotion, working with government agencies (public affairs), publicity campaigns, and paid advertising.

The need for PR developed in the late 19th century, when big business found it had a very poor public image. Early public relations practitioners, such as Ivy

Box 14.6
MEDIA LITERACY
Declaration of Principles of the Public Relations Society of America

This declaration serves as a preamble to the Public Relations Society of America's Code of Professional Standards for the Practice of Public Relations. The Code was adopted by the PRSA Assembly in 1988 to replace the Code of Ethics in force since 1950 and revised in 1954, 1959, 1963, 1977, and 1983.

Members of the Public Relations Society of America base their professional principles on the fundamental value and dignity of the individual, holding that the free exercise of human rights, especially freedom of speech, freedom of assembly and freedom of the press, is essential to the practice of public relations.

In serving the interests of clients and employers, we dedicate ourselves to the goals of better communication, understanding and cooperation among the diverse individuals, groups and institutions of society.

We pledge:

To conduct ourselves professionally, with truth, accuracy, fairness and responsibility to the public;

To improve our individual competence and advance the knowledge and proficiency of the profession through continuing research and education;

And to adhere to the articles of the Code of Professional Standards for the Practice of Public Relations as adopted by the governing Assembly of the Society.

Ledbetter Lee and Edward L. Bernays, helped to elevate PR from an activity of merely getting publicity for a client to one involving a systematic effort to represent clients favorably to the public and to research public perceptions adequately.

The federal government got into the public relations business in World War I when it appointed the Creel Committee to present the U.S. war effort to the public in a favorable light.

During the Great Depression of the 1930s, businesses failed to make the most of PR efforts at a time when they needed them most. The U.S. government again cranked up public relations efforts during World War II by creating the Office of War Information. This agency survives today as the U.S. Information Agency.

Issues management and crisis management play a major role in the activities of public relations practitioners in today's corporate world. More than 200,000 people work in public relations today, and there are several hundred PR firms. In addition, almost all major companies and government agencies have PR personnel on their payrolls.

The mass media rely on public relations practitioners for information to keep our society informed. The public is served by PR practitioners who accurately interpret the activities of their corporate or government clients.

Although public relations is a respectable profession today, with its own code of ethics, many people who call themselves PR practitioners still do not adhere to the principles of the profession and often use the same dubious tactics early press agents used. The Public Relations Society of America now administers a Universal Accreditation Program in an attempt to improve the image and quality of those working in the field.

Find a review of *Key People and Concepts*, a message board for *Practicing Media Literacy* questions, self tests, and more at: www.mhhe.com/wilson.

Thought Questions

1. If you were the chief executive officer of a major chemical company that was criticized for making toxic substances, how would you combat the negative image?

2. Select a company and determine what types of issues-management concerns the PR staff should monitor.

3. List some examples of spin doctoring in recent political campaigns.

4. Should PR firms take on controversial clients such as those handled by Hill & Knowlton? Why or why not?

5. Do you think the Public Relations Society of America should seek legislation requiring all PR practitioners to be licensed? Why or why not?

Notes

1. Georgann Koelln of *Knight Ridder* Newspapers, "Hot Hype in Action," *Fresno Bee*, June 21, 1999, p. C1.

2. *Ibid.*

3. Philip Lesly, ed., *Public Relations Handbook* (Englewood Cliffs, NJ: Prentice Hall, 1971), p. xi.

4. Rex F. Harlow, "Building a Public Relations Definition," *Public Relations Review*, Winter 1976, p. 36.

5. First World Assembly of Public Relations Associations, Mexico City, Mexico, 1978.

6. Philip Lesly, "Report and Recommendation: Task Force on Stature and Role of Public Relations," *Public Relations Journal*, March 1981, p. 30.

7. Edward L. Bernays, *Public Relations* (Norman, OK: University of Oklahoma Press, 1952), p. 84.

8. Quoted in Don R. Pember, *Mass Media in America,* 4th ed. (Chicago: Science Research Associates, 1983), p. 292.

9. Frank Wylie, "The New Professionals," speech to the First National Student Conference, Public Relations Student Society of America, Dayton, Ohio, October 24, 1976 (published by Chrysler Corporation), p. 5.

10. Herb Schmertz with William Novak, *Good-bye to the Low Profile: The Art of Creative Confrontation* (Boston: Little, Brown, 1986), pp. 16–17.

11. Edward L. Bernays, "The Engineering of Consent," *Industry,* December 1978, pp. 12–13, 36.

12. Mission Statement, Burson-Marsteller Global Perception Management Firm, www.bm.com.

13. Irwin Ross, *The Image Merchants* (Garden City, NY: Doubleday, 1959), p. 31.

14. Lawrence G. Foster, "The Role of Public Relations in the Tylenol Crisis," *Public Relations Journal*, March 1983, p. 13.

15. "It's in the Journal. But This Is Reporting?" *Columbia Journalism Review,* March/April 1980, pp. 34–36.

16. Schmertz, *Good-bye to the Low Profile,* pp. 82–83.

17. *APME Guidelines* (New York: Associated Press Managing Editors Association, 1969), p. 42.

18. Quoted from an address at a Public Relations Society of America convention, June 25, 1990, Palm Desert, California.

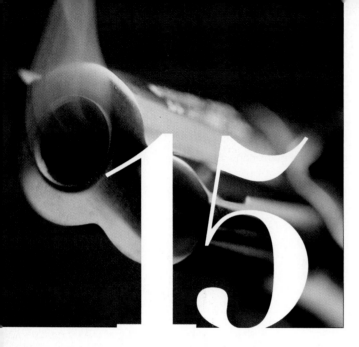

Media Ethics

Journalists must be free of obligation to any interest other than the public's right to know the truth.

—The Society of Professional Journalists

Moviegoers watching Steven Spielberg's *The Lost World: Jurassic Park* knew that those dinosaurs running around the screen weren't real. But toward the end of the film, the television newscaster reporting on the havoc being wreaked by the prehistoric monsters certainly looked real. That's because it really was Bernard Shaw of the Cable News Network (CNN), and he is just one of many legitimate television anchors and reporters who have been appearing in the movies. ● Many of these reporters work for stations in the Los Angeles area and make a little money on the side doing cameos for the movies, but in recent years CNN has been prominent in many movies, from *The Lost World* and *Contact* to *Air Force One* and *The Peacemaker*. Some journalists have condemned this blurring of the line between actual news reporters and Hollywood fiction. There was even dissension at CNN over Shaw's crossover into the movies, with some saying that he was trading credibility for visibility. But others felt that Time Warner, the owners of CNN, had accomplished an acceptable product-placement triumph. After all, Time Warner owns Warner Bros. studios. With all of the media mergers in recent years, there has been a lot of crossover promotion for various corporation products. ● There are those who feel the use of real news reporters in fictional stories is bad because the public already has a difficult time distinguishing between entertainment and reality. But others feel that as long as journalists are portrayed in an accurate manner, it's okay. After all, the major television network anchors are not afraid to appear on the various television talk shows and make jokes with the hosts (Dan Rather singing railroad songs on *The Late Show with David Letterman*, Tom Brokaw being humorous on *The Tonight Show with Jay Leno*, and Peter Jennings appearing often on *Live with Regis and Kathie Lee*). ● NBC's *Dateline* host Jane Pauley has said she's a real journalist and would never portray a fictional one on TV on or the movies because "it blurs the line." According to Pauley, "Viewers are confused enough about the hair and the makeup and the glamour. We already confuse them so much without crossing the line and suddenly becoming make-believe."[1] CNN's Larry King disagrees, saying that reporters take themselves too seriously and pointing out that moviegoers are hip enough to figure out that if they're in a movie, the reporters are part of the fiction. King made his comments at about the time he was appearing as himself in an estimated eight movies set for release.[2] • While ABC, CBS, and NBC say they will not allow their news anchors or reporters to appear in movies, there has been no stopping the network sports reporters from making such appearances. ABC's Howard Cosell appeared in Woody Allen's 1971 film *Bananas* while more recently CBS's Jim Nantz was in the 1997 Kevin Costner movie *Tin Cup*, and NBC's Bob Costas joined ABC's Al Michaels in the 1999 film *BASEketball*. • The networks may be squeamish about having their top-line news stars appearing in fictional movie stories, but *television* fiction doesn't seem to bother them. Such people as NBC's Katie Couric, ABC's Joan Lunden, and CBS's Lesley Stahl appeared as themselves on the sitcom *Murphy Brown*. It would appear that as far as the networks are concerned, ethics are not a consistent thing. In this chapter, we'll examine some of the ethical issues which have plagued the mass media over the years.

NEWS MEDIA ETHICS

Although all areas of the mass media face tough ethical decisions and are constantly being criticized for perceived failures in performance, three areas seem to receive the most criticism: coverage of news events, blurring of content, and advertising and entertainment. Let's first examine ethical decisions in covering news.

It is not unusual for television programs in the Los Angeles area to be preempted by the station's coverage of a high-speed police chase. It doesn't make any difference if the suspect is wanted for a bank robbery or for running a stoplight; as long as there's a chase, the TV news departments will send up their helicopters to provide live coverage of the action. The fact that LA residents are familiar with this pattern is what caused a problem for the stations in 1998. That's when Daniel V. Jones, upset with his health maintenance organization (HMO), took police and TV news choppers on a chase along various LA freeways. After traffic had been stopped in the area, Jones got out of his pickup truck and spread his protest banner on the highway overpass so that the helicopters above could show his message to the viewers. A short time later, Jones set fire to his truck, then took a shotgun and killed himself on live television. Seven Los Angeles stations—two of which had interrupted children's programming—and MSNBC cable aired the incident.

@ Practicing Media Literacy

Have you ever watched a real police chase on television? How long did you remain watching?

The death caused much soul-searching among the media. Tom Goldstein, the dean of the Columbia Graduate School of Journalism, wrote in *TV Guide* that this was "the latest evidence of the steady erosion of the distinction between news and entertainment."[3] Several Los Angeles stations vowed to begin providing a six-second delay when televising high-speed chases. Others said they would use more discretionary judgment in when to cut away from such incidents.

A similar situation occurred in 1994 when a television station in Alexandria, Louisiana, provided live coverage of a standoff between police and a deputy sheriff who had fatally shot his wife several hours earlier. Police had evacuated people from nearby buildings and blocked the streets as the suspect sat on a bench agonizing with a priest for two hours. Then, as the cameras continued to deliver the scene to homes around the city, the man placed the barrel of a .45 to his jaw and pulled the trigger. His body slumped as the cameras showed the blood splattering. The news director for the TV station later said they had not televised a suicide. They had reported a story that had left the downtown area in danger, and the public needed to be aware of it. Although he said about 80 percent of the calls to the station had been in favor of airing the scene, the station elected not to play the tape of the shooting on later newscasts and declined requests from other stations for copies of the video.

On January 22, 1987, 30 reporters and camera technicians gathered in the Pennsylvania state capitol of Harrisburg for a news conference that state treasurer R. Budd Dwyer had called to announce his resignation. He had been convicted the previous month on bribery charges.

The 47-year-old politician appeared nervous and sweaty as he delivered a rambling speech in which he referred to his 22-year political career in the past tense. He told the reporters he was innocent and criticized the prosecutor, judge, governor, justice system, and media, which he said had feasted on him during his legal troubles. Then Dwyer pulled a .357 magnum from a manila envelope, stuck the gun barrel in his mouth, and blew his head off in front of the horrified onlookers.

What resulted was not just a sensational news story but some serious ethical questions as well. How vividly should the journalists who witnessed the event describe the scene? How much detail should be shown in photographs and television tapes? Some television stations showed the entire scene in living color. Others showed the event right up to the placing of the gun barrel in Dwyer's mouth; they then froze the picture but continued the sound through the blast of the gun and the horrified gasps of those in attendance. Some print journalists merely reported that Dwyer had shot himself, while others described in detail what they had seen. Those who did not spare the grisly details were criticized by many of their fellow journalists and members of the

"Live" TV cameras in the courtroom broadcast this reaction of Richard Alan Davis as he was convicted of the kidnap/murder of young Polly Klass in California. However, most TV stations did not use the shot in later newscasts and there was much debate in the newsroom of the San Francisco Chronicle *before it was decided to run this picture on the front page the next day (see Box 15.7).*

public for going too far. Those criticized defended their actions by stating that as reporters they had a duty to tell and show what happened.

A survey of radio, television, and print news professionals conducted by the Radio–Television News Directors Foundation found that while many news executives and reporters welcomed the changing technology in the industry, they also feared it has its downside. Key concerns centered on the increasing ability to broadcast stories live and the ability to alter audio and video images. Being faster with the news presents many ethical problems. As one television station manager told the survey, "Our ability to process information at an ever-increasing rate of speed will necessitate the institution of fail-safe editorial procedures to prevent unauthorized/unedited/unchecked content from airing."[4]

According to Columbia's Goldstein, "News is more than just the current, the dramatic, the titillating, the extraordinary. News is what is important and meaningful, a definition too often forgotten in the rush to grab ratings." (See Box 15.1)[5]

Accuracy and Fairness

getting it right
truth

At the top of the list of journalistic responsibilities are accuracy and fairness. Accuracy means **getting it right,** while fairness means pursuing the **truth** with both vigor and compassion, and reporting information without favoritism, self-interest, or prejudice.[6]

On the surface, accuracy and fairness seem like noble ideals. But even the highest journalistic principles can cause problems in day-to-day implementation. Accuracy sometimes gets in the way of fairness. For example, to be accurate should you use the real names of people in news stories? What if the person is a rape victim? Would revealing the name be fair to the traumatized victim?

The pictures of rescue efforts following the bombing of the federal building in Oklahoma City had tremendous impact. Some people were critical of the newspaper pictures, but felt that the TV images were acceptable because they were fleeting.

In writing a story for a family newspaper or an evening television newscast, would you have used explicit language found in 2 Live Crew's album *As Nasty As They Wanna Be* to describe the controversy? It certainly would be accurate, but would it be fair to the parents of children who might be reading or listening? Would it be fair to adults who find such language offensive?

Some people believed the pictures shown in newspapers following the bombing of the federal building in Oklahoma City in 1995 were too graphic. However, many of those same critics thought the scenes shown

Box 15.1
MEDIA LITERACY
Ethics in Journalism: A Thing of the Past?*

As the 21st century began, many people inside and outside the news media thought the term "journalism ethics" had, perhaps, become an oxymoron.

Certainly the conduct of the media in reporting the sex scandal involving President Bill Clinton and White House intern Monica Lewinsky gave credence to that view.

A widely reported study by Princeton Survey Research Associates showed that, in the early days of the scandal, more than 40 percent of news coverage by magazines, newspapers, and TV involved not factual reporting, but analysis or opinion by journalists themselves.

Only about one percent of all the reporting was based on two or more named sources. Forty percent of the stories based on anonymous sources came from only one source.

Contrast that with guidelines established in the 1970s by the *Washington Post* and accepted by journalistic organizations during coverage of the Watergate break-in involving the Nixon Administration. The *Post* decreed that its reporters Bob Woodward and Carl Bernstein could only use information from an anonymous source if it was confirmed by a second, independent anonymous source.

So what happened?

In a word—competition. Too much of it for the news media to withstand.

In the year 2000, the news media were involved, to their detriment, in a 24-hour news cycle. "All news, all the time" became the norm, thanks to the national presence of the Cable News Network (CNN), CNBC, MSNBC, and the Fox News Channel (FNC). Numerous big cities across the United States also had local 24-hour cable news channels. In addition, the major broadcast TV networks had amortized prohibitive news-gathering costs by expanding coverage from their evening newscasts to such prime time vehicles as *Dateline*, *20/20*, and *48 Hours*.

That glut of information programming, along with the cable news channels and the rise of such Internet gossips as Matt Drudge, forced editors and publishers to increase the pressure on reporters to "be first" and "react faster" to any kind of breaking story.

For example, during the early days of the Clinton–Lewinsky scandal, news media "reporting" frequently involved the airing or printing of information that another news media outlet originated. There was no attempt to verify such information—the imperative was to get it on the air or in print as quickly as possible.

Indeed, by the end of the 20th century, the reporting of gossip or unverified information increased exponentially. In some newsrooms, the fact that a source said something, no matter how wild or unprovable the allegation, was enough for it to be reported. Standards of accuracy or taste frequently were sacrificed by news organizations seeking to remain competitive.

In the early 1990s, a tabloid newspaper named the victim in a widely publicized case in which a member of the Kennedy family was accused of rape. *NBC Nightly News* and the *New York Times* followed suit, each saying the name had been made public and was, therefore, fair game. Critics—who noted the *Times* and NBC had routinely protected the identity of rape victims in the past—called this a case of journalism's traditional "bottom feeders" (tabloids) setting the agenda for the industry's most respected entities.

Where does journalism go from here? Serious reporters must make the case to their public that values such as fairness, balance, and assiduous fact-checking are indispensable. Given the vast array of nontraditional information sources now available—including Internet websites where unverified rumors are posted as facts and inflammatory talk-radio hosts who masquerade as journalists—it is not at all certain that the public will care about serious reporting.

If that becomes the case, then "journalism ethics" truly will be an oxymoron.

*By Dennis Hart, a former TV news executive in San Francisco, Detroit, Atlanta, Phoenix, Buffalo and Fresno

on television were acceptable because they went by quickly, while the newspaper pictures were frozen on the front pages of many newspapers across the nation.

The Oklahoma City bombing also raised an issue concerning fairness. Shortly after the bombing, there were reports that one of the suspects was believed to be from

@   **Practicing Media Literacy**
How far do you think the media should go in presenting the visual aspects of a story to the public?

the Middle East. Many Middle Eastern visitors to this country at that time later reported that people were looking at them strangely; some were even stopped by police for questioning, and citizens from that part of the world had received a bad reputation. No one from the Middle East was ever arrested or charged with the crime. In fact, two American citizens were later taken into custody. It was a case of the media jumping on a story with very few facts available.

A similar situation occurred in 1996 when a bomb went off in a park in Atlanta during the summer Olympics. For a few days following the incident, Richard Jewell, a security guard who had found the bomb before it went off, was considered a hero. Then the FBI leaked a story to the media that Jewell had become a suspect in the case. The media began relentless coverage of every move Jewell made. Cameras and reporters camped out in his yard as FBI agents searched his residence; news vans followed him as he went to FBI headquarters for questioning; and there was much speculation as to his motives for planting the bomb.

Some observers believed the Jewell story served two purposes: (1) The FBI got what it wanted—the appearance of being quick to identify a suspect in the case—and (2) the media got what they wanted—headlines and ratings. The problem was that Jewell's reputation was being ruined even though no official charges had been made. Months later, the FBI announced that Jewell was no longer a suspect.

But for Jewell, the case wasn't over yet. Following the news that he was no longer an FBI suspect, he sued the *Atlanta Journal-Constitution*, as well as CNN and NBC. Atlanta attorney Peter Canfield, whose firm represents the newspaper, later noted that Jewell didn't sue the FBI for making him its chief suspect, but went after the *Journal-Constitution* for reporting that information. Saying that the newspaper's coverage of the investigation was fair and accurate, Canfield asked:

> Should the *Journal-Constitution* have been sure that Jewell was the FBI's chief suspect before reporting that? Yes, and the newspaper was. Should the *Journal-Constitution* have explained why Jewell had become the FBI's chief suspect? Yes, and it did. What Jewell calls "a vicious assault" by the *Journal-Constitution* on him was, in fact, accurate reporting of information sworn to by the FBI that convinced a federal magistrate to authorize the extensive searches of Jewell's premises and belongings.
>
> Should the *Journal-Constitution* have actively questioned FBI theories as to Jewell's guilt? Yes, and it did; in fact, it did so more than any other news organization.
>
> In the end, Jewell received a clearance letter from the FBI and a congressional inquiry into the FBI's tactics. If the *Journal-Constitution* and other responsible media had not aggressively reported on the investigation, the outcome could well have been very different.[7]

Both NBC and CNN reached out-of-court settlements with Jewell, NBC paying an estimated $500,000. Despite agreeing to an unspecified amount in its settlement, CNN continued to maintain that its coverage provided a "fair and accurate review" of the events surrounding the bombing and the Jewell investigation. As for Jewell himself, there were reports that his attorneys were talking with HBO and a Hollywood movie studio about a possible deal to tell his side of the story. *Daily Variety*, citing unidentified sources, reported that he was considering offers in the mid-six-figure range from three studios. More than a year after the incident, Attorney General Janet Reno offered an apology to Jewell for the news

@   **Practicing Media Literacy**
Do you think Richard Jewell is justified in suing media outlets or do you feel that the media handled the story properly?

leaks, and less than two months later he helped open the 1997 season for NBC's *Saturday Night Live* program, appearing in a skit in which he got to belt a Janet Reno impersonator in the stomach.

There was also the incident just before the 1996 NFL playoffs when authorities in Texas reported two members of the Dallas Cowboys football team had been accused of rape. The media, including talk radio programs nationwide, ran with the story and had the two players all but convicted of the crime. However, police later reported that the woman who had filed the rape charges was now being charged with filing a false report, adding that no evidence was found implicating the two Cowboys.

Should the media have made these stories as big as they were since no arrests had been made? It's not realistic to expect the media to wait until arrests occur, especially if law enforcement officials are leaking the names of suspects. But some form of restraint seems to be needed.

Columbia dean Goldstein noted that no one seems to have come up with a way to stop this herd mentality in the media. But he offered a few possible solutions:

> Journalists need training in criminal procedure so they understand what evidence is required for a search warrant or arrest. Gatherings in which journalists and law-enforcement officials educate each other about their work—so popular in the 1970s—need to be revived.
>
> Prosecutors must learn how to apologize if someone is accused falsely. And the government must also learn to keep its secrets, especially in criminal investigations. Like it or not, journalists cannot guarantee the truth of what investigators say. They can only strive to report accurately what investigators say.
>
> Journalists must learn restraint, especially in competitive situations. They must apologize on-air when they have overstepped the boundaries of taste and decency.[8]

Once an error has been made by the news media, how should it be corrected? Some television and radio stations will not acknowledge a mistake while others, if the mistake was large enough, will offer an apology on the air. Most newspapers in the United States now run a box somewhere in the paper to correct previous errors. These boxes, sometimes called "Setting It Straight" or "Errata," are often placed in prominent locations, but other times are buried deep in the newspaper where they aren't easily found.

When Britain's largest selling daily newspaper ran an 11-year-old photograph revealing a breast of Sophie Rhys-Jones, the soon-to-be bride of England's Prince Edward, the paper was castigated strongly by Buckingham Palace, the office of the Prime Minister, and other London newspapers. So the *Sun* ran an apology under the headline "Sorry, Sophie." The paper went on to tell the princess-to-be that she wouldn't have to worry; the *Sun* would run nothing else which might offend her. The controversial picture of Rhys-Jones was featured on the front page of the *Sun*, while the apology was carried on page 13.

Honesty and Integrity

Not all ethical dilemmas deal with accuracy and fairness. Honesty and integrity also come into play. In 1998, *Boston Globe* columnist Mike Barnicle came under fire when it was revealed that he had passed off some jokes from a book by comedian George Carlin as his own work in one of his columns. The newspaper suspended him without pay for two months. Just two months earlier, another *Boston Globe* writer, award-winning metro columnist Patricia Smith, had resigned after it was found that many of her columns had contained fictional quotes and people. Barnicle was quick to point

leaks

@   Practicing Media Literacy

Do you think that it is common for the media to make up stories?

out that his offense was nothing compared to what Smith had done. "No one's reputation is ruined; there are no fatalities left in the rear-view mirror," he said.[9] Within two weeks, Barnicle resigned from the *Globe* when charges arose that he had fabricated a 1995 tear-jerker column about two children hospitalized with cancer.

That same year, editors at *The New Republic* apologized to readers after finding that a former reporter had invented all or part of 27 of the 41 articles he had written for the magazine. "We offer no excuses for any of this," the editors wrote, "only our deepest apologies to all concerned." The editors noted that six of the stories could be considered entirely or nearly made up, while others blended fact with fiction. As for reaction from the readers, editor Charles Lane said that comments had varied. "I don't believe lasting damage has been done to the credibility of the magazine although certainly this is not the kind of episode we'd like."[10]

The Cincinnati Enquirer published an apology across the top of the front page of its Sunday edition in June of 1998, adding that it had agreed to pay Chiquita Brands International a settlement of more than $10 million. The action was an attempt to keep the Gannett newspaper from being sued for a series of articles that were critical of the fruit company's business practices. The articles were partially based on some 2,000 internal voice mails that were said to have been illegally obtained by a reporter for the paper. The reporter was fired and later entered a plea of guilty to intercepting voice mail from Chiquita. However, as we discussed in Chapter 4, it is still unclear just how much of the information reported in the *Enquirer* story was inaccurate.

But it wasn't only newspapers finding themselves in the spotlight over honesty and integrity issues; television and magazines also came under fire. In what some described as the worst embarrassment in its 18-year history, CNN retracted a story it had run which charged that U.S. troops had used lethal nerve gas to kill American defectors during an air raid into Laos during the Vietnam war. In a statement released by the chairman of the CNN News Group, it was explained that an independent investigation commissioned by CNN found that the story could not be supported with sufficient evidence and CNN couldn't even confirm that American defectors had been targeted. *Time* magazine, which is a part of the same conglomerate that owns CNN, also printed a retraction since the magazine had published a print version of the story. However, officials at *Time* stressed that CNN alone bore the responsibility for both the television report and the printed article.

The controversy became public when CNN's military analyst, retired Major General Perry Smith, resigned in protest while calling the story "sleazy." Journalists at both *Time* and CNN said that the story was broadcast and published despite complaints and memos from journalists inside both organizations who were concerned after seeing the piece before it was released. The two CNN producers who developed the story refused to resign and were subsequently fired. Pulitzer Prize–winning correspondent Peter Arnett reportedly received a reprimand. Arnett tried to distance himself from the story, saying he had not contributed anything to it but had only served as the narrator for the piece. He later left the cable news channel after network executives decided to exercise an exit clause in his contract.

The study that brought on the controversy showed no willful deception or illegality on the part of the producers; instead the report said that the story was the result of a more subtle process of **distortion.** The report indicated that the problem began when available evidence could not support the conclusions being drawn and

distortion

continued when sources were led to believe that unseen evidence supported their own suspicions. The report was also critical that the journalists refused to give more than a passing nod to a series of denials by witnesses that the event could have taken place. The two fired CNN reporters issued a 78-page rebuttal to the study and continued to vigorously defend their work, saying they had many other sources on tape who could further support their claims. Meanwhile, the Pentagon said there was no evidence to support the story, and Secretary of Defense William Cohen called the reports irresponsible. One former Green Beret sergeant filed a $100 million defamation suit against *Time*, CNN, and correspondent Arnett.

In another case, Denver television reporter Wendy Bergen aired a series on illegal dogfights. Entitled "Blood Sport," the four-part series showed pit bulls attacking one another and contained interviews with purported fans and dog trainers boasting about the activity. It was later revealed that the dogfights had been **staged.** The viewers had been deceived, and Bergen was convicted on three felony charges in connection with the taped pit bull fights.[11]

staging

Reporters for an Oklahoma City television station managed to avoid prosecution when they registered Boo-Boo Kitty, Phred the Dog, and other family pets to vote. When station KOCO-TV notified the election board secretary that the reporters were going to test the voter registration system, they were warned not to break any laws. When the story of the pet registration was aired, authorities asked county and federal prosecutors to investigate. The district attorney's office later ruled that the case lacked any criminal intent and, even if criminal intent had been an essential element in the case, there probably would be no prosecution because a jury simply would not convict.

In 1997, in a costly verdict against the practice of using hidden cameras to get a story, a North Carolina jury decided that the ABC television network had to pay more than $5.5 million in damages to the Food Lion supermarket chain. The action was unusual because Food Lion had not sued for libel, nor did it contest in the court the accuracy of an ABC *Prime Time Live* broadcast five years earlier alleging unsanitary practices at some of the chain's stores. Instead, the federal jury had found ABC guilty of fraud and trespassing because two of the program's producers lied to get jobs as Food Lion clerks and then used miniature **hidden cameras** to shoot footage inside the stores. The amount of the judgment was later reduced to $315,000, but the whole case was eventually thrown out by an appeals court. The case also stimulated some spirited discussion among television journalists. According to the creator and boss of CBS's *60 Minutes*, Don Hewitt, hype and promotion have supplanted reporting and legwork as networks search for ratings. According to Hewitt, the most overworked gimmick is one that he claims responsibility for pioneering in the early days of *60 Minutes*, the hidden camera. He singled out ABC News as being "drunk on hidden cameras. You don't want to overdo it. After a while, it starts to get silly."[12] But ABC News president David Westin disagreed, saying that ABC has very tight guidelines and hidden cameras were being used sparingly. Meanwhile, a year after the initial court ruling in its favor, Food Lion announced that it was closing 61 stores in three states and laying off more than 3,000 workers because the damaging report on ABC News had kept the grocery store chain from gaining a foothold in those areas. And in 1998, the California State Supreme Court ruled that reporters who used hidden recording devices in pursuit of a story could be sued for invasion of privacy.

hidden cameras

@ **Practicing Media Literacy**

Do you feel the networks are overusing hidden cameras to get stories? Do you support the use of hidden cameras?

Was freelance reporter Jonathan Franklin right or wrong when he posed as a mortician in 1991 and entered the mortuary at Dover Air Force Base, the sole Desert Storm casualty processing center, to determine whether the government was underestimating the number of casualties during the Persian Gulf War? Franklin had exhausted other efforts to get an accurate account of the war dead. When he got inside the morgue, he found there were "about 200" combat deaths, in contrast to the official Pentagon figure of 55. Newspapers that ran Franklin's story said the **deception** was justified because (1) there were no other means by which to report the story and (2) the information in the story was politically vital to readers, with important public policy ramifications.[13]

deception

The end of the 20th century has seen much new technology, but this rapid development has created problems in the areas of honesty and integrity. There have been instances of using the Internet to help sell bootlegged concert recordings (see Chapter 11). Copyright laws have also been violated on the Internet, generating international hearings in Vienna regarding the establishment of standards. The wide-open public usage of this far-reaching tool of communication has created many ethical problems (see Box 15.2).

Photographic Accuracy

Journalists have long held that photographs should accurately reflect the event being portrayed. However, occasionally photographers are tempted to make pictures more eye appealing by changing the angle of the shot or cropping out certain details. The Society of Professional Journalists' code of ethics states that "photographs and telecasts should give an accurate picture of an event and not highlight an event out of context."

New computerized technology, however, has made this ethical issue a concern once again. For example, CBS News was accused of sacrificing journalistic ethics for the sake of business when it superimposed digital images of the network logo over that of a competitor during *The CBS Evening News with Dan Rather* on the eve of the year 2000 in New York's Times Square. Those watching the newscast that night saw a billboard advertising CBS News in the picture behind Rather. If they thought it was a well-placed piece of billboard advertising, they were wrong. The truth is the logo was covering NBC's large Astrovision screen in Times Square and a Budweiser ad.

Rather later said that the action was "a mistake" that he regretted. "There is no excuse for it," he said. "I did not grasp the possible ethical implications of this and that was wrong on my part."[14] However, CBS executives defended the action, pointing out that the technology is used regularly to display the CBS logo on buildings, cabs, and even on horse-drawn carriages outside the studio where *The Early Show* originates each morning. A producer of that show defended the practice, saying that it doesn't press the boundaries of ethical guidelines or "distort the content of the news."[15] Said CBS Television president Leslie Moonves, "Anytime there's an NBC logo up on our network, we'll block it again."[16]

> **@   Practicing Media Literacy**
>
> Do you think it is acceptable for a network to use this technology to alter the images being seen by the viewers?

Inserting digital images into your television picture is now relatively common in sports broadcasts. Advertising messages are often shown on the wall behind the batter in baseball telecasts, with advertisers changing every few batters. The technology allows "**virtual advertising**" to reach specific audiences. For example, in the national telecast of a game between the New York

virtual advertising

Box 15.2

MEDIA WATCH

The World Wide Web: Are There Ethics in Gossip?

The World Wide Web is an extension of the local coffeehouse or barbershop where people can gossip or just chat, speculate, and argue. There's also another similarity: A lot of erroneous information is passed along as fact.

Before the technological advances of the 20th century, people read the same newspapers and magazines, watched the same news on the three television networks, or caught up on local community events from the local radio station. Everyone shared a common denominator. But on the Internet, that common link doesn't exist. There are many windows into news events all around the world, and the public tends to believe the information available to be true, just because it's there.

Within weeks or even days after a major event, dialogue on the Internet begins to include an element of speculation and wild conjecture, and the line between the credible and the incredible, between fact and fiction, is no longer viable.

The Internet is still so new that it's perceived to be powerful, truthful, and far reaching, with many people giving it a high level of trust—a much higher trust, in fact, than they would give to their government leaders or to the traditional news media.

This also presents a problem for the media, which have been turning to the Internet as a valuable information resource. But just how much of this information is valid, reliable, or even usable?

When a TWA flight from New York to Paris went down off the coast of Long Island speculation abounded as to what might have caused the crash. While the FBI and investigators for the National Transportation Safety Board spent months sifting through the retrieved pieces of the aircraft for clues, the Internet was jumping with a variety of theories. What was interesting was that many web users indicated that when given a choice between what the FBI, the NTSB, or the news media were saying and what information was available online, the Internet was considered more reliable.

A media leaders forum, sponsored by the Louisiana State University School of Mass Communication, found that a slim margin of media executives felt that journalists could quote from conversations "overheard" on Internet discussions. Since the web has become a forum for heated debate, journalists faced the dilemma of whether such "chat room" discussions should be treated as private dialogues (similar to telephone conversations) or as open discussions with the Internet serving as a public forum. Some 35 of the 63 media executives polled said that reporters don't need permission to use the comments, but the stories should clearly indicate where the quotes originated. Eighteen of the executives said they would not use a quote without permission.

Every newsroom has editors and producers who serve as filters for information before it's presented to the public. This careful editing process does not occur on the Internet. Yet this is preferable to some people. They don't want someone else deciding what they should be told about news events. They would rather decide for themselves—even if their decisions are based on erroneous information.

Mets and the San Francisco Giants, an ad for Con Edison can be inserted for New York viewers, while Pacific Gas & Electric could have its ad inserted for the Bay Area audience. Many networks are now using a yellow line inserted during football telecasts to indicate how far a team has to go to get a first down.

While the placement of products in movies or on television programs has been going on for some time (see Chapter 9), the technology now exists to insert such products *after* the filming has been completed. For example, when a movie is shown in theaters and the hero is drinking from a can of Coke, you know that Coke paid for that placement. When the movie appears on television or video, the can may be a Pepsi product because a new deal has been made with the advertiser. Product logos have also been removed from movies being shown on television so that the products wouldn't conflict with something being advertised during the TV commercial breaks.

But the move of the new technology into the area of news has raised ethical questions. "When there's new technology, the ethical rules have to be restated or firmed up," said Richard Kaplar, vice president of The Media Institute, a nonprofit think tank in Washington, D.C. "There are bigger implications in terms of eroding people's confidence in what they see on the screen."[17] *Broadcasting & Cable* magazine editor Harry Jessell said, "You would think that a TV news organization would not tamper with video, especially live video. Viewers should be able to rely on the fact that what they are seeing is actually there."[18] But that type of concern didn't seem to bother ABC news in 1994 when it placed reporter Cokie Roberts in an overcoat in front of a picture of the Capitol and made it appear that she was actually standing in front of the Capitol building during her report, when she was actually in the ABC News studio some distance away. Roberts and her producer were reprimanded and the network apologized on the air.

The new technology is not raising ethical questions with just the television industry. A computerized digital processor, known as Scitex, is currently in use at many major daily newspapers. It can move, add, or subtract images in any photograph. Concerns about abuses of this new device surfaced in 1989 when the *St. Louis Post-Dispatch*'s director of imaging and technology decided to remove a can of Diet Coke from a front-page photograph because he did not want to give the product free advertising. However, the altered photograph became an issue in the *St. Louis Journalism Review* (a press watchdog publication) when the journal pointed out that the ethical standards of accuracy in photographs had been violated.

Digital technology has also had an effect on the world of television advertising. In 1991, Diet Coke brought several deceased entertainers back to life for an ad campaign. Viewers saw the likes of James Cagney, Cary Grant, Louis Armstrong, and Groucho Marx singing and dancing in a modern setting to promote the merits of Diet Coke, even though they had been dead for many years. Their images had been digitally removed from old movies and transposed to the new setting of a modern television commercial.

In 1996, actor John Wayne (who died in 1979) began appearing in a television commercial wearing a general's uniform and claiming a six-pack of Coors Light beer from a drill sergeant. Wayne's image had been taken from a 1966 film, *Cast a Giant Shadow,* and digitally moved into a commercial created around a scene from the movie. While Wayne never mentions the product by name, the script for the commercial was written around dialogue from the film so that he appeared to be an actual participant. Coors later mixed scenes of Wayne from other movies with current actors to make him a participant in a new series of commercials. Like the Diet Coke commercials, the Coors Light spot drew heavy criticism from media critics—but the use of the new technology continued. By 1997, such deceased performers as Jackie Gleason and Fred Astaire were appearing in commercials that portrayed them endorsing products that weren't even available while they were alive. By Super Bowl XXXIV in January of 2000, Federal Express was using the late Judy Garland and scenes from the 1939 film *The Wizard of Oz* to sell its services.

Another type of controversy surfaced in 1989 when *TV Guide,* which had recently been purchased by tabloid king Rupert Murdoch, ran a cover photograph of a slim-looking Oprah Winfrey. It was later revealed that Oprah's head had been superimposed on the body of Ann-Margret. Readers felt deceived, and *TV Guide* said it would not happen again.

Journalists again come down on both sides of digital manipulation of photographs using the **Scitex technology.** Opponents believe it manipulates reality, supporters

Scitex technology

argue that it merely enhances the quality and impact of the photographs and that photographers have been doing this in their darkrooms since photography's early days. There are those who have proposed an icon be placed in the corner of a picture to let the reader know when the photo has been altered. The argument against that practice has been that with just the icon there, the reader will not know exactly how the picture has been altered and will wonder whether the scene in front of the house has only had a telephone wire removed from the top of the shot or if some of the participants in the picture have been either digitally added or removed.

> **@   Practicing Media Literacy**
> Would you support the use of an icon to identify digitally altered pictures? Would you oppose such an icon? Would you support a ban on all digital altering of news pictures?

New technology has posed other ethical issues. In 1996, EarthWatch, the weather graphics company that had introduced "3D fly-through" graphics for weather reports four years earlier brought out the next step in graphics, which permitted real-time animations for both weather and news. EarthWatch announced that 1,000 frame animations that would have required hours to render could now be created and aired within seconds. Stations could now produce 3D images of a news scene using a simulated helicopter perspective with a photo-realistic virtual-reality city skyline. Broadcasters were told the system could simulate fires and explosions, and permit the user to recreate accidents in near real time, getting compelling visuals on the air to tell the story before the actual video arrives from the scene. Obviously, some newspeople, educators, and media ethics specialists expressed great concern that television news would no longer present actual visuals of news events but instead computer-generated images from the world of virtual reality.

TV Reenactments

On a segment of *World News Tonight* in 1989, ABC News displayed two grainy photos that it said depicted an American diplomat handing a briefcase to a "known Soviet agent on the streets of a European capital." The man ABC identified as the diplomat had been under an official espionage investigation. However, it was later revealed that the photo did not show the diplomat or a Soviet agent but was a staged reenactment using actors. ABC acknowledged that it was a "terrible mistake" not to inform the viewers about the simulation.

TV simulations or reenactments by actors became commonplace during the last decade of the 20th century. Their popularity climbed with the development of tabloid TV, particularly such shows as *A Current Affair, Inside Edition, Hard Copy, Rescue 911, America's Most Wanted,* and *Unsolved Mysteries.* Soon such documentaries as *Fatal Passions* were using reenactments to show murders being committed. But the lines between the genres were blurred. Were these news broadcasts? Public affairs shows? Or just entertainment programs?

In 1993 NBC staged a reenactment for its newsmagazine *Dateline* to depict the hazards of a gas tank on a General Motors pickup truck. The truck had been the subject of a civil lawsuit in Florida claiming that a faulty gas tank had caused a driver to burn to death when the tank exploded after a collision. To ensure that the tank would explode on the TV program, NBC placed remote-controlled incendiary devices under the vehicle so it would burst into flames on impact. General Motors challenged the ethics of this decision.

NBC also got into trouble for using a video showing dead fish in streams to substantiate the charges of a forest service employee who said that overcutting forest land in the Clearwater National Forest was killing fish. NBC apparently couldn't find any dead fish in Clearwater streams, so it showed a video of dead fish from streams in another location.

News or Titillation?

A recent trend in television news that has spread to establishment newspapers as well is the sensationalistic coverage of titillating news stories. Led by the tabloid TV shows and tabloid newspapers, the mainstream press seems to be forsaking its ethical commitments to balanced news coverage and jumping on the entertainment bandwagon (see Box 15.3).

ABC News faced this dilemma when Bill Clinton was running for president in 1992. When Gennifer Flowers held a news conference to announce she had been Clinton's extramarital lover for some 12 years, ABC elected not to carry the story since the only evidence was her statement, and Clinton had denied the charge when asked about it by an ABC reporter. However, the story was fed out by many other news sources, and ABC soon found that everybody, including its own affiliated stations, was carrying the story. The next evening, with absolutely no new evidence being provided—only the original charge made by Flowers at the news conference— ABC and Peter Jennings reported the story. They had been forced to reverse the original news judgment based on what the competition was doing and what the people were watching.

In 1996, the supermarket tabloid *Star,* which was the first to break the Gennifer Flowers story, again shocked the Clinton presidential campaign by revealing the sexual activities of one of the president's top advisers, Dick Morris. The *Star* described Morris as being beguiled by prostitute Sherry Rowlands, a call girl whom Morris had allowed to listen in on private phone conversations with the president. Was this more smutty journalism intended only for readers of the tabloids? No; the exposé received widespread coverage in all of the establishment media, as did the prompt resignation of Morris.

By the time special prosecutor Kenneth Starr was ready to release his report on the relationship between President Clinton and a White House intern in late 1998, the media were in a feeding frenzy. The story made the front page of newspapers across the country; television newscasts, both network and local, led with the story; newspapers were trying to be first with the information on their web pages, and the news magazines had the full story within days. The frenzy continued throughout the president's impeachment trial in 1999, with the media reporting more than just the charges and the defense, but also the graphic details of the relationship. Despite the fact that many were complaining that the media were involved in overkill, circulation figures and ratings went up as Americans continued to seek the salacious information.

The question of news versus titillation has been a big part of newsroom discussions as journalists scramble to reach an audience. One classic case came in Florida, where a Telemundo cable network reporter was visiting a cemetery with the mother of a teenage girl who had recently died. As they were walking, the mother's estranged husband suddenly ran up and fatally shot her several times as the camera was running. The footage was shown on numerous television stations across the nation, and even one of the television networks ran it on its evening newscasts. But the question was: Would those stations and the

@   **Practicing Media Literacy**

Did you go to a website to read the transcript of Kenneth Starr's charges against President Clinton in the Lewinsky case?

The age-old cliché "It sells newspapers" has long been used as an excuse for justifying sensational and titillating news in the media. The statement seems to render a moral judgment of disgust while tolerating (and, of course, reading and viewing) the media's coverage of such news stories.

But do the media have a responsibility to give the public what it needs to function in today's world? Or should they go by the newsstand sales and ratings, giving the public what it wants? And what exactly does the public want? Important information about a reduction in the national debt? The latest information regarding a military coup in a South American nation? Sensational stories about sexual activities in the White House? Titillating news/gossip about the frolicking of Hollywood's biggest stars?

The media are businesses, and to survive they must give their customers what they want. Tabloid newspapers have had a successful following since their beginnings; the *National Enquirer* is the largest-selling newspaper in the country. When Rupert Murdoch introduced tabloid TV on his new Fox network and in syndication with *America's Most Wanted* and *A Current Affair,* the programs showed successful ratings. This sparked a series of clones, such as *Hard Copy, Inside Edition,* and many others. Why did these programs develop? Because the viewing audiences watched them. These successes led the regular evening news broadcasts to start competing by also featuring some of the more lurid and titillating news stories.

The ethical issue here is a business decision: Is the customer always right? Is it the job of a business to give the customer what he or she wants? Or should the businesses be leaders that attempt to change consumer behavior by refusing to give consumers what they want and instead giving them what they (the businesses) think they should have? In our consumer culture, it is highly unlikely that the latter approach will succeed.

So is the content of the mass media solely the responsibility of media executives? Are the ethical decisions limited to those who determine the content of the mass media? Or do we, the consumers of the mass media, have an ethical responsibility to exercise some judgments as to what media content should be? If we truly do not want to see the content of the media dominated by sensational and titillating news, we could change the emphasis on this content by rejecting the media that carry it and letting our desire for more socially responsible news and information be known to the media executives.

Ethical decision making is the responsibility of all of us.

---

network have even reported the Florida murder if they didn't have the video to go with it? The answer in most cases would be no; the story had little or no impact on viewers in other parts of the nation. But it *was* good video, and therefore it was shown despite its lack of relevance to viewers across the country.

Checkbook Journalism

Another ethical situation has become an increasing concern with the expansion of tabloid journalism into television. This is the practice of paying news sources for stories and photographs. Sensational tabloid newspapers have paid for news for years, but mainstream news agencies have shunned the practice. However, with the emergence of tabloid TV, major network news agencies have been offering money for stories. Often the allure of quick cash causes ordinary people to sell information that is damaging to friends and family.

Take the tragic murder of Nicole Brown Simpson. Her sister, Dominique Brown, admitted in 1996 that she had sold five photos of her sister to the *National Enquirer* for $32,500. Two of the pictures sold to the supermarket tabloid during the murder trial of

O.J. Simpson showed Nicole sunbathing topless, while another showed one of her children visiting her gravesite. The allure of easy money from certain segments of the media made Brown do something quite distasteful to other members of her own family.

The Simpson trial was the scene of another instance of checkbook journalism that could have had an effect on the trial. During the preliminary hearing, a prosecution witness testified that he had accepted money from the *National Enquirer* for his story about selling a knife to Simpson that was similar to the one used in the murders. Because of this, the prosecution decided not to use the witness during the regular trial. However, the question was raised as to what effect this type of checkbook journalism—paying witnesses for their stories prior to a trial—would have on the American judicial system.

A Dallas television station came under fire in 1996 after the station ran a dimly lit video in which Dallas Cowboys wide receiver Michael Irvin was shown sitting in a car talking about buying and using cocaine. KXAS-TV was heavily criticized for furnishing the camera for a paid informant to secretly shoot the scene of Irvin. The station paid the informant $6,000 for the rights to the tape. While some felt that it was good journalism to get the story, others felt there was a problem in the fact that the station did not immediately reveal that it had paid for the video. "The sin is not in paying the money," said then-president of the Radio–Television News Directors Association (RTNDA) David Barlett. "The sin is in not disclosing it."[19] A Columbia University ethics professor added one more problem to the mix for the station, pointing out that if somebody comes in and says a crime is going to be committed, the station should inform the authorities rather than videotaping it and showing it during a ratings period.

> @ **Practicing Media Literacy**
>
> Do you think it is acceptable for the media to pay for story information?

Accepting Gifts

Another aspect of media ethics that has undergone rethinking in recent years is the acceptance of gifts or *freebies*. For many years, one of the rewards of being a journalist was the numerous **perks** (perquisites) that came in the line of duty. Reporters often received free travel, theater passes, and athletic-event passes in return for stories. Reporters were often treated to lavish parties with free drinks and expensive hors d'oeuvres preceding many annual news and promotional events. Of course, the reporters were expected to write about the activities to which they were invited. Journalists also routinely received free books, music albums, and tapes to review.

perks

Around such holidays as Christmas, many newsrooms were piled high with gifts from news sources and newsmakers. A bottle of expensive liquor or a turkey from the mayor to the city desk was commonplace at Christmas.

In 1959, the payola scandal rocked the radio and recording industries when it was revealed that many disk jockeys had been receiving cash or gifts in exchange for promoting records on the air. Journalists who covered the scandal started wondering about their own attitudes toward gifts. How were they supposed to retain their credibility if they were accepting free travel, tickets, and gifts from their news sources? Could a reader be expected to believe a rave review about a play knowing that the critic had been treated to free tickets and a lavish opening-night party by the play's producers?

The Society of Professional Journalists revised its code of ethics to prohibit journalists from accepting gifts. A 1983 survey by the society found that 75 percent of the newspapers and broadcast stations responding had policies regarding gifts. The policies varied greatly: Some news institutions prohibited the acceptance of any gifts, while others set a monetary limit on them. The *Beaver Falls News-Tribune* in Pennsylvania, for example, allowed employees to keep a bottle of liquor but required that they return a case.

Today some newspapers pay for everything their reporters attend, and even the White House now bills journalists for the price of a tourist-class airline ticket and for meals when reporters travel with the president on Air Force One. Policies of the *Detroit Free Press* regarding the acceptance of gifts, books, or records states clearly that nothing of value will be accepted "from news sources or from sources whose activities are, or are likely to be, the subject of news coverage by the *Free Press*." The *Orange County* (California) *Register* policy states that gifts may be accepted only if they are of "inconsequential value" and that free meals and tickets may be accepted if they surround an event to be covered by the reporter.[20]

Conflicts of Interest

For years journalists have been reporting on the conflicts of interest of other people, particularly politicians. However, journalists are subject to similar conflicts themselves. Can a reporter who is active in the Democratic party, for example, cover political campaigns objectively? Can religious editors fairly report on developments in their own churches? Can a financial reporter write about a company in which he or she owns stock? Can a news agency, such as a newspaper chain or television network, that has corporate holdings in other business endeavors objectively report about one of its subsidiaries (see Box 15.4)?

One of the top-selling books in 1996 was *Primary Colors* (later made into a movie starring John Travolta), an unflattering novel that appeared to be based on the 1992 presidential campaign of Bill Clinton. What made the novel even more intriguing to book buyers was the fact that its author was anonymous. Great pains were taken to protect the identity of the author, causing the guessing games to increase in Washington, D.C., and across the nation.

When the finger pointed to *Newsweek* political columnist Joe Klein, he adamantly denied being the author. At one point, he publicly berated a political columnist at *New York* magazine, questioning the professionalism of the magazine's editor-in-chief when it printed a comparison of the book's style with Klein's prose as analyzed by a Shakespearean scholar at Vassar. However, by July of that year, handwriting analysis in the *Washington Post* finally exposed Klein as the author.

However, new questions arose as Klein admitted his authorship of the controversial book. Was it ethical for a journalist to lie to peers to preserve his or her anonymity? Was his action primarily to help book sales? In reporting the revelation of Klein's authorship, *Newsweek* writer Larry Reibstein called the situation "an embarrassing black eye for Klein and *Newsweek*, at least in journalistic circles."[21] Many of Klein's critics called him a liar who had damaged his and journalism's credibility by repeatedly and vigorously denying authorship of the book—in part, they said, for his own commercial gain. A *New York Times* editorial called Klein's actions "corrupt," and NBC News Washington bureau chief Tim Russert said, "The public looks at us as people who make judgments about character. When they see one of us lying, it hurts everyone."[22]

Also a target of criticism was *Newsweek* editor Maynard Parker, who was one of the few—along with Klein's agent and his wife—who knew the columnist was the author of *Primary Colors*. While the denials were being issued, Parker even allowed an

Box 15.4

MEDIA WATCH
Controversy in the Los Angeles Times *Newsroom*

The pressure for the media to make a profit has been heightened in recent years with the high cost of mergers and corporate takeovers. As a result, newsrooms have seen a reduction in staff and an increase in advertising. And, when there's an increase in advertising, it often means a smaller window for actual news content.

This means that the news media must be sensitive to how that dwindling space is actually used. Reporters are also concerned that editorial decisions are increasingly being affected by business interests.

So it wasn't surprising that the *Los Angeles Times* published a special 168-page special issue of its Sunday magazine devoted entirely to the new Staples Center, a downtown sports arena. However, when it was learned that the paper had split the advertising profits with Staples Center, many reporters at the *Times* felt that the action violated journalistic principles of editorial independence and constituted a conflict of interest. More than 300 editors and reporters at the paper signed a petition demanding that the publisher apologize for the action and begin a "thorough review of all other financial relationships that may compromise the *Times* editorial heritage."[*] The journalists were concerned that the newspaper's integrity and credibility had been compromised at a time when public confidence in the media was continuing to drop.

Times publisher Kathryn Downing did issue an apology, and she and her boss, Times Mirror CEO Mark Willes, acknowledged that it had been a mistake to make the profit-sharing arrangement. However, Willes also pointed out that newspapers that don't take appropriate risks to meet the challenge of a rapidly changing media environment are doomed to die.

Those in the *Times* newsroom still weren't happy. There were calls for the resignations of both Downing and Willes. Some reporters and editors were also upset that they weren't even aware of the arrangement between the paper and Staples Center until they read about it in the *Wall Street Journal* and the *New York Times*. Former *Los Angeles Times* publisher Otis Chan-

dler, whom some consider the man most responsible for lifting the paper from mediocrity to excellence, was so upset by the action that he issued a letter strongly critical of the newspaper's management and asked that it be read aloud to the newsroom staff.

What could management do to ease the rebellion in its newsroom and restore public confidence? In addition to the public apology by the publisher, Downing asked that the staff develop a set of guidelines to cover such situations in the future. A little more than two months later, the guidelines were issued, including a provision that "themed advertising sections or pages produced by or on behalf of the *Times*' business partners or advertisers—including those commonly known as 'advertorial' or 'banner pages'—must be readily distinguishable from news content by clear labeling, distinctive typography and graphics, as determined by the editor."[**]

That same day, the *Times* published a 14-page supplement written by the paper's Pulitzer Prize-winning media critic David Shaw which examined all aspects of the controversy. The piece was edited by a former *Times* editor who had retired several years earlier. To preserve the independence of the story, no one else at the paper was allowed to see it before it was published, except for an executive news editor, a copy chief, and a copy editor who were handpicked by Shaw and the former editor. None of the principals in the story, including CEO Willes, publisher Downing, or the editor of the paper, had any say in its scope, content, or presentation.

Will the publicity and controversy surrounding the *Times* serve as a warning to other news media to be cautious in this area? Probably not. Other news organizations have had similar ties for many years now, and a poll published by *Editor & Publisher* showed that 51 percent of the 60 publishers taking part indicated they had no problem with the *Times*' profit-sharing arrangement.

[*]David Shaw, "Special Report: Crossing the Line," *Los Angeles Times*, December 20, 1999, p. V1.

[**]Ibid., p. V14.

item to appear in *Newsweek*'s "Periscope" section speculating that the anonymous author may have been a speechwriter for former governor Mario Cuomo of New York.

As the revelation and criticism made headlines across the nation, Klein offered a defense in a column in *Newsweek* in which he acknowledged that his critics "have a

case" and agreed that he had said "some things I'll probably always regret." But he added that he believed the decision he had made was "justifiable."[23]

Was it justifiable for a member of the media to lie to his colleagues about being the author of a best-selling novel? Some might point to the figures available when Klein's authorship was revealed: The hardback had gone through 19 printings, totaling 1.2 million copies; it had been on the *New York Times* best-seller list for 20 weeks, nine of them as number one; rights to the book had been sold to 21 foreign publishers; rights to the paperback edition had been sold to Warner books for $1.5 million; and movie rights had been sold for $1.5 million.

In 1993 a story appeared in the *New York Times* stating that an anonymous source close to Judge Kimba M. Wood, whom President Clinton was considering for appointment as attorney general until it was revealed that she had hired an illegal immigrant as a baby-sitter, claimed the White House had lied about its knowledge of the illegal activity of the judge. The next day, it was revealed that the anonymous source was a *Time* magazine political columnist who was also the husband of the Judge Wood. Did the *Time* reporter have a conflict of interest?

When a Kansas congressman called for a congressional order to require General Electric, the nation's second-largest defense contractor, to sell off its NBC network, he asked how NBC could objectively report on such matters as the Strategic Defense Initiative without appearing to have a conflict of interest.[24] Today NBC is still owned by General Electric, while Viacom and Westinghouse own CBS and Disney Corporation owns ABC.

When General Motors challenged the rigging of the GM truck explosion on NBC's *Dateline,* the network admitted its error and apologized within days. Previously, NBC had been known to spend millions of dollars to defend itself in the courts against any charges of error or libel. Many speculated that the apology came so quickly—at the expense of the credibility of NBC News—because General Electric was also in the business of making automobile components that it sold to General Motors. NBC's parent company could have lost a major contract as well as a libel suit.

In 1992 a San Antonio, Texas, television station came under fire when it was disclosed that several employees had been working for a congressional candidate who was on leave from the station where he worked as a public affairs producer. The candidate's wife was a news anchor at the station. The station employees defended their actions, saying the activities were part of their "private lives," but management said it was poor judgment. The candidate's wife also took a leave of absence.[25]

> @ **Practicing Media Literacy**
>
> Were the rights of those reporters as citizens being infringed upon by their employers?

Withholding Information

Another aspect of ethics that plagues journalists is when to withhold information. Not everything that happens in our culture is reported—nor should it be. Deciding what facts to include in or omit from a story is often not easy. Should a reporter write about a discovery that a prominent civic leader is having an affair? If a high-ranking government official is killed in an automobile accident and a number of pornographic magazines are found in the car, should that be reported? Should the fact that a person committed suicide or died of AIDS be included in the obituary?

In 1992, retired tennis star Arthur Ashe believed his privacy had been invaded when confronted by a *USA Today* reporter who told him he had better confirm the rumor that he had AIDS or the newspaper would print the story anyway. Ashe had contracted HIV from a blood transfusion while undergoing heart surgery in the 1980s. He called a news conference to confirm the rumor, but he also blasted the media for forcing him to make the issue public. Of particular concern to him was the effect the disclosure would have on his young daughter in view of public attitudes toward AIDS. The newspaper claimed that even though Ashe had retired 12 years earlier, it was an important news story because he was the most prominent African-American male tennis player in history and was a spokesperson for various public causes.

Many were outraged by the newspaper's intrusion into Ashe's private life and the disregard for his family. Others believed reporting stories about famous people who have contracted AIDS in ways other than sexual activity and drug usage would help to break the stigma often associated with the disease. Ashe died of AIDS in 1993.

The AIDS issue became an important one during the 1980s as the epidemic grew. Many newspapers developed policies on the subject. Usually a newspaper will mention AIDS if it is a cause of death of a prominent person, such as the widely reported deaths of entertainers Rock Hudson and Liberace. If the person is not

When a reporter from USA Today *told former tennis star Arthur Ashe that he was going to run a story that Ashe had AIDS, the retired athlete held a news conference to criticize the media for forcing him to admit that he had contracted HIV from a blood transfusion.*

well known, some newspapers will respect the wishes of the family. A common practice among many newspapers when running obituaries of gay AIDS victims is to refrain from mentioning the cause of death but to include the victim's lifelong companion among the survivors. The *Washington Post*, however, refuses to run an obituary if the cause of death is not given by the family, and it presses hard for the true cause when AIDS is suspected.

But what happens if AIDS is not the cause of death, yet a coroner's report turns up the fact that the well-known victim had AIDS or human immunodeficiency virus (HIV)? This ethical dilemma hit the newspaper industry close to home in 1989 when C. K. McClatchy, chairman of the Sacramento-based McClatchy newspaper chain, died of a heart attack while jogging. When contacted by the coroner, McClatchy's doctor reported that the publisher had tested positive for HIV. When this fact was revealed to the Sacramento press, the McClatchy papers decided against running it, citing the fact that it was not a cause of death. The rival Sacramento *Union* and one TV station ran the story, as did the prestigious *Los Angeles Times*. Most other news outlets ignored the story.

> @ **Practicing Media Literacy**
>
> Do you think there are times when it is acceptable for the media to withhold information from the public in their stories?

When the editor of the San Antonio *Light* died in February 1989 of cryptococcal meningitis, which often is AIDS related, the newspaper mentioned the AIDS connection in the second paragraph along with profiles of the editor, his funeral, and a column discussing why the paper mentioned the cause of death. In the column, the editor's wife, also a journalist, said that as a journalist she understood the decision, but as a wife she could not accept it.

Another common practice among journalists is not to reveal the names of rape victims. Sometimes this practice leads to problems, for example when the rape victim is prominent or the assault occurred during a highly newsworthy crime spree. But is withholding the victim's name and details about the crime the right ethical decision? An Iowa rape victim didn't think so, and for five days in 1990 her name, photograph, and graphic details of her rape and subsequent experience as a witness at her assailant's trial appeared in the *Des Moines Register*. The victim and the female editor believed newspapers don't do enough to publicize the brutality of rape.

The much publicized rape trial of William Smith, a member of the Kennedy family, also caused problems for the media. The case was televised on the Court TV cable channel and was covered by all the networks. When the victim was called to the stand to testify, the media did not use her name, and they covered her face with a blue dot to protect her anonymity. However, when the supermarket tabloid the *National Enquirer* revealed her name in one of its stories, *NBC Nightly News with Tom Brokaw* followed up by identifying her on the air. Their justification was that the *Enquirer* had made the name public information. *The New York Times* used the same reasoning when it began using her name. Following the trial, in which Smith was acquitted, the victim granted interviews with the media and agreed to appear on camera without the blue dot.

Do you withhold information if the subject of the news story threatens to commit suicide? Often such threats are made merely to kill a story. But what if the person is serious? Do you place human life above a story? What if there is not threat of a suicide when you decide to go with the story? That was the case in 1996, when Navy admiral Jeremy Boorda killed himself after learning that two *Newsweek* reporters were on their way to question him about whether some of the military decorations he wore were authorized.

Most news organizations have a policy of not reporting suicides for fear that doing so will incite other unstable individuals to take their own lives. However, that policy is not in effect if the suicide victim is well known.

Invasion of Privacy

Still another ethical problem for news media personnel is the question of invasion of privacy (see the legal discussion of this issue in Chapter 4). Often the press intrudes into people's private lives while pursuing a story. Television news crews have received the heaviest criticism in this area. Many viewers become irate when they see a TV reporter shove a microphone into the face of a grief-stricken person and ask how he or she feels about the loss of a loved one (see Box 15.5).

The death of Princess Diana in a Paris car crash in 1997 caused a tremendous backlash against tabloid publications, freelance photographers known as paparazzi and the media in general for their thirst for headlines. Initial reports following the crash indicated that the princess was in a car being pursued by paparazzi on motorcycles, and that may have been what caused the accident.

At her funeral, Diana's brother, Earl Spencer, delivered the eulogy, in which he said:

> There is no doubt that she was looking for a new direction in her life at this time. She talked endlessly of getting away from England, mainly because of the treatment she received at the hands of the newspapers.
>
> I don't think she ever understood why her genuinely good intentions were sneered at by the media, why there appeared to be a permanent quest on their behalf to bring her down. It is baffling. My own, and only, explanation is that genuine goodness is threatening to those at the opposite end of the moral spectrum.
>
> It is a point to remember that of all the ironies about Diana, perhaps the greatest is this: that a girl given the name of the ancient goddess of hunting was, in the end, the most hunted person of the modern age.

While freelance photographers, known as paparazzi, were initially blamed for the accident which killed Britain's Princess Diana, tabloid publications in general came in for much criticism for the way they had sensationalized her life—and death.

> ## Box 15.5
> ## MEDIA LITERACY
> *Covering the News vs. the Invasion of Privacy*

As television covered an earthquake in Los Angeles extensively, the cameras were present when a fire department rescue worker informed a mother that her husband and 14-year-old son had died in a collapsed apartment building. The mother's grief was broadcast live to millions of people. Photos of the incident appeared in the next morning's newspapers and on the covers of national newsmagazines.

Other live television action footage showed many injured victims of the disaster on stretchers as emergency workers rushed them to hospitals. Some were only partially clad, as they had been trapped in their beds when the earthquake struck at 4:31 A.M.

While many lauded Los Angeles television crews and print journalists for their extensive coverage of the tragedy, others were highly critical of the coverage, believing that cameras should not have intruded into a mother's moment of grief and should not have stripped the dignity from other victims. They thought television and newspaper coverage could have given a complete story of the tragedy from overviews of the disaster scenes without using closeups of the dead, injured, and grieving.

What do you think? Do journalists have an obligation to give readers and viewers *all* the details, or are overviews sufficient? Can journalists really bring to readers and viewers the true impact of such tragedies without giving the private details of the human side of the experience? Journalists are constantly asked to make these tough ethical decisions.

> She would want us today to pledge ourselves to protecting her beloved boys, William and Harry, from a similar fate. And I do this here, Diana, on your behalf. We will not allow them to suffer the anguish that used regularly to drive you to tearful despair.[26]

A short time later, leading British newspapers promised that they would protect the two sons from the type of hounding by photographers that Princess Di had suffered. Britain's best selling newspaper, the tabloid *Sun,* said it had "no intentions of carrying photographs which invade the privacy of Princes William and Harry."[27] Lord Rothermore, whose company publishes the *Daily Mail, Mail on Sunday,* and *Evening Standard,* announced that he had "instructed my editors that no paparazzi pictures are to be purchased without my knowledge and consent."[28] Similar positions were taken by *The Independent* and the tabloid *Mirror.* The *Sunday Mirror* had recently paid $400,000 for pictures of Diana kissing her companion, Dodi Fayed, who was also killed in the car crash.

In this country, the *National Enquirer* announced that it had turned down color pictures of the princess trapped alive inside the car after it crashed. The asking price was $250,000. But the tabloid type headlines ("Di Goes Sex-Mad" screamed one such headline) continued in several publications, including the *Enquirer,* causing several national grocery store chains and independent stores to pull the tabloids from their shelves during the period of mourning. A *Los Angeles Times* poll showed that 69 percent of the public approved a boycott of tabloids until they curtailed the activities of the paparazzi who were stalking celebrities. The poll also reported that 85 percent wanted tabloid editors to refuse to purchase pictures taken by paparazzi.

When Chelsea Clinton, the 17-year-old daughter of President and Mrs. Bill Clinton, entered Stanford University as a freshman, the White House asked the media not to hound her but to give her the privacy that any other college student would receive. The editor of the *Stanford Daily* said that she and her managing editors had established a policy that after her first day on campus, Chelsea would be treated as a regular student, not as a celebrity. The media generally agreed to give her some space.

However, as Joan Ryan of the *San Francisco Chronicle* reported, no question was too trivial, no detail too minor as Hillary Rodham Clinton's spokeswoman met with the media on Chelsea's first day of college. What kinds of questions were asked? "Are the Clintons paying full tuition?" "What was the chemistry between Chelsea and her roommate?" "How many boxes did she bring?" "What was the first family wearing?" "Did she bring a bike?" and "Were there plants?" Wrote Ryan, "Such banal questions are asked only of celebrities, whose most ordinary actions inspire extraordinary interest. Chelsea Clinton, clearly, is a celebrity."[29]

Less than a month after the start of classes, a columnist for the *Stanford Daily* was fired for writing about the Clinton daughter. The column was about how her arrival affected the campus, but the student editor killed it. When the columnist refused to revise it, he was fired. Saying that he was being wrongfully silenced, the columnist said the student newspaper's policy would have "a chilling effect, shutting down conversation that should be able to go on in an opinion column."[30] He added that his column had not violated the paper's policy because he hadn't written about Chelsea's private life; his column was about the impact the Clintons, their Secret Service agents, and the media were having on the campus.

Bay Area journalism professors noted that the decision not to run the column was not a First Amendment issue, but rather was an editorial decision which happens all the time. In an editorial, the *San Francisco Chronicle* wrote: "The Constitution does not protect your column from being killed by the editor. It protects your column from government authorities—whether low-level bureaucrat or a certain student's high-powered dad—who might want to make that decision for your editor."[31]

Across the bay a few months later, the *Daily Californian*, the student newspaper at the University of California at Berkeley, apologized for a column in that paper which identified Chelsea Clinton's dormitory at rival Stanford and urged Cal students to "show your spirit on Chelsea's bloodied carcass."[32] The author of the column, which urged Cal students to seize the Stanford campus prior to the upcoming "Big Game" between the two rivals, said it was just a satire aimed at poking fun at Stanford and its elitist students. A few days later, the columnist reported that Secret Service agents had searched his apartment claiming that the search and investigation were instigated by an angry Hillary Rodham Clinton. The Secret Service emphatically denied the accusation, explaining that it was required by law to investigate when comments of that type were made regarding members of the first family.

Attempts by the media to report inside information about average families have also drawn criticism. In 1996, a Fresno, California, television reporter announced on the early news that he would have an interview later that night with the mother of a missing girl who was feared dead. Throughout the evening, the station was flooded with phone calls from irate viewers accusing the station of invading the privacy of the grieving mother and criticizing television reporters for their callousness. When the interview was aired on the later newscast—and on all subsequent newscasts—the anchors took great pains to explain to viewers that the mother had called the station and requested the interview so that she could make a last-ditch appeal for the return of her missing daughter. It was a case of a television station being burned by the image the media have when it comes to covering the reactions of people involved in tragedies.

Take the case of the 20-year-old son of Oklahoma governor David Walters in 1991. His arrest and pleading of no contest to a misdemeanor charge of possessing drug paraphernalia evoked wide media coverage. If he had not been the son of the governor, the news media most likely would not have covered the story. Shortly afterward, he committed suicide. Many believed his death was directly related to the intense and intrusive news coverage of his arrest. His parents claimed the University of Oklahoma student was hounded by the press at his Norman, Oklahoma, apartment while trying to attend classes. Does the element of "**prominence**" (one of the criteria for judging newsworthiness) justify extensive coverage of a misdemeanor charge against a governor's son when it would not be newsworthy for an ordinary citizen? Should children of prominent people be allowed to live private lives?[33] The political protest activities of Amy Carter, daughter of former president Jimmy Carter, were reported in the early 1990s, and the media extensively covered her wedding in 1996—some 15 years after her father had left office.

prominence

Diversity

A growing concern regarding news media ethics centers around the new sensitivity to diversity in our culture. According to Black, Steele, and Barney in *Doing Ethics in Journalism,* "Diversity is clearly a part of accuracy and fairness, whether it relates to avoiding stereotypes or redefining news to better reflect a multicultural society."[34]

Journalists in a multicultural society must ensure that their coverage of news events is sensitive to ethnic diversity, racism, religious differences, homophobic attitudes, and individuals who are physically or mentally challenged. These sensitivities must be exercised in hiring practices by the media, in deciding on stories to be covered, in assigning reporters to stories, and in the way stories are reported and edited. It is also important that the news media give a voice to the voiceless.

Covering Wars

During the 1990s, ethical decisions have come into question from what appears to be an overzealous effort on the part of the news media to cover wars. For example, when the United States engaged in the Persian Gulf war in 1991, the news media took advantage of satellite technology to broadcast Scud missile attacks live and report on bombings from the scenes.

When the United States began its preparations for an infantry battle in the Iraqi desert, CNN requested permission to install uplinks to satellites to broadcast the battles as they occurred. The government turned down the request. Was this a suppression of news? Or was the government correct in trying to protect the families and loved ones of U.S. soldiers who might have been shown dying live and in color on national TV?

When U.S. marines landed on the beach in Mogadishu, Somalia, in 1992, they were greeted not by enemy fire but by hordes of U.S. TV cameras, microphones, and reporters anxiously awaiting their arrival. Had enemy troops been awaiting them, would the presence of TV cameras and lights have interfered with the Marines' ability to protect themselves and win the battle? What kinds of ethical issues should news media personnel consider when they balance the public's right to know with the need to protect human life and national security? The news media came in for some heavy criticism when the network newscasts showed the dead body of an American soldier being dragged through the streets of Mogadishu. The picture also made the cover of *Newsweek.* Those opposed to the picture said it was an invasion of privacy and was not fair to the mourning members of the victim's family. However, others

@ **Practicing Media Literacy**
Do you think television should be allowed to broadcast war battles live?

When U.S. military
Special Forces landed
on the beach at
Mogadishu, Somalia,
they were greeted by
members of the media
who were already on
the scene before the
military landed.

believed the picture needed to be shown to demonstrate the horrors of war and to question the Clinton administration's handling of the situation in Somalia.

Double Standards?

Although journalists today are more concerned about their ethical behavior than at any time in American history, they are still often criticized for adhering to a double standard. Former Mobil Oil vice president Herb Schmertz, in his critique of the media, *Goodbye to the Low Profile,* charged that the press is the only institution in the United States that avoids public scrutiny:

> Whenever those in the news media have been challenged, they have grown righteously indignant. Basking in the glow of Watergate, members of the press have refused to acknowledge that they are ever on the wrong track. Never mind that reputations have been tarnished by untrue stories. Never mind that bad laws have been passed because of zealous crusading that hasn't always portrayed the whole picture. The rush into print or onto the air with evermore sensational scandals and conspiracies was, for a time, all-consuming. In the short run, it sold newspapers and it sold advertising. But in the long run, the public will ultimately be tired of it.[35]

USA Today editorialized on this subject by asking the following question:

> Journalism is a high calling. The First Amendment to the Constitution makes the news media free to serve democracy, inform the public, promote debate and scrutinize and criticize the conduct of public officials. Some have described these rights and responsibilities of the news media as a "watchdog" role. But who watches the watchdog?[36]

Contrary to Schmertz's assertion and *USA Today*'s question, some news media do serve as watchdogs for their own institutions. Some newspapers employ ombudsmen who operate independently of management to investigate and answer public complaints about certain stories. Others, such as the *Los Angeles Times*, have media critics on their staffs to report on media practices and shortcomings.

Social Responsibility

As discussed in the four theories of media operation section in Chapter 5, social responsibility is the preferred system for the news media to function under in our society. It is also a voluntary system in American society. In addition to serving society better, the news media must be socially responsible for selfish reasons. If they are to remain an important information source in our American culture, the media must be a credible source of information. To be credible, they must be socially responsible, and social responsibility includes adherence to strict ethical standards (see Box 15.6) and dedication to disclosing the truth about all institutions, including one's own (see Box 15.7). There are also times when the media make mistakes. Social responsibility means admitting mistakes and, if necessary, offering an apology for them.

It is important that the news media begin thinking about its image in the years ahead. As the 20th century was ending, a survey by the Freedom Forum Media Studies Center found that 88 percent of the public—almost nine out of every 10 Americans—believed that reporters often or sometimes use unethical or illegal techniques to get a story. In addition, 76 percent said they believed journalists often or sometimes plagiarize material, and 66 percent said they believed stories are made up and passed off as real.[37] This is yet another low point for the media in the eyes of the public they serve, and it will take a concentrated effort to improve that image.

> **@ Practicing Media Literacy**
> How do you rate the news media in the areas of ethics, plagiarism, and truth in reporting?

MEDIA ETHICS AND ECONOMICS

Other ethical considerations arise from the fact that the American mass media are businesses designed to make a profit.

Advertiser Influence

One fairly frequent problem occurs when advertisers, who pay the bills and produce the profits for the media, want to control their content. In the South during the civil rights movement of the 1960s, for example, some newspapers sympathetic to the civil rights cause were forced to change their positions or go out of business as the result of economic **boycotts** instigated by readers and advertisers who opposed civil rights.

boycotts

Another case occurred in Texas in the 1960s when a newspaper publisher ran several stories about the illegal activities of one of the community's leading citizens. The stories revealed how this individual, a friend and confidant of President Lyndon Johnson, had defrauded the government out of millions of dollars in grain subsidies. Community leaders reacted to these stories by starting another newspaper in the town and persuading all the local businesses to boycott the paper that ran the exposé. Even though the stories led to a jail term for the community leader, the crusading publisher was forced out of business.

A front-page story in the *Hartford* (Connecticut) *Courant* exposing high-powered sales techniques used by automobile dealers ran on the same day a big "President's Week" auto sales ad campaign began appearing in the newspaper. The angry auto

Box 15.6
MEDIA WATCH
Principles of Ethical Conduct for Newsrooms

In the summer of 1999, the Gannett newspaper chain issued its Principles of Ethical Conduct for Newsrooms. Gannett publishes *USA Today* and numerous local newspapers across the nation. Here are some of its highlights.

WE ARE COMMITTED TO:
Seeking and reporting the truth in a truthful way

- We will dedicate ourselves to reporting the news accurately, thoroughly and in context.
- We will be honest in the way we gather, report and present news.
- We will be persistent in the pursuit of the whole story.
- We will keep our word.
- We will hold factual information in opinion columns and editorials to the same standards of accuracy as news stories.
- We will seek to gain sufficient understanding of the communities, individuals and stories we cover to provide an informed account of activities.

Serving the public interest

- We will uphold First Amendment principles to serve the democratic process.
- We will be vigilant watchdogs of government and institutions that affect the public.
- We will provide the news and information that people need to function as effective citizens.
- We will seek solutions as well as expose problems and wrongdoing.
- We will provide a public forum for diverse people and views.
- We will reflect and encourage understanding of the diverse segments of our community.
- We will provide editorial and community leadership.
- We will seek to promote understanding of complex issues.

Exercising fair play

- We will treat people with dignity, respect and compassion.

- We will correct errors promptly.
- We will strive to include all sides relevant to a story and not take sides in news coverage.
- We will explain to readers our journalistic processes.
- We will give particular attention to fairness in relations with people unaccustomed to dealing with the press.
- We will use unnamed sources as the sole basis for published information only as a last resort and under specific procedures that best serve the public's right to know.
- We will be accessible to readers.

Maintaining independence

- We will remain free of outside interests, investments or business relationships that may compromise the credibility of our news report.
- We will maintain an impartial, arm's length relationship with anyone seeking to influence the news.
- We will avoid potential conflicts of interest and eliminate inappropriate influence on content.
- We will be free of improper obligations to news sources, newsmakers and advertisers.
- We will differentiate advertising from news.

Acting with integrity

- We will act honorably and ethically in dealing with news sources, the public and our colleagues.
- We will obey the law.
- We will observe common standards of decency.
- We will take responsibility for our decisions and consider the possible consequences of our actions.
- We will be conscientious in observing these Principles.
- We will always try to do the right thing.

Box 15.7
MEDIA WATCH
A Case Study in Questioning Your Newsroom's Actions

When Richard Alan Davis was convicted of the kidnapping and murder of a 12-year-old northern California girl, his reaction to the verdict caused many ethical discussions in newsrooms across the country. After the verdict had been read, Davis turned to the cameras in the courtroom, puckered his lips, winked, and then made obscene gestures toward the cameras with both hands.

While the television stations covering the verdict live sent the picture out as it happened, they still had to decide whether to use the footage again in later newscasts. Other stations later received the video and had to make the same decision. Only one newspaper photographer was in the courtroom at the time, and he got the shot, but newspapers everywhere debated whether or not to use it and, if so, where to place it.

The *San Francisco Chronicle,* which served the area where both the kidnapping and trial had taken place, elected to carry the picture of Davis with his middle fingers extended as a three-column color shot on the front page. The overwhelming majority of people who wrote or called the paper objected to the picture. Television stations that carried the footage in their newscasts were also inundated with calls and letters of protest.

To many, Davis's action was considered a final insult to both the victim's family and the American judicial system, and they accused the news media of assisting him in this insult. Others questioned whether the picture was even news, charging the media with pandering to low standards.

The *Chronicle* responded by saying that it ran the picture because of its compelling news value. A University of California at Berkeley journalism instructor, William Drummond, wrote an op-ed piece for the paper stating that he believed the picture deserved to be shown. "Was it news?" he asked. "Of course. Should it have been shown? Yes." But Drummond added that before such a picture is shown, the news media need to attach "substantial warnings and explanations. It's a simple matter of courtesy, like saying 'excuse me.'"

Drummond, a former correspondent for the *Los Angeles Times* and National Public Radio, also wrote that in the aftermath of the Davis photo,

[M]any news executives are doing some real soul-searching, because some of the time-honored axioms of journalism don't seem to work any more. It's high-time for just such a top-to-bottom rethinking.

The old-time editors of the green-eyeshade era never felt accountable to the public.

The adage, "The public has a right to know," was the sure-fire way to end ethical discussions. For years, newsrooms were steeped in the culture of disclosure.*

Drummond noted that "competition created the culture of disclosure, forcing decisions based on the assumption that you'd lose audience if the other guys had something you didn't." But *how* the media handle these visuals is also important and should be given thorough consideration in all newsrooms.

*Quoted in William Drummond, "How the Press Handled Davis Photo," *San Francisco Chronicle,* July 2, 1996.

dealers protested, and the publisher sent a letter of apology to the dealers and their advertising agencies expressing his anger that the story had appeared without his knowledge. The publisher's reaction to the story had a chilling effect on the editorial department of the newspaper.

In 1996, the newly launched cable network the History Channel came under much criticism when it announced it would carry a series of hour-long documentaries recounting the histories of different corporations. What drew the criticism for the proposed *The Spirit of Enterprise* series was the fact that the programs were to be produced by each corporation featured. The first episode, spotlighting Boeing, was almost completed, and further programs featuring General Motors, AT&T, and DuPont were in the works when the project was canceled because of charges that the programs could not be objective if the subjects were involved in their production.

That same year, the CNBC cable channel announced a weekly series that would examine the impact of technology on people's lives. It was to be sponsored by IBM, which also had final approval of the program's contents. Also blurring the line between news–entertainment and advertising were a series of commercials and infomercials that were designed to look like news reports and talk shows. For example, many stations carried 60-second reports featuring what appeared to be news anchors discussing some of the films currently running in theaters. What the viewing public may not have known was that all of the films featured in these minireports were from Disney Corporation, the sponsor for these commercials.

But such disguise of commercials wasn't new. In 1994, a prime time special on the newly opened Treasure Island casino and resort in Las Vegas was aired on NBC. The program was produced by the owner of Treasure Island. In addition, many of the networks and cable channels were carrying prime time specials on the making of many of the big-budget Hollywood movies produced by the studios releasing the films. Said Betsy Frank, executive vice president of Zenith Media Services, "As advertisers look for new ways to break through the clutter on the Web and in television, you are going to see a greater push to do this kind of thing."[38]

PR for Advertisers

Some newspapers go out of their way to cater to advertisers. In small towns, for example, many newspapers run stories that are not really newsworthy but instead are publicity pieces for major advertisers. This type of story is called an ***advertorial.*** In his book *The News at Any Cost: How Journalists Compromise Their Ethics to Shape the News,* Tom Goldstein cited several examples of advertorials:

> In a 1983 issue of the *Reporter,* a weekly in Walton, New York, in a news column adjacent to an advertisement for the Imperial Restaurant, there was an article on the renovations that had been completed at that building. There was a picture of the new entry way with this caption: "From a newly paved parking lot one now may enter Walton's Imperial Restaurant under a new canopy to a new entrance. Foyer includes a large hanging area for coats." A weekly in a neighboring town, the *Hancock Herald,* ran a picture of the Delaware Land Office in the spring of 1984 with the caption explaining that the real estate firm had a new "outlook" on Hancock as a result of "thermo-pane windows installed on the first floor in the front to replace the old windows that had become leaky." The office is run by a frequent advertiser.[39]

Such advertiser-generated hype is not limited to small-town journalism. Take a look at the real estate section of your nearest metropolitan newspaper. Most likely you will find the ads surrounded with "news" stories that report in glowing terms how wonderful some of the real estate developments in the area are and how fantastically they are selling. These stories appear even when the real estate market is depressed. Such articles often are written not by journalists but by publicists for the developers or by advertising personnel at the newspaper.

Even the *Los Angeles Times,* which is regarded as one of the nation's best newspapers, runs real estate hype sections and special regional advertising supplements that look like any other section of the newspaper. Even though these sections are labeled in small print as advertising supple-

---

advertorial

@ **Practicing Media Literacy**

Do you feel that advertisers have an influence on the news you receive?

ments, many readers believe the "news" stories in these supplements (which are actually verbatim news releases) are as legitimate as any others.

Although profitable, such practices raise some ethical questions and tend to cloud a newspaper's credibility. Is the reader getting a true picture of real estate developments in the area? Has media hype influenced people to make bad real estate investments in second-home markets? Can a reader trust his or her newspaper if certain sections peddle a developer's rosy view of reality as fact?

Television Content

The influence of advertisers on TV content, particularly children's programs, raises serious ethical concerns as well. Is it ethical for toy manufacturers to produce shows that are essentially 30-minute-long commercials for their toy or doll lines? Children, who have a difficult enough time distinguishing between commercials and programs, are now being targeted throughout the program by these product-oriented theme shows. Some wonder if this is ethical television programming or industry exploitation of its most impressionable audience.

As the 21st century began, a new source of influence on television program content was revealed. Many were surprised when it was revealed that the White House had been making suggestions about the content of television scripts in an attempt to send an antidrug message to viewers. The little-known financial agreement allowed the networks to reduce the number of public service announcements they were required by law to broadcast, since those free announcements take up valuable commercial inventory for the free spots.

Among the many program scripts reviewed in advance by White House drug policy officials were *ER*, *Chicago Hope*, and *Beverly Hills 90210*. Representatives of the White House Office of National Drug Control Policy acknowledged that they had made some programming suggestions to the networks. Although the networks were participating in the reviews voluntarily as a means of improving profits, they insisted that they never gave content control of their programs to the government.

Many in the media expressed anger and concern that a government agency was being allowed to review the scripts of entertainment programs in advance, even if it was designed to curtail the drug problem in this country. Network executives at ABC-TV say they stopped trying to collect government financial credits for inserting antidrug messages into their programs when White House drug advisers began asking to see the scripts before they were broadcast. A spokesman for ABC said that during the previous season, government officials were satisfied with just evaluating programs after they had been aired.

The heads of several Hollywood studios producing prime time TV shows for the networks said they were angry that they had not been informed about the arrangement the networks had with the government. Newspapers across the country carried editorials saying that the government should not be allowed to dictate the content of television programs. The *New York Times* editorialized that in allowing government review of content in return for financial rewards, "the networks are crossing a dangerous line they should not cross. On the far side of that line lies the possibility of censorship and state-sponsored propaganda."[40] Within days, the *Times* admitted that the paper also had a cooperative relationship with the Drug Control

> **@ Practicing Media Literacy**
> Do you feel it is acceptable for government representatives to review the scripts of the television programs you watch before they are aired? Do you think it is okay to insert antidrug messages in such programs?

office. White House officials said that three newspapers, the *Times, Washington Post,* and *USA Today,* had been granted financial credits that reduced the amount of public service advertising they were required to provide. In the case of the *Times,* it had agreed to produce some 30,000 booklets as part of its Newspapers in Education program to guide New York area teachers on dealing with drug abuse. In exchange, the paper received $200,000 in financial credits, allowing it to cut back on donating valuable advertising space for public service ads. "I knew absolutely nothing about this," said the editor of the *Times* editorial page, Howell Raines, when the paper's involvement in the program was revealed. "There was no involvement by editorial employees of the *Times* and no advance content review . . . which is the critical issue where the networks are involved."[41]

Direct-Response Sales

Another concern emerged when cable systems and satellites started carrying home-shopping channels, which consist entirely of direct-response advertising. The hard sell of these programs encourages impulse buying—on credit—and consumers can incur unreasonable, even unimaginable debts if they are not careful. This situation has the potential to become very serious when new technology on the horizon allows viewers to place an order by merely pushing a button on a hand-held response terminal hooked up to a two-way television set. Virtual-reality shopping sprees may also be the catalyst to send consumers into debtor chaos.

Chain Ownership

The growing number of mass media owned by large chains also poses some ethical questions. Do chain-owned media owe their allegiance to the communities they serve, or are they solely responsible to their parent corporations headquartered in other areas?

In 1977, Panax Corporation told its 8 daily and 40 weekly newspapers to run two stories critical of President Jimmy Carter on their front pages. When two of the editors refused, offering instead to run them as opinions on the editorial page, they were fired for insubordination. Despite community protests, the editors were not reinstated. Panax even refused to run letters to the editor protesting the firings.

When media baron Rupert Murdoch purchased a number of newspapers in the United States, including the *New York Post,* he turned some of them into sensationalizing publications to boost circulation. This action demonstrates that he was more interested in making a profit than providing quality journalism.

MEDIA ETHICS AND ENTERTAINMENT

Entertainment in the mass media also generates some serious ethical questions. Some of the more passionately discussed issues in this decade have been violence, explicit language, and sex in recorded music, on radio and television shows, and in the movies.

Congress attempted to address the problem of violence on our streets in 1993 by going after the television industry to get it to eliminate violence in its programming. The industry responded by placing **warning labels** at the beginning of violent shows. But even that wasn't enough for Congress and, in 1996, the new Telecommunications Act was passed, which included the requirement that future television sets contain the V-chip to allow parents to block out programs containing sex and violence.

warning labels

The vulgarity and violence in songs by popular rap artists and the inclusion of songs written by mass murderers have recently caused controversy. Rapper Snoop Doggy Dogg's gangsta rap album *Doggystyle* sold 800,000 copies during the first week of its release in 1993 while the rapper was free on $1 million bail awaiting trial on charges of being an accomplice to murder. His bodyguard was charged with a drive-by shooting while Dogg was in the car. The publicity helped the sale of his albums, which were filled with violence and vulgarity.

Guns N' Roses produced a hit album in 1993 called *The Spaghetti Incident*, which featured a song, "Look at Your Game, Girl," written by convicted killer Charles Manson. The inclusion of the song on the album was heavily criticized by law enforcement and victim rights groups, as well as by the head of the recording company that produced the album, entertainment mogul David Geffen. The band later justified its inclusion of the song by citing a court order that directed the royalties from the song to the son of one of Manson's victims. The song earned $62,000 in royalties for every one million copies sold.

Is **artistic freedom** the paramount factor in releasing albums of questionable content and origin? Or does the recording industry have an obligation to exercise social responsibility?

artistic freedom

The ABC television network came in for its fair share of criticism during the 1990s by airing such shows as *NYPD Blue*, which featured violence and nudity, and *Civil Wars*, in which actress Mariel Hemingway did a nude photo shoot. In addition, Hemingway was involved in much controversy when a character she played on the *Roseanne* situation comedy was involved in a female-female kiss with the star's character, Roseanne Conner. In 1997, stand-up comic Ellen DeGeneres received much publicity when she and her character on the ABC television series *Ellen* came out of the closet and announced they were gay. As a result of many of these trends in television programming, the networks were the focus of many concentrated boycotts and letter-writing campaigns orchestrated by the religious right. The Reverend Jerry Falwell called DeGeneres "Ellen Degenerate."

In addition to the relatively recent concern about what is good taste and how far the networks and popular music will go to challenge those standards, there is longstanding controversy over the way TV entertainment distorts cultural reality.

The Cone Effect

One way to understand better how the media influence our perceptions and often distort our view of reality is to examine how we as individuals interact with the media. One of the best diagrams of this process is Edward Jay Whetmore's *cone effect*.[42]

According to Whetmore, all entertaining programming exaggerates and magnifies real life to make it more entertaining and interesting. He calls what results from this process *constructed mediated reality* (CMR). To be worthy of our attention, CMR is made sexier, funnier, more intense, more violent, and more colorful than real life. After all, who would want to read a novel or watch a TV show that was only as interesting as everyday life?

Next the constructed mediated reality is transmitted through a mass medium, such as a book or television set, to the audience. CMR consumers then interpret the messages at a perceptual level. Whetmore calls this perceived mediated reality (PMR). We each interpret the mediated reality differently. An African-American ghetto child, for example, would interpret an episode of *Family Matters* or *In Living Color* differently than a middle-class white child would.

After people perceive this mediated reality in their own way, based on their own frames of reference (see Chapter 1), they eventually incorporate it into their own lives. This can lead to distortions if a person perceives media reality—for example, permissive sexuality on soap operas—to be the norm in modern society and changes his or her own behavior accordingly. With the cone effect in mind, let's look at the issue of media distortion of cultural reality.

Distortions of Cultural Reality

There is a concern that the media give us distorted perceptions of the morals and activities of our own culture. Such charges have been leveled since the novel entered the popular culture in the early days of mass communication. Concern has progressively intensified, however, as the media's influence has become more pervasive.

Comic books came under criticism as early as the 1930s. As the youth culture enthusiastically embraced this new medium, parent groups started calling for a reduction of violence in comic books. Some people predicted that if actions weren't taken, the nation's youth would grow up with a distorted view of reality and a permissive attitude toward violence. The criticism was not totally unfounded. Many youngsters were injured by blows to the head from cap guns and other childhood accidents caused when they reenacted comic book adventures. The comic book industry was finally forced to adopt a code of ethics in 1954.

Concern about comic books and movies all but vanished in the 1950s, when parents and other advocacy groups turned their attention to the new, more pervasive medium of television. Children's television entertainment started out with such innocent shows as *Kukla, Fran and Ollie, Howdy Doody, The Mickey Mouse Club,* and *Time for Beanie*. But then television started running old movie cartoons on Saturday mornings exclusively for children. Shows that featured the Roadrunner and the Coyote, Popeye, Tom and Jerry, Bugs Bunny, and numerous other characters were now seen for the first time as violence ridden. People started questioning whether a five-year-old's perception of reality would be distorted when he or she saw the Coyote walk away unharmed after being squashed by boulders and falling off cliffs. In addition, many of the old Westerns, featuring Gene Autry, Roy Rogers, Hopalong Cassidy, and Lash LaRue, were now being seen in the home on television. The made-for-television Western series became extremely popular in the late 1950s and early 1960s, but this genre had all but disappeared from the networks by the end of that decade. However, as cable began to flourish, one cable channel began running many of these old westerns—from *The Lone Ranger* and *Gunsmoke* to *The Cisco Kid* and *Bonanza*—on weekends. A national organization later cited this channel as being the most violent on television on Saturday and Sunday afternoons. The cable channel was known at that time as the CBN, the Christian Broadcasting Network. It is now known as The Family Channel.

During the 1980s, violence-oriented Saturday children's shows continued with such programs as *He-Man and the Masters of the Universe, G.I. Joe: A Real American Hero, Transformers, She-Ra: Princess of Power,* M.A.S.K. (*Medical Armored Strike Command*), *Thunder Cats, Voltron,* and *Rambo*.

Concern over violence spread to other forms of TV entertainment as well. Westerns, police shows, and detective shows all became targets for critics. The networks, anxious over this new wave of accusations, started toning down violent programs and canceling violence-oriented shows. With its rating system now in place, the motion picture industry was quick to pick up the violence themes and intensify them. As the

V-chip and its corresponding rating system became a reality for television in the latter part of this decade, many expressed concern that the producers of television programs would use the rating system to make the shows even more violent, using the justification that the viewing public was now being warned of the more violent content.

Another source of alarm was the distorted picture of American culture painted by both television entertainment and TV news. When sociologists investigated the causes of riots in American ghettos in the mid-1960s, they started getting answers that pointed a finger at television. Some ghetto residents indicated they were rebelling against the establishment because they felt cheated by the system. Their frustrations were traced to hours of watching such television shows as *Father Knows Best, Leave It to Beaver,* and *The Adventures of Ozzie and Harriet,* which all showed happy, white, middle-class families living in comfortable homes with modern furniture, refrigerators, and spacious fenced yards.

The Simpsons are an example of the dysfunctional families portrayed on television today—a far cry from the happy, middle-class families seen on the TV of the 1950s and '60s.

By the end of the 20th century, this criticism of negative influences on our culture by television focused on cartoon shows, such as MTV's *Beavis and Butt-head* and Fox's *The Simpsons.* The 15-year-old cartoon characters on MTV were blamed for encouraging antisocial behavior among the young and even for causing deaths from fires set after the cartoon characters proclaimed that "Fire is cool." Some critics believed the Simpson family did not portray American family life in a suitable fashion. After the consumer culture began selling popular Bart Simpson T-shirts with the slogan "Underachiever and Proud of It," school districts went into action, banning the wearing of such apparel.

Soap Operas

A mainstay of daytime television from the beginning, the soap opera has also been a target of criticism. Do soap operas provide an innocent escape into the troubled lives of others, or do they, as some have charged, distort our view of reality? Do they reflect changes in our culture, or do they cause them? Is the level of permissive sex and adultery in modern soap operas in line with the level that exists in society, or is it an exaggeration? If there are distortions, how do they affect average people when they filter the PMR into real life? Is there a relationship between the tremendous increase in herpes, AIDS, and teenage pregnancies and the escalation of casual sex on television?

In 1994, the key creative players in the world of soap opera, including head writers, executive producers, and network programming heads, gathered in Los Angeles for what was described as a **soap opera summit.** This was daytime drama's first industry-wide conference, and it was called to discuss how soap operas can affect U.S. attitudes toward reproduction behavior (or sex in the soaps).

Organizers of the event said that the soaps, with their long-term stories and strong viewer identification with the characters, have a greater ability to deliver a message to

soap opera summit

viewers than any other form of programming. During the session, it was stressed that the conference was not designed to advocate prochoice or proabortion stances or even one manner of birth control over another; rather it was intended to reevaluate the way soaps deal with sexual responsibility.

Those involved in the production of television soap operas met with population experts to discuss such issues as teen pregnancy, male sexual irresponsibility, and female empowerment. As a result of the session, story lines on many of the soaps began dealing with these issues with obvious messages for the viewer. For example, on the popular CBS soap *The Young and the Restless,* a high school football player bragged about his sexual conquest with a female student, even though it wasn't true. Before the story line had been completed, the girl had told him off in a popular high school diner, explained to him that women have the right not to be treated in such a manner, and threw a drink in his face.

However, a professor at the University of Washington later released a survey showing that when the male character on a soap opera finally ends up in bed with a female character, the partners are unlikely to discuss methods of safe sex. The study, released by the Kaiser Family Foundation, showed that of 594 acts of sexual behavior dealt with during five weeks of soap operas, only 58 either depicted or discussed birth control planning or the consequences of unprotected sex. However, the study of some 97 hours of programming from the 10 daily soap operas did show only 6.1 acts of sexual behavior per hour compared to 6.6 acts per hour recorded during a study two years earlier. *Sexual behavior* was defined as any flirting, caressing, kissing, or sexual intercourse that was either discussed, implied, or performed by the characters.[43]

Some media critics also worry that the exportation of such prime time soaps as *Dallas, Dynasty, Beverly Hills 90210,* Party of Five and *Melrose Place* to other countries give people in foreign lands a distorted view of Americans. Many foreigners, for example, are led to believe all Americans are rich, beautiful, promiscuous, and successful.

Docudramas

The docudrama, which dramatizes an actual event, has sparked considerable controversy since the 1980s. It didn't take long before critics were asking where the facts left off and fiction began.

This controversy intensified in the 1990s when all three major networks broadcast a different docudrama (called *schlockudramas* by critics) based on the Amy Fisher story, in which a high school teenager was convicted of shooting her lover's wife. Each version gave a dramatized and different point of view about the news story. All three programs scored large ratings.

In 1987 two television networks aired different docudramas of the same sensational case, making people wonder which was closer to the truth. In January CBS broadcast *At Mother's Request,* a miniseries about a woman who talked her son into killing her wealthy father because he wouldn't give her money. Then, in the spring, NBC televised its version, *Nutcracker: Money, Madness, Murder,* also as a well-promoted miniseries. For many of these programs, the networks carry a brief disclaimer at the opening indicating that certain events and characters have been fictionalized.

Eight months after a Boston man killed himself to avoid arrest on suspicion of murdering his pregnant wife, and before a grand jury could deliver the results of its investigation, CBS broadcast a docudrama based on the case: *Good Night, Sweet Wife: A Murder in Boston.* The family of the victim, Carol Stuart, issued a statement reported widely in the news media that it was "very disturbing that the movie was made without their consent or participation and that such a movie is being broadcast while there is still a sitting grand jury, before anyone, even our family, knows the outcome of the criminal investigation."

When HBO broadcast the docudrama *The Tragedy of Flight 103: The Inside Story*, Pan American World Airways issued a strong statement reported in *Time* claiming the program contained a "reckless disregard for the facts," was an "outright fabrication," and was a "work of fiction and a cheap shot."

The ethical problem with docudramas stems from television's dual role as both an information medium and an entertainment medium. To get high ratings and audience shares (the percentage of TV sets in use that are tuned to a particular program), television—as has always been the case with the motion picture industry—has too often been willing to stretch the truth to be more entertaining.

TV Sex and Explicit Language

The increase in themes about casual sex and suggestive and titillating language in TV sitcoms has generated much media criticism. Fox's *Married . . . With Children* was attacked for its sexual content and mockery of traditional family values. In 1989 a Detroit woman, Terry Rakolta, launched a campaign against the program urging advertisers to stop their sponsorship. Senator Jesse Helms called the program "trash." Stephen Bochco's introduction of the first R-rated program on television, *NYPD Blue*, in the early 1990s also came in for much criticism because of its explicit language and partial nudity. Many groups called for a boycott of the program and its advertisers, and several ABC stations across the country, including one in Dallas, refused to carry it. However, by the second year of the show, most of those stations, led by the Dallas affiliate, had changed positions and begun broadcasting the program.

The advent of MTV in the 1980s caused alarm and dismay among critics who claimed that many of the music videos were advocating sexual violence. Sexually violent themes in music lyrics as well have been a concern of media critics. Some contend that such sexual exploitation by the music industry may erode the progress women have made in their quest to avoid being stereotyped as sex objects.

Others contend that sex scenes in the media seldom show pleasant, enjoyable lovemaking in a romantic context. Instead, they note, most of them involve some sort of violence or unpleasantness, and media programming often suggests that participants should be punished in some way for their sexual activity.

Coping with the problem of sex and sexual violence in the media is complex. Allowing pressure groups to force governmental censorship might open the door to widespread censorship of any unpopular idea. The answer seems to lie in responses to the following questions: Is there any real harm in the content of media entertainment? And if there is, should the producers of constructed mediated reality exercise more social responsibility in creating this entertainment? Social scientists have been wrestling with the first question for decades and have generated a great deal of media effects research suggesting a variety of answers (see Chapter 16).

> **@ Practicing Media Literacy**
>
> Do you think this type of depiction will eventually change cultural attitudes toward the relationship between sex and love?

Although social responsibility seems to be the key ingredient for all mass-media operations, Congress thought it wasn't enough when it revised the Telecommunications Act in 1996. The requirement of the V-chip in all newly manufactured television sets was seen as the answer to the problem by placing the responsibility of determining what programs children watch in the hands of parents. But concern still exists as to whether parents are willing to take on that responsibility or just leave it to the people who create television programs. If our culture is to have high standards, those who shape that culture through the mass media must be extremely careful to adhere to the highest ethical practices.

SUMMARY

The mass media have come under fire in recent years for failing to practice high moral and ethical standards. The major areas of criticism focus on the news media, the blurring of content, and advertisements and media entertainment.

Although journalists today are more concerned about ethical standards than ever before, they are still severely criticized for operating under a double standard: They hold other institutions accountable for anything less than high ethical practices while refusing to criticize or examine their own practices. Areas of concern are accuracy and fairness, honesty and integrity, doctoring photographs, staging news events, focusing on titillation rather than real news, checkbook journalism, accepting gifts, conflicts of interest, poor judgment when faced with decisions to withhold information, covering cultural diversity, coverage of wars, and invasion of people's privacy.

The media also have been criticized for questionable ethical standards related to their business activities. Advertisers' attempts to control media content is a problem that has plagued the media for years. Those who pay the bills and produce the profits often believe they should have a say in the media's editorial and entertainment content. Sometimes advertisers threaten to boycott the media if they don't get their way. Some media often run advertorials, news items that are publicity pieces for advertisers. Real estate sections of most newspapers are filled with advertiser hype disguised as news stories. Although these practices are profitable, they raise ethical concerns about the credibility of the news medium.

Some concerns also have been raised about television's new home-shopping channels and direct-response advertising. It is feared that excessive impulse buying by consumers could result if interaction with the television set becomes commonplace. The trend toward large chain ownership of most community newspapers also threatens community journalism. Corporate dictates expressed without concern for local community sensitivities could change American journalism.

Many ethical questions are arising in the area of media entertainment. Distortions of cultural reality have become a concern. Docudramas, sitcoms, and soap operas are just some of the program genres criticized. Violence and sex in media content are also concerns. Such issues have led the government to require a V-chip in all new television sets so that parents can block out sexual and violent programming.

All of these ethical concerns about the mass media highlight the point that a successful medium in American popular culture should be a socially responsible one.

Find a review of *Key People and Concepts*, a message board for *Practicing Media Literacy* questions, self tests, and more at: www.mhhe.com/wilson.

Thought Questions

1. Do the media have an obligation to deliver what the people want to know regardless of content?

2. Do the media have an obligation to avoid broadcasting news about violent or unscrupulous acts which might incite people to model or mimic those acts?

3. What do you think of the various approaches the news media use in reporting AIDS-related stories? How would you handle such stories if you were a newspaper editor?

4. Should news media continue the practice of omitting names of rape victims? How is such a practice justified when the names of other violent-crime victims are included in stories? Does withholding names downplay the severity of rape as a violent crime?

5. What guidelines should be established for news-media coverage of wars? Who should establish them, and how?

Notes

1. "Pauley Won't Act, but King Will," *Fresno Bee*, July 23, 1997, p. A2.

2. Ibid.

3. Tom Goldstein, "Dramatic Footage, Yes—But Is It News?" *TV Guide*, May 23–29, 1998, p. 41.

4. Radio Television News Directors Foundation, *The Future of News: Defining the Issues* (Washington, DC: RTNDF, 1995).

5. "Dramatic Footage," *TV Guide*, p. 41.

6. Jay Black, Bob Steele, and Ralph Barney, *Doing Ethics in Journalism: A Handbook with Case Studies* (Greencastle, IN: Sigma Delta Chi Foundation and Society of Professional Journalists, 1993), p. 43. (This quote and a number of the case studies cited in this chapter can be found in this publication.)

7. Peter C. Canfield, "Atlanta Paper Defends Its Report," *San Francisco Chronicle*, April 29, 1999, p. A27.

8. Tom Goldstein, "Rush to Judgment?" *TV Guide*, October 5, 1996, p. 37.

9. "Second *Boston Globe* Columnist Crosses Ethics Boundaries; Resignation Is Sought," *Baltimore Sun*, August 6, 1998, p. 4A.

10. *"New Republic* Apologizes for Fabrications," *Fresno Bee*, June 13, 1998, p. A8.

11. Black, Steele, and Barney, *Doing Ethics in Journalism*, p. 49.

12. "*60 Minutes* Executive Criticizes Hidden Cameras," *Palm Springs Desert Sun*, October 1997.

13. Black, Steele, and Barney, *Doing Ethics in Journalism*, pp. 109–110.

14. Bill Carter, "CSB Is Divided over the Use of False Images in Broadcasts," *New York Times*, January 13, 2000, p. C1.

15. Alex Kuczynski, "On CBS News, Some of What You See Isn't There," *New York Times*, January 12, 2000, p. A1.

16. "CBS Is Divided," *New York Times*, p. C1.

17. "CBS Logo Use Raises Questions," Associated Press in the *Fresno Bee*, January 13, 2000, p. C1.

18. "TV Manipulation: CBS' Fake Ads Undermine Credibility," *Fresno Bee*, January 22, 2000, p. B6.

19. Jay B. Lewis, "Station's Role in Irvin Tapes Receives Mixed Reviews," *Fort Worth Star-Telegram*, May 14, 1996.

20. Black, Steele, and Barney, *Doing Ethics in Journalism*, pp. 95–101.

21. Larry Reibstein, "End of the Game," *Newsweek*, July 29, 1996, p. 74.

22. Margaret Carlson, "Say It Ain't So, Joe," *Time*, July 29, 1996, p. 85.

23. Joe Klein, "A Brush with Anonymity," *Newsweek*, July 29, 1996, p. 76.

24. Dennis McDougal, "Congress Takes off the Gloves at TV Hearings," *Los Angeles Times*, April 30, 1987, p. 1.

25. Black, Steele, and Barney, *Doing Ethics in Journalism*, pp. 86–87.

26. "Text of Eulogy by 9th Earl Spencer," *Fresno Bee*, September 7, 1997, p. A15.

27. "Diana: Prince Charles Fought Queen's Wishes," *Fresno Bee*, September 9, 1997, p. A8.

28. Ibid.

29. Joan Ryan, "Media's Hunger Makes a Celebrity of Chelsea," *San Francisco Chronicle*, September 20, 1997, p. A1.

30. Bill Workman, "Chelsea Columnist Gets the Ax," *San Francisco Chronicle*, October 2, 1997, p. A18.

31. "Showdown at the *Stanford Daily*," *San Francisco Chronicle*, October 3, 1997, p. A24.

32. "UC Berkeley Paper Apologizes for Chelsea 'Satire,'" *Fresno Bee*, November 24, 1997, p. A3.

33. Black, Steele, and Barney, *Doing Ethics in Journalism*, pp. 175–176.

34. Ibid., p. 121.

35. Herb Schmertz with William Novak, *Goodbye to the Low Profile: The Art of Creative Confrontation* (Boston: Little, Brown, 1986), p. 94.

36. *USA Today*, April 5, 1984, p. 10a.

37. "Survey Questions Journalists' Ethics," *Fresno Bee*, October 17, 1998.

38. Richard Zoglin, "A Show for Our Sponsor," *Time*, June 17, 1996, p. 101.

39. Tom Goldstein, *The News at Any Cost: How Journalists Compromise Their Ethics to Shape the News* (New York: Simon & Schuster, 1985), pp. 91–92.

40. "Television's Risky Relationship," *New York Times*, January 18, 2000, p. A26.

41. Howard Kurtz, "Drug Office Deal Included Newspapers," *Washington Post*, January 20, 2000, p. C1.

42. Edward Jay Whetmore, *Mediamerica: Form, Content and Consequences*, 5th ed. (Belmont, CA: Wadsworth, 1995), pp. 10–12, 170–171.

43. Tom Whitmore, "Soap Opera Sex Ignores Consequences, Educator Says," *Fresno Bee*, September 8, 1996, p. A8.

16

Media Research, Effects, and Consequences

Logical consequences are the scarecrows of fools and the beacons of wise men.

—**Thomas Henry Huxley,** 1874

As the 20th century drew to a close, there were a number of shootings at schools across the country, topped off with what has been termed by some as "the massacre at Columbine High School" in Littleton, Colorado. The finger of blame was immediately aimed in many different directions, but the overall target was the mass media. ● Some said video games had led to the violence among young people; others said it was the violence on television and in the movies, and there were those who blamed the violence portrayed in much of today's popular music. In Washington, D.C., politicians joined in the search to find a cause for what has made America one of the most violent nations in the world. ● President Bill Clinton held a summit on youth violence less than a month after the Columbine shootings, saying that the session was going to be about finding answers, not assigning blame. Invited to attend the session were members of the film industry, broadcast and cable television, and the recording industries, as well as representatives of computer software companies and the Internet. Also invited were parents, young people, religious leaders, law enforcement officials and teachers. The biggest result of the three-hour meeting was the announcement that a nonprofit foundation would be established and a national campaign similar to campaigns aimed at reducing teenage pregnancy would be launched aimed at curtailing violence among young people. ● However, in Congress, attempts to regulate program content were defeated. One proposal would have required TV programmers, movie producers, video game makers, and record companies to join together in creating a universal labeling system to identify products that contained violent content unsuitable for children. Another defeated proposal would have made it a crime to sell explicit violent or sexual material to minors under 17. ● The reaction to the violence among young people has not changed over the years. There have been summits held before with a lot of discussion but not much of substance coming out of the sessions. There have been attempts to pass legislation to cut back on the violence portrayed in the media, but the fear of having such legislation overturned by the courts on First Amendment grounds usually prevailed. There have also been threats from the public to boycott television programs, movies, and recordings that send out violent messages, but ratings and sales have stayed high. And there have been calls for the media to regulate themselves to cut back on the violence being presented.   •   But not much has changed, even with a television content ratings system that had been in place for several years prior to the shootings at Columbine.   •   Despite decades of studies relating to violence in the media, there has been little action taken in dealing with the problem. Over the years, media research has focused on three major themes: (1) the effects of violence in the mass media on the American culture, (2) the effects of erotica in the media on our culture, and (3) the effects of the mass media on children. This chapter will examine those studies, as well as the overall effects and consequences of the media on our society.

EARLY MEDIA RESEARCH STUDIES

Early media-effects research was based on the magic bullet theory, which assumed that a given message reaches every eye and ear immediately and directly in the same way and that all responses are similar. It wasn't until the 1930s that research began showing that individual differences play a role in how people respond to media.

Payne Fund Studies

The first major research efforts on media effects began in 1929 with a series of 12 studies on the impact of motion pictures on our society. Sponsored by the well-respected Payne Fund, the studies examined such topics as how motion picture morals compared with American moral standards, whether there was a link between films depicting crime and actual crime and delinquency reported in the community, and how motion pictures affected the behavior of children.

Although these studies did not come up with conclusive proof that motion pictures were damaging to our culture, the results, particularly the conclusion that teenagers had been greatly influenced by the movies, did bring pressure to bear on the government and the industry. In an effort to head off government censorship, the industry responded by strengthening the production code of the Motion Picture Producers and Distributors of America (see Chapter 9).

Cantril Study

Radio became the next mass-communication medium to undergo media-effects research. When Orson Welles's 1938 radio drama "War of the Worlds" caused more than a million Americans to panic over the belief that Martians were invading the earth, researchers went into action to find out why a radio drama, clearly identified as such, could have fooled so many people. A study conducted by Hadley Cantril at Princeton University found that critical thinking skills were a key factor. Individuals with better education were less likely to believe the broadcast was real. It also listed the excellent quality of the broadcast and political tensions in Europe as contributors to the panic.

Lazarsfeld Study

The next major study, conducted in 1940 by Paul Lazarsfeld, sought to determine if the mass media, particularly radio, were influencing the way people made political choices at election time. The study concluded that other people, known as *opinion leaders,* not the mass media, influenced most people's political decisions. The study did find, however, that the opinion leaders read newspapers more, listened to radio news shows, and in general were better informed than the average person. Of course, this study was done before television came on the scene and politicians learned the power of the image over the message.

opinion leaders

Delinquency and Violence

Since the very first Payne studies, society and researchers have been concerned about the effects the mass media might have on children. A particularly important question is whether violence in the mass media causes delinquency and violent behavior in children and teenage viewers. As delinquent behavior and the number of violent crimes by youths rose in the 1980s, this question was the focus of a great deal of debate by the 1990s.

When comic books entered the popular culture in the late 1930s as a youth-oriented entertainment medium (see Chapter 6), action–adventure characters such as Superman became popular with young people. As previously discussed, more than one youngster was injured while imitating the actions of comic book heroes. In 1952, Congress got into the business of studying media effects when Senator Estes Kefauver held hearings into the causes of juvenile delinquency. When the same committee held hearings during the 1954–55 session of Congress, it concluded that violent programming in large amounts could be potentially harmful to children.

In addition to the **Kefauver hearings,** two other U.S. senators held subcommittee hearings on juvenile delinquency and the media during the 1960s. They issued a warning that young people could develop antisocial behavior from watching too much televised violence. The National Commission on the Causes and Prevention of Violence, appointed by President Lyndon Johnson in 1968, concluded that a constant diet of violent behavior on television had an adverse effect on human character and attitudes. The commission stressed the need for more significant research in this area.

Kefauver hearings

The surgeon general, at the urging of Senator John Pastore, also became involved in studying TV violence as a possible public health hazard. An advisory committee issued *Television and Social Behavior: The Surgeon General's Report* and a summary report entitled *Television and Growing Up: The Impact of Televised Violence.* Both reports became involved in political controversy over the committee's membership selection and research decisions, much as the Meese Commission on obscenity did in 1986 (see Chapter 4).

Less controversial research by Wilbur Schramm, Jack Lyle, and Edwin Parker found that violence did affect children but the process was not a simplistic action–reaction activity; rather, it was a complex phenomenon that created different reactions among a variety of children under similar and different situations. The study said,

> **@ Practicing Media Literacy**
> Why do you think that all of these studies over the years have had little impact on media content?

For some children, under some conditions, some television is harmful. For other children, under the same conditions, or for the same children under other conditions, it may be beneficial. For most children, under most conditions, most television is probably neither harmful nor particularly beneficial.[1]

Four Theories of Violence

As research on the relationship between violence and the media continued, different schools of thought developed. The "catharsis theory" suggests that we relieve frustrations and potential violent behavior vicariously by watching violence in the media.[2]

The "aggressive cues theory" contends that TV violence increases excitement levels in viewers and triggers already learned behavior, resulting in repetition of violent acts in real-life situations. A similar theory, the "reinforcement theory," suggests that TV violence reinforces behavior already existing in individuals. According to this theory, a violent individual perceives violence on television as real-life occurrences, while a nonviolent person sees it as entertainment.[3]

Finally, the "observational theory" contends that we can learn violent behavior from watching violent programs. Albert Bandura and his colleagues advanced the observational theory through their studies of children interacting with "Bobo" dolls. The experiments, using different groups of children, found that those who were shown pictures depicting abusive conduct with the doll imitated that behavior.[4]

The aggressive cues theory was supported by the research of Leonard Berkowitz, who conducted aggression-machine experiments in which subjects were asked to administer an electric shock to another person whenever he or she gave a wrong answer to a question. Those administering the shocks had a choice of how strong to make the electrical charge. The studies showed that both children and college students participating in the research administered stronger shocks after they were exposed to TV violence.[5] Since both the Bandura and Berkowitz studies demonstrated a relationship between TV violence and aggressive behavior in the laboratory setting, they were widely quoted by groups advocating the reduction of violence on television.

Many of the studies on violence in the media used researcher George Gerbner's violence index, a technique that counts the number of violent acts in a TV program.[6] This content analysis continues to show high levels of violence in TV programming. However, many studies have disagreed as to just what constitutes violence: should slapping a person trying to steal a kiss or the implied threat of violence be considered in such research? A study released in 1990 showed that violence in children's television programming climbed dramatically during the previous three years. The study, conducted under the auspices of the University of Pennsylvania's Annenberg School of Communications, also found that prime time levels of violence remained high but unchanged from those earlier in the decade.[7] As mentioned earlier in this book, the American Medical Association (AMA) released a report in 1996 saying that television and movie violence were partly responsible for an increase in violent crime among children between ages 13 and 17. According to the AMA study, such violence rose 126 percent between 1976 and 1992.

> @   **Practicing Media Literacy**
>
> Do you agree with the concept that some people are already violent and media violence merely reinforces those feelings or triggers violent actions?

> @   **Practicing Media Literacy**
>
> What do you consider to be an act of violence in an entertainment program?

Television News and Violence

In 1998, delegates to the American Psychological Association's annual meeting were told that children were often frightened by watching television news stories about murders, kidnappings, and even natural disasters. The convention report also indicated that as the children grew older, the more fearful they became.

Some 33 percent of parents with children in kindergarten through sixth grade reported that their children had been frightened or upset by a TV news story during the previous year, often suffering nightmares or sleeplessness. Some were said to be afraid to leave their homes.

While researchers at the APA meeting were critical of television news for playing up blood and gore on the evening news when it could be viewed by youngsters, they also conceded that there was no clear evidence that watching TV news does any permanent psychological damage. They also could not draw a link between media content and the apparent increase in such real-life tragedies as the school shootings which had been going on around the country. The general feeling was that children younger than 8 should not watch news shows at all and youngsters between the ages of 8 and 12 should have their news viewing limited by their parents. Said one of the researchers: "I don't think children should be entirely shielded from the world, but television news just isn't the best way for children to learn about the world."[8] TV newscasts are not required to use the television content rating code that entertainment programs must display.

Obscenity and Pornography

In addition to the effects of TV program violence on children, the effects of pornography in the culture have generated interest. As previously discussed (see Chapter 4), government commissions on obscenity and pornography came up with opposite conclusions in 1970 and 1986. However, a number of other studies have dealt with this issue.

In 1980, a five-year longitudinal study of *Playboy* and *Penthouse* found a significant increase in depictions of rape, bondage, and sadism.[9] Studies by Donnerstein and Hallam in 1978[10] and K. A. Baron in 1979[11] indicated that pornography can stimulate violent behavioral tendencies. Other studies have shown that the highest levels of sexual arousal occur in response to sexually violent pornography[12] and that a substantial number of male students observed in studies on pornography found the idea of rape attractive.[13] However, since all of these studies were conducted among male college student volunteers, care must be taken not to apply the results to sex offenders or any other group without further research.

> **@ Practicing Media Literacy**
> Do you feel uncomfortable with the increase in sexual content in the media in recent years? Do you consider it pornographic?

Still, some researchers suggest that sexual violence shown in the media promotes its occurrence in real life. Research led J. H. Court to conclude that the increase in media sexual violence had caused a rise in sexual attacks on women in the Western world.[14]

TELEVISION'S EFFECTS ON THE CULTURE

The question of violence on TV has been around nearly as long as the medium itself. Many critics claim that TV violence increases violence in our society and that the increase of violence in our culture is a direct result of television. Others maintain that television merely reflects the violence that already exists in our culture.

Information-Imitation Theory

The information-imitation theory contends that TV violence plays a prominent role in causing bizarre and violent behavior in society. It is believed that some people (usually mentally unbalanced individuals) observe information and activities in the media and then proceed to imitate what they see. Several specific cases illustrating this theory have received a great deal of discussion and have fueled the arguments for eliminating violence on TV.

Fuzz, which first appeared as a book written by Evan Hunter under the pseudonym Ed McBain, was made into a movie starring Burt Reynolds and Raquel Welch. No public outcry developed over the book or the movie. However, when the movie was shown on television, it generated a great deal of concern. Some groups, objecting to a scene in the film in which a group of juvenile delinquents pour gasoline over a skid row vagrant and set him on fire, attempted to prevent the movie from being shown by a major television network.

The night after the movie was shown on national television, a woman who had run out of gas in Boston and was carrying a can of fuel back to her car from a corner service station was accosted by a gang of juveniles. They poured the gasoline over her and set her on fire. Several nights later, a vagrant sleeping along railroad tracks in Florida was doused with gasoline by a gang of youths and set on fire.

When the motion picture *The Deer Hunter,* which features numerous intense scenes of people playing Russian roulette, was shown on TV, more than 20 deaths of people playing the deadly game were reported. No such incidents were reported during the theatrical run of the film.

Major motion pictures, such as The Deer Hunter *with Robert DeNiro, did not cause many incidents of copycat violence when shown in theaters. However, the situation is different when they are shown on TV. Is this because television has more influence or is it because TV is more accessible?*

Following an NBC-TV network showing of the movie *Born Innocent,* which contains a prison scene in which a female inmate, played by Linda Blair, is raped with the handle of a plumber's helper, a San Francisco girl was raped with a Coke bottle by several other girls who said they got the idea while watching the TV movie. The victim's mother sued NBC and the local TV station, but the court ruled that television could not be held responsible for how some people reacted to scenes in an entertainment program.

Several years later, a Florida teenager was on trial for murder. His defense attorney claimed the youngster was driven to commit the act by watching too much violence on television. The court found the youth, not the TV industry, guilty of the murder.

A number of researchers have linked aggressive behavior and television viewing. In one such study, the National Institute of

Mental Health concluded that "the scientific support for the causal relationship [between violence on TV and aggressive behavior] derives from the convergence of findings from many studies, the great majority of which demonstrate a positive relationship between televised violence and later aggressive behavior."[15]

As a result of some of these studies, television reduced some of its violent content. The violent Westerns of the 1950s and 1960s have, for the most part, vanished from network television (but are still available on cable). Detective shows such as *Starsky and Hutch* were taken off the air for being too violent. They were replaced, however, by action–adventure shows, such as *The A-Team*, that used "make-believe" violence. Some psychiatrists and psychologists charged that shows such as *The A-Team* created a false view of violence by showing the use of automatic rifles, hand grenades, and other weapons without ever injuring or killing anyone. Without such consequences, they contended, the viewer will seriously underestimate the impact of violence in real life. By the year 2000, the TVLand cable channel was showing reruns of *The A-Team*, promoting it as the violent program where no one gets hurt.

In the fall of 1993, NBC, ABC, CBS, and Fox began placing parental advisory notices at the beginning of TV shows containing violence. The effort was a response to congressional criticism of the levels of violence on TV. Critics of TV violence were not satisfied with these efforts and indicated they were similar to placing a warning notice on a toxic smokestack rather than cleaning up the pollution. As a result, the Telecommunications Act of 1996 introduced the **V-chip** to America, as well as a more specific rating system for television programs (see Box 16.1).

> **@ Practicing Media Literacy**
>
> Do you feel content warnings at the beginning of violent programs are useful in alerting viewers as to what's to come or do they alert young people that the program's violence may be what they want to watch?

V-chip

TV Cartoons and Children

Saturday morning cartoon shows continue to be one of the main targets for antiviolence advocates. A report by the National Coalition on Television Violence reported that there was a "deluge of high-action, violent cartoon shows" aimed at children. Dr. Thomas Radecki, head of the coalition and a psychiatrist, said, "We can only pump so much violence into our people before we explode."[16] However, others maintain that they grew up watching the cartoons of the Road Runner and Tom and Jerry on television and have managed to live normal adult lives.

> **@ Practicing Media Literacy**
>
> Did you watch television cartoon programs as a youngster? What, if any, impact do you think they had on you? If they didn't have much impact, why do you think that was the case? Did parental training have anything to do with it?

Children and Alcohol

Parents and other groups are concerned about other issues on TV besides violence. They are also bothered by some nonviolent content. Research by the National Council on Alcoholism, for example, found that before a child reaches age 18, he or she will watch someone drink alcohol on television an average of 100,000 times. George Gerbner, former dean of the Annenberg School of Communications at the University of Pennsylvania, pointed out that having a drink is an effective dramatic device for TV.

A study released early in the year 2000 suggested that television programs and commercials which glamorize alcohol consumption promoted drinking in some teens.

From the Smurfs to Pokemon, *children are easily influenced by what they see on TV. Children are then known to put pressure on their parents to buy the many items related to their favorite TV shows.*

Researchers pointed out that television viewing was linked to teen drinking among those young people who think that alcohol would make them happy and popular. However, it was also pointed out that those teenagers tended to find television to be an accurate reflection of reality, possibly because they also saw their parents drinking. ✓

Children and TV Commercials

Another concern regarding TV's influence on children developed in the 1980s when commercial enterprises began exploiting children by reaching into actual program content to sell their products. This concern developed after the FCC began deregulating the television industry in the 1980s. This hands-off policy toward TV encouraged toy makers to begin producing their own programs, a practice that had been abandoned after the quiz show scandal of 1959. Such toy manufacturers as Hasbro, Milton Bradley, Mattel, Coleco, Kenner, Tomy, Tonka, Selchow & Righter, and even CBS Toys joined forces with animation houses to produce children's shows that featured planned and existing toys. These product-oriented entertainment shows were in reality 30-minute commercials. Because youngsters had difficulty telling the difference between the program content and the commercials, the FCC began requiring the networks to provide both written and oral **announcements** when they were breaking for a commercial ("We'll return to our program after these messages") and when they returned ("And now, back to our program").

announcements

Early program-length commercials featured such lovable dolls as Strawberry Shortcakes and the Smurfs, but by 1985 they included such aggression-oriented products as He-Man and the Masters of the Universe, G.I. Joe: A Real American Hero, Transformers, She-Ra: Princess of Power, M.A.S.K. (Medical Armored Strike Command), Thunder Cats, Voltron, and Rambo. By the 1990s, we had the Mighty Morphin Power Rangers and the Teenage Mutant Ninja Turtles. Children, who at early ages have difficulty distinguishing between commercials and programs, now found there *was* no difference. All of these preceded the Pokemon craze that led the youth movement into the 21st century.

Concerns over Physical Effects

Concerns about the effects of TV on children are as old as the medium itself. Early concerns centered around physiological effects (will staring at a picture tube ruin a child's eyesight?) as well as emotional or psychological effects. Numerous studies have been conducted over the years to examine TV's impact on children. A 1998 U.S. Department of Agriculture seminar on childhood obesity supported an earlier study in Tennessee that found that excessive TV viewing by children lowers their metabolism and causes obesity. Saying that there was a record 10 million overweight children in the United States, the experts pointed to TV as the number-one problem in creating young **couch potatoes.** Researchers noted that children who watch a lot of television gain weight due to a lack of activity and the consumption of junk food while sitting in front of the tube.

couch potatoes

Since July 1, 1999, television sets manufactured with screens 13 inches or larger have been required to include the V-chip. The Telecommunications Act of 1996, approved by Congress and signed into law by President Clinton, mandated the use of the V-chip to help parents determine which programs contained too much sex or violence for their children. The V-chip allows for programs to be blocked from the TV screen by parents, based on the rating information provided to them by the television programmers.

But a study released by the Kaiser Family Foundation just months before the V-chip sets started coming off the line showed that while parents were concerned that their children were being exposed to too much sex or violence in the TV shows they watched, only four out of 10 had ever seen or heard anything explaining how the V-chip or the ratings system worked. According to the survey, only five of the 11 ratings categories (TV-G, TV-PG, TV-14, V, and L) were understood by a majority of parents; less than half of the parents knew that sitcoms, children's shows, talk shows and soap operas were even rated, and among parents with children under 10, only 17 percent could name one of the ratings used to identify shows specifically designed for children.

As a result of the findings, the Center for Media Education and the Kaiser Family Foundation announced a national campaign to educate parents about the V-chip and the TV ratings system. The campaign included the distribution of free booklets for parents on how these new tools actually worked, as well as a guide for viewers on how to watch television with children.

It's a well-known fact in the advertising business that sex sells. The motion picture industry learned years ago that violence also sells, and people will pay money to see such violent films as *The Texas Chainsaw Massacre, Friday the 13th, Nightmare on Elm Street,* and the three *Scream* movies. But since the early days of television in the late 1940s and early 1950s, the viewing public has often complained about too much sex and violence coming into their homes by means of this new technology.

However, it wasn't until the 1990s that the television industry agreed to take part in a study of violence on TV. But the study found in 1996 that based on some

3,000 hours of programming, only five series contained violence in what was considered a large number of episodes, and of those five series, two had already been canceled. The study, conducted by UCLA, also reported that only four children's programs contained what was described as "sinister combat violence," and that was down from seven the previous year. As for theatrical movies shown on television during the previous season, 33 were deemed excessively violent, down from 50 the year before.

Rather than counting acts of violence or rating programs, the UCLA study looked at violence in context. For example, such programs as *NYPD Blue* and *Law and Order* were praised for their realistic depictions of urban life and the consequences of crime and violence, while the Fox network's *New York Undercover* was criticized for using popular music tracks during the violent scenes, thereby glorifying the criminals by making them appear to be the stars of an MTV video.

However, the UCLA study also noted a new and disturbing trend: Graphic reality specials, such as "When Animals Attack," "When Disaster Strikes," "The World's Most Dangerous Animals," "The World's Wildest Police Chases," "Forces of Nature," and "Close Call: Cheating Death," all depicted real-life violence. In fact, the program, broadcast on the Fox network, was cited by NBC programming official Don Ohlmeyer as being nothing more than a snuff film.

But even before the V-chip was being installed, the rating system proposed by representatives from the networks, studios, and producers was the subject of complaints and controversy. With the process overseen by the Motion Picture Association of America (MPAA), which had its own system for rating theatrical movies, the group made its recommendations for the new system to eventually work with the V-chip. But within months of its implementation, some—including the Clinton Administration—were saying that the initial ratings (TV-G, TV-PG, TV-14 and TV-MA) were not enough.

While the new rating proposal was considered to be an improvement over what was used before—nothing—many found the system to be a disappointment. A survey by the National Parent Teachers Association showed that parents wanted a system that would give

continued

them more information about the sexual, violence, and language content on specific programs. Pressure was applied for the networks to add some sort of content codes to be shown with the acceptable viewing age guidelines, so that parents would have the information needed to control the viewing of their children. However, most broadcasters were fearful of labeling programs as having sex or violence, as this might cause advertisers to pull out of such programs.

Two other concerns were being expressed: one, that children with their computer knowledge and video game skills would soon be able to break through the V-chip when parents were away, and two, that television producers, knowing that they now had to rate their programs with violent content would use that as an excuse to increase the level of violence ("Well, we warned the viewers at the start of the show!").

Finally, most of the networks agreed to list S, V, L, and D with their ratings (NBC declined to do so) but, as was found in the Kaiser study, the average viewer still didn't know what the letters meant. Do you? For the record S means "sexual content," V is for "violence," L is for "offensive language" and D is for "sexually suggestive dialogue."

Positive Effects Research

Most research seems to indicate that children do learn behavior and that television does play a role in teaching that behavior. Some research has been conducted on the positive effects of television on children. These studies focused on prosocial programs developed for children, such as *Sesame Street, The Electric Company, Mister Rogers' Neighborhood, Fat Albert and the Cosby Kids, The Harlem Globetrotters' Popcorn Machine,* and *Shazam*. All these programs were developed to impart positive social values. Of these, the most extensively researched has been *Sesame Street*, which attempts to teach rudimentary reading and counting skills as well as social skills. Much of the research suggests that children do learn from the program, but disadvantaged children—the target audience—are the least likely to watch it.

In her book *Mind and Media*, Patricia Greenfield says that children often take well-known TV characters as examples to be imitated. She points out that the day after Fonzie took out a library card on the popular television show *Happy Days*, the number of children applying for library cards in the United States increased fivefold. She contends that TV can be a very positive force in the lives of children if it is used constructively and if parents actively see to it that their children interact with the programs' content through discussions and parental explanations.[17]

parental involvement

Such **parental involvement** is not always possible, however. Recent changes in our culture regarding the traditional nuclear family are creating new problems. The traditional family in which the father works and the mother stays home has been replaced with situations where either both parents work or the household consists of a single parent raising the children. For example, in 1960, 17 percent of American mothers returned to work within a year of their children's birth. The number rose to 53 percent by the 1990s. In 1960, 1 percent of children under 18 experienced divorce. By the 1990s the number had climbed to 50 percent, with 25 percent of children under 18 living in one-parent families. These conditions created a new kind of child in the United States: the "latchkey kid." Millions of American children today go home from school to fend for themselves, and they usually do so in front of the television set.

Many observers of this new trend contend that today's American child no longer obtains his or her cultural values

@   **Practicing Media Literacy**

Do you agree with those who feel that the television set has replaced the family unit in passing on cultural values to young people?

For many decades, there has been concern about the effects the mass media have on children. Of particular concern is whether violence in the media causes violent behavior among young people.

from the traditional family structure but instead gets them from the mass media. And some critics say that what they are getting is a popular culture filled with sex and violence.

Child psychiatrist Robert Coles says that what children do with television depends on the nature of their own lives. He points out that a child who has an unstable family life may be more vulnerable to the emotional and moral power of TV, while a child with a stable home life will not "likely be sucked into the moral wasteland that one finds while watching certain programs." What matters, he says, "is not only the quality of television programming for our young people (or their parents) but the quality of American family life."[18]

TV VIOLENCE AT THE END OF THE CENTURY

By the decade of the 1990s, the concern over violence in the media had come to a head. Concerns about constitutional consequences of curbing violence, which hinted at censorship, seemed to have diminished as such liberals as Attorney General Janet Reno, Senator Paul Simon of Illinois, Representative Edward Markey of Massachusetts, and the Reverend Jesse Jackson began speaking out for controls against media violence. Some media executives began to voluntarily take action. Television networks began including warning labels at the beginning of shows with violent content. This was not enough, however, and the television industry was forced to establish a rating system for its programs as the V-chip was introduced to allow parents control of the programs that could be viewed in their homes.

Touchstone Films ordered the removal of a scene where macho football players prove their manhood by lying in the middle of a highway at night in the movie *The Program*. This action came after several deaths occurred when young men tried to prove their own manhood by imitating the scene.

The new concern about violence in television was sparked by a growing amount of violence in American society and the increasing evidence showing that viewing violence increased aggressive behavior among heavy viewers. According to a survey by the American Psychological Association called "Big World, Small Screen," 1,000

The violence shown on some TV shows, such as NYPD Blue, is thought by some to be acceptable because it also shows the results of the violence. However, others feel that society is becoming desensitized to violence because we've seen so much of it on television over the years.

consensus

studies, reports, and commentaries concerning the impact of television violence had been published since 1955, and the accumulated research clearly demonstrated a correlation between viewing violence and aggressive behavior.[19]

Among the major studies reaching this conclusion were those conducted by the National Commission on the Causes and Prevention of Violence (1968), the Surgeon General's Report (1972), the National Institute of Mental Health's Study (1982), the U.S. Attorney General's Task Force on Family Violence (1984), and the American Medical Association study (1996).

This **consensus** prompted child experts, psychologists, and the medical community to begin treating television violence as a serious public health issue, similar to smoking and drunk driving. They believed the public needed to be educated about TV violence for its own safety and well-being.

The public also believes a strong correlation exists between violence on television and violence in the streets. A poll by the *Los Angeles Times* found that four out of five Americans believed violence in television entertainment programs has directly contributed to violence in our society. Of the 79 percent who said there is a connection between TV violence and society's increasing violence, two-thirds said they believed it was a significant cause.[20]

Even scholars were taking the concern of violence in the media seriously. St. John's University sponsored an international conference on violence in the media in New York City. In organizing the conference, the university noted that over 3,000 scholarly studies had indicated a direct causal relationship between excessive violence on television and in other media and the development of aggression in viewers. While acknowledging that other causative agents may share the responsibility for the high rate of violent crimes in our society, they said "there is no question that the media have a major impact on this particular problem."

The conference brought together media professionals, government officials, and academics from around the world and in many disciplines, such as psychology, sociology, criminal justice, communications, journalism, and health care, to explore and identify the relationship between the media and violence in society.

VIOLENCE IN MUSIC

Although violence in television programming has received the most attention by researchers and concerned citizens, the increase in violence in music, and in music videos in particular, has also become a target for concern in recent years (see Chapter 11). Although specific songs with explicit lyrics, such as Ice-T's "Cop Killer," have caused public outrage, little study has been done of the relationship between violence in music and an increase in violence among young people. As mentioned in Chapter 15, there was some public outcry about rapper Snoop Doggy Dogg's gansta rap album *Doggystyle*, which sold 800,000 copies during the first week of its release while the rapper was free on $1 million bail awaiting trial on charges of being an accomplice to murder, and the inclusion of a song by convicted mass killer Charles Manson in Guns N' Roses' hit album *The Spaghetti Incident*. But there were no boycotts or major protests, and Snoop Doggy Dogg's album went on to sell 5 million copies.

However, by the final years of the 20th century, the popularity of gangsta rap albums that glorified life in the "hood," including senseless drive-by shootings, was increasing. Some of the music videos produced to promote these gangsta rap albums graphically glorified violence on the streets. In "Gangsta Lean," for example, four young men mourn the gang-related death of a "homie" while sipping 40-ounce bottles of beer and reminiscing about how they used to hang out. The four toast other dead friends and their pals in prison. Lyrics include "My boys in the pen who ain't never gonna see the street again" and "It don't matter what they were doing. Banging, slangin'. But they ain't here no more."

In Ultramagnetic MC's "Raise It Up," another group of young men rap about pulling out a Smith & Wesson pistol. Another rap video showed a large group of young people, some with small children, gathered around Dr. Dre in "Nothin' but a G Thang" with one person displaying a gun tucked in the back of his pants. "Steady Dippin'," by Bloods and Crips, shows a rapper holding a gun in front of a group of young people, all flashing gang signs. Although increased pressure mounted to get radio stations to ban or edit some of the violence and explicit language in rap songs, very little attention was directed toward gangsta rap videos that were being played on three cable outlets: MTV, Black Entertainment Television (BET), and the request-video jukebox station The Box (see Box 16.2).

Rap artists have fought the efforts to censor their music, but very little research has been done to study its effects. What seems to be lacking are studies that cross over media boundaries and examine the cumulative effects of all the images and messages in our society. More longitudinal studies (studies conducted over a long period of time) that examine our **total media environment** would give us some insights into the total effects on individuals, particularly young people, of exposure to a variety of mass-media images during their formative years.

> **@ Practicing Media Literacy**
>
> Do you feel that recording artists should have the freedom to say anything in their songs, even if those songs present a negative image of our society and the people?

total media
environment

Box 16.2
MEDIA WATCH
Violence and Popular Music

The popularity of rap music did not diminish during the final years of the 20th century. This, despite the fact that many organizations and public figures had been protesting the violent and abusive content of many of the songs. For example, a variety of police, politicians, and community leaders have expressed anger at the popular gangsta recordings and videos that they say show youths and young adults, predominantly African-Americans, rapping about shooting police officers, drinking large bottles of beer, smoking marijuana, carrying guns, and treating women in an abusive manner. They claim that young fans of such recording artists as Tupac Shakur, Snoop Doggy Dogg, DRS, Eazy-E, Ultramagnetic MCs, and Mista Grimm are exposed to negative and one-sided images of African-American life.

Although the rappers defend their work by saying they are rapping only about what is happening in the street, African-American leaders claimed the music reflects only a small percentage of African-American life and the recordings and videos distort the black experience and reflect on it negatively. Leaders in the Inglewood (California)–based organization Stop the Violence–Increase the Peace Foundation claim the videos are making heroes out of gang members. Parents claim the music is undoing years of good child rearing.

Executives at MTV, BET, and The Box claimed the controversy was just a fabrication and young viewers are smart enough to distinguish between music the rap and real life. They passed it off as just being "show business." However, as the controversy intensified, the three cable outlets began to take steps to counterbalance the violent images. MTV began airing an antiviolence public service campaign, while The Box began running a "Violence Sucks" ad campaign. Black Entertainment Television put the word out to the music industry that it

The American Medical Association is one of the many organizations expressing concern that violence in the media—from radio and recordings to movies and television—is a serious public health issue, similar to smoking and drunk driving.

could produce all the videos it wanted with guns but those videos would receive very limited airtime on the BET network.

CULTURAL CONSEQUENCES

Throughout this book, we have explored how the mass media shape and change our culture. Western civilization changed slowly until the invention of the printing press in the 15th century. Then change, assisted by mass communication, became more rapid. After the forces of industrialization, democratization, and public education emerged in the 19th century, the expansion of the old and development of new mass media accelerated rapidly. As a result, our popular culture was radically transformed.

During the past 25 years, the development of new communication technologies has been analogous to a giant snowball gathering speed as it rolls down a steep mountain, and it is safe to assume this phenomenon is only beginning to gain momentum. As these new technologies find their place in our culture, we will see dramatic changes in our lifestyles. Whether these changes will have a positive or negative impact on our culture remains to be seen.

Form vs. Content

All technological change affects the form—the "hardware"—of the mass media. From our discussions of media ethics in Chapter 15, we might conclude that the content of the mass media, the all-important "software," has not kept pace.

What will happen if the same media content—distortions of reality through exaggerated entertainment programs, tasteless sitcoms, and more casual sex and sexual violence—is disseminated through larger and better television sets and home information centers? Will the transfer of newspaper and magazine material from print to television and computer screens mean anything if the information is no more socially responsible than it is today? Will the transmission of hundreds of TV channels into our homes by satellite or fiber optics advance our culture if the focus remains on entertainment rather than on education and we continue to see the same old reruns?

If the content of our culture is to keep pace with its form, major changes need to be made in the mass media. We have learned that the media shape our culture. Perhaps it's time that we in the culture take a more active role in shaping the media. Before we do this, however, we must keep in mind the importance of the media in our free society and make sure we maintain the delicate system of checks and balances among the judicial, legislative, and executive branches of government that our nation's founders set up. Helping to protect this system is an additional check that was added by the Bill of Rights: a free press.

Despite the various regulations placed on the American mass media (see Chapter 4), the media in this country remain the most free in the world. This must continue to be the case if American democracy is to survive.

Importance of a Free Press

The concept that a free press is an inherent part of a free society was based on the philosophies of John Milton, Andrew Hamilton, James Madison, Thomas Jefferson, and others. As Hamilton said in his closing arguments at the John Peter Zenger trial in 1735, "a free press is a cause of **liberty**—the liberty both of exposing and opposing arbitrary power by speaking and writing the truth."

liberty

Our democracy depends on a free press to keep us informed. The temptation of government leaders, the courts, and consumers to regulate our mass media is great. Thus, it is important that we recognize the importance of keeping our mass media free from unreasonable restraints.

Just keeping the media free is not good enough, however. Free yet irresponsible mass media that are insensitive to the needs and desires of their culture are almost as useless as a system of mass media under strict government control. This is particularly true if the mass media lose their credibility with the public.

The proliferation of news media and the development of better news-gathering technology at the start of the 21st century has presented some problems, however. The success of several cable news channels and online information providers has fragmented the television audience with the public getting different, and sometimes erroneous, information from a larger number of sources. At the same time, total newspaper circulation in the nation has fallen by almost 5.5 million. And the actions of some news organizations in covering some of the sensational stories of the day has caused many Americans to have a negative view of the news media. A survey by Pew Research Center for The People and The Press reported that the number of people with negative views toward the media had increased significantly. The study found that a majority of the people polled considered the media inaccurate, unfair, and intrusive.[21]

> ## @ Practicing Media Literacy
>
> How do you view the job being done by the print and electronic media—Good, Fair, or Poor? Do you think the media are losing their credibility?

Several prominent news people have spoken out on the issue. Former CBS anchor Walter Cronkite sees the race for ratings and profits as being responsible for both print and broadcast journalism sinking to new depths in the minds of the public. Cronkite pointed out that the increase in 24-hour news channels has been good for the viewers because they now should be able to find at least one channel doing serious news. As he put it, "The networks do news now as entertainment."[22] Noting that reporters are better educated and more informed than they were 30 or 40 years ago, Cronkite said that the product is worse because the corporations that own the media are driven to make excessive profits.

However, ABC's Ted Koppel says that television news is no better or worse than it was 30 or 40 years ago; there's just more of it. According to Koppel, the driving force then, as it is now, was ratings and money, and the challenge for the news media is maintaining high standards of quality and integrity at the same time as they are trying to attract the largest number of viewers.

When CBS showed video of Dr. Jack Kevorkian on *60 Minutes* as he injected fatal drugs into one of his patients to assist in his suicide, the program came in for much criticism. Newspaper editorials across the country questioned whether it was really newsworthy or an attempt by Kevorkian to escalate his crusade to legalize assisted suicides. *60 Minutes* correspondent Mike Wallace later said that he and the program had been used by Kevorkian to further his cause, but added that this was good because it helped to stimulate the debate about euthanasia in this country. The end result of the controversial showing on *60 Minutes*? The program finished fourth in the week's ratings, the top show for the network that week, helping CBS to pull even with NBC in the critical November 1998 ratings sweeps period.

While some people feel that the increase in television news outlets has led to sensationalized news as stations and networks compete for ratings, others—such as NBC's Tom Brokaw—feel that it has allowed for more in-depth news coverage.

NBC news anchor Tom Brokaw thinks that the technology has changed television news, but feels that the change has been for the better. Since most people are already familiar with the day's top stories because of the 24-hour news channels and the Internet, he says the networks are becoming more analytical and are mixing in longer, more in-depth discussions of the issues facing our society.

But others feel that the struggle for ratings leads television journalists to follow like lemmings when someone hits on a juicy story, and the feeding frenzy begins. Many cite the situation when ABC's Diane Sawyer got an interview with Olympic skater Tonya Harding and CBS sent Connie Chung to follow Harding around in hopes of also getting an interview. Robin Dorian, formerly with the TV tabloid show *A Current Affair*, commented "When you see Connie Chung hanging out at a skating rink, you know networks have changed the way they're covering the news."[23] Said Morley Safer of CBS's *60 Minutes*, "So much crap passes as information that, not only does the audience sometimes miss the distinction between news and crap, the editors sometimes miss the distinction."[24]

As a society, we should not tolerate shoddy, arrogant, irresponsible, or inadequate performances from any of our mass media. Likewise, society should not let business interests in the media forsake social responsibility in exchange for financial gains.

Consumer Awareness Needed

It is the **obligation** of each of us to become aware, concerned, skeptical, and demanding. We should be aware of just how well our mass media are or are not performing in terms of social responsibility and high ethical standards. We should be concerned about inadequate performances. We should be skeptical of any movements to strengthen external regulations of the mass media (whether from government, the courts, or organized consumer groups). And, most importantly, we should constantly demand that our mass media perform with the utmost responsibility and concern for the quality of our culture. For this reason, there are some groups who are seeking a return to the family viewing hour, where network programs run between 8 and 9 P.M. each day would be acceptable for all age groups to watch (see Box 16.3).

obligation

The fact that the mass media in the United States are businesses dependent on making a profit is important to remember. In any business enterprise, the consumer is the most important element in the sales transaction. Without the consumer there is no sale. Television shows must be watched, news articles must be read, magazines and books must be purchased, and advertised products must sell if the mass media are to stay in business.

If we were more **discriminating** in our **consumption** of the mass media, we might influence the media's content. The numbers of people listening to radio and watching television are closely monitored. When a show's ratings slip, the program is canceled. TV ratings, like newspaper and magazine circulations, determine the advertising revenues a medium generates. The mass media pay close attention to what the majority of people in the culture think. We are the ones who determine whether a place in our culture exists for them. If they fail to give us what we want and demand, we have the power to phase them out of existence.

discriminating
consumption

Thus, if the content of the mass media remains less than of the highest quality, the fault is partially ours. Television, for example, will continue to give us questionable programming with high doses of sex and violence if that is what the people are willing to watch. Sex and violence will continue to dominate movies, videos, and magazines if that is what continues to sell. Whether or not the quality of mass-media content keeps pace with the new technological advances depends on each of us.

> **@   Practicing Media Literacy**
> Do you consider yourself a discriminating media consumer?

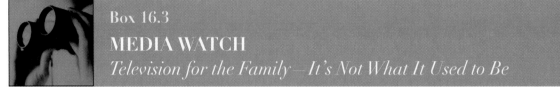

Box 16.3
MEDIA WATCH
Television for the Family — It's Not What It Used to Be

Television has come a long way from those days in the early 1950s when the lead character on the popular sitcom *I Love Lucy* was banned from saying the word *pregnant* when she found that she was expecting. By the 1970s, a New York radio station found itself in trouble for playing a George Carlin comedy recording of seven dirty words that you wouldn't hear on TV.

Today, such terms as *boobs*, *turd* and *pissed* are commonplace on television, even on programs aired as early as 8 to 9 P.M., a zone once considered the family viewing hour. That was when the networks voluntarily agreed to carry only programs that could be shared by the entire family. The family hour concept was later thrown out by the courts.

Since then, the television networks have implemented a rating system to warn viewers of a program's content, but there are those who feel that such on-screen warnings really don't fix the problem of what's really wrong with television: The shows are offensive. As the 20th century was drawing to a close, the Parents Television Council (PTC), an organization affiliated with conservative L. Brent Bozell's Media Research Center, reported that there had been a marked increase in the foul language, sexual content, and violence during that 8 to 9 P.M. hour. According to the PTC, more than two-thirds of the programs scheduled in that hour contained sexual material that parents might find objectionable, and nearly half of the programs featured coarse language. The survey found that the Fox television network was the most objectionable, airing such programs as *Melrose Place* and *Cops* in the eight o'clock

hour. NBC ranked second in terms of total objectionable content, followed by UPN, WB, ABC, and CBS.

But the survey studied only the broadcast networks and didn't take into account the many cable programs available for viewing. One of the most criticized cable shows was a cartoon program, *South Park*, which is the only series to carry a rating of TV-MA on a regular basis. Research has shown that even at its later viewing hour, 20 percent of its viewers are 17 years of age or younger.

Meanwhile, the Parents Television Council also launched a series of newspaper ads across the country featuring television personality Steve Allen and charging in bold headlines that TV was leading children down a moral sewer. The ad was an appeal to parents to let advertisers know that they weren't happy with the content of today's television programs. The organization is also seeking a return to the family viewing hour.

Even TV comedian Bill Cosby challenged television viewers to think before they let their children watch the tube. Cosby refuted the argument that the networks regularly use, that television doesn't influence people. "If that's true," he said, "why do they have commercials? Why am I sitting here with Jell-O pudding?"* But Cosby also pointed out that the viewers themselves bear the responsibility for the content of the shows they watch, saying that there's violence and sex on TV because people tune in to watch it.

*"Bill Cosby Urges TV Control," *Fresno Bee*, October 9, 1997, p. A2.

SUMMARY

Numerous research studies on the effects of mass media on individuals and on our culture have been conducted over the years. The concern over media content began with the motion pictures in the 1920s and led to the first major media effects studies, the Payne Fund studies, conducted in 1929.

Other major research included the Cantril study, which focused on the panic that occurred from the radio broadcast "War of the Worlds." The Lazarsfeld study investigated the influence of the media on presidential elections and found that opinion leaders were more influential than direct media contact.

Numerous studies have been conducted on the influence of media violence on children. Since television has become the most dominant mass medium, it has been the focus of most of the media-effects research in recent years.

Over the years, a consensus has developed that high levels of violence viewing in the media cause aggressive behavior. Many psychologists, child experts, and the medical community have started treating violence on television as a serious public health issue, similar to smoking and alcohol abuse. Action by Congress to bring about program ratings for violence and sexual content as well as the introduction of the V-chip have been among the largest attempts to control such programming on television.

In recent years, there has been a growing concern over a previously ignored area of media influence: recorded music. Violence in music videos has become a serious concern among some organizations, particularly in the African-American community.

Whether socially responsible mass-media content will keep pace with the media's rapidly expanding technology remains to be seen. If our culture is to advance with its technology, Americans must play an active role in demanding responsible content while bearing in mind the importance of a free and independent system of mass media to the American democracy.

Find a review of *Key People and Concepts,* a message board for *Practicing Media Literacy* questions, self tests, and more at: www.mhhe.com/wilson.

Thought Questions

1. Do you believe pornography causes an increase in crimes against women? If not, why not? If so, what should be done about it?

2. Should sex and violence be reduced on television and in the movies? If so, how can it be done without government censorship? If not, how do we protect children from such programming?

3. Are sex and violence scenes on MTV and in recorded music harmful to young people? Why or why not?

4. Is the replacement of the church and family with television as a socializing influence for the very young a healthy development in our culture? If not, how can we correct the problem?

5. Are current efforts by fundamentalist religious groups and concerned parents to censor the media a positive or negative development in our culture? Explain your answer.

Notes

1. Wilbur Schramm, Jack Lyle, and Edwin Parker, *Television in the Lives of Our Children* (Stanford, CA: Stanford University Press, 1961), p. 13.

2. Seymour Feshbach, "The Stimulating vs. Cathartic Effects of a Vicarious Aggressive Experience," *Journal of Abnormal and Social Psychology* 63 (1961), pp. 381–385.

3. Joseph Klapper, *The Effects of Mass Communication* (New York: Free Press, 1960).

4. Albert Bandura and Richard Walters, *Social Learning and Personality Development* (New York: Holt, Rinehart & Winston, 1963).

5. Leonard Berkowitz, *Aggression: A Social Psychological Analysis* (New York: McGraw-Hill, 1962).

6. George Gerbner, Larry Gross, Michael Morgan, and Nancy Signorielli, "The Mainstreaming of America: Violence

Profile Number 11," *Journal of Communication*, Summer 1980.

7. Shawn Pogatchnik, "Kids' TV Gets More Violent, Study Finds," *Los Angeles Times*, January 26, 1990, p. F1.

8. Kim Curtis, Associated Press, "Television News about Crime Scares Children, Psychologists Report," *Fresno Bee*, August 18, 1998, p. B4.

9. N. M. Malamuth and B. Spinner, "A Longitudinal Content Analysis of Sexual Violence in the Best-Selling Erotica Magazines," *Journal of Sex Research* 16 (1980), pp. 226–237.

10. E. Donnerstein and J. Hallam, "Facilitating Effects of Erotica on Aggression Against Women," *Journal of Personality and Social Psychology* 36 (1978), pp. 1270–1277.

11. K. A. Baron, "Heightened Sexual Arousal and Physical Aggression: An Extension to Females," *Journal of Research in Personality* 13 (1979), pp. 91–102.

12. N. M. Malamuth, M. Heim, and S. Feshbach, "Sexual Responsiveness of College Students to Rape Depictions: Inhibitory and Disinhibitory Effects," *Journal of Personality and Social Psychology* 38 (1980), pp. 399–408.

13. N. M. Malamuth, S. Haber, and S. Feshbach, "Testing Hypotheses Regarding Rape: Exposure to Sexual Violence, Sex Differences, and the 'Normality' of Rapists," *Journal of Research in Personality* 14 (1980), pp. 121–137.

14. J. H. Court, "Pornography and Sex Crimes: A Reevaluation in Light of the Recent Trends Around the World," *International Journal of Criminality and Penology* 5 (1977), pp. 129–157.

15. *Television and Behavior: Ten Years of Scientific Progress and Implications for the Eighties*, Vol. 1 (Rockville, MD: U.S. Department of Health and Human Services, 1982), pp. 89–90.

16. "Why Children's TV Turns Off So Many Parents," *U.S. News & World Report*, February 18, 1985, p. 65.

17. Patricia Marks Greenfield, *Mind and Media: The Effects of Television, Video Games and Computers* (Cambridge, MA: Harvard University Press, 1984), pp. 25–70.

18. Robert Coles, "What Makes Some Kids More Vulnerable to the Worst of TV?" *TV Guide*, June 21–27, 1986, p. 7.

19. Neil Hickey, "How Much Violence? What We Found in an Eye-opening Study," *TV Guide*, August 22, 1992, p. 12.

20. Daniel Cerone, "Most Say TV Violence Begets Real Violence," *Los Angeles Times*, December 18, 1993, p. 1.

21. "News Media Again Sink in Public Opinion," *Fresno Bee*, March 21, 1997, p. A8.

22. James Brady, "Personality Profile," *Parade* magazine, December 15, 1996, p. 16.

23. Peter Johnson, "Stars of TV News See Standards Declining," *Palm Springs Desert Sun*, March 10, 1997, p. D4.

24. Ibid.

Glossary

ABC American Broadcasting Company; a television network that began as a radio network in the 1940s after NBC was forced to sell one of its two radio networks in 1943.

Acta diurna "Daily acts"; news sheets posted in public places by the government during the Roman Empire.

Advertorial Advertising copy written in the form of a news story. Sometimes placed in news columns of special sections of newspapers labeled "advertising supplement" or used as editorial copy in magazines.

AFP Agence France-Presse; a Paris-based French news wire service organized in 1945.

Agenda setting A process whereby the mass media shape our awareness of people and events by establishing what is important for us to think about.

Age of Enlightenment A movement that began in Germany in the 18th century and prompted great intellectual activity that advanced philosophy, education, and culture.

Alien and Sedition Acts Laws passed in 1798 to silence critics of the government. These laws, which lasted only two years, represented the first U.S. government effort to restrict freedom of the press following the ratification of the First Amendment in 1791.

AM radio Amplitude modulation; a form of radio transmission in which sound waves modulate the length (or amplitude) of the carrier wave.

Amekaji A Japanese term meaning "American casual"; used to describe the trend among Japanese youth to give up traditional Japanese values as a result of influences from American mass media, particularly recorded music and music videos.

AP The Associated Press; the oldest American news wire service, founded in 1848.

A-T-R A model of how advertising works; stands for *awareness, trial,* and *reinforcement.*

Audio book A book reproduced, often in abridged form, on audiocassette. By the 1980s, all major publishing houses had audio book divisions that were showing rapid growth for the industry.

Authoritarian theory A theory of the press asserting that the rulers of society should control what is disseminated to the public in the mass media. Authoritarian theory has an offshoot, Soviet communist theory. See **Libertarian theory.**

Backmasking A controversial technique of inserting words and phrases into recorded music that can be heard only if the music is played backward.

Ballpark A term used by sociologists to describe the early development of the American pastime of baseball to help socialize the new nation of immigrants that was developing in industrial America.

BBC British Broadcasting Corporation; the public broadcasting system in the United Kingdom. It was founded in the 1920s during the early days of radio broadcasting, and in 1936 it became the first system to begin regular television broadcasting.

Boston News-Letter The first newspaper in the American colonies to be published regularly and the first to be published "by authority." Boston postmaster John Campbell was the publisher.

British invasion A term used to describe British rock groups bringing their version of American rock-'n'-roll to U.S. audiences. The invasion began with the Beatles' U.S. tour in 1964.

Cable TV A system of sending and receiving TV signals by wire. Cable systems usually receive signals by satellite at a central facility and relay them by cable to homes for a monthly fee.

Canon 35 A court regulation that restricts the use of cameras, tape recorders, and microphones in the courtrooms.

CBC Canadian Broadcasting Corporation; the official English-language broadcasting system in Canada.

CBS Columbia Broadcasting System; founded in 1927 under the name United Independent Broadcasters/Columbia.

CD-ROM A compact disc that is loaded with printed materials for easy computer access to information.

CD-ROMs are replacing reference books in many scholarly libraries. ROM stands for "read only memory."

Chain ownership   The publishing of two or more newspapers in different communities by the same company.

Channel   A term for the way we send a message. In mass communication, it refers to any one of the mass media.

Channel noise   Anything that externally interferes with a message in the communication process.

Chapbooks   Forerunners to the novel, these were pocket-size books made available to the semiliterate after the 15th-century invention of movable type.

CNN   Cable News Network; a 24-hour television news network launched by Ted Turner in 1980.

Communication   A process involving the sorting, selecting, and sharing of symbols to help receivers elicit from their own minds a meaning similar to that in the mind of the communicator.

Cone effect   A concept used to describe how the mass media influence our real lives. Developed by Edward Jay Whetmore, the cone effect describes how media content begins with real life, is exaggerated to make it interesting, and is then transmitted through one of the mass media to individuals, who in turn perceive the material according to their own frames of reference and filter it back into their own lives.

Corantos   Predecessors of the newspaper that consisted of a single sheet of paper containing current news. They first appeared in Germany in 1609 and in England in 1621.

CP   Canadian Press; the only news wire service in Canada. It is similar to our Associated Press.

Crisis management   A public relations activity that reacts to corporate crises and disasters by attempting to place a positive angle on the publicity that results from the disaster. It often involves showing the company taking strong, positive actions to correct the problem.

Cult   A subcultural group or movement that usually rejects and refuses to conform to mass-cultural activities or attitudes.

Cultural industries   Commercial enterprises that sell not only items for use in our mass culture but items for the many subcultures as well.

Cultural niches   A reference to the fact that as all new communication technologies develop, they must first find an acceptance or use in the culture before they become part of the mass culture.

Culture   Everything that occurs in a society; all the customs and practices handed down from generation to generation.

Customized textbooks   Textbooks specifically produced for a particular class by combining a variety of chapters from more than one textbook. The instructor of the course selects the chapters, and the publisher assembles the product.

Cyberpunk   A 1990s term for a subculture that fuses humans and computers. Taken from the words *cybernetics*, the science of communication and control theory, and *punk*, or antisocial rebellion.

Demographic breakout   A magazine production technique that enables advertisers to insert ads in only a portion of a given issue. Advertisers can target their ads to specific demographic groups, such as doctors, students, executives, or people earning more than a specified income.

Desktop publishing   The use of a personal computer to write, edit, typeset, design graphics, and lay out pages of a publication.

Digital compression   A system of converting the analog signals of television into digital video signals. The process allows 10 TV signals to be broadcast in the space previously reserved for one channel.

Digital sound   A sound converted electronically into a numerical system to achieve better sound reproduction.

Direct broadcasting satellites (DBS)   A powerful satellite system that sends signals directly to homes with small, relatively inexpensive receiving dishes.

Direct mail   Computerized mailings that can send different messages to different audiences. One of the most effective methods of disseminating information on political candidates and issues.

Docudrama   A form of dramatic TV presentation based on a current or historical event.

Drive time   A term referring to the time most people commute to and from work. During this period, usually from 6 to 10 A.M. and 3 to 7 P.M., radio stations in urban areas have their largest audiences.

DuMont   A TV network operating in the early days of television. Named after Allen B. DuMont, a pioneer in the development of TV receivers.

Electronic cottages   A term for the homes of telecommuters, people who work at home connected to an office by computer terminal.

EPS cycle   The three stages through which most mass media evolve: the elitist stage, when a medium is restricted to the educated, aristocratic, and wealthy; the popular stage, when a medium is consumed by the masses; and the specialized stage, when a medium caters to a variety of specific groups.

Equal-time provision   A Federal Communications Commission requirement that all bona fide political candidates have equal opportunity to use the airwaves. (Also known as Section 315.)

Fairness doctrine   A 1949 Federal Communications Commission ruling that required broadcasters to air both sides of controversial issues. In 1987 the FCC abolished the rule, calling it unconstitutional.

FCC freeze   A freeze on new television stations placed by the Federal Communications Commission in 1948 to allow time to allocate frequencies throughout the country. The freeze was lifted in 1952.

Federal Communications Commission (FCC)   A government agency established in 1934 to regulate wire and radio broadcasting; its authority was later expanded to include television. It took over the duties of the Federal Radio Commission.

Federal Radio Commission (FRC)   A government agency established in 1927 to regulate the airwaves and allocate frequencies for broadcasting.

Feedback   Any observable response from a receiver to a sender of a message sent in the communication process.

Fiber optics   Tiny, flexible glass strands capable of carrying 100,000 telephone or 100 broadcast signals on a cable the width of a human hair.

Flacks   A derogatory term occasionally used by journalists to refer to public relations practitioners.

FM radio   Frequency modulation; a form of radio transmission in which sound waves modulate the frequency of the carrier wave.

Folk culture   The culture of ordinary (nonelite) people during the Middle Ages. *Popular culture* is the term used to describe today's folk culture.

Fotonovel   A book that is part text, part picture book, and part comic book. Usually the content is a spinoff of a popular movie or television show.

Frame of reference   The set of individual experiences that each person has and uses to form an understanding in the communication process. (Sometimes called a *field of experience*.)

Freebie   A gratuity; usually tickets, passes, musical recordings, or books given to journalists by people seeking press coverage.

Freedom of Information Act (FOIA)   Legislation passed in 1966 to give the news media and public access to the files of federal government agencies.

Gag order   Court-imposed restriction on what attorneys and/or court officials may say to the media during a legal proceeding.

Gatekeeping   The process whereby numerous people become involved in determining what news, information, or entertainment will reach a mass audience.

Gazetta   Printed sheets of current news in Venice, which sold for a coin called a *gazetta*, prior to the development of newspapers. When newspapers began developing in the 17th century, many were named "Gazette."

Glasnost   The policy of "openness," established in the 1980s by Communist Party secretary Mikhail Gorbachev, that began the process of developing a free press in the former Soviet Union.

Graphic novel   A spinoff of the comic book that became popular in the 1980s. This book form consists of original, self-contained stories told in comic book format.

Green marketing   A trend among advertisers to appeal to the growing concern about the environment by designing products and advertising campaigns to be more environmentally sensitive.

Group communication   The act of conducting interpersonal communication in group settings.

Hard news   The factual account of significant news events. See **Soft news.**

High-definition television (HDTV)   An extremely clear television signal transmitted at 1,125 lines per picture (as opposed to the current 525 lines per picture in U.S. broadcasts), allowing excellent reception on larger-than-life TV screens. May one day be used to transmit motion pictures to theaters via satellites.

Holography   A process of using lasers to split light beams to create three-dimensional images. May some day be used in television signal transmission.

How-to book   A specialized book giving advice on how to do something. How-to books cater to a wide range of interests.

Hybrid TV   A 1980s TV genre, introduced by Steven Bochco, that borrows techniques from a variety of television genres, including soap operas, TV dramas, action/adventure shows, urban Westerns, and sitcoms.

IBA   Independent Broadcasting Authority; the government agency in the United Kingdom that regulates television and radio broadcasting.

Industrial Revolution   The social and economic upheavals of the 18th and 19th centuries that transformed America from an agrarian society to a mechanized, production-oriented culture.

Infomercials   Television commercials designed as informational programs, usually 30 minutes in length. Topics range from moneymaking ideas to weight loss programs. Political candidates also use them in campaigns.

Information-imitation theory   The theory that TV violence plays a prominent role in causing bizarre and violent behavior in society by leading some individuals to imitate the violent behavior they observe.

Information overload   A term used to describe a situation where a person is overwhelmed by too much information.

Information processing   The way information is managed or used by communicators and consumers of the information.

Instant book   A book produced in only a few days or weeks so it can be sold while the news event it describes is still topical.

Interactive TV   The result of merging computer and television technology to allow viewers to interact with TV programs.

Internal specialization   A term describing a general-interest magazine that carries a variety of articles and allows readers to specialize by selecting articles of interest; an example is *Reader's Digest*. See **Unit specialization.**

Internet   A computer network of networks throughout the world that can intercommunicate by virtue of applications, gateways, routers, and bridges to provide a wide variety of services to users.

Interpersonal communication   Face-to-face communication that takes place between individuals.

Interpretive reporting   A reporting style that developed in the 1930s to provide background for complex stories.

Intrapersonal communication   A term used for the act of talking to oneself.

Invasion of privacy   The publishing or broadcasting of information that violates a person's right to be left alone.

Inverted pyramid   A style of organizing news stories in which the essential material is placed at the beginning and subsequent paragraphs provide information in declining order of importance.

Investigative reporting   News reporting that digs below the surface to uncover important information, usually about political corruption or other wrongdoing.

Issues management   A public relations activity that attempts to identify and correctly interpret issues before they become problems. See **Crisis management.**

Kinescope   The process used in the early days of television to preserve "live" programs for later showing in other time zones; a special camera filmed the show directly off of a television screen.

Kinetoscope   A four-foot-high box used to show motion pictures in the 19th century. The device, which allowed one person at a time to view the pictures, became a penny arcade attraction.

Libel   Published or broadcast information that damages an individual's reputation. There are three defenses against a libel suit: truth, privileged information, and fair comment and criticism.

Libertarian theory   The theory that the press should serve the governed (people), not the governors. Libertarian theory has an offshoot, the social responsibility theory. See **Authoritarian theory.**

Low-power television (LPTV)   A system that can transmit television signals at lower cost to a small geographic area (usually a 15–20 mile radius). Can be used to provide special-interest programming in metropolitan areas.

Mass communication   A process whereby professional communicators use technological devices to share messages over some distance to influence and inform large audiences.

Mass culture   The things in our culture that are mass-produced and/or shared through the mass media. See **Popular culture.**

Mass-market paperback   Usually a romance, Western, or mystery novel that is mass-produced (a million copies or more) and mass-distributed. It is usually smaller in size than other paperbacks and printed on cheaper paper.

Message   In the communication process, whatever the source or communicator attempts to share with someone else.

Metropolitan newspaper   Also called the *penny press*, a newspaper with a style of reporting designed for ordinary people that moved the press from the elite culture into the popular culture.

Miniseries   A multipart TV drama that runs for several consecutive nights. A popular TV genre, it is used to disrupt regular viewing habits and allow networks to promote their other programming during commercial breaks.

Morph   A motion composite that changes one image into another (used in music videos by such artists as Michael Jackson; in movies, such as Arnold Schwarzenegger's *Terminator* films; and for the opening credits of TV's "Roseanne").

Motivational research (MR)   Advertising research based on Freudian psychology; used to develop advertising strategies.

MP3   A digital audio file. On a computer, the format enables music to be compressed into a manageable file size which is easy to store and transfer.

MTV   Music Television; a cable network launched by Warner-Amex in 1981 to bring 24-hour-a-day music videos to 12-to-23-year-olds. It is now owned by Viacom.

Muckrakers   A term coined by President Theodore Roosevelt to describe reporters who specialized in exposing scandals and corruption.

NBC   National Broadcasting Company; founded in 1926 as a subsidiary of Radio Corporation of America (RCA), it is the oldest broadcasting network in America.

News ploys   News events staged by public relations practitioners or political consultants to get free publicity for their clients. Sometimes called *media events*.

Noise   See **Channel noise, semantic noise,** and **psychological noise.**

Nonfiction novel　Book based on a true story but written in the style of a novel, often with invented dialogue and made-up scenes.

Novelization　The basing of a book on a successful movie; the opposite of making a book into a movie.

Op-ed page　The page opposite the editorial page, where guest columns and other opinion materials not necessarily representing the views of the newspaper management usually appear.

Opinion leader　A person who influences the thinking of others; usually someone who is better informed by the mass media than the average person.

Papyrus scrolls　A format used for books in which a paperlike material made from the papyrus plant found in the Nile Valley area was used to write on and then was rolled up on two rods. The scrolls could be spread out and read by scholars.

Pay-per-view　The requirement by cable TV channels of a special fee to access specific programs, usually movies and sporting events. It is predicted that in the future many additional sporting activities, including the Super Bowl, will be available only on pay-per-view channels.

Pay TV　Special entertainment channels, such as HBO, Showtime, and Disney, that cable operators provide for an additional charge.

PBS　Public Broadcasting System; a noncommercial television system established by the Public Broadcasting Act of 1967.

Penny press　Term first used in the 1830s to describe new American newspapers aimed at the popular culture and selling for 1 cent. See **Metropolitan newspaper.**

People meter　A hand-held, remote-control device used by TV rating services to measure the size and demographics of a television audience.

Personalized book　A book, usually for children, whose text is stored in a computer. When a purchaser supplies specified personal data, the computer prints out a book with these facts included in the plot.

Pictorial prints　The first form of mass-produced images for popular markets. Renaissance artists, led by Albrecht Dürer, began mass-producing their art using woodcuts, metal engravings, and the printing press.

Political consultants　People trained in opinion polling, advertising, or public relations who package political candidates and/or issues and sell them to the public.

Popular culture　The culture of everyone in a society. This culture is so pervasive that we seldom notice it. See **Mass culture.**

Popular press　The popular national tabloid newspapers in the United Kingdom.

Press agents　People who design and execute plans to stage events and plant stories to get publicity in the news media for their clients.

Prime time　The three viewing hours on television with the biggest audiences: 7 to 10 P.M. central and mountain time zones, 8 to 11 P.M. in eastern and Pacific areas.

Prior restraint　The ability of the government to prevent something from being published or broadcast. Such activity is usually prohibited by the First Amendment.

Prodigy　A computer information service that provides access to database information via personal computers and modems.

Product brokers　People who arrange for the use of their clients' products in movies and TV shows.

Propaganda devices　Techniques used to sell products or points of view by appealing to one's emotions rather than intellect.

Protestant Reformation　The 16th-century religious revolt against the Catholic church that led to the establishment of Protestant churches. This was the first major social movement to use printing, the new invention of mass communication, to further its cause.

Psychographics　A kind of advertising research that gathers information on people's interests, needs, values and lifestyles.

Psychological noise　Internal factors that can lead to misunderstanding a message, including selective exposure, selective perception, and selective retention.

Public access　The use afforded by some cable TV operators to the public of cable channels for public service programming. Uses often include public instruction by school districts, community forums, and broadcasting of local city council meetings.

Public relations　The business of creating favorable images for clients; includes press agentry, promotion, public affairs, spin doctoring, publicity, opinion research, and advertising.

Publick Occurrences　The first newspaper published in the American colonies. Published by a former English publisher, Benjamin Harris, the September 25, 1690, edition of the newspaper became the last because it was published without the permission of the colonial governor.

Quality press　The elite-oriented national newspapers in the United Kingdom, usually found in broad-sheet (full-size) formats as opposed to the tabloid popular press.

Ratings　Percentage of all households having television sets that watch a particular program, whether or not the sets are turned on. See **Share.**

Receiver　In the communication process, the person who receives the message being shared.

Red Channels   A 1950s report on the alleged communist infiltration of the motion picture and broadcast industries. Published by a group called Counterattack, it accused 151 radio and television personalities of having communist leanings; many of them lost their jobs.

Regional breakouts   Copies of a magazine that are circulated only in a designated geographic region. Magazine advertisers can lower their advertising costs by designating that their ads run only in certain regions.

Reuters   British news wire service, similar to our Associated Press wire service, organized in the 1850s.

Satellite   An electronic relay system that orbits 22,300 miles above the equator; it receives signals from earth, recharges them on a transponder, and sends them back to earth to be received by anyone with the proper receiving dish.

Section 315   A requirement of the Federal Communications Commission that broadcasters give bona fide political candidates equal opportunities for air time on their stations.

Selective exposure   A form of psychological noise that causes people to expose themselves to information that reinforces rather than opposes their general beliefs or opinions.

Selective perception   A form of psychological noise that causes people to see, hear, and believe only what they want to see, hear, and believe.

Selective retention   A form of psychological noise that causes people to remember things that reinforce their beliefs and opinions better than things that oppose them.

Semantic noise   A form of message interference that occurs when the message gets through exactly as sent but is not understood because terms used are unclear in meaning and outside the receiver's frame of reference.

Share   The number of TV sets specifically turned on at a given time and tuned to a specific program. Also see **Ratings.**

Sitcom   Situation comedy, a popular and long-enduring genre of broadcast entertainment. Although a major ingredient of today's TV programming, the sitcom originated on radio in the 1920s.

Soap opera   A broadcasting genre that originated on radio and now provides popular entertainment for both daytime and sometimes prime time television. Named after the original radio sponsors, soap companies such as Procter & Gamble.

Social responsibility theory   An offshoot of the libertarian theory of the press that contends that the press is socially responsible to keep a democratic nation well informed.

Soft news   Feature stories or background information about entertaining items of interest. It includes everything from lifestyle articles to personality profiles and Dear Abby–type columns. Sometimes called "fluff journalism," soft news accounts for most of the content in today's newspapers.

Source   The person in the communication process who shares information, ideas, or attitudes with others.

Soviet communist theory   An offshoot of the authoritarian theory of the press stating that the mass media should be state owned and operated to best serve the government.

Specialization   A trend in the mass media whereby the medium moves out of the popular stage and begins appealing to a narrowly focused target audience. Although magazines are the most specialized of the mass media, nearly all magazines in the American culture have entered the stage of specialization.

Spin doctor   A public relations person who specializes in getting the news media to put a special angle or "spin" on news stories so that clients are shown in a favorable light.

Subliminal advertising   A technique of hiding images in advertisements; these imbeds are supposed to appeal to the emotional instincts of sex, fear, and death, triggering a subconscious response that causes the person to remember the ad.

Subliminal message   A message dropped into recorded music just below the decibel level at which it can be heard consciously and intended to be received by the subconscious mind.

Sunshine laws   Laws that give the news media and the public access to government agencies. They usually require the public agencies to hold open meetings and make their printed documents available. These laws are based on the premise that the public's business should be conducted in public.

Symbols   Words, pictures, or objects used in the communication process to elicit meaning in the mind of the receiver of the message.

Tabloid   Any half-size newspaper; often used to refer to sensational publications, such as the *National Enquirer.*

Tabloid TV   Sensational or titillating TV programs that began in the 1980s with such productions as "Hard Copy" and "A Current Affair." Soon others were copying the format with such programs as "American Journal" and "Inside Edition." Sometimes called "trash TV."

TASS   *Telegrafnoie Agentsvo Sovetskovo Soyuza;* the official news agency in the Russian republic.

Teenzines   Youth-oriented magazines that feature pictures, stories and profiles of rock stars. Although most of these publications are targeted at 11-to-13-year-old girls, some are aimed at boys in the same age group.

Telecommuting   A trend in urban lifestyles that encourages employers to reduce traffic congestion and air pollution by making it possible for some employees to work at home using computer terminals, modems, faxes, and telephone lines.

Teleshopping channels   Cable TV channels that sell merchandise to viewers, who telephone their orders and credit card numbers on 1-800 lines. Teleshopping channels feature a wide variety of products at volume discounts.

Teletext   A system that provides one-way interactive viewing of printed text carried on the unused space of TV signals. A special converter on the TV set is required to receive these signals.

Televangelism   Programs on broadcast and cable TV featuring preachers who use the airwaves as an electronic version of old-fashioned tent revivals.

Truth boxes   Newspaper articles that analyze political ads for accuracy. The process, started in the 1990s, allows a reader to see whether political advertising claims are true or false.

Two-step flow theory   A theory developed by Paul Lazarsfeld to describe the opinion-leader concept: (1) the mass media influence certain individuals, and (2) these individuals personally influence others.

Two-way cable   A cable TV system that allows the consumer to respond to programming by sending messages back to the cable station.

Underground press   Alternative or counterculture newspapers published in the 1960s and early 1970s to promote the ideas and cultural reflections that were being ignored by the Establishment press; an outgrowth of the youth subculture.

UNESCO   United Nations Educational, Scientific, and Cultural Organization, which has been trying to regulate the way world news media operate in less developed countries.

Unit specialization   A term used to describe a magazine that targets a specialized audience; *Surfer* and *Personal Computing* are examples. See **Internal specialization.**

UPI   United Press International; a private news service that was formed in 1958 by the merger of United Press (1907) and International News Service (1909). This American company was purchased in the 1990s by a Saudi Arabian family.

Urban Western   A term applied to the police, doctor and detective action/adventure shows that supplanted the Westerns on television in the 1960s.

VALS   Values and lifestyles; psychographic research by SRI International that categorizes Americans into eight different lifestyles. Advertisers use VALS to determine the target audiences for their products.

Vaudeville   A 19th-century entertainment form that developed to meet the new leisure-time needs created by the Industrial Revolution. It was live theater, consisting of comedy skits and musical acts. Although no longer around, its influence is still seen on modern-day television.

Video compression   The use of digital technology to compress video signals so that 10 times the number of pictures can be squeezed into space previously required for one signal.

Video disc player   A playback unit that uses prerecorded video discs shaped much like phonograph records or audio CDs.

Video magazine   Material that magazine publishers, in a new trend, are now making available on videocassettes. The tapes for VCR use sell for about $5 and contain about two hours of material, including 20 minutes of advertising.

Videocassette recorder (VCR)   A videotape recorder that can record TV programs and play prerecorded movies.

Virtual Reality (VR)   The result of using computer-sensory technology to deepen a person's immersion in computer-generated simulation; first developed for use in flight training. The person usually wears a helmet or sits in a booth equipped with viewing screens that replicate stereoscopic vision.

Vote video   A prerecorded videocassette used to promote political candidates and issues.

Wood block printing   Printing books from wooden blocks that have been carved with the images and words of each page; a process that preceded moveable type.

World Wide Web (WWW)   A front end to information located throughout the Internet, allowing a single point of entry to most Internet sources and services accessible through computer and telephone lines.

Yellow journalism   A derogatory term used to describe American journalism during the turn-of-the-century circulation war between William Randolph Hearst and Joseph Pulitzer, when sensational headlines and stunt reporting were common. The name derives from a feud between Hearst and Pulitzer over the use of the "Yellow Kid" comic strip.

Zapping   Using fast-forwarding to eliminate commercials from TV programs recorded on VCRs.

Zipping   Using a remote-control device to flip from one TV channel to another during commercials.

Index

Photo Credits

CO 1   Corbis Images
1-1   Erich Lessing/Art Resource
1-2   Les Stone/Sygma
1-3   Photofest
1-4   Gamma Liaison
1-5   Jim Bourgh/Gamma Liaison
1-6   Wide World Photos

CO 2   Corbis Images
2-1   The British Museum, London
2-2   Hulton Getty Pictures/Gamma Liaison
2-3   Courtesy of the NY Historical Society, NYC
2-4   Corbis Bettmann
2-5   The Bettmann Archive
2-6   Photofest
2-7   Courtesy of NBC
2-8   Associated Press
2-9   Corbis/Sygma
2-10   Photofest

CO 3   PhotoDisc
3-1   Hulton Getty Picture Library/Gamma Liaison
3-2   Associated Press
3-3   Associated Press
3-4   Everett Collection
3-5   Associated Press
3-6   Associated Press
3-7   Everett Collection
3-8   Associated Press

CO 4   PhotoDisc
4-1   1971 by the New York Times company. Reprinted by permission.
4-2   Sygma
4-3   Associated Press
4-4   Michael Ferguson/Globe Photos
4-5   Associated Press
4-6   Gamma Liaison
4-7   Associated Press

CO 5   PhotoDisc
5-1   The Grancer Collection
5-2   Les Stone/Sygma
5-3   Michael Newman/Photo Edit
5-4   Bettmann Archive
5-5   Associated Press

5-6   (L) CBS Archive photo, (R) Les Stone/Sygma
5-7   Associated Press
5-8   Associated Press
5-9   Rick Maimon/Sygma
5-10   John Chiasson/Gamma Liaison
5-11   D. Kirkland/Sygma

CO 6   PhotoDisc
6-1   Brown Brothers
6-2   The Granger Collection
6-3   Photofest
6-4   Photofest
6-5   David Young Wolff/Photo Edit
6-6   Ciboux/Gamma Liaison
6-7   J. Ohlinger/Sygma

CO 7   Corbis Images
7-1   Brown Brothers
7-3   The Granger Collection
7-4   The Granger Collection
7-5   The Granger Collection
7-6   Robert Brenner/Photo Edit
7-7   Spencer Grant/Photo Edit
7-8   Bill Aron/Photo Edit
7-9   UPI/Bettmann

CO 8   Brian Smith/Stock Boston
8-1   The Granger Collection
8-2   Associated Press
8-3   Michael Newman/Photo Edit
8-4   Michael Newman/Photo Edit
8-5   Cotrell/Gamma Liaison
8-6   M. Dwyer/Stock Boston
8-7   Michael Newman/Photo Edit
8-8   Gregory Pace/Corbis/Sygma
8-9   Gamma Liaison

CO 9   Corbis Images
9-1   The Bettmann Archive
9-2   The Granger Collection
9-3   The Granger Collection
9-4   The Granger Collection
9-5   The Granger Collection
9-6   The Bettmann Archive
9-7   Gamma Liaison
9-8   Sygma
9-9   Sygma

CO 10	Corbis Images
10-1	Gamma Liaison
10-2	Associated Press
10-3	The Granger Collection
10-4	The Bettmann Archive
10-5	The Everett Collection
10-6	Sygma
10-7	Kramer/The Image Works
10-8	Gamma Liaison
CO 11	Corbis Images
11-1	Topham/The Image Works
11-2	Associated Press
11-3	Nina Leer/Life Magazine/ TIME WARNER INC.
11-4	Sygma
11-5	Associated Press
11-6	Photofest
11-7	Bettmann Newsphoto
11-9	Associated Press
11-10	Associated Press
CO 12	Corbis Images
12-1	Bettmann
12-2	David Young Wolff/Photo Edit
12-3	Photofest
12-4	Photofest
12-5	Robert Visser/Sygma
12-6A	Associated Press/Wide World Photos
12-6B	Barbara Alper/Stock Boston
12-7	Shooting Star
12-8	The Everett Collection
12-9	Associated Press/Wide World Photos

CO 13	Corbis Images
13-1	Jed Jacobsohn/Gamma Liaison
13-2	Culver
13-3	Jonathan Elderfield/Gamma Liaison
13-4	Jonathan Elderfield/Gamma Liaison
13-5	Reuters/Bettmann
13-6	Jonathan Nourok/Photo Edit
13-7	Associated Press/Wide World Photos
CO 14	Corbis Images
14-2	Bettmann
14-3	Allan Tannenbaum/Sygma
14-4	Corbis/Bettmann
14-5	Reproduced with permission of Pepsi Co Inc.
CO 15	PhotoDisc
15-0	Gamma Liaison
15-1	Les Stone/Sygma
15-2	Sygma
15-3	Doug Bauman/Gamma Liaison
15-4	David Young Wolff/Photo Edit
15-5	Associated Press/Wide World Photos
15-6	Sygma
CO 16	Corbis Images
16-1	The Everett Collection
16-2	Michael Newman/Photo Edit
16-3	Bob Daemmrich/Stock Boston
16-4	The Everett Collection
16-5	Owen Franken/Stock Boston
Box 16-2	Billy Barnes/Stock Boston